TEXTBOOK

Public International Law

THIRD EDITION

ALINA KACZOROWSKA
BCL, DEA, Ph D, Barrister at the Paris Bar,
Senior Lecturer in Law, University of the West Indies,
Faculty of Law, Cave Hill Campus, Barbados

OLD BAILEY PRESS

OLD BAILEY PRESS
at Holborn College, Woolwich Road,
Charlton, London, SE7 8LN

First published 2002
Third edition 2005

© Holborn College Ltd 2005

ISBN 1 85836 607 0

British Library Cataloguing-in-Publication.
A CIP Catalogue record for this book is
available from the British Library.

Acknowledgement
The publishers and author would
like to thank the Incorporated
Council of Law Reporting for
England and Wales for kind
permission to reproduce extracts
from the Weekly Law Reports, and
Butterworths for their kind
permission to reproduce extracts
from the All England Law Reports.

Printed and bound in Great Britain

Contents

The historical development of international law – Definition of international law – The nature of international law – Machinery for enforcement of international law – Situations to which international law is relevant

Introduction – Treaties – Custom – The relationship between treaties and custom – General principles of law – Judicial decisions – The writings of publicists – Other sources of international law – The International Law Commission – Soft law – Ius cogens

Introduction – The relationship between international law and municipal law – The application of municipal law before international tribunals – The application of international law in UK courts – EC law in UK courts

Introduction – The criteria for statehood – Independent states – Dependent states – Special cases – Mandates and trusteeship territories – International organisations – Individuals

Introduction – Recognition in international law – Recognition of governments – Recognition in municipal law

The doctrine of equality of states – Legal consequences of sovereign equality or independence – Domestic jurisdiction

Contents

Preface

As in previous editions of this work, I have in this edition sought to present the fundamental aspects of public international law in a clear, easy to understand and simple style.

It has been written with an awareness not only of the sweeping changes in international law in the last two decades, but also of the implications for international law of George W Bush's so-called 'war on terror'.

Whilst this book stands very well on its own, my companion work, *Public International Law: 150 Leading Cases*, provides a convenient source of reference to the cited cases.

Changes in this edition from the 2003 second edition reflect new and significant developments in public international law, the most important being the implications of the military intervention by the USA, the UK and their allies, despite the lack of legal backing from the UN Security Council and despite the lack of any evidence as to the possession of weapons of mass destruction in Iraq. Although Saddam Hussein's regime has gone, the consequences of the unlawful use of force by the US and its allies against Iraq will continue to hang over the international legal system for many years to come. Another current major concern is the search for equilibrium between protecting against the threat of international terrorism and safeguarding the international protection of human rights. In this respect US detention policy, under which hundreds of detainees from around 40 countries have been held at the US base in Guantanamo Bay and at other undisclosed places on the ground of their possible link with Al-Qaeda, remains in legal limbo: it has been questioned by the international community and challenged by the US judiciary, including the US Supreme Court. Even the release of detainees raises controversy because they are not afforded any protection against torture, execution and other serious human rights abuses if returned to their countries.

In this book, in addition to the above, I also discuss the situation in the Middle East after the death of Yasser Arafat, whose greatest achievement was the reconstitution of the shattered, defeated Palestinian people into a proud and self-confident nation. I also comment on new disarmament initiatives aimed at eliminating weapons of mass destruction; the adoption by the European Summit held on November 2004 of the Hague programme, which constitutes a further step in the establishment of a Common European Asylum System; the adoption of Protocol 14 by the Committee of Ministers of the Council of Europe during May 2004 which reforms, once again, the functioning of the control system under the

European Convention on Human Rights; and the continued hostility of the US government towards the newly established International Criminal Court.

Changes in this edition were also necessitated by recent decisions delivered by the International Court of Justice, ie: in the *Case Concerning Oil Platforms: Islamic Republic of Iran* v *USA* (2003) 42 ILM 1334, in the *Case Concerning Avena and Other Mexican Nationals: Mexico* v *USA* (2004) 43 ILM 581 and in the *Advisory Opinion on the Legal Consequences of the Construction of a Wall by Israel in the Occupied Palestinian Territory* (2003) 43 ILM 1009. Decisions rendered by other international and national courts and tribunals are also examined.

The updating of this edition has been accompanied by improvements in analysis, coverage and exposition throughout the book, whilst retaining the topical structure of the previous edition.

This work owes a great deal to many people. I would like to thank Chris Ireland, of Horsey Lightly Fynn Solicitors of Newbury, London and Bournemouth, for reviewing the entire manuscript and offering many useful suggestions. I would like to convey my sincere gratitude to my friends at the Old Bailey Press: my editor, Vanessa Osborne, for her competence, patience and encouragement throughout the production of this work; and Professor Cedric Bell for his constant support and savoir faire in connection with all matters of importance.

I hope this book will be your friend in understanding the ever-changing but always interesting landscape of public international law.

Account has been taken of changes in the law up to 1 January 2005.

Alina Kaczorowska

Note: some recent material can be found on the Internet. The most useful websites are:

For the United Nations: http://www.un.org
For the International Law Commission: http://www.un.org/law/ilc
For the ICJ: http://www.icj-cij.org
For the ECHR: http://www.echr.coe.int
For the ICTY: http://www.un.org/icty
For the ICTR: http://www.ictr.org
For the ICRC: http:/ www.icrc.org
For the ECJ: http: //www. curia.eu.int/jurisp
For the American Society of International Law: http://www.asil.org

Table of Cases

Table of National Statutes

Table of Treaties

Including Covenants, Treaties, Conventions, ICJ Statute and UN Charter etc

Table of Other Documents

Agreements, Declarations, Resolutions etc

1

History and Nature of
International Law

1.1 The historical development of international law

1.2 Definition of international law

1.3 The nature of international law

1.4 Machinery for enforcement of international law

1.5 Situations to which international law is relevant

1.1 The historical development of international law

It is impossible to fix a precise date or a period in history to mark the beginning of international law as it predates recorded history! It began when a politically organised group came into contact with another group and was prepared to treat that group as equal and, at the same time, felt the need to develop a system of rules to regulate their relations. Evidence of rules and procedure regarding international law dates back over 5,000 years. Around 2100 BC a solemn treaty was signed between the rulers of Lagash and Umma (small city states in Mesopotamia) which defined boundaries between them. In 1400 BC the Egyptian Pharaoh Rameses II concluded a Treaty of Peace, Alliance and Extradition with the King of Cheta, which recognised territorial sovereignty over certain areas of each ruler and provided for the extradition of refugees and the exchange of ambassadors: C Fenwick, *International Law*, 4th ed, New York: Appleton-Century Crofts, 1965, pp5–6. The grand empires of Egypt, Mesopotamia, Persia, Assyria and Chaldea, as well as small Hebrew monarchies and the Phoenician city states, concluded treaties based on the equality of signatories and the principle 'pacta sunt servanda' (agreements are to be kept). Ancient Greece adopted two institutions from the oriental civilisations – the technique of treaties and the art of diplomacy – and added its own: international arbitration.

The most influential of all ancient civilisations, the Roman civilisation, before its period of expansion and conquest, made treaties with Latin cities under which Latins and Romans were given rights in each other's courts and promised mutual co-operation. Once Rome became an empire the Romans organised their relations

1

with foreigners on the basis of ius fetiale and ius gentium. Ius fetiale consisted of religious rules which governed Roman external relations and formal declarations of war which, inter alia, recognised the inviolability of ambassadors and was at the origin of the distinction between just and unjust war. Ius gentium was the Roman solution (as Rome expanded) to the necessity of regulating legal relations between Roman citizens and foreigners. A special magistrate, the praetor peregrinus, was appointed in 242 BC who created law (called ius gentium) acceptable to both Roman citizens and foreigners. This law was the first truly international law, although it essentially regulated relations between private individuals. It was based on the commercial law in use in Mediterranean trade, ius civile (law applicable to relations between Roman citizens), in its less formalistic version, and on principles of equity and bona fides (good faith). The distinction between ius civile and ius gentium was obliterated when Roman citizenship was granted to all male inhabitants of the Empire in 212 AD. However, ius gentium did not disappear but became an essential part of Roman law and has thus greatly influenced all European legal systems and, through them, public international law. From ancient Rome international law has also inherited the doctrine of the universal law of nature known as 'natural law', which was developed by Stoic philosophers of ancient Greece and adopted by the Romans. This doctrine considered law as the product of right reason emanating from assumptions about the nature of man and society. Because natural law is the expression of right reason inherent in nature and man, and discoverable by reason, it applies universally. Cicero in his *De Republica* gave the following definition of natural law:

> 'True law is right reason in agreement with Nature; it is of universal application, unchanging and everlasting; it summons to duty by its commands, and averts from wrongdoing by its prohibitions ... There will not be different laws at Rome and at Athens, or different laws now and in the future, but one eternal and unchangeable law will be valid for all nations and for all times.'

The doctrine of natural law is regarded as a precursor to the concept of human rights.

There is disagreement as to whether and to what extent the Middle Ages contributed to the development of international law. Some argue that papal leadership in all matters and the voluntarily recognition of feudal suzerainty of the papacy were incompatible with the existence of international law, particularly as at its height in the twelfth and thirteenth centuries the medieval Church was omnipresent and the distinction between Church and 'states' as separate entities had disappeared. Indeed, the basic premise of international law which requires co-existence of equal and independent communities was missing. Others claim that 'the pyramidal structure of feudalism culminating in Pope and Emperor as spiritual and temporal heads of Western Christendom, was hardly ever fully realised. It left ample scope for relations on a footing of equality between what were often in fact independent states. This applied especially to kingdoms like England and Scotland which existed on the fringe of the Holy Roman Empire. Even within the Empire, relations between the more powerful feudal princes, independent knights and free cities were regulated by rules which in all but form were indistinguishable from those of international law and formed a system of quasi-international law': G Schwarzenberger, *A Manuel of International Law*, 5th ed, New York: Praeger, 1967, p6. There is no doubt that the confrontation between the papacy and German emperors over the ultimate authority in the Christian empire which lasted for centuries contributed to the revival of legal studies in Italian universities. Indeed, in their confrontation, both sides invoked legal arguments based on Roman law and canon law, blended with natural law, to bolster their claims. Treaties, principles and standards which were elaborated by medieval Christian world became, at a later stage, the origins of international customary law.

In the Middle Ages two sets of truly international law developed – the lex mercatoria and the maritime customary law – to deal with problems that transcended national boundaries.

With the revival of trade in the tenth century merchants started to travel throughout Europe in order to sell, buy and place orders for various goods. These commercial activities required the establishment of a common legal framework. Out of necessity the European merchants created their own rules of conduct and fair dealing which formed the lex mercatoria.

Also, in the Middle Ages maritime customs and usages were formed. The high seas were no-man's land, but with the development of maritime commerce it became necessary to establish some rules and standards. The rules of the sea, based on the Rhodian Sea Law, a codification undertaken under the Byzantine empire, were compiled into widely recognised collections such as the Consolato del Mare, composed in Barcelona in the mid-fourteenth century, the Rolls of Oleron in the twelfth century, the English Black Book of the Admiralty and the Maritime Code of Visby. These codifications become accepted throughout Europe.

The Middle Ages also saw the rise of nation states. First, there were the microscopic Italian city states which with increasing wealth and prestige were searching for legal justifications to accommodate their demands for independence. The Italian School of Law represented by Bartolus (1314–1357) and Baldus (1327–1400) responded to their needs. Although the treatment of international law was fragmentary the Italian School conceived the law of nations as a universal and natural law applicable between independent princes and free commonwealths. Towards the end of the medieval period the Spanish School of International Law represented by Francesco de Vitoria (circa 1486–1546) added its ideas to international law. De Vitoria in his *Reflectiones de Indis Noviter Inventis* confirmed the universal validity of international law and it application in the Americas. He considered that the Indians were the true owners of the land but justified the Spanish colonial expansion on the inferiority of their civilisation.

The period from the Peace Treaty of Westphalia (1648) to the Congress of Vienna (1815) is considered as the period of formation of 'classical' international law.

Indeed, international law in its modern version begins with the break up of the feudal state-system and the formation of society into free nation states. This is commonly traced back to the Peace Treaty of Westphalia (1648) which brought to an end the Thirty Years War in Europe.

The Treaty of Westphalia 1648, which is often referred to as the constitutional treaty of Europe, recognised the principle of sovereignty, territorial integrity and equality of states as independent members of an international system. Since then a state defeated in war may be deprived of some of its territory but in general is allowed to continue as an independent state. Also, after the Thirty Years of War, one of the bloodiest in history until World War II, European rulers established a system of balance of power aimed at preventing wars. This system lasted until the French Revolution and Napoleonic Wars.

The concept of sovereignty is at the centre of the international system. It justifies the authority of kings over their subjects and places the supreme power within the state. But since all states are equally sovereign it also conveys the idea of independence. The claim of a state to be sovereign does not mean that the power of the state is subject to no limitations. The obvious limitation is territorial: any state is finite and necessarily has boundaries. Beyond the scope of its boundaries, where its writ does not run, the independence of each state presupposes that of the others. Sovereignty as a concept is decisive in distinguishing Europe from the rest of the world. In the East the decline of empire spelt anarchy and created a power vacuum which led to colonial subjugation. In Europe power was devolved to states who were content simply to rule themselves rather than to succeed to the imperial mantle. The growing relationship between sovereign states provides the customary source of international law.

The intellectual support for new ideas was provided by scholars, in particular the Anglo-Dutch School represented by Hugo Grotius and Alberto Gentilli. Alberto Gentilli, an Italian Protestant who fled to England to avoid prosecution, was the first to separate international law from theology and ethics. Grotius, who is considered as the founder of the modern theory of natural law, acknowledged Gentilli's contribution to his work but further divorced international law from theology by exploring the hypothetical argument that natural law would have validity even if there were no God or if God was not interested in human affairs. Grotius's second innovation was that he treated his law as deductive and independent of experience. In respect of international law in his work *Mare Liberum* (*The Free Sea* (1609)) he advocated the freedom of the seas. He argued that it would be against natural law to rule over the sea as no country was able to monopolise control over the ocean because of its immensity, lack of stability and lack of fixed limits. His principal work *De Jure Belli ac Pacis* (*On the Law of War and Peace* (1625)) constituted the first systematic treatment of positive international law. He considered war as violating natural law but accepted its necessity. He supported the idea of a 'just war' which according to him was a war to obtain a right. War was of a punitive character, conducted against state crimes, when conciliation had failed. He considered religious war as unjust because religion was a matter of inner conviction which could not be forced on anyone. He believed that war should be regulated. In his work *Ptolegomena* he stated that:

> 'I saw in the whole Christian world a license of fighting at which even barbarious nations might blush. Wars were begun on trifling pretexts or none at all, and carried on without any reverence for law, Divine or human. A declaration of war seemed to let loose every crime.'

Consequently he put emphasis on moral conduct during wars. Non-combatants should be protected, hostages and prisoners treated humanly, property protected from wanton destruction. The topics of neutrality, treaties and diplomatic practice were examined in his works. He also discussed methods for peaceful settlement of international disputes. He recognised sovereign states as the basic units of international law and the law of nations as universally accepted, and emphasised that a civil right which derives from the laws of a sovereign state is inferior to a right based on the law of nations because 'the law of nations is more extensive rights, deriving its authority from the consent of all, or at least of many nations'.

His works were very popular with his contemporaries and appealed to subsequent generations. His law of nature was further developed by the German jurist Samuel von Pufendorf and the seventeenth century English philosophers Thomas Hobbes and John Locke. In the nineteenth century the principle of utility – according to which the object of all legislation must be the 'greatest happiness of the greatest number' – developed by Jeremy Bentham and legal positivism (according to which law is based simply on 'the command of the ruler') formulated by John Austin rejected the doctrine of natural law as unprovable. However, after World War II the idea that there are some higher standards than positive law revived the interest in natural law.

From the Congress of Vienna held in 1815 to the outbreak of World War I international law was based on five principles: sovereignty, balance of power, legitimacy (in the sense of restoration of 'legitimate' governments to power and of prevention of political revolutions), nationality (which relegated the principle of legitimacy as nations aspiring to achieve national unity replaced the system of the old regime, based exclusively upon the aristocracy, with a system of governments elected by people from all classes of society) and equality. The Congress of Vienna ended 25 years of Napoleonic war in Europe. The Congress was convened by the four European powers which had defeated Napoleon. Its main objective was to establish a balance of power of political forces in Europe which would ensure lasting peace and to maintain the status quo in Europe by repressing political revolutions. At the Congress the five powers (France joined in 1818) promised to meet periodically over the next 20 years to discuss common problems and to co-operate on major issues to prevent war. This so-called Concert of Europe which developed out of the Congress of Vienna was mostly successful in preserving peace in Europe for almost a century. It constituted the first serious attempt in modern times to establish an international mechanism to maintain peace. The system of periodic meetings also began a new diplomatic era in Europe which was marked by the adoption of numerous treaties, inter alia, establishing the neutrality of Switzerland (1815) and Belgium (1831), laying down general rules for the navigation of rivers (1815) (and specific regulations for the Rhine), and a number of treaties aimed at restricting human suffering during international armed conflicts (this matter is examined elsewhere in the book). During that period state practice produced the framework for modern international law dealing with recognition of states, which achieved prominence in the attitude of the United Kingdom and the United States to the independence of Greece. Rules governing state responsibility were also developed.

The classical system of international law was described by Grewe in the following terms:

'... the basic and characteristic feature of the classical system was its close commitment to the modern sovereign state as the sole subject of international law. Deriving from this basic structure, two other elements helped to form the shape of the classical system: the unorganised character of the international community, composed of a multitude of sovereign states as legally equal, if de facto unequal members; and the acceptance of war as the ultimate instrument of enforcing law and safeguarding national honour and interest': W G Grewe in R Bernhardt, *Encyclopaedia of Public International Law*, Vol II, 8th ed, 1995, pp839–40.

The twentieth century witnessed two inhuman ideologies at work – Nazism and Communism – and two World Wars. In response a different system of international law has been introduced which is examined in this book.

1.2 Definition of international law

There are many definitions of international law. In *SS Lotus Case: France* v *Turkey* (1927) PCIJ Rep Ser A No 10, 18 the PCIJ provided the following definition:

'International law governs relations between independent states. The rules of law binding upon states therefore emanate from their own will as expressed in conventions [treaties] or by usages generally accepted as expressing principles of law established in order to regulate the relations between these co-existing independent communities or with a view to the achievement of common aims.'

In *Trendtex Trading Corporation* v *Central Bank of Nigeria* [1977] 1 All ER 881 at 901 and 902 an English judge gave a definition of international law in terms of its impact on English law:

'I know no better definition of it than that it is the sum of rules or usages which civilised states have agreed shall be binding upon them in their dealing with one another.

It is quite true that whatever has received the common consent of civilised nations must have received the assent of our country, and that to which we have assented along with other nations in general may be called international law, and as such will be acknowledged and applied by our municipal tribunals when legitimate occasion arises for those tribunals to decide questions to which doctrines of international law may be relevant.'

The American Law Institute in the Official Draft of the Restatement of the Foreign Relations Law of the United States provided the following definition:

'International law ... means those rules of law applicable to a state or international organisations that cannot be modified unilaterally by it': §1, at 1, 3rd ed, St Paul, MN: American Law Inst Publishers, 1987.

The definition formulated by the US Department of State and the American Law Institute emphasises the evolving nature of international law. It states that:

'International law is the standard of conduct, at a given time, for states and other entities thereto. It comprises the rights, privileges, powers, and immunities of states and entities invoking its provisions, as well as the correlative fundamental duties, absence of rights, liabilities, and disabilities. International law is, more or less, in a continual state of change and development. In certain of its aspects the evolution is gradual; in others it is avulsive. International law is based largely on custom, eg, on practice, and whereas certain customs are recognised as obligatory, others are in retrogression and are recognised as non-obligatory, depending upon the subject matter and its status at a particular time': I M Whiteman, *Digest of International Law*, Washington, DC: US Department of State, 1963.

The definition provided by Shearer is the most comprehensive. It states that:

'International law may be defined as that body of law which is composed for its greater part of the principles and rules of conduct which states feel themselves bound to observe, and therefore, do commonly observe in their relations with each other, and which includes also:
(a) the rules of law relating to the functioning of international institutions or organisations, their relations with each other, and their relations with states and individuals; and
(b) certain rules of law relating to individuals and non-states so far as the rights or duties of such individuals and non-state entities are the concern of the international community.'

See *Starke's International Law*, 11th ed, London: Butterworths, 1994, p3.

1.3 The nature of international law

The question of whether or not international law is law at all may be examined at two levels. First, people believe that states have little respect for international law and have no incentive to comply with it in the absence of world government. This belief springs from the common misconception that international law is broken with impunity. But the same could be said of any legal system. In English criminal law, where prosecutions are brought by the police, around 60 per cent of crimes known to the police are never solved, and there must be a large number which are never reported in the first place. The breaches of international law are more spectacular than the comparatively staid law of international co-operation. Moreover, people imagine that international disputes are not necessarily governed by international law, just as disputes between individuals are not necessarily governed by national law.

Second, at the theoretical level, the existence of international law has been challenged by the positivist theory. John Austin, the great nineteenth-century positivist, argued that international law is not really law because it has no sovereign. He defined laws 'properly so called' as commands of a sovereign. According to him a sovereign is a person who receives obedience of the members of an independent political society and who, in turn, does not owe such obedience to any person. Rules of international law did not qualify as rules of positive law by this test and not being commands of any sort were placed in the category of laws 'improperly so called'.

The reply of any international lawyer would be to ask what legal system does conform to Austin's concept. In the United States the separation of powers does not admit a single sovereign, and in the United Kingdom the legislature is not the only source of law-making. His criticism of international law is largely based on his peculiar conception of law. But it must be conceded that his definition of law does not invalidate his criticism and he does expose one shortcoming which international law has always suffered: the lack of effective enforcement mechanisms.

1.4 Machinery for enforcement of international law

In municipal systems the machinery for enforcement is centralised in the government authority. In international law it is of necessity decentralised, since the primary subjects of international law are sovereign states.

Professor Kelsen, the Austrian-American legal philosopher who formulated a kind of positivism known as the 'pure theory' of law and was the main representative of the monist school in international law, argued that international law does have machinery for enforcement. Traditionally, in a decentralised society enforcement of laws is accomplished through self-help. The legal order leaves enforcement to the individuals injured by the delict or illegality. He stated that although it may appear that the individuals take law into their own hands, they may nevertheless be considered as acting as organs of the community.

Kelsen's argument is not without historical attraction. Until the 1928 Kellogg-Briand Pact, the use of force did constitute a recognised method of enforcing international law. However, the use of force, except in self-defence, is now illegal. The problem therefore arises as to what to put in place of force as a means of enforcement.

The system established under the UN Charter was designed to ensure that member states obey and respect international obligations deriving from the Charter. The Cold War and its rigid division of the world distorted the potential of the UN system. However, since the end of the Cold War the enforcement powers of the UN have been reinvigorated even though the UN is not a law-enforcing agency.

Nevertheless, the scope of enforcement actions taken by the UN is steadily growing. Within its function of maintaining international peace and security the Security Council has found that it must act in situations involving serious and continuous violation of human rights. In addition the punishment of notorious abusers of human rights has become a concern of the Security Council. The establishment of the two Criminal Tribunals – the International Criminal Tribunal for the Former Yugoslavia and the International Criminal Tribunal for Rwanda – on the basis of the Security Council resolutions illustrates this point. Also, an ad hoc Special Court for Sierra Leone was set up jointly by the Government of Sierra Leone and the United Nations to try those who bear the responsibility for serious violations of international humanitarian law and Sierra Leoneon law committed in the territory of Sierra Leone after 30 November 1996. Furthermore, the UN has ratified an agreement with Cambodia with a view to creating an internationally assisted tribunal in Cambodia to try Khmer Rouge leaders responsible for the Cambodia genocide of 1975–1979 in which approximately 1.7 million people lost their lives. Finally, the establishment of the International Criminal Court which, at the time of writing is in the course of moving from the preparatory stage to the judicial stage, will contribute to the creation of a more comprehensive and effective system of enforcement of human rights: see Chapter 19.

The Security Council's use of sanctions, both involving use of force and those not involving use of force has been more frequent and more effective than ever before: see Chapter 17.

States are more active in apprehending and trying persons responsible for grave violations of human rights as exemplified by a growing number of cases before courts in Belgium, France, Austria, Germany, etc. It may be said that this new development has been, to some extent, initiated and inspired by the decision of the House of Lords in the *Pinochet* case but, unfortunately, this has suffered a major setback as a result of the ICJ's judgment in *Case Concerning the Arrest Warrant of 11 April 2000: Democratic Republic of Congo* v *Belgium* (2002) 41 ILM 536: see Chapter 9.

Moreover, the Articles on Responsibility of States for Internationally Wrongful Acts adopted by the International Law Commission in August 2001, and approved by the UN General Assembly in December 2001, reinforce the system of remedies available to a state injured by a violation of legal obligations by another state. The ILC Articles legitimate the recourse to counter-measures against a delinquent state whilst strictly defining their scope. The Articles introduce the 'aggravated responsibility' which allows any state to seek compensation on behalf of the victims of serious and widespread human rights violations and to apply counter-measures when a delinquent state is breaching a peremptory norm of international law: see Chapter 10.

Another important factor contributing to the enforcement of international law is the growing awareness of ordinary people of their rights under international law. This has two dimensions. On the one hand, they fight for their rights against totalitarian governments and, on the other hand, governments appeal to public opinion for support in the case of breaches of international law by a state. Pressures which are exercised by public opinion on governments, whether their own or foreign, should not be underestimated.

The existence of international law should not be viewed exclusively in the context of enforcement. Individuals obey municipal law for many reasons, only one of them is the fear of being punished. Individuals and states obey legal rules because those rules are considered as appropriate and right.

No country can totally disregard international law, although this occurred during the 1966–76 Cultural Revolution in the People's Republic of China! International law was no longer considered as an academic subject, all law lectures and professors were dismissed. When the Cultural Revolution ended in 1976 China's leaders, in the light of China's isolation, decided to join the international community in order to conduct relations with other governments. In 1982 more liberal views were taken and the President of the Chinese Society of International Law in Beijing announced that China had abandoned its parochial view of international law. Thus international law is essential for the existence of any state and no state can afford to stand alone.

1.5 Situations to which international law is relevant

If it is accepted that international law does exist, what form does it take? It is suggested that international law is relevant at three separate levels in international relations: the level of co-operation, co-existence and conflict.

Co-operation

States are naturally interdependent in many ways and international law facilitates co-operation. States have a common interest in an international postal system, eradicating disease by means of common rules as to vaccination, etc. These are areas where action on an international scale is essential and, in general, states obey these rules of international law.

Co-existence

States have to co-exist with one another and a means of doing this is to define their relationship by making treaties and other consensual agreements. At this level, Professor Schwarzenberger argued, obedience is high and the law is generally effective. Several reasons have been suggested for this fidelity. The concept of reciprocity plays an important part in a state's strategy. Both medium- and long-term strategies are involved. The former is illustrated by an example of a state thinking of extending its territorial waters, but not doing so because it may encourage other states to do the same. In the long term all states have an interest in international stability, so there is an incentive not to rock the boat excessively.

Conflict

The role of international law is confined to two main functions: the technical rules of conduct and the keeping of the breach to a minimum.

For example, many of the rules of warfare exist in an unwritten form but some of the rules are embodied in international conventions, particularly the Hague and Geneva Conventions. All these rules are included in manuals of military law for use by commanders in the field. Breach has important psychological impact. States will try to keep violations of international law to the minimum. A good example of this psychological impact is evidenced in the US blockade of Cuba. In the Suez crisis, Sir Partick Dean, the Foreign Office Legal Adviser, and the Lord Chancellor were consulted throughout.

2

Sources of International Law

2.1   Introduction

2.2   Treaties

2.3   Custom

2.4   The relationship between treaties and custom

2.5   General principles of law

2.6   Judicial decisions

2.7   The writings of publicists

2.8   Other sources of international law

2.9   The International Law Commission

2.10 Soft law

2.11 Ius cogens

2.1 Introduction

The question of where to find sources of international law, bearing in mind that the international community has neither a constitution nor legislature, is usually answered by reference to art 38 of the Statute of the International Court of Justice (ICJ). This provision, adopted from the same article in the Statute of the Permanent Court of International Justice (PCIJ) which operated under the auspices of the League of Nations, provides:

'(1) The Court, whose function is to decide in accordance with international law such disputes as are submitted to it, shall apply:
(a) international conventions, whether general or particular, establishing rules expressly recognised by the contesting states;
(b) international custom, as evidence of a general practice accepted as law;
(c) the general principles of law recognised by civilised nations;
(d) subject to the provisions of Article 59, judicial decisions and the teaching of the most highly qualified publicists of the various nations, as subsidiary means for the determination of rules of law.

(2) This provision shall not prejudice the power of the Court to decide a case ex aequo et bono, if the parties agree thereto.'

Five distinct sources can be identified from art 38 of the Statute of the ICJ:

1. international treaties;
2. international custom;
3. the general principles of law;
4. judicial decisions;
5. the writings of publicists.

There is also an incidental source, ie equity. While there is little doubt that art 38 does embody the most important sources of international law, it provides an incomplete list of them because, on the one hand, it envisages sources of international law from a strictly jurisdictional perspective and, on the other hand, being a text adopted more than 80 years ago, it does not take into account the evolution of international law.

Article 38 has been criticised for a number of reasons. For example, it treats judicial decisions and the writing of publicists as being of equal importance, while in practice judicial decisions have more weight than the writings of publicists. There is also a discrepancy between the English and the French texts of art 38 as to the role of judicial decisions and the writing of publicists which is considered as 'auxiliary' in French and as 'subsidiary' in English, terms which do not have the same meaning. Furthermore, art 38 is worded very generally and thus provides little assistance in resolving the issue of a hierarchy of sources. Although art 38 indicates an order of importance, which in practice the Court may be expected to observe, it does not address the issue of a conflict between different sources of law. Therefore, it operates without any problem when there is, for example, no treaty between the parties to a dispute but there is a customary rule. The situation is more complex where a treaty and a customary rule of international law provide an opposite solution. This is particularly acute when a customary rule has the status of ius cogens. Another criticism which may be added to art 38 is that it does not reflect the evolution of international law. Thus, the reference to international principles 'recognised by civilised nations' appears today as at best archaic, and at worst insulting.

Acts of international organisations which have greatly contributed to the formation of international law are not mentioned in art 38. Moreover, the concept of ius cogens, recognised by the Vienna Convention on the Law of Treaties 1969 and endorsed by the ICJ and other international and national courts and tribunals, which plays a fundamental role in modern international law is not a part of art 38.

However, whatever the shortcomings of art 38 it provides a starting point for any discussion of sources of international law.

It should be noted that the distinction between formal and material sources appears inappropriate in relation to international law. Salmond explained the distinction between formal and material sources in the following words:

'A formal source is that from which a rule derives its force and validity ... The material sources, on the other hand, are those from which is derived the matter, not the validity of the law. The material source supplies the substance of the rule to which the formal source gives the force and nature of law': *Jurisprudence*, 10th ed, London: Sweet and Maxwell, 1947, p151.

For example, a rule will be binding if it meets the requirements of a custom, which is a formal source of international law, and its substance will be indicated by state practice, which is the material source of the custom.

The peculiarity of international law calls into question a clear distinction between substantive and procedural elements of a rule of international law. As Professor Brownlie stated it is difficult to maintain the distinction between formal and material sources taking into account that material sources 'consist simply of quasi-constitutional principles of inevitable but unhelpful generality. What matters is the variety of material sources, the all-important evidence of the existence of consensus among states concerning particular rules of practice': *Principles of Public International Law*, 5th ed, Oxford: Oxford University Press, 1998, p2.

2.2 Treaties

Treaties represent a source of international law, the importance of which is ever increasing. The effect of a treaty on the formation of rules of international law depends upon the nature of the treaty concerned. A distinction is sometimes made between law-making treaties, ie those treaties which lay down rules of general or universal applications, and treaty contracts, eg a treaty entered into between two or only a few states, dealing with a particular matter concerning those states exclusively. While this distinction may be helpful in distinguishing treaties – usually multilateral – which are general in nature and which establish common principles of law, from those – usually bilateral – which focus more on the regulation of particular conduct (eg trade), it is important to bear in mind that a treaty of whatever kind is a direct source of obligation for the parties. The binding force of a treaty comes from the consent of the parties, not from the subject matter or form of the treaty.

Law-making treaties

Since the middle of the nineteenth century there has been a great increase in the number of law-making treaties primarily due to the inadequacy of custom in meeting the demands of states for rules regulating the industrial and economic changes which have taken place. These treaties deal with a wide range of activities. For example, the Red Cross conventions, the protection of submarine cables, the suppression of the slave trade, international waterways, the pacific settlement of international dispute, the control of narcotics, nationality and statelessness.

These are all matters which called urgently for international statute law and where it would have been impossible to rely on the eventual emergence of customary rules.

Treaty contracts

Treaty contracts, unlike law-making treaties, are usually concerned to regulate a narrow area of practice between two states (eg trade agreements). Such treaties may lead to the formation of general international law through the operation of the principle governing the development of customary rules in the following ways.

1. A series of treaties laying down a similar rule may produce a principle of customary international law to the same effect.
2. A rule contained in a treaty originally concluded between a limited number of parties may subsequently be accepted or imitated as a general rule.
3. A treaty may have evidential value as to the existence of a rule which has crystallised into law by an independent process of development.

The essential characteristics of treaties

The essential characteristic of a treaty as a source of law is that it becomes binding on the parties to it by virtue of their consent. While there may be limited circumstances in which a treaty may create rights or duties for third states (see arts 34–37 of the Vienna Convention on the Law of Treaties 1969), it remains the case that a treaty, qua treaty, will only be binding as between its parties.

While treaties will, in most cases, be written instruments concluded between states, the term applies equally to unwritten agreements and to agreements between states and international organisations (eg the Convention on the Privileges and Immunities of the United Nations 1946) and between international organisations. Agreements between states and private parties, while exhibiting many of the characteristics of treaties, and frequently subject to the same rules of interpretation, are generally described by some other terms, eg concessions.

Many treaties, particularly those of a multilateral nature designed to establish general rules of common application, exhibit a mixture of 'legislative' characteristics. There may, for example, be provisions which purport to codify existing rules of customary law, eg art 55 of the Convention on the Law of the Sea 1982 which provides for the recognition of the Exclusive Economic Zone. Equally, a treaty provision may crystallise a developing rule of law, firmly establishing on a legal footing a situation which had hitherto been part of the practice of a limited number of states, eg the Geneva Convention on the Continental Shelf 1958 which placed on a legal footing the practice that had developed amongst some states since 1945 to claim an area of sea-bed off their coast. Finally, treaty provisions may generate rules of law independently of the previous practice of states, eg art 2(4) of the United Nations Charter which prohibits the threat of or the use of force in international relations.

2.3 Custom

The ICJ in the *Asylum Case: Columbia* v *Peru* (1950) ICJ Rep 266 described custom as a 'constant and uniform usage, accepted as law', ie those areas of state practice which arise as a result of a belief by states that they are obliged by law to act in the manner described.

Brownlie lists the following in a non-exhaustive list of the material sources of custom: diplomatic correspondence, policy statements, press releases, the opinions of official legal advisers, official manuals on legal questions (eg manuals of military law), executive decisions and practices, orders to naval forces, etc, comments by governments on drafts produced by the International Law Commission, state legislation, international and national judicial decisions, recitals in treaties and other international instruments, a pattern of treaties in the same form, the practices of international organs, and resolutions relating to legal questions in the United Nations General Assembly: *Principles of Public International Law*, 5th ed, Oxford: Oxford University Press, 1998, p5.

Custom may be either general or regional. General customs are those customary rules binding upon the international community as a whole. Local or regional customs are those applicable to a group of states or just two states in their relations inter se.

In the *Right of Passage Over Indian Territory Case (Merits): Portugal* v *India* (1960) ICJ Rep 6 the ICJ accepted the argument that a rule of regional custom existed between India and Portugal. The Court said:

> 'With regard to Portugal's claim of a right of passage as formulated by it on the basis of local custom, it is objected on behalf of India that no local custom could be established between only two states. It is difficult to see why the number of states between which a local custom may be established on the basis of long practice must necessarily be larger than two. The Court sees no reason why long continued practice between two states accepted by them as regulating their relations should not form the basis of mutual rights and obligations between the two states.'

Local customs may supplement or derogate from general customary international law.

As indicated above, the ICJ in the *Asylum Case* described custom as a constant and uniform usage, accepted as law. The Court did not, however, go on to describe what degree of uniformity of practice and over what duration would be sufficient for the practice to meet the requirement of 'constant and uniform'. Nor did the Court give any indication as to the evidence that would be required before a constant and uniform practice would become a rule of customary law. For example, there is probably a constant and uniform practice to salute the ranking officers in the armed forces of another friendly state. However, it is unlikely that this practice would be regarded as a rule of law. It is rather a rule of comity. In determining which examples of practice are to be regarded as embodying rules of law it is important, therefore, to determine whether that practice is 'accepted as law' by the state carrying out the act. That is, state practice will only be transformed into customary law when the state concerned is conducting itself in the belief that the action is required by law. This element of subjective intention can, however, be extremely difficult to ascertain in practice.

Following the *Asylum Case*, four questions remained for consideration.

1. What duration of practice is required?
2. How uniform and consistent must the practice be to give rise to a rule of law?
3. How is the Court to determine the subjective element in practice, ie an acceptance that the practice is based on law?
4. How general must the practice be in order to bind third states?

Duration of the practice

The jurisprudence of the ICJ indicates that no particular duration is required for practice to become law provided that the consistency and generality of a practice are proved.

In the *North Sea Continental Shelf Cases: Federal Republic of Germany* v *Denmark; Federal Republic of Germany* v *The Netherlands* (1969) ICJ Rep 3 it was recognised that there is no precise length of time during which a practice must exist; simply that it must be followed long enough to show that the other requirements of a custom are satisfied:

'Although the passage of only a short period of time is not necessarily, or of itself, a bar to the formation of a new rule of customary international law on the basis of what was originally a purely conventional rule, an indispensable requirement would be that within the period in question, short though it might be, state practice, including that of states whose interests are specially affected, should have been both extensive and virtually uniform in the sense of the provision invoked – and should moreover have occurred in such a way as to show a general recognition that a rule of law or legal obligation is involved.'

Uniformity and consistency of the practice

It is clear that major inconsistencies in practice will prevent the creation of a rule of customary international law. In the *Asylum Case* the ICJ noted that:

'The facts brought to the knowledge of the Court disclose so much uncertainty and contradiction, so much fluctuation and discrepancy in the exercise of diplomatic asylum and in the official views expressed on different occasions; there has been so much inconsistency in the rapid succession of conventions on asylum, ratified by some states and rejected by others, and the practice has been so much influenced by considerations of political expediency in the various cases, that it is not possible to discern in all this any constant and uniform usage, accepted as law ...'

However, complete uniformity is not required and minor inconsistencies will not prevent the creation of a customary rule provided that there is substantial uniformity. In the *North Sea Continental Shelf Cases*, the Court noted only that state practice should be 'both extensive and virtually uniform'. This question of the uniformity and consistency of practice was returned to by the Court in the *Nicaragua Case: Nicaragua* v *US (Merits)* (1986) ICJ Rep 14 where the ICJ indicated that it was not necessary that all state practice be rigorously consistent in order to establish a rule of custom. It would suffice that conduct in general was consistent with the rule and that instances of practice inconsistent with the rule be treated as breaches of that rule rather than as recognition of a new rule.

Acceptance of the practice as law – opinio juris sive necessitatis

To assume the status of customary international law the rule in question must be regarded by states as being binding in law, ie that they are under a legal obligation to obey it.

In this way customary rules of international law may be distinguished from rules of international comity which are simply based upon a consistent practice of states not accompanied by any feeling of legal obligations, eg the saluting by a ship at sea of another ship flying a different flag.

The distinction between those international rules which create a legal obligation and those which simply permit a state to act in a certain way was illustrated in the *SS Lotus Case: France* v *Turkey* (1927) PCIJ Rep Ser A No 10.

The question before the Court was whether Turkey had the jurisdiction to try the French officer of a French merchant ship which had, through his alleged negligence, collided with a Turkish merchant ship on the high seas, causing loss of life.

Turkey argued before the Court that in the absence of a rule to the contrary, there was a permissive rule empowering her to try the officer. France, however, argued that there was a customary rule imposing a duty on Turkey not to try the officer as previous practice showed that 'questions of jurisdiction in collision cases ... are but rarely encountered in the practice of criminal courts ... in practice prosecutions only occur before the Courts of the state whose flag is flown'.

The Court rejected the French argument, stating:

'Even if the rarity of the judicial decisions to be found among the reported cases were sufficient to prove in point of fact the circumstances alleged by the Agent for the French Government, it would merely show that states had often, in practice, abstained from instituting criminal proceedings, and not that they recognised themselves as being obliged to do so; for only if such abstention were based on their being conscious of having a duty to abstain would it be possible to speak of an international custom. The alleged fact does not allow one to infer that states have been conscious of having such a duty ...'

Can opinio juris or intention be presumed from the general practice of states or must it be strictly proved?

In the *North Sea Continental Shelf Cases* (see above) the ICJ required that opinio juris be strictly proved:

> 'Not only must the acts concerned amount to a settled practice, but they must also be such, or be carried out in such a way, as to be evidence of a belief that this practice is rendered obligatory by the existence of a rule of law requiring it. The need for such a belief, ie the existence of a subjective element, is implicit in the very notion of the opinio juris sive necessitatis. The states concerned must therefore feel that they are conforming to what amounts to a legal obligation. The frequency, or even habitual character of the acts is not in itself enough. There are many international acts, eg in the field of ceremonial and protocol, which are performed almost invariably, but which are motivated only by considerations of courtesy, convenience or tradition, and not by any sense of legal duty.'

A number of the dissenting judges, however, took issue with this strict requirement. Judge Sorenson, echoing comments made years earlier by Sir Hersch Lanterpacht, argued that because of the difficulty in establishing opinio juris, uniform conduct should be taken as implying the requisite intention unless the contrary was established. Judge Tanaka, in contrast, proposed that opinio juris be inferred from evidence of a need for that rule in the international community. In the *Nicaragua Case*, the majority of the Court accepted that, in cases where a rule of customary law existed alongside a rule of treaty law with similar content, opinio juris could be deduced by examining the attitude of the parties to the particular convention. This approach has, however, come in for widespread criticism on the grounds that it confuses two different sources of obligation – a treaty, binding because of the express consent of the parties, and custom, which only becomes law when practice and intention are separately proved. Given the practical difficulties in establishing opinio juris, however, it seems likely that the Court will place increasing emphasis on determining the extent of the practice and will be ready to infer opinio juris from those examples of practice that confirm that the actions in issue are not merely casual acts or acts dictated by international comity.

Generality of the practice

The recognition of a particular rule as a rule of international law by a large number of states raises a presumption that the rule is generally recognised. Such a rule will be binding on states generally and an individual state may only oppose its application by showing that it has persistently objected to the rule from the date of its first formulation.

In the *Anglo-Norwegian Fisheries Case: UK* v *Norway* (1951) ICJ Rep 116, for example, the Court, rejecting the UK argument that the ten-mile closing line for bays was a rule of customary international law, went on to observe that even if it had acquired the status of a rule of customary international law '[i]n any event the ... rule would appear to be inapplicable as against Norway, in as much as she has always opposed any attempt to apply it to the Norwegian coast.'

However, universality is not required to create a customary rule and it will be sufficient if the practice has been followed by a small number of states, provided that there is no practice conflicting with that rule. Therefore, rules of customary law can exist which are not binding on all states: the practice may be limited to a small group of states, or a state may contract out of a custom in the process of formulation.

In the *Asylum Case*, the ICJ stated:

'The Columbian Government has finally invoked "American international law in general" … it has relied on an alleged regional or local custom particular to Latin American states.

   The Party which relies on a custom of this kind must prove that this custom is established in such a manner that it has become binding on the other Party. The Columbian Government must prove that the rule invoked by it is in accordance with a constant and uniform usage practised by the states in question, and that this usage is the expression of a right appertaining to the state granting asylum and a duty incumbent on the territorial state. This follows from Article 38 of the Statute of the Court, which refers to international custom "as evidence of a general practice accepted as law".'

The Court having commented on the uncertainties and contradictions disclosed by the practice of the states concerned continued:

'The Court cannot therefore find that the Columbian Government has proved the existence of such a custom. But even if it could be supposed that such a custom existed between certain Latin American states only, it could not be invoked against Peru which, far from having by its attitude adhered to it, has, on the contrary, repudiated it by refraining from ratifying the Montevideo Conventions of 1933 and 1939, which were the first to include a rule concerning the qualification of the offence in matters of diplomatic asylum.'

The identity crisis 'of international customs'

Many writers argue that customary international law is suffering from an 'identity crisis'. This results from, on the one hand, the de-emphasising of material practice as a constitutive element of international custom and, on the other hand, the tendency to 'count' the articulation of a rule twice, not only as an expression of opinio juris but also as state practice. The inconsistences in the reasoning of the ICJ in the *Nicaragua Case* confirm this tendency: F Kirgis, 'Custom on a Sliding Scale' (1987) 81 AJIL 146.

2.4 The relationship between treaties and custom

As indicated above, treaty provisions will frequently have a close relationship with custom. This relationship flows in both directions: treaties may give rise to rules of custom and treaties may reflect pre-existing or evolving rules of custom. In the *North Sea Continental Shelf Cases* the argument advanced on behalf of Denmark and

The Netherlands was that, even though Germany was not party to the Geneva Convention on the Continental Shelf 1958 and was not, therefore, bound by art 6 of that Convention in respect of the delimitation of the shelf, a rule of customary law of similar content had developed since the adoption of the Convention.

The Court accepted that a provision in a treaty could indeed generate a rule of customary law which would become binding on third parties. However, it indicated that this process is not to be lightly inferred. The Court continued to lay down a number of conditions that would have to be satisfied before the process could be accepted.

1. The provision should be of a fundamentally norm-creating character.
2. While a very widespread and representative participation in the Convention would suffice, such participation must include those states whose interests would be specially affected by the provision in question. A treaty rule could not become binding on third parties as a rule of custom if those third parties had not shown their consent to the rule.
3. Within the period of time since the adoption of the Convention, state practice, including that of states whose interests are specially affected, must have been both extensive and virtually uniform.

In other words, for a treaty provision to become binding as a rule of customary international law, the party invoking the rule must be in a position to show that the rule meets all the general requirements for the creation of customary law.

This approach by the Court was further advanced by Judge Arechaga who suggested that a treaty may reflect custom in one of three ways:

1. it may be declarative of custom, ie it may codify a pre-existing rule of customary law;
2. it may crystallise a rule of custom in statu nascendi, ie in the process of development;
3. it may serve to generate a rule of custom in the future; ie a treaty rule may come to be accepted as a rule of custom.

The process of concluding a treaty will of itself have important consequences for the content of the rule of custom. In the first case above, for example, it is likely that the process of codification will alter the content of the customary rule. The very act of putting down in words what had hitherto been a flexible, unwritten rule will exert an influence on the content of that rule. Equally, the process of interpreting and amending a rule of treaty law will be different from that relating to custom. The fact that a treaty purports to codify custom does not mean, therefore, that the content of the rule will remain the same.

In the second case – that of crystallisation – the act of concluding the treaty may be an important example of state practice. The treaty-making process, with its detailed discussions on the content of the rule and inevitable compromises between parties, may see the content of the emerging rule change. The objective of certainty in the treaty provisions may thus be achieved at the expense of the flexibility of the rule of custom.

The argument in the *North Sea Continental Shelf Cases* discussed above provides an example of generative treaty provisions. A more recent example arose in the context of the *Nicaragua Case*. In that case the ICJ accepted that art 2(4) of the United Nations Charter – a treaty provision prohibiting the threat of or the use of force – had, together with other instruments such as General Assembly resolutions, the effect of generating a rule of customary law of similar content to art 2(4) which existed side by side with the treaty provisions.

The relationship of treaty law to customary law is important in one other respect. In the event of a conflict between a rule of treaty and a rule of custom which rule prevails? While it nevertheless is generally accepted that art 38(1) of the Statute of the International Court of Justice does not create a strict hierarchy of sources of law, it is possible to discern a number of principles and propositions relating to the hierarchy of sources:

1. general rules of interpretation apply; eg the principles of lex posterior – a new treaty replaces an old treaty (see art 30 of the Vienna Convention on the Law of Treaties 1969) – and lex specialis – a special rule prevails over a general rule – will be relevant in the event of conflicting treaty provisions;
2. the *North Atlantic Fisheries Arbitration: US* v *Great Britain* (1910) 11 RIAA 167 establishes the principle that developments in customary law will not relieve a state of its obligations under a treaty;
3. Article 103 of the UN Charter provides that the Charter is to prevail over any inconsistent treaty obligations – a number of commentators have suggested that this provision would apply equally to inconsistent customary law;
4. perhaps the clearest proposition is that to be found in arts 53 and 64 of the Vienna Convention on the Laws of Treaties 1969 which provides that a treaty that is in conflict with a rule of ius cogens – peremptory rules of international law – will be void. In such circumstances, therefore, rules of custom will prevail over inconsistent treaty provisions.

These propositions not withstanding, the better view is probably that whether the Court will apply a rule of custom or conflicting rule of treaty law will depend largely on the circumstances of the case in issue.

2.5 General principles of law

Article 38(1)(c) of the Statute of the ICJ refers to 'the general principles of law recognised by civilised nations'. Sir Hersch Lauterpacht noted that this provision was first introduced into the Statute of the PCIJ by the Commission of Jurists charged with drawing it up in order to avoid the problem of 'non-liquet' – the argument that a court could not decide a matter because there was no law on the subject: Lauterpacht, *International Law*, vol 1, Cambridge: Cambridge University Press, 1970, p69 et seq. If there is no treaty relevant to the dispute, or if there is no rule of customary international law that can be applied, the Court is directed to apply general principles of law.

The meaning and scope of art 38(1)(c)

There is little agreement as to the precise significance of the phrase.

In the course of discussion by the Advisory Committee of Jurists on art 38(1)(c) Lord Phillimore, the author of that provision, stated that:

'The general principles referred to ... those which were accepted by all nations in foro domestico, such as certain principles of procedure, the principle of good faith, and the principle of res judicata, etc': procès-verbal of the Committee (1920), p335.

Oppenheim states that: 'The intention is to authorise the Court to apply the general principles of municipal jurisprudence, in particular of private law, insofar as they are applicable to relations of state'.

In this way private law, being in general more developed than international law, has provided a reserve store of legal principles upon which international law can draw. The inclusion of art 38(1)(c) has therefore been seen as a rejection of the positivist doctrine, according to which international law consists solely of rules to which states have given their consent, and as affirming the naturalist doctrine whereby if there appeared to be a gap in the rules of international law recourse could be had to general principles of law, ie to natural law. For example, the writers of the seventeenth and eighteenth centuries, when dealing with questions as to the acquisition of territory, turned for assistance to the rules of Roman private law.

The difficulty in evaluating the role of these general principles, however, is that art 38(1)(c) does not make clear if it is referring to general principles of international law recognised by civilised nations or general principles of law in the broadest sense, including principles of private law which have their counterpart in most developed legal systems.

References by international tribunals to general principles of law

It is difficult to establish the precise extent to which general principles have been used by international tribunals as specific reference to such sources is rarely made in their judgments. However, some references do exist. For example: In the *Chorzow Factory Case (Indemnity) (Merits): Germany* v *Poland* (1928) PCIJ Rep Ser A No 17, 29 the Permanent Court of International Justice stated that 'the Court observes that it is a principle of international law, and even a general concept of law, that any breach of an engagement involves an obligation to make reparation'.

In the *Eastern Carelia Case (Advisory Opinion)* (1923) PCIJ Rep Ser B No 5 the Court referred to the independence of states as being a 'fundamental principle of international law'.

Some examples of municipal principles of law adopted by international tribunals

Res judicata: *United Nations Administrative Tribunal Case* (1973) ICJ Rep 166

The ICJ referred to the 'well established and generally recognised principle of law [that] a judgment rendered by a judicial body is res judicata and has binding force between the parties to the dispute'.

Estoppel: *Temple of Preah Vihear Case* (1962) ICJ Rep 6

The ICJ was asked to rule that Cambodia and not Thailand, had sovereignty over the Temple of Preah Vihear. In 1904 the boundary between Cambodia (then a French protectorate) and Thailand (then Siam) was determined by a treaty between France and Siam under which a map was prepared which placed the Temple in Cambodia. The Siamese received and accepted the map without protest and in 1930 a Siamese Prince actually paid a state visit to the disputed area where he was officially received by the French authorities.

The Court with reference to these facts stated that:

'Even if there were any doubt as to Siam's acceptance of the map in 1908, and hence of the frontier indicated thereon, the Court would consider, in the light of the subsequent course of events, that Thailand is now precluded by her conduct from asserting that she did not accept it.'

Circumstantial evidence: *Corfu Channel Case*: *United Kingdom* v *Albania* *(Merits)* (1949) ICJ Rep 4

The ICJ remarked that 'this indirect evidence is admitted in all systems of law, and its use is recognised by international decisions'.

Other examples of municipal principles adopted by international tribunals include prescription; the rule that no man may be judge in his own suit, etc.

The application by international tribunals of general principles

As illustrated above, international tribunals have not been slow in having recourse to general principles of law in the absence of other rules of international law or in order to complement their application. There remains, however, the question of the manner in which these rules are applied. Are they, for example, imparted into international law directly from one or other municipal legal system? This issue was addressed by Lord McNair in his Separate Opinion in the *South West Africa Case* (1950) ICJ Rep 128 in which South Africa's obligations under the mandate were considered. Drawing analogies with the municipal concept of a trust, McNair, however, indicated that international law would not import 'lock, stock and barrel' principles found in municipal legal systems. It was rather a question of finding legal principles appropriate to the case in issue and to apply them in a manner consistent with international law.

A similar approach has more recently been adopted by the European Court of Justice (ECJ) in its protection of fundamental rights within the Community legal order. The Treaty of Rome provides no explicit protection for fundamental human rights. In many cases, however, fundamental rights are safeguarded by the laws and constitutions of the member states. In *Internationale Handelsgesellschaft GmbH* v *Einfuhr und Vorratsstelle für Getriede und Futtermittel* Case 11/70 [1970] ECR 1125 the ECJ confirmed that fundamental rights formed part of the general principles of law protected by the Court. While, however, the protection of these rights may be inspired by the constitutional traditions of the member states, the application of these principles must be ensured within the framework, and according to the objectives, of the Community.

Apart from the manner of application of general principles, the question also arises as to the ambit of the search before a principle can be applied as a general principle of law. Would it be sufficient, for example, that a principle was found in one municipal legal system? If not, how common must be the principle to be accorded the status of a general principle? The better view seems to be that there is no hard and fast rule on the matter. Much will depend on the nature of the case before the Court, the parties to the case and any special agreement concluded giving the Court or tribunal jurisdiction. In the *LIAMCO* v *Libya* (1981) 20 ILM 1, for example, the arbitration agreement provided that the tribunal should apply principles common to Libyan law and international law and, failing this, general principles of law. Arbitrator Mahmassani, in applying this clause, looked at principles of law found in common law and Arab legal systems.

2.6 Judicial decisions

Article 38(1)(d) of the Statute of the ICJ directs the Court to apply:

'... subject to the provisions of Article 59, judicial decisions ... as subsidiary means for the determination of rules of law.'

Article 59 of the Statute of the Court provides that:

'The decision of the Court has no binding force except between the parties and in respect of that particular case.'

There is, therefore, no binding authority of precedent in international law, and international court and tribunal cases do not make law. Judicial decisions are not, therefore, strictly speaking a formal source of law.

It can be argued, however, that if an international tribunal is unable to discover an existing treaty or customary rule relevant to a dispute, any rule which the tribunal adopts in deciding the case will, in theory at least, form a new rule of international law. The question is whether the new rule is a rule of customary law or whether the tribunal's decision may itself, be regarded as a source of international law.

Several decisions of the ICJ have introduced innovations into international law which have subsequently won general acceptance.

In the *Anglo-Norwegian Fisheries Case: UK* v *Norway* (1951) ICJ Rep 116 Norway had promulgated a series of decrees claiming as the baseline of Norwegian territorial waters the general line of the Skjaergaard – a series of islands and rocks stretching along Norway's north-western coast, often at a considerable distance from the mainland. As a result a large area of what was formerly high seas became enclosed as Norwegian national waters and closed to British fishing.

The UK contested the legality of Norway's acts before the ICJ. The Court held that the method of baselines employed by Norway was not contrary to international law given, inter alia, the special geographical facts involved and the economic interests peculiar to the region.

The Court in effect, therefore, created a new rule of international law for the delimitation of the territorial sea in those parts of the world where peculiar geographical and economic factors are present.

In *Reparations for Injuries Suffered in the Service of the United Nations* (1949) ICJ Rep 174 the ICJ was asked to advise whether the United Nations had the right to present a claim on the international plane against a state for injuries suffered by United Nations officials in the performance of their duties. The Court decided that the United Nations could claim damages under international law against a state responsible for injuries suffered by its officials.

The Court's decision that such a power could be implied from the express functions entrusted to the Organisation was clearly an extension of the rights of the Organisation as laid down in the Charter and thus created a new principle in international law.

Judicial precedent and the Statute of the Court

Article 59 of the Statute was intended to prevent the Court from establishing a binding system of judicial precedent.

In the *Certain German Interests in Polish Upper Silesia Case* (1926) PCIJ Rep Ser A No 7 the Court stated that:

> 'The object of [Article 59] is simply to prevent legal principles accepted by the Court in a particular case from being binding on other states or in other disputes.'

In its practices the Court has, however, of necessity followed previous decisions in the interests of judicial consistency, and has where necessary distinguished its previous decisions from the case actually being heard. This is well illustrated by the *Interpretation of Peace Treaties Case* (1950) ICJ Rep 65 in which the General Assembly of the United Nations requested an advisory opinion regarding the interpretation of the peace treaties with Bulgaria, Hungary and Rumania. The three states refused to take part in the proceedings before the Court and it was argued that, following the *Eastern Carelia Case (Advisory Opinion)* (1923) PCIJ Rep Ser B

No 5, the Court should decline to give an advisory opinion. In the *Eastern Carelia Case* the Court had held it to be a fundamental principle that a state could not, without its consent, be forced to submit its dispute to arbitration or judicial settlement.

The Court in rejecting this argument said:

'Article 65 of the Statute is permissive. It gives the Court the power to examine whether the circumstances of the case are of such a character as should lead it to decide to answer the Request. In the opinion of the Court, the circumstances of the present case are profoundly different from those which were before the Permanent Court of International Justice in the *Eastern Carelia Case* [Advisory Opinion No 5], when that Court declined to give an Opinion because it found the question put to it was directly related to the main point of dispute actually pending between two states, so that answering the question would be substantially equivalent to deciding the dispute between the parties, and that at the same time it raised a question of fact which could not be elucidated without hearing both parties.

... the present Request for an Opinion is solely concerned with the applicability to certain disputes of the procedure for settlement instituted by the Peace Treaties, and it is justifiable to conclude that it in no way touches the merits of those disputes.'

Decisions of national courts

Article 38(1)(d) of the Statute of the Court is not confined to international decisions. Although not in the same category as international courts and tribunals, the decisions of municipal courts do have some evidential value. It should also be noted that decisions of municipal courts will form part of the practice of a state for the purposes of deciding on rules of custom.

Additionally, municipal decisions may be important sources of material on sovereign and diplomatic immunity and the laws of prize.

2.7 The writings of publicists

Article 38(1)(d) directs the Court to apply:

'The teachings of the most highly qualified publicists of the various nations, as subsidiary means for the determination of rules of law.'

Although this source only constitutes evidence of customary law, learned writings can also play a subsidiary role in developing new rules of law.

The contributions of writers such as Grotius, Bynkershoek and Vattel were very important to the formulation and development of international law, and writers of general works, such as Oppenheim, Hall, Hyde, Guggenheim and Rousseau, have international reputations. Although it is sometimes argued that some writers reflect national and other prejudices, their opinions are used widely by legal advisers to states, arbitral tribunals and courts. Their value has been described by Gray J of the US Supreme Court, in *The Paquete Habana* 175 US 677 (1900) at 700, as follows:

'International law is part of our law, and must be ascertained and administered by the courts of justice of appropriate jurisdiction, as often as questions of right depending upon it are duly presented for their determination. For this purpose, where there is no treaty, and no controlling executive or legislative act or judicial decision, resort must be had to the customs and usages of civilised nations; and as evidence of these, to the works of jurists and commentators who by years of labour, research, and experience have made themselves peculiarly well acquainted with the subjects of which they treat. Such works are resorted to by judicial tribunals, not for the speculations of their authors concerning what the law ought to be, but for trustworthy evidence of what the law really is.'

2.8 Other sources of international law

As indicated at the outset, the sources of law enumerated in art 38(1) of the Statute are often regarded as comprising the sum of the traditional sources of international law. Increasingly, however, this approach is subject to limitation as international courts and tribunals look to additional sources to give them guidance on the law. Many of these 'new' sources may be squeezed within existing headings. Given the evolution of international law and the changes taking place in international society it may, however, be more sensible to look to such sources as additional sources of law. The most important of these sources of law are as follows.

General Assembly resolutions (GARs) and resolutions of other international organisations

There is often confusion in the approach by many writers to the question of whether GARs constitute a source of international law. Under the provisions of the Charter the majority of such resolutions have no direct legal effect (unlike decisions of the Security Council which, under art 25, are binding). However, it is clear that some resolutions embody a clear consensus of the international community. Other resolutions may be very significant in influencing the development of international law and practice.

Attempt is often made to fit GARs into the parameters of either treaty or custom. Clearly, such resolutions do not conform to the formal requirements of a treaty and it may perhaps be unrealistic to apply treaty rules on interpretation, amendment etc, to them. Equally, GARs do not on their face meet the requirements laid down for customary law – constant and uniform usage accepted as law. The compromise is to regard GARs – and resolutions of other international bodies – as evidence of customary law. The weight of the evidence would be determined by considering all the relevant factors surrounding the adoption of the resolution in question – the degree of support for the resolution; whether or not that support was widespread amongst ideologically or politically divided groups; the intention of states in voting for the resolution as illustrated by the debates; the form of words used, etc. This approach was adopted by arbitrator Dupuy in *Texaco* v *Libya* (1977) 53

ILR 389 in which he considered the legal effect of two General Assembly resolutions: GAR 1803 (XVII) on the Permanent Sovereignty over Natural Resources and GAR 3281 (XXIX), the Charter of Economic Rights and Duties of States. Although GAR 3281 was adopted 12 years after GAR 1803 with very strong support from developing states – 120 votes in favour, six against (Belgium, Denmark, the Federal Republic of Germany, Luxembourg, the UK and the US) and ten abstentions – Dupuy concluded that it was GAR 1803 that reflected existing customary law. The reasoning behind this was that GAR 1803 had achieved wide support from both the capital-importing (developing) states and capital-exporting (Western) states. GAR 1803 was therefore illustrative of a broad consensus between the groups likely to be affected by its provisions. In contrast, GAR 3281 had received virtually no support from capital-exporting states. To be regarded as evidencing customary law, a resolution must be seen to have gathered support from a broad cross-section of the international community.

A further example where resolutions of the General Assembly were held to be reflective of customary international law arose in the *Nicaragua Case: Nicaragua* v *US (Merits)* (1986) ICJ Rep 14. In that case the majority of the Court considered that GAR 2625 (XXV), the Declaration on Principles of International Law Concerning Friendly Relations and Co-operation among States, was illustrative of customary law. While there is little dispute about the relative importance of this resolution, or about the broad measure of support it achieved (it was adopted by consensus), some commentators have voiced concern at the manner in which the Court accepted that the resolution could be evidence of both state practice and opinio juris for the purposes of establishing custom. Any acceptance of this dual characteristic of such resolutions would have the effect of elevating GAR to a form of 'instant custom'. This approach remains highly controversial.

Equity

Equity is most frequently regarded as coming within the concept of general principles of law discussed above. Certainly, this will be true in many respects as has been illustrated in the context of the doctrine of estoppel and good faith generally. It is clear, however, that international tribunals have resorted to equity or equitable principles quite apart from general principles derived from municipal law. Perhaps the best example of this wider definition of equity is to be found in the concept of 'relevant circumstances' employed by the Court in cases of maritime delimitation. Resort to equity in these circumstances may be more easily assimilated with resort to principles of fairness and justice. It is nevertheless important to stress that equity in this context remains an element of a legal decision. It must be contrasted with the ex aequo et bono provision in art 38(2) of the Statute of the ICJ. In the *Gulf of Maine Case: Canada* v *US* (1984) ICJ Rep 246 the Court held that while the latter would permit a Court or tribunal to examine socio-economic and political considerations, equity as a component of a legal decision would involve the Court in taking a decision on the basis of legal reasoning.

Other sources of law

Treaties not yet in force

While the provisions of a treaty not yet in force will not be binding qua treaty provisions they may be persuasive as between those states that have signed and ratified the treaty. Note also that art 18 of the Vienna Convention on the Law of Treaties 1969 imposes a positive obligation on a state that has indicated its consent to be barred from defeating the object and purposes of a treaty.

Draft treaties and texts adopted by the International Law Commission

While such 'sources' of law are often regarded as writings of publicists, the significance of such attempts at the codification or development of international law require, perhaps, that they be considered as an independent 'source' or evidence of law.

International trade practice and usage

A number of commentators have suggested that there is a developing body of lex mercatoria which may be applied by international courts and tribunals in the case of disputes involving questions of international trade.

2.9 The International Law Commission

Customary rules lack precision and are difficult to evidence. The idea of codification of customary rules originates from the time of the Vienna Congress of 1815 when the participating states felt a need for codifying rules in areas of great importance to them, such as the legal regime of international rivers, the prohibition of slavery and the regulation of diplomatic relations. This was further developed by private societies and institutions such as the Institute de Droit International and the International Law Association, both founded in 1873. The two Hague Peace Conferences of 1899 and 1907 accomplished an enormous task by codifying the most important customary rules relating to the conduct of war. World War I prevented the third Hague Peace Conference from ever taking place. After World War I the Assembly of the League of Nations set up the first permanent organ – the Committee of Experts – to examine matters 'sufficiently ripe' for regulation through international conventions. Three areas were selected by the Committee of Experts – nationality, the territorial sea and some aspects of state responsibility – as being ready for codification. The League of Nations convened the Hague Codification Conference in 1930 which produced rather unsatisfactory results as only certain aspects of nationality were agreed by the participating states to be regulated by international conventions.

At the 1945 San Francisco Conference when the Charter of the United Nations was being discussed the idea of directly investing the United Nations with full legislative powers was rejected, but the proposal to have a body entrusted with the codification of international law was viewed with favour. The General Assembly was invited to initiate studies to 'encourage the progressive development of international law and its codification'. The General Assembly responded by setting up a Committee entrusted with examining the matter. On the basis of a report from the Committee the General Assembly adopted Resolution 174 (II) in November 1947 establishing the International Law Commission (ILC). At its first session in 1949 the ILC reviewed topics for possible study and decided to select fourteen topics for codification:

1. recognition of states and governments;
2. succession of states and governments;
3. jurisdictional immunities of states and their property;
4. jurisdiction with regard to crimes committed outside national territory;
5. regime of the high seas;
6. regime of territorial waters;
7. nationality and statelessness;
8. treatment of aliens;
9. right of asylum;
10. law of treaties;
11. diplomatic intercourse and immunities;
12. consular intercourse and immunities;
13. state responsibility;
14. arbitral procedure.

This list was considered as provisional, but in fact has become the Commission's basic long-term programme. Out of the 14 topics the Commission has submitted final drafts of, or reports on, all but four. These are:

1. recognition of states and governments;
2. jurisdiction with regards to crimes committed outside national territory;
3. treatment of aliens;
4. right of asylum.

In respect of items (2) and (3) of the list of topics not yet examined, the ILC, at its fifty-sixth session held in the summer of 2004, decided to include the topic 'expulsion of aliens' in its current programme of work, and agreed to include the topic 'obligation to extradite or prosecute' (aut dedere aut judicare) in its long-term programme of work.

Under the Statute of the ILC the General Assembly as well as Members of the UN and other authorised agencies are entitled to refer topics for study to the ILC, although the ILC may also choose topics for codification. However, requests from the General Assembly have priority over other proposals. The ILC has studied, or is studying, a number of topics referred to it by the General Assembly, for example:

1. formulation of the Nuremberg principles;

2. the question of defining aggression;
3. a Draft Code of Crimes against Peace and Security of Mankind;
4. the question of the protection and inviolability of diplomatic agents and other persons entitled to special protection under international law;
5. the law and practice relating to reservations to treaties, etc.

The ILC is made up of 34 members elected by the General Assembly from candidates nominated by the member states of the UN. They serve in their individual capacity and are independent of any government. They are elected on the basis of equitable geographical distribution so as to represent the major legal systems of the world. The ILC holds its sessions in Geneva and meets annually in open session for 12 weeks. The Commission elects its officers for each session, consisting of a Chairman, First Vice-Chairman and Second-Vice Chairman of the Drafting Committee and a General Rapporteur who is charged with the task of drafting the Commission's annual report to the General Assembly. They form the Bureau of the ILC and together with former chairmen and special rapporteurs they constitute the Enlarged Bureau which meets in private and has an overall recommendation function. The ILC also has a Planning Group made up of 11 members and a Drafting Committee made up of 14 members.

The two main tasks of the ILC are the codification of international law, which is defined as the more precise formulation and systematisation of the existing customary rules of international law, and the progressive development of international law, which involves the creation of new rules of international law either by means of the regulation of a new topic or by means of the revision of the existing rules. The second task normally requires the preparation of international conventions. When a topic for study is selected by the ILC, it appoints a special rapporteur who is entrusted with the task of preparing a report on the subject. At this stage governments may be requested to provide texts of law, statutes, judicial decisions and diplomatic correspondence relevant to the topic under consideration. The special rapporteur submits a report, normally in the form of draft articles with commentaries, which are discussed by the Commission. Once the Commission reaches an agreement on the provisional draft articles it submits it to the General Assembly and to the governments for their written observations. Under the current procedure the governments have about one year to reply. The observations are received by the special rapporteur who in the light of these prepares a new report. The ILC on the basis of the report and observations of governments and the General Assembly (Sixth Committee) adopts a final draft which is forwarded to the General Assembly and which contains a recommendation regarding further action. Such action may consist of the adoption of the report by resolution, or of the recommendation of the draft for the conclusion of a convention or the convening of an international conference with a view to the conclusion of a convention.

The number of international conventions and resolutions prepared by the ILC is impressive. The ILC has fulfilled its task of developing and codifying international law with great professionalism and dedication.

2.10 Soft law

It has been submitted that international law consists of rules of varying degrees of force. Some of them, for example rules in international treaties, contain binding obligations while others, such as acts of international organisations, for example resolutions or declarations of the General Assembly, contain standards of behaviour or ideals which the international community aspires to achieve but are not binding. The influence of non-binding rules on the development of international law and on state practice is considerable, although these rules cannot be classified as law in the positive sense. There is an agreement that both types of rules should be considered as law, although a distinction should be made between the two. Non-binding rules are called 'soft law' whilst binding rules are considered as 'hard law'.

'Soft law' has many advantages. It allows states to participate in the creation of new rules without the necessity of implementing them into national law. In many areas, such as the protection of the environment, states are not ready to accept binding obligations at a particular time but are gradually taking measures to conform with international standards.

2.11 Ius cogens

The introduction of ius cogens, or peremptory rules, into international law was inspired by the national law analogy which firmly establishes the hierarchy of legal rules.

Many municipal laws make a distinction between imperative rules, that is rules referring to public order from which no derogation is permitted, and others which parties in their private transactions can ignore and replace according to their wishes (ius dispositivum). The consequence of a breach of an imperative rule is nullity. In the hierarchy of norms, imperative rules are superior to any other rules. Their superiority is evidenced by the fact that their violation entails nullity of the transaction concerned. The transposition of this idea into international law entails that some rules of international law are fundamental or of a higher order as being rules of international public order. This idea has been advanced by Grotius, who made a reference to ius strictum, and further developed by the modern school of natural law.

When the International Law Commission was preparing the Draft Articles on the Law of Treaties it carefully examined the matter of peremptory rules and decided to introduce them into international law. Article 53 defines a peremptory norm as:

'... a norm accepted and recognised by the international community of states as a whole as a norm from which no derogation is permitted and which can be modified only by a subsequent norm of general international law having the same character.'

Therefore states cannot deviate from a peremptory rule. A new state must accept it. It cannot be changed without the approval of the international community as a whole. Article 53 provides that a treaty in conflict with a peremptory norm is void.

The ius dispositivum nature of most rules of international law is based on the fact that a group of states may substitute one conventional rule for another. A peremptory rule cannot be derogated from. The prohibition is absolute. The legal consequences of violation of a peremptory rule and other rules of international law has been examined by the ILC in its Draft Articles on State Responsibility 1980: see Chapter 10.

The 1969 Vienna Convention does not freeze the rules of ius cogens. To the contrary, its art 64 highlights the evolutive nature of ius cogens. It states that 'if a new peremptory norm of general law emerges, any existing treaty which is in conflict with that norm becomes void and terminates'.

When the ILC was preparing the Draft of the 1969 Convention on the Law of Treaties it refrained from suggesting a list of peremptory rules. However, later in art 19 of the Draft Articles on State Responsibility, which article was subsequently deleted and does not appear in the final version, the ILC provided some indications as to what should be considered as peremptory rules. The ILC, first, defined an international crime as an internationally wrongful act which results from the breach by a state of an obligation 'so essential for the protection of fundamental interests of the international community that its breach is recognised as a crime by that community as a whole' and, second, provided some examples of international crimes such as:

1. serious breaches of the law on peace and security, such as that prohibiting aggression;
2. serious breaches of the right to self-determination;
3. serious breaches of international duties on safeguarding human rights (eg slavery, genocide, apartheid);
4. serious breaches of obligations to protect the environment such as those prohibiting massive pollution of the atmosphere or the seas.

The ILC in its commentary on art 40 of the Articles on State Responsibility 2001 noted that the concept of ius cogens had been recognised in international practice, in the jurisprudence of international and national courts and in legal doctrine. Whilst the ILC refused to provide an exhaustive list of peremptory norms, it did give examples of such rules. These were: the prohibition of aggression; the prohibition of slavery and the slave trade; the prohibition of genocide; the prohibition of racial discrimination; the prohibition of apartheid; and the prohibition of torture. The ILC noted that rules recognised by the ICJ as being intransgressible in character (some rules of international humanitarian law: see *Legality of the Threat or Use of Nuclear Weapons (Advisory Opinion)* (1996) ICJ 226) and those which give rise to an obligation to the international community as a whole to act in order to ensure their respect (ie the right to self-determination: see *East Timor Case: Portugal v Australia* (1995) ICJ Rep 90 and *Legal Consequences of the Construction of a Wall in the Occupied Palestinian Territory (Advisory Opinion Delivered by the International Court of Justice on 9 July 2004)* (2004) 43 ILM 1009) should be regarded as peremptory norms.

The international community has not agreed on any list of peremptory rules. In the *Barcelona Traction, Light and Power Co Ltd Case (Second Phase): Belgium v Spain* (1970) ICJ Rep 4 at paras 33–34 the ICJ made a distinction between mere bilateral obligations and the obligations of a state 'towards the international community as a whole'. The ICJ stated that:

> 'Such obligations derive, for example, in contemporary international law, from the outlawing of acts of aggression, and of genocide, as also from the principles and rules concerning the basic rights of the human person, including protection from slavery and racial discrimination.'

In the advisory opinion the ICJ noted that the obligations violated by Israel included certain erga omnes obligations. The Court specified those erga omnes obligations as being the right of the Palestinian people to self-determination (*East Timor Case*) and certain obligations under international humanitarian law which are so fundamental that they must be observed by all States, irrespective of whether or not a State is a contracting party to the Geneva Conventions. Those obligations under international humanitarian law, because they constitute intransgressible principles of customary international law, have acquired an erga omnes character. With regard to the construction of the wall by Israel in the Occupied Palestinian Territory, the erga omnes character of the above obligations requires that no State must recognise the illegal situation created by the construction of the wall in the Occupied Palestinian Territory, and that all States must abstain from rendering any aid or assistance in maintaining the situation resulting from such construction, and must bring to an end any impediment (resulting from the construction of the wall) to the exercise by the Palestinian people of their right to self-determination.

In the *Nicaragua* case the ICJ regarded the prohibition of the use of force as being 'a conspicuous example of a rule of international law having the character of ius cogens'.

The International Tribunal for the Former Yugoslavia in *Furundzija* IT–95–17/1 'Lasva Valley' (1999) 38 ILM 317 recognised that the prohibition of torture had acquired the status of ius cogens. This should be viewed, however, in the light of the judgment of the ICJ in the *Case Concerning the Arrest Warrant of 11 April 2000: Democratic Republic of Congo v Belgium (Preliminary Objections and Merits)* (2002) 41 ILM 536, and the judgment of the European Court of Human Rights in *Al-Adsani v United Kingdom* (2002) 34 EHRR 11 in which state immunity was maintained in respect of high-ranking officials who were accused of committing acts of torture whilst in office. The ICJ in the *Arrest Warrant* case above avoided any reference to the prohibition of torture as being a peremptory norm. Judge Al-Khasawneh, in his dissenting opinion, criticised the judgment on the ground, inter alia, that the ICJ failed to recognise the prohibition of torture as being of ius cogens character and consequently as taking precedence over the rules on immunity: see the section on ius cogens and human rights in Chapter 12.

On a national level, the Swiss Conseil d'Etat in 1995 annulled a national referendum intended to revise the Swiss Constitution on the ground that the proposed revision would call into question art 33 of the Geneva Convention Regarding the Status of Refugees 1951, which article had acquired the status of ius cogens: J-F Flauss, 'Le contrôle de la validité internationale des initiatives populaires en Suisse' (1995) RFDC 625.

In the light of the above there is no doubt that the concept of ius cogens is recognised under public international law, although it still raises many controversies taking into account uncertainty surrounding its content, the manner in which new rules of ius cogens may be created, and the process of recognition of ius cogens by the international community, etc.

3

International Law and Municipal Law

3.1 Introduction

3.2 The relationship between international law and municipal law

3.3 The application of municipal law before international tribunals

3.4 The application of international law in UK courts

3.5 EC law in UK courts

3.1 Introduction

The relationship between international law and municipal law gives rise to two main problems. First, the theoretical question as to whether international law and municipal law are part of a universal legal order (monist doctrine) or whether they form two distinct systems of law (dualist doctrine).

Second, the situation where there exists a conflict between the rules of international law and the rules of municipal law before an international tribunal, or before a municipal court.

3.2 The relationship between international law and municipal law

The relationship between international law and municipal law is of more than just academic interest. As well as the jurisprudential issues concerning the relationship between the two systems of law (eg whether they form part of one all-embracing legal system but with different spheres of operation or whether they form two distinct systems) it will often be important to determine the scope of application of rules of international law before domestic tribunals and vice versa.

At the jurisprudential level, the relationship between international law and municipal law has been cast in terms of the monist/dualist debate. At the level of the practical application of international law before UK courts, this debate is cast in terms of the incorporation/transformation debate. While these debates are important, it is in the nature of things that they focus on general issues. The actual relationship between international law and English law can only be properly understood by examining the jurisprudence of English law on the matter of the application of treaties, custom and other sources of international law in the English courts.

Public international law leaves each country to decide on the relationship between international and municipal law. In this respect, there are two theories: dualist and monist.

Dualism

The dualist doctrine considers international law and municipal law as two independent and separate systems. It is based on the view that international law is the law applicable between sovereign states and that municipal law applies within a state to regulate the activities of its citizens. On this basis, neither legal system has the power to create or alter rules of the other.

Where there is a conflict between international law and municipal law, municipal courts following the dualist doctrine would give precedence to municipal law.

In respect of an international treaty, the dualist theory entails that a duly ratified international treaty produces legal effect only at the international level, that is, it is only binding on the contracting states. In order to be applied by national courts it is necessary to transform an international treaty into the state's legal system to enable it to take effect at the national level. The reception of international law by municipal law constitutes the most important feature of the dualist doctrine. However, once an international provision is implemented in national law, it is applied by national courts as any other municipal provision and not as an international one.

Monism

Monism considers international law and municipal law to be both part of the same legal order and emphasises the supremacy of international law even within the municipal sphere. Its advocates, such as the late Sir Hersch Lauterpacht, considered a supreme universal law a more trustworthy repository of civilised values than the municipal law of the nation state and thus better equipped to protect international human rights: see *International Law: Collected Papers*, Cambridge: Cambridge University Press, 1957, pp151–177 and *International Law and Human Rights*, Hamden, Conn: Archen, 1968.

Under the monist doctrine the unity between international and municipal law means that international treaties automatically become law within a contracting state. It is directly applicable. There is no need for reception of an international treaty as it becomes an integral part of national law of a contracting state once the procedure for its ratification is completed. An international provision is applied by municipal courts as such and not as a provision of domestic law.

The Fitzmaurice doctrine

Sir Gerald Fitzmaurice sought to overcome the conflict between the monist and dualist schools by challenging their common premise that there exists a common field in which the two legal orders both simultaneously have their spheres of activity: 'The General Principles of International Law Considered from the Standpoint of the Rule of Law' 92 Recueil des Cours (1957–11), p5 et seq.

He argued that the two systems do not come into conflict as systems since they operate in different spheres, each being supreme in its own field. Formally, therefore, international and domestic law as systems can never come into conflict.

There may, however, occur a conflict of obligations, or an inability on the part of the state on the domestic plane to act in a manner required by international law. In such cases if nothing can be, or is, done to deal with the matter, it does not invalidate the local law, but the state will, on the international plane, have committed a breach of its international law obligations for which it will be internationally responsible.

On a practical level, whether or not the municipal courts follow the monist, dualist or Fitzmaurice approach to the relationship of international law and municipal law, the matter will be determined by the constitutional law of the state concerned. Thus, the constitutions of many of the civil law states of continental Europe provide expressly that customary international law is to be regarded as part of the domestic law of the state concerned. So, for example, art 10 of the Italian constitution provides that 'Italian law shall be in conformity with the generally recognised rules of international law'.

Common law traditions have also largely accepted this principle in the case of customary international law. In the UK, for example, the accepted view is still probably that customary law forms part of the law of the land to be applied by English courts unless it is in conflict with a provision of statute.

As with customary law, the reception of treaty law into domestic law will be determined by the constitutional traditions of the state concerned. Once again, many of the civil law states of continental Europe accept as a general premise that treaties may be directly applicable by the courts of that state. The approach of common law systems is frequently more confusing. In the United States, for example, a treaty may only be ratified with the approval of two-thirds of the Senate (unlike the UK where no parliamentary involvement is required for the conclusion of a treaty). Although the constitution provides that treaties shall be the 'supreme law of the land', US courts have since developed the distinction between 'self-executing' and 'non-self-executing' treaties. Thus, self-executing treaties, which confer certain rights upon citizens, rather than being primarily a 'compact between independent nations', will be applied by US courts in the same way as with federal laws. Not so the case with respect to non-self-executing treaties. Whether or not a treaty should be regarded as self-executing is, however, frequently a matter of debate.

In the UK, as is discussed below, constitutional convention dictates that only treaties that have been incorporated into domestic law by Act of Parliament may be given effect by UK courts. In the last analysis, therefore, the relationship between international law and municipal law at the level of municipal courts, is determined by the municipal law of the state concerned.

3.3 The application of municipal law before international tribunals

The general rule is that in the event of conflict between international obligations and national law, the international law prevails. The Draft Declaration on Rights and Duties of States prepared by the International Law Commission, which was adopted in 1949 by the UN General Assembly in art 13 of Resolution 375(IV), provides that:

> 'Every State has the duty to carry out in good faith its obligations arising from treaties and other sources of international law, and it may not invoke provisions in its constitutions or its laws as an excuse not to perform this duty.'

In respect of international treaties, art 27 of the 1969 Vienna Convention on the Law of Treaties states:

> 'A party may not invoke the provision of its internal law as justification for its failure to perform a treaty. This rule is without prejudice to art 46.'

The exception embodied in art 46 applies only in exceptional circumstances, that is, when a State's consent to a treaty is invalidated by a 'manifest' violation of its internal law and concerns 'a rule of its internal law of fundamental importance'.

There is ample judicial and arbitral authority for the rule that a state cannot rely upon the provisions or deficiencies of its municipal law to avoid its obligations under international law. Some examples are listed below.

Alabama Claims Arbitration *(1872) Moore, 1 Int Arb 495*

During the American Civil War, a number of ships were built in England for private buyers. The vessels were unarmed when they left England but it was generally known that they were to be fitted out as warships by the Confederates in order to attack Union shipping. These raiders caused considerable damage to American shipping. The US sought to make Great Britain liable for these losses on the basis that she had breached her obligations as a neutral during the War in contravention of the 'Three Rules of Washington'.

Great Britain argued, inter alia, that under English law as it then stood, it had not been possible to prevent the sailing of vessels constructed under private contracts.

In rejecting the British argument the arbitrators had no hesitation in upholding the supremacy of international law:

'... the government of Her Britannic Majesty cannot justify itself for a failure in due diligence on the plea of insufficiency of the legal means of action which it possessed. ... It is plain that to satisfy the exigency of due diligence, and to escape liability, a neutral government must take care ... that its municipal law shall prohibit acts contravening neutrality.'

Polish Nationals in Danzig Case *(1932) PCIJ Rep Ser A/B No 44*

In this case the Permanent Court of International Justice stated that:

'It should ... be observed that ... a state cannot adduce as against another state its own constitution with a view to evading obligations incumbent upon it under international law or treaties in force. Applying these principles to the present case, it results that the question of the treatment of Polish nationals or other Persons of Polish origin or speech must be settled exclusively on the basis of the rules of international law and the treaty provisions in force between Poland and Danzig.'

UN Headquarters Agreement Case *(1988) ICJ Rep 3*

The principle of international law that international law prevails over municipal law was reaffirmed by the ICJ in its Advisory Opinion in the *UN Headquarters Agreement Case*. The principle of primacy of international law over municipal law before international tribunals applies to all aspects of a state's municipal law, to its constitutional provisions, its ordinary legislation and to the decisions of its courts.

LaGrand Case: Germany *v* United States of America *(2001) 40 ILM 1069 and* Case Concerning Avena and Other Mexican Nationals: Mexico *v* United States of America *(2004) 43 ILM 581*

In the above cases the ICJ examined the US constitutional rule of 'procedural default' under which a procedural failing which has not been argued at State level cannot be argued at federal level. In *LaGrand* the ICJ stated that although the rule itself did not violate art 36 of the 1963 Vienna Convention on Consular Relations its application to the *LaGrand* case was in breach of that provision. The procedural default rule prevented a German national from raising a claim on appeal (which had not been raised in earlier proceedings) based on failure of the competent USA authorities to comply which their obligations to provide the requisite consular information 'without delay' set out in art 36(1), thus preventing the person from seeking and obtaining consular protection from the relevant German authorities. Subsequent to the judgment in *LaGrand* the USA did not revise the above rule. In *Avena* the ICJ agreed with the submission of Mexico that the USA, by failing to revise the procedural default rule in the light of its implications for defendants seeking to rely on the Vienna Convention in appeal proceedings, the USA had failed to provide 'meaningful and effective review and reconsideration of convictions and sentences impaired by a violation of art 36(1)' of the Convention.

The conflict between a state's municipal law and its international obligations does not necessarily affect the validity of that law on the municipal plane. Thus, a municipal act contrary to international law may be internally recognised as valid but other states will be under no duty to recognise its external effects.

3.4 The application of international law in UK courts

Customary international law

Can English law have regard to rules of customary international law? In the event of a conflict, which rule prevails? Two approaches are in evidence here: the doctrine of transformation, ie that customary international law only forms part of English law to the extent that it has been made part of English law by Act of Parliament, judicial decision or established usage; and the doctrine of incorporation, ie that rules of customary international law are automatically part of English law as long as they are not inconsistent with Acts of Parliament or authoritative judicial decision.

The doctrine of incorporation

The traditional rule is that, provided they are not inconsistent with Acts of Parliament or prior authoritative judicial decisions, rules of customary international law automatically form part of English law. The doctrine of incorporation is supported by a long line of authority.

In *Buvot* v *Barbuit* (1737) Cases Talbot 281 Lord Chancellor Talbot declared: 'That the law of nations, in its full extent was part of the law of England'.

Holdsworth described the approach of the English courts as follows:

'It would, I think, have been admitted that, if a Statute or a rule of the common law conflicted with a rule of international law, an English judge must decide in accordance with the statute or the rule of common law. But, if English law was silent, it was the opinion of both Lord Mansfield and Blackstone that a settled rule of international law must be considered to be part of English law, and enforced as such.'

The doctrine of transformation

It has been argued by some writers that in some cases decided since 1876, the doctrine of incorporation has been displaced by that of transformation, ie customary international law forms a part of the law of England only in so far as it has been accepted and made part of the law of England by Act of Parliament, judicial decision or established usage.

In *R* v *Keyn* (1876) 2 Ex D 63 the *Franconia*, a German ship, collided with the *Strathclyde*, a British ship in British territorial waters. The defendant, the German captain of the *Franconia*, was prosecuted for the manslaughter of a passenger on board the *Strathclyde* who was drowned as a result of the collision. The defendant was found guilty. However, the question whether an English court had jurisdiction to try the case was reserved for the Court of Crown Cases Reserved which decided by seven votes to six that it did not.

The majority was of opinion that the English court did not have jurisdiction in the absence of an Act of Parliament granting such jurisdiction. This decision has been interpreted as supporting the 'transformation' approach and as displacing the doctrine of incorporation.

However *Keyn* remains an ambiguous precedent, the true ratio decidendi being difficult to establish from among the eleven different judgments delivered.

Lauterpacht, commenting on the case observed:

'... it cannot be said that this judgment amounts to a rejection of the rule that international law is a part of the law of England. Writers seem to forget that the main issue of the controversy in the case was not the question whether a rule of international law can be enforced without an Act of Parliament; what was in dispute was the existence and the extent of a rule of international law relating to jurisdiction in territorial waters.'

In *West Rand Central Gold Mining Co* v *R* [1905] 2 KB 391 Lord Alverstone CJ, in an obiter statement while appearing to support the principle of transformation, noted that:

'It is quite true that whatever has received the common consent of civilised nations must have received the assent of our country, and that to which we have assented along with other nations in general may properly be called international law, and as such will be acknowledged and applied by our municipal tribunals.'

However, these words would seem to rest on an assumption that the doctrine of incorporation holds good. Indeed, Oppenheim regards the case as 'a reaffirmation of the classical doctrine', ie of incorporation.

In *Mortensen* v *Peters* (1906) 8F (Ct of Sess) 93 the judgment of Lord Dunedin, Lord Justice-General, contains the following dictum:

'It is a trite observation that there is no such thing as a standard of international law extraneous to the domestic law of a kingdom, to which appeal may be made. International law, so far as this Court is concerned, is the body of doctrine ... which has been adopted and made a part of the law of Scotland.'

This statement is understood to be in favour of the transformation doctrine.

A remark made by Lord Justice Atkin in *Commercial and Estates Company of Egypt* v *Board of Trade* [1925] 1 KB 271 is also regarded as supporting the doctrine of transformation:

'International law as such can confer no rights cognisable in the municipal courts. It is only insofar as the rules of international law are recognised as included in the rules of municipal law that they are allowed in municipal courts to give rise to rights and obligations.'

In *Chung Chi Cheung* v *The King* [1939] AC 160 Lord Atkin, delivering the opinion of the Privy Council, stated:

> 'It must always be remembered that, so far, at any rate, as the courts of this country are concerned, international law has no validity, save insofar as its principles are accepted and adopted by our own domestic law. There is no external power that imposes its rule upon our own code of substantive law or procedure.
>
> The courts acknowledge the existence of a body of rules which nations accept amongst themselves. On any judicial issue they seek to ascertain what the relevant rule is, and having found it, they will treat it as incorporated into the domestic law, so far as it is not inconsistent with rules enacted by statutes or finally declared by their tribunals.'

Lord Denning MR followed the transformation approach of Lord Atkin in the case of *Thakrar* v *Secretary of State for the Home Office* [1974] QB 684.

The current approach

Three years after his decision in *Thakrar*, Lord Denning reversed his views on the relationship between customary international law and English law. In *Trendtex Trading Corporation* v *Central Bank of Nigeria* [1977] QB 529 he put the argument in these terms:

> 'A fundamental question arises for decision: what is the place of international law in our English law? One school of thought holds to the doctrine of incorporation. It says that the rules of international law are incorporated into English law automatically and considered to be part of English law unless they are in conflict with an Act of Parliament. The other school of thought holds to the doctrine of transformation. It says that the rules of international law are not to be considered as part of English law except in so far as they have been already adopted and made part of our law by the decisions of the judges, or by Act of Parliament, or long established custom. The difference is vital when you are faced with a change in the rules of international law. Under the doctrine of incorporation, when the rules of international law change, our English law changes with them. But, under the doctrine of transformation, the English law does not change. It is bound by precedent.
>
> As between these two schools of thought, I now believe that the doctrine of incorporation is correct. Otherwise I do not see that our courts could ever recognise or change the rules of international law.'

Since *Trendtex* it has been generally accepted that, in so far as customary international law is concerned, the doctrine of incorporation applies. Some doubt has, however, been cast on this view following the decision by the House of Lords in the *International Tin Council Cases* [1990] 2 AC 418. Although the issue directly in point was not one of customary law, the dismissal by the Lords of a subsidiary argument involving recourse to custom, with reference that custom was a 'rule of construction', has led some commentators to remark that English law has reverted to a strongly dualist approach. Given the complexity of the litigation and the fact that a rule of customary law was not directly in issue, the better view is probably that the decisions of the Lords on the *International Tin Council Cases* do not radically alter the situation one way or another. Insofar as custom is concerned, it probably remains correct to say that the prevailing doctrine is that of incorporation.

The dictum of Lord Denning in *Trendtex* has been followed in a number of more recent cases which support the proposition that the doctrine of incorporation has been adopted as the prevailing principle of English law. Certainly, the courts have been reluctant to apply principles of the common law which conflict with customary international law. For example, in *Westland Helicopters Ltd* v *Arab Organisation for Industrialisation* [1995] 2 All ER 387, Colman J reaffirmed the doctrine of incorporation and stated:

> 'Inasmuch as the common law rule is at large before this court, there is, in my judgment, every reason in principle why the approach of the common law should be consistent with that of public international law unless there is some controlling common law principle to the contrary; for it is part of English public policy that our courts should give effect to clearly established rules of international law.'

In the light of this principle, the court refused to apply a rule of construction in English common law which, it was claimed, would allow a member state of an international organisation to continue the existence of that organisation even after the other participating states had issued a declaration ordering its liquidation. Instead, the court found that the proper constitutional law of the organisation, in common with all international organisations, was public international law. Therefore, customary principles of law were applied to determine whether the organisation was wound up or continued in the guise of another organisation established under the domestic laws of one of its participants.

Various judgments in the *Pinochet* case provide support for the doctrine of incorporation, for example Lord Lloyd stated that the principles of customary international law 'form part of the common law of England' ([2000] 1 AC 61) whilst Lord Millet emphasised that 'customary international law is part of the common law' (*R* v *Bow Street Metropolitan Stipendiary Magistrate, ex parte Pinochet Ugarte (No 3)* [2000] 1 AC 147). Further, Scottish law recognises that customary international law forms an integral part of Scots law (cases of *John Donnelly* and *Lord Advocate's Reference No 1 of 2000* (2001) SLT 507: see S Neff, *International Law and Nuclear Weapons in Scottish Courts* (2002) 51 ICLQ, 171).

Situations in which English courts cannot apply customary international law

There are situations in which English courts cannot apply customary international law.

If there is a conflict between customary international law and an Act of Parliament, the Act of Parliament prevails

In *Mortensen* v *Peters* (1906) 8 F (JC) 93 the appellant was a Dane and the master of a Norwegian ship. He was convicted by a Scottish court of otter trawling contrary to a bye-law issued by The Fishery Board for Scotland. He argued that the bye-law was in contravention of a rule of international law limiting territorial waters to bays and estuaries of no greater breadth of ten miles.

His appeal against conviction was dismissed unanimously by a full bench of 12 judges. The Lord Justice-General, Lord Dunedin said:

> 'In this Court we have nothing to do with the question of whether the Legislature has or has not done what foreign powers may consider a usurpation in a question with them. Neither are we a tribunal sitting to decide whether an Act of the Legislature is ultra vires as in contravention of generally acknowledged principles of international law. For us an Act of Parliament duly passed by Lords and Commons and assented to by the King is supreme, and we are bound to give effect to its terms.'

Where such matters as the status of a foreign state or the identity of a Head of State, the extent of territorial jurisdiction, or the existence of a state of war, are in issue

English courts accept a certificate signed by the Foreign Secretary as being conclusive of such questions. The determination in the Foreign Office Certificate is treated by the courts as conclusive and therefore no independent judicial determination will be entered into by the courts.

Note, however, that the UK Government is no longer issuing certificates regarding the formal recognition of foreign governments (see Chapter 5).

The 'act of state' doctrine

Under English constitutional law an alien injured abroad by an act authorised or subsequently ratified by the Crown has no remedy in the English courts.

Treaty rules and their relation to English law

In the UK, the conclusion and ratification of treaties are within the prerogative of the Crown. Parliament has no part in this process. If the courts could apply treaties in municipal law, the Crown would be in a position of being able to alter English law without parliamentary consent. To forestall this, treaties are only part of English law if an enabling Act of Parliament has been passed.

In *The Parlement Belge* (1878–79) 4 PD 129 Sir Robert Phillimore reaffirmed, in that part of the first instance decision which still stands, that the Crown cannot by entering into a treaty alter the law of England.

If such an Act is not passed by Parliament, the treaty is nevertheless still binding on the UK from the international point of view.

There is a distinction, therefore, between the effects of a treaty in international law and the effects of a treaty in municipal law. The treaty is effective in international law when ratified by the Crown. But if the treaty alters the law of England it has no effects in municipal law until an Act of Parliament is passed giving it effect.

The general rule that an English court may not look at an unincorporated treaty has been confirmed by a number of decisions. In the *International Tin Council Cases* [1990] 2 AC 418 the House of Lords confirmed the rule that an English court could not examine the International Tin Agreements to establish the liability or otherwise of member states of the International Tin Council. This rule has since been strictly interpreted by the Court of Appeal in *Arab Monetary Fund* v *Hashim (No 3)* [1990] 2 All ER 769 where it held that the decision by the House of Lords in the *International Tin Council Cases* precluded the court from having reference to and applying the provisions of a treaty establishing the Arab Monetary Fund. In this case, the Arab Monetary Fund had legal personality, owned assets and conducted business in the UK. The UK was not a party to the treaty of establishment. However, owing to the English constitutional rule requiring transformation in respect of treaties, the Court held that it could not have regard to the treaty. Each of the three Lord Justices of Appeal however remarked on the obvious injustice of the result, indicating that it was up to Parliament to legislate to change the matter.

In the case of *ex parte Amnesty International* (1998) The Times 11 December the Divisional Court rejected a submission based on a duty arising under art 7 of the 1984 Torture Convention on the ground that the duty arose under international law and had not been incorporated into municipal law. This approach was confirmed by the House of Lords in *R* v *Bow Street Metropolitan Stipendiary Magistrate, ex parte Pinochet Ugarte (No 3)* [1999] 2 WLR 827: see Chapter 9.

In respect of ratified but unincorporated treaties there is an ongoing discussion as to whether or not developments in administrative law might have some effect on the traditional approach which consists of rejecting the idea that such treaties cannot be a source of legal rights and duties. There is much debate in administrative law as to whether the concept of 'legitimate expectation' is founded upon: (a) a future interest; or (b) a past representation; or (c) established criteria: *R* v *Secretary of State for the Home Department, ex parte Asif Mahmood Khan* [1984] 1 WLR 1337. Regardless of its precise judicial basis the theory has begun to develop that a ratified but unincorporated treaty might give rise to a 'legitimate expectation' that the executive branch will act in accordance with the treaty. Such an approach has found favour in some jurisdictions (*Minister of State for Immigration* v *Teoh* (1995) 128 ALR 353) and its supporters argue that it prevents the executive branch from speaking with two voices. In *R* v *Uxbridge Magistrates' Court, ex parte Admi and Others* (1999) The Times 12 August (QBD) the court endorsed this approach. In this case Mr Admi was prosecuted on a charge of using false documents. Two others were convicted in similar circumstances. All three claimed that they were using false documents because they were fleeing from persecution in their own country and were in the process of seeking asylum in the UK and therefore should be protected under the Geneva Convention Regarding the Status of Refugees 1951. An application for judicial review was made, arguing that:

1. all three were protected under art 31 of the 1951 Convention;

2. the criminal proceedings against Mr Admi should be stayed; and
3. the convictions against the other two individuals should be quashed.

The court allowed the applications on the grounds that although the 1951 Convention was ratified by the UK but not incorporated into English law the act of ratification created for the purposes of administrative law a legitimate expectation in the applicants that its terms would be respected. Furthermore, the Parliament indicated in s2 of the Asylum and Immigration Appeals Act 1993 that nothing in the immigration rules 'shall lay down any practice which would be contrary to the Convention'. The court also stated that in future it was desirable that questions of prosecution of those claiming asylum should be decided by the Home Office rather than the Crown Prosecution Service because the substance of the matter related to immigration control and asylum rather than the general application of the criminal law.

Treaties and the interpretation of statutes in the UK

It is a general principle of British constitutional law that in the case of a conflict statute prevails over treaty.

However, as a rule of construction where domestic legislation is passed to give effect to an international convention, there is a presumption that Parliament intended to fulfil its international obligations.

In *Salomon* v *Commissioners of Customs and Excise* [1967] 2 QB 116 a provision of a statute being ambiguous, the court had to consider whether recourse could be had to a treaty, which the provision was intended to implement, to interpret the provision.

Diplock LJ stated:

'... if the terms of the legislation are not clear but are reasonably capable of more than one meaning, the treaty itself becomes relevant, for there is a prima facie presumption that Parliament does not intend to act in breach of international law, including therein specific treaty obligations; and if one of the meanings which can reasonably be ascribed to the legislation is consonant with the treaty obligations and another or others are not, the meaning which is consonant is to be preferred.'

Lord Diplock went on to hold that provided there is cogent extrinsic evidence that the statute was intended to give effect to a particular international convention, then that convention may be consulted as an aid to interpretation of the statute.

In *R* v *Chief Immigration Officer, ex parte Bibi* [1976] 1 WLR 979 the point at issue was whether immigration rules made under the Immigration Act 1971 should be interpreted and applied by immigration officers in accordance with the right to family life in art 8 of the European Convention on Human Rights.

Lord Denning MR stated:

'The position as I understand it is that if there is any ambiguity in our statutes, or uncertainty in our law, then these courts can look to the Convention as an aid to clear up the ambiguity and uncertainty, seeking always to bring them into harmony with it. Furthermore, when Parliament is enacting a statute, or the Secretary of State is framing rules, the courts will assume that they had regard to the provisions of the Convention, and intended to make the enactment accord with the Convention: and will interpret them accordingly. But I would dispute altogether that the Convention is part of our law. Treaties and declarations do not become part of our law until they are made law by Parliament.'

On the basis of the existing case law it emerges that in the interpretation of international agreements the court will be guided by the following principles.

1. The court will give a purposive construction to the Convention taken as a whole: *Fothergill* v *Monarch Airlines Ltd* [1981] AC 251.
2. Cautious use will be made of travaux preparatoires.
3. The court will take into consideration the interpretation of the given Convention by courts in other contracting states.
4. The court will be most anxious to ensure that decisions in different contracting states are, as far as possible, kept in line with each other.
5. The court will not give a judgment which would create domestic remedies that would undermine the working of the Convention.

In *Sidhu* v *British Airways plc* [1997] 2 WLR 26 (HL) Mr Sidhu brought an appeal against the decision of the Court of Appeal on the ground that he was entitled to bring a claim at common law in the following circumstances. Mr Sidhu and members of his family were passengers on a British Airways flight from London to Kuala Lumpur via Kuwait on 1 August 1990. When the plane landed in Kuwait on 2 August 1990 the passengers and crew were detained by the invading Iraqi forces. They were not released until 21 August 1990. Mr Sidhu brought an action in the county court in England in 1993 against British Airways (BA) for negligence and personal injury. BA argued that the claim was statute-barred under the Warsaw Convention and in particular by its art 29 which places a two–year time limit on such claims. Mr Sidhu submitted that his claim was brought at common law independent of the provisions of the Convention. The county court and the Court of Appeal rejected the claim on the ground that it could only be brought under the Convention and therefore was time-barred. On the basis of the above-mentioned principles the House of Lords rejected the appeal.

The above rule of construction does not, however, extend to the interpretation of subordinate legislation. In *R* v *Secretary of State for the Home Department, ex parte Brind* [1990] 1 All ER 469 (confirmed by the House of Lords: [1991] 1 AC 696) the Court of Appeal refused to apply this principle in an application by a number of journalists for judicial review of the right of the Home Secretary to issue directives to broadcasting authorities prohibiting the broadcast of statements by proscribed terrorist organisations in Northern Ireland. The applicants contended that the directives were unlawful because they violated art 10 of the European Convention on Human Rights, which provides that the right to freedom of expression includes the freedom 'to receive and impart information and ideas without interference by public authorities'. According to the applicants, the Home Secretary was obliged to exercise his powers in a manner consistent with the European Convention.

While the court was prepared to acknowledge the existence of a presumption that statutes and primary legislation should be interpreted in a manner consistent with the international obligations of the UK, it was not prepared to accept that this principle extended to the interpretation of secondary legislation or executive action. The court held that, where Parliament has delegated subordinate legislative powers to ministers or other functionaries, it has enacted the primary legislation in full knowledge of the obligations of the UK. Parliament has therefore had an opportunity to draft the primary legislation in light of the obligations of the UK and if no express reference was made in the delegation to the terms of an international agreement, no such restraints could be imposed on the discretion of the Minister exercising the power.

The court therefore concluded that an extension of this principle of construction to subordinate legislation would involve 'imputing to Parliament an intention to import international conventions into domestic law by the back door, when it has quite clearly refrained from doing so by the front door'.

3.5 EC law in UK courts

EC law is neither foreign nor external to the legal systems of the member states. To the contrary, it forms an integral part of national laws. Its peculiar position is due to the manner in which it penetrates into the national legal order of the member states. The three fundamental principles developed by the Court of Justice of the European Communities (ECJ) – that is, direct applicability, direct effect and supremacy of Community law – strengthen the autonomy of EC law and determine the degree of its integration into the national laws of the member states, as does the fourth which goes side by side with those three, that is the principle that establishes a member state's liability for damage to individuals caused by a breach of Community law for which that member state is responsible.

Community law endorses the monist theory. This approach derives from the nature of the Community. Only a monist system is compatible with the idea of European integration. In *Costa* v *ENEL* Case 6/64 [1964] ECR 585 the ECJ emphasised its peculiar nature by stating that the member states have created:

'... a Community of unlimited duration, having its own institutions, its own personality, its own legal capacity and capacity of representation on the international plane and, more particularly, real powers stemming from a limitation of sovereignty or a transfer of powers from the states to the Community, the member states have limited their sovereign rights, albeit within limited fields, and have thus created a body of law which binds their nationals and themselves.'

This confirmation is even more evident in the following passage extracted from the same decision in which the ECJ held that:

> 'By contrast with ordinary international treaties, the Treaty has created its own legal system which, on the entry into force of the Treaty, became an integral part of the legal systems of the member states and which their courts are bound to apply.'

As a result, Community law cannot tolerate national divergencies as to relations vis-à-vis international law since the dualist system jeopardises the attainment of the objectives of the Treaty and is contrary to the spirit and objectives of Community law. Member states may preserve the dualist system in relation to international law but it is excluded in relations between Community law and national law. As a result, Community law becomes an integral part of national law without any need for its formal implementation (apart from directives which often require further implementing measures on the part of a member state) and national judges are bound to apply it. Furthermore, Community law occupies a special place in the domestic legal systems of the member states as it is applied as Community law and not as municipal law.

After years of hesitation, the House of Lords fully recognised the fundamental principles of EC law mentioned above in a number of judgments in the *Factortame* saga: *R* v *Secretary of State for Transport, ex parte Factortame (No 3)* [1990] 2 AC 85.

4

International Personality

4.1 Introduction

4.2 The criteria for statehood

4.3 Independent states

4.4 Dependent states

4.5 Special cases

4.6 Mandates and trusteeship territories

4.7 International organisations

4.8 Individuals

4.1 Introduction

International personality refers to the capacity to be a bearer of rights and duties under public international law. The traditional view is that the only subjects of international law are sovereign states. They alone have capacity to make claims on the international plane in respect of breaches of international law, capacity to make treaties and other binding international agreements, and enjoy privileges and immunities from national jurisdiction. This traditional view has been challenged with the development and proliferation of international organisations. As a result, it is now accepted that international organisations can have a measure of international personality. However, international personality is unlimited only in respect of sovereign states. Limited international personality applies to dependent states or international organisations. The International Court of Justice has recognised the diversity of international personality by stating that 'the subjects of law in any legal system are not necessarily identical in their nature or in the extent of their rights': Advisory Opinion in *Reparations for Injuries Suffered in the Service of the United Nations* (1949) ICJ Rep 174.

Increasingly, there is a trend towards accepting private persons, whether legal or natural, as having limited international personality for the purposes of carrying out a limited category of transactions.

4.2 The criteria for statehood

Independent states remain the primary subjects of international law as they occupy the central position in the international community. In order to be regarded as an independent state an entity must satisfy certain criteria. The accepted definition of what constitutes the criteria for statehood is laid down in art 1(1) of the Montevideo Convention on Rights and Duties of States 1933 which provides:

> 'The state as a person of International Law should possess the following qualifications:
> (a) a permanent population;
> (b) a defined territory;
> (c) government;
> (d) capacity to enter into relations with other states.'

(28 AJIL, Supp, 75.)

The simultaneous occurrence of these elements creates a sovereign entity possessing international personality. However, the absence of some of these elements over a period of time does not necessarily deprive a state of its international personality.

The criteria set out by the 1933 Montevideo Convention have been clarified and developed by international law, first by academics who, on the basis of states' practices, have identified further elements that should be included within the criteria for statehood, and, second, by the Badinter Arbitration Commission which was established by the European Community to respond to the break up of the former Yugoslavia and the subsequent unilateral declarations of independence of its former republics. The EC decided that if the former republics wished to be recognised by the EC as independent states they had to apply to the EC which would then refer their applications to an Arbitration Commission chaired by Robert Badinter (as a result the Commission has become known as the Badinter Commission). The Badinter Commission prepared guidelines for possible recognition of the republic of Yugoslavia which were officially adopted by the EC: see the text of the EC Guidelines on Recognition adopted on 17 December 1991, H Hannum (ed), *Documents on Autonomy and Minority Rights*, Dordrecht/Boston/London: Martinus Nijhoff Publisher, 1993, p85. Although the Badinter Commission's main concern was the recognition of states, its decisions have also influenced the criteria for statehood.

A permanent population

A state cannot exist without population. The requirement of 'a permanent population' refers to a stable community. There is no prescribed minimum number of people making up the population. When Nauru became independent its estimated population was 6,500 people. The criterion of population is not affected if the population of a state is nomadic, that is, it constantly changes its place of residence because of its nomadic mode of life. The nomadic tribes on the Kenya-Ethiopia borders have been a changing element of each nation's population for centuries. The transient nature of their population has never affected their qualification as independent states. International law does not require the population to be homogeneous. The notion of a nation state is of historical interest only. It is not necessary that the population is made up of nationals. The determination of nationality is one of the attributes of a state but not an element of its definition. Therefore, nationality is dependent upon statehood and not the reverse. The criterion of a 'stable population' refers to a group of individuals living within a certain geographical area.

The matter whether a very limited population will preclude the creation of a state was examined by the UN 'Special Committee of Twenty-Four' which was asked to interpret the right to self-determination of colonial people in the context of extremely small colonial populations. The smallest entity which was examined by the Committee was Pitcairn Island with a population of 90 inhabitants occupying an area of five square kilometres. The Committee reaffirmed the right of the people of Pitcairn Island to self-determination but warned them that in deciding their political future they should take into consideration 'the Territory's tiny size, its small and decreasing population, mineral resources and dependence on postage stamps for the bulk of its revenue': UN Doc A/9623/Add 5 (Part III) (1974), 6–7.

A defined territory

A fixed territory constitutes a basic requirement for statehood. Jessup, in his arguments submitted in favour of the admission of Israel to the United Nations, stated that 'The reason for the rule that one of the necessary attributes of a state is that it shall possess territory is that one cannot contemplate a state as a kind of disembodied spirit': 3 UN SCOR (383 mtg, 41) (1948). There is no requirement that the frontiers of the state be fully defined and undisputed, either at the time it comes into being or subsequently. The state of Israel was admitted to the United Nations in 1949, though the final delimitation of its boundaries had not yet been settled. Many of the states created after World War I were recognised by the Allied powers, although their boundaries were only drawn up in the subsequent peace treaties.

What is important is the effective establishment of a political community. In the Case of *Deutsche Continental Gas-Gesselschaft* v *Polish State* (1929) 5 AD 11 the German-Polish Mixed Arbitral Tribunal held that:

> 'In order to say that a state exists and can be recognised as such ... it is enough that ... [its] territory has a sufficient consistency, even through its boundaries have not yet been accurately delimited.'

Therefore, there is no state without an area of land being generally defined. For that reason a 'nomad state' cannot exist. International law does not require any minimum size for a territory. For example, the Vatican City occupies only 0.44 square kilometres.

Government

A government, or at least some governmental control, is required for qualification as a state. The government must maintain some degree of order and stability. According to Shaw this criterion:

> '... should be regarded more as an indication of some sort of coherent political structure and society, than the necessity for a sophisticated apparatus of executive and legal organs. The requirement relates to the nineteenth century concern with "civilisation" as an essential of independent statehood and ignores the modern tendency to regard sovereignty for non-independent peoples as the paramount consideration, irrespective of administrative conditions': *International Law*, 2nd ed, Cambridge: Cambridge University Press, 1986, p128.

However, once a government has been established, the absence of governmental authority does not affect the existing state's right to be considered as a state. States have often survived periods of anarchy, civil war and hostile occupation.

Capacity to enter into relations with other states

This requirement mentioned by the Montevideo Convention has been challenged by many authors as being a consequence of statehood not a prerequisite. Indeed, the capacity of an entity to enter into relations with other states derives from the control the government exercises over a given territory, which in turn is based on the actual independence of that state. The essence of the capacity to enter into relations with other states is independence. As Lauterpacht said:

> '... the first condition of statehood is that there must exist a government actually independent of that of any other state ... If a community, after having detached itself from the parent state, were to become, legally or actually, a satellite of another state, it would not be fulfilling the primary conditions of independence and would not accordingly be entitled to recognition as a state': *International Law: Collected Papers*, Cambridge: Cambridge University Press, 1975, p487.

In the *Island of Palmas Arbitration: The Netherlands* v *US* (1928) 2 RIAA 829 the Permanent Court of Arbitration clearly stated that 'Sovereignty ... signifies independence. Independence ... is the right to exercise ... to the exclusion of any other state, the functions of a state.'

Sovereignty is described as the supreme power of the state over its territory and inhabitants, independent of any external authority. The supreme power exists only inside the independent state not outside. However, a state may be limited in the exercise of its sovereignty, for example as a result of economic dependence, or because it has surrendered by treaty some of its competences to another state. Limitations of its competences do not limit a state's sovereignty. They only impose restrictions on the exercise of sovereignty. Consequently, a state remains independent as long as it has not given up its independence to any other state, since only an entity 'which is subjected to international law through the intermediary of a foreign state is not a sovereign state under international law': M S Korowicz, *Some Present Aspects of Sovereignty in International Law*, Leyden: A W Sijthoft, 1961, p108. Therefore, if a state has neither abandoned its independence to another state, nor is subject to the intermediary of any other state, nor dependent economically on another state such a state is a direct subject of international law.

In respect of independence it is necessary to distinguish between independence as a criterion for statehood and as a qualification for the continued existence of a state. Indeed, once a state is established it can reduce its independence through agreements and treaties with other states or international organisations. International law identifies two elements evidencing the existence of independence.

1. The entity exists separately within established boundaries. This emphasises the link between territory, population, government and independence. All four criteria must be present for the purposes of statehood.
2. The entity is not subject to any other authority except international law.

Independence as a criterion for statehood can be formal or actual. Formal independence refers to the situation where a state has control over all its functions or competences (the so-called kompetenz kompetenz), whilst actual independence is described as 'the minimum degree of real government power at the disposal of the authorities of the putative state, necessary for it to qualify as independent': J Crawford, *The Creation of States in International Law*, Oxford: Clarendon Press, 1979, pp56–57.

The relationship between formal and actual independence of an entity will indicate to what extent such entity satisfies the criteria for statehood. In this circumstance a number of possibilities may arise.

1. Formal independence may be combined with the actual ability to exercise independence. The entity will satisfy the fourth criterion and its recognition should pose no problem.
2. Formal independence exists but actual independence is missing. The entity will not meet the fourth criterion and should not be recognised as a state.
3. Formal independence is missing but the entity exercises some degree of actual independence. In such a case the fourth criterion is not satisfied. It will be difficult to recognise such an entity, although the circumstances of each case may provide justification for its recognition, eg colonial people exercising the right to self-determination.

The legality of origin of a state

Some authors argue that an additional criterion should be added to those mentioned above: that is the legality of origin of a state. A putative state which is created in violation of international law, and which exists because of such violation, should be denied recognition. A putative state will be illegal if it has been created in violation of any of the following three norms of international law: the prohibition of aggression and of the acquisition of territory by force; the right to self-determination; and the prohibition of racial discrimination and apartheid.

Article 2(4) of the UN Charter which prohibits aggression and the acquisition of territory by force has the status of ius cogens. Consequently, no entity created in breach of this rule should be recognised by the international community. This is illustrated by the case of Manchukuo, a puppet state created by Japan subsequent to its 1931 invasion of Manchuria. The League of Nations sent the Lytton Commission to Manchukuo to observed the situation. It reported:

> 'In the Government of Manchukuo Japanese officials are prominent and Japanese advisers are attached to all important Departments. Although the premier and his ministers are all Chinese, the heads of the various Boards of General Affairs, which, in the organisation of the new state, exercise the greatest measure of actual power, are Japanese. At first they were designated as advisers, but recently those holding the most important posts have been made full government officials on the same basis as the Chinese': League of Nations Publication, 1932, VIIA, 12.

The League of Nations adopted the recommendations of the Commission and decided not to recognise Manchukuo.

Similarly, when the independent Turkish Republic of Northern Cyprus was proclaimed by Turkish Cypriots in 1983 it was not recognised by any state but Turkey since the entity was created as a result of the illegal Turkish military intervention in 1974. Although there have been some examples which challenged the view that an entity founded on a breach of the prohibition of aggression and the use of force will not be recognised by the international community (eg the recognition of Bangladesh as a result of the 1971 invasion of East Pakistan by India which within three months was recognised by 90 states), it seems that the UN will strongly oppose such recognition. The EC in its Declaration on the Recognition of New States in Eastern Europe and in the Soviet Union 1991 clearly stated that 'its member states will not recognise entities which are the result of aggression'.

When new entities are created in breach of the right to self-determination and the prohibition of racial discrimination and apartheid the international community will refuse to recognise them as states and thus effectively deny these entities personality under international law even though the other criteria for statehood are satisfied. When Rhodesia, a British colony, unilaterally declared its independence on 11 November 1965 the UN called its members not to recognise the white minority racist government on the ground that the new state was created in breach of the principle of self-determination. In respect of South Africa the creation of the homeland states of Transkei, Ciskei, Bophutatswana and Venda without the consent of the black population was condemned by the international community.

Some authors argue that the criterion of legality should be rejected because 'the criterion of effective government leaves the choice of the form of government to the population of the state, but does not punish it with disappearance of the statehood if the government violates a norm of ius cogens': J Duursma *Self-determination, Statehood and International Relations of Micro-States*, Leyden: A W Sijthoft, 1994, p111. It is difficult to agree with this view given that an entity which, at its creation, violates fundamental norms on which the international community is based can hardly, as a sovereign state, be expected to respect those norms. The cases of Rhodesia and the homeland states of South Africa clearly indicated that new entities were created without the consent of the people and subsequently disintegrated as a result of internal conflicts.

The criteria for statehood were not frozen by the Montevideo Convention 1933. Since then the criterion of legality of origin of a state has been widely accepted. Possible future additions to the 1933 Montevideo criteria may be taken from the EC Declaration on the Recognition of New States. Although the Guidelines were applied in respect of recognition of new states, some of their principles are relevant to the criteria for statehood. It is submitted that the following principles should be included in the criteria for statehood.

1. Respect for the provisions of the United Nations Charter, the Final Act of Helsinki and the Charter of Paris, especially with respect to the rule of law, democracy and human rights. This element would ensure that a state is 'adult' enough to be a member of the international community.
2. Guarantees for the rights of ethnic and national groups and minorities. This would ensure that such groups are incorporated into the structure of a state from its inception.

4.3 Independent states

Independent states possess unlimited international personality. However, they may enter into various agreements with other states which may affect their international personality.

Composite states

The following types of composite state can be identified.

Federation

In a federation two or more states unite to such an extent that they abandon their separate organisation. Governmental responsibilities are divided between the federal authority and the constituent members of the federation. Usually, the federal government is entrusted with exclusive competence in foreign affairs while the member states have competences in respect of internal domestic matters.

Consequently, only the federal state is regarded as a state under international law and will possess international personality. There is a general principle that member states of the federation cannot enter into separate relations with foreign states. The United States and Canada are example of this type of state. However, there are some federal constitutions which give member states of the federation a limited capacity to enter into international relations. In such circumstances, the member state is simply acting as a delegate of the federal state. Such a situation may create separate personality in international law. For example, in 1944 the constitution of the USSR was amended to allow the Ukrainian SSR and Byelorussian SSR, both of which were member states of the USSR, to conclude treaties on their own behalf and become members of the United Nations alongside USSR.

Confederation
In a confederation two or more independent states decide to unite for their mutual welfare and the furtherance of their common aims. A central government is created that has certain powers, mostly in external affairs, and component states retain their powers for domestic purposes. The central government acts upon the member states, not upon the individuals. Each member state is fully sovereign and independent and thus possesses international legal personality. Examples of confederations are: Switzerland (1291–1848), The Netherlands (1581–1795), the US (1776–1788) and Germany (1815–1866). A later example is provided by the Confederation of Independent States (CIS) which was created after the collapse of the Soviet Union and comprises Russia and its former republics apart from Latvia, Lithuania, Estonia and Georgia which all declined membership of the CIS. The main purposes of the CIS are to co-ordinate its members' policy in respect of foreign relations, defence, immigration, environmental protection, law enforcement and economic matters. The armed forces of the members of the CIS and nuclear weapons based on their territories are under a single, unified command.

A confederation, because of its loose structure, normally, with time, transforms itself into a unitary state or a federation.

Personal union
This occurs when two or more states decide to have the same Head of State whilst remaining separate states with distinct international personalities. Great Britain and Hanover formed a personal union from 1714 to 1837. However, a personal union may take various forms. In the case of the Channel Islands – Jersey, Guernsey, Alderney and Sark – each is united in a personal union with the British monarch. Each island has sovereignty over its territory, population, administration and judiciary entirely free of the control of the British Parliament, but their external affairs are conducted by the UK. They have no international personality.

Real union
In a real union two or more states share one or more state organs. Whether or not

members of a real union enjoy international personality depends upon internal arrangements between them and the attitude of third states towards them. An example of a real union was provided by the Austro-Hungarian dual monarchy from 1723 to 1849 and 1867 to 1918.

Commonwealth of Nations

The Commonwealth of Nations, formerly known as the British Commonwealth of Nations (the term British was dropped in 1946), merits special attention. The Commonwealth is a free association of sovereign states who have decided to maintain ties of friendship and co-operation with the UK and recognise the British monarch as a symbolic head of their association. The Commonwealth has no international personality: its members, sovereign states, are subjects of international law. The Commonwealth was established by the Statute of Westminister 1931 which recognised that some British colonies and dependencies, taking into account the large degree of self-government granted to them, had a special status within the British Empire. With decolonisation the Commonwealth redefined its objectives. It allowed its members to resign from membership (which was done by the Irish Republic in 1948, South Africa in 1961 and Pakistan in 1972), but the majority of the former British colonies choose to remain within the Commonwealth. The activities of the Commonwealth relate to trade, investment, education, sport etc, and are co-ordinated through its Secretariat located in London. The Commonwealth provides a forum for discussion for its members, including meetings of the heads of governments which take place every two years.

4.4 Dependent states

In *Customs Regime between Germany and Austria Case* (1931) PCIJ Rep Ser A/B No 41, in a separate opinion, Anzilotti J provided some clarifications as to the meaning of 'dependent state' in the context of international law. He stated that:

> 'These are states subject to the authority of one or more other states. The idea of dependence therefore necessarily implies a relation between a superior state (suzerain, protector, etc) and inferior or subject state (vassal, protégé, etc); the relation between the state which can legally impose its will and the state which is legally compelled to submit to that will.'

There are different forms of dependency and therefore in some situations a dependent state will retain its international personality, in others it will lose it.

Colonies

Under the traditional rules of international law colonies were not regarded as possessing international personality. The exercise of their international relations was under the effective control of the colonial power. However, colonies in the process of becoming independent states may have limited capacity to enter into international relations. For instance, before its independence the British colony of Singapore was authorised to enter into commercial treaties and to join international organisations subject to the veto of the UK. Another example is provided by India when it became an original member of the League of Nations.

With the emergence of the principle of self-determination international law has recognised that some 'pre-independent states' and national liberation movements have a limited international personality. In 1974 the Palestine Liberation Organisation (PLO) was granted an observer mission status at the UN, which is normally reserved to sovereign states which are non-members of the UN. The head of the PLO was invited to address the General Assembly and representatives of the PLO have attended conferences and meetings organised under the auspices of the UN. Similarly, the South West African People's Organisation (SWAPO) was recognised by the General Assembly as representing the people of Namibia.

Protectorates

Protectorates are of historical interest as they no longer exist on the international scene. A distinction must be made between protected territories and protected states.

Protected territories

In the nineteenth century it was the practice of certain European states to create 'protectorates' over certain primitive areas of Africa and Asia by entering into treaties of protection with the local ruler. The effect of such agreements was that, while the local ruler retained control of his territory's internal affairs, foreign affairs were placed exclusively in the hands of the protecting power. Examples in British Africa included Northern Rhodesia and Nyasaland.

Protectorates did not have international personality before the protectorate was created. They acquired limited personality when they began to operate at international level. Once the protecting power was removed and the protectorate started to act independently from the protecting power it became an independent state and as such possessed international personality. This is illustrated by the case of Kuwait which became a British protectorate in 1899. It was gradually given responsibility for its own international relations and this position was formally recognised by the UK in 1961 although, at that time, Kuwait had already achieved statehood independently of formal recognition by the UK.

Protected states

Protected states are those states which have enjoyed international personality but subsequently surrendered their international competence to one or more protecting states. Protected states retain their original personalities as states in international law notwithstanding any subsequent treaty of protection.

Morocco was a protectorate of France and Spain from the beginning of the twentieth century. The General Act of Algeciras of 7 April 1907 governing relations between France and Morocco guaranteed 'the Sovereignty and the Independence of His Majesty the Sultan, the integrity of his Domains, and economic liberty without inequality'. Morocco surrendered to France the right to institute administrative, judicial, educational, financial and military reforms. France could maintain its military presence without permission of the Sultan. The treaty was concluded for an unlimited period and the Sultan had no right to terminate it. In 1912, by the Treaty of Fez, Morocco made another arrangement with France whereby France undertook to exercise certain sovereign powers in the name and on behalf of Morocco, and all of the international relations of Morocco. Notwithstanding this, the ICJ in the *Case Concerning Rights of Nationals of the United States of America in Morocco* (1952) ICJ Rep 176 held that the Treaty of Fez 1912 was an international treaty and that Morocco, even under the protectorate, had retained its international personality despite the fact that France exercised certain sovereign powers in the name of, and on behalf of, the Sultan in both internal and external affairs.

Satellite states

After World War II the 'liberation' of the central and eastern European states by the Red Army from German occupation gave the Soviet Union military and political control of these countries. However, the political and economic power exercised by the USSR and the military presence of the Red Army within the territory of the satellite states did not affect their international personality. Furthermore, the USSR was always very careful to eliminate any semblance of de jure dependency in relation to satellite states. Nevertheless, in reality there were no doubts that the satellite states were not fully sovereign, particularly after the Soviet invasion of Hungary in 1956 and Czechoslovakia in 1968.

Condominium and co-imperium

In condominium two or more states exercise joint sovereignty over the same territory and its inhabitants. The territory under condominium has no international personality. The best example of condominium was the Anglo-French condominium of the New Hebrides constituted in 1906. This arrangement was said to create ' a region of joint influence ... each of the two Powers retaining sovereignty over its nationals ... and neither exercising a separate authority over the group'. The territory achieved its independence in 1980 as the state of Vanuaty.

Co-imperium is different from condominium. The best example is provided by Germany after 1945. After the defeat of Germany the victors decided neither to annex the enemy territory nor to establish an international territory but to govern it jointly as a distinct international entity. The Allied powers decided to divide Germany into four occupation zones: Berlin was jointly controlled by the four powers and the Control Council, an inter-Allied government which acted on behalf of Germany and was empowered to enter into international agreements. The state of Germany was never dismantled and the situation during co-imperium was described as 'akin to legal representation or agency of necessity'.

Free cities

By virtue of an agreement, normally a peace treaty, some territories may be endowed with a limited international personality. The Free City of Danzig (now Gdansk) was created by the Treaty of Versailles 1919 and the 1920 agreement between the Free City of Danzig and Poland. It occupied 1,890 square kilometres and had 356,000 inhabitants. In art 100 of the Treaty of Versailles Germany renounced all its rights and title to Danzig in favour of the Allied powers. Article 102 provided for the establishment of the Free City of Danzig under the protection of the League of Nations. The relationship between Poland and the Free City of Danzig was regulated in art 104 of the Treaty of Versailles, which stated that an agreement between Poland and the Free City of Danzig which shall come into force at the time of the establishment of the Free City would ensure:

1. the inclusion of the Free City into the Polish Customs frontier and the establishment of a free area in the port;
2. free use and service of all waterways, docks, basins etc for Polish imports and exports;
3. the control of Poland over the administration of the Vistula and of the whole railway system within the Free City, except streets and railways which serve the primary needs for the Free City, and of postal, telegraphic and telephonic communication between Poland and the port of Danzig;
4. that Polish citizens and other persons of Polish origin and speech will not be discriminated against within the Free City;
5. that the Polish government will conduct foreign relations of the Free City and be in charge of the diplomatic protection of all citizen of the city when abroad.

The agreement between Poland and the Free City of Danzig was signed on 9 November 1920 and entered into force on 15 November 1920. The legal status of the Free City was described in its constitution, which provided for a Parliament exercising legislative, executive and administrative powers, as well as a Senate representing the Free City within the limits set out by the treaties. Although Poland was entrusted with the foreign affairs of the Free City, she had no right to initiate or to impose international agreements contrary to the interests of the Free City. The High Commissioner appointed by the League of Nations, who had his headquarters in Danzig, had a general power of supervision in respect of implementation of the League's decisions and resolutions concerning the Free City, and was entitled, in the first instance, to settle disputes between the Free City and Poland. He also had the right of veto in respect of international agreements which, according to the League of Nations, were in breach of the status of the Free City.

From the point of view of international law the Free City of Danzig was neither an independent state nor subordinate to any sovereign state. It was legally dependent on the League of Nations and Poland and as such possessed a limited international personality. The Free City was organised as a state, it had its own constitution, flag and currency, and was entitled to grant citizenship to inhabitants of Danzig. The PCIJ recognised that the Free City had international personality, except in so far as the treaty obligations arising from its special relationship with Poland and the League of Nations: *Free City of Danzig and the ILO* (1930) PCIJ Rep Ser B No 18 and *Polish Nationals in Danzig Case* (1932) PCIJ Rep Ser A/B No 44, 23–24.

In the 1947 Peace Treaty with Italy a similar arrangement was envisaged for Trieste but never came into being.

Diminutive states

Extremely small states such as Monaco, Andorra, San Marino and Liechtenstein exist somewhere between being independent and dependent states! Each is regulated under different arrangements. For example, Andorra is governed by two co-princes, the President of the French Republic and the Spanish Bishop of Urgel. And Monaco has various arrangements with France and may de facto be considered as her satellite. Nevertheless, these states are recognised by other states as sovereign states and are members of many international organisations, including the UN.

4.5 Special cases

There are a number of entities that enjoy a special status under international law. They do not satisfy the criteria for statehood but are, nevertheless, recognised as states by the majority of states. Examples are the Holy See and the Sovereign Military Hospitaller Order of Malta. Also limited international personality may, in certain circumstances, be conferred upon insurgents and belligerents.

The Holy See and the Vatican City

The Holy See enjoys a special status in international law. It has no population; there are around 500 persons residing in the Vatican City, of which fewer than 70 are Vatican citizens. Any inhabitant of the Vatican, irrespective of whether or not he is a citizen of the Vatican, can be expelled at any time from its territory. The reason is that residence is dependent upon the official position which the person holds. Consequently, the Vatican does not have a fixed population within the meaning of the criterion for statehood. From 1870 to 1929 the Holy See had no territory, it occupied de facto the Vatican palaces which were regarded as a part of Italy. In 1929 the Holy See signed the Lateran Treaty with Italy under which diplomatic relations were established between them, and the 'City of Vatican' was granted to the Holy See as its sovereign territory. The Lateran Treaty expressly stated that all customary inhabitants of the Vatican, irrespective of their citizenship, were subject to the sovereign authority of the Holy See while on the territory of the Vatican City.

Notwithstanding this the Holy See has always been recognised as possessing international personality. Even during the period when the Holy See lacked any sovereign territory it entered into international agreements (concordats) with many independent states. The Holy See has its diplomatic representations in many countries, and is a member of many international organisations.

The Sovereign Military Hospitaller Order of Malta

The order was founded as a religious military order of the Roman Catholic Church during the Crusades. In 1312 it was given the Island of Rhodes by the Pope which was lost to the Turkish Sultan in 1532. In 1530 the Order became a vassal of the King of Sicily and was given the Islands of Malta and Gozo, which it lost in 1798. In 1834 the Order established itself in Rome as a humanitarian organisation.

In 1446 Pope Nicholas V acknowledged the Grand Master of the Order as a 'sovereign prince'. From the time of its establishment in Rhodes the Order has always maintained diplomatic relations with other states and has been consistently treated as a sovereign state despite its lack of territory or population. Its Knights are citizens of other states. Italy, where the Order is located, has recognised the Order as a sovereign state in a number of legislative and administrative acts as well as in decisions of its judiciary. The Italian Council of state excluded the Order from the application of the 1866 royal decree suppressing religious orders. In 1921 the Grand Master and Grand Chancellor of the Order were exempted from customs duties in the same way as any Head of State or government. From 1956 Italy established full diplomatic relations with the Order, although the Grand Master has been accreditated to Italy since 1929. The relationship between the Order and Italy is based on the Note delivered by the Order's ambassador to Italy on 11 January 1969, which was endorsed by the government of Italy. In the endorsement the Italian government recognised the Grand Master as a foreign Head of State and the institutions of the Order were granted judicial personality and diplomatic immunity in respect of its property situated in Italy. The Order has also been recognised as a sovereign state by the Italian judiciary. In 1947 the Roman Court of Cassation held that the Order, being a subject of international law, was exempt from executive proceedings and therefore the Italian employment law did not apply to the employees of the Order's Grand Magistery and the Italian Association of Knights. In 1974 the Italian Court of Cassation ruled that the Order 'constitutes a sovereign international entity, equivalent in all respects, even though without territory, to a foreign state, and with which Italy has normal diplomatic relations, so that it is beyond doubt, as this Supreme Court has already pointed out, that it is entitled to the juridical treatment accorded to foreign states and thus also to the jurisdictional exemption within the after-mentioned limits and with regard to the activity concerning the performance of its public objectives': see G I Draper, *Functional Sovereignty and the Sovereign Military Hospitaller Order of Saint John of Jerusalem, of Malta*, Annales de L'Ordre Souverain Militaire de Malte, 1974, pp78–86.

The Order has established diplomatic relations with more than 80 states and has lesser relations with five other states, has its own postal service, issues passports which are internationally recognised, is a member of numerous international organisations, since 1994 has a status of a permanent observer to the UN, enters into treaties and international agreements with many independent states, possesses its own fleet of hospital aircraft carrying its flag, is independent from other states and jurisdictions except in religious matters in which the Order is subordinated to the Holy See. Its decorations (a Bailiff Grand Cross of Honour and Devotion, and the Collar Pro Merito Melitense) have been accepted by Heads of State or government.

Insurgents and belligerents

Limited international personality may be granted to some insurgent groups and belligerents during armed conflicts when they exercise de facto control over a part of a national territory, provided the requirements contained in the 1977 Additional Protocol I to the four 1949 Geneva Conventions are satisfied. The main objective of such recognition is to ensure the compliance of the parties involved in an armed conflict with international humanitarian law and the protection of human rights.

4.6 Mandates and trusteeship territories

Mandates and trusteeship territories are dealt with elsewhere in this book: see Chapter 7, section 7.13. Currently, there are no trusteeship territories. Under a Compact of Free Association, which entered into force on 1 October 1994, the last trusteeship territory, Palau, became associated with the United States.

The status of the people inhabiting such territories was defined by Judge Ammoun in the *Namibia Case* (1971) ICJ Rep 16, at 68, in the following terms:

> 'Namibia, even at the periods when it had been reduced to the status of a German Colony or was subject to the South African Mandate, possessed a legal personality which was denied it only by the law, now obsolete ... It nevertheless constituted a subject of law ... possessing national sovereignty but lacking the exercise thereof ... sovereignty ... did not cease to belong to the people subject to mandate. It had simply, for a time, been rendered inarticulate and deprived of freedom of expression.'

Consequently, such territories could not be regarded as attaining full legal personality until independence was achieved.

4.7 International organisations

An international organisation must satisfy three conditions to have legal capacity under international law: it must be a permanent association of states, created to attain certain objectives, having administrative organs; it must exercise some power that is distinct from the sovereign power of its member states; and its competences must be exercisable on an international level and not confined exclusively to the national systems of its member states.

Legal personality of international organisations

The leading judicial authority on the personality of international organisations is contained in the Advisory Opinion of the ICJ in the *Reparations for Injuries Suffered in the Service of the United Nations* (1949) ICJ Rep 174. This case concerned the assassination on 17 September 1948 of the UN chief truce negotiator, a Swedish national, Count Folke Bernardotte, and of the UN observer, a Frenchman, Colonel André Sérot, by Jewish terrorist organisations while on an official mission for the UN. They were murdered in the eastern part of Jerusalem, which was under Israeli control, at the time when Israel had proclaimed its independence but was not yet admitted to the UN. The UN considered that Israel had neglected to prevent or punish the murderers and wished to make a claim for compensation under international law. The General Assembly sought the advice of the ICJ as to the legal capacity of the UN to make such a claim. The Court held that the UN possessed a judicial personality on the international plane and was therefore capable of presenting such a claim with a view to obtaining reparation due in respect of the damage caused to both its assets and its agents (the so-called functional protection). The ICJ stated that:

> 'In the opinion of the Court, the organisation was intended to exercise and enjoy, and is in fact exercising and enjoying, functions and rights which can be explained on the basis of the possession of a large measure of international personality and the capacity to operate upon an international plane. It is at present the supreme type of international organisation, and it could not carry out the intentions of its founders if it was devoid of international personality ...
>
> Accordingly, the Court has come to the conclusion that the organisation is an international person. That is not the same thing as saying that it is a state, which it certainly is not, or that its legal personality and rights and duties are the same as those of a state. Still less is it the same thing as saying that it is a "super-state", whatever that expression may mean. It does not even imply that all its rights and duties must be upon that plane. What it does mean is that it is a subject of international law and capable of possessing international rights and duties, and that it has capacity to maintain its rights by bringing international claims.'

It must be remembered, however, that when states create an international organisation they set it up for specific purposes and in this respect legal personality must be treated as being relative to those purposes. Therefore, in order to determine whether an organisation has legal competence to perform a particular act both its express and implied purposes and functions must be taken into consideration. As the ICJ emphasised:

> 'Under international law, the organisation must be deemed to have those powers which, though not expressly provided in the Charter, are conferred upon it by necessary implication as being essential to the performance of its duties.'

Consequently, the question whether an international organisation possesses international personality can only be answered by examining its functions and powers expressly conferred by, or to be implied from, its constitution and developed in practice. Relevant factors may include the following.

Status under municipal law

Most treaties setting up international organisations contain a clause providing for them to enjoy legal personality under the municipal laws of its contracting states. Usually the clause is similar to art 104 of the Charter of the United Nations which states that:

> '... the organisation shall enjoy in the territory of each of its members such legal capacity as may be necessary for the exercise of its functions and the fulfilment of its purposes.'

It is doubtful that international personality can be deduced from such a grant of municipal personality, although some writers have argued that the granting of this personality may be a recognition of that status.

Treaty-making power

The most important attribute of an international organisation in respect of international personality is the right to enter into international agreements with states who are not members of it on matters within the organisation's competence. Treaty-making power is strong evidence of international personality.

International claims

If the constitution of the organisation provides for the settlement of disputes by arbitration or other international adjudication this may be of relevance in deciding its status, the power to present claims on the international plane being one of the basic rights of international personality.

General powers

It is apparent from the Advisory Opinion in the *Reparations for Injuries Suffered in the Service of the United Nations* case (above) that the whole powers of the organisation must be considered. These will therefore include those implied powers which must be conferred on an organisation in order for it to perform the duties required under its constitution.

Recognition

The most important aspect of conducting international relations for international organisations is their recognition by third states and other international organisations.

If international personality is conferred on the organisation, either expressly or impliedly, its members, by signing the constitutional instrument, ipso facto recognise it in their domestic legal order. A distinction, however, must be made between monist and dualist states. In monist states international law forms part of municipal law and as such can be relied upon before national courts. In dualist states an international agreement must be incorporated into municipal law in order to produce legal effects at national level. The House of Lords in the *International Tin Council Cases* [1990] 2 AC 418 stated that '[the] ITC as a matter of English law owes its existence to the Order in Council. That is what created the ITC in domestic law.' Consequently, an international organisation of which the UK is a member acquires its personality in the UK in two ways: through the adoption of an Order in Council which confers upon such an organisation 'legal capacities of a body corporate'; or through the enactment of specific legislation by the UK Parliament in respect of a given organisation.

The situation is more complicated in respect of non-member states. Subjects of international law are entitled to use their discretion. In the absence of recognition, acts of a new entity in international law would not be opposable by those who refuse to recognise it. In this respect it is interesting to note that the European Communities were not recognised by the Soviet Union and the central and eastern European countries of the former Soviet bloc associated within the Council for Mutual Economic Co-operation (COMECON). The COMECON refused to deal with the Communities even in those areas in which the EEC had exclusive competence. This situation should have logically resulted in the severance of all relations between them. The member states of the EEC favoured a more 'political solution', that is, individual member states were allowed to conclude co-operation agreements with eastern European countries under the supervision of the Community: OJ L208 (1974). This problem disappeared with the establishment of official relations between the EEC and the COMECON. They were formalised in the Joint Declaration of 21 June 1988 of the EEC and the COMECON which implicitly recognised the Community: OJ L157 (1988).

An example of an international organisation is the European Community (EC). Member States have conferred distinct legal personality on both the EC and the EA (European Atomic Energy Community). The new EU Constitution, in its Art I–1, provides that the European Union (EU) shall have international legal personality.

The extent of the European Communities' competences has been determined by the member states in the original Treaties as amended over the years and clarified by case law of the European Court of Justice. The Communities have been granted the capacity to enter into relations and to conclude treaties with third states and other organisations. Further, the Communities, and especially the most active and important among them, the EC, are the only international organisations that possess and exercise an independent power to make binding decisions which affect member states, their nationals and corporate bodies situated within the European Union and (in some circumstances) outside it. The Communities, to a certain extent, exercise powers similar to sovereign states; they have power to regulate the activities of people and to control the use of property within the territory of the Union.

The Communities have the capacity to conclude treaties with third states and international organisations (ius tractatus), to engage in diplomacy (ius missionis) and to sue an individual state for injuries to it and to be sued.

The status of international organisations in municipal law

The status of international organisations in national law has become a matter of increasing importance. The extent of the rights and duties of international organisations in the UK was clarified by the House of Lords in *Arab Monetary Fund* v *Hashim (No 3)* [1991] 1 All ER 871. The AMF was established by an international agreement among 20 Arab states and the Palestine Liberation Organisation. Under art 2 of the treaty creating the AMF it was granted 'independent judicial personality' which included the rights to own, contract and litigate. The headquarters of the organisation was in Abu Dhabi, and in 1977 the United Arab Emirates (UAE) passed legislation incorporating the treaty into its national law, thereby conferring legal personality within the UAE on the organisation.

Hashim, a former director-general of the Organisation, was alleged to have absconded with approximately US $50 million in assets belonging to the Fund. In 1988 Hashim was found resident in the UK and the Fund raised an action against Hashim, and a number of banks which had allegedly assisted in laundering a substantial part of the embezzled proceeds, for recovery of the stolen money. The defendants argued that the claimant possessed no legal personality, being an international organisation established under a treaty to which the UK was not a party, and therefore had no standing to bring the action.

The House of Lords made a number of interesting statements concerning the legal personality of international organisations in English law. Most importantly, it held that the UK was not obliged to recognise an entity created by a treaty to which it was not a party. However, the fact that the British government had not accorded recognition to an international organisation was not necessarily a bar to it having legal personality in English law. Ultimately, the House of Lords held that the Fund could not have legal personality in English law unless the treaty creating it had been incorporated into English law. The Fund, therefore, had no legal existence in English law.

The commencement and continuation of the action was allowed not on the ground that the AMF possessed legal personality, but by virtue of the conflict of laws principle that entities which possess legal personality in municipal law of a foreign state are entitled to raise actions by virtue of their status as foreign legal entities.

The United Kingdom courts have also had to interpret the constitutional documents of international organisations in private litigation before them. The most significant case was *Westland Helicopters Ltd* v *Arab Organisation for Industrialisation* [1995] 2 All ER 387. In 1975 the Arab Organisation for Industrialisation (AOI) was established by a treaty between four Arab states: Egypt, the United Arab Emirates, Qatar and Saudi Arabia. Its purpose was to facilitate the creation of an Arab arms manufacturing industry. The treaty afforded the AOI international personality and expressly provided that its operations were not to be subject to the domestic laws of any of its member states.

In 1979 Egypt signed a peace agreement with Israel, an act condemned by the Arab world. As part of the recriminations, the three Gulf states issued a declaration calling for the termination of the AOI and the liquidation of its assets. A committee was then set up in Riyadh for that purpose, although the Egyptian government refused to participate in that process. Instead, the Egyptian government enacted a law which purported to take control of the organisation. This law provided that the organisation would continue as a legal person under the law of Egypt and that its powers, privileges and immunities would be derived from that legislation.

Westland, a UK helicopter manufacturer, had entered into an agreement with the AOI to set up a joint venture company, called the Arab Helicopter Co, which would manufacture and repair Lynx helicopters under licence. Financing for this operation came from the substantial share capital and deposits made by the member states and lodged in various foreign banks. After the liquidation declaration, Westland informed the four governments that it considered the joint venture at an end and claimed compensation from the AOI liquidation tribunal in Riyadh. No compensation was forthcoming, so Westland applied for arbitration before the ICC in Geneva and was successful. The company then applied to the English courts for garnishee orders against six British banks holding funds on behalf of the AOI. The Egyptian AOI intervened in these proceedings, claiming that it was the legitimate successor organisation to the 1975 AOI and that it should be granted standing to be heard. The court therefore had to decide if the Egyptian AOI was, in law, the successor organisation to the 1975 AOI.

The court found that the issue of succession was to be decided in terms of the treaty setting up the organisation in 1975. The terms of this agreement were to be interpreted under public international law which was the proper law of the organisation's constitution. It would be contrary to the principle of the comity of nations for the English court to impose the domestic law of one member state over the organisation, particularly when the founding treaty expressly provided that it was not to be subject to national legal systems of the participating states.

The case demonstrates that the UK courts are prepared, in certain circumstances, to interpret the constitutional documents of international organisations in order to settle disputes. In doing so, the courts acknowledge that public international law is the proper law under which such constitutional documents are to be construed.

4.8 Individuals

Under public international law some provisions of international treaties may confer rights on individuals or impose some obligations upon them. This possibility was recognised for the first time by the Permanent Court of International Justice (PCIJ) in the *Case Concerning Competences of the Courts of Danzig (Advisory Opinion)* (1928) PCIJ Rep Ser B No 15, in which it was held that an exception to the principle that individuals are not subjects of international law arises if the intention of the contracting parties was to adopt a treaty which creates rights and obligations for individuals capable of being enforced by municipal courts. The PCIJ emphasised that this intention must be express and not inferred from the treaty since this kind of international treaty constitutes an exception to a general principle. Such treaties are defined under international law as 'self-executing'. They become automatically part of the national law of the contracting parties and are directly applicable by the national courts.

International law has increasingly conferred direct rights and duties upon individuals. Article 3 of the Draft Code of Crimes against the Peace and Security of Mankind ((1987) ILC YB, vol II, Part II, 13) provides that:

> '[An individual] is a person in international law, though his capacity may be different and less in number and substance than the capacities of states. An individual, for example, cannot acquire territory, he cannot make treaties, and he cannot have belligerent rights. But he can commit war crimes, and piracy, and crimes against humanity and foreign sovereigns and he can own property which international law protects, and he can have claims to compensation for acts arising ex contractu or ex delicto.
>
> Any individual who commits a crime against the peace and security of mankind is responsible for such crime.'

The international criminal responsibility of individuals is examined in depth in Chapter 19. Their access to international bodies and tribunals in the case of human rights abuses, at both international and national levels, is discussed in Chapter 12.

It is important to note that a number of international treaties have provided for states to recognise the international personality of individuals in the case of trade or investment disputes. These treaties were originally agreed to encourage foreign investment in developing countries by ensuring that investors would have access to an international tribunal. The best known is the Washington Convention Establishing the International Centre for the Settlement of Investment Disputes between States and Nationals of Other States 1965.

It is also important to emphasise that under EC law natural and legal persons have direct access to the Court of Justice of the European Communities (ECJ) to challenge acts adopted by the Community institutions, to force those institutions to act and to bring actions for damages caused by the institutions or by their servants in the performance of their duties. Furthermore, directly effective Community law creates rights and obligations for EC nationals enforceable before national courts.

5

Recognition

5.1 Introduction

5.2 Recognition in international law

5.3 Recognition of governments

5.4 Recognition in municipal law

5.1 Introduction

The international community is subject to a process of continuous change. The collapse of the Soviet Union and subsequent emergence of 15 new states, the break-up of the Socialist Federal Republic of Yugoslavia (SFRY) from which five states have emerged, the division of Czechoslovakia into two new states – the Czech Republic and Slovakia – all go to show that nothing on the world's political stage is ever static. New states may be created, existing states may disappear, territorial changes may take place. Moreover, revolutions, uprisings and coups d'etat may sweep aside existing governments and replace them with new regimes.

Under international law important legal consequences flow from these new factual situations for the entity concerned, whether a new state or a government. In order to fully operate on the international plane it must be recognised by other states. Recognition of a new entity may be defined as a discretionary function exercised unilaterally by the government of a state acknowledging the existence of another state or government or belligerent community.

State practice shows that the birth of a new state, the establishment of a new government and territorial changes are in general recognised by other states. However, it can also happen that a state may expressly withhold recognition. Recent recognition practice in respect of new states established after the collapse of the Soviet Union and the break up of the SFRY demonstrates that recognition of a state is not a matter governed by law but by an issue of policy, and that political considerations are paramount in respect of the recognition of new states. Recognition, as exemplified above, is more than ever an instrument of foreign policy, a means of expressing either approval or disapproval of the new situation. In the light of state practice regarding the recognition of the Baltic states, Russia, the former republics of the Soviet Union and states that emerged from the ruins of the

SFRY it is clear that recognition is a political act, that this topic is one of the most confusing areas of international law and that the rules of recognition are far from being certain.

Usually, once a new entity has been recognised, a recognising state will not retract its recognition if the requirements of statehood continue to be fulfilled. However, if a recognising state refuses to recognise a new government this refusal will not challenge the existence of a state. The matter of recognition of a new government arises normally when a new government comes to power by unconstitutional means. Therefore, a state may be recognised by a recognising state but its government may be denied recognition.

Recognition is important for two reasons. First, at the level of international law it shows that the recognised state possesses the attributes of statehood and that the recognising state is willing to engage in foreign relations with the recognised state. The recognition of a new government signifies that it is an effective government and that the recognising state expresses its willingness to initiate, or to continue, relations with that new government. State practice also includes the recognition of 'belligerency'. Second, at the level of municipal law, it will usually be entities that are recognised that will be accorded rights and have obligations under the law concerned.

5.2 Recognition in international law

Recognition is the willingness to deal with the new state as a member of the international community or with the new government as the representative of the state. Recognition is a matter of intention and may be express or implied. The act of recognition may be effected expressly, by a formal announcement or by a bilateral treaty of recognition, or, in some circumstances, impliedly through any act indicating an intention to effect recognition.

Express recognition

A formal announcement may take the form of a public statement, a congratulatory message on attainment of independence or a simple diplomatic note delivered to the entity which is to be recognised.

Express recognition may be granted by a bilateral treaty formally regulating the relations between the two states. This has been the method usually employed by the UK when establishing the independence of its colonial or other dependent territories as exemplified by the treaty the UK government and the provisional government of Burma signed on 17 October 1947 which expressly recognised 'the Republic of Burma as a fully independent sovereign state'.

Implied recognition

It is possible under certain circumstances for recognition to be implied from the conduct of one state towards another. It has been stated, however, that the recognition, by implication, must be unequivocal and clearly indicate that a recognising state has a clear and inescapable intention to do so. Lauterpacht was of the opinion that, in the case of recognition of states, only the 'conclusion of a bilateral treaty regulating comprehensively the relations between the two states, the formal initiation of diplomatic relations and, probably, the issue of consular exequaturs' would justify recognition by implication.

State practice shows that recognition is not implied:

1. by the fact that a state has become party to a multilateral treaty to which an unrecognised state was already a party;
2. by the fact that a state remains a party to a multilateral treaty after an unrecognised state becomes a party;
3. by the establishment of unofficial representatives;
4. by exchange of trade missions with the unrecognised state;
5. by the presentation of an international claim against, or by payment of compensation to, an unrecognised state;
6. by entering into negotiations with an unrecognised state. For example, at the Geneva Conference on Korea and Indo-China the US government entered into negotiations with communist China for the release of captured US airmen. The US delegation stated:

   > 'The United states government has made the decision to authorise informal United states participation in this meeting because of its obligations to protect the welfare of its citizens ... United states participation in these conversations in no way implies United states accordance of any measure of diplomatic recognition to the Red Chinese regime.'

   In practice many states are, for various reasons, forced to negotiate with unrecognised regimes. To avoid embarrassment such negotiations normally take place in secret;
7. by the admission of the unrecognised state to an international organisation, in respect of those states opposing the admission;
8. by the presence of the state at an international conference in which the unrecognised state participates.

Collective recognition

Collective recognition may arise in two contexts, the first being in situations where recognition is accorded collectively by a group of states, for example by a peace treaty, as illustrated by the Treaty of Versailles which recognised new states emerging after the end of World War I. The second when an entity is admitted as a new member of the UN.

Article 4 of the Charter of the United Nations sets out the conditions and the procedure for admission. Article 4(1) requires that a new member must love peace, must accept the obligations deriving from the Charter and must be able and willing to carry out those obligations. Under art 4(2) the absolute masters of the admission procedure are the Security Council and the General Assembly. The Security Council will verify whether the conditions laid down in art 4(1) are fulfilled by the applying entity, and at the recommendation of the Security Council the General Assembly will adopt a final decision. Despite the criteria for admission set out in art 4(1) an applying entity is not entitled to challenge a decision refusing its admission to the UN under procedural law. This was recognised by the ICJ in the *Case Concerning the Application of the Convention on the Prevention and Punishment of the Crime of Genocide: Bosnia and Herzegovina v Yugoslavia (Preliminary Objections)* (1996) ICJ Rep 1. While it is clear that non-admission does not act as an effective denial of the statehood of the entity concerned, and that admission to membership does not establish that the entity concerned has been recognised in so far as the bilateral relationship between the entity and each existing member is concerned, it is clear from state practice that admission to membership will be prima facie evidence of statehood.

In is important to note that the United Nations has acquired a function which was not envisaged in the Charter: a collective legitimation or, in its absence, collective illegitimation of new states as exemplified in the cases of Rhodesia and Palestine. In response to the Unilateral Declaration of Independence of Southern Rhodesia in 1965 the UN called upon its members not to recognise the new state, even though the purported state of Rhodesia fulfilled the traditional criteria of statehood. The non-recognition was justified on the ground that Rhodesia was created in violation of the fundamental principles of the UN: the prohibition of racial discrimination and apartheid and the right of people to self-determination.

On 15 November 1988 the Palestinian National Council at its extraordinary session in Algiers adopted a Declaration Creating the state of Palestine in the Land of Palestine with a Capital at Jerusalem. The State of Palestine did not satisfy the criteria for statehood as it had no defined territory and consequently no government exercising effective control over it. Despite that the General Assembly officially acknowledged the proclamation of independence of Palestine in December 1988 and approximately 100 states have recognised a new State of Palestine. The justification for the recognition of the state of Palestine was based on the right of the people of Palestine to self-determination.

In the case of Rhodesia the Security Council Resolution 221 (1966) was adopted under Chapter VII and thus was binding on all members of the United Nations, whilst in the case of Palestine the General Assembly Resolution 43/177 on Palestine had no binding force. Both decisions of the political organs of the UN have produced important legal consequences for the entities seeking recognition. In practice, Rhodesia was denied international personality and rejected by the international community, while the recognition of Palestine as a state, even though this perpetuated a legal fiction, has contributed to its progress towards an independent state.

The effects of recognition in international law

Recognition confers the legal status of a state under international law upon the entity seeking recognition. Such an entity becomes a subject of international law, initially vis-à-vis states recognising it and subsequently upon its admission to the UN as a member of the international community. Important legal effects derive from recognition.

There are two theories as to the legal effects of recognition: the constitutive theory and the declaratory theory. The state practice in respect of recognition of new states in the former Soviet Union and in the former Socialist Federal Republic of Yugoslavia has shown that there is no legal duty to recognise an entity which otherwise satisfies the criteria for statehood and therefore has challenged the very premise of the declarative theory.

Declaratory theory

The declaratory theory states that recognition is a mere formality serving no legal purpose. States exist as a matter of fact and the granting of recognition is merely an acknowledgment of that fact. Thus the position of an entity under international law stems from its actual control over territory and not from its recognition or non-recognition by the members of the international community. The declaratory theory was endorsed by the mixed arbitration tribunal in *Deutsche Continental Gas-Gesellschaft* v *Polish State* (1929) 5 AD 11. It was stated that:

> '... according to the opinion rightly admitted by the great majority of writers on international law, the recognition of a state is not constitutive but merely declaratory. The state exists by itself (par lui-même) and the recognition is nothing else than a declaration of this existence, recognised by the state from which it emanates.'

The objection to the declaratory theory is that it reduces recognition to an empty formality. The fact that a state possesses the attributes of statehood is not a guarantee that it will discharge its obligations under international law. Furthermore, its illegality of origin would not prevent it from being a state.

It is submitted that the declaratory theory is now obsolete. states have no duty to recognise a new state merely because it possesses all the factual attributes of statehood. State practice in respect of recognition of new states which have emerged after the collapse of the Soviet Union and the Socialist Federal Republic of Yugoslavia has conclusively rejected the declaratory theory.

Constitutive theory

The constitutive theory originates in the nineteenth century and is based on the positivist view of international law. According to the constitutive theory a state may possess all the formal attributes and qualifications of statehood but unless recognition is accorded it will not acquire international personality. This is exemplified by the case of the German Democratic Republic which was not recognised by the western powers until 1973. The subsequent recognition had a constitutive effect as far as the western powers were concerned and converted the Republic from an illegal Soviet 'puppet regime' into a state with full international rights and obligations.

There are several defects inherent in the constitutive theory.

1. New states are without rights and obligations under international law until recognised.
2. State practice shows that recognition is primarily a political act on the part of the states. Why should the legal status of an entity be dependent upon the performance of such a political act?
3. State practice shows that it may not be possible to ignore completely an unrecognised entity. For instance, while the US did not recognise Communist China, it nevertheless had to enter into negotiations with it on several occasions and thereby acknowledged its existence.
4. How many members of the international community must recognise the new entity?
5. Is existence relative to those states which do extend recognition?

The drawbacks of the constitutive theory have been particularly evident in the case of non-recognition of some of the states established after the break-up of the former Yugoslavia. They are examined below.

Under the constitutive theory recognition is of a purely political nature. The decision of a recognising state is therefore based on political expediency. Inevitably, therefore, there will arise situations in which an entity is recognised as a state by some members of the international community, but denied recognition by others – as exemplified by the cases of Munchukuo and the German Democratic Republic (GDR). Manchukuo was recognised by El Salvador, Germany, Hungary, Italy and Japan. Other states, including the US and those of the League of Nations, denied recognition on the ground that Manchukuo was a puppet state of Japan seized from China by illegal force. The GDR was denied recognition by the western powers for many years on the ground that it was a mere dependent territory of the Soviet Union and not a sovereign and independent state. The UK did not recognise the GDR until February 1973.

The application of the constitutive theory clearly demonstrates its drawbacks in the case of Yugoslavia.

The Socialist Federal Republic of Yugoslavia (SFRY) comprised six republics: Slovenia, Croatia, Serbia, Bosnia-Herzegovina, Montenegro and Macedonia, plus two autonomous regions – Kosovo and Vojvodina. All attempts to impose the national identity of Yugoslavia upon the people living within this territory failed; the only factor that had kept the various ethnic groups together was the 'towering political dominance' of President Tito. His death in 1980 resulted in a lack of political leadership and control, and over the next decade the SFRY had begun the process of dissolution. On 25 June 1991 both Croatia and Slovenia declared their independence. The new states attempting to oust the Yugoslav National Army from their territories were met by armed resistance. Violence followed. The European Community (EC), as a principal mediator in the conflict, requested both Republics to agree to a three-month review on the implementation of their declarations of independence. In August, after widespread violence in Croatia, the EC decided to establish both a Peace Conference on Yugoslavia and an Arbitration Commission made up of five presidents from various constitutional courts of the EC countries (named the Badinter Commission after the name of its chairman). After the expiry of the three-month moratorium Slovenia and Croatia formally seceded from Yugoslavia. This, and the unilateral declarations of independence of Ukraine and Byelorussia in July 1991, prompted the EC to establish a coherent policy regarding recognition of new states. On 16 December 1991 the EC foreign ministers meeting in Brussels issued two declarations – a Declaration on the Guidelines on the Recognition of the New States in Eastern Europe and in the Soviet Union and a Declaration on Yugoslavia. These two documents have significantly influenced the rules on recognition under international law. The Guidelines set out the following requirements for recognition.

1. Respect for the provisions of the UN Charter, the Final Act of Helsinki and the Charter of Paris, especially with respect to the rule of law, democracy and human rights.
2. Guarantees for the rights of ethnic and national groups and minorities in accordance with the commitments subscribed to in the framework of the Conference on Security and Co-operation in Europe (CSCE).
3. Respect for the inviolability of all frontiers, which may only be changed by peaceful means and by common agreements.
4. Commitment to settle by agreement or arbitration all issues concerning state secession and regional disputes.
5. Acceptance of all relevant commitments with regard to disarmament and nuclear non-proliferation, as well as to security and regional stability.
6. It also contained a clause stating that the EC countries 'will not recognise entities which are the result of aggression'.

Further requirements were laid down with regard to the Yugoslav Republics wishing to be recognised by the EC. They were required to apply to the EC for recognition by 23 December 1991. Their applications would then be submitted to the Arbitration Commission. Upon its recommendation a decision would be taken by the EC on 15 January 1992. Moreover, the applications would have to declare:

1. that they wished to be recognised as independent states;

2. that they accepted commitments contained in the 1991 EC Guidelines as mentioned above;
3. that they agreed to accept obligations respecting human rights and the rights of national and ethnic groups;
4. that they supported the continued effort of the UN and EC to resolve the Yugoslav crisis;
5. that they had no territorial claim towards any neighbouring EC member state.

The Republics of Slovenia, Croatia, Bosnia-Herzegovina and Macedonia applied for recognition through the Badinter Commission. In mid-January 1992 the EC granted recognition to the states of Slovenia and Croatia despite the fact that the Badinter Commission had found that Croatia did not satisfy the requirements laid down in the EC Guidelines, namely the Croation constitution did not contain sufficient guarantees in respect of the protection of human rights, especially relating to the status of minorities. The President of Croatia wrote a letter to the Badinter Commission confirming Croatia's acceptance of these obligations and thus satisfying the requirements of the Guidelines. Within the next few days, following the recognition of Slovenia and Croatia by the members of the EC, others such as Australia, Argentina, Canada and a number of European countries granted their recognition. Within a few months both countries were recognised worldwide by Japan, the US, China, India, etc. On 22 May 1992 they were admitted to the United Nations.

The recognition of Bosnia-Herzegovina by the EC was subject to an additional condition. The Badinter Commission recommended a referendum which would demonstrate whether the people of Bosnia-Herzegovina wished to constitute a sovereign and independent state. The referendum was duly held and with a turnout of 63.4 per cent almost all were in favour (99 per cent). At that time the tension in Bosnia-Herzegovina was growing as the Yugoslav National Army was there ready to defend the Serbian minority. On 7 April 1992 the US and the EC recognised Bosnia-Herzegovina. Subsequently, other countries also recognised. At the time of recognition the situation in Bosnia-Herzegovina deteriorated. The President of Bosnia-Herzegovina was kidnapped by the Yugoslav army upon his arrival from a peace conference in Lisbon. He was later released in exchange for a commitment guaranteeing safe passage out of Sarajevo for the Yugoslav army but the fight had already started. Bosnia-Herzegovina at the time of recognition was torn by violence and its government had no control over its territory.

In the case of Bosnia-Herzegovina its recognition as a state was prompted by the fact that the principles of non-intervention and the prohibition of the use of force were not applicable to Bosnia-Herzegovina before its recognition as a state. As other former republics it was regarded as a constituent part of the SFYR and the conflict between the Yugoslav National Army and the Bosnian moslems was seen as an internal conflict to which only the provisions of humanitarian law relating to civil wars were applicable and general rules on the protection of human rights. By recognising Bosnia-Herzegovina, notwithstanding the fact that the criterion of effective government was not satisfied (as the government of Bosnia-Herzegovina had control only over a small part of the national territory), the EC and the US, by way of a legal fiction, conferred on Bosnia-Herzegovina international legal personality and the status of a state with all ensuing consequences. These consequences being: the protection of its territorial integrity and political independence, the prohibition of intervention from other states, the prohibition of the use of force, the application of the full Geneva regime to the armed conflict taking place on its territory, the obligation of peaceful settlement of international disputes, etc.

The case of Bosnia-Herzegovina illustrates the importance of recognition and at the same time demonstrates the political nature of the act of recognition, thus evincing the fact that the declarative theory on recognition has been rejected by the international community.

The recognition, or rather non-recognition by the EC, of Macedonia in January 1992 was also based on political considerations. Macedonia satisfied all the criteria for statehood. The Badinter Commission recommended its recognition but the EC declined on account of Greek opposition regarding the name and the flag of Macedonia. Neither Macedonia nor Greece were willing to change their position. Only Bulgaria and Turkey recognised Macedonia. The breakthrough came in August 1992 with Russian recognition dictated by the concern about the security and stability of the Balkan region. Recognition as a political act has interesting implications in respect of Macedonia. On 27 April 1992 the Assembly of the SFRY enacted the constitution of the Federal Republic of Yugoslavia (FRY) proclaiming that the SFRY was transformed into the FRY, a state comprising two republics – Serbia and Montenegro. On the one hand the FRY had no claims in respect of Macedonia, on the other hand Macedonia was not recognised as a state. Under international law Macedonia became terra derelicta and was therefore, in theory, open to (military) intervention by a third state. The EC countries decided that this could not be permitted, especially taking into account the general situation in the Balkan region, and consequently recognised Macedonia as a state in 1993. Because of its status as terra derelicta the only protection that could be given to Macedonia by international law was under Chapter VII of the UN Charter, which empowers the Security Council, in the event of a military conflict occurring between Macedonia (an unrecognised entity) and a member of the United Nations, to use its powers to force a member state to respect the prohibition of the use of force. This is in conformity with the definition of aggression contained in General Assembly Resolution 3314 (XXIX) which states that every state enjoys protection 'without prejudice to questions of recognition or to whether a state is a member of the United Nations'. Therefore, only the procedural rules of Chapter VII of the Charter of the UN extend the protection provided by the prohibition of the use of force to new states not universally recognised.

The EC set an interesting precedent by inviting entities wishing to be recognised as states to apply for recognition. The requirements for recognition went beyond the traditional criteria for statehood but conformed with the existing state practice and the requirements for admission to the United Nations. The EC was seeking a commitment from entities waiting to be admitted to the international community in respect of the protection of human rights, especially concerning the protection of minorities, the rule of law and democracy. Consequently, what, for the existing states, would amount to the violation of the prohibition of intervention in internal affairs was required as a precondition for recognition in respect of new states. This clearly demonstrates that the constitutive theory on recognition has been endorsed by states and that an entity wishing to be recognised is not a subject of international law and thus has no international personality, with the ensuing consequences that some fundamental principles such as the prohibition of the use of force or the prohibition of intervention in internal affairs are not applicable to it before its recognition. Moreover, the EC, by acting in unison, has altered national policies on recognition of states by its member states including the UK.

It is also interesting to note that most states were in the context of the Yugoslav conflict waiting for formal recognition to be accorded by the EC before themselves recognising the new European states.

Lauterpacht argued that there was a legal duty imposed upon the existing states to grant recognition when a new entity satisfied the factual criteria for statehood. He stated that:

> 'In the absence of an international organ competent to ascertain and authoritatively to declare the presence of requirements of full international personality, states already established fulfil that function in their capacity as organs of international law. In thus acting they administer the law of nations. This legal rule signifies that in granting or withholding recognition states do not claim and are not entitled to serve exclusively the interests of their national policy and convenience regardless of the principles of international law in the matter': *Recognition in International Law*, New York: AMS Press, 1978, p6.

State practice has clearly challenged his opinion and demonstrates that there is no legal obligation imposed upon existing states to recognise an entity only because it satisfies the actual requirements of statehood.

5.3 Recognition of governments

The recognition of new states necessarily involves the recognition of new governments which have effective control over their territory. The situation is different when, in a state that has previously been recognised as a state, a government changes through unconstitutional means, by violence (eg a coup d'etat) or with foreign help. The distinction between the recognition of a state and the recognition of governments introduces a measure of confusion into the law of recognition but has some theoretical justification in the light of the two above-examined theories on recognition. However, the clear rejection of the declaratory theory in respect of the recognition of a state makes this distinction unnecessary and artificial. The recognition of a new government is based on political considerations. As in the recognition of new states, recognition of new governments may be lawfully withdrawn or withheld. The effects in municipal law of the non-recognition of a state or of its government are the same, save in the case where there is more than one authority requesting recognition as the government of the entity concerned.

There is no legal duty imposed upon states to recognise new governments. Examples include the non-recognition by the US and the Allied powers of the Tinoco regime that ruled Costa Rica between 1917 and 1919 and the non-recognition by the UK until 1921 (and by the US until 1933) of the Soviet government which came into power in 1919.

Approaches to the recognition of governments

Three approaches have been applied in respect of recognition of governments.

1. *An objective approach*, under which a state recognises a new government on a factual basis, namely that the new government has effective control over that state's territory and that this control seems likely to continue, without giving any judgment on the legality of that government or any approval. This approach is illustrated by the attitude of the UK government towards the Kadar government established in Hungary after the 1956 uprising. The Under Secretary of State for Foreign Affairs stated:

    > 'Her Majesty's Government have never taken any special step to recognise the Kadar Government ... They have ... continued to maintain a diplomatic mission there and to accept a Hungarian Mission in London. Generally speaking, Her Majesty's Government's policy in the matter of recognition of governments is to face facts and acknowledge de facto a government which has effective control of the territory within its jurisdiction, and of the inhabitants within that territory. Such de facto recognition does not constitute a judgment on the legality of the government concerned, still less does it imply approval of it.'

2. *A subjective approach*, under which a state by recognising a new government expresses its approval and endorses the policy of that new government. The US has always used the recognition of a new government as a powerful political tool.

3. *The Estrada doctrine*. As a response to the use of recognition by powerful nations as a means of extracting some concessions from new governments of small nations the 'Estrada doctrine' was put forward by the Mexican foreign minister, Genaro Estrada, in 1930. (Genaro Estrada's statement of this doctrine is reprinted in (1931) 25 AJIL, Supp, 203.) He rejected the doctrine of recognition of new governments because

    > '... it allows foreign governments to pass [judgment] upon the legitimacy or illegitimacy of the regime existing in another country, with the result that situations

arise in which the legal qualifications or national status of governments or authorities are apparently made subject to the opinion of foreigners.'

This approach avoids the disadvantages of the subjective and the objective approach. Indeed, if non-recognition can be an expression of disapproval of the new government then it can be argued that recognition may be interpreted as implying approval of the new government even in cases where no such approval was intended. The Estrada doctrine rejects the need for express and formal declarations granting recognition of governments. The doctrine has gained increasing support. In 1977 the US announced that it would no longer issue formal declarations of recognition of new governments and therefore recognition would be implied from any dealings between the governments.

In the UK in April 1980 the Foreign Secretary made a similar announcement. He emphasised that the practice of making a formal announcement, which was a simply neutral formality, recognising a new government had been sometimes misunderstood, despite explanations to the contrary, and was interpreted as implying approval.

De jure and de facto recognition

The terms 'de jure' and 'de facto' recognition have been traditionally applied to recognition of governments. The terms reflect the quality of the government rather than that of the act of recognition. De facto recognition of a new government is an interim step taken where there are doubts as to the legitimacy and the stability of the new government. The 1980 statement of the Foreign Secretary has changed the UK approach regarding recognition of new governments and thus made irrelevant the distinction between de facto and de jure recognition.

There are, however, many examples from pre-1980 practice which were based on this distinction. In particular two situations stand out where a distinction of this nature has been made.

1. Where a de facto authority is exercising the powers of government in an area under the nominal control of the existing de jure government of a state.

    In *Luther* v *Sagor* [1921] 3 KB 532 Bankes LJ described the distinction as follows:

    'A de jure government is one which in the opinion of the person using the phrase ought to possess the powers of sovereignty, though at the time it may be deprived of them. A de facto government is one which is really in possession of them, although the possession may be wrongful or precarious.'

For example, the UK recognised the government of the Soviet Union de facto in 1921 and de jure in 1924. In 1936 after the invasion of Abyssinia by Italy, Emperor Haile Selassie continued for two years to be recognised by the British government as the de jure government of Abyssinia.

2. Where the de jure government has ceased to exist and the recognised de facto authority is the only government of the state, but de jure recognition is withheld because of doubts as to the regime's degree of permanence, or as a sign of disapproval.

For example, in the case of Abyssinia, although Haile Selassie was recognised as the de jure government, de facto recognition was extended to the Italian regime following its occupation.

De facto recognition has been used by the UK as an expression of disapproval and has also been employed where the original de jure government has ceased to exist. For instance, Baltic states which were recognised as independent states in the early 1920s were invaded and subsequently forcibly annexed to the Soviet Union in 1940. In 1967 the UK Foreign Secretary stated that 'Her Majesty's Government recognises that Latvia, Lithuania and Estonia have been incorporated de facto into the Soviet Union but have not recognised this de jure'.

5.4 Recognition in municipal law

International lawyers frequently draw a distinction between the effects of recognition in municipal law in the case of states or governments. In general, there is little merit in making this distinction for a number of reasons. First, it will often be difficult in practice to distinguish between non-recognition of states and governments at the international level. For example, was the non-recognition by the UK of the Soviet Union prior to 1924 a failure to recognise the Soviet state or the Soviet government? Similarly, was the non-recognition of the Smith regime in Rhodesia post-UDI in 1965 a refusal to recognise an illegal government or a withholding of recognition from the Rhodesian state? At first sight these questions may appear straightforward. In truth, though, they are more complex.

Second, the distinction between non-recognition of states and governments for the purposes of municipal law is seldom significant because the effect of non-recognitions in either case will invariably be the same. Thus, it will make little difference whether entity 'X' or its government is not recognised. In either case, 'X' will not be entitled to claim sovereign immunity before English courts or to sue in this country. The reason why non-recognition will have the same effect in the case of a state or its government is that a state is invariably represented on the international plain by its government. The importance of this relationship draws attention, therefore, to the one set of circumstances when it will be important to distinguish between non-recognition of a state or its government for the purposes of municipal law, ie when the state in question remains recognised while the authority in control of the state is an illegal authority with which the third state has had no dealings.

Such a situation arose following the Iraqi invasion of Kuwait. While it was clear that the state of Kuwait remained a recognised entity, it was equally apparent that the Iraqi-imposed administration was not recognised. At one level, therefore, the non-recognition of the illegal administration was fatal to the international standing of the state. However, the attempts which were made by the deposed, but still recognised and legitimate, government of Kuwait to retain a measure of international personality to act on behalf of the state on the international level was successful. In these circumstances (ie where there are competing authorities in respect of the same state) it will be important to distinguish between the non-recognition of a state and its government.

Recognition of states in English law

Generally, English courts will not recognise a foreign state unless the UK Foreign Office certifies that it has been recognised by the British government.

The effects of recognition of a state in English law are as follows.

A recognised state has sovereign immunity and cannot be sued in the English courts without its consent

In *Duff Development Company* v *Government of Kelantan* [1924] AC 797 the House of Lords had to decide whether Kelantan, a state in the Malay Peninsula then under the protection of Great Britain, was an independent state so that it could claim state immunity in the English courts. The Under Secretary of State for the Colonies submitted a letter stating: 'Kelantan is an independent state in the Malay Peninsula … His Majesty the King does not exercise or claim any rights of sovereignty or jurisdiction over Kelantan'.

The above Colonial Office statement was accepted as binding by the court. Lord Dave said that 'it is the duty of the Court to accept the statement of the Secretary of state thus clearly and positively made as conclusive upon the point'.

An unrecognised state cannot sue in an English court and is not recognised for the purposes of conflict of laws

It is a rule of English conflict of laws that in cases of dispute over title to property, English courts will apply the lex situs, ie the laws of the state where the property is situated. In *Carl Zeiss Stiftung* v *Rayner and Keeler Ltd* [1964] 3 All ER 326 the court had to consider the validity of title to property based upon legislative and administrative acts of the German Democratic Republic. At the time of the case, the German Democratic Republic was not recognised by the British government who considered East Germany as being under the de jure control of the USSR.

The Court of Appeal therefore refused to apply East German law. Diplock LJ said that where English rules of private international law made reference to a foreign system of law, that law would only be regarded as effective in so far as it was:

'… made by or under the authority of those persons who are recognised by the Government of the United Kingdom as being the sovereign Government of the place where the thing happens.'

The correctness of this decision notwithstanding, the consequences of the application of this rule of law could potentially be very harsh. As in *Adams* v *Adams (Attorney-General Intervening)* [1971] P 188, where the UK courts refused to recognise a divorce granted by the Rhodesian courts, this strict conflicts approach could lead to hardship in the day-to-day transactions of ordinary people.

With this in mind the House of Lords reversed the decision of the Court of Appeal in *Carl Zeiss (No 2)* [1967] 1 AC 853. Two approaches to the problem of the non-recognition of East Germany were in evidence in their Lordships' decision. In the first place Lord Wilberforce indicated that, non-recognition notwithstanding, English courts should in some circumstances recognise the administrative acts of a non-recognised state. These comments pre-empted those of Lord Denning in *Hesperides Hotels* v *Aegean Turkish Holidays Ltd* [1978] 2 All ER 1168 (HL) (reversing [1978] QB 205 (CA)). In the second place the approach preferred by the majority of the Lords, was for the court to rely on a legal fiction. Thus, the Lords accepted that the East German government was an administration or subordinate authority controlled by the Soviet Union. As the Soviet Union was recognised by the UK government, the English courts could grant recognition to the acts of its local authority, normally the East German government.

It was therefore possible for the House to accept the acts of the unrecognised German Democratic Republic as being those of a subordinate authority of the USSR.

Lord Reid explained what would be the effect of a strict application of the rule of non-recognition:

'We must not only disregard all new laws and decrees made by the German Democratic Republic or its Government, but we must also disregard all executive and judicial acts done by persons appointed by that Government because we must regard this appointment as invalid. The results of that would be far reaching. Trade with the Eastern Zone of Germany is not discouraged, but the incorporation of every company in East Germany under any new law made by the German Democratic Republic or by the official act of any official appointed by its Government would have to be regarded as a nullity so that any such company could neither sue nor be sued in this country. Any civil marriage under any such new law or owing its validity to the act of any such official would also have to be treated as a nullity so that we should have to regard the children as illegitimate; and the same would apply to divorces and all manner of judicial decisions whether in family or commercial questions. That would affect not only the status of persons formerly domiciled in East Germany but also property in this country the devolution of which depended on East German law.'

Although the strict application of the rule that non-recognition equals non-existence was avoided by the House of Lords on the particular facts of the *Carl Zeiss Case*, nevertheless it may have effect in respect of other unrecognised states which may be called in question before the English courts.

The possibility of strict applications of the rule has attracted a great deal of criticism.

In *Hesperides Hotels* v *Aegean Turkish Holidays Ltd* [1978] QB 205 the plaintiff, a Greek Cypriot, owned two hotels which, following the Turkish invasion of 1974, were being run by Turkish Cypriots with the approval of the Turkish Cypriot administration which governed the part of Cyprus in which the hotels were located. The Court of Appeal rejected the plaintiff's action in trespass for lack of jurisdiction on the basis of English conflict of laws rules. The UK continues to recognise the pre-invasion government of Cyprus as the de jure government of the whole of Cyprus and does not recognise the Turkish administration de jure or de facto. Lord Denning stated, obiter:

> 'If it were necessary to [do so] ... I would unhesitatingly hold that the Courts of this country can recognise the laws or acts of a body which is in effective control of a territory even though it has not been recognised by Her Majesty's Government de jure or de facto: at any rate, in regard to the laws which regulate the day-to-day affairs of the people, such as their marriages, their divorces, their leases, their occupations, and so forth; and furthermore that the Courts can receive evidence of the state of affairs so as to see whether the body is in effective control or not.'

Recognition of governments in English law

In the past the English courts applied the same reasoning to the recognition of governments as they did to the recognition of states. The Foreign Office certificate of recognition being evidence of the government's existence.

If a government was not recognised, it was not entitled to sovereign immunity

A plea of immunity can be raised by an authority recognised as being in de facto control of territory, even if the proceedings are brought by the de jure sovereign.

The *Arantzazu Mendi* [1939] AC 256 case arose out of the Spanish Civil War. In June 1937, shortly before the Basque region of Spain fell to the Nationalist insurgents, the Spanish Republican government issued a decree requisitioning all ships registered in Bilbao, including the *Arantzazu Mendi* owned by the respondent Spanish company and which was at sea when the decree was issued. In March 1938 the Nationalist government issued a decree requisitioning ships registered in Bilbao. The respondent company did not oppose this second requisition and agreed to hold the ship, then in the Port of London, for the Nationalists. The Republican government then issued a writ for possession of the *Arantzazu Mendi* on the basis of its 1937 decree. The Nationalist government sought to have the writ set aside on the ground that it impleaded a sovereign state.

On the question whether the Nationalist government of Spain was a sovereign state the judge at first instance directed a letter to be written to the Secretary of state for Foreign Affairs as to the status of the Nationalist authorities. In reply it was stated that His Majesty's Government recognised Spain as a sovereign state and recognised the government of the Spanish Republic as the only de jure government of Spain or any part of it. The reply also stated that:

'5. His Majesty's Government recognises the Nationalist Government as a Government which at present exercises de facto administrative control over the larger portion of Spain.
6. His Majesty's Government recognises that the Nationalist Government now exercises effective administrative control over all the Basque Provinces of Spain.
7. His Majesty's Government have not accorded any other recognition to the Nationalist Government.
8. The Nationalist Government is not a Government subordinated to any other Government in Spain.
9. The question whether the Nationalist Government is to be regarded as that of a foreign Sovereign state appears to be a question of law to be answered in the light of the preceding statements and having regard to the particular issue with respect to which the question is raised.'

The court held that the Foreign Office letter established that the Nationalist government of Spain at the date of the writ was a foreign sovereign state and could not be impleaded. Lord Atkin stated:

'... this letter appears to me to dispose of the controversy. By "exercising de facto administrative control" or "exercising effective administrative control", I understand exercising all functions of a Sovereign Government, ie maintaining law and order, instituting and maintaining acts of justice, adopting or imposing laws regulating the relations of the inhabitants of the territory to one another and to the Government ... That the decree, therefore, emanated from the Sovereign in that territory there can be no doubt. There is ample authority for the proposition that there is no difference for the present purposes between a recognition of a state de facto as opposed to de jure. All the reasons for immunity which are the basis of the doctrine in international law as incorporated into our law exist.'

If a government was not recognised it could not sue or be sued in an English court

In *City of Berne* v *Bank of England* (1804) 9 Ves 347 it was held that an unrecognised government has no locus standi in English courts.

The question of the locus standi of an unrecognised government has arisen more recently before the English courts. In *GUR Corp* v *Trust Bank of Africa Ltd* [1986] 3 WLR 583 the question in issue was whether the government of the Republic of the Ciskei could be joined to the proceedings as third party. In the Queen's Bench Division Steyn J, after receiving a certificate from the Foreign Office indicating that:

'Her Majesty's Government does not recognise the "Republic of Ciskei" as an independent sovereign state, either de jure or de facto, and does not have any dealings with the "Government of the Republic of Ciskei" ',

held that the government of the Republic of Ciskei had no locus standi before English courts.

The case did not end there. On appeal, counsel for the Trust Bank, which sought to have the government of the Ciskei joined as third party, successfully argued, on the precedent of *Carl Zeiss*, that the government of the Republic of

Ciskei was 'a subordinate body set up by the Republic of South Africa to act on its behalf' and that, as such, it had locus standi before the courts of the UK.

The effect of this decision is to avoid, by the use of a legal fiction, doing an injustice to private parties in the conduct of their day-to-day activities.

If a government was not recognised its laws were not applied in English courts

In *Luther* v *Sagor* [1921] 1 KB 456 the defendant company purchased in 1920 a quantity of timber from the then recently constituted Soviet government of Russia. The plaintiff Russian company claimed title to the timber on the ground that it had come from a factory in Russia that had been owned by it before being nationalised by the Soviet government in 1919. The plaintiff argued, inter alia, that the decree should not be recognised by the English court because the Soviet government had not been recognised by Great Britain. Roche J held:

'If a foreign Government, or its sovereignty, is not recognised by the Government of this country the Courts of this country either cannot, or at least need not, or ought not, to take notice of, or recognise such foreign Government or its sovereignty ... I am not satisfied that His Majesty's Government has recognised the Soviet Government as the Government of a Russian Federative Republic or of any Sovereign state or power. I therefore am unable to recognise it, or to hold it has sovereignty, or is able by decree to deprive the plaintiff company of its property.'

On appeal this decision in favour of the plaintiff was reversed in the light of the intervening recognition of the Soviet government by the British government. This recognition was held to be retroactive and dated back to the actual coming into being of the recognised entity, which in this particular case was when the Soviets seized power in 1917. The decree confiscating the timber could therefore be recognised.

However, in the Court of Appeal, Bankes LJ stated that so far as the first instance decision was concerned: 'Upon the evidence which was before the learned judge I think that his decision was quite right'.

If a government was not recognised it was not entitled to the property of the state which it claimed to govern

Haile Selassie v *Cable and Wireless Limited (No 2)* [1939] 1 Ch 182: in 1935 Italy invaded Abyssinia and formally annexed the territory on 9 May 1936. Prior to the invasion the plaintiff had made a contract with the defendants for the transmission of wireless messages between Abyssinia and Great Britain. In 1937 the plaintiff commenced proceedings to recover money due under the contract. At this time the plaintiff was still recognised by Great Britain as the de jure sovereign although Italy was recognised as the de facto government.

The question before the court was stated as follows:

'Does the fact that the Italian Government has been and is recognised by the British Government as the de facto Government of Ethiopia vest in the Italian Government the right to sue for and obtain judgment in an English court for a debt formerly due to and recoverable by the plaintiff as the sovereign authority of Ethiopia, the debt being due to the plaintiff as Emperor of Ethiopia and the British Government recognising the plaintiff as the de jure Emperor of Ethiopia?'

At first instance Bennett J held that the plaintiff had not been divested of the right to sue for the debt in spite of the fact that the British government recognised the Italian government as the de facto government of virtually the whole of Abyssinia.

The defendants had relied, inter alia, on *Luther* v *Sagor* to establish the exclusive power of the de facto government. The learned judge distinguished the case, saying:

'I think the only point established by [*Luther* v *Sagor*] is that where the Government of this country has recognised that some foreign Government is de facto governing some foreign territory, the law of England will regard the acts of de facto Government in that territory as valid and treat them with all the respect due to the acts of a duly recognised foreign Sovereign state. It is clear I think that the acts so treated are acts in relation to persons or property in the territory which the authority is recognised as governing in fact.

It was not suggested in that case nor was anything said in it which supports the view that on or in consequence of such recognition a title to property in this country vests in the de facto Government and that a title vested in a displaced Government is divested ... The present case is not concerned with the validity of acts in relation to persons or property in Ethiopia. It is concerned with the title to a chose in action – a debt, recoverable in England.'

While an appeal by the defendants was pending the British government recognised the King of Italy as de jure Emperor of Ethiopia.
Sir Wilfrid Greene MR stated:

'It is not disputed that in the Courts of this country, His Majesty the King of Italy as Emperor of Abyssinia is entitled by succession to the public property of the state of Abyssinia and the late Emperor of Abyssinia's title thereto is no longer recognised as existent ... that right of succession is to be dated back at any rate to the date when the de facto recognition of the King of Italy as the de facto Sovereign of Abyssinia took place ... in December 1936 ... Now that being so the title of the plaintiff to sue is necessarily displaced.'

The question of claim to property also arose in *Republic of Somalia* v *Woodhouse Drake and Carey (Suisse) SA* [1992] 3 WLR 744. In this case, the incumbent government of Somalia purchased a cargo of rice for delivery at the port of Mogadishu. However, prior to delivery, the government was overthrown and a provisional government established. In the meantime, the cargo was not delivered to its port of destination due to fighting.

The provisional government of Somalia raised an action for recovery of the price of the undelivered goods and the court had to consider whether the provisional government had standing to bring the action.

Hobhouse J examined four criteria in order to decide whether the plaintiffs existed as the government of the state of Somalia: They were:

1. whether the plaintiffs were the constitutional government of the state;
2. the degree, nature and stability of administrative control, if any, that the plaintiffs maintained over the territory of the state;
3. whether Her Majesty's government had any dealings with the provisional government and, if so, what were the nature and extent of those dealings; and
4. the extent of the international recognition afforded by the world community as the government of the state.

The evidence submitted by the provisional government of Somalia failed to satisfy these criteria and the claim to the price of the consignment was rejected.

However, the withdrawal of de jure recognition and the retrospective effect of the granting of de jure recognition to the successor, did not affect the validity of the transactions already completed by the previous sovereign.

In *Gdynia Ameryka Linie Zeglugowe Spolka Akcyjna* v *Boguslawski* [1953] AC 11 the government of National Unity in Lublin became the de facto government of Poland on 28 June 1945, and at midnight 5–6 July 1945 the British government accorded de jure recognition to this government. Before this the Polish government-in-exile in London had been recognised de jure by Great Britain. The question at issue was whether the de jure recognition of the government of National Unity of 5–6 July had retroactive effect on the validity of acts done by the government-in-exile in London, in respect of the Polish merchant marine fleet and personnel under its control.

The Foreign Office certificate stated that the question of the retroactive effect of recognition of a government was a question of law to be decided by the courts. Their Lordships were unanimous in upholding the validity of the actions of the government-in-exile. Although the recognition of the government of National Unity in Lublin might be retroactive in its effect so far as Poland was concerned where the government had effective control, it could not apply retroactively to events over which it had no control, such as the actions taken in London prior to midnight 5–6 July by the government-in-exile.

In *Civil Air Transport Inc* v *Central Air Transport Corporation* [1953] AC 70 (PC) Viscount Simon stated that 'Primarily … retroactivity or recognition operates to validate acts of a de facto government which has subsequently become the new de jure government and not to invalidate acts of the previous de jure government'.

It is important to note the decision of the British government in April 1980 to abandon the practice of expressly recognising foreign governments has introduced an element of uncertainty into this particular area of the law.

In the House of Lords in May 1980, the Foreign Secretary, Lord Carrington, was asked:

'How in future, for the purposes of legal proceedings, it may be ascertained whether, on a particular date, Her Majesty's Government regarded a new regime as the government of the state concerned?'

The Foreign Secretary replied:

'In future cases where a new regime comes to power unconstitutionally our attitude to the question whether it qualifies to be treated as a government will be left to be inferred from the nature of the dealings, if any, which we may have with it, and in particular on whether we are dealing with it on a normal government-to-government basis.'

Possible problems in the implementation of the new policy

The abandonment of express recognition of foreign governments may give rise to several problems for the judges when deciding whether an entity qualifies to be treated as a government.

1. The Foreign Office may not make available to the judges details of its dealings with the foreign government.
2. If such details are made available it may be difficult for the judges, in the absence of diplomatic experience, to infer from the nature of those dealings whether or not the foreign government qualifies to be treated as a government.
3. If a government is in firm control of a state, it may be unjust to refuse to apply its laws in an English court solely because the British government refuses to have dealings with it.
4. The extent of a government's control over its territory, and not the extent of its dealings with the British government, remains the best test of its international status.
5. If the courts were to adopt the control test and the Foreign Office refused to provide the judges with details of a particular government's control over its territory, the judges may have difficulty in deciding whether such control does in fact exist.

The matter of recognition of a foreign government was examined in *Sierra Leone Telecommunications Co Ltd* v *Barclays Bank plc* [1998] 2 All ER 821. In this case Sierra Leone Telecommunications Co Ltd (Sierratel), incorporated in Sierra Leone, wholly owned by the government of Sierra Leone and controlled by it, held a US dollar account at Barclays Bank in London. The relevant bank mandate had been drawn up in July 1996 and provided for four signatories. In May 1997 the democratically elected government of President Kabbah was ousted in a military coup and replaced by a military junta. The ministers in the government of President Kabbah fled to the Republic of Guinea. The UK government had continued to deal with President Kabbah and had been active in demanding the restoration of the democratic government. The military regime was condemned by the UN, the Commonwealth, the Organisation of African Union (OAU) and the European Union.

In December 1997 Barclays Bank in London received a letter purportedly from Sierratel in Freetown which stated that a board meeting had resolved that the original bank mandate be suspended. The London Bank was faced with a dilemma as whether to respect the wishes of the original signatories to the mandate or whether to accept the new instructions emanating from the head office of Sierratel.

The Sierra Leone High Commissioner in London, who remained loyal to President Kabbah, began proceedings seeking a declaration that the London Bank account remained subject to the original mandate of July 1996.

The court held that the claimant was entitled to the declaration. The court stated that the question whether the military junta in Sierra Leone was to be regarded as the recognised government was to be tested by applying the criteria set out by Hobhouse J in *Republic of Somalia* v *Woodhouse Drake and Carey (Suisse) SA* (above). The court took into consideration the facts:

1. that the British government was continuing to deal with President Kabbah and had been active in seeking the restoration of his constitutional and democratic regime;
2. that the military junta did not have effective control beyond Freetown and could not be said to be in control of the entire country;
3. that the military regime had been condemned by the Commonwealth and the OAU;
4. that UN sanctions against the regime had been given force of law by delegated legislation in the UK.

The application of the criteria established in the Republic of Somalia to the above facts convinced the court that the military junta was not the government of Sierra Leone and thus lacked the legal capacity under the Sierra Leone constitution to alter the board of directors of Sierratel or to suspend the bank mandate.

This case indicates that, whatever the difficulties of English courts in deciding whether or not to accord recognition to governments, the criteria set out by Hobhouse J in the *Republic of Somalia* case represent sensible and workable guidelines. They are likely to become the governing orthodoxy on the matter.

6

Sovereignty and Equality of States

6.1 The doctrine of equality of states

6.2 Legal consequences of sovereign equality or independence

6.3 Domestic jurisdiction

6.1 The doctrine of equality of states

The doctrine of equality of states was introduced into the theory of international law by the naturalist writers. As de Vattel stated in 1758:

> 'A dwarf is as much a man as a giant; a small republic is no less a sovereign state than the most powerful kingdom': *de Droit des Gens, ou Principes de la Loi Naturelle*, Paris: J-P Aillaud, 1830, p47.

The doctrine recognises that all states are equal in law despite their obvious inequalities in other respects: inequality of size, wealth, population, strength or degree of civilisation. This principle of sovereign equality of states has found expression in the Charter of the United Nations, art 2(1) of which states: 'The Organisation is based on the principle of the sovereign equality of all its Members'.

The doctrine of equality may become seriously misleading. It cannot, for instance, mean that all states have equal rights, and that the legal notion of equality must therefore be limited in practical terms. The need for international co-operation in such areas as international peace and security and in economic and social matters has led states to accept limitations upon their national equality in relation to other states. For instance, politically the Great Powers have always exercised a primacy among states. Today this is illustrated by the Security Council of the United Nations in which certain states are given both permanent membership and a privileged voting position.

The better view today, therefore, is that the doctrine of sovereign equality of states is more accurately described as the independence of states. It has been suggested that it is difficult to find any consequence flowing from the doctrine of sovereign equality which does not equally flow from, and is not better explained by, the fact that states are independent.

6.2 Legal consequences of sovereign equality or independence

Certain practical consequences flow from the legal equality or independence of states.

Each state has a prima facie exclusive jurisdiction over a territory and the permanent population living there

States have a duty of non-intervention in the area of exclusive jurisdiction of other states:

1. no state can claim jurisdiction over another;
2. the courts of one state do not as a rule question the validity of the official acts of another state in so far as these acts purport to take effect within the latter's jurisdiction;
3. municipal courts will not exercise jurisdiction over a foreign sovereign in his public capacity.

Membership of international organisations is not obligatory, but as regards states who are members of such organisations:

1. when a question arises which has to be settled by consent, every state has a right to a vote and to one vote only;
2. the vote of the weakest state has as much weight as the vote of the most powerful.

Jurisdiction of international tribunals depends on the consent of the parties

In the *Eastern Carelia Case* (1923) PCIJ Rep Ser B No 5 the Permanent Court of International Justice stated that it is 'well established in international law that no state can, without its consent be compelled to submit its disputes with other states either to mediation or to arbitration, or to any other kind of pacific settlement'.

These principles were restated by the United Nations Special Committee on Principles of International Law Concerning Peaceful Relations and Co-operation among States in 1964:

'All states enjoy sovereign equality. As subjects of international law they have equal rights and duties:
(a) states are juridically equal;
(b) each state enjoys the rights inherent in full sovereignty;
(c) each state has the duty to respect the personality of other states;
(d) the territorial integrity and political independence of the state are inviolable;
(e) each state has the right freely to choose and develop its political, social, economic and cultural systems;

(f) each state has the duty to comply fully and in good faith with its international obligations, and to live in peace with other states.'

6.3 Domestic jurisdiction

One important consequence of the doctrine of sovereign equality of states is the principle that certain matters are within the exclusive competence of states and are not subject to international obligations. Thus, for example, such matters as the granting of nationality and a state's treatment of its own nationals within its territory are not subject to interference by other states or international organisations.

The principle is expressly stated in the Charter of the United Nations, art 2(7) of which provides:

'Nothing contained in the present Charter shall authorise the United Nations to intervene in matters which are essentially within the domestic jurisdiction of any state or shall require the Members to submit such matters to settlement under the present Charter; but this principle shall not prejudice the application of enforcement measures under Chapter VII.'

In practice art 2(7) has been given a narrow interpretation by the organs of the United Nations. They have claimed the inherent power to determine their own competence and therefore to undertake preliminary investigations to ascertain whether a particular matter is 'essentially within the domestic jurisdiction of any state'.

In practice the organs have taken action on a wide range of topics, despite protests from the states concerned that such matters were wholly within their domestic jurisdiction. These include such matters as human rights violations, the principle of self-determination and colonialism. The organs have expressed the view that if a matter is contrary to the purposes and principles of the Charter of the United Nations, or if it endangers international peace and security, then their competence to deal with the matter overrides any plea of domestic jurisdiction under art 2(7).

7

Territorial Sovereignty

7.1 Introduction

The occupation of territory and the exclusive exercise of jurisdiction therein is one of the essential elements of state sovereignty.

Territorial sovereignty was described in the *Island of Palmas Arbitration: The Netherlands* v *US* (1928) 2 RIAA 829 as being 'the right to exercise therein, to the exclusion of any other state, the functions of a sovereign'.

The concept of territory

The territory of a state is the foundation of its factual existence and the basis for the

98

exercise of its legal powers. The territory of a state comprises all land areas, including subterranean areas, waters, including national rivers, lakes, the territorial sea appurtenant to the land and the sea-bed and subsoil of the territorial sea and the airspace over the land and the territorial sea. Territorial sovereignty may be exercised over various geographical features analogous to land territory including islands, islets, rocks and reefs.

Other forms of territorial sovereignty

It is sometimes said that territorial sovereignty is indivisible, but there have been numerous instances in international practice both of division of sovereignty and of distribution of the components of sovereignty.

Titular, residual and distributed sovereignty

No territory, unless it be terra nullius, is without sovereignty and some entity must be isolated as sovereign. The entity which has the ultimate capacity of disposing of the territory may be said to possess 'titular' or 'residual' sovereignty: the entity which exercises plenary power over the territory but lacks the capacity of ultimate disposal may be said to possess 'effective' sovereignty. The two together, residual and effective powers, make up the totality of sovereignty.

Similarly, two or more entities may exercise divided functions, and this may give rise to either dual, divided or distributed sovereignty depending upon whether the actors must act jointly or may act separately within defined spheres of competence.

Residual sovereignty

Oppenheim describes this form of sovereignty as 'nominal'. It occurs when a grantor cedes the administrative competence of a territory to a foreign power by treaty during a time of peace. Thus Japan placed the Ryukya Islands under US administration under art 3 of the Treaty of Peace 1951, while retaining residual sovereignty in the islands: R Jennings and A Watts (eds), *Oppenheim's International Law*, 9th ed, vol I, Harlow: Longman, 1992, pp567 and 568.

Condominium

According to Oppenheim, condominium occurs when two or more states, under the joint tenancy, exercise sovereignty conjointly over a piece of territory and its inhabitants.

The best example was the Anglo-French Condominium of the New Hebrides constituted in 1906. This arrangement was said to create 'a region of joint influence ... each of the two Powers retaining sovereignty over its nationals ... and neither exercising a separate authority over the group'.

Indeterminate sovereignty

It may be that a piece of territory which is not a res nullius nevertheless has no determinate sovereign. This would apply for instance in a situation where a sovereign has renounced his sovereignty and the coming into being of a new sovereign or an interregnum is postponed until a certain condition is fulfilled, or there is a dispute as to who the new sovereign is. An example is that of Japan's renunciation of any right to Formosa (now Taiwan) and the subsequent claims of both the Communist regime which controlled mainland China and the Nationalist government installed in Taiwan to represent the whole of China, including Taiwan. Neither government has ever submitted that Taiwan was a separate state. As a result Taiwan appears to be a non-state territorial entity which is de jure part of China but under separate administration.

Terminable and reversionary sovereignty

Territorial sovereignty may be defeasible by operation of law, for example, by reversion on the failure of a condition under which sovereignty was transferred. This situation could come into being in Monaco where independence is subject to there being no vacancy in the Crown of Monaco. Otherwise Monaco will revert to France.

The notion of reversionary sovereignty was applicable for example to the mandate system established under the League of Nations whereby the principal powers who placed their territories under mandate retained a reversionary interest in the territory until it attained independence.

Other territorial regimes

In addition to territorial sovereignty three other territorial regimes are recognised by international law.

1. Territory not subject to the sovereignty of any state or states and which possesses a status of its own (eg mandate and trust territories).
2. The res nullius, being land legally susceptible to acquisition by states but not as yet placed under territorial sovereignty.
3. The res communis, consisting of the high seas and also outer space, which is not capable of being placed under the sovereignty of any state.

7.2 The acquisition of territory

Traditional international law distinguishes several modes by which sovereignty can be acquired over territory. They were originally based on Roman law rules regarding acquisition of property. The Roman law analogy was well suited to the system of absolute monarchy prevalent in Europe during the formative years of European expansion in the sixteenth and seventeenth centuries where the Prince was regarded as 'owner' of his state's territory. However, with the decline of private law notions in the eighteenth and nineteenth centuries the analogy with the Roman law rules became less distinct and today, under current international law, it can be argued that such an analogy serves no useful purpose and indeed gives a distorted view of current practice.

The five modes by which territory has traditionally said to have been acquired are: occupation; prescription; accretion; cession; and conquest. These modes are not, however, exclusive or exhaustive. In practice it is unlikely that any single mode would be evident in isolation. The modes are interrelated and in complex cases may be used in conjunction to the extent that no one mode appears dominant. In addition, these modes do not adequately describe the acquisition of territory by newly independent states exercising a right to self-determination. It must also be borne in mind that the traditional modes of acquisition of territory found a place in legal reasoning during the formative stages of international law. In a number of cases it will, therefore, still be evident that these modes are based on a Western perception of the status of the territory prior to acquisition. As is illustrated in more detail below, acquisition of territory by occupation, for example, is based on the fundamental perception that the territory was previously terra nullius, ie not under the sovereignty of any state. By terra nullius it was, however, implied that the territory was not under the sovereignty of any other recognised state, ie one of the small club of state entities to which international law was deemed to have application. It would not defeat a claim for acquisition by occupation to show that the territory in question was inhabited.

The historical origins of the traditional modes of acquisition of territory thus makes it important to examine disputed claims to sovereignty in the light, also, of contemporary principles of international law.

7.3 Occupation

This is an original mode of acquisition whereby a state acquires sovereignty over a terra nullius (ie territory not under the sovereignty of any state). The territory may be new land having previously never belonged to any state. It may have been abandoned by the former sovereign or it may have been occupied by a people lacking the social and political organisation necessary to constitute a sovereign state under international law. For example, the existence of the Australian aborigines notwithstanding, Australia was regarded as terra nullius at the time of its original settlement by the UK.

What constitutes occupation?

Territory is occupied when it is placed under effective control which is a relative concept varying according to the nature of the territory concerned. For instance, it will be much easier to establish effective control over territory which is uninhabited than over territory which is inhabited albeit by a primitive people.

In the *Legal Status of Eastern Greenland Case: Norway* v *Denmark* (1933) PCIJ Rep Ser A/B No 53 the Permanent Court of Justice said:

> '... a claim to sovereignty based not upon some particular act or title such as a treaty of cession but merely upon a continued display of authority, involves two elements each of which must be shown to exist: the intention and will to act as Sovereign; and some actual exercise or display of such authority.'

These two elements are examined below.

The intention and will to act as sovereign

Brownlie argues that the intention and will to act as sovereign is a subjective criterion involving the imputation of a state of mind involving a legal assessment and judgment to those ordering various state activities. He says, therefore, that this approach expects too much and is unrealistic in seeking a particular and coherent intention in a mass of activity by numerous individuals.

This requirement of animus possidendi also leads to problems where there are competing acts of sovereignty. Today all habitable areas of the earth fall under the dominion of some state and, therefore, the importance of acquisition by occupation lies not in the acquisition of new territory but the solving of boundary disputes and competing claims based on past occupation. So in cases where there are competing acts of sovereignty the subjective requirement of the animus possidendi of the competing states may be inconclusive. In such cases the determination of the matter relies on objective elements of state activity, ie the actual manifestations of sovereignty.

The intention to act as sovereign as a requirement of effective occupation is important in three respects.

1. The activity must be that of the state or its authorised agent and not that of a mere individual.
2. The activity must not be exercised by consent of another state.
3. The activity taken as a whole must have no other explanation but the assumption of pre-existing sovereignty.

Effective exercise or continued display of authority

Possession must give the occupying state control over the territory concerned and there must be some display of state activity consistent with sovereignty. The traditional view is one of occupation in terms of settlement and close physical possession. However, under current international law what constitutes the necessary degree of control will vary with the circumstances of the case.

In the *Island of Palmas Arbitration*: *The Netherlands* v *US* (1928) 2 RIAA 829 the

US claimed the Island of Palmas which lies half-way between the Philippines and what was then the Dutch East Indies. The US founded its title upon the 1898 Treaty of Paris by which Spain ceded the Philippine Islands to the US. In this Treaty the island of Palmas was described as forming part of the Philippines. However, the island was actually under Dutch control. The issue was therefore whether sovereignty over the island belonged to Spain at the time she purported to cede the island to the US.

The arbitrator held that even if Spain did originally have sovereignty over the island the Dutch had administered it since the early eighteenth century, thereby supplanting Spain as the sovereign. He stated that:

'... the continuous and peaceful display of territorial sovereignty (peaceful in relation to other states) is as good as a title ...

Manifestations of territorial sovereignty assume, it is true, different forms, according to conditions of time and place. Although continuous in principle, sovereignty cannot be exercised in fact at every moment on every point of a territory. The intermittence and discontinuity compatible with the maintenance of the right necessarily differ according as inhabited or uninhabited regions are involved, or regions enclosed within territories in which sovereignty is incontestably displayed or again regions accessible from, for instance, the high seas.'

The learned arbitrator found ample expression of the Dutch arguments based upon peaceful and continuous display of state authority over the island. These included the close link existing since 1677 between the people of the island and The Netherlands via the Dutch East India Company and the unchallenged peaceful display of Dutch sovereignty from at least 1700 to the outbreak of the present dispute in 1906.

In *Clipperton Island Arbitration: France* v *Mexico* (1932) 26 AJIL 390 the arbitrator stated that 'the actual and not the nominal, taking of possession is a necessary condition of occupation', and the taking of possession consisted of an exercise of state authority sufficient in the circumstances of the territory concerned, ie the inaccessible and uninhabited nature of the island. So that in the particular case an offshore geographical survey of the uninhabited island, a landing by a small shore party, followed by a declaration of sovereignty published in a Honolulu journal were held to be sufficient to support the French claim.

In the *Legal Status of Eastern Greenland Case* (above) the dispute arose out of the action of Norway in proclaiming its occupation of parts of East Greenland in 1931. Denmark argued that Danish sovereignty extended to the whole of Greenland. On the evidence submitted the Court was satisfied that Denmark's intention to claim title to the whole of Greenland was established, at least after 1721. It was, therefore, necessary to next discover some actual exercise or display of authority by Denmark over the disputed territory. The following factors were submitted in evidence.

1. The absence, until 1931, of any competing claim by another state.
2. The character of the country – the arctic and inaccessible nature of the

uncolonised parts of the territory where it would be unreasonable to demand a continuous exercise of authority.
3. The numerous Danish legislative and administrative acts purporting to apply to the whole of Greenland.
4. Treaties with other states acquiescing to the Danish claim to the territory.
5. The granting of a trade monopoly and the granting of trading, mining and other concessions.

The Court held that this pattern of activity between 1721 and 1931 was sufficient to establish Danish title to the whole of the territory.

An example of this more modern and practical approach to occupation was provided by the Anglo–French dispute involving the *Minquiers and Ecrehos Islands Case: France* v *UK* (1953) ICJ Rep 47. In appraising the relative strength of the opposing claims to sovereignty over the Ecrehos the Court stated that it 'attaches, in particular, probative value to the acts which relate to the exercise of jurisdiction and local administration and to legislation'. The Court referred to the exercise of criminal jurisdiction, the holding of inquests, the collection of taxes and to a British Treasury Warrant of 1875 including the 'Ecrehos Rocks' within the Port of Jersey.

A further example of the development of this approach is provided by the *Rann of Kutch Arbitration: India* v *Pakistan* (1968) 7 ILM 633. In the case of a traditional agricultural economy the tribunal was able to concede that grazing and other economic activities by private landholders may provide acceptable evidence of title.

The critical date
Bound up with the issue of the continuous display of authority is the question of the date at which sovereignty comes to be assessed. This 'critical date' is the date beyond which further evidence of the exercise of sovereign authority will not be allowed. This judicial technique is important for two reasons. First, it establishes a point beyond which the parties will not be called upon to provide evidence of authority. Particularly in cases of uninhabited or sparsely inhabited territories it would make little sense to require that the display of authority be constantly in evidence. Second, in the case of disputed territories where the dispute arises in respect of the initial circumstances of acquisition rather than the display of authority thereafter, the critical date will be important in determining which factors are to be taken into account by the court or tribunal. In the *Taba Arbitration* (1988) 80 ILR 226, for example, involving a boundary dispute between Egypt and Israel in the area of the Sinai along the Gulf of Aqaba, the Tribunal determined that '29 September 1923, the date of the formal entry into force of the Mandate, is the appropriate date in the circumstances'.

While the critical date will invariably be apparent from the facts of the case, its determination by the court or tribunal, particularly in the face of conflicting evidence from the parties, may be of great significance to the merits of dispute. The choice of one or other date may, for example, preclude a party from adducing particular evidence or may alter the case from one of occupation to one of prescription. The choice of the critical date is thus a useful practical tool available to the court to restrict or broaden the scope of the argument.

A state may ratify an act by one of its nationals purporting to appropriate territory on its behalf. The activities of chartered companies and corporations to which powers of acquisition and government may have been delegated by the state will also be regarded as state activity in relation to the acquisition of territory.

7.4 Acquisitive prescription

Prescription

Like occupation this is based on effective control over territory, but whereas occupation is acquisition of terra nullius, prescription is the acquisition of territory which belongs to another state.

Oppenheim describes prescription as:

'The acquisition of territorial sovereignty through continuous and undisturbed exercise of sovereignty over it during such a period as is necessary to create, under the influence of historical development, the general conviction that the present condition of things is in conformity with international order': R Jennings and A Watts (eds), *Oppenheim's International Law*, 9th ed, vol I, Harlow: Longman, 1992, p706.

According to Brownlie:

'The essence of prescription is the removal of defects in a putative title arising from usurpation of another's sovereignty by the consent and acquiescence of the former sovereign': *Principles of Public International Law*, 5th ed, Oxford: Oxford University Press, 1998, p151.

Generally, however, prescription as to title to territory is ill-defined and indeed some writers deny it recognition altogether. Learned writers have, however, described three categories of situations in which the doctrine of prescription may operate: immemorial possession; competing acts of sovereignty; cases of acquiescence.

Immemorial possession

This is the presumption of a legal title in cases where the original basis of title is uncertain. It has been argued, however, that this cannot be a true case of prescription since the origin of the possession is unknown.

Competing acts of sovereignty

In practice the difference between occupation and prescription in claims based upon the nominal exercise of sovereignty may be impossible to ascertain. The very point at issue may be whether the territory was terra nullius or whether it was subject to previous sovereignty. In the *Island of Palmas Arbitration* (above), for example, the court did not make clear whether the island was under Spanish sovereignty before the Dutch began to exercise control.

When faced with competing claims, international tribunals often decide in favour of the state which can prove a greater degree of effective control over the disputed territory, without basing their judgment on any specific mode of acquisition. Again, therefore, in such cases references to prescription may be misleading.

Acquiescence

A combination of the passage of time and the implied acquiescence of the alleged dispossessed sovereign are the basis of prescriptive rights.

The four requirements for acquisitive prescription

1. Possession must be exercised a titre de soverain. There must be a display of state authority and the absence of any recognition of sovereignty in another state.
2. Possession must be peaceful and uninterrupted. What conduct is sufficient to prevent possession from being peaceful and uninterrupted? Any conduct indicating a lack of acquiescence, eg protest. Effective protests prevent acquisition of title by prescription.

    In the *Chamizal Arbitration: US v Mexico* (1911) 5 AJIL 782 the US laid claim to an area of Mexican territory which had become joined to US territory by the movement of the Rio Grande southwards, inter alia, on the ground of uninterrupted possession. The claim failed because Mexico had made a number of protests to the US, and indeed as a result of the protests a convention had been signed in an attempt to settle 'the rights of the two nations with regard to the changes brought about by the action of the waters of the Rio Grande'. Therefore in the opinion of the commissioners, diplomatic protests by Mexico prevented title arising.

    However, it is doubtful whether diplomatic protests alone are sufficient to preserve the rights of a dispossessed sovereign. There must be some serious expression of protest, eg the severing of diplomatic relations or the imposition of sanctions as a retaliation. The matter should be raised before the United Nations and reinforced by a bona fide suggestion that the dispute be submitted to arbitration or judicial settlement.

    In the *Minquiers and Ecrehos Islands Case* (above) the UK argued that French protests against British legislation applying to the disputed islands were ineffective, inter alia, on the ground that they should have been reinforced by pressure to have the matter submitted for determination by an international tribunal.

    This will be particularly relevant where the parties are bound by treaty providing for the settlement of their legal disputes by the Permanent Court of Arbitration.

    However, while some jurists do regard protest as merely effecting a postponement for a reasonable period of the process of prescription while advantage is taken of the available machinery for the settlement of international disputes, this approach can be criticised. Should failure to resort to certain organs be penalised by loss of territorial rights? Is it proper to demand all territorial disputes to be referred to international arbitration? Should procedural requirements be introduced into the concept of acquiescence?

3. The possession must be public. If there is to be acquiescence then there must be publicity.

4. The possession must persist. The effective control necessary to establish title by prescription must last for a longer period of time than the effective control which is necessary in cases of occupation. Unlike the situation under municipal law there is no fixed period in international law. The length of time required, therefore, is a matter of fact depending on the particular case.

Historical consolidation

Whatever limitation may exist in cases of adverse possession there will come a time when there will be created a belief that however wrongful the original taking, or whatever protests have been made, the present condition of things should not be disturbed.

The doctrine was first expressed in the *Anglo-Norwegian Fisheries Case: UK* v *Norway* (1951) ICJ Rep 116 with reference to the Norwegian decrees which had the effect of extending the area of internal waters through the use of straight baselines as the base points for the delimitation of the territorial sea. The exercise of sovereignty claimed by Norway was, therefore, over res communis and, therefore, general acquiescence of all foreign states was necessary.

The Court commented:

'Since ... these ... constitute ... the application of a well defined and uniform system, it is indeed this system itself which would reap the benefit of general toleration, the basis of an historic consolidation which would make it enforceable as against all states.'

De Visscher cites the decision as an example of the 'fundamental interest of the stability of territorial situations from the point of view of order and peace'.

According to De Visscher's doctrine, consolidation differs from prescription, occupation and recognition:

'... consolidation differs from acquisitive prescription ... in the fact that it can apply to territories that could not be proved to have belonged to another state. It differs from occupation in that it can be admitted in relation to certain parts of the sea as well as of land. Finally, it is distinguished from international recognition ... by the fact that it can be held to be accomplished ... by a sufficiently prolonged absence of opposition either, in the case of land, on the part of states interested in disputing possession or, in maritime waters, on the part of the generality of states.'

In addition, historic consolidation also takes cognisance of other special factors including economic interests and resources.

Criticisms of the doctrine of consolidation

Jennings points out that, however important consolidating factors might be, it is still the fact of possession which is the foundation of the process of consolidation. The process cannot begin until actual possession is enjoyed and this is a necessary prerequisite in order to prevent evidence of an alleged political right or claim to have title transferred, being adduced as the foundation of a legal title.

7.5 Accretion

A state has the exclusive right of sovereignty over any additions made to its territory as a result of silting or other deposits or resulting from the formation of islands within its territorial waters. Although not of great importance it can be of significance where a state boundary follows the course of a river. Where a boundary river undergoes a sudden change of course (avulsion) this will not change the boundary line which will remain usually the centre line of the former main channel.

In the *Chamizal Arbitration* (above) the question arose as to which state had title to the tract of land between the old and the new river beds. The boundary commission held that the part of the tract that had occurred by accretion belonged to the US, ie the US had acquired title by accretion. That part of the land that had resulted from a flood, in contrast, remained with Mexico.

In *Louisiana* v *Mississippi* (1940) 282 US 458 the United states Supreme Court applied international law principles to a boundary dispute between the two federal states. The Court held that the gradual erosion of soil from the Mississippi bank and its deposit on the Louisiana bank between 1823 and 1912 passed title to Louisiana. But when the river suddenly changed course in 1913 across the accretion of the previous 90 years this did not divest Louisiana of the territory already acquired. This change was an avulsion and therefore the pre-1913 boundary remained.

7.6 Cession

This is the transfer of territory, usually by treaty, from one state to another, the treaty forming the legal basis of sovereignty. It may be either gratuitous or for some consideration, eg the sale to the US by Denmark of the Danish West Indies in 1916.

Cession is an example of a derivative title. If there were defects in the ceding state's title, the purported cession from the previous sovereign cannot cure the defect.

In the *Island of Palmas Arbitration* (above) the US claimed that by the Treaty of Paris 1898 it acquired title to the island of Palmas from Spain. However, the Arbitrator found that at the time of the purported transfer of the island in 1898 sovereignty over the island lay not with Spain but with The Netherlands. Spain could not transfer more rights than she herself possessed. Therefore since Spain had no title to the island in 1898, the US could not acquire title from Spain.

In order to effect a valid cession there should normally be both a treaty and an actual transfer of possession: *Iloilo Case* (1925) 4 RIAA 158. The Treaty of Paris, signed on 10 December 1898, provided that on exchange of ratifications, Spain should evacuate the Philippines in favour of the US. However, on 24 December local insurgents forced the Spanish to withdraw and it was not until 10 February that American troops captured Iloilo from the insurgents. On the following day the insurgents set fire to the town damaging property of British subjects. The British-American tribunal hearing claims for damaged property held that as the treaty did not take effect until ratification on 11 April, the transfer of de jure sovereignty to the US, and its resulting obligations, did not commence until that date.

There is, however, no need for a transfer of possession if the state to which the territory is ceded is already in possession. Similarly, in cases such as Lombardy which was ceded by Austria to France in 1860 and then immediately retroceded by France to Italy, there was no requirement for France to actually enter into possession.

7.7 Conquest

Under traditional international law conquest was recognised as a means of acquiring territory even in the absence of a treaty of cession, but the acquisition of territory by conquest was not lawful until hostilities had come to an end. Therefore, in the absence of a peace treaty evidence was necessary that all resistance by the enemy state and by its allies had ceased so that there were no longer forces in the field to free the occupied territory from the control of the conquering power. Thus, the German annexation of Poland during World War II was invalid, because Poland's allies continued to struggle against Germany.

Even when a state has been completely subjugated there would be no transfer of sovereignty in the absence of an intention to annex it. Thus, in 1945 the victorious Allies expressly disclaimed the intention of annexing Germany, although they had occupied all German territory and defeated her Axis allies.

While acquisition of territory by conquest may have been acceptable during the period when there was no legal restriction upon the right of a state to wage war, it is now generally accepted that the Covenant of the League of Nations, the Pact of Paris, and, more importantly, art 2(4) of the United Nations Charter restrict the ability of a state to acquire territory by conquest.

The effect of the change

Once the proposition is accepted that an aggressor state cannot acquire territory by conquering another state through the illegal use of force, it follows that an aggressor cannot now acquire territory by conquest alone and that any treaty of cession imposed by the victor on the vanquished will be invalid.

Can an 'innocent party' to a war still acquire territory by conquest?

Can a state acting in self-defence acquire territory by conquest? The Soviet view was that states acting in self-defence may impose sanctions on a defeated aggressor: in particular, they are empowered to take away part of the territory of the aggressor in order to prevent a recurrence of the aggression.

However, the Declaration on Principles of International Law Concerning Friendly Relations and Co-operation among States in Accordance with the Charter of the United Nations, passed by the General Assembly in 1970, suggests otherwise:

> 'The territory of a state shall not be the object of military occupation resulting from the use of force in contravention of the provisions of the Charter. The territory of a state shall not be the object of acquisition by another state resulting from the threat or use of force.'

So any threat of or use of force, whether in contravention of the United Nations Charter or not, invalidates the acquisition of territory. For example, both the General Assembly and the Security Council of the United Nations have repeatedly declared that Israel is not entitled to annex any of the territory it captured following the war of June 1967. The Security Council affirmed in 1968 that the 'acquisition of territory by military conquest is inadmissible' and that all measures taken by Israel in the occupied territories were invalid and ineffective to change the status of that territory.

But it must be remembered that as long as the international community of states is not determined to prevent aggressors from enjoying their spoils the principle that an aggressor cannot acquire a good title to territory is liable to produce serious discrepancy between the law and the facts. It will depend upon political rather than legal circumstances.

The invasion of Goa 1961

Portugal retained this colony on the Indian subcontinent until it was invaded by India and incorporated into its own territory. This illegal use of force by India and the subsequent annexation of Goa received the approval of many members of the United Nations and there was no condemnation of the act by either the Security Council or the General Assembly.

It can be argued that India has obtained a basis of title which, even if there is no express recognition of the fact, will become consolidated over a relatively short period of time, by the acquiescence of the international community into a fully valid title.

Consider the case of Namibia, one of the last instances of conquest. If the ICJ had not declared South Africa's occupation of the territory illegal and if there had been no opposition to this state of affairs, would the international community have eventually acknowledged the reality of South Africa's title?

Similarly with the Falkland Islands. If Britain had not repossessed the islands by force would the illegal Argentinian invasion and occupation have eventually been regarded by the international community as confirming Argentina's claim to sovereignty over the islands?

The invasion of Kuwait 1990

On 2 August 1990 Iraqi armed forces invaded Kuwait and subsequently the Iraqi government announced its intention to establish a 'comprehensive and eternal merger' between the two states. On 8 August, Iraq again declared its intention to annex Kuwait and that it would become the nineteenth province of Iraq and instructed all foreign diplomats to leave Kuwait. Foreign embassies and consulates were closed by the Iraqi authorities.

In response, the UN Security Council adopted Resolution 662 (1990) of 9 August 1990, which declared that the 'annexation of Kuwait by Iraq under any form and whatever pretext has no legal validity and is considered null and void'. The Resolution also called upon all states to refrain from extending recognition to the purported annexation and to abstain from any actions that could be construed as indirect recognition of the annexation.

This Resolution was ignored by Iraq and preparations were made by the Iraqi government to declare Kuwait as its nineteenth province. The Security Council therefore adopted a second Resolution relating to the Iraqi claim to have acquired the territory of Kuwait by means of conquest and annexation. Specifically referring to the obligations of Iraq under international law, Security Council Resolution 664 (1990) reaffirmed that the annexation of Kuwait by Iraq was null and void and demanded that the government of Iraq rescind its orders for the closure of the diplomatic and consular missions in Kuwait and the withdrawal of immunity of their personnel.

Both these Resolutions are evidence that the acquisition of territory by means of annexation and conquest is no longer a valid method of obtaining title under international law.

7.8 Other circumstances relevant to the acquisition of territory

Contiguity

Contiguity alone is not a basis of title. However, it is a fact which may influence the decision of an international tribunal in cases, for instance, where sovereignty has not been exercised uniformly in every part of the territory or where only the coast of a barren territory has been occupied or in cases where it is desired to give effect to principles of geographic unity. For example, in the *Legal Status of Eastern Greenland Case* where Danish sovereignty over the whole of Greenland was conferred, the actual areas of the disputed territory settled by Denmark were few.

Contiguity is also the basis of the law concerning territorial waters, the contiguous zone and the continental shelf.

Recognition, acquiescence and estoppel

Although they are not strictly speaking modes of acquisition they do play an important role in the acquisition of territory in the sense that they may provide evidence of control where there are competing acts of possession.

Recognition

Recognition refers to the attitude of third states. This may take the form of a unilateral express declaration or may occur in treaty provisions with third states. In the *Legal Status of Eastern Greenland Case* (above) the Court referred to treaties between Denmark and states other than Norway as constituting evidence of recognition of Danish sovereignty over Greenland in general.

Recognition and acquisition by conquest

Although states are no longer permitted to acquire territory by conquest the invalidity of such territorial acquisitions may be cured by recognition, subject to certain conditions.

1. The recognition must take the form of an express statement and cannot be implied.
2. The recognition must be de jure and not merely de facto.
3. The recognition must be acknowledged not only by the victim but also by third states.

Acquiescence

This applies to the attitude of the dispossessed state and is inferred from its failure to protest in circumstances where protest might reasonably be expected against the exercise of control by its opponent. Recognition or acquiescence by one state has little or no effect unless it is accompanied by some measure of control over the territory by the other state. So, for instance, failure to protest against a purely verbal assertion of title unsupported by any degree of control does not constitute acquiescence.

Estoppel

Recognition or acquiescence may give rise to an estoppel. In the context of international disputes over territory the rule would mean that a state which had recognised another state's title to particular territory would be estopped from denying the other state's title if the other state had taken some action in reliance on the recognition.

Novation

This is a distinct mode of acquisition defined by Verzijl as follows:

> 'It consists in the gradual transformation of a right in territorio alieno, for example a lease, or a pledge, or certain concessions of a territorial nature, into full sovereignty without any formal and unequivocal instrument to that effect intervening': *International Law in Historical Perspective*, vol 3, Leyden: Sijthoff, 1970, p384.

For example, British claims to British Honduras (Belize) resulting from the

Treaty of Paris 1763 allowing British nationals to cut compeachy wood in the Spanish territories bordering the Bay of Honduras.

Discovery

It was believed in the sixteenth century that discovery alone conferred a complete title to territory and such discovery was usually accompanied by symbolic acts such as the planting of a flag. The modern view, however, is that discovery merely gives an option to the discovering state to consolidate its claim by proceeding to effective occupation within a reasonable time. This was the view stated by the arbitrator in the *Island of Palmas Arbitration*.

Symbolic annexation

Symbolic annexation has been defined by Brownlie as:

> 'A declaration or other act of sovereignty or an act of private persons duly authorised or subsequently ratified by a state, intended to provide unequivocal evidence of the acquisition of sovereignty over a parcel of territory or an island': *Principles of Public International Law*, 5th ed, Oxford: Oxford University Press, 1998, p145.

In the *Clipperton Island Arbitration* (above) a declaration of French sovereignty was proclaimed and subsequently published by a duly authorised Lieutenant in the French navy, while cruising near the island on 17 November 1858. It was held that in the absence of any effective rival claim and taking into account the inaccessible and uninhabited nature of the island, that France acquired the island when sovereignty was proclaimed and that the purported annexation, though symbolic in form, had legal effect.

Boundary treaties

The vast majority of states have fixed their borders with neighbouring states by means of bilateral treaties which determine the respective territories. Periodically, disputes arise between states over the precise delimitations set down in this type of agreement and states make claims over portions of territory which are considered by adjacent states as their territory. In such circumstances, the treaties establishing the borders must be interpreted and applied by an impartial international body such as the International Court of Justice. For example, in *Case Concerning Land, Island and Maritime Frontier Disputes: El Salvador v Honduras, Nicaragua Intervening* (1992) ICJ Rep 92 El Salvador and Honduras submitted a long-standing dispute over an area of territory on the border between these states to the International Court for resolution.

Treaties defining borders have a special status in international law. Borders established by such agreements have a permanence that exists independently from the fate of the agreements which sets them out. This principle has been affirmed by the International Court in the *Case Concerning the Territorial Dispute: Libyan Arab*

Jamahiriya v *Chad* (1994) ICJ Rep 6. After an armed conflict caused by competing claims to an area of border territory, Libya and Chad agreed to refer the dispute regarding the location of their mutual border to the Court. A Treaty of Friendship and Good Neighbourliness 1955 had been negotiated between the newly independent state of Libya and France as the colonial administrator of the territory which subsequently became Chad. In the treaty, a border had been set down between the two countries but the treaty was expressed to be of limited duration. The Court considered the matter and concluded that the border was definitively agreed in the 1955 Treaty to which Chad was a party as the successor state to the French administered territory. The subsequent actions of the parties supported this determination. The fact that the treaty was only concluded for a limited period – 20 years – was not relevant because treaties setting down borders create demarcations which endure independently of the agreement establishing them. In the words of the Court:

> 'The establishment of this boundary is a fact which, from the outset, has had a legal life of its own, independently of the fate of the 1955 Treaty. Once agreed, the boundary stands, for any other approach would vitiate the fundamental principle of the stability of boundaries, the importance of which has been repeatedly emphasised by the Court.'

Uti possidetis

Uti possidetis, a principle first developed among the Spanish colonies of Latin America, provides that the old colonial boundaries will be recognised as the borders of the newly independent ex-colonial states. This principle was adopted by the Organisation of African Unity in a resolution of 1964 which provides that all states should respect the colonial boundaries. The function of this principle is to preserve the territorial integrity of newly independent states. The principle was followed by the Court in its judgment on the boundary dispute in *Burkina Faso* v *Republic of Mali* (1986) ICJ Rep 554.

The principle was again followed in the *Case Concerning Land, Island and Maritime Frontier Dispute* (above), which involved a dispute between El Salvador and Honduras concerning the land frontiers between their respective territories. Both parties agreed that the matter should be resolved according to the principle of uti possidetis and the Court determined the disputed boundaries by applying this principle. The original colonial boundaries were, therefore, transformed into international frontiers.

7.9 The acquisition of territory in polar regions

The polar regions create unique problems in the context of territorial acquisition. The Arctic comprises the northern polar region encompassing approximately 20 million square kilometres, half of which consists of ocean almost entirely covered by ice. The remainder is made up of territories and islands belonging to Canada, the US (Alaska), Russia, Norway, Finland, Sweden, Denmark (Greenland) and Iceland. Initially, these 'Arctic Eight' states claimed their sovereignty over regions beyond their land territories, inter alia, on the basis of a sector theory. According to this theory all land lying within the triangle between the east–west extremities of a state contiguous to the Pole and the Pole itself should be subject to that state's dominion, unless the territory already belongs to another state. The sector theory was examined by the Permanent Court of International Justice (PCIJ) in *Legal Status of Eastern Greenland Case: Norway* v *Denmark* (1933) PCIJ Rep Ser A/B No 53. The PCIJ stated that whilst the sector theory does not give title which would not otherwise arise, if necessary state activity occurs in the claimed territory such activity represents a reasonable application of the principle of effective occupation. The international community has never accepted the sector theory, which was finally dismissed by the 1986 UN Convention on the Law of the Sea. The Convention affords coastal countries an economic zone extending 370 kilometres from their shore.

The Arctic has great military importance for the US and Russia. Also, the economic potential of the Arctic shelf areas, which are rich in oil, gas and other natural resources, has prompted territorial claims to the Arctic. Canada alone is facing a number of actual or potential disputes relating to its control of the Arctic region: for example, as regards the status of the Northwest Passage which Canada claims constitutes part of its internal waters but the US, the EU and possibly Japan regard as being an international strait; relating to the delimitation of a maritime boundary between Alaska and Yukon; concerning the delimitation of the northern continental shelf to which Russia and the US may submit their claims; relating to an existing dispute over Hans Island, a small island between northern Greenland and Ellesmere Island, to which Denmark asserts its claim, etc. Further, under the terms of the 1958 Convention on the Law of the Sea, a contracting state must determine the limits of its continental shelf within ten years of its ratification. The claim is submitted to the Commission on the Limits of the Continental Shelf, an international panel, for review. Once this process is completed and provided that there are no counter claims from neighbouring states, the claimant state is granted its claim. At the time of writing, no nation has secured territorial rights to the Arctic in this manner but Russia has submitted its claim and Denmark must submit its claim in 2005. Canada and the US have not ratified the Convention and as such have not submitted their claims. Global warming has added a new urgency to competition for coastal states' rights to the Arctic. This region is warming twice as fast as the rest of the planet. It is likely that the North Pole could be ice-free in summertime by the end of the century. Apart from the treasure of natural resources, which the thaw may make accessible, this environmental disaster may create a northwest passage, cutting thousands of miles of the shipping routes between the Atlantic and Pacific Oceans and providing new fishing grounds for the claimant states.

Despite the existing legal controversies the Arctic Eight have been willing to co-operate in respect of environmental matters. The first major development was the conclusion of the 1973 Agreement on the Conservation of Polar Bears, followed in 1991 by the creation of the Arctic Environmental Protection Strategy (AEPS) and the establishment of the Arctic Council in 1996.

Antarctica

Antarctica has a surface area of more than 14 million square kilometres. The UK, Russia and the US all claim to have discovered Antarctica. Explorers reached the continent in the late eighteenth century. The whaling and sealing industry was developed in the nineteenth century. The last uncharted and unclaimed land on earth became a target of scientific explorations around the turn of twentieth century. The first territorial claim was made by the UK. In the Letters Patent of 21 July 1908 the UK claimed a large portion of Antarctica with a view to controlling the whaling industry. Subsequently six nations submitted territorial claims to Antarctica: Australia, Chile, France, New Zealand and Norway (claimant states including the UK). Their claims were based on various grounds: occupation, contiguity, the sector theory, discovery, exploitation and historic rights. The claimant states recognised each other's claims, whatever the legal basis, except when claims overlapped.

After World War II five countries (non-claimant states) stated that they would neither assert nor recognise any territorial claims to Antarctica. These five were: Belgium, Japan, South Africa, the US and the USSR.

The above, combined with the claim of the USSR to maintain its bases in Antarctica and numerous territorial disputes by South American countries with the UK, emphasised the need for a more permanent solution at an international level. The Antarctic Treaty of 1959, which entered into force on 23 June 1961, provided such a solution. The 1959 Treaty 'freezes' all claims to territorial sovereignty in Antarctica. Art IV of the 1959 Treaty states:

> 'No acts or activities taking place while the present Treaty is in force shall constitute a basis for asserting, supporting or denying a claim to territorial sovereignty in Antarctica or create any rights of sovereignty in Antarctica. No new claim, or enlargement of an existing claim to territorial sovereignty in Antarctica shall be asserted while the present Treaty is in force.'

The Treaty is of unlimited duration. To ensure compliance with the Treaty, the contracting parties provided for the inspection of 'all areas of Antarctica, including all stations, installations and equipment within those areas'.

Apart from imposing a moratorium on territorial claims, the Treaty ensures that Antarctica is used for peaceful purposes only and that freedom of scientific investigation and co-operation is preserved.

On the basis of the 1959 Treaty a system of management of the continent was set up, often referred to as the Antarctic Treaty System (ATS), which over the years has developed new policies to respond to changing circumstances, in particular, to ensure the protection of the environment in Antarctica. Additional components of the ATS include: The 1972 Convention for the Conservation of Antarctic Seals, the 1980 Convention on the Conservation of Antarctic Marine Living Resources, the 1988 Convention on the Regulation of Antarctic Mineral Resource Activities and the 1991 Protocol on Environmental Protection to the Antarctic Treaty.

7.10 Restrictions on the transfer of territory

States may enter into treaty agreements not to alienate certain areas of territory under any circumstances or they may contract not to transfer territory to a particular state or states. An obligation not to acquire territory may also be undertaken. By the State Treaty of 1955 Austria agreed not to enter into political or economic union with Germany. By the Treaty of Utrecht 1713, Great Britain agreed to offer Gibraltar to Spain before attempting to transfer sovereignty over Gibraltar to any other state.

However, it is doubtful whether a breach of such treaty not to alienate or acquire territory will affect the title of the grantee of such territory.

7.11 Intertemporal law

As a result of changes in the law relating to the acquisition of territory, problems have arisen as to which legal regime should be applied when determining title. For example, should title to territory acquired by conquest in the nineteenth century be assessed according to the rules relating to conquest at the time (title would be lawful) or according to the law on conquest today (title would be unlawful)?

The general rule – known as the principle of intertemporal law – is that title should be assessed according to the rules of law that prevailed at the time of the acquisition of territory. In the *Island of Palmas Arbitration*, however, Arbitrator Huber suggested that title to territory needed to be confirmed against the changing standards of international law, ie he appears to suggest that title should be assessed by reference to current rules rather than by reference to the rules existing at the time of the acquisition. A number of writers have argued that the modified rule developed by Huber would be highly disruptive, as every state would constantly have to review and confirm its title. Huber's interpretation should, therefore, probably best be seen in terms of the facts of the case in issue, ie as discovery only formed an incomplete title, whether or not title had been 'made good' had to be assessed by reference to the law as it applied to subsequent possession.

7.12 The loss of territory

The loss of territory may occur in the following circumstances.

1. By treaty of cession – a transfer of rights by one state to another.
2. By prescription.
3. Where a new state is created which by definition will cause another state or states to lose territory.
4. By abandonment (derelicto) – a state may by its conduct or by express admission acquiesce in the extension of another state's claim to its territory. In such cases absence of a reasonable level of state activity may cause loss of title. It has been argued that dereliction requires both a physical abandonment and an intention to abandon dominion. For reasons of stability, however, abandonment is not to be presumed and certainly in the case of remote and uninhabited areas it would seem that international tribunals require little in the way of maintenance of sovereignty. Such a rule was applied in the *Clipperton Island Arbitration* and was referred to in the *Legal Status of Eastern Greenland Case*. In less inhospitable territories it may well be, however, that dominion will only remain if a physical manifestation of sovereignty subsists.

7.13 The external territorial rights of a state

A state may have powers to regulate the foreign relations of a protectorate, a trusteeship territory, other colonial possessions, or the territory of another state.

Mandates and trusteeship territories

State authority over mandated or trusteeship territories cannot be described in terms of sovereignty. As was stated in the *South West Africa Cases (Second Phase)* (1966) ICJ Rep 6, the territory of the non-self-governing community is held on trust by the administering power and cannot be considered as part of the territory of that power.

Colonies

These have usually been considered as under the sovereignty of the colonial power even where, as in the case of the British colonies, they were not incorporated as part of the UK. Thus matters concerning the internal affairs of the territories were regarded by the UK as falling within its domestic jurisdiction.

Leases

Examples include the grants made by China in favour of France, Russia, Germany and Great Britain in 1898, the best known being the 'New Territories' attached to

Hong Kong. Such leases amount to a transfer of sovereignty by the grantor for the period of the lease. Such a lease is a right in rem. It attaches to the territory and remains enforceable against the territory even if the territory subsequently passes under the dominion of another state.

Use and possession granted in perpetuity

In 1903 Panama granted to the US 'in perpetuity the use, occupation and control' of the Panama Canal Zone. In such a case residual sovereignty remains with the grantor.

Leases of military bases

The status of such bases is doubtful and would depend upon the terms of the actual treaty which granted the disposition. It is unlikely, however, that they create real rights under international law and are best considered as leases in the municipal sense.

Servitudes

By treaty or otherwise a state may have acquired rights over the territory of a neighbouring state, eg a right to exercise a right of way. Such rights may be divided into two categories.

1. Rights benefitting the international community: international servitudes may exist, not for the benefit of a single state but for the benefit of the international community.

    In the *Aaland Islands Case* (1920) LNOJ Spec Supp No 3, 3 Russia had entered into a treaty obligation in 1856 not to fortify the Aaland Islands. Although the islands lay near Stockholm, Sweden was not a party to this treaty. In 1918 the islands became part of Finland which started fortifying them. Sweden complained to the League of Nations. It was decided that Finland had succeeded to Russia's obligations and that Sweden could claim the benefit of the 1856 Treaty, although she was not a party to it. The treaty was designed to preserve the balance of power in Europe and could, therefore, be invoked by all the states which were 'directly interested', including Sweden.

2. Rights benefitting only a single state: these include mining rights, rights to run an oil or gas pipeline across a neighbouring state, rights to take water for irrigation, rights of way, etc.

    In the *Right of Passage over Indian Territory Case (Merits): Portugal* v *India* (1960) ICJ Rep 6 it was held that Portugal had a right of passage over Indian territory between the coastal district of Daman and the 'enclaves' in respect of private persons, civil officials and goods in general, and this right was binding on India.

However, international tribunals seem reluctant to find servitudes in favour of a single state where those servitudes are of an economic nature. For example, in the *North Atlantic Fisheries Arbitration: US* v *Great Britain* (1910) 11 RIAA 167, it was held that a treaty between the US and Great Britain (the Newfoundland Coast Fishing Treaty 1818), granting the inhabitants of the US the liberty to take fish from the sea off Newfoundland, did not create a servitude preventing Great Britain from limiting the fishing rights of all persons, including US nationals, in the area concerned. However, if evidence of the intention to create such a servitude is found to exist on the part of the state granting it then it will be upheld.

7.14 Assessment

At the outset of this discussion relating to acquisition of territory mention was made of the fact that the traditional modes of acquisition of territory are unhelpful in explaining the most significant form of acquisition of territory during the post-war period, ie acquisition by newly independent states.

Although the acquisition of territory by newly independent states can be explained in terms of cession or prescription, such analysis fails to take into account the developments in international law since the late 1950s which have underpinned the independence movement. Most significant among these developments has been the recognition of a right to self-determination which has a specific content going beyond the broad principles outlined in, inter alia, art 1(2) of the United Nations Charter and common art 1 of the International Covenant on Civil and Political Rights 1966 and the International Covenant on Economic, Social and Cultural Rights 1966.

A second important limitation is that the traditional approach gives little mention to the fact that title in international law is a *relative* rather than absolute concept. In the *Legal Status of Eastern Greenland Case*, for example, the PCIJ was concerned to assess the strength of the Danish claim relative to that of Norway. This is not to say that a state's control over its own territory will always be open to challenge. Rather, it is a recognition of the fact that disputes over territory arise in the context of competing claims. In these circumstances, the function of the Court is to determine which of the competing claims has greater merit, not which of the claims is good against the world at large.

Given these two substantive limitations regarding the traditional modes of acquisition, any assessment of current entitlement can only take place on the basis of a full analysis of the circumstances of the dispute.

Note: for a discussion about the right to self-determination:see Chapter 14 below.

8

Jurisdiction

8.1 Introduction

8.2 Territoral principle

8.3 Nationality principle

8.4 Protective principle

8.5 Passive personality principle

8.6 Universal jurisdiction

8.7 Concurrent jurisdiction

8.8 Extraterritorial application of competition law – the 'effects doctrine'

8.1 Introduction

The jurisdiction of a state describes the power of a state under international law to exercise its authority over persons and property by the use of its municipal law. It includes both the power to prescribe rules (prescriptive or legislative jurisdiction) and the power to enforce them (enforcement or prerogative jurisdiction). Described in these terms, jurisdiction is fundamental to the concept of sovereignty. It describes both the extent of sovereign powers and the scope or limitation of those powers at international level.

Jurisdiction is, therefore, the aspect of state sovereignty which relates to the legislative, executive and judicial competence of a state. There are three groups of powers:

1. the power to legislate in respect of persons, property and events;
2. the power of physical interference exercised by the executive (arrest, seizure of property, etc);
3. the power of the state's courts to hear cases concerning persons, property and events.

It is essential to distinguish between these three groups of powers and in particular between the executive and the judicial competence of a state. The governing principle – one of the fundamental tenets of the concept of sovereignty – is that a state cannot take measures on the territory of another state by way of enforcement of its national laws without that other state's consent. For example, a person may commit an offence in England and then escape to Brazil. The English courts have jurisdiction to try him, but the English police cannot enter Brazilian territory and arrest him. If they did, this would be contrary to the well established rule of international law that one state may not commit acts of sovereignty on the territory of another state. So persons may not be arrested, police investigations may not be mounted, summonses may not be served, on the territory of another state except under the terms of a treaty or with other consent.

The necessity of exercising jurisdiction in an international context arose when the internationally community of states had to deal with troublesome problems of penal jurisdiction. In 1935 the Harvard Law School conducted an extensive study on jurisdiction in the light of, on the one hand, the increasing need for co-operation between states and, on the other hand, the problem arising from conflicts between states which wanted to exercise their jurisdiction to prosecute the same criminals: *The Research in International Law of the Harvard Law School, Jurisdiction with Respect to Crime* (1935) 29 AJIL (Special Supplement). The Harvard study identified five traditional bases under which a state is allowed to regulate an individual's conduct occurring wholly or partially beyond its borders. They are:

1. the territorial principle;
2. the nationality principle;
3. the protective principle;
4. the passive personality principle;
5. the universality principle.

Of these, according to the Harvard study, the principles most widely accepted were territoriality and nationality. The Harvard researchers also found evidence in state practice for the protective and universality principles. Although some evidence of passive personality was apparent, the researchers were of the opinion that this was insufficient to bring it within the ambit of customary law.

8.2 Territorial principle

The essence of this principle is that every state has jurisdiction over crimes committed in its own territory. This principle has been widely recognised. Normally, the application of the principle will be straightforward. An individual, present within a state, committing a crime in that state, will be subject to the enforcement jurisdiction of that state. In two circumstances, however, the application of the territorial principle will be more complicated – where an offence, commenced within the territory of another state but is completed in the territory of the state concerned and where the offence is commenced within the territory of the state concerned but only completed in the territory of another state.

The 1935 Harvard Research Convention approached this problem by providing that a state would have territorial jurisdiction in respect of acts which occur in whole or in part within the territory of the state. 'In part' was defined as an essential constituent element of the act in question. Thus, whether the act commenced in the territory (subjective jurisdiction) or was completed in the territory (objective jurisdiction) the state concerned would be able to exercise its authority.

Objective territoriality, ie jurisdiction on the grounds that the act was completed in the state in question, received general support in the *SS Lotus Case: France* v *Turkey* (1927) PCIJ Rep Ser A No 10. The *SS Lotus* was a French ship that collided on the high seas with a Turkish collier, the *Boz-Kourt*, which sank with loss of life. When the *SS Lotus* reached Constantinople, the French officer of the watch at the time of the collision was arrested, tried and convicted of involuntary manslaughter, before a Turkish court. France protested about the legality of the Turkish action and the PCIJ was asked to decide whether Turkey had acted in conflict with international law by instituting proceedings and thereby exercising criminal jurisdiction. By the casting vote of the President, the Court decided that Turkey had not acted in conflict with the principles of international law by exercising such jurisdiction.

France had put forward two main contentions:

1. that international law did not allow a state to take proceedings with regard to offences committed by foreigners abroad;
2. that international law recognised the exclusive jurisdiction of the flag state over events occurring on board a ship on the high seas.

The second contention was rejected. The Court reserved its opinion on the first point but went on to hold that:

> '... the offence produced its effects on the Turkish vessel and consequently in a place assimilated to Turkish territory in which the application of Turkish criminal law cannot be challenged, even in regard to offences committed there by foreigners.'

The majority of the Court, therefore, by assimilating the Turkish vessel to Turkish territory, brought the case under the principle of the objective territorial jurisdiction.

8.3 Nationality principle

The competence of the state to prosecute and punish its nationals on the sole basis of their nationality is based upon the allegiance which the person charged with the crime owes to the state of which he is a national. It is now universally accepted that a state may prosecute its nationals for crimes committed anywhere in the world.

In *Joyce* v *Director of Public Prosecutions* [1946] AC 347 the accused, William Joyce, was charged with treason under the Treason Act 1951 for having made propaganda broadcasts to the UK from Germany during World War II. Joyce was a US citizen born in the US of Irish parents but he had spent most of his adult life in England. It was contended that because the accused was a US citizen he did not owe allegiance to the Crown and could not, therefore, be guilty of committing treason.

The House of Lords accepted that allegiance was necessary and found that the accused, who also held a British passport, still in force at the time of his broadcasts, was entitled to protection by the Crown and, therefore, owed the Crown allegiance. The fact that the passport had been obtained by fraud was immaterial.

It is, however, recognised that the application of the nationality principle may create parallel jurisdiction, ie jurisdiction by more than one state, and possible double jeopardy in cases of dual nationality or where the territorial and national jurisdiction overlap. Many states, therefore, place limitations on the nationality principle. For instance, English courts may only claim such jurisdiction in the case of serious offences such as treason, murder and bigamy. The UK does not, however, challenge the application of the principle by other states in less serious criminal cases.

8.4 Protective principle

Almost all states assume jurisdiction to punish acts prejudicial to their security, even when they are committed by aliens abroad. Such acts, not necessarily confined to political matters, include spying, plots to overthrow the government, forging currency, immigration and economic offences.

For example, art 7 of the French Criminal Code provides:

> 'Every foreigner who is outside the territory of the Republic and renders himself guilty, either as perpetrator or accomplice of a felony or misdemeanour against the security of the state or the counterfeiting of the seal of the state or current national monies may be prosecuted and tried according to the provisions of French law if he is arrested in France or if the Government obtains his extradition.'

The protective principle was accepted by the courts as providing alternative bases for jurisdiction in both the *Joyce* case and the *Eichmann* case (*Attorney-General of the Government of Israel* v *Eichmann* (1961) 36 ILR 5). In the latter case, the court assimilated the state of Israel – which did not exist at the time of the offences – to the Jewish people, holding that the protective principle permitted the Israeli court to exercise jurisdiction in respect of crimes against the Jewish people.

Although most states use this principle to some extent, thereby confirming its legitimacy, there is nevertheless always the danger that some states may abuse the principle by giving a very broad interpretation to the concept of protection.

For example, Nazi Germany decreed that it would endanger the racial composition of its nation if a German married a non-Aryan. On that basis a Jew who married a German girl in Czechoslovakia was charged under the relevant German law.

The growth in international terrorism and drug smuggling has made the courts of the Western democratic countries less hostile to the reception of the protective principle of jurisdiction. Even the courts of the common law countries, which have traditionally rejected the protective principle, have been compelled to have a change of heart.

This change of policy was most evident in the Privy Council decision in *Liangsiriprasert* v *United States Government* [1990] 3 WLR 606. This case involved the extradition of a Thai national from Hong Kong to the US on charges of drug smuggling. However, the defendant had been lured into Hong Kong territory by an American agent posing as a fellow smuggler and the defendant had committed no offence under Hong Kong law. The charges used as grounds for extradition related to offences outside the territory and in fact the only connection of the defendant with the territory was his physical presence.

The Privy Council rejected the contention that the courts could not exercise jurisdiction to extradite the defendant to the US. The court continued to reject the notion that the protective principle could not be relied upon by pointing out that:

> 'Unfortunately in this century crime has ceased to be largely local in origin and effect. Crime is now established on an international scale and the common law must face this new reality. Their Lordships can find nothing in precedent, comity or good sense that should inhibit the common law from regarding as justiciable in England inchoate crimes committed abroad which are intended to result in the commission of criminal offences in England ...'

The court, however, qualified its decision by deciding that the charge in question could be construed as involving illicit trade in drugs which could be considered to amount to a potential conspiracy to traffic drugs in Hong Kong. But, despite this qualification, the decision signals a definite change of policy on the part of the British courts towards the acceptance of the protective principle.

8.5 Passive personality principle

According to this principle a state has jurisdiction to punish aliens for harmful acts committed abroad against its nationals. This has been described as the most difficult principle to justify in theory, and while some states such as Italy and Turkey claim jurisdiction on this ground others, such as the UK and the US, tend to regard it as contrary to international law.

Although this principle was in evidence in state practice, it was not indicated as one of the accepted bases of jurisdiction in the Harvard Research Convention 1935 because of opposition from the common law countries. In the *SS Lotus Case*, for example, although the Court ultimately did not have to decide on jurisdiction under the passive personality principle because they had already accepted the principle of territoriality, all of the dissenting judges expressly rejected the application of the passive personality principle.

Despite this opposition, however, passive personality has been successfully relied upon as an alternative basis for jurisdiction in a number of cases. In *US* v *Yunis* (1989) 83 AJIL 94, for example, involving the prosecution in the US of a Lebanese national for his alleged involvement in the hijacking of a Jordanian airliner in the Middle East, the US-based jurisdiction in part on passive personality. The only nexus between the aircraft and the US was the presence of a number of US nationals on the flight. The court nevertheless accepted that passive personality did provide an appropriate basis for jurisdiction.

Similarly, although this issue did not come before the courts, the US based its extradition request in the *Achille Lauro* incident on the fact that the victim murdered by the hijackers of the Italian pleasure cruiser off the Egyptian coast was a US national.

The principle of passive jurisdiction has gained a new impetus following the judgment of the ICJ in the *Case Concerning the Arrest Warrant of 11 April 2000: Democratic Republic of Congo* v *Belgium* (2000) ICJ Rep 3. This is evinced by the decisions of the Spanish Supreme Court in the *Guatemala Genocide Case* (2003) 42 ILM 686 and in the *Peruvian Genocide Case* (2003) 42 ILM 1200. The Court decided by a majority of eight to seven not to apply the principle of universal jurisdiction as a basis for the prosecution in Spain of former Guatemalan officials and former Peruvian officials for acts of torture committed respectively in Guatemala and in Peru, and decided instead to apply the passive personality principle. The Supreme Court, relying on recent decisions of German and Belgian courts, limited the jurisdiction of Spanish courts over the most serious international crimes, such as genocide and torture, to cases where there is a close connection between the victim of the crime and Spanish nationality. These connections include: that victims were of Spanish nationality or citizenship; that victims or their survivors have dual nationality (the country were the crime was committed and Spanish nationality); and that victims or their survivors have some close familial lineage of Spanish origin.

8.6 Universal jurisdiction

Under this principle a state may exercise jurisdiction in respect of persons accused of international crimes committed anywhere in the world and irrespective of the nationality of the perpetrator and of the victim. The reasoning behind this principle is that some crimes are so universally repugnant that their perpetrators are considered as hostis humani generis or enemies of all mankind. The prosecuting state acts, therefore, on behalf of all states.

There are two approaches to the exercise of universal jurisdiction: one which requires the presence of the perpetrator within the arresting state, the so-called forum deprehensionis, and one which considers that a state may exercise jurisdiction regardless of whether or not the alleged offender is in its custody. Under the second approach, the obvious problem is that when an offender is not present within the jurisdiction, unless the court is prepared to conduct proceedings in absentia, such a state must make a request for his extradition to a state where he is present. The most famous example of universal jurisdiction exercised regardless of the presence of the perpetrator within the jurisdiction is provided by the case of the former dictator and President of Chile, Augusto Pinochet. His extradition was requested by Spain when he was undergoing medical treatment in the UK. The Law Lords in the UK ruled that he was not immune as a former Head of State from charges of systematic torture in Chile and therefore his extradition to Spain for a trial there based on universal jurisdiction could proceed: see Chapter 9.

Based on universal jurisdiction Belgian law allows a Belgian prosecuting judge to issue an international arrest warrant against a person accused of committing international crimes. Such warrant was issued on 11 April 2000 against Abdulaye Yerodia Ndombasi, the then Minister for Foreign Affairs of the Democratic Republic of Congo (DRC), for serious violations of international humanitarian law. On 17 October 2000 the DRC filed an application before the ICJ against Belgium challenging the arrest warrant. The government of Belgium being less revolutionary than its judiciary tried to remove the case from the ICJ agenda arguing that Mr Yerodia no longer had ministerial responsibility and that Belgium was undertaking a review of the relevant legislation.

The ICJ rejected both arguments (ICJ, Order of 27 June 2001).

On 14 February 2002 the ICJ delivered its judgment in the above case: see *Case Concerning the Arrest Warrant of 11 April 2000: Democratic Republic of the Congo v Belgium* (2002) 41 ILM 536. The ICJ ruled that under international customary law serving foreign ministers when abroad enjoy absolute immunity from criminal jurisdiction and inviolability. They are protected from 'any act of authority' by another State irrespective of whether they are in a foreign territory in an 'official' or 'private' capacity, whether the acts were performed before or during the period of office and whether or not they were performed in an official or private capacity. This rule applies also in the situation where a Minister for Foreign Affairs is accused of having committed international crimes.

The majority of the ICJ rejected any distinction between acts performed in an official capacity and those performed in a private capacity, or acts performed before or during the holding of the office of foreign minister. The dissenting judges, Higgins, Kooijmans and Buergenthal, submitted that the failure of the majority of the ICJ to distinguish between so-called 'functional immunity' and 'personal immunity' for the purpose of determining what acts are protected by sovereign immunity did not reflect state practice, as evidenced by judgments in *Attorney-General of the Government of Israel v Adolf Eichmann* (1961) 36 ILR 5 and *R v Bow Street Metropolitan Stipendiary Magistrate, ex parte Pinochet Ugarte (No 3)* [1999] 2 WLR 827 (HL) and international treaties such as the Charter of the International

Military Tribunal and the Statutes of the International Criminal Tribunal for the Former Yugoslavia (ICTY), the International Criminal Tribunal for Rwanda (ICTR) and the International Criminal Court (ICC).

The majority of the ICJ noted that immunity does not mean impunity since immunity from jurisdiction does not affect individual criminal responsibility. Accordingly, an individual can be held responsible:

1. before the courts of his own country; or
2. when his state waives immunity and allows another state to bring him to justice; or
3. after he ceases to hold public office he may be tried by any state which has jurisdiction under international law to do so; and
4. in the future he may be brought before the ICC.

The dissenting judges were sceptical as to the likelihood of an individual being held liable for international crimes under the above circumstances.

The implications of the judgment of the ICJ are far reaching. First, the judgment entails that state officials such as Heads of State or foreign ministers, after leaving office, can be made accountable for international crimes committed while in office in a situation where such crimes are regarded as acts committed in a 'private capacity'! This is in effect opposite to the decision of the House of Lords in the *Pinochet* case. It also means that international crimes committed by state officials would not be attributable to the state but to individuals, and thereby other states would be prevented from relying on state responsibility against the offending state in respect of those acts: see M Spinedi, 'State Responsibility v Individual Responsibility for International Crimes: Tertium Non Datur?' (2002) 13 EJIL 895.

Second, the ICJ declined to examine the matter of whether or not Belgium was entitled to enact national legislation under which its municipal courts had universal jurisdiction in respect of international crimes. Even though the Congo decided to withdraw its original argument challenging the legality of the Belgian law under international law, the ICJ could have taken the opportunity to clarify the issue of universal jurisdiction. The majority of the ICJ ruled that under the non ultra petita rule the Court was bound to abstain from deciding issues not included in the submissions of the parties. This was challenged by dissenting judges who considered that the Court was not prevented from examining issues relevant to the case, even if they were not raised by the parties. The dissenting judges considered that the principle of jura novi curia could supersede the non petita rule and thereby the ICJ had inherent competence to decide on the relevant issues of international law irrespective of submissions of the parties to the proceedings.

Another implication of the above judgment is that Belgium was required to revise the relevant legislation. Following from this the 1992 and 1999 Belgian legislation concerning the punishment of grave breaches of humanitarian law, on the basis of which the Belgian courts could and did exercise universal jurisdiction, was twice amended in 2003, on 23 April 2003 and on 5 August 2003. As a result of these amendments Belgian courts are now allowed to ascertain jurisdiction in cases concerning grave breaches of humanitarian law in situations where the victim is a national of Belgium or has resided in Belgium for at least three years. Prosecution is excluded in respect of persons enjoying immunity under international law, such as Heads of State, heads of government and ministers of foreign affairs while they are in office, and other persons enjoying immunity from civil and criminal proceedings as recognised under international law or granted on the basis of international treaties to which Belgium is a contracting party. Under the amendments no act in furtherance of commencing criminal proceedings will be allowed against any person who has been officially invited to Belgium by the Belgian authorities or by an international organisation located in Belgium during the period of stay of such a person in Belgium. (Amendment to Law of 15 June 1993 [7 August 2003] (English Translation) (2003) 42 ILM 1258.)

Notwithstanding the fact that the judgment of the ICJ applies only to the case at issue, and therefore is binding between the parties to the proceedings, it is likely that not only Belgium but other states will have to review their national legislation in the light of the above judgment, taking into account the statement of the ICJ that persons enjoying immunity must be protected from 'any authority' by another state that would prevent them from exercising the functions of their office.

The above judgment is very disappointing from the point of view of the development of international human rights. It confirms that political power means protection and immunity. While in office notorious abusers of human rights instead of being prosecuted are protected by international law. (For an examination in depth of the above judgment see: A Cassese, 'When May Senior State Officials be Tried for International Crimes? Some Comments on the *Congo* v *Belgium* Case' (2002) 13 EJIL 853.)

It is interesting to note that in October 2002 Africa Legal Aid (AFLA) has initiated the drafting of the Principles on Universal Jurisdiction in Respect of Gross Human Rights Offences in order to assist African and other governments, human rights organisations and legal practitioners in their attempts to pursue international justice, and advocacy and lobbying initiatives in respect of prosecution of gross violation of human rights. The AFLA initiative constitutes a response to the lack of prosecutions for the gross violations of human rights in Africa.

The Principles provide for universal jurisdiction in respect of gross human rights offences committed during armed conflict and in peacetime. Rationae personae they apply not only to natural persons but also to legal entities. To the list of international crimes contained in the Rome Statute of the International Criminal Court the Principles add offences such as acts of plunder and gross misappropriation of public funds, trafficking in human beings and environmental crimes which have 'major adverse economic, social or cultural consequences'.

The principle of universal jurisdiction raises two important questions:

1. what crimes are considered as international crimes; and

2. whether a prosecuting state is entitled to base its jurisdiction on international customary law or whether specific domestic legislation needs to be enacted to provide the legal basis for its jurisdiction.

International crimes

Offences which may be tried under the principle of universal jurisdiction are those which are considered sufficiently heinous to be crimes against the entire community of nations and therefore their repression becomes a matter of international public policy.

Article 404 of the Restatement (Third) of the Foreign Relations Law of the United States provides a list of universal crimes. (Restatements are prepared by the American Law Institute; they have no official standing, although courts and writers often use the Restatement to resolve legal problems.) Article 404 states that:

> 'A state has jurisdiction to define and prescribe punishment for certain offences recognised by the community of nations as of universal concern, such as piracy, slave trade, attacks on or hijacking of aircraft, genocide, war crimes, and perhaps certain acts of terrorism.'

According to the Restatement the above list is based on customary law. Universal jurisdiction for additional offences is provided by international treaties. The above list is very controversial. It is, at the same time, too broad and too restrictive. It is too restrictive because some crimes not mentioned in art 404 of the Restatement (Third) are seen as violating the rules of ius cogens and therefore should be included in the list – for example, torture and the crime of aggression. It is too broad because there is no sufficient evidence based on state practice to consider some crimes, such as attacks on, or hijacking of, aircraft, as crimes in international customary law. Moreover, some international norms such as the prohibition of genocide, the use of force in international relations contrary to the UN Charter or the prohibition of torture, have acquired a status of ius cogens. The Restatement (Third) makes no distinction between international crimes which violate ius cogens and international crimes which breach other norms of international customary law.

Important clarifications in determining crimes which should be considered as international crimes are provided by the Statutes of both the International Criminal Tribunal for the Former Yugoslavia (ICTY) and the International Criminal Tribunal for Rwanda (ICTR). It may be implied that since both Tribunals were established on the basis of Security Council resolutions the international community considers crimes falling within the jurisdiction of both courts as international crimes. The ICTY may adjudicate cases involving grave breaches of the 1949 Geneva Conventions, violations of the laws or customs of war, genocide and crimes against humanity. The ICTR jurisdiction covers genocide, crimes against humanity, violations of art 3 common to the 1949 Geneva Conventions and the 1977 Additional Protocol II to the 1949 Geneva Conventions.

The Statute of the International Criminal Court, which sets out only the most serious violations of international law, provides that the International Criminal Court has jurisdiction rationae materiae in respect of genocide, war crimes, crimes against humanity and the crime of aggression.

It is submitted that the following offences are recognised under customary international law as international crimes: piracy, slavery, crimes against peace, war crimes, crimes against humanity, genocide and torture.

Piracy

Customary international law allows a state to try pirates. This offence is usually committed on the high seas rather than within the territorial waters of any nation. The nationality and passive personality principles are not practical alternatives because it is be difficult to establish the nationality of the pirates and the state apprehending the pirates will not necessarily be the state of the victims. Piracy as an offence in international law is defined in art 15 of the Convention on the High Seas 1958:

> 'Piracy consists of any of the following acts:
> 1. Any illegal acts of violence, detention or any act of depredation, committed for private ends by the crew or the passengers of a private ship or private aircraft, and directed:
> (a) on the high seas, against another ship or aircraft, or against persons or property on board such a ship or aircraft;
> (b) against a ship, aircraft, persons, or property in a place outside the jurisdiction of any state;
> 2. Any acts of voluntary participation in the operation of a ship or an aircraft with knowledge of facts making it a pirate ship or aircraft;
> 3. Any act of inciting or of intentionally facilitating an act described in sub-para 1 or sub-para 2 of this article.'

This definition of piracy in international law (piracy jure gentium) must be distinguished from definitions provided under municipal law which may differ.

Slavery

The first attempt at international level to protect human rights concerned the abolition of slavery which was legal under national laws at the end of eighteenth century. England outlawed slavery in the *Somersett Case* in 1772 (see M Meltzer, *Slavery: A World History*, New York: Da Capo, 1993), and established herself as a leading international advocate of its abolition. In the 1814 Treaty of Paris, France and the UK agreed to co-operate in the suppression of the traffic in slaves. In 1815 the major European states endorsed the prohibition of the slave trade at the Congress of Vienna. The first multinational treaty abolishing slavery, the slave trade and introducing measures for their suppression both in Africa and on the high seas, including the right to visit and search ships suspected of being involved in the slave trade, their confiscation and the punishment of their master and crew, was the Anti-Slavery Act adopted by the Brussels Conference of 1890 and ratified by 18 states, including, the US, Turkey and Zanzibar.

The most comprehensive international instrument abolishing slavery and the slave trade was adopted under the auspices of the League of Nations. The Convention on the Abolition of Slavery and the Slave Trade 1926 declared as its main objective: 'the complete suppression of slavery in all forms and of the slave trade by land and sea'.

War crimes and crimes against humanity

War crimes were first recognised as crimes under international law by the 1907 Hague Convention and the Geneva Convention Relating to the Amelioration of the Condition of the Wounded and Sick in Armies in the Field 1949. After World War II the Statute of the International Military Tribunal (IMT) at Nuremburg declared them crimes under international law. In 1946 the UN General Assembly (GA) adopted unanimously Resolution 95 (I) entitled Affirmation of the Principles of International Law Recognised by the Charter of the Nuremberg Tribunal and asked the International Law Commission (ILC) to codify these principles. In its resolution the GA confirmed the customary nature of the provisions contained in the Charter of the IMT as the GA had only 'affirmed' the principles which already existed before the IMT recognised them in both its Charter and its Judgment. In 1950 the ILC adopted a report on the 'Principles of International Law Recognised in the Charter of the Nuremberg Tribunal and in the Judgment of the Tribunal'. Its Principle VI codifies the three categories of crimes set out in the Charter of the IMT as crimes under international law. The four 1949 Geneva Conventions and the two 1977 Additional Protocols further define war crimes and impose a duty on a contracting state to extradite or to try alleged offenders and punish them if appropriate under the principle of universal jurisdiction. The Statutes of the ICTR and ICTY and the International Criminal Court recognise war crimes and crimes against humanity as international crimes.

The most spectacular example of a state relying on the principle of universality was the trial of Adolf Eichmann who was illegally abducted by members of the Israeli secret service, by order of the then Prime Minister, David Ben-Gurion, to stand trial in Israel. He was charged under the Nazi and Nazi Collaborators (Punishment) Law 1950 with 15 counts of war crimes and crimes against humanity. Under the Nazi regime Eichmann, by his own admission, was in charge of 'cleansing' or forcing the emigration of 150,000 Jews from Austria. From 1942 he was one of the main persons responsible for Hitler's 'final solution', ie the systematic execution of some six million Jews. After the war he escaped to Argentina and lived there with his family for ten years before being abducted. He was found guilty by the Israeli court and was executed on 31 May 1962.

Eichmann challenged the jurisdiction of the Israeli court on the grounds that: he was illegally abducted and Israel had no right to hold him; he was charged with crimes that did not exist at the time he committed them; and he stood trial in a country that did not exist at the time of the commission of the alleged crimes. All his arguments were rejected. The court stated that the crimes committed by

Eichmann were international crimes in nature and therefore it applied the universality principle of jurisdiction.

The court stated that:

'The crimes defined in this [Israeli] law must be deemed to have always been international crimes, entailing individual criminal responsibility: customary international law is analogous to the common law and develops by analogy and by reference to general principles of law recognised by civilised nations, these crimes share the characteristics of crimes ... which damage vital international interests, impair the foundations and security of the international community, violate universal moral values and humanitarian principles ... and the principle of universal jurisdiction over "crimes against humanity" ... similarly derives from a common vital interest in their suppression. The state prosecuting them acts as agent of the international community, administering international law': *Attorney-General of the Government of Israel* v *Eichmann* (1961) 36 ILR 5 (District Court of Jerusalem).

A later example of a state exercising universal jurisdiction is provided by the first trial (concerning Rwandan genocide) held by a Belgian court under the Belgian law providing for universal jurisdiction (now amended). On 8 June 2001 four accused (two Rwandan nuns, Sister Gertude, who was tried under her full name of Consolata Mukangango, and Sister Maria Kisito, tried as Julienne Makabutera, and two other ethnic Hutu militants, Alphonse Higaniroa, a businessman and former Rwandan transport minister, and Vincent Ntezimana, a University professor) were found guilty of international crimes arising from the Rwandan genocide. All were sentenced to at least 12 years' imprisonment. The two Roman Catholic nuns were accused of aiding the massacre of 6,000 Tutsis in April and May 1994. Sister Gertrude was a mother superior at a convent in the town of Sovu. She collaborated with a local militia leader to kill Tutsis who sought sanctuary in the convent. Both nuns were accused of forcing Tutsis to leave the convent when armed Hutu militia were gathering outside the convent waiting to massacre them. Sister Maria Kisito was accused of providing jerry cans filled with petrol to local Hutu militias to help them to set fire to up to 700 people who refused to leave the convent and were locked in a garage at the convent's health clinic. The two Hutu militants were accused of helping to plan massacres and of spreading ethnic hatred. All four pleaded not guilty.

The legal basis of the charges are still unclear. The 1993 Belgian Law provided for universal jurisdiction in respect of grave breaches of the Geneva Conventions and Additional Protocols I and II and abolished the distinction between international and internal conflicts. It applied irrespective of the place of commission of offences, or the nationality of the victim or alleged offender. The 1999 Belgian Law extended universal jurisdiction to genocide and crimes against humanity. All reports of the news media and international human rights organisations denied that charges of genocide or crimes against humanity were brought against the accused. Apparently these charges were not brought because of the non-retroactivity of the 1999 Law. It seems that charges were brought under the 1993 Law, bearing in mind that genocide and crimes against humanity may be implied from the Geneva Conventions and their Additional Protocols. Further, following from the fact that genocide and crimes against humanity are international crimes recognised under customary international law, Belgian courts may in any event assume jurisdiction independently of any legislation. Moreover, S Smis and K Van der Borght submitted that the travaux preparatoires to the 1993 law indicated that the Belgian legislator had already incorporated the crime of genocide into the 1993 Law and the express inclusion of acts of genocide in the 1999 Law was not intended to produce any legal effect but had 'symbolic and educational value of declaring genocide a crime in itself' in order to 'call the issues by their proper name': 'Act Concerning the Punishment of Grave Breaches of International Humanitarian Law' (1999) 38 ILM 918.

Between 500,000 and 800,000 ethnic Tutsis and moderate Hutus were killed in Rwanda in 1994. The Belgian trial was a triumph for justice and a step towards the ending of the impunity of human rights' abusers. The offenders were not Heads of States or high-ranking governmental officials. They were found guilty by a civil jury made up of 12 ordinary people, which included a hairdresser, a lorry driver and a university professor.

However, the amendments to the 1993 and 1999 Belgian legislation have destroyed their revolutionary character with regard to the punishment of grave breaches of humanitarian law. Under their amended versions the jurisdiction of Belgian courts will be based on the passive personality principle or on three years residence in Belgium by a victim of such crimes.

Genocide

The crime of genocide is relatively recent in origin. It evolved from crimes against humanity. In 1948 the General Assembly adopted the Convention on the Prevention and Punishment of the Crime of Genocide. In its art II the Convention defines genocide as involving 'intent to destroy, in whole or in part, a national, ethnical, racial or religious group', such as killing members of the group, causing serious bodily or mental harm to them, deliberately inflicting on the group conditions of life calculated to bring about its physical destruction in whole or in part, imposing measures intended to prevent births within the group and forcibly transferring children of the group to another group. Article IV of the Convention establishes the obligation to punish not only 'rulers' or 'public officials' but also 'private individuals'. Article VI confers jurisdiction to punish the offenders on both municipal and international courts. The Convention classifies genocide as a crime under international law irrespective of whether it is committed in time of peace or in time of war. The ICJ in its Advisory Opinion concerning *Reservations to the Convention on the Prevention and Punishment of the Crime of Genocide* (1951) ICJ Rep 15 recognised genocide as a crime in customary law.

The Appeals Chamber of the ICTY provided important clarifications on the definition of the crime of genocide in *Krstic* IT–98–33 'Srebenica – Drina Corps', Judgment of 19 April 2004 (Appeals Chamber) (see Chapter 19).

Torture

The prohibition of torture has been recognised by the ICTY as having a status of ius cogens. In *Furundzija* 1T–95–17/1 'Lasva Valley' (1999) 38 ILM 317 the ICTY stated that:

> 'Because of the importance of the values it protects, [the prohibition of torture] has evolved into a peremptory norm or ius cogens, that is, a norm that enjoys a higher rank in the international hierarchy than treaty law and even "ordinary" customary rules. The most conspicuous consequence of this higher rank is that the principle at issue cannot be derogated from by states through international treaties or local or special customs or even general customary rules not endowed with the same normative force … Clearly, the ius cogens nature of the prohibition against torture articulates the notion that the prohibition has now become one of the most fundamental standards of the international community. Furthermore, this prohibition is designed to produce a deterrent effect, in that it signals to all members of the international community and the individuals over whom they wield authority that the prohibition of torture is an absolute value from which nobody must deviate.'

The UN General Assembly has adopted a large number of resolutions recognising torture as a crime under international law. Lord Browne-Wilkinson in *R v Bow Street Metropolitan Stipendiary Magistrate, ex parte Pinochet Ugarte (No 3)* [1999] 2 WLR 827 stated that torture was 'an international crime in the highest sense' long before the 1984 Torture Convention recognised it as such. Moreover, the Republic of Chile accepted that the prohibition of torture has the status of ius cogens.

However, subsequent to the judgment of the ICJ in the *Case Concerning the Arrest Warrant of 11 April 2000: Democratic Republic of the Congo v Belgium* (2002) 41 ILM 536 the prohibition of torture as a norm of ius cogens has been considerably weakened. If the prohibition of torture is, indeed, the highest norm in the hierarchy of norms of international law it prevails over the rule which gives Heads of State, when in office, immunity from jurisdiction in a situation where they are accused of serious human rights abuses, in particular acts of torture. The ICJ in the above judgment decided otherwise. The Court clearly stated that under customary international law a minister of a foreign state, for as long as he remains in office, enjoys absolute immunity from any act of authority by another state, regardless of the gravity of the charges involved. Accordingly, national courts have followed the above judgment of the ICJ and have, on the ground of state immunity, dismissed civil lawsuits alleging, among other things, torture by Heads of State and other high ranking state officials. Recent examples include:

1. the dismissal of proceedings against the President of Zimbabwe, Robert Mugabe, by the US Court of Appeals for the Second Circuit (*Tachiona* v *United States*, 386 F 3d 205 US App Lexis 20879 (2nd Cir; 6 October 2004) (Tachiona II));
2. the dismissal of proceedings against Jiang Zemin, former President of the People's Republic of China, who was served with process whilst in office but subsequently departed from the office of President. The fact that Jiang Zemin

was no longer in office did not change the outcome of the case. The US Court of Appeals for the Seventh Circuit ruled that the US government's assertation of immunity on behalf of Zemin was conclusive and must be accepted by the court (*Wei Ye* v *Jiang Zemin*, 383 F 3d 620 2004 US App; Lexis 18944 (7th Cir; 8 September 2004)).

However, it is also interesting to note a recent judgment of the English Court of Appeal delivered on 28 October 2004 in *Jones* v *The Ministry of the Interior of the Kingdom of Saudi Arabia* (2004) EWCA Civ 1394. Although the Court of Appeal dismissed proceedings against the Ministry of the Interior of the Kingdom of Saudi Arabia in which the appellant alleged that he had been systematically tortured whilst he was detained in prison in Saudi Arabia, in respect of the master's refusal to permit service out of the jurisdiction against Saudi Arabian nationals who had been allegedly involved in systematic torture of the appellants in their official capacity as police or prison officers and in an official context, the appeal was allowed against that refusal. The Court of Appeal held that the personal immunity from proceedings in the UK under s1(1) of the State Immunity Act 1968 did not extend to blanket subject matter immunity in respect of state officials alleged to have committed acts of torture. The Court stated that in determining whether an individual claim against a state official allegedly involved in acts of torture should proceed a court should consider and balance at the same time all relevant factors, including state immunity and jurisdiction.

Universal jurisdiction based on customary international law

The matter of a distinction between customary international law and a treaty basis for exercising universal jurisdiction by a prosecuting state is of considerable importance even though all international crimes mentioned in art 404 of the Restatement (Third) have been the subject of international conventions imposing a duty upon a contracting state to either extradite or prosecute the offender.

Whether or not a prosecuting state may exercise universal jurisdiction solely on the basis of customary international law depends on the relationship between its municipal and international law. In monist countries international law forms part of national law. Consequently, no domestic legislation is needed to be enacted in respect of crimes under customary international law. The situation is different in dualist countries. In two cases decided by the Federal Court of Australia (dualist country) the court had to determine whether the international customary norm, whereby international law prohibits genocide, was part of Australian law. In *Nulyarimma* v *Thompson* [1999] FRC 1192 (held together with *Buzzacott* v *Hill* (below), an appeal was lodged against a decision refusing to issue warrants for the arrest of the Prime Minister of Australia, John Howard, and other officials. The warrant was sought on the ground that these persons by preparing and supporting the 'Ten Point Plan' and the Native Title Amendment Act 1998 had committed the crime of genocide. In *Buzzacott* v *Hill*, the issue concerned an application to strike out proceedings instituted by Kevin Buzzacott on behalf of the Arabunna people against the Australian Minister for the Environment and the Australian Minister for Foreign Affairs and Trade for failure to apply for world heritage listing for the Arabunna people's land in the Lake Eyre region. The claimant submitted that this failure amounted to an act of genocide. In both cases the Federal Court of Australia held that the international customary norm prohibiting genocide was not recognised in Australian law and, therefore, proceedings could not be brought in an Australian court unless specific domestic legislation was first enacted.

In his dissent, Merkel J, relying on *Attorney-General (Israel)* v *Eichmann* (above) and the case of *Pinochet Ugarte,* stated that in respect of universal crimes having the status of ius cogens there is no need for the Australian Parliament to legislate in order to incorporate international custom into municipal law because the universality and the ius cogens status of the norm results in vesting jurisdiction in all states.

Other dualist countries, for example Canada and New Zealand, favour a different approach. There customary international law is considered as part of municipal law without the necessity of transformation by legislation unless it is in conflict with statutory law.

Another difficulty may arise in countries which accept that international law forms part of municipal law but special legislation is required for national courts to exercise jurisdiction in respect of international crimes. Under US law no person can be tried in the federal courts for international crimes unless Congress enacts a statute defining such crimes and providing for their punishment.

According to Amnesty International approximately 120 states have legislation 'providing for' universal jurisdiction over war crimes, crimes against humanity, genocide and torture. However, in many states such legislation requires amendments to reinforce its provisions. It is suggested that the main problem is the lack of political will to prosecute human rights' abusers rather than the absence of appropriate legislation.

Since the establishment of the ICTR and the ICTY national prosecutors in many countries – including Austria, Belgium, Denmark, France, Germany, Mexico, The Netherlands, Senegal, Spain, Switzerland, the UK and the US – have carried out investigations based on universal jurisdiction or have arrested suspects at the request of states conducting such investigations.

The ratification of the Statute of the International Criminal Court by contracting states requires amendments to the municipal law of such states, namely the establishment of universal jurisdiction in respect of international crimes. This may be a strong incentive for many states to amend their legislation in this area.

However, as the Spanish Supreme Court emphasised in the *Guatemala Genocide Case* (2003) 42 ILM 686 the principle of universal jurisdiction is loosing its strength. The Court noted that:

'Today there is significant support in doctrine for the idea that no particular State is in the position to unilaterally establish order, through resort to criminal law, against everyone and the entire world, without there being some point of connection that renders legitimate the extension of extraterritorial jurisdiction.'

Universal jurisdiction based on treaties

Treaties define international crimes and contain specific provisions in respect of the international jurisdiction of contracting states. A contracting state exercises its jurisdiction on the basis of the terms of the treaty rather than on any generally accepted principle of customary international law. The key element of most of the treaties dealing specifically with crimes of an international nature, for example the Hague Convention for the Suppression of Unlawful Seizure of Aircraft 1970 or the Rome Convention for the Suppression of Unlawful Acts against the Safety of Maritime Navigation 1988, are as follows.

1. The provision of definitions of international crimes.
2. The establishment of an obligation on a contracting state to make acts considered as international crimes offences under their municipal legal systems.
3. The requirement that a contracting state must be in a position to establish jurisdiction over these crimes. Invariably, territoriality and nationality are indicated as mandatory bases of jurisdiction. Other principles are permitted as optional grounds of jurisdiction.
4. The offences created are deemed to be extraditable offences.
5. The imposition of a duty on a contracting state to either extradite or prosecute the offender.

Defects in establishing jurisdiction over persons accused of crimes specified in multilateral treaties were highlighted in the *Case Concerning Questions of Interpretation and Application of the 1971 Montreal Convention Arising from the Aerial Incident at Lockerbie (Provisional Measures): Libya v UK* (1992) ICJ Rep 3. Libya sought from the ICJ an order for interim protection to prevent the Security Council from imposing sanctions in response to the refusal of the Libyan authorities to extradite two of its nationals suspected of carrying out the destruction of Pan Am Flight 103 which exploded when flying over the Scottish town of Lockerbie. All 234 passengers were killed, as well as 16 crew members and 11 residents of Lockerbie.

The application was based on the contention made by Libya that the matter was governed by the Montreal Convention for the Suppression of Unlawful Acts against the Safety of Civil Aircraft 1971 and not an issue that constituted a threat to international peace and security justifying the Security Council's decision to adopt sanctions.

The Montreal Convention specifies that if a person suspected of a terrorist act is arrested in the territory of a contracting party, that state is required to prosecute the accused for the offences or, alternatively, it must extradite the accused to any contracting state that is seeking to exercise jurisdiction over the accused. Thus, the state in which an accused person is found has the option of prosecuting or extraditing to a requesting state.

Since the accused were Libyan nationals, Libya opted to conduct the prosecution itself and refused to extradite the suspects to either the UK or the US. Both the UK and the US feared that the trial of the accused in Libya would be a sham, and the accused would escape proper trial. Hence, both states sponsored the Security Council Resolution imposing sanctions in an attempt to compel Libya to extradite as opposed to conducting the trial itself.

Libya's application was designed to secure provisional measures to protect its rights under the Montreal Convention.

Three days after the closing of oral hearings by the ICJ the Security Council adopted Resolution 748 which went further than previous resolutions as it called for coercive measures to be applied against Libya, involving the severance of all economic, commercial and diplomatic links by all member states of the UN if the two suspects were not released to stand trial. It was at that time that the ICJ refused to grant provisional measures to protect Libya from sanctions. The ICJ refused the application on the ground, inter alia, that Libya was required to carry out the decisions of the Security Council in accordance with art 25 of the UN Charter. To permit Libya to rely on the 1971 Montreal Convention would have been inconsistent with the principle that the UN Charter prevails over the inconsistent terms of any international agreements. In the end the Court could not protect the rights conferred upon Libya by the Convention because there were no longer any rights to protect in the light of the Security Council Resolution 748. The ICJ held that:

> 'Whatever the situation previous to the adoption of that resolution, the rights claimed by Libya under the Montreal Convention cannot now be regarded as appropriate for protection': (1992) ICJ Rep 3 at 15.

While in this particular case Libya was not allowed to avoid its UN Charter obligations, the existence of alternative grounds for exercising jurisdiction will clearly cause problems when one of two or more states permitted to exercise jurisdiction has a connection with the accused such as nationality. Since the international community is increasingly employing multilateral treaties as a means of establishing jurisdiction over persons accused of perpetrating cross-border offences, this is regrettable.

8.7 Concurrent jurisdiction

The existence of different grounds of jurisdiction inevitably means that several states may have concurrent jurisdiction. Where more than one state has jurisdiction it seems that priority to exercise enforcement jurisdiction depends solely upon custody.

The matter of concurrent jurisdiction is illustrated by the disagreement between Saudi Arabia and the US in respect of the indictment on 21 June 2001 by a US federal grand jury of 13 Saudi Arabian nationals and one Lebanese national in connection with the bombing in 1996 of a building in Saudi Arabia which was used as a barracks for US military service personnel. A bomb left in a truck near the building exploded killing 19 members of the American military services and wounding nearly 400 others in an apartment building. The bombing was allegedly committed by a terrorist organisation and was intended to drive the US out of the Persian Gulf.

Saudi Arabia claimed that it had exclusive jurisdiction in the matter: *New York Times*, 23 June 2001, A6.

In the above situation Saudi Arabia could have asserted jurisdiction under either the territorial or the nationality principles since the bombing took place in its territory and the accused were nationals of Saudi Arabia. However, the US had strong arguments in exercising concurrent jurisdiction:

1. the victims were nationals of the US and thus it may invoke the passive personality principle;
2. although universal jurisdiction is not widely accepted in respect of acts of terrorism, the US could try to justify its jurisdiction on the ground that the offenders are in the custody of the US.

Neither the US nor Saudi Arabia are contracting parties to the UN Convention for the Suppression of Terrorist Bombings 1997 which entered into force in May 2001. As at 20 October 2003 the Convention had been ratified by 123 states. The Convention has, however, some significance for the non-contracting parties because it expresses the need to suppress acts of terrorism and codifies general principles in this area, including the issue of jurisdiction. The Convention recognises that the state of nationality of victims is entitled to prosecute the offenders. It also sets out grounds for universal jurisdiction: a contracting state must prosecute the offenders if it decides not to extradite them to a state with a more direct interest. Further, the Convention states that it does not exclude the exercise of any criminal jurisdiction established by a contracting state in accordance with its domestic law.

8.8 Extraterritorial application of competition law – the 'effects doctrine'

The traditional principles establishing jurisdiction have been the subject of some debates in the context, largely, of business transactions which are deemed to have a national interest dimension. So, for example, if two foreign companies enter into an agreement abroad to co-ordinate their pricing policy for goods marketed in the territory of state X, the question may arise as to whether the agreement infringes the municipal law in that state and, if so, whether state X is in a position to do anything about it.

First analysis may suggest that such situations fall neatly within the scope of the territorial principle. The act in question has been completed within the territory of the state seeking to exert its authority over the parties concerned. Such an interpretation, however, involves a fundamental and controversial extension of the application of the territorial principle. The PCIJ in the *SS Lotus Case: France* v *Turkey* (1927) PCIJ Rep Ser A No 10 accepted the principle of objective territoriality, ie jurisdiction based on the territoriality of the place of completion. However, as is evident from the facts of that case, it was intrinsic to objective territoriality that there existed a direct and immediate link between the initiation and completion of the act. A number of commentators have noted that remoteness will defeat a claim to jurisdiction based on objective territoriality.

In the example above the matter of remoteness between the initiating act and the act of completion is clearly at issue. The initiating act would be the anti-competitive agreement on pricing policy. This may well be prima facie unlawful. It is, however, not clear that there is a direct and immediate link between that act and any result flowing therefrom within the territory of the state concerned.

The problem posed by the limited scope of the objective territorial principle led the US courts to develop what has become known as the 'effects doctrine' of jurisdiction. The doctrine was first applied in *US* v *Aluminium Co of America* (1945) 148 F 2d 416 where the question at issue was whether a Canadian company could be liable under US anti-trust legislation. The US court held that it did have jurisdiction as the acts in question were intended to have effect within the US and did indeed have such effect.

This doctrine has since undergone a measure of refinement in the case law of US courts. In *Timberlane Lumber Co* v *Bank of America* (1976) 549 F 2d 597 the issue was whether foreign companies, acting outside the US, could be subject to US anti-trust jurisdiction. The Court of Appeals held that it was too simplistic to look only at the effect that the agreement in question would have on trade within the US. This approach failed to take into account the interests of other states. The Court indicated, therefore, that a balancing of interests approach should be applied to determine whether the US courts should assume jurisdiction. This balancing of interest approach was further developed in the *Mannington Mills* v *Congoleum Corporation* (1979) 595 F 2d 1287 where the court indicated a number of factors that should be taken into account before jurisdiction could be assumed. This weighing of competing interests required the US court before which the case was heard to consider such matters as the nature of the alleged violation, the nationality of the parties, the interests of other states and the effect of an assumption of jurisdiction.

The 'competing interests' or 'reasonableness' approach is now clearly recognised in US jurisprudence as a legitimate basis of jurisdiction.

The Court of Justice of the European Communities (ECJ) endorsed the extraterritorial application of EC competition law in the *Wood Pulp* cases in which it delivered two judgments, one dealing solely with jurisdictional issues (*Ahlström and Others* v *EC Commission (Re Wood Pulp Cartel)* Joined Cases 89, 104, 114, 116, 117 and 125–129/85 [1988] ECR 5193; [1988] 4 CMLR 901) and the other with the substance of the claim: [1993] 4 CMLR 407.

In *Re Wood Pulp Cartel* [1998] ECR 5193; [1988] 4 CMLR 901 the Commission found more than 40 suppliers of wood pulp in violation of Community competition law despite the fact that 40 out of 42 undertakings were not resident within the European Community (there were 11 undertakings from the US, six from Canada, 11 from Sweden, 11 from Finland, one from Norway, one from Spain and one from Portugal). Non-EC undertakings were making sales into the Community in a variety of ways, including via agents, branches and subsidiaries located there. Fines were imposed on 36 of the undertakings for violation of art 81(1) EC. A number of them appealed to the ECJ against the decision. One of their arguments was that EC competition law was not capable of having extraterritorial effect and therefore the fines were unlawful.

The ECJ confirmed the extraterritorial application of EC competition law. The applicants argued that the Commission's decision was incompatible with public international law, taking into account that the application of EC competition rules was founded exclusively on the economic repercussions within the Common Market of conduct restricting competition which was carried out outside the Community. The ECJ replied that:

> 'It should be observed that an infringement of art [81 EC], such as the conclusion of an agreement which has had the effect of restricting competition within the Common Market, consists of conduct made up of two elements: the formation of the agreement, decision or concerted practice and the implementation thereof. If the applicability of prohibitions laid down under competition law were made to depend on the place where the agreement, decision or concerted practice was formed, the result would obviously be to give undertakings an easy means of evading these prohibitions. The decisive factor is therefore the place where it is implemented.'

The extraterritorial application of EC competition law is expressly provided in Merger Regulation 4064/89 which applies to undertakings from outside the EC if three conditions are met, that is, that it must be foreseeable, and that the intended concentration will have both an immediate and substantial effect in the Community: *Gencor Ltd* v *EC Commission* Case T–102/96 [1999] All ER (EC) 289.

The extraterritorial application of any national law, as well as EC competition law, creates many problems. The investigation of alleged breaches outside the territory of the European Union often necessitates the co-operation of competent authorities of a third state. Even more challenging is the actual enforcement outside the Community territory of decisions of Community competition authorities because a third state, where the offending undertaking is located, has no obligation to co-operate, to assist foreign authorities or to recognise and enforce their decisions. In this respect it is often left to the offending undertakings to plead guilty and pay the fine. This means that the undertaking concerned will co-operate in investigations only when forced and that only powerful countries or blocks of countries will successfully enforce their decisions against an offending undertaking and consequently obtain compensation, although in the context of a global economy the anti-competitive conduct of an undertaking may affect millions of consumers living all over the world. In this respect, the proceedings of the US anti-trust authorities against Hoffmann–La Roche and other pharmaceutical giants participating in a conspiracy to eliminate competition in the pharmaceutical sector worldwide is very instructive. Hoffmann–La Roche, a Swiss-based pharmaceutical multinational, was a leader of a worldwide conspiracy to fix, raise and maintain prices for the most commonly used vitamins (ie A, B2, B5, C, E and Beta Carotene), to allocate market shares of such vitamins worldwide and to 'allot' contracts to supply vitamin pre-mixes to customers in the US, by rigging the bids for those contracts. The conspiracy lasted from January 1990 to February 1999. As Joel I Klein, Assistant Attorney-General in charge of the Department of Justice Anti-trust Division, emphasised:

> 'During the life of the conspiracy, virtually every American consumer paid artificially inflated prices for vitamins and vitamin-enriched foods in order to feed the greed of those defendants and their co-conspirators who reaped hundreds of million of dollars in additional revenues': see US Department of Justice press release of 20 May 1999, http://www.usdoj.gov/atr/public/press_release /1999/2450.htm.

During the investigation the personnel concerned of Hoffmann–La Roche and other participating undertakings lied to the US anti-trust authorities in attempts to cover-up the conspiracy. Only when faced with evidence provided by Rhone-Poulenc SA, a French pharmaceutical company which also participated in the conspiracy (but decided to co-operate with US anti-competition authorities in order to qualify for protection from criminal proceedings under the US Corporate Leniency Program), did Hoffmann–La Roche plead guilty, agree to pay the highest criminal fine ever imposed of $500 million and agree to co-operate with the investigation. The company director in charge of worldwide marketing, Dr Sommer, a Swiss citizen, also agreed to submit to the jurisdiction of the US courts and pleaded guilty to charges which resulted in his serving a four-month prison term and paying a $100,000 fine. Money received from the fines was deposited into the Crime Victims Fund in the US. This is designated to provide financial compensation to US victims of crime and to provide other benefits in the US. However, millions of consumers outside the US, also victims of the conspiracy, will never be compensated, either directly or indirectly!

Extraterritorial application of Community competition law is contrary to international comity and fairness and encourages confrontation between countries rather than co-operation in resolving competition issues. This is even more obvious in the context of the global economy, taking into account that anti-competitive conduct of undertakings may have a worldwide impact.

The best solution is to establish a progressive and global approach towards the unification of substantive competition law at international level. So far this solution has not been very successful, although this matter has attracted the attention of the World Trade Organisation (WTO). Talks on competition rules were agreed at the 2001 Ministerial Conference in Doha (WT/MIN/01/DEC/1) but there is still no consensus among member states as to the WTO being an appropriate arena for the formulation of any global rules on competition policy. In particular, developing countries resist any attempt to put competition policy on the agenda for the next world trade round (see A Choudry, 'Another Corporate Steal? The Proposed WTO Competition Policy', www.ased.org).

In the meantime the European Community has decided to enter into bilateral competition co-operation agreements. They increase the effectiveness of enforcement of competition law and reduce the risk of conflicting, or incompatible, decisions being reached by two competition authorities in individual cases. So far the EC has concluded agreements with the US, Canada and Japan.

9

Immunity from Jurisdiction

9.1 Introduction

9.2 State immunity

9.3 Diplomatic immunity

9.4 Quasi-diplomatic privileges and immunities

9.1 Introduction

Under international law certain categories of persons and bodies are immune from the jurisdiction of municipal courts. These are as follows.

1. Foreign sovereigns and foreign states enjoy sovereign immunity (state immunity). The extent of state immunity from the European perspective was set out in the European Convention on State Immunity 1972 which was given effect in the UK by the State Immunity Act 1978.

2. Diplomatic agents of a foreign state in the United Kingdom enjoy diplomatic immunity. The scope of diplomatic immunity was the subject of the Vienna Convention on Diplomatic Relations 1961, adopted on 16 April 1961 by the UN Conference on Diplomatic Intercourse and Immunities. It entered into force on 24 April 1964. The Diplomatic Privileges Act 1964 implements the Convention in the UK.

3. The International Organisations Acts 1969 and 1981 regulate the extent of exemptions from the jurisdiction of English courts of representatives of such organisations: *Standard Charter Bank* v *International Tin Council* [1987] 1 WLR 641.

4. Although consular officers of a foreign state are not diplomatic representatives, they also enjoy some measure of immunity from the jurisdiction of the English courts. This matter is governed by the Consular Relations Act 1968 which implements the Vienna Convention on Consular Relations 1963.

5. Special statutory limitations on jurisdiction are provided by international conventions such as, inter alia, the Carriage of Goods by Air Act 1961, the Carriage of Goods by Road Act 1965, the Carriage of Passengers by Road Act 1974, the Nuclear Installations Act 1965, etc.

145

The principle underlying the doctrine of immunity from jurisdiction developed as a natural extension of the immunity of the individual sovereign. Its scope has changed over the centuries. From the concept of an absolute immunity covering all actions of a foreign state and reflecting the medieval personification of a state and its ruler, it has become subject to a number of limitations both ratione personae and rationae materiae.

Diplomatic immunity has evolved from state immunity. For centuries kings and other Heads of State appointed their agents to represent their interests in other states. Ancient Greece first established the inviolability of the persons of heralds who were intermediaries bringing messages between warring states. In the Middle Ages papal diplomacy conducted through papal legates and nuncii contributed to the development of diplomacy as secular rulers started to follow the example of the Holy See in modelling the conduct of international relations. From the twelfth century agents representing foreign rulers were called ambassadors. Italian city states, in particular Venice, conducted the most extensive diplomatic relations. During the period of the crusades Venice entered into commercial relations with Byzantium and endorsed some of its practices. For example, Venice started to give its agents written instructions and established an archive containing a registry of all diplomatic documents. Its agents also reported on the conditions in the host country. This practice was followed by other Italian city states and later by France and Spain. Diplomatic rules, procedures and protocols were established in the sixteenth century when foreign ambassadors began to reside permanently in host capitals. In 1626 Cardinal Richelieu established the first Ministry of External Affairs. He regarded diplomacy as a continuous process of negotiations which should ensure that national interests, not rulers' wishes or dynastic considerations, were pursued by diplomats. He believed that the reason d'etat should be recognised and acted upon by those in charge of international relations. The Peace Treaty of Westphalia 1648 terminating the Thirty Years War was the first major meeting of Heads of State in Europe but diplomats were in charge of its preparations. Four years before its signature they were working together and became well acquainted with each other. Experience gained by representatives of European rulers during negotiations of the Peace Treaty of Westphalia served as a base for the establishment of networks of embassies and legations throughout Europe. By seventeenth century diplomacy had become a profession for the aristocracy. From the Peace Treaty of Westphalia until the development of modern means of communication and transportation diplomats played a principal role in conducting international relations and enjoyed a large measure of autonomy in a host state.

9.2 State immunity

The basic principle behind the doctrine of state immunity is that since states are independent and equal they should not be subjected to the jurisdiction of other states without their consent.

In *De Haber* v *Queen of Portugal* (1851) 17 QB 196 the claimant issued writs in the UK against the defendant and a number of agents of the Portuguese government, claiming that the Portuguese government had wrongfully received money which was in fact due to him. The defendant succeeded in having all further proceedings stayed.

Lord Campbell LJ stated that: 'to cite a foreign potentate in a municipal court ... is contrary to the law of nations and an insult which he is entitled to resent'.

Basis of state immunity and non-justiciability

State immunity rests upon two principles.

1. The principle of par in parem non habet jurisdiction em: legal persons of equal standing cannot have their disputes settled in the courts of one of them.

   This is founded upon the principle of sovereign equality and independence of states and rests upon the historical proposition that a sovereign could not himself be sued before his own municipal courts, so the sovereign of another state was similarly exempt from the jurisdiction of the local law.

   This principle is based upon the immunity of the sovereign. It is possible, therefore, for a sovereign to waive this immunity, in which case the municipal courts of the other state may exercise jurisdiction.

2. The principle of non-intervention in the internal affairs of other states.

   Under this principle there are issues which are essentially non-justiciable and, therefore, the municipal court has no competence to assert jurisdiction.

   In *Buck* v *Attorney-General* [1965] Ch 745 the Court of Appeal refused to make a declaration on the validity or otherwise of the constitution of Sierra Leone as created by Order in Council at independence. The Court held that it had no jurisdiction to make such a declaration. In this respect Diplock LJ said:

   '... the application of the doctrine of sovereign immunity does not depend upon the persons between whom the issue is joined, but upon the subject matter of the issue. For the English court to pronounce upon the validity of a law of a foreign sovereign state within its own territory, so that the validity of that law becomes the res of the res judicata in the suit, would be to assert jurisdiction over the internal affairs of that state. That would be a breach of the rules of comity. In my view, this Court has no jurisdiction so to do.'

The evolution of the concept of state immunity

The concept of absolute immunity was endorsed and explained by Chief Justice Marshall of the United States Supreme Court in *Exchange* v *McFaddon* (1812) 7 Cranch 116 in the context of a dispute involving the ship, the *Exchange*, whose ownership was claimed by both the government of France and a number of US nationals. In this case it was held that:

> 'The full and absolute territorial jurisdiction being alike the attribute of every sovereign, and being incapable of conferring extraterritorial power, would not seem to contemplate foreign sovereigns nor their sovereign rights as its objects. One sovereign being in no respect amenable to another; and being bound by obligations of the highest character not to degrade the dignity of his nation, by placing himself or its sovereign rights within the jurisdiction of another ...'

The need to impose restrictions on state immunity had become apparent with the development of international trade at the end of the nineteenth century when states became increasingly involved in commercial activities. The emergence of Communist states in the twentieth century further accentuated this tendency as Communist states and their trading organisations entered into commercial dealings with foreign individuals and companies. They had no remedy under their national laws if a dispute arose because a foreign state or its trading organisation could rely on the concept of sovereign immunity and claim immunity from the judicial process of the courts of that state. The growing pressure toward establishing a more realistic and pragmatic approach led to a distinction between the public acts of a state (acts jure imperii) and private acts such as trading and commercial activities (acts jure gestionis). A state could rely on its immunity only in relation to acts jure imperii. The Supreme Court of Austria in *Dralle v Republic of Czechoslovakia* (1950) 17 ILR 165 endorsed this distinction. Other states have followed. Under the auspices of the Council of Europe, European states confirmed this restrictive approach to the concept of state immunity in the European Convention on State Immunity 1972 which was implemented in the UK by the State Immunity Act 1978 and entered into force on 22 November 1978. Even before the State Immunity Act 1978 became operational the UK courts endorsed the new approach in two cases: *The Philippine Admiral* [1977] AC 373 and *Trendtex Trading Corporation Ltd v Central Bank of Nigeria* [1977] 2 WLR 356. This was confirmed by the House of Lords in *I Congreso del Partido* [1981] 2 All ER 1064, a case concerned with the pre-1978 Act common law.

The matter whether or not new restrictions can be imposed on state immunity was answered in the affirmative by the Hellenic Supreme Court in its judgment of 4 May 2000. In *Prefecture of Voiotia v Federal Republic of Germany* Case No 11/2000 (2001) 95 AJIL 95 the Hellenic Supreme Court decided that Germany could not rely on state immunity in respect of acts jure imperii in breach of ius cogens.

In this case the Greek district court awarded damages of nearly 9.5 billion drachmas as indemnity for atrocities, including murder and destruction of private property, committed by the Germany occupation forces in the village of Distomo on 10 June 1944. The Hellenic Supreme Court upheld the appeal.

The Supreme Court based its decision on the customary nature of the tort exception to sovereign immunity. The Court found evidence of this new restriction on state immunity.

1. In art 11 of the European Convention on State Immunity 1972, which provides that a state cannot claim immunity from jurisdiction of a court in another state in proceedings for redress for injuries to persons including wilful bodily harm, negligent bodily harm and manslaughter, or to damage to property 'irrespective of whether the tort was carried out by the contracting state jure imperii or jure gestionis'. The Court stated that the European Convention codified the pre-existing customary law in Europe on state immunity. Although the Convention has only been ratified by eight states including Germany but excluding Greece, the Court did not regard the Convention's limited popularity as challenging its conclusions.
2. In art 12 of the 1991 Draft Articles on Jurisdictional Immunities of States and Their Property prepared by the International Law Commission and its commentary.
3. In art 2(2)(e) of the Draft Articles attached to the Resolution on 'Contemporary Problems Concerning the Immunity of States in Relation to the Questions of Jurisdiction and Enforcement' adopted by the Institut de Droit International at its 1991 Basel session.
4. The judgment cited, inter alia, relatively recent national legislation of many states: s1605(a)(5) of the US Foreign Sovereign Immunities Act 1976; s5 of the UK State Immunity Act 1978; s6 of the Canadian Sovereign Immunity Act 1985; s13 of the Australian State Immunity Act 1985: s6 of the South African Foreign State Immunity Act 1981; and s7 of the Singapore State Immunity Act 1979.
5. In case law – the Court cited the case of *Letelier* v *Republic of Chile* 488 F Supp 665 (DDC 1980) and *Liu* v *Republic of China* 892 F 2d 1419 (9th Cir 1989).

The main problem for the Court was to overcome the exclusion contained in the above-cited international instruments concerning torts committed in situations involving armed conflicts. In order to exclude the application of the exception the Court characterised the facts of the cases in the following manner:

> 'In case of military occupation that is directly derived from an armed conflict and that, according to the by now customary rules of art 43 of the Regulations concerning the Laws and Customs of War on Land attached to the 1907 Hague IV Convention, do not bring about a change in sovereignty or preclude the application of the laws of the occupied state, crimes carried out by organs of the occupying power in abuse of their sovereign power do not attract immunity.'

The Court noted that among crimes not covered by immunity were 'reprisals against a specific and limited number of innocent and wholly uninvolved citizens for specific sabotage acts carried out by underground groups'. The Court looked at the facts of the case and found that the tort committed by the German occupation forces was directed against innocent civilians who had not been involved in resistance which had resulted in the death of German soldiers taking part in a terror operation directed against the local population. Acts committed by the German occupation forces were therefore hideous murders and constituted an abuse of the sovereign power of the German Third Reich. Moreover, those acts violated the rules of peremptory international law contained in art 46 of the Regulations attached to the Hague IV Convention. For that reason the Court decided that Germany had tacitly waived the privilege of immunity and that the Greek courts had jurisdiction to try the case.

There was strong dissident opinion from a minority of the Court. Five members of the Court challenged the customary nature of the tort exception to state immunity. They argued that there was no evidence that such a rule acquired the status of customary law. They stated that the European Convention neither at the time of its conclusion nor at the time of the judgment constituted codification of customary law and that other international instruments were merely proposals and had not been transformed into international conventions because of the lack of consensus of the international community restricting the scope of state immunity with regards to acts jure imperii. This was the main reason why national legislation incorporating such an exception was enacted by a number of states. Consequently, the case law cited by the majority referred to national law rather than to international law applied by the domestic courts of some states. Also the interpretation of the armed conflict clause was rejected by four members of the Court. They argued that even the European Convention expressly preserves immunity in situations involving armed forces since the use of force is certainly the best example of acts jure imperii. Even though the military action of the German occupying forces was in breach of ius cogens there is no exception to the sovereign immunity of the German state 'since there is no customary rule according to which such a breach would engender a tacit waiver of sovereign immunity'.

The above case is of major interest. The Hellenic Supreme Court was one of the first to reject the theory of the absolute immunity of states. Its decision in *Voiotia* (above) may inaugurate a new restrictive approach to state immunity for acts jure imperii based on the violation of ius cogens. There is certainly a strong analogy between *Voiotia* and the case of *Pinochet Ugarte (No 3)* (below) in which the House of Lords restricted the scope of personal immunity, ruling that the violation of ius cogens entails personal criminal liability in cases which otherwise would be described as jure imperii.

The decision of the Hellenic Supreme Court focused on the rule which was breached by the offending state. The rule in question has the status of ius cogens. Consequently, the Court reasoned that the violation of a peremptory rule must be sanctioned. This is the weakest point in the arguments presented by the Court, that is the connection between the violations of ius cogens and its result, namely a tacit waiver of immunity by the offending state. However, the International Law Commission's Articles on State Responsibility 2001 provides important arguments supporting the decision of the Hellenic Supreme Court: see Chapter 10.

English judicial practice regarding state immunity

English judicial practice regarding state immunity will be examined in two parts. The first will focus on the restrictions imposed on the scope of absolute immunity of a state. The second will deal with further restrictions concerning immunity of Heads of State for acts performed in the exercise of their official duties, which acts are in breach of ius cogens. The case of Augusto Pinochet, the former President of Chile, will be examined in some detail.

Limitations imposed on the absolute immunity of a state

Whereas absolute immunity always attached itself to a sovereign in relation to his public acts, it remained for most of the nineteenth century unsettled whether the immunity attached to him was absolute. In *The Charkich* (1873) LR 4 A & E 59 Sir Robert Philimore held that a vessel owned by the Khedive of Egypt forfeited its immunity because it was chartered to a private individual and engaged in commercial activity. This approach, founded on a division between acts jure imperii and jure gestionis, did not survive the century!

In *The Parlement Belge* (1878–79) 4 PD 129 the defendant ship was owned by the King of Belgium. It was a mail boat engaged in channel crossings. In this case Philimore remained faithful to his reasoning in *The Charkich*: because it was involved in a commercial enterprise the mail boat was not to be accorded immunity. His decision was reversed by the Court of Appeal, but the rule adopted by him may have been far wider than was necessary. The Court of Appeal had the option of deciding that the vessel was primarily operating for the public benefit, the carrying of cargo and passengers being secondary to the carrying of mail. However, the principle applied by the Court of Appeal was that of absolute immunity resting on the theory of the independence of states.

This principle was confirmed in *The Porto Alexandre* [1920] P 30. This ship had gone aground in the Mersey and had been refloated with the assistance of three tugs. The tug owners could not obtain payment and so issued a writ in rem against the ship itself. The facts were that the ship had been requisitioned by the Portuguese government, but was being employed entirely for carrying cargoes for private individuals. A claim of immunity was upheld. The judges in the Court of Appeal were aware of the blatant injustice of the decision, but demurred that they had no alternative in the light of the strong dicta in *The Parlement Belge*. Strong dicta (particularly in the judgment of Lord MacMillan) is also evident in the case of *The Cristina* [1938] AC 485.

Foreign governmental agencies like the United States Shipping Board and the Tass News Agency were accorded immunity by the English courts, but in 1957 in *Baccus SRL* v *Servicio Nacional del Trigo* [1957] 1 QB 438 the Court of Appeal went further. The defendant was a department of the Spanish Ministry of Agriculture but, according to expert advice, was an independent legal personality. Nevertheless, the majority of the Court of Appeal upheld the plea of immunity, even though it was in Spanish law a separate company and the subject matter of the dispute was a commercial transaction.

The above cases are of interest in that they illustrate the power of the doctrine of precedent where there appears to be little room for flexibility. The virtue of flexibility is that it can take account of changes in public policy. In this area the change in public policy was the increase of state activity in commerce, and the emergence of Communist states and their increasing participation in international commerce.

The doctrine of absolute immunity was justifiable when it applied to a sovereign in person, but when great corporations receive immunity on account of the fact that they are state controlled the whole doctrine must be called into question.

The stranglehold of precedent was, however, broken in 1975 with the case of *The Philippine Admiral* [1977] AC 373. The ship was owned by the Philippine Reparation Commission, an agency of the Philippines government, but it was being operated at the relevant time by the Liberation Steamship Company under a conditional sale agreement with the Commission. The company had employed the ship for normal commercial purposes. The Privy Council refused to uphold the plea of immunity.

This was followed in *Trendtex Trading Corp* v *Central Bank of Nigeria* [1977] QB 529 where the Central Bank of Nigeria claimed sovereign immunity. Lord Denning MR concluded that by then international law recognised the doctrine of restrictive immunity and that a distinction must be drawn between acts jure imperii and acts jure gestionis. The only satisfactory test was to look to the functions and control of the organisation. It was necessary to examine all the evidence to see whether the organisation was under governmental control and exercising governmental functions.

At common law, therefore, the British courts abandoned the doctrine of absolute immunity in respect of both actions in rem and actions in personam, thereby anticipating the enactment of the State Immunity Act 1978.

The *Pinochet* case

The judgments of the House of Lords in the *Pinochet* saga established a new restriction on state immunity. This restriction is based on the violation of a peremptory rule of customary international law. The majority of the House of Lords found that the Criminal Justice Act 1988 removed immunity from a former Head of State in respect of acts carried out in the exercise of his official functions as a Head of State (that is acta jure imperii normally covered by sovereign immunity irrespective of whether or not a Head of State is still in office or has ceased to be Head of State) if these acts were in breach of ius cogens. However, the House of Lords in *R* v *Bow Street Metropolitan Stipendiary Magistrate, ex parte Pinochet Ugarte (No 3)* [1999] 2 WLR 827 ruled that Pinochet could be extradited only for torture committed in Chile after 8 December 1988, the date on which the 1984 Torture Convention entered into force in the UK, it at that time already being in force in Chile and Spain. From that date Augusto Pinochet's immunity from prosecution, as a former Head of State, was removed since only at that point did his acts of torture in Chile become international crimes under the UK law as well as in international law. This construction reflects the relationship between English municipal law and international law. In his obiter remarks Lord Browne-Wilkinson said that:

'The ius cogens nature of the international crime of torture justifies states taking universal jurisdiction over torture wherever committed ... I have no doubt that long before the Torture Convention of 1984 state torture was an international crime in the highest sense.'

All three judgments in *Pinochet* rendered by the House of Lords attracted a wide degree of comment and attention and have been the subject of political debate in several countries. It is impossible within the confines of this work to analyse in detail all the legal questions raised by the decisions of the House of Lords. For that reason the treatment of the subject will be limited to the most important aspects of each judgment.

The facts of the case were as follows. Augusto Pinochet was President of the military junta which overthrew the government of President Allende and ruled Chile from 11 September 1973 until June 1974. From 1974 until March 1999 Augusto Pinochet, although unelected, held office as President of Chile. He was at all material times a Chilean national and had never held Spanish citizenship. Throughout this period Chilean nationals and citizens of Spain, Switzerland, France and other countries were arbitrarily imprisoned and tortured and up to 4,000 persons disappeared or were killed as part of a government policy to eliminate political opposition.

In 1998 Pinochet came to the UK to receive medical treatment. During his stay in the UK Spain applied for a warrant to extradite him to face charges of genocide, attempted murder, torture, hostage-taking and conspiracy. Two provisional warrants were issued in October 1998 for his arrest in London pursuant to s8(1) of the Extradition Act 1989. The first warrant alleged the murder of Spanish citizens in Chile in the period between September 1973 to December 1983. The second warrant related to events in the period 1973 until 1979 and concerned allegations of torture, the taking of hostages and conspiracy to murder.

Pinochet asked the Divisional Court to judicially review the issue of the warrants and sought an order of certiorari to quash the issue of both warrants. On his behalf, Clive Nicholls QC advanced the following arguments:

1. that the first warrant was bad in law because it did not disclose an extraditable crime having regard to the provisions of ss2(1)(a) and 3(a) of the Extradition Act 1989 and s9 of the Offences against the Person Act 1861;
2. that in respect of both provisional warrants the issue was unlawful because the courts in the UK had no jurisdiction to exercise authority over the applicant as a former sovereign having regard to the provisions of ss1, 14(1), 20(1) and 23(3) of the State Immunity Act 1978 and ss1, 2 and arts 29, 31 and 39 of Sch 1 of the Diplomatic Privileges Act 1964;

3. that a number of technical arguments were raised in respect of the second warrant as to (a) procedure and (b) whether the offences disclosed were criminal offences in England at the relevant dates.

On behalf of the Crown Prosecution Service (and the Spanish government seeking extradition) it was argued that immunity under the 1978 Act and the 1964 Act did not extend to a class of criminal acts contrary to international law and the accepted moral law, namely crimes against humanity, genocide, torture and the taking of hostages.

The matters were decided by the Divisional Court and the case was reported as *R v Evans and Others, ex parte Pinochet Ugarte* (1998) The Times 3 November. The application was granted and relief given by certiorari to quash both warrants.

The Crown Prosecution Service and the Spanish government appealed in respect of the determination that Augusto Pinochet was entitled to immunity from proceedings as a former Head of State. Prior to the hearing in the House of Lords their Lordships permitted Amnesty International, the Medical Foundation for the Care of Victims of Torture and Human Rights Watch to make oral and written representations. It was broadly accepted that the House of Lords would be required to rule on four particular questions concerning immunity. The relevant questions were as follows.

1. Was Pinochet entitled at common law to immunity as a former Head of State? This would depend on whether he was entitled to such immunity under the rules of customary international law.
2. Was Pinochet entitled to immunity under Part I of the State Immunity Act 1978? If not, did Part I restrict any immunity at common law?
3. Was Pinochet entitled to immunity as a former Head of State under Part III of the State Immunity Act 1978?
4. Was this a case in which the court ought to decline jurisdiction on the basis that the issues raised were non-justicable?

The majority of the House of Lords held that Augusto Pinochet did not enjoy immunity from extradition proceedings because:

1. no immunity arose at common law because no immunity arose under customary international law in respect of acts of torture and hostage-taking;
2 no immunity arose under Part I of the State Immunity Act 1978 by reason of the provisions of s16(4);
3. no personal immunity arose under Part III of the State Immunity Act 1978;
4. the matters alleged were justiciable in particular because Parliament had legislated to outlaw torture and hostage-taking: *R v Evans and Others, ex parte Pinochet Ugarte (No 1)* [1998] 3 WLR 1456.

On 9 December 1998 the Home Secretary gave permission for the extradition of Pinochet to Spain. In the meantime the ruling of the House of Lords was challenged by Pinochet on the ground that it was discovered that one of the Law Lords, although not a member of Amnesty International, was an unpaid director and chairman of Amnesty International Charity Ltd, which was controlled by Amnesty International. As mentioned above in *Pinochet (No 1)*, Amnesty International was allowed to intervene in the proceedings and was permitted both to make written representations and to be represented by counsel. Pinochet requested the House of Lords to set aside the earlier judgment on the ground of apparent bias by the judge.

On 17 December 1998 in *R* v *Bow Street Metropolitan Stipendiary Magistrate, ex parte Pinochet Ugarte (No 2)* [1999] 2 WLR 272, a differently constituted House of Lords set aside the earlier ruling and directed that there should be a fresh hearing on the issue of immunity. Lord Browne-Wilkinson in giving judgment stressed the following points:

1. that the House of Lords possessed an inherent jurisdiction to set aside an earlier order that might have caused injustice;
2. that it was a fundamental principle of English law that no man should be a judge in his own cause;
3. that the fundamental principle set out by Lord Hewart LCJ in *R* v *Sussex Justices, ex parte McCarthy* [1924] 1 KB 256 was not capable of being subject to fine distinctions;
4. that in the present case there was a real danger or reasonable suspicion of bias – that is to say that there was an appearance of bias, not actual bias;
5. that the concept of an 'interest in proceedings' could extend to a non-pecuniary interest;
6. that where a person was a director of a company closely associated to a party in proceedings, he should not sit in those proceedings;
7. Pinochet was entitled to the judgment of an impartial and independent tribunal on the question as to whether he enjoyed immunity.

In *R* v *Bow Street Metropolitan Stipendiary Magistrate, ex parte Pinochet Ugarte (No 3)* [1999] 2 WLR 827 the House of Lords by a majority of six to one (Lord Goff dissenting) held the following.

1. Section 2 of the Extradition Act 1989 required that the alleged conduct that was the subject of the extradition request should be a crime in the UK at the time the offence was committed. Extraterritorial torture did not become a criminal offence in the UK until s134 of the Criminal Justice Act 1988 came into effect on 29 September 1988. It therefore followed that all allegations of torture prior to that date which did not take place in Spain were not extraditable offences.
2. In principle a Head of State had immunity from the criminal jurisdiction of the UK for acts done in his official capacity as Head of State by virtue of s20 of the State Immunity Act 1978 when read with art 39(2) of Sch 1 to the 1964 Diplomatic Privileges Act. However, torture was an international crime and after

the coming into effect of the 1984 Torture Convention it was a crime of universal jurisdiction.

3. Since the Convention had been ratified by Spain, Chile and the UK by 8 December 1988 and the Convention was in effect from 1987 there could be no immunity for offences of torture or conspiracy to torture from 8 December 1988 at the latest.

4. Extradition proceedings on the charges of torture and conspiracy to torture could therefore proceed.

It is doubtful whether a more complex case in international law has ever reached the House of Lords. As Lord Browne-Wilkinson said, 'the interaction between the various issues is complex'. The seven judgments in *Pinochet (No 3)* run to over 100 pages.

The original charges of murder had been deleted by Bingham LCJ, while the Home Secretary deleted the genocide charge. Other charges had been added prior to the second hearing in the House of Lords.

The double criminality rule in extradition proceedings requires that the conduct be an offence in both the requesting state and the requested state. The important question is the operative date. The understandable desire to avoid any retroactive element makes it sensible to fix the date as the date of the offence. Since the rule is contained in a statute it is reasonable to assume that this was the intention of Parliament when enacting s2 of the Extradition Act 1989. In these circumstances it was inevitable that the House of Lords would have to delete those extraterritorial charges of torture that arose prior to the date when s134 of the Criminal Justice Act 1988 came into effect, ie 29 September 1988.

This left the charges relating to torture after 29 September 1988. In respect of this matter there were four possible approaches:

1. to examine whether any rule of customary international law provided for immunity;
2. to examine the statutory provisions;
3. to consider whether the immunity was rationae materiae or rationae personae;
4. to consider the effect of the 1984 Torture Convention.

In respect of the first two approaches the majority felt that immunity arose either by virtue of rules of customary international law or under the terms of s20 of the State Immunity Act 1978 as read with s2 and arts 29, 31, and 39 of Sch 1 of the Diplomatic Privileges Act 1964. In respect of such immunity the question arises as to whether it is rationae personae or rationae materiae. In the circumstances of the case the majority rightly categorised it as rationae materiae. This means that the alleged acts of torture were carried out by Pinochet in his official capacity. Lord Millet was of the opinion that: 'These were not private acts. They were official and governmental or sovereign act by any standard.' This opinion was shared by the majority of the Law Lords. Consequently, Pinochet was prima facie entitled to immunity rationae materiae in respect of them. However, such immunity is that of the state and not the individual and is thus only capable of being waived by the state (*Zoernsch* v *Waldock* [1964] 2 QB 352, but contrast with the decision of the Hellenic Supreme Court in *Voiotia* (above)).

Because of s134 of the Criminal Justice Act 1988 it was possible to remove the sovereign immunity in respect of the former Head of State. It provides a specific exception to the immunity rationae materiae of a former Head of State in the case of acts of torture as defined therein. Thus, it is the nature of the offence that permits removal of the immunity. In this respect Lord Browne-Wilkinson stated:

> 'Finally, and to my mind decisively, if the implementation of a torture regime is a public function giving rise to immunity rationae materiae, this produces bizarre results ... If immunity ratinae materiae applied to the present case, and if the implementation of the torture regime is to be treated as official business sufficient to found an immunity for the former Head of State, it must also be official business sufficient to justify immunity for his inferiors who actually did the torturing. Under the Convention the international crime of torture can only be committed by an official or someone in an official capacity. They would all be entitled to immunity. It would follow that there can be no case outside Chile in which successful prosecution for torture can be brought unless the state of Chile is prepared to waive its right to officials' immunity ... In my judgment all these factors together demonstrate that the notion of continued immunity for ex-Heads of State is inconsistent with the provisions of the Torture Convention.'

The majority of their Lordships held that any immunity rationae materiae was displaced at the latest at the time when the 1984 Torture Convention had come into effect in all of Spain, Chile and the UK. Thus, they argued that after 8 December 1988 no immunity arose in international law in respect of any torture charge. In other words, the 1984 Torture Convention had the effect of displacing any existing immunity. In *R* v *Evans and Others, ex parte Pinochet Ugarte (No 1)* the House of Lords ruled that the loss of immunity applied to all the offences allegedly committed by Pinochet, including torture, the taking of hostages and conspiracy to murder, but (after the above was set aside) in *R* v *Bow Street Metropolitan Stipendiary Magistrate, ex parte Pinochet Ugarte (No 3)* the majority of the House of Lords decided to limit justiciability to those crimes alleged to have been committed after the Torture Convention had been incorporated into UK domestic law and was in force in Spain, Chile and the UK.

Pinochet was not extradited to Spain and returned to Chile after the UK Home Secretary refused his extradition on medical grounds! In August 2000 the Chilean Supreme Court removed immunity from prosecution under Chilean law in respect of Pinochet. He was indicted on charges of kidnapping arising out of the disappearance of 19 political opponents in the first months of his leadership in 1973. On 9 July 2001 the panel of three judges of the Santiago Appeals Court found him, on the basis of dementia, unfit to face any trial. On appeal on 26 August 2004, the Supreme Court of Chile held that Pinochet was fit to face trial. It is highly likely that the decision of the Supreme Court was influenced by the release of a report by the US Senate's Permanent Subcommittee on Investigations providing details concerning Pinochet's personal involvement in financial operations with Riggs National Bank from 1996 to 2002. The report disclosed that although Pinochet had, in 2001, been declared to be suffering from dementia he carried out several financial transactions through offshore corporations in the Bahamas relating to his assets at the Riggs National Bank. In Chile there are more than 230 lawsuits outstanding against him, filed by families of more than 3,000 people that disappeared or were tortured.

The most important contribution of the Law Lords is that until their judgments in *Pinochet* the peoples of the world were convinced that political power meant protection and immunity. The judgment of the House of Lords has proved that it is possible for those such as Pinochet to be brought to trial. However, the controversial judgment of the ICJ in the *Case Concerning the Arrest Warrant of 11 April 2000: the Democratic Republic of Congo v Belgium* (2002) 41 ILM 536 will certainly weaken the worldwide movement to end immunity for the worst abusers of human rights while in office. Even before the above judgment was rendered a federal court of the US upheld sovereign immunity in respect of a serving Head of State, Jean-Bertrand Aristide: *Lafontant v Aristide* 844 F Supp 128 (East Dist NY) (1994). Also, claims against Robert Mugabe, the President of Zimbabwe, and Stan Mudenge, Foreign Minister of Zimbabwe, individually and as officers of the Zimbabwe African National Union-Patriotic Front (ZANU-PF) brought by a group of citizens of Zimbabwe alleging that the defendants planned and executed a campaign aimed at intimidating and suppressing their political opponents, namely the Movement for Democratic Change in Zimbabwe, by resorting to murder, torture and other inhuman acts were dismissed by the US Court of Appeal for the Second Circuit on 6 October 2004. The Court of Appeal upheld the finding of a lower court that Mugabe and Mudenge were entitled to diplomatic and Head of State immunity but reversed the part of the judgment relating to the claim against ZANU–PF. The lower court had held that they were not entitled to diplomatic immunity as agents of ZANU–PF (*Tachiona v Mugabe* 169 F Supp 2d 259 (SDNY) 2001). The Court of Appeal disagreed and held that on the grounds of art 29 of the Vienna Convention on Diplomatic Relations, as applied to Mugabe and Mudenge through art IV, s11(g) of the UN Convention on Privileges and Immunity, they were immune from the service of process as agents for ZANU–PF (*Tachiona v US* 386 F 3d 205 (2004)).

The decision of the highest court of Belgium, the Court of Cassation, in the case of Ariel Sharon, currently the Prime Minister of Israel, regarding his role in the Sabra and Shatila refugee camp massacres in Lebanon in 1982, according to which Sharon can be prosecuted only after he leaves office, confirms that serving Heads of State and other high officials while in office are unlikely to be prosecuted (*HSA Et Al, SA Et Al (Decision Related to the Indictment of Ariel Sharon, Amos Yaron and Others)* (2003) 42 ILM 596).

The State Immunity Act 1978

The position of English law on state immunity is regulated by the State Immunity Act (SIA) 1978.

This Act, broadly implementing the provisions of the European Convention on State Immunity 1972, embodies the restrictive theory of immunity accepted by the Court of Appeal in *Trendtex*. The approach of the Act is, however, to affirm the general principle of absolute immunity in s1(1) and then go on to indicate a number of exceptions to this rule. This approach can also be found in the US Foreign Sovereign Immunities Act 1976.

Section 2 of the SIA 1978 lays down general provisions regarding waiver of immunity. It confirms that immunity is lost when a state submits to the jurisdiction of the courts in the UK. The submission may be made after a dispute has arisen or by a prior written agreement. Section 2(3) provides that a state will be deemed to have waived immunity in cases where it has instituted proceedings. Under s13, however, a state must give a separate waiver of immunity before execution and enforcement of a judgment can take place against any state property not in use for commercial purposes.

The most important exceptions to the basic rule of absolute immunity are set out in s3, which provides that a state will not be immune in respect of proceedings relating to commercial transactions or obligations which under contract stand to be performed in whole or in part in the UK. Section 3(3) defines commercial transactions as:

> '(a) any contract for the supply of goods or services;
> (b) any loan or other transaction for the provision of finance and any guarantee or indemnity in respect of any such transaction or of any other financial obligation; and
> (c) any other transaction or activity ... into which a state enters or in which it engages otherwise than in the exercise of sovereign authority.'

A transaction that falls within any one of these definitions will be a commercial transaction for the purpose of the Act with the exception that a contract of employment is not to be regarded as a commercial transaction within the meaning of the section. Contracts of employment are specifically covered by s4 which provides, inter alia, that a state will not be able to claim immunity in respect of such a contract made in the UK or in respect of work to be performed in whole or in part in the UK.

Other substantive provisions of the Act establish exceptions to absolute immunity in the case of:

1. proceedings for personal injury, death or loss or damage to tangible property in the UK (s5);
2. proceedings relating to any interest in or possession or use of immovable property in the UK (s6);
3. proceedings relating to patents or trademarks registered or protected in the UK (s7);

4. proceedings relating to a state's membership of a body corporate, unincorporated association or partnership which has members other than states and one which is incorporated or constituted under UK law or controlled from or has its principal place of business in the UK (s8);
5. proceedings in the UK courts with respect to arbitration to which the state has agreed to submit (s9);
6. actions in rem against a ship belonging to a state or actions in personam for enforcing a claim in connection with such a ship (s10); and
7. proceedings in respect of liability for VAT, customs and excise duties, agricultural levies or rates in respect of premises occupied for commercial purposes (s11). Immunity from indirect taxes does not, however, extend to liability for income tax payable by foreign governments on earnings from investments in the UK: see *R v IRC, ex parte Camacq Corp* [1990] 1 All ER 173.

The leading case dealing with the application of the 1978 Act in the context of commercial transactions is *A Company Limited v Republic of X* [1990] 2 Lloyd's Rep 250. This case involved an attempt to obtain an injunction to prevent the disposal of assets held in the UK by a government of a state X in both bank accounts and property in order to enforce any decree obtained from an action for payment for the price of a consignment of rice ordered by the government of state X.

The defendants argued that such action was incompetent because of the immunity conferred by s1(1) of the 1978 Act, despite the exception in s2(1) of the statute which allows jurisdiction when a government of a foreign state has submitted to adjudication or arbitration in England. The contract of sale provided for the exercise of such jurisdiction and the claimants argued that this was sufficient to found jurisdiction in the English courts.

The court agreed with the submission of the claimants and held that the intention and purpose of the clause in the contract was to place state X in the same position as a private individual for the purposes of legal proceedings. However, the action was dismissed because, even if the claimants were successful, no decree could be enforced against the assets of state X in the UK without the consent of the government of that state.

In *Al-Adsani v Government of Kuwait* [1996] 1 Lloyd's Rep 104; (1996) 100 ILR 465 (CA) the claimant, a British passport holder and Kuwaiti citizen, alleged that he was kidnapped, taken to prison in Kuwait and beaten by security guards. He brought an action against a particular sheikh and the government of Kuwait. At first instance it was held that the government was entitled to state immunity under the State Immunity Act 1978. On appeal it was argued that:

1. immunity did not apply to acts prohibited by international law;
2. torture was contrary to international law and in particular to the 1984 Torture Convention and other human rights treaties;
3. torture is a criminal offence by virtue of the Criminal Justice Act 1988.

The Court of Appeal rejected the appeal in March 1996. In December 1996 the House of Lords refused leave to appeal. In March 1997 the claimant, having exhausted domestic remedies, lodged an application to the European Commission of Human Rights under the European Convention on Human Rights (ECHR). In March 1997 the claimant, having exhausted domestic remedies, lodged an application to the European Commission of Human Rights under the ECHR: Application No 35763/97. The application was forwarded to the European Court of Human Rights. The Court:

1. held unanimously that there had been no violation of art 3 of the Convention;
2. held by nine votes to eight that there had been no violation of art 6(1) of the Convention: *Al Adsani* v *United Kingdom* (2002) 34 EHRR 11.

In respect of art 6(1), which guarantees the right of access to courts, the European Court of Human Rights confirmed that this right is not absolute. Some limitations are allowed provided that they do not restrict or reduce access to a national court in such a manner or to such an extent as to impair the very essence of the right: *Waite and Kennedy* v *Germany* (2000) 30 EHRR 261. Those limitations must pursue a legitimate aim and must be proportionate to the objective sought to be attained by a contracting state. Therefore, the Court had to determine whether or not a limitation was justified on the basis of the doctrine of sovereign immunity.

The Court accepted that the application of the doctrine of sovereign immunity, under which a state grants sovereign immunity to another state in respect of civil proceedings, had pursued the legitimate aim of complying with international law to promote comity and good relations between states.

The issue of proportionality was, however, more controversial. The starting point in the deliberations of the European Court of Human Rights was that the ECHR must be interpreted in accordance with international law, in particular art 31(3) of the Vienna Convention on the Law of Treaties 1969 which provides that in the interpretation of a treaty account must be taken of 'any relevant rules of international law applicable in the relations between the parties'. Consequently, the ECHR had to take into consideration relevant rules of international law, in particular those relating to the grant of state immunity. The Court stated that generally recognised rules of public international law on state immunity could not, in principle, be considered as imposing a disproportionate restriction on the right of access to a court. Nevertheless, this case was unusual in that the applicant's claim was related to torture, the prohibition of which has acquired the status of ius cogens in international law and accordingly prevails over treaty law and other rules of international law.

The European Court of Human Rights examined in depth the new developments in international law in respect of the prohibition of torture as a norm of ius cogens, but nevertheless stated that:

'... the Court, while noting the growing recognition of the overriding importance of the prohibition of torture, does not accordingly find it established that there is yet acceptance in international law of the proposition that States are not entitled to immunity in respect of civil claims for damages for alleged torture committed outside the forum State. The 1978 Act, which grants immunity to States in respect of personal injury claims unless the damage was caused within the United Kingdom, is not inconsistent with those limitations generally accepted by the community of nations as part of the doctrine of State immunity.'

Consequently, the European Court of Human Rights held that there was no violation of art 6(1) of the ECHR by the UK and that the UK was entitled under the State Immunity Act 1978 to grant immunity to a foreign state in respect of personal injury claims when the damage occurred outside the forum state.

In *Holland* v *Lampen-Wolfe* [2000] 1 WLR 1573 the House of Lords considered that the State Immunity Act 1978 did not apply to the circumstances and based its judgment on state immunity at common law. The facts of the case are simple. The claimant was a US citizen and a professor at a US university that provided courses at a number of US military bases in Europe. From 1991 the claimant taught courses on international relations at a military base in England that was operated by the US under the terms of the NATO alliance. The defendant was a US citizen who was responsible for educational programmes at a military base in Yorkshire and was employed by the US Department of Defence. In March 1997 pursuant to his duties the defendant wrote a letter to the university's European programme director in Germany stating that the claimant had been subject to criticism by students and that the writer questioned her professional competence. The letter concluded with a request that another tutor be appointed to replace her.

Following the letter the claimant issued a writ for defamation. The defendant applied in the High Court to Master Trench for the setting aside of the writ on the ground that as an employee of the US Department of Defence he was immune from the jurisdiction of the court. The Master set aside the writ. The claimant appealed. The appeal was subsequently rejected by the High Court, the Court of Appeal and the House of Lords. The House of Lords reached the same conclusions as the Court of Appeal in *Littrell* v *United States of America (No 2)* [1995] 1 WLR 82. The appeal was unanimously rejected by the House of Lords on the grounds that although the State Immunity Act 1978 did not apply on the facts the defendant was entitled to immunity at common law.

This case raises a number of interesting issues.

1. By virtue of s16(2) of the State Immunity Act 1978, which provides that the Act 'does not apply to proceedings relating to anything done by or in relation to the armed forces of a state while present in the United Kingdom and, in particular, has effect subject to the Visiting Forces Act 1952', the House of Lords decided that the 1978 Act could not apply to the circumstances.

2. The Law Lords found that the applicable law was the common law on state immunity as stated in the *I Congreso del Partido* [1981] 2 All ER 1064 which was decided before the entry into force of the State Immunity Act 1978. The *I*

Congreso case endorsed the restrictive doctrine of state immunity based on the distinction between acts jure imperii and jure gestionis. Therefore, the question to be decided by the House of Lords was whether the tort was covered by the *I Congreso* case and if so to determine the nature of the acts. The House of Lords ruled that the *I Congreso* case applied not only to contract but also to tort.

3. The crucial matter was to classify whether tort claims were attached to acts jure imperii or jure gestionis. The House of Lords, in determining the issue, decided to take into consideration the whole context of the claim, including the place where the educational programme was being provided and the person to whom it was provided as well as its beneficiaries. The unanimous conclusion reached by the House of Lords was that the letter in question was classified as an act jure imperii and therefore covered by state immunity at common law.

4. The House of Lords confirmed that its decision was in line with art 6(1) of the ECHR. In this respect Lord Millet stated:

> 'At first sight [the right to a fair trial] may appear to be inconsistent with the doctrine of comprehensive and unqualified state immunity in those cases where it is applicable. But in fact there is no inconsistency. This is not because the right guaranteed by article 6 is not absolute but subject to limitations, nor is it because the doctrine of state immunity serves a legitimate aim.'

The decision of the House of Lords is in conformity with the case law of the European Court of Human Rights which has acknowledged in a number of cases that the right to access to the court is not absolute: *Golder* v *United Kingdom* (1979–80) 1 EHRR 524; *Osman* v *United Kingdom* (2000) 29 EHRR 245. Moreover, in *Vearncombe* v *United Kingdom and Germany* (1989) 59 DR 186, which raised similar issues to *Holland* v *Lampen-Wolfe*, the Commission rejected the application and confirmed that a German court had no jurisdiction on the ground of state immunity.

Remedies

Section 13 of the 1978 Act establishes the general rule that relief may not be given against a state by way of injunction, specific performance or order for the recovery of land or other property and that the property of a state shall not be subject to enforcement save where the state concerned has consented to such measures being taken. This principle of absolute immunity in respect of enforcement is, however, subject to an important limitation in the case of 'property which is for the time being in use or intended for use for commercial purposes': s13(4). Section 13(5) provides that the head of the state's diplomatic missions shall be deemed to have the authority to certify whether or not the property in question is in use or intended for use for commercial purposes. Such a certificate shall constitute sufficient evidence unless the contrary is proved.

The issue of execution and enforcement was considered in *Alcom* v *Republic of*

Colombia [1984] 2 WLR 750 where the question arose as to whether the claimants could enforce an order for execution against monies in a bank account in the name of the Colombian mission in the UK. The House of Lords, refusing enforcement, accepted a certificate from the head of the mission under s13(5) that the funds were not used for the day-to-day running of the mission and were thus not property used for commercial purposes within the meaning of the section.

Entities entitled to claim immunity

The immunities and privileges conferred by the 1978 Act apply to any foreign state. Section 14(1) of the statute identifies the following bodies as eligible for protection:

1. the sovereign or other Head of State of a country when acting in a public capacity;
2. the government of a state;
3. any department of the government of a state.

By s21 of the Act, a certificate from the Secretary of State is deemed to be conclusive of the matter whether an entity falls into one or other of these categories. Such a certificate should, however, be distinguished from other instruments which set out the UK government's position on such matters. For example, in *Coreck Maritime GmbH* v *Sevrybokholodflot* 1994 SLT 893, the Scottish Court of Session declined to accept as conclusive letters issued by the Foreign Office summarising the legal consequences of the dissolution of the USSR and which stated that Russia was to be considered as the successor state to the USSR.

In modern international life there are many entities which are related to states or conduct quasi–state activities and which raise the issue whether they are entitled to the protection under the 1978 Act. These are referred to in the Act as 'separate entities'. These are bodies or organisations which are distinct from the executive organs of the government of a state and which are capable of suing or being sued in the courts of the UK. Whether or not an entity is a 'separate entity' or a department of government will probably be determined in accordance with the municipal law of the state concerned.

The test for whether such a body can benefit from the immunities of the Act is set out in s14(2), which provides that a separate entity is immune from the jurisdiction of the courts of the United Kingdom if, and only if:

1. the proceedings relate to anything done by the entity in the exercise of sovereign authority; and
2. the circumstances are such that a state would have been so immune.

This rather inelegant formula was applied by the Court of Appeal in *Kuwait Airways Corporation* v *Iraqi Airways Co* [1994] ILPr 427.

The facts were that after Iraq invaded Kuwait in 1990, ten commercial aircraft belonging to Kuwait Airways Corporation (KAC) were forcibly confiscated by the

Iraqi Airways Corporation (IAC), a state-owned corporation. The confiscation of the aircraft was ordered by the Iraqi Minister of Transport and the aircraft were seized from Kuwait territory and removed to Iraq where they were indefinitely retained. Subsequently, Iraq enacted legislation (RCC Resolution 369) granting IAC ownership of the confiscated aircraft. During the Gulf War, four of these aircraft were destroyed as a result of the Coalition bombing of an airfield in Iraq, whilst the rest of them were evacuated to Iran and after the Gulf War returned to KAC by Iran in exchange for £20 million for the cost of keeping, sheltering and maintaining them.

In 1991, the plaintiffs issued a writ in the English courts in an attempt to recover compensation for the appropriation of the planes. Both the IAC and Iraq itself were cited as defendants. The question was whether or not IAC was immune under English law from civil action under s14(2) of the State Immunity Act 1978 as a 'separate entity' exercising sovereign authority in circumstances where the state itself would have been immune.

The Court of Appeal applied the two criteria set out in s14(2) and concluded that the essential test was whether the circumstances of the confiscation of the aircraft related to acts done by the defendants in the exercise of sovereign authority, namely that of Iraq. The claimants had alleged that the defendants wrongfully removed the aircraft from Kuwait and continued to wrongfully interfere with them after obtaining unlawful possession and control. These acts were considered by the Court of Appeal to be acts jure imperii or, in other words, acts done by, or on the instructions of, a sovereign state in the exercise of its sovereign authority. The Court construed the function of IAC as that of a dutiful accomplice of Iraq in the forcible confiscation of the aircraft. The fact that the defendants intended to use the aircraft for commercial purposes did not alter the essential nature of the act. As a result, IAC was entitled to the immunity conferred by s14(2). The claimants appealed to the House of Lords.

A majority of the Law Lords (three to two) (*Kuwait Airways Corporation* v *Iraqi Airways Company* [1995] 1 WLR 1147) held that the defendants were not immune in respect of all actions occurring after the purported transfer of ownership, as such actions were not done in the exercise of sovereign authority but as 'owner'.

The House of Lords found that the taking of the aircraft and their removal from Kuwait to Iraq constituted an exercise of governmental power by the state of Iraq. However, the immunity was removed after RCC Resolution 369 was enacted by Iraq which nationalised Kuwaiti aircraft and conferred on IAC the right to use them. As Lord Goff explained, the fact that RCC Resolution 369 was a governmental act by the state of Iraq could not of itself render IAC's consequent retention and use of the aircraft a governmental act. A separate entity of a state which receives nationalised property from the state cannot ipso facto claim sovereign immunity in respect of a claim by the former owner, though it may well be able to plead, by way of defence, that its actions were not unlawful. In these circumstances the determination of damages that KAC could claim caused considerable controversy, which was finally decided by the House of Lords on 16 May 2002: see *Kuwaiti Airways Corporation* v

Iraqi Airways Company [2002] UKHL 19. KAC was awarded only the damages for expenses it paid to Iran in respect of five, out of six, aircraft transferred there and no damage was awarded in respect of the four aircraft that were destroyed by the Coalition during the Gulf War.

As well as government departments and 'separate entities', the property of a state's central bank or other monetary authority is not to be regarded as intended for use for commercial purposes in respect of execution and enforcement proceedings. However, the fact that a state or embassy of a state has lodged sums in accounts with commercial banks does not protect those accounts from exposure to normal commercial risks. Thus, in *Re Rafidain Bank* [1992] BCC 376; [1992] BCLC 301, the courts refused to protect sums lodged by Iraq and the Iraqi embassy from a petition for liquidation.

Waiver of immunity

Waiver of immunity is covered by ss2 and 13 of the 1978 Act. The position regarding the waiver may be summarised as follows.

1. A state may waive its immunity from jurisdiction either expressly or by conduct. Such waiver may occur by treaty, diplomatic communication or by actual submission to the jurisdiction in respect of those proceedings and all matters incidental to them.
2. If a foreign sovereign comes to the court as claimant, or appears without protest as defendant in an action, he has submitted to the jurisdiction in respect of those proceedings and all matters incidental to them.
3. Even if the sovereign waives his immunity and a decision is given against him, it is not possible for the successful claimant to execute the judgment against the sovereign. A separate act of waiver of immunity from execution will be necessary before execution can be levied.
4. Whether the foreign sovereign appears as a claimant or defendant, he submits not only to the jurisdiction of the court of first instance, but also to all necessary stages of appeal.
5. The submission must be a genuine act of submission in the face of the court.

9.3 Diplomatic immunity

Diplomatic immunity is 'essential for the maintenance of relations between states and [is] accepted throughout the world by nations of all creeds, cultures and political complexions' *US Diplomatic and Consular Staff in Iran: US* v *Iran* (1980) ICJ Rep 3 at 24. Diplomatic relations are based on mutual consent between the sending state and the receiving state. Since a state is both a receiving and a sending state the rules on diplomatic immunity are universally respected and rarely breached (for example, during the Iran-US crisis, where US diplomats were held hostages from 1979 to 1981, no country supported Iran's actions). The protection of the representatives of another state is necessary to ensure that they can perform their international political functions without fear of prosecution. In England the first statute in this area, the Diplomatic Privileges Act 1708 was passed as a result of the arrest and detention of the Russian Ambassador and his coach by the English authorities in order 'to prevent like insolence for the future': see *Empson* v *Smith* [1965] 2 All ER 881 at 883 discussing the case law on this subject. In the UK rules in force on diplomatic immunity are embodied in the Diplomatic Privileges Act 1964, which is based on the Vienna Convention on Diplomatic Relations 1961 which was approved by the UN Conference on Diplomatic Intercourse and Immunities held in 1961. The Vienna Convention on Diplomatic Relations came into force on 24 April 1964 and has been ratified by more than 150 states.

Functions of missions

The functions of diplomatic missions are specified in art 3 of the Vienna Convention. They consist, inter alia, in representing the sending state in the receiving state, protecting the interests of the sending state and its nationals, gathering, by lawful means, information about conditions and developments in the receiving state and reporting them to the government of the sending state, negotiating with the government of the receiving state and promoting friendly relations in all areas between both states.

Staff of the mission

Under the Diplomatic Privileges Act 1964 the common law rule of absolute immunity was abolished and a qualified immunity now applies even to the head of the diplomatic mission. The 1964 Act divides the staff of a diplomatic mission into three categories as to the extent of immunity they enjoy.

1. The first category comprises 'diplomatic agents', such as the head of the mission or chargé d'affaires, and members of his diplomatic staff – counsellors, attachés, secretaries. Provided they are not nationals or permanent residents of a receiving state they are entitled to complete immunity from (in both official and private acts) criminal, civil (including divorce petition: *Shaw* v *Shaw* [1979] Fam 62) and administrative jurisdiction, and from measures of execution except in three cases:

   a) in actions relating to private immovable property located in the UK, provided it is not held on behalf of the sending state for the purposes of the mission (s16(1)(b) State Immunity Act 1978);

   b) in actions relating to succession in which the diplomatic representative is an executor, administrator, heir or legatee as a private person;

   c) in actions relating to any professional or commercial activity exercised by the diplomatic representative in the UK outside his official functions: Diplomatic Privileges Act 1964, Sch 1, art 31.

This immunity is also granted to the family of a diplomatic agent which forms part of his household, unless they are nationals of a receiving state: Diplomatic Privileges Act 1964, Sch 1, art 37(1); *Re C* [1959] Ch 363; and *R* v *Guildhall Magistrates' Court, ex parte Jarren-Thorpe* (1977) The Times 6 October.

2. The second category encompasses the members of the administrative and technical staff of the mission, which includes clerks, typists, translators, radio and telephone operators etc and their families which form part of their household provided they are neither nationals nor permanent residents of the receiving state. The second category does not enjoy immunity from civil and administrative jurisdiction in relation to acts performed outside the course of their duties: Diplomatic Privileges Act 1964, Sch 1, art 37(2).

3. The third category comprises members of the service staff such as butlers, maids, cooks, chauffeurs, porters, cleaners. Provided they are not nationals or permanent residents of a receiving state, they only enjoy immunity from the civil jurisdiction in respect of acts performed in the course of their duties.

Expulsion of individual diplomats

A receiving state is entitled at any time and without any explanation to declare a head of mission or members of his diplomatic staff as unacceptable – ie persona non grata. In this event the sending state normally recalls the diplomat concerned. However, if no such step is taken the receiving state may refuse to consider him as being a member of the mission. The declaration of persona non grata may be made either before or after the diplomat's arrival in the territory of the receiving state. There are two main reasons for which a diplomat may be declared persona non grata: his personal behaviour, such as the commission of a criminal act or anti-social conduct; or an abuse of his diplomatic status when he acts as a spy or in any other manner endangers the security and other interests of the receiving state. Also a receiving state may declare a diplomat persona non grata as a retaliation against a sending state which has so declared one of its own diplomats. This practice is quite common.

Inviolability of diplomatic agents

All diplomats as well as members of their families forming part of their households, provided they are not nationals or permanent residents of a receiving state, enjoy personal inviolability. A receiving state must treat them with due respect and is bound to ensure complete protection of all members of a foreign mission and their families against physical violence, and from attacks on their dignity and freedom.

Inviolability is extended to a private residence of a diplomat, his papers, correspondence and his property.

Inviolability of the mission, its records and communication

Article 1(1) of the Vienna Convention defines 'premises of the mission as':

> '... the buildings or parts of buildings and the land ancillary thereto, irrespective of ownership, used for the purposes of the mission including the residence of the head of the mission.'

The premises of the mission are inviolable: art 22 of the Vienna Convention. They may not be entered by agents of the receiving state without the permission of the head of mission. This rule is universally accepted and was applied by the High Court when it refused to issue a writ of habeas corpus in respect of the incident in 1896 concerning a Chinese refugee Sun Yat Sen who was held against his will in the Chinese mission in London.

The receiving state is bound to take all appropriate measures to protect such premises against intrusion and damage and to prevent any disturbance of the peace of the mission or impairment of its dignity. This obligation is embodied in art 22 of the Vienna Convention.

The most flagrant violation of this provision occurred after the overthrow of the Shah of Iran in 1979. On 4 November 1979 the US embassy in Teheran was overrun by hundreds of Iranians who were demonstrating at the embassy gate. They seized diplomats, consuls and marine personnel there and occupied the premises of the embassy. The embassy personnel was physically threatened and refused all communication with either US officials or relatives. Also the US consulates in other Iranian cities were subject to similar attacks.

On 22 November several hundred thousand demonstrators converged on the embassy in Teheran and the Iranian government, once again, did not intervene or assist the hostages. Some of them were released, others were removed to an unknown location outside the premises of the embassy.

The US government instituted proceedings against Iran before the ICJ alleging violations by Iran of the Vienna Convention on Diplomatic Relations 1961, the Vienna Convention on the Prevention and Punishment of Crimes against Internationally Protected Persons 1973 and the US–Iran Treaty of Amity 1955.

Iran refused to participate in the proceedings before the ICJ but presented its official position in correspondence sent to the Court, in which it stated that the matter of the hostages of the US embassy in Teheran was secondary or marginal in the light of 25 years of interference of the US in the internal affairs of Iran, namely that crimes were committed by the US – such as the preparation by the CIA of the coup d'etat in 1953 which overthrew the lawful government of Dr Mossadegh and resulted in the restoration of the Shah and his regime and subsequent subjugation of Iran's interest in all matters to the US – which led to a shameless exploitation of Iran contrary to international law and humanitarian norms. Iran asked the ICJ not to take cognisance of the case.

On 15 December 1979 the ICJ issued an order indicating provisional measures to be taken by Iran, that is the immediate release of all hostages.

In its judgment the ICJ disagreed that the detention of US diplomats was a secondary matter and emphasised the importance of the legal principle involved in the dispute. The Court confirmed that it had compulsory jurisdiction under the protocols to the two Vienna Conventions to which both states were the contracting parties as well as under the US-Iran Treaty of Amity 1955. Moreover, the ICJ stated that under the ICJ Statute and its Rules of Procedure there was no provision contemplating that the Court should decline jurisdiction merely because a dispute had other aspects, however important. The ICJ held that although the attacks on the US embassy and consulates at Tabiz and Shiraz could not be imputable to the Iranian state, nevertheless Iran was not free of responsibility. The Iranian government was in breach of the above-mentioned Conventions as well as 'long-established rules of general international law' for failure to take appropriate measures to ensure the protection of the US embassy and consulates, their staff, their archives, their means of communications and the freedom of movement of the members of staff. The Court emphasised that this failure was due to 'more than negligence or lack of appropriate means'.

The Court ordered Iran to immediately release all hostages and make reparations to the US.

Iran did not comply with the judgment, but the dispute was subsequently settled through negotiations. Under the International Convention against the Taking of Hostages 1979 all hostages were released after 15 months of captivity and the Iranian-United States Claims Tribunal was established to deal with claims of US nationals against Iran. A special fund created from a portion of Iranian government assets in the US frozen by President Carter at the begining of the hostage crisis was set aside to satisfy the claims.

Cessation of immunities and privileges

Under art 39(2) of the Vienna Convention immunities and privileges normally cease at the moment when a diplomat leaves the receiving country, or on the expiry of a resonable time in which to do so, even in the case of armed conflict. Therefore, the termination of his functions in a receiving state does not coincide with the cessation of immunity. It extends for a reasonable time to allow a diplomat to complete his arrangements to leave the receiving state.

In respect of the cessation of immunities it is important to make a distinction between functional and personal immunities. The functional immunity referes to acts and transactions performed by a diplomat in his official capacity. The personal activities concern all private activities of a diplomat for which he is immune from jurisdiction of the receving state during his mission. Functional immunity continues to subsist in respect of acts already done by him in the exercise of his official duties (art 39 of the Vienna Convention) but not in respect of acts done in his private capacity. Therefore, if after the termination of his diplomatic functions and his subsequent return to his country he goes back to a receiving state as a private individual he may be accountable for his personal activities and may be arrested and brought to trial there.

The matter of functional immunity as well as the relationship between diplomatic and state immunity was examined in *P* v *P (Diplomatic Immunity: Jurisdiction)* (1998) The Times 2 March (CA). In this case a US diplomat who worked as a cultural attaché to the US Embassy in London was ordered by the US government to return to the US with his family. Shortly after the termination of his functions his wife commenced divorce proceedings in London. During the custody proceedings the family returned to the US but his wife went under protest having beforehand issued an originating summons in the English court seeking a declaration under s8 of the Child Abduction and Custody Act 1985 that the removal of the children from the UK by her husband was a wrongful removal within the meaning and terms of art 3 of the Hague Convention on the Civil Aspects of International Child Abduction 1980.

The US government was given leave to intervene and sought dismissal of the proceedings on the grounds of diplomatic immunity and sovereign immunity.

The divorce proceedings were set aside on the basis of diplomatic immunity enjoyed by the husband. Under the Diplomatic Privileges Act 1964 a cultural attaché is regarded as a diplomatic agent and thus he is exempt from the civil and criminal jurisdiction of the English courts in respect of both his official and private acts. In *Shaw* v *Shaw* [1979] Fam 62 it was held that civil proceedings include a divorce petition.

However, the matter whether the husband could rely on his status of a diplomatic agent when he removed his children at the end of the diplomatic posting was assessed in the light of art 39(2) of the Vienna Convention on Diplomatic Relations 1961 which provides that:

'When the functions of a person enjoying privileges and immunities have come to any end, such privileges and immunities shall normally cease at the moment when he leaves the country, or on expiry of a reasonable period in which to do so, but shall subsist until that time, even in case of armed conflict. However, with respect to acts performed by such a person in exercise of his function as a member of the mission, immunity shall continue to subsist.'

In *P* v *P* his Lordship, Sir Stephen Brown, President of the Family Division, emphasised that diplomatic privileges and immunities were functional in character, aimed at ensuring the efficient performance of the functions of diplomatic missions as representing states, and not to benefit individual diplomats. His Lordship held that removal of children from the UK by a father at the end of his diplomatic posting could not be construed as an act performed in the exercise of a diplomat's functions within the scope of art 39(2) of the Vienna Convention on Diplomatic Relations 1961.

However, the jurisdiction of the English court was also challenged on the ground of state immunity. The husband was ordered by the government of the US to leave the UK with his family. The court found that his action in removing the children was of a governmental nature and therefore subject to state immunity from legal proceedings in the UK. His return to the US occurred in compliance with the direct order of the US government, his employer. It was an act of a governmental nature and as such subject to state immunity from legal proceedings in the UK.

Foreign diplomats and their families are not entitled to the right to residence or to expedited immigration procedure after the expiry of the secondment to their mission. If they remain in the UK it is without the leave of the immigration authorities: *R* v *Secretary of State for the Home Deparment, ex parte Bagga* [1990] 3 WLR 1013.

Waiver of immunity

Artilce 32(1) of the Vienna Convention provides that it is for the sending state to waive immunity at its discretion and under art 32(1) 'Waiver must always be express'.

However, s2(3) of the Diplomatic Privileges Act 1964 provides that the waiver by the head of a mission shall be deemed to be a waiver by the state he represents. But there is nothing in the Act to suggest that a subordinate official requires approval from his state or the head of his mission before waiving his immunity by taking proceedings in the English courts. But a subordinate member of the staff of a mission cannot, by appearing as defendant in an action, waive an immunity which is primarily that of his state and not his own.

Article 32(4) provides that if he commences proceedings, a diplomatic agent is precluded from invoking immunity from jurisdiction in respect of any counterclaim directly connected with the principal claim. Article 32(4) provides that waiver of immunity from civil or administrative jurisdiction shall not be held to imply waiver in respect of the execution of the judgment, for which a separate waiver shall be necessary.

9.4 Quasi-diplomatic privileges and immunities

Consuls, although representatives of their states in another state, are not accorded the degree of immunity within the receiving state enjoyed by diplomatic agents. Their functions are varied and include the protection of the interests of the sending state and its nationals, the development of economic and cultural relations, the issuing of passports and visas, the registration of births, marriages and deaths and the supervision of vessels and aircraft attributed to the sending state.

However, while as a general rule a consul is not immune from local jurisdiction, under the provisions of the Consular Relations Act 1968, which gives effect to the Vienna Convention on Consular Relations 1963, a consul does enjoy a limited degree of immunity in respect of his official functions. Article 41 of the Convention provides that:

'1. Consular officers shall not be liable to arrest or detention pending trial, except in the case of grave crime and pursuant to a decision by the competent judicial authority.

2. Except in the case specified in paragraph 1 of this article, consular officers shall not be committed to prison or liable to any other form of restriction on their personal freedom save in execution of a judicial decision of final effect.

3. If criminal proceedings are instituted against a consular officer, he must appear before the competent authorities. Nevertheless, the proceedings shall be conducted with the respect due to him by reason of his official posistion and, except in the case specified in paragraph 1 of this article, in a manner which will hamper the exercise of consular functions as little as possible. When, in the circumstances mentioned in paragraph 1 of this article, it has become necessary to detain a consular officer, the proceedings against him shall be instituted with the minimum delay.'

The Convention provides that career consuls (as opposed to honorary consuls) are exempted from taxation and customs duties in the same way as diplomats. Consular premises, archives and documents are made inviolable and are given exemption from taxation. Immunity and protection afforded by customary law are maintained.

10

State Responsibility for Wrongful Acts

10.1 Introduction

All legal systems provide for consequences arising from failure to observe obligations imposed by their rules. International law is no different in that every state which is in breach of the obligations imposed upon it by international law must bear responsibility for that breach. In the *Spanish Zones of Morocco Claims: Great Britain v Spain* (1925) 2 RIAA 615 Judge Hubert said that:

> 'Responsibility is the necessary corollary of a right. All rights of an international character involve international responsibility. If the obligation in question is not met, responsibility entails the duty to make reparations.'

Traditionally, responsibility of states for internationally wrongful acts was based on customary rules originating from the practice of states as applied by the PCIJ and ICJ and by international arbitral tribunals. Only a very limited number of international treaties contained provisions providing for liability of a contracting state for violations of their provisions. An example of such an international treaty is art 3 of the Hague Convention IV Respecting the Laws and Customs of War on Land 1907 which states that the violation of the Regulations annexed to the Convention by a contracting state gives rise to liability. By virtue of this provision, a contracting state is required to pay compensation in respect of all wrongful acts committed by its armed forces.

The matter of state liability was on the agenda of the League of Nations. A Codification Conference convened under the auspices of the League of Nations in 1930 at the Hague to codify rules in a number of areas, including rules on state responsibility, failed to produce any internationally binding instruments with regard to state responsibility. The Hague Conference showed a deep disagreement between participating states in respect of state responsibility for the treatment of aliens. Some states wanted to apply 'national' treatment, others were in favour of the application of the 'minimum standard' principle.

In the assessment of traditional customary law on state responsibility the following conclusions can be reached: it focused on the treatment of aliens; it contained gaps; and it was unclear on a number of important issues, such as whether a state could be liable irrespective of any fault or intention on the part of an agent of a state whose conduct caused injury (subjective theory) or whether its liability arose when an unlawful act attributable to a state constituted a breach of international law without any necessity to show some fault or intention on the part of the official concerned (objective theory). Moreover, an injured state was allowed to resort to armed force without first requesting reparation. If the offending state failed to make reparation the injured state was free to decide whether to use peaceful means to resolve the matter or whether to enforce its right to reparation by using military or economic force.

The rules on state responsibility have evolved. The development of human rights resulted in the establishment of a common international standard of treatment of aliens thus resolving the disagreement between supporters and opponents of both the 'national treatment' and the 'minimum treatment'. The use of force in international relations was banned and the principle of peaceful settlement of international disputes has modified the manner in which the injured state is allowed to exercise its right to reparation. Moreover, in respect of certain activities – such as the use of, and experiments with, nuclear technology, the exploration of space, etc – only the principle of strict or absolute liability of a state is appropriate because, on the one hand, it is impossible to prove the commission of a wrongful act taking into account the precautions which are normally taken and, on the other hand, it is unrealistic to prohibit such activities altogether. International co-operation in the prevention of disasters arising from such activities is paramount. This is particularly developed in the area of nuclear activities.

The topic of state responsibility has been greatly clarified and developed by the International Law Commission (ILC). At its first session in 1949 the ILC selected the matter of state responsibility for future codification. The ILC adopted a final text of the Draft Articles on Responsibility of States for Internationally Wrongful Acts at its 53rd session held in August 2001: A/CN4/L602/Rev 1. In December 2001 the UN General Assembly recommended the Articles to the attention of governments and attached them to its Resolution 56/83 (10 December 2001). The Articles were prepared under the leadership of special rapporteurs – Alberto Ago (1962–1979), Willem Riphagen (1979–1986), Gaetano Arangio-Ruiz (1987–1996) and James Crawford (1997–2001). The basic concepts of the Articles, its structure and content were prepared by Alberto Ago. His successors improved and substantially revised the initial Draft. Its final version comprehensively deals with the most important aspects of state responsibility for wrongful acts, including the definition of such an act, the consequences of an internationally wrongful act, the circumstances precluding wrongfulness, the rights of an injured state, the means of reparation at its disposal and the circumstances in which it is allowed to resort to countermeasures. Moreover, the ILC has made three essential contributions to the development of rules on state responsibility.

1. Alberto Ago introduced a distinction between 'primary rules', which impose certain rules of conduct (obligations to do or not to do), and 'second level rules' which define consequences of internationally wrongful acts attributable to a state. Primary rules are of a substantial nature as they define international obligations of a state in each particular context. Secondary rules contain principles which govern state responsibility. The ILC Articles are is solely concerned with 'second level rules'.

2. The ILC promotes two regimes of state responsibility – 'ordinary responsibility' and 'aggrieved responsibility' – whilst maintaining the unitary nature of a wrongful act. The emphasis is on the character of the obligation breached. Aggrieved responsibility occurs when a state breaches peremptory norms of international law.

3. Damage has been dissociated from the wrongful act and is no longer considered as a constituent element. The Special Rapporteur explained this solution as follows:

> 'It will be a matter for the primary rule in question to determine what is the threshold for a violation: in some cases this may be the occurrence of actual harm, in others a threat of such harm, in others again, the mere failure to fulfil a promise, irrespective of the consequences of the failure at the time. Similarly, it will be a matter for the primary rules and their interpretation to specify what are the range of interests protected by an international obligation, the breach of which will give rise to a corresponding secondary obligation of reparation': *Fourth Report on State Responsibility*, Mr James Crawford, Special Rapporteur, A/CN4/517, para 28.

The dissociation of damage from a wrongful act will allow the secondary rules to cover all possible breaches of primary rules without excluding responsibility of the delinquent state in cases where there is no damage or the damage is not compensable.

10.2 The theories of responsibility

International law makes no distinction between tortious and contractual liability. The breach of a treaty or customary obligation will give rise to the same remedy, usually an award of damages or a declaration. The matter of whether states may be criminally liable is very controversial. The ILC adopted at the first-reading of the Draft text of the Articles on Responsibility of States for Internationally Wrongful Acts, art 19 of which referred to international crimes and thus made a distinction between 'international delicts' and 'international crimes'. At the second reading of the Draft, which began in 1998, the ILC, in the light of comments from governments, deleted art 19 and the term 'crime' disappeared from the Draft. The ILC decided that internationally wrongful acts should form a single category. The idea embodied in art 19 has been dealt with differently. In the Final Version, Chapter III of Part II refers to serious breaches of obligations under peremptory norms of general international law, and art 41 of the ILC Articles deals with some particular consequences of such breaches which will be added to the general consequences attached to 'ordinary' breaches of international law.

The basis of responsibility

There are two theories as to the basis of state responsibility: the 'risk' or 'objective theory' of responsibility and the 'fault' or 'subjective theory' of responsibility.

Objective responsibility

The principle of strict liability on the part of states has been followed both in state practice and in the jurisprudence of the PCIJ and ICJ and that of arbitral tribunals. Objective responsibility relies on the premise that a state is liable once an unlawful act which violates an international obligation has taken place, regardless of any fault or intention on the part of the official concerned.

In the *Caire Claim: France* v *Mexico* (1929) 5 RIAA 516 Caire, a French national, was killed in Mexico by Mexican soldiers after they had demanded money from him which Caire was unable to obtain. He was subsequently arrested, tortured and killed. France, on his behalf, presented a claim against the Mexican government before the Franco-Mexican Claims Commission. The Commission found the Mexican government liable for the actions of its military personnel regardless of the fact that they were acting without orders and against the wishes of the commanding officer. The President of the Franco-Mexican Claims Commission applied the doctrine of objective responsibility and explained its meaning in the following terms:

> '... the doctrine of the "objective responsibility" of the state, that is the responsibility for the acts of the officials or organs of a state ... may devolve upon it even in the absence of any "fault" of its own ... The state also bears an international responsibility for all acts committed by its officials or its organs which are delictual according to international law, regardless of whether the official organ has acted within the limits of its competence or

has exceeded those limits ... However, in order to justify the admission of this objective responsibility of the state for acts committed by its officials or organs outside their competence, it is necessary that they should have acted, at least apparently, as authorised officials or organs, or that, in acting, they should have used powers or measures appropriate to their official character.'

Subjective responsibility

Subjective responsibility originates from the Grotian view that culpa or dolus malus provide the proper basis of state responsibility in all cases.

The term culpa is used to describe types of blameworthiness based upon fault arising from any sort of conduct from negligence to recklessness. The view that culpa or fault is a necessary basis for state responsibility has been supported in some arbitral awards.

In *Home Missionary Society Claim: United States of America* v *Great Britain* (1920) 6 RIAA 42 the collection of a new tax imposed by Britain in 1898 on the natives of the Protectorate of Sierra Leone led to serious and widespread revolt during which missions were attacked and either destroyed or damaged and some missionaries were murdered. The tribunal dismissed the claim brought by the US against the UK. It stated that:

> 'It is a well established principle of international law that no government can be held responsible for the act of rebellious bodies of men committed in violation of its authority, where it is itself guilty of no breach of good faith, or of no negligence in suppressing insurrection.'

This statement has often been invoked by the supporters of the subjective doctrine as justifying its existence, whilst its opponents argue that the case involved the specific topic of a state's responsibility for the acts of rebels rather than establishing a general rule on a state's responsibility based on culpa.

In addition to the above the supporters of the doctrine of subjective responsibility relied on the judgment of the ICJ in the *Corfu Channel Case (Merits)* (1949) ICJ Rep 4 in which the fault was assessed in the form of knowledge. In this case the UK argued that Albania had laid the mines which cause the sinking of a British warship in Albanian territorial waters. However, the lack of evidence in this respect forced the UK to reformulate its argument whereupon the UK government submitted that the mines could not have been laid without the knowledge or connivance of the Albania authorities. The ICJ stated:

> 'It cannot be concluded from the mere fact of the control exercised by a state over its territory and waters that state knew, or ought to have known, of any unlawful act perpetrated therein, nor that it necessarily knew, or should have known, the authors. This fact, by itself and apart from other circumstances neither involves prima facie responsibility nor shifts the burden of proof.'

Assessment

Of these two approaches, the objective school appears to have wider support.

However, a number of writers have argued that to see state responsibility exclusively in the light of either of these two approaches is misleading. The better view, according to Brownlie, is that:

'... the content of a particular duty ... will not depend upon a general principle but upon the precise formulation of each obligation of international law. The relevance of fault, the relative "strictness" of the obligation, will be determined by the content of each rule': *The System of the Law of Nations: State Responsibility*, Part 1, Oxford: Clarendon Press, 1983, p40.

This also emphasises the necessity of examining the 'the secondary level rules' in the context of primary rules.

The ILC gives preference to the objective theory in its arts 1 and 2. Article 1 provides that 'Every internationally wrongful act of a state entails international responsibility', whilst art 2 specifies an internationally wrongful act as being an action or omission on the part of a state which:

1. is attributable to a state under international law; and
2. constitutes a breach of an international obligation.

Articles 1 and 2 do not mention any fault on the part of a state. The notion of fault or culpa is particularly inappropriate in respect of state responsibility for wrongful acts because, first, it requires the discovery of the intentions or motives of a wrongful act and, second, it misunderstands the main purpose of imposing responsibility on a state which consists of restoring equality of states vis-à-vis their international obligations which has been disturbed by the commission of a wrongful act.

However, the ILC Articles have not completely abandoned subjective responsibility. Lack of fault may still be invoked as an excuse and thus preclude state responsibility in certain circumstances. A state may rely on the defence of necessity to preclude the wrongfulness of its act provided that act did not contribute to the situation of necessity. The definition of necessity is very strict and presupposes an absolute impossibility of taking any other course of action than that which led to the violation of an international obligation. Necessity may excuse the wrongful act but a state may still be obliged to make compensation.

Fault is taken into account in the determination of the amount of compensation. Article 39 of the ILC Articles specifies that if the injured state has contributed to the injury by wilful or negligent action or omission the amount of reparation should be reduced accordingly.

Also fault in the form of knowledge and not as wrongful intent or negligence is incorporated in Chapter IV of the ILC Articles dealing with responsibility of a state in connection with the commission of a wrongful act by another state. Under this Chapter a state is internationally responsible if it has knowledge of the circumstances of a wrongful act of another state and notwithstanding this provides aid and assistance to that state (art 16), or directs and controls another state in the commission of a wrongful act (art 17) or coerces another state to commit such an act: art 18.

10.3 Imputability

State responsibility is engaged by the acts or omissions of individuals. It is a fundamental matter of responsibility, therefore, to distinguish those acts that are attributable to a state from those which are not. Attribution has the effect of indicating that the act in question is an act of the state concerned.

The matter of attribution may arise in any of the following:

1. the acts of the state and its officials;
2. the acts of private persons;
3. the acts of insurrectionaries.

Acts of the state and its officials

A state can only act through its organs and representatives. The organs and representatives of a state include the following: the executive and administration; the judiciary; the legislature; the armed forces; and federal states and its component states.

The general rule regarding state organs and officials is found in art 4 of the ILC Articles which provides that:

> '1. The conduct of any state organ shall be considered an act of that state under international law, whether the organ exercises legislative, executive, judicial or any other functions, whatever position it holds in the organisation of the state, and whatever its character as an organ of the central government or of a territorial unit of the state.
> 2. An organ includes any person or entity which has that status in accordance with the internal law of the state.'

The position of an official, whether superior or subordinate, will involve the same measure of responsibility. In the *Massey Case: United States of America* v *Mexico* (1927) 4 RIAA 155 a US national was murdered in Mexico by a Mexican named Saenz. Saenz was later arrested, but escaped from prison when the assistant warder allowed him to leave. The Mexican government argued that it was not liable for this denial of justice because it stemmed from the misconduct of a minor official who was acting in violation of Mexican law and his duty. Commissioner Nielson stated that:

> 'To attempt by some broad classification to make a distinction between some "minor" or "petty" officials and other kinds of officials must obviously at times involve practical difficulties. Irrespective of the propriety of attempting to make any such distinction at all, it would seem that in reaching conclusions in any given case with respect to responsibility for acts of public servants, the most important considerations of which account must be

taken are the character of the acts alleged to have resulted in injury to persons or to property, or the nature of functions performed whenever a question is raised as to their proper discharge.'

Article 6 of the ILC Articles provides that the conduct of an organ placed at the disposal of a state by another state shall be considered an act of the former state, if that organ was acting in the exercise of elements of governmental authority of the former state. Under this provision, for example, the conduct of the Privy Council, which acts as the highest appeal body for some Commonwealth countries, will not be attributable to the UK but to the country at the disposal of which it has been placed.

Liability of the state for ultra vires acts of organs and officials

A state is responsible for ultra vires acts of its organs or officials if committed within the scope of their apparent authority.
Article 7 of the ILC Articles provides that:

'The conduct of an organ of a state or of a person or entity empowered to exercise elements of the governmental authority shall be considered an act of the state under international law if the organ, person or entity acts in that capacity, even if it exceeds its authority or contravenes instructions.'

Article 7 embodies a well established customary rule that wrongful acts may be imputed to the state when its organs or its officials act beyond their legal capacity but act to all appearances as competent officials or organs.
In two cases, *The Jessie* (1921) RIAA 57 and *The Wonderer* (1921) RIAA 68, the US was held responsible for the acts of its revenue officers in the exercise of their right of visit and search over British ships on the high seas. The officers had acted in good faith but had exceeded their powers under the relevant Anglo–American agreement. Although acting outside their actual authority, the tribunal confirmed that so long as the officers were acting within the scope of their duties then the state would be responsible.
In the *Union Bridge Company Claim: United States of America* v *Great Britain* (1924) 6 RIAA 138 the facts of the case were that in 1899, shortly after the outbreak of war between Great Britain and the Orange Free State, a British official of the Cape Government Railway appropriated neutral property under the mistaken belief that it was not neutral. The arbitration tribunal held that:

'... liability is not affected either by the fact that [the official appropriated the property] under a mistake as to the character and ownership of the material or that it was a time of pressure and confusion caused by war, or the fact, which, on the evidence, must be admitted, that there was no intention on the part of the British authorities to appropriate the material in question.'

The official acted within the scope of his general duty, and liability was, therefore, attributed to the British government.

In the *Youmans Case: United States of America* v *Mexico* (1926) 4 RIAA 110 a group of three US nationals was being attacked by a Mexican mob. Troops sent to protect them joined in the attack, which resulted in the death of the Americans. The Mexican government argued that as the soldiers had acted in complete disregard of its instructions, Mexico could not be responsible for the deaths.

The Commission rejected the Mexican argument that the soldiers having disregarded their orders were acting in a private capacity. The Commission stated:

> 'We do not consider that the participation of the soldiers in the murder ... can be regarded as acts of soldiers committed in their private capacity when it is clear that at the time of the commission of these acts the men were on duty under the immediate supervision and in the presence of a commanding officer. Soldiers inflicting personal injuries or committing wanton destruction or looting always act in disobedience of some rules laid down by superior authority. There could be no liability whatever for such misdeeds if the view were taken that any acts committed by soldiers in contravention of instructions must be considered as personal acts.'

A distinction exists between the case law and art 7 of the ILC Articles in that the cases stress the requirement of apparent authority, while art 7 is silent on this issue. This notwithstanding, it is probably the case that some notion of apparent authority or use of official powers will be necessary for a claim to be founded. In *Yeager* v *Iran* (1987) 17 Iran-USCTR 92 the Iran-US Claims Tribunal disallowed a claim by a US national to recover money extorted from him by an Iranain official at the time of his expulsion from Iran as the act concerned was beyond the scope of the apparent authority of the official in question.

The acts of private persons

The ILC Articles provide for two situations in which a state may be responsible for unlawful acts committed by private persons, first when their conduct is directed or controlled by a state (art 8) and, second, when their conduct is acknowledged and adopted by a state as its own: art 11.

The first situation can be illustrated by the *Nicaragua Case: Nicaragua* v *US (Merits)* (1986) ICJ Rep 14 in which the question arose as to whether the acts of the Contras could be attributed to the US. In considering the matter the ICJ had to determine the relationship between the Contras and the US government. The Court stated that it was not sufficient to establish that the US government financed, organised, trained, supplied and equipped the Contras as well as providing logistical assistance in terms of selecting targets and planning their operations. The Court stated that:

> 'For this conduct to give rise to legal responsibility of the US, it would in principle have to be proved that the state had effective control of the military or paramilitary operations in the course of which the alleged violations [of human rights and humanitarian law] were committed. The Court does not consider that the assistance given by the US to the

Contras warrants the conclusion that these forces are subject to the US to such an extent that any acts they have committed are imputable to that state.'

The second situation is illustrated by the *Hostages Case* (1980) ICJ Rep 3 in which the ICJ held that Iran, by adopting the acts of the revolutionary guards, became responsible for them. However, in respect of the first phase of the taking of the US embassy and of the hostages, which acts had been carried by the revolutionary guards, the Court was quite clear that even congratulatory and approving statements made by the Iranian leadership did not have the effect of attributing the acts to the state. It was only when, on 17 November 1979, Ayatollah Khomeini issued a decree which maintained the occupation of the US embassy and the detention of hostages until the US handed over the Shah for trial in Iran that the acts were adopted by the state and therefore responsibility arose.

Liability for the acts of insurrectionaries

The development of the law in this area has been complicated by the fine line between insurrection and mob violence. In the case of mob violence, the contention has long been that a state would be liable for failure to take the necessary measures. In the case of insurrections such a view was less certain as a number of writers argued that a state engaged in repressing insurgents was not responsible for harm caused to foreigners.

Lord McNair stated five principles regarding the responsibility of lawful governments for the consequences of insurrection and rebellion.

1. A state on whose territory an insurrection occurs is not responsible for loss or damage sustained by a foreigner unless it can be shown that the government of that state was negligent in the use of, or in the failure to use, forces at its disposal for the prevention or suppression of the insurrection.

    In the *Sambaggio Case: Italy* v *Venezuela* (1903) 10 RIAA 499 a claim presented by an Italian national for damages caused by unsuccessful revolutionaries in Venezuela was rejected on the following grounds:

    a) revolutionaries are not agents of government, and no natural responsibility exists;
    b) their acts are committed to destroy the government, and no one should be held responsible for acts of an enemy attempting his life;
    c) the revolutionaries were beyond governmental control, and the government cannot be held responsible for injuries committed by those who have escaped its restraint.

2. This is a variable test, depending on the circumstances of the insurrection.
3. A state is not responsible for damage resulting from military operations directed by its lawful government unless the damage was wanton or unnecessary.

4. A state in not responsible for loss or damage caused by the insurgents to a foreigner after that foreigner's state has recognised the belligerency of the insurgents.
5. A state can usually defeat a claim in respect of loss or damage sustained by resident foreigners by showing that they have received the same treatment in the matter of protection or compensation, if any, as its own nationals.

Article 10 of the ILC Articles encompasses the general proposition that a state will not be responsible for acts of any insurrectionary movement. The position changes if the movement subsequently becomes the government of the state or establishes a new state in part of the territory of a pre-existing state. In such cases the new government formed by the insurgents will be responsible for the acts of the movement during the insurgency. It will also bear responsibility for any acts committed by the previous government.

A number of cases on the responsibility of the state in respect of insurrection were submitted to the Iran-US Claims Tribunal. In *Short v Iran* (1987) 16 Iran-USCTR 76 a US national was forced to leave Iran after threats from private persons during the revolution. He claimed against Iran for wrongful expulsion. The Tribunal, while accepting that the revolutionary government was liable for acts committed during the revolution, held that Iran was not responsible for acts of private persons who had no status within the revolutionary movement. He would have been able to recover had he been compelled to leave by revolutionary officials. In a dissenting opinion, the US member of the Tribunal queried how to distinguish between mere enthusiastic supporters and members of the revolutionary movement. In *Yeager v Iran* (1987) 17 Iran – USCTR 92 the applicant was expelled by revolutionary guards. The Tribunal decided in his favour since these acts were clearly attributable to the new government.

10.4 Direct and indirect international wrongs

An indirect wrong arises when a state is in breach of an obligation owed to a national of another state, eg an unlawful expropriation of private property. In contrast, a direct wrong arises when one state is in direct breach of an obligation owed to another state – ordinary responsibility. The ILC Articles introduces a new category of direct international wrong which arises when a state is in direct breach of ius cogens and thus in a breach of an obligation owed to the international community as a whole – aggrieved responsibility. These two categories of direct international wrongs are dealt with below.

10.5 Direct international wrong: aggrieved responsibility

Article 19 of the Draft adopted at the first reading in 1996 dealt with international crimes. The Draft defined an international crime as:

'... an internationally wrongful act which results from the breach by a state of an international obligation so essential for the protection of fundamental interests of the international community that its breach is recognised as a crime by that community as a whole.'

Article 19 identified some of these crimes as being:

1. serious breaches of the law on peace and security, such as aggression;
2. serious breaches of the right to self-determination, such as the establishment or maintenance by force of colonial domination;
3. serious breaches of international duties on safeguarding the human, such as slavery, genocide and apartheid;
4. serious breaches of an obligation to protect the environment, such as massive pollution of the atmosphere or the seas.

Article 19 was strongly criticised. Many states felt that the seriousness of the breach of an obligation was not a matter of kind but of degree. On the one hand, breaches other then those set out in art 19 may also be very serious in terms of their consequences and, on the other hand, there are other ways of imposing a stricter form of responsibility for serious breaches of international law without introducing the distinction between international crimes and international delicts. Moreover, in the context of other articles of the Draft, art 19 gave rise to many problems, especially in respect of the consequences attached to international crimes, the definition of an injured state, etc. For the above-mentioned reasons the ILC, at its session in 1998, decided to put aside art 19 and to consider 'whether the systematic development in the draft articles of key notions such as obligations (erga omnes), peremptory norms (ius cogens) and a possible category of the most serious breaches of international obligation could be sufficient to resolve the issues raised by art 19': *First and Second Reports on State Responsibility*, James Crawford, UN Doc A/CN 4/490 & Adds 1–7 (1998), para 331.

As a result, art 19 was deleted, the term 'international crime' was abandoned and the distinction between criminal and delictual responsibility was abolished. The problems raised in connection with art 19 have been dealt with in a manner more consistent with other ILC Articles. The notion of international crimes is envisaged through the concept of peremptory norms and obligations to the international community as a whole. Peremptory rules are expressly or implicitly invoked in the context of non–derogability, whilst international obligations to the international community as a whole are expressed through the wide determination of the legal interests of injured states which invoke the responsibility of another state.

Chapter III of the ILC Articles deals with serious breaches of obligations under peremptory norms of international law. Article 40(2) states:

'A breach of such obligation is serious if it involves a gross or systematic failure by the responsible state to fulfil the obligation.'

The general definition of a wrongful act remains the same in respect of both 'ordinary' and 'aggrieved responsibility' of a state. However, for aggrieved responsibility additional requirements are set out in art 40(2).

First, the obligation which has been breached by a state must be of ius cogens character, that is it must concern the most fundamental values protected under international law. Second, it must be serious, that is it must involve a gross or systematic breach of that obligation. Therefore, sporadic, or minor breaches, are not covered by art 40(2).

The requirement that the obligation breached must be owed to the international community as a whole, that is its erga omnes character, is present in a number of articles contained in Chapter III of the ILC Articles relating to the implementation of the international responsibility of a state. It is further emphasised by the right given to any state, whether injured or not, to enforce the erga omnes obligation. Moreover, some obligations are imposed on all states other than the delinquent state. In this respect art 41 of the ILC Articles requires:

1. all states to co-operate to bring the breach to an end through lawful means;
2. all states not to recognise the situation created by such a breach;
3. all states not to provide any aid or assistance to the delinquent state in maintaining the situation so created.

The possibility for states other then the injured state to invoke and enforce the responsibility of the delinquent state constitutes the main legal consequence of the commission of a wrongful act in cases of aggrieved responsibility. In this respect the distinction between an injured state and other states is vital. Article 42 defines an injured state in the following terms:

'A state is entitled as an injured state to invoke the responsibility of another state if the obligation breached is owed to:
(a) that state individually; or
(b) a group of states including that state, or the international community as a whole, and the breach of the obligation:
(i) specifically affects that state; or
(ii) is of such a character as radically to change the position of all the other states to which the obligation is owed with respect to the further performance of the obligation.'

Article 42(b)(ii) refers to the so-called 'integral obligations' which, the Special Rapporteur noted, 'operates in an all-or-nothing fashion': A/CN4/517§38. The consequences of the breach of an 'integral obligation' are envisaged in art 60(2)(c) of the Vienna Convention on the Law of Treaties 1969. In such an event any party, other than the defaulting party, is entitled to suspend the operation of the whole treaty or part of it in respect to all other parties to the treaty because its breach by a defaulting party radically changes the position of every other party. In other words, the treaty is devoid of its substance and its further performance is purposeless. Examples of integral treaties are the non-proliferation treaty, the Antarctic Treaty, the disarmament treaties, etc. The compliance of all contracting parties with integrated obligations ensures their effectiveness. There are a very limited number of such treaties but, according to the Special Rapporteur, their importance justifies the granting of the status of an injured state to a contracting party when another contracting party is breaching an integral obligation. Within this meaning human rights treaties can never be considered as integrated treaties taking into account that a breach of their provisions by one contracting party has no effect on the performance of obligations by all other parties. To the contrary, a contracting state cannot justify the suspension of, for example, the ECHR on the account that another contracting party has violated fundamental rights and freedoms guaranteed under the ECHR.

The rights given to any state to invoke the responsibility of the delinquent state entitle that state to:

1. demand the cessation of the international wrongful act and assurances and guarantees of non–repetition; and
2. claim reparation in the interest of the injured state or of the beneficiaries of the obligation breached, for example in respect of victims of gross violations of human rights.

The ILC Articles also allow any state to take countermeasures. This may occur in two situations: when a state acts on behalf of the injured state and when no state is 'injured'. In the first situation an injured state must give its consent and any actions of a state acting on its behalf must be confined to the scope of the consent. The second situation concerns in particular violations of human rights' obligations owed to the international community as a whole which are committed against nationals of the delinquent state. Any state may take lawful countermeasures acting in the interests of the beneficiaries of the obligation breached: art 54 of the ILC Articles. All limitations on the taking of countermeasures by an injured state set out in the ILC Articles apply in such event.

10.6 Direct international wrongful acts: ordinary responsibility

The following are examples of direct wrongful acts by one state against another.

Breach of treaty

A breach of a treaty by a state is a breach of an obligation owed by that state to the other party to the treaty whereby that other party suffers a direct wrong.

In the *Chorzow Factory Case (Indemnity): Germany* v *Poland* (1928) PCIJ Rep Ser A No 17 the PCIJ stated that it was 'a principle of international law that the breach of an engagement involves an obligation to make reparation' and that reparation was therefore 'the indispensable complement of a failure to apply a convention'.

Damage to state property

If a state through its acts or omissions is the direct cause of damage to the property of a foreign state, then it is liable to make reparation for the damage caused.

For example, in December 1999 the US and China agreed on $28 million in damages payable to China for the mistaken bombing of the Chinese embassy in Belgrade by NATO forces led by the US. At the same time, China agreed to pay $2.87 million in damages to the US for mob damage of the US diplomatic mission in China during demonstrations subsequent to the above-mentioned bombing.

In the *Corfu Channel Case: United Kingdom* v *Albania (Merits)* (1949) ICJ Rep 4 the ICJ held Albania responsible for the loss of life and the damage sustained by UK warships which were struck by mines laid in Albanian territorial waters. On 22 October 1946 a squadron of British warships, the cruisers *Mauritius* and *Leander* and the destroyers *Saumarez* and *Voltage*, left the port of Corfu and proceeded northwards through a channel in the North Corfu Strait previously swept for mines.. Outside the Bay of Saranda, the *Saumarez* struck a mine and was heavily damaged. Whilst towing the damaged ship, the *Voltage* struck a mine and was much damaged. The ICJ emphasised that the laying of the minefield 'could not have been accomplished without the knowledge of the Albanian government'. Albania, by failing to notify all ships and especially the approaching UK warships of the existence of a minefield in its territorial waters, breached 'certain general and well recognised principles, namely: elementary considerations of humanity ... the principle of the freedom of maritime communication; and every state's obligation not to allow knowingly its territory to be used for acts contrary to the rights of other states'.

Failure to respect the territorial rights of other states

A failure to respect the territorial rights of another state may consist of a straightforward breach of the prohibition of the use of force contained in art 2(4) of the Charter of the United Nations which will give rise to 'aggrieved responsibility' of the offending state or it may occur in other ways.

The unlawful arrest of a wanted criminal on the territory of another state

In the *Attorney-General of the Government of Israel* v *Eichmann* (1961) 36 IRL 5 Eichmann, who played a key role in the planning and the execution of the Nazi 'final solution' consisting of the extermination of some six million Jews, was found in Argentina in 1960 by the Israeli Secret Service and abducted without the knowledge of the Argentinian government. Argentina complained to the Security

Council which adopted a resolution stating that 'acts such as that under consideration, which affect the sovereignty of a member state ... endanger international peace and security' and requested the government of Israel to make appropriate reparations to the government of Argentina.

Illegal flights in the airspace of another state
In the U-2 incident of May 1960 (see Lissitzyn (1962) 56 AJIL 135 and Wright (1960) 54 AJIL 836) a US aircraft engaged in espionage activities over the Soviet Union was forced to land on Russian soil. The US did not protest at the shooting down of the aircraft and the subsequent trial of the pilot.

The carrying out of activities in the territorial waters of a state
In the *Corfu Channel Case: United Kingdom* v *Albania (Merits)* (1949) ICJ Rep 4 the ICJ held that the Royal Navy, in carrying out minesweeping operations in Albanian territorial waters, violated the sovereignty of the Albanian Peoples Republic.

By allowing toxic fumes to escape into the territory of another state
In the *Trail Smelter Arbitration: United States of America* v *Canada* (1938 and 1941) 3 RIAA 1905 a Canadian company began smelting lead and zinc at Trail, on the Columbia River about ten miles from the US-Canadian border, on the Canadian side. By 1930 over 300 tons of sulphur, containing considerable quantities of sulphur dioxide, were being emitted daily. Some of the fumes were being carried down the Columbia River valley and across into the US where they were allegedly causing considerable damage to land and other interests in the state of Washington. The US claimed compensation, and the matter was referred to the International Joint Commission.

The Tribunal found that 'under the principles of international law ... no state has the right to use or permit the use of its territory in such manner as to cause injury by fumes in or to the territory of another or the properties of persons therein'.

Insult to the state

Such acts are generally termed 'insults to the flag' and constitute international wrongs for which the state responsible should make suitable reparations. An example is provided by the *I'm Alone: Canada* v *United States of America* (1935) 3 RIAA 1609. In this case, the *I'm Alone*, a British schooner, registered in Canada, was ordered to heave to by a US coastguard vessel, on suspicion of smuggling liquor at the time of prohibition in the US. She fled, and when more than 200 miles from the US coast was fired upon and sunk, with the loss of the boatswain and the cargo.

The Arbitration Commission, to which the case was referred, found that the sinking of the vessel was unlawful. It was also established that the vessel was de facto owned by citizens of the US and therefore no compensation ought to be paid in respect of the ship or cargo. However, the Commission considered that the

United States ought to formally acknowledge the illegality of its act, apologise to His Majesty's Canadian government and further pay the sum of $25,000 to that government as material compensation.

In the majority of such cases a public apology and an undertaking to punish those responsible for the act will constitute adequate amends.

10.7 Indirect international wrongs: the treatment of aliens

Vattal stated that an injury to a citizen is an injury to the state. This relationship between the individual and his state gives rise to two principles.

1. The state is responsible for the acts of its citizens of which its agents know or ought to know and which cause harm to the legal interests of another state.
2. The state has a legal interest in its citizens and in protecting this interest the state may call to account those harming its citizens.

In the *Mavrommattis Palestine Concessions Case (Jurisdiction): Greece* v *United Kingdom* (1924) PCIJ Rep Ser A No 2, 12 the Court said:

'... it is an elementary principle of international law that a state is entitled to protect its subjects, when injured by acts contrary to international law committed by another state, from whom they have been unable to obtain satisfaction through the ordinary channels. By taking up the case of one of its subjects and by resorting to diplomatic action or international judicial proceedings on his behalf, a state is in reality asserting its own right – its right to ensure, in the person of its subjects, respect for the rules of international law.'

Failure to protect these principles, therefore, may lead the injured state to exercise its right of diplomatic protection. The injured state may make a claim through diplomatic channels against the offending state or, failing satisfaction, may present a claim on the international plane.

The defendant state's duties are owed not to the injured alien, but to the alien's national state. Thus: (1) the claimant state may refrain from making a claim; (2) the claimant state may abandon its claim; (3) the claimant state is under no obligation to pay any compensation obtained to its injured national.

In *Rustomjee* v *The Queen* (1876) 1 QBD 487 money had been paid to Great Britain by China as compensation for damage suffered by British nationals in China. Lush J stated:

'No doubt a duty arose as soon as the money was received to distribute that money amongst the persons towards whose losses it was paid by the Emperor of China; but then the distribution when made would be, not the act of an agent accounting to a principal, but the act of the Sovereign in dispensing justice to her subjects. For any omission of that duty the Sovereign cannot be held responsible.'

International treatment of aliens

Much of the controversy regarding the treatment of aliens stems from the difference in approach between those states that consider that there is an 'international minimum standard' of treatment which must be accorded to aliens by all states irrespective of how they treat their own nationals and those that argue that aliens may only insist upon 'national treatment', ie treatment equal to that given by the state concerned to its own nationals.

The standard of national treatment

The principle of national treatment has been favoured by the newer and developing states. For example, it has received support in Latin America and today many of the post-colonial Afro-Asian states support the principle. The main justifications for granting aliens equality of treatment under the local law have been stated as follows: to give the alien a special status would be contrary to the principles of territorial jurisdiction and equality of states; and by residing in the particular state the alien is deemed to have submitted to both the benefits and the burdens incidental to residence in that state, ie he takes conditions as he finds them.

The standard does not apply to every area of activity.

Customary international law recognises that in certain areas of activity states may treat aliens less favourably than their own nationals.

For example, aliens may be restricted in: the ownership of property; participation in public life and politics; the taking of employment; and receiving legal aid and welfare benefits.

In the UK for instance, an alien may not own a British ship, may not vote in parliamentary elections and may face restrictions in joining the civil service.

The international minimum standard

The older and more economically developed states of Western Europe and North America have generally supported the international minimum standard of treatment of aliens. This principle is also supported by the great majority of international tribunals.

In the *Neer Claim: United States of America* v *Mexico* (1926) 4 RIAA 60 the US claimed that Mexico had failed to exercise due diligence in finding and prosecuting the murderer of a US national. In rejecting the claim the Commission expressed the applicable standard as follows:

> '... the propriety of governmental acts should be put to the test of international standards ... the treatment of an alien, in order to constitute an international delinquency, should amount to an outrage, to bad faith, to wilful neglect of duty, or to an insufficiency of governmental action so far short of international standards that every reasonable and impartial man would readily recognise its insufficiency. Whether the insufficiency proceeds from deficient execution of an intelligent law or from the fact that the laws of the country do not empower the authorities to measure up to international standards is immaterial.'

The treatment of aliens and fundamental human rights

The national standard of treatment and the international minimum standard of treatment reflect conflicting economic and political interests. The International Law Commission in its Debate on the Second Report on State Responsibility in 1957 attempted to move away from this conflict by linking the question of the protection of aliens to the rapidly developing law regarding the protection of human rights in general.

The Rapporteur – the Cuban jurist Garcia Amador – proposed in art 1 of his second report that:

> '1. The state is under a duty to ensure to aliens the enjoyment of the same civil rights, and to make available to them the same individual guarantees as are enjoyed by nationals [national standard]. These rights and guarantees shall not, however, in any case be less than the "fundamental human rights" recognised and defined in contemporary international instruments [international minimum standard].
> 2. In consequence, in case of violation of civil rights, or disregard of individual guarantees, with respect to aliens, international responsibility will be involved only if internationally recognised "fundamental human rights" are affected.'

This proposal would have made substantial inroads upon the domestic jurisdiction of states and was felt to be quite unacceptable in the light of current state practice. Furthermore, it was felt by non-European states that the 'fundamental human rights' protected were reflective of Western European standards and ideals, and were not necessarily suitable for the Third World states, with their particular economic, social and political problems. However, with the rapid growth of international instruments dealing with human rights since 1956, there is a growing body of opinion that this approach is now correct. Thus, the standard of treatment to be accorded to non-nationals should be the standard established by the international law of human rights.

Admission and expulsion of aliens

These are matters essentially within the domestic jurisdiction of states.

A state may refuse to admit aliens or may impose conditions or restrictions upon their admission.

In *Attorney-General for Canada* v *Cain* [1906] AC 542 the Judicial Committee of the Privy Council stated:

> 'One of the rights possessed by the supreme power in every state is the right to refuse to permit an alien to enter that state, to annex what conditions it pleases to the permission to enter it, and to expel or deport from the state, at pleasure, even a friendly alien, especially if it considers his presence in the state opposed to its peace, order and good Government, or to its social or material interests.'

Providing the state acts in good faith it may exercise the power of expulsion at its discretion. However, certain exceptions do exist which limit this discretion:

1. expulsion may constitute the crime of genocide or may infringe the rule of non-discrimination under customary international law;
2. there may be no right of expulsion where persons by long residence have acquired effective nationality of the foreign host state.

Denial of justice

The term 'denial of justice' has been given widely differing interpretations by international tribunals and its precise meaning is, therefore, uncertain and controversial. In its widest sense it has been equated with any wrongful treatment of aliens for which the respondent state would be accountable. In its narrow sense it has been used to cover only those situations in which foreigners have either been refused access to the local courts, or where such access has been hindered.

A definition somewhere between these two views is that contained in the Harvard Draft Convention on the Responsibility of States for Damage Done in Their Territory to the Person or Property of Foreigners 1929.

Article 9 states:

> 'Denial of justice exists when there is a denial, unwarranted delay or obstruction of access to courts, gross deficiency in the administration of judicial or remedial process, failure to provide those guarantees which are generally considered indispensable to the proper administration of justice, or a manifestly unjust judgment. An error of a national court which does not produce manifest injustice is not a denial of justice.'

This draft has been criticised as being too general. It is this generality which has resulted in the wide interpretation given to the term 'denial of justice' and has led to its erratic application and uncertainty of meaning.

The international standard of denial of justice

It is generally agreed that if 'denial of justice' is to achieve a degree of certainty and be used as a basis of international responsibility then it must be defined in terms of an international law standard.

The international standard is founded upon two principles:

1. it is no defence to show that an alien has been treated no worse than nationals of the respondent state if the standard of treatment is lower than the minimum standard required by international law;
2. if the local standards of the administration of justice are higher than those of the minimum standard required by international law, the alien must receive the benefit of that higher standard and not the international minimum, ie there must be no discrimination.

However, when the special circumstances of many states are taken into account it is obvious that any international standard will be a variable concept. Allowance must be made for derogation from the international standard in special circumstances.

Special measures may have to be introduced by a state to meet an emergency, eg war, rebellion or other civil disorder. Some account may also have to be taken of the special difficulties involved in administering justice in the underdeveloped, less stable parts of the world. For example, inadequate communications may make the local police and judicial authorities virtually autonomous from the central authorities of the state.

The international standard and local conditions

If the international standard is not to impose unreasonably high standards on the less developed states, the standard must take into account local conditions and not be a reflection of those standards applied in the more advanced Western states.

The problem is illustrated by the cases involving injury to American nationals heard by the Mexican–United States Claims Commission.

In many cases before the Commission, Mexico argued that if foreigners came to work in Mexico they must accept life as they found it and should not be entitled to more favourable treatment than that enjoyed by Mexican nationals. This defence was usually rejected. For example, in *Roberts Claim: United States of America* v *Mexico* (1926) 4 RIAA 77 the Commission found:

> '... the jail in which he was kept was a room thirty five feet long and twenty feet wide with stone walls, earthen floor, straw roof, a single window, a single door and no sanitary accommodation, all the prisoners depositing their excrement in a barrel kept in a corner of the room ... 30 or 40 men were at times thrown together in this single room ... the prisoners were given no facilities to clean themselves ... the room contained no furniture ... they were afforded no opportunity to take physical exercise ... the food given them was scarce, unclean, and of the coarsest kind. The Mexican Agent ... stated that Roberts was accorded the same treatment as that given to all other persons, and with respect to the food Roberts ... was given "the food that was believed necessary, and within the means of the municipality".
>
> Facts with respect to equality of treatment of aliens and nationals may be important in determining the merits of a complaint of mistreatment of an alien. But such equality is not the ultimate test of the propriety of the acts of authorities in the light of international law. That test is broadly speaking whether aliens are treated in accordance with ordinary standards of civilisation. We do not hesitate to say that the treatment of Roberts was such as to warrant an indemnity on the ground of cruel and inhuman imprisonment.'

The failure of international law to establish a compromise between the international standard and local conditions led the South American states to reject the international minimum standard and adopt instead the standard of national treatment when dealing with aliens.

The Panamanian Draft on the Rights and Duties of States 1947 provided that foreigners were not entitled to claim rights 'different from, or more extensive than, those enjoyed by nationals'.

However, this approach has had to be adapted to meet the developments in international human rights generally, and today even the advocates of the national standard of treatment accept the need for some limitation on the application of their municipal laws so as not to contravene fundamental human rights.

The International Law Commission Revised Draft on International Responsibility of the State for Injuries Caused on its Territory to the Person or Property of Aliens 1961 reflects this changing attitude.

Article 1 provides:

> '... aliens enjoy the same rights and the same legal guarantees as nationals, but these rights and guarantees shall in no case be less than the "human rights and fundamental freedoms" recognised and defined in contemporary international instruments.'

The requirement of 'bad faith'

There may be no denial of justice where the failure arises through deficiencies in the administration of justice, unless those deficiencies are such as to raise a presumption of bad faith.

In the *Neer Claim: United States of America* v *Mexico* (1926) 4 RIAA 60 the US claimed that Mexico had failed to exercise due diligence in finding and prosecuting the murderer of a US national. In rejecting the claim the Commission said there was:

> '... a long way between holding that a more active and efficient course of procedure might have been pursued on the one hand, and holding that this record presents such a lack of diligence and of intelligent investigation as constitutes an international delinquency on the other hand.'

However, this may be contrasted with *Janes Claim: United States of America* v *Mexico* (1926) 4 RIAA 82, where the Commission stated that in its opinion:

> 'Carbajal, the person who killed Janes, was well known in the community where the killing took place. Numerous persons witnessed the deed. The slayer, after killing his victim, left on foot. There is evidence that a Mexican police magistrate was informed of the shooting within five minutes after it took place ... Eight years have elapsed since the murder and it does not appear from the records that Carbajal has been apprehended at this time ... there was clearly such a failure on the part of the Mexican authorities to take prompt and efficient action to apprehend the slayer as to warrant an award of indemnity.'

10.8 Expropriation of foreign property

A state may restrict or place conditions upon the acquisition of certain kinds of property by aliens. In the absence of such restrictions an alien is free to acquire and enjoy title to property in accordance with the provisions of the local law.

Expropriation, or the compulsory taking of private property by the state has always been considered as a ground for diplomatic intervention as constituting a breach of international law. Whereas in the nineteenth century the problem was usually one of the destruction or expropriation of the property of one individual, today it is likely to be one of general expropriation of all foreign property, or the expropriation of all property in certain key areas of the state's economy, eg railways, banks, oil companies and mines.

The acquisition and control of property by aliens is of considerable political importance to states. The economies of many states, both underdeveloped and developed, are dominated by foreign companies and foreign investors. Many states resent this foreign dominance and see it as a threat to their independence and as inhibiting their freedom to implement their chosen economic and social policies.

The problem has become particularly acute following the spread of socialism and the emergence of the post-colonial states in Asia and Africa who resent the interests retained by their former colonial powers and seek ways to sever their former colonial ties completely.

The rules of expropriation

Although it is generally agreed that expropriation may occur, the wide divergence of political and economic beliefs among states has resulted in little agreement as to the rules to be applied in cases of expropriation.

The Communist countries believe that states may expropriate the means of production, distribution and exchange without paying any compensation, ie confiscation.

The developing states believe the matter should be left to the expropriating state to regulate at its discretion and in accordance with its national law.

Western capital-exporting states have, however, advocated an international minimum standard based on three principles: the principle of non-discrimination; the principle that the expropriation most be for a public purpose; and the principle that expropriation must be followed by adequate compensation.

Non-discrimination based on nationality

While the requirement of non-discrimination is not expressly stated in either of the principal international instruments dealing with this question (see below), it is based on a general principle of good faith and has been widely upheld in arbitral awards such as *BP* v *Libya* (1974) 53 ILR 297 and *LIAMCO* v *Libya* (1981) 20 ILM 1. In *Aminoil* v *Kuwait* (1982) 21 ILM 976 Kuwait was pursuing a general policy of nationalisation but was doing so in stages. At the time of the nationalisation of Aminoil, a Japanese company operating in the same region was left unaffected. Aminoil alleged discrimination. This was, however, rejected by the Tribunal on the grounds that there were legitimate reasons for the nationalisation not having included the Japanese company. To establish discrimination a company would, therefore, have to show that it had been singled out on the basis of its nationality. The most striking example of this arose in the *BP* case in which Libya expressly stated that it was expropriating BP's assets in response to what was regarded as improper action by the British government in the Gulf. The expropriation thus arose directly as a result of the British nationality of BP.

Public purpose

In the *Certain German Interests in Polish Upper Silesia Case* (1926) PCIJ Rep Ser A No 7, 22 the Court acknowledged that 'expropriation for reasons of public utility, judicial liquidation and similar measures' was permissible in international law.

This is stated as a requirement in GAR 1803 (XVII) but not in GAR 3281 (XXIX) (see below). There has thus been some debate as to whether this forms part of the international law test of lawfulness. Arbitrator Lagergren in *BP* accepted that this was a requirement of international law. In that case, the Libyan nationalisation of BP took place in the context of a specific anti-British policy. The nationalisation was, therefore, unlawful because it 'was made for purely extraneous political reasons' rather than as part of a policy of public utility. In the *LIAMCO* award, however, arbitrator Mahmassani expressly rejected the notion that international law included a public policy test.

As in the *BP* case, there will frequently be an overlap between the non-discrimination requirement and the public purpose principle. In *BP*, for example, the Libyan nationalisation decree was contrary to both principles: 'the taking ... violates public international law as it was made for purely extraneous political reasons and was arbitrary and discriminatory in character'. This does not clarify, however, whether Lagergren saw non-discrimination as part of the public policy test or a separate test in its own right. In *LIAMCO*, Mahmassani accepted the non-discrimination principle but rejected the public policy requirement. These decisions can be reconciled only if it is accepted either that the two principles form part of the same test or that, while they are separate tests, the public policy principle will be easily satisfied on evidence that the act in question was motivated other than by purely political considerations.

Compensation

While there is general acceptance that there is a requirement to compensate in the case of expropriation the standard of the compensation required has been much in issue. The debate has focused on the divide between those seeking an international standard of compensation and those in favour of a standard of compensation determined in accordance with the municipal law of the state concerned.

Those in favour of an international standard of compensation have pointed to numerous examples of state practice in support of the proposition. US Secretary of State Hull, in 1940, argued that the right to expropriate was 'coupled with and conditioned on the obligation to make adequate, effective and prompt compensation'.

In the *Anglo-Iranian Oil Company Case (Interim Measures)* (1951) ICJ Rep 81 at 83 the UK pleaded the following before the ICJ:

'... it is clear that the nationalisation of the property of foreigners, even if not unlawful on any other ground, becomes an unlawful confiscation unless provision is made for compensation which is adequate, prompt and effective ... By "adequate" compensation is meant "the value of the undertaking at the moment of dispossession, plus interest to the day of judgment" ... There have, in fact, been pronouncements that prompt compensation means immediate payment in cash. Thus in the arbitration between the United states and Norway relating to the requisitioning of contracts for the building of ships in the United states, it was held: the Tribunal is of opinion that full compensation should have been paid ... at the latest on the day of the effective taking ... The Government of the United Kingdom is, however, prepared to admit that deferred payments may be interpreted as satisfying the requirement of payment in accordance with the rules of international law if: (a) the total amount to be paid is fixed promptly; (b) allowance for interest for late payment is made; (c) the guarantees that the future payments will in fact be made are satisfactory, so that the person to be compensated may, if he so desires, raise the full sum at once on the security of the future payments ... The third requirement is summed up in the word "effective" and means that the recipient of the compensation must be able to make use of it. He must, for instance, be able, if he wishes, to use it to set up a new enterprise to replace the one that has been expropriated or to use it for such other purposes as he wishes ... The compensation ... must be freely transferrable from the country paying it and, so far as that country's restrictions are concerned, convertible into other currencies.'

Similarly, GAR 1803 (XVII) on the Permanent Sovereignty over Natural Resources indicates a requirement to pay 'appropriate compensation ... in accordance with international law'. While the definition of what was meant by 'appropriate' was left unstated, it was generally accepted that the resolution firmly established an international standard of compensation. The international standard argument has been put in numerous cases since that resolution (eg *Texaco*, *BP*, *Aminoil*).

There are nevertheless exceptions to the compensation rule in the case of:

1. treaty provisions;
2. confiscation as a penalty for crimes;
3. legitimate exercise of police power;
4. measures of defence;
5. seizure by way of taxation;
6. destruction of property of neutrals arising from military operations;
7. taking of enemy property as reparations.

In opposition, developing states have argued in favour of a standard of compensation set by the municipal law of the state concerned. They point in particular to GAR 3281 (XXIX) – the Charter of Economic Rights and Duties of States – which provides, in para 2(c), that 'where the question of compensation gives rise to a controversy, it shall be settled under the domestic law of the nationalising state'.

In terms of this debate, the weight of opinion would appear to rest with an international standard of compensation. The arbitrator in *Texaco* v *Libya* (1977) 53 ILR 389, following an assessment of the two GA resolutions, came to the conclusion that GAR 1803 reflected customary law while GAR 3281 did not. This conclusion notwithstanding, the debate on the international versus domestic standard of compensation, has lost much of its vigour for two main reasons:

1. in an attempt to encourage foreign investment in order to stimulate economic growth, a large number of developing states have been willing to conclude bi-lateral investment agreements containing clauses that subject the agreement to international law and that provide for the submission of any dispute to international settlement;
2. the growth in the number of cases involving questions of compensation before international tribunals is leading to the development of specialised rules on the payment of compensation.

Much in the same way as international human rights instruments are establishing a common body of rules and standards applicable to the treatment of aliens, so it is likely that the jurisprudence of international tribunals will give rise to specialised rules and agreed standards of compensation.

The General Assembly Resolution on Permanent Sovereignty over Natural Resources 1962 (GAR 1803 (XVII))

Widespread nationalisation following World War II and the emergence of the new post-colonial states in Africa and Asia has led to a dramatic shift in international opinion regarding the expropriation of foreign property. This Resolution of the General Assembly illustrates the emerging attitudes of the developing states by emphasising that foreign ownership of the means of production should not deprive a state of its sovereignty or its ability to control and plan its economy.

The General Assembly in the above resolution declares that:

'1. The right of peoples and nations to permanent sovereignty over their natural wealth and resources must be exercised in the interest of their national development and of the well-being of the people of the state concerned;

2. The exploration, development and disposition of such resources, as well as the import of the foreign capital required for these purposes, should be in conformity with the rules and conditions which the peoples and nations freely consider to be necessary or desirable with regard to the authorisation, restriction or prohibition of such activities;

3. In cases where authorisation is granted, the capital imported and the earnings on that capital shall be governed by the terms thereof, by the national legislation in force, and by international law. The profits derived must be shared in the proportions freely agreed upon, in each case, between the investors and the recipient state, due care being taken to ensure that there is no impairment, for any reason, of that state's sovereignty over its natural wealth and resources;

4. Nationalisation, expropriation or requisitioning shall be based on grounds or reasons of public utility, security or the national interest which are recognised as overriding purely individual or private interests, both domestic and foreign. In such cases the owner shall be paid appropriate compensation in accordance with the rules in force in the state taking such measures in the exercise of its sovereignty and in accordance with international law. In any case where the question of compensation gives rise to a controversy, the national jurisdiction of the state taking such measures shall be exhausted. However, upon agreement by Sovereign states and other parties concerned, settlement of the dispute should be made through arbitration or international adjudication;

5. The free and beneficial exercise of the sovereignty of peoples and nations over their natural resources must be furthered by the mutual respect of states based on their Sovereign equality;

6. International co-operation for the economic development of developing countries, whether in the form of public or private capital investments, exchange of goods and services, technical assistance, or exchange of scientific information shall be such as to further their independent national development and shall be based upon respect for their sovereignty over their natural wealth and resources;

7. Violation of the rights of peoples and nations to sovereignty over their natural wealth and resources is contrary to the spirit and principles of the Charter of the United Nations and hinders the development of international co-operation and the maintenance of peace;

8. Foreign investment agreements freely entered into by, or between sovereign states shall be observed in good faith; states and international organisations shall strictly and conscientiously respect the sovereignty of peoples and nations over their natural wealth and resources in accordance with the Charter and the principles set forth in the present resolution.'

As suggested above, para 4 of the Resolution would seem to reflect the Western states' position regarding expropriation.

The Charter of Economic Rights and Duties of States 1974 (GAR 3281 (XXIX))

This Charter, adopted by a Resolution of the General Assembly of the United Nations, reflects the viewpoint of the developing states on the matter of expropriation of foreign property. The Charter illustrates the great strength of support for the developing states' viewpoint present within the United Nations.

Article 2 of the Charter provides:

'1. Every state has and shall freely exercise full permanent sovereignty, including possession, use and disposal, over all its wealth, natural resources and economic activities.

2. Each state has the right:

(a) To regulate and exercise authority over foreign investment within its national jurisdiction in accordance with its laws and regulations and in conformity with its national objectives and priorities. No state shall be compelled to grant preferential treatment to foreign investment;

(b) To regulate and supervise the activities of transnational corporations within its national jurisdiction and take measures to ensure that such activities comply with its laws, rules and regulations and conform with its economic and social policies. Transnational corporations shall not intervene in the internal affairs of a host state. Every state should, with full regard for its sovereign rights, co-operate with other states in the exercise of the right set forth in this sub-paragraph;

(c) To nationalise, expropriate or transfer ownership of foreign property in which case appropriate compensation should be paid by the state adopting such measures, taking into account its relevant laws and regulations and all circumstances that the state considers pertinent. In any case where the question of compensation gives rise to a controversy, it shall be settled under the domestic law of the nationalising state and by its tribunals, unless it is freely and mutually agreed by all states concerned that other peaceful means be sought on the basis of the Sovereign equality of states and in accordance with the principle of free choice of means.'

As will be evident, the two resolutions differ in a number of important respects. While both accept that there is a right to nationalise, GAR 1803 specifies the requirement of public utility whereas GAR 3281 does not. Both acknowledge the requirement for compensation to be paid. GAR 1803, however, specifies that this should accord with international law while GAR 3281 establishes a domestic standard of compensation.

The status of these resolutions was reviewed by arbitrator Dupuy in *Texaco* (above). In contrast to GAR 1803, which had the support of both developed and developing states, GAR 3281 had little or no support from industrialised nations (ie the investors).

The Charter was adopted by 120 votes to six, with ten abstentions. The states voting against were Belgium, Denmark, the Federal Republic of Germany, Luxembourg, the UK and the US. The abstaining states were Austria, Canada, France, Ireland, Israel, Italy, Japan, The Netherlands, Norway and Spain. The nature of this opposition to the Charter was regarded by Dupuy as being of sufficient size and significance to deny it the status of customary international law.

Disguised expropriation

This may involve placing a company under 'temporary' government control which is then maintained indefinitely, or by more subtle processes of discrimination against foreign companies. These may take the form of controls on prices or profits, promoting nationally owned competition or creating delays in the granting of licenses, supplying equipment, manpower etc. This question was considered by the Iran-US Claims Tribunal in *Starrett Housing Corporation* v *The Government of the Islamic Republic of Iran* (1984) 23 ILM 1090. The Tribunal concluded that any significant interference with property rights, such that these rights were rendered useless, would amount to an expropriation even though there was no actual change in ownership or legal title. Thus, the appointment by Iran of a temporary manager, with a right to control and use the assets of the housing project, amounted to a taking. The question was raised again in *Elettronica Sicula SpA (ELSI): US* v *Italy* (1989) ICJ Rep 14. The US argued that the taking of property would include not only an outright expropriation but also any unreasonable interference with the use, enjoyment or disposal of that property. While the court did not rule directly on this point, it implied that any act that amounted to a significant deprivation of interest would satisfy the requirement of a taking.

National monopolies

Legislation may be enacted by a state establishing a national monopoly in certain areas of the economy thereby restricting or excluding foreign competition.

For instance, in 1973 Mexico introduced legislation under which certain areas – petroleum and hydrocarbons, exploitation of radioactive minerals and nuclear energy, certain mining activities, electricity, railways, telegraphic and wireless communications – were 'reserved exclusively for the state'.

Other activities – radio and television, gas distribution, forestry, transport – were reserved exclusively to Mexican nationals and companies.

Limited foreign participation was to be allowed in certain other areas – secondary petrochemicals, exploitation and use of minerals.

Investment protection

Many developing countries in order to attract new investment have passed laws, or in some cases inserted provisions into their constitutions, guaranteeing foreign investments against expropriation or providing for payment of compensation in the event of expropriation.

Some developing states have also entered into treaties with developed countries with respect to foreign investment guarantees and payment of compensation in the event of expropriation.

Other Western states, including the US and the UK, encourage their nationals to invest in developing countries by insuring their nationals against the risk involved in such investment, in return for a small premium.

The available methods of settling investment disputes have been supplemented by the Convention on the Settlement of Investment Disputes Between States and Nationals of Other States 1965. This established an International Centre for the Settlement of Investment Disputes, under the auspices of the International Bank for Reconstruction and Development.

The Centre was established to settle investment disputes by conciliation and arbitration and has jurisdiction over:

> '... any legal dispute arising directly out of an investment, between a contracting state ... and a national of another Contracting state, which the parties to the dispute consent in writing to submit to the Centre'.

As at 20 November 2004, 141 states had ratified the Convention, including the US, the UK, the majority of Western states and most Afro-Asian states.

The Calvo clause

It has long been the practice of many Latin American governments to insert a 'Calvo clause' when making concession contracts with aliens, under which the alien agrees not to seek the diplomatic protection of his own state and submits any matters arising from the contract to the local jurisdiction.

Many governments deny the validity of such clauses on the principle that a clause in a private law contract cannot deprive a state of the right of diplomatic protection, or deny an international tribunal jurisdiction.

For example, in the *North American Dredging Company Case* (1926) 4 RIAA 26, one of the terms of the contract between the American company and the Mexican authorities provided:

'The contractor and all persons who, as employees or in any other capacity, may be engaged in the execution of the work under this contract either directly or indirectly, shall be considered as Mexicans in all matters, within the Republic of Mexico, concerning the execution of such work and the fulfilment of this contract. They shall not claim, nor shall they have, with regard to the interests and the business connected with this contract, any other rights or means to enforce the same than those granted by the laws of the Republic to Mexicans, nor shall they enjoy any other rights than those established in favour of Mexicans. They are consequently deprived of any rights as aliens, and under no conditions shall the intervention of foreign diplomatic agents be permitted, in any matter related to this contract.'

The Mexican/US General Claims Commission held that by agreeing to such a clause, an individual could not:

'... deprive the Government of his nation of its undoubted right of applying international remedies to violations of international law committed to his damage. Such Government frequently has a larger interest in maintaining the principles of international law than in recovering damage for one of its citizens in a particular case, and manifestly such citizens cannot by contract tie in this respect the hands of his Government.'

Generally, a breach of a private law contract will not be an international wrong unless there is a denial of justice in the course of exhausting local remedies. In practice, therefore, the effect of the Calvo clause in arbitration has, in the absence of a denial of justice, been to prevent contractual disputes becoming inter-state proceedings.

Breaches and annulment of state contracts

The general view is that in the absence of a denial of justice, a breach of contract does not create state responsibility on the international plane. Most contracts between states and aliens are governed by municipal law (usually the municipal law of the contracting state). However, in some circumstances it is possible for contractual obligations to create state responsibility over and above that arising from a denial of justice.

The following factors may give a contract an international character thereby creating state responsibility on the international plane.

Legislative interference

The contracting government may legislate in such a way as to make the contract worthless. For example, it may impose export or currency restrictions, or it may legislate to annul the contract or otherwise alter its existing contractual obligations. By so acting it can be argued that the state is taking the matter out of the field of private law and is creating an issue of international character.

In the *Norwegian Loans Case: France* v *Norway* (1957) ICJ Rep 9 French nationals had purchased bonds issued by two Norwegian banks on behalf of the Norwegian state. The bonds stipulated in gold the amount of the borrower's obligation and the borrower could only discharge the substance of his debt by the payment of the gold value of the redeemed bond. The Norwegian government introduced legislation prohibiting the convertibility of Norwegian currency into gold and suspending all payments in gold.

Although the Court, after upholding a preliminary objection raised by Norway, did not decide upon the merits of the dispute, individual judges did comment upon Norway's international responsibility under the bond agreements.

Judge Read was of the opinion that when the bondholders purchased the Norwegian bonds the transaction was solely within the jurisdiction of the municipal law. However, the passing of the Norwegian legislation and the suspension of payments in gold raised the question 'whether Norway could, in conformity with the principles of international law by legislative action unilaterally modify the substance of the contracts'. In the opinion of Judge Read the action of the Norwegian government, which breached the contracts, automatically 'internationalised' the dispute and became prima facie a breach of international law.

Where the contract is internationalised

Most contracts between states and aliens are governed by the municipal law of the debtor state. However, it is possible for a state to enter into a contract which is either expressly or by implication subject to some foreign system of law.

In *R* v *International Trustee for Protection of Bondholders Aktiengesellschaft* [1937] 2 All ER 164 the House of Lords held that while the fact that a state is a party to a contract is a factor of general significance in determining the applicable law, nevertheless it is not of itself conclusive. It may still be possible to infer from the circumstances as a whole that the contract is governed by some other legal system.

In *Texaco* v *Libya* (above) arbitrator Dupuy set out three ways in which a contract could be internationalised:

1. if there was an express choice of law clause subjecting the contract to general principles of law (or international law);
2. if there was a clause providing that in the event of a dispute the matter was to be submitted to international arbitration;
3. if the agreement was in the nature of an 'international development agreement', that is, agreements which continue over a long period of time and involve investment in the developing country in question.

A contract may also become internationalised if it contains a 'stabilisation' clause, ie a clause purporting to restrict the right of the state to unilaterally vary the terms of the contract. This will invariably also include a clause subjecting the contract to international or general principles of law.

Contracts of a quasi-public nature

It has been argued that contracts of a quasi-public nature entered into between a state and a foreign individual are governed not by municipal law but by general principles of international law. In this respect the contract is internationalised. This internationalisation may be by express choice of the parties or may be inferred by the Court from the circumstances of the case.

This proposition that contracts between states and non-international persons can, either expressly or by implication, be subject to international law has been supported in several commercial arbitrations involving concessions granted to oil companies: see, eg, *Abu Dhabi Arbitration: Sheikh of Abu Dhabi* v *Petroleum Development (Trucial Coast) Ltd* (1951) 18 ILR 144.

This case concerned a dispute over the interpretation of the terms of an oil concession contract granted by the Sheikh of Abu Dhabi in 1939. The sole arbitrator had to decide firstly upon the law governing the contract.

The contract was made in Abu Dhabi and was wholly to be performed in that country. If any municipal system of law were applicable therefore it would prima facie be that of Abu Dhabi. But as the arbitrator pointed out:

'... no such law can reasonably be said to exist. The Sheikh administers a purely discretionary justice with the assistance of the Koran; and it would be fanciful to suggest that in this very primitive region there is any settled body of legal principles applicable to the construction of modern commercial instruments.'

Nor could the arbitrator see any basis on which the municipal law of England could apply:

'On the contrary (the substance) of the agreement ... repels the notion that the municipal law of any country, as such, could be appropriate. The terms ... invite, indeed prescribe, the principles rooted in the good sense and common practice of the generality of civilised nations – a sort of "modern law of nations".'

The 'modern law of nations'

Two theories have been advanced in order to identify this 'modern law of nations'.

This is a new system of international commercial law based upon general principles of law derived from municipal systems

The system provides a choice of law that can be used to reconcile the interests of the state on the one hand and the foreign individual on the other. Breach of the contract by the state concerned is not a breach of international law giving rise to a claim on the international plane but simply a breach according to the law of the contract. Therefore, because the system of law is not international law in its true sense there is no conflict with the principle that international law only governs relations between entities having international personality.

If one of the parties to the contract is endowed with international personality then it is possible for that contract to be governed by public international law

In theory, therefore, a breach of such a contract governed by 'international law' would amount to a breach of an international obligation.

In the *Lena Goldfields Arbitration* (1929–30) 5 AD 3 the tribunal had to consider the law governing a concession granted by the Soviet Union to a British company. Under the concession agreement, it was provided that the parties should base their relations 'on the principle of good will and good faith as well as on reasonable interpretation of the terms of the Agreement'.

The majority of the tribunal accepted the argument of the complainant company that in regard to performance of the contract inside the Soviet Union, Russian law was applicable but that for other purposes:

> '… the general principles of law such as those recognised by art 38 of the Statute of the Permanent Court of International Justice … should be regarded as "the proper law of the contract".'

Does a reference to 'general principles of law' in such a contract mean 'international law'? With regard to these contracts, McNair stated:

> 'If then, as is submitted, one can reasonably infer that the parties do not regard the national law of either of them as affording an adequate or appropriate legal system within which these contracts can operate, and if we may also assume that they contain an international element, what legal system can be regarded as appropriate to govern them? What is the legal system which best satisfies the intention of the parties? One can truly infer from these contracts – both from what they do say and from what they do not say – the parties are groping after some legal system which is not the territorial law of either party.
>
> The answer to these questions is not that these contracts are governed by public international law stricto sensu, for this system is an inter-state system – jus inter gentes. It is true that a corporation operating in a foreign country can be said to be under the protection of public international law because it can invoke the diplomatic protection of its own government if it should meet with wrongful treatment at the hands of the government of the country in which it is operating; but that is not the same thing as saying that the contract is governed by public international law. My submission is that in contracts of this type the parties, if they specify no particular legal system, intend that their contracts should be governed by the general principles of law recognised by civilised nations.'

In the *Aramco Arbitration* (1963) 27 ILR 117, under the arbitration agreement between Saudi-Arabia and the Arabian American Oil Company (Aramco), the Tribunal was required to decide disputes over the concession agreement in accordance with Saudi Arabian law in so far as matters within the jurisdiction of Saudi Arabia were concerned, and in accordance with the law deemed by the tribunal to be applicable in so far as matters beyond the jurisdiction of Saudi Arabia were concerned.

The Tribunal stated that as the concession was not an agreement between two states but between a state and a private American Corporation, it could not be governed by public international law. The tribunal found that the concession agreement itself constituted 'the fundamental law' of the parties and in so far as doubts might remain as to the content or meaning of the agreement, it was 'necessary to resort to the general principles of law and to apply them in order to interpret, and even to supplement, the respective rights and obligations of the parties'.

The *Aramco Arbitration,* therefore, strongly supports the view that contracts of a concessionary type not governed by the municipal law of the grantor state are subject to general principles of law and not international law.

Breach of a commercial contract is not ipso facto a breach of international law.

If the principle is accepted that the proper law in such cases is not public international law, a breach of a commercial contract subject to general principles of law is not ipso facto a breach of international law. Such a case would only assume an international character if: a state that is a party to an 'international contract' refuses to go to arbitration as required by the contract; or refuses to abide by the tribunal's ruling.

Internationalisation of a contract by a collateral understanding or treaty arrangement between states

In some cases a treaty specifically lays down that a particular contract between one of the states which is a party to the treaty and nationals of the other state which is a party to the treaty shall be performed, or that rights under the contract shall be recognised. In such cases a breach of the contract by the state concerned is, therefore, a breach of an international obligation owed to the other state.

Many of the capital–exporting states have entered into such bilateral agreements to promote and protect investments by their nationals in a number of developing states.

Breach of contract and expropriation

Some writers contend that if a state exercises its executive or legislative authority to destroy contractual rights then the act comes within the ambit of expropriation and will lead to state responsibility on that basis.

10.9 Admissibility of state claims

A case involving the treatment of aliens brought before an international tribunal may be lost on a preliminary objection by the defendant state, which, if successful, will stop all proceedings in the case.

The principal factors giving rise to a preliminary objection are as follows.

1. Non-compliance with the rules regarding nationality of claims.
2. Failure to exhaust local remedies.
3. Unreasonable delay in bringing the claim.
4. Waiver of the claim.
5. Improper behaviour by the injured alien.

Nationality of claims

The general rule on the nationality of claims is that a state may only assert an international claim on behalf of one of its nationals. Article 44 of the ILC Articles provides that the responsibility of a state may not be invoked if the claim is not brought in accordance with any applicable rule relating to nationality of claims. Rule I of the UK Rules Applying to International Claims provides that 'Her Majesty's Government will not take up the claim unless the claimant is a UK national and was so at the date of the injury': see UKMIL (1983) 54 BYIL 520.

The rule was stated by Oppenheim as follows:

'... from the time of the occurrence of the injury until the making of the award the claim must continuously and without interruption have belonged to a person or to a series of persons: (a) having the nationality of the state by whom it is put forward, and (b) not having the nationality of the state against whom it is put forward': R Jennings and A Watts (eds); *Oppenheim's International Law*, 9th ed, Harlow: Longman, 1992, pp512–513.

The requirement of continuity, evident in the rule, has been criticised on two main grounds: that it allows incidental matters, eg a change of nationality by operation of law, to defeat a valid claim; and if an injury to the individual is an injury to the state of origin, then the wrong matures at the time of the injury and should not be affected by any subsequent change in the status of the individual.

In many cases, the question of the nationality of the injured party will be complicated by additional factors. Two situations are of particular importance:

1. where the injured persons is a national of more than one state;
2. where the injured person has a stronger link with the respondent state than with the national state seeking to exercise diplomatic protection.

Protection in cases of dual nationality

Position where the individual is also a national of the respondent state – the test applicable in such cases is that of 'dominant nationality'.

In the *Canevaro Case: Italy v Peru* (1912) 11 RIAA 397 the Arbitral Tribunal was asked to decide whether Italy could claim on behalf of Raphael Canevaro who had both Italian and Peruvian nationality.

The Tribunal held that:

'Whereas, as a matter of fact, Raphael Canevaro has on several occasions acted as a Peruvian citizen, both by running as a candidate for the Senate where none are admitted except Peruvian citizens and where he went to defend his election, and also especially by accepting the office of Consul General of The Netherlands, after soliciting the authorisation of the Peruvian Government and then of the Peruvian Congress ... under these circumstances, whatever Raphael Canevaro's status may be in Italy with respect to his nationality, the Government of Peru has a right to consider him as a Peruvian citizen and to deny his status as an Italian claimant.'

This principle denying admissibility in the case of dual nationals found support in art 4 of the Hague Convention on Certain Questions Relating to the Conflict of Nationality Laws 1930. Rule III of the UK Rules on International Claims further provides that 'Her Majesty's Government will not normally take up [the] claim [of] a UK national if the respondent state is the state of his second nationality'.

These examples of state practice notwithstanding, a number of cases have sought to modify the rule against dual nationality. In the *Mergé Claim* (1955) 22 ILR 443, for example, the US brought a claim under the Italian Peace Treaty 1947. The claimant was, however, of both US and Italian nationality and the Treaty, which permitted claims on behalf of 'United States nationals', contained no provisions governing the case of dual nationality. The Commission decided that the question whether the US could bring the claim against Italy must be decided according to 'the general principles of international law' and agreed that these included the principle of the dominant and effective nationality. The Commission gave the following examples of dominant US nationality:

'(i) Children born in the United States of an Italian father when the children have habitually lived there;
(ii) Italians who, having acquired United States nationality by naturalisation and having thus lost their Italian nationality, later re-acquire it by Italian law by staying in Italy for more than two years though without the intention of residing there permanently;
(iii) American women married to Italian nationals where the family has had habitual residence in the United States and the interests and the permanent professional life of the head of the family were established in the United States;
(iv) A widow who at the termination of her marriage transfers her residence from Italy to the United States when her conduct, especially with regard to the raising of her children shows her new residence to be of a habitual nature.'

The principle of dominant and effective nationality has since been upheld in two important cases before the Iran-US Claims Tribunal, namely, *Esphahanian* v *Bank Tejarat* (1983) 2 Iran-USCTR 157 and *Case A/18* (1984) ILR 75. Despite these decisions, however, it is by no means clear that the principle of dominant and effective nationality has become part of customary law.

Position where the individual is the national of a third state as well as of the claimant state – the practice of international tribunals seems to treat an individual's connection with a third state as immaterial.

In the *Salem Case: Egypt* v *United States of America* (1932) 2 RIAA 1161 the Tribunal stated that it is the practice of several governments, where two powers are both entitled by international law to treat a person as their national, that neither of these powers can raise a claim against the other in the name of such person.

Accordingly Egypt could oppose the American claim if they could bring evidence that Salem was an Egyptian subject and that he acquired American nationality without the express consent of the Egyptian government.

'In the opinion of the Arbitral Court the Egyptian government is unable to bring such evidence. Indeed from the circumstances it must be assumed that Salem was not an Egyptian subject but a Persian subject when he acquired American nationality ...

It is beside the point to ask whether Salem lost his Persian nationality or not by the acquisition of American nationality. ... Whatever may be the true interpretation, the Egyptian government cannot set forth against the United states the eventual continuation of the Persian nationality of George Salem; the rule of international law being that in a case of dual nationality a third power is not entitled to contest the claim of one of the two powers whose national is interested in the case by referring to the nationality of the other power.'

In the *Mergé Claim* (above) the Italian-US Conciliation Commission accepted the principle that the respondent state could not raise the second dominant nationality of a third state:

'United States nationals who do not possess Italian nationality, but the nationality of a third state can be considered "United States nationals" under the Treaty, even if their prevalent nationality was the nationality of the third state.'

Position where an individual has close ties with, but not the nationality of, the respondent state – in the *Nottebohm Case: Liechtenstein v Guatemala* (1955) ICJ Rep 4 Nottebohm was born in Hamburg and held German nationality by birth. In 1905 he went to Guatemala, took up residence there and made that country the headquarters of his business activities. He had business connections in Germany and sometimes went there on business. He also paid a few visits to a brother who had lived in Liechtenstein since 1931. In 1939 Nottebohm applied for admission as a national of Liechtenstein. His request was granted and his passport was issued, the three years' residence requirement being waived. Nottebohm returned to Guatemala and when Guatemala later declared war on Germany he was interned and his property confiscated.

In 1951 the government of Liechtenstein instituted proceedings before the ICJ in which it claimed restitution and compensation on the ground that the government of Guatemala had 'acted towards the person and property of Mr Friedrich Nottebohm, a citizen of Liechtenstein, in a manner contrary to international law'.

The Court held that Liechtenstein was not entitled to exercise diplomatic protection and present a claim to the Court on behalf of Nottebohm against Guatemala because there was no genuine link between Nottebohm and Liechtenstein:

'At the time of his naturalisation does Nottebohm appear to have been more closely attached by his tradition, his establishment, his interests, his activities, his family ties, his intentions for the near future to Liechtenstein than to any other state? ...

He had been settled in Guatemala for 34 years. He had carried on his activities there.

It was the main seat of his interests. He returned there shortly after his naturalisation, and it remained the centre of his interests and of his business activities. He stayed there until his removal as a result of war measures in 1943. He subsequently attempted to return there, and he now complains of Guatemala's refusal to admit him. There, too, were several members of his family who sought to safeguard his interests.

In contrast, his actual connections with Liechtenstein were extremely tenuous. No settled abode, no prolonged residence in that country at the time of his application for naturalisation: the application indicates that he was paying a visit there and confirms the transient character of this visit by its request that the naturalisation proceedings should be initiated and concluded without delay. No intention of settling there was shown at that time or realised in the ensuing weeks, months or years – on the contrary, he returned to Guatemala very shortly after his naturalisation and showed every intention of remaining there … There is no allegation of any economic interests or of any activities exercised or to be exercised in Liechtenstein and no manifestation of any intention whatsoever to transfer all or some of his interests and business activities to Liechtenstein …

These facts clearly establish, on the one hand, the absence of any bond of attachment between Nottebohm and Liechtenstein and, on the other hand, the existence of a long-standing and close connection between him and Guatemala, a link which his naturalisation in no way weakened …'

It is, however, important to bear in mind that the ICJ decided that Liechtenstein could not bring a claim against Guatemala. It did not decide that Liechtenstein could not bring a claim against a third state with which Nottebohm had no connection. Thus, for example, a claim by Liechtenstein against, say, Japan may well have been admissible, the link of nationality serving to establish Liechtenstein's interest in exerting diplomatic protection.

Position where the individual while not being a national of a third state nevertheless has a close connection with a third state – if the 'genuine link' theory of the *Nottebohm Case* is now the paramount aspect of diplomatic protection, then a 'genuine link' with a third state might be of greater significance than actual nationality of a third state.

However, it must be remembered that the *Nottebohm* decision is of limited application. This fact was recognised by the Italian-US Conciliation Commission in the *Flegenheimer Claim* (1958) 25 ILR 91.

In the opinion of the Commission:

'… it is doubtful that the International Court of Justice intended to establish a rule of general international law in requiring, in the *Nottebohm* case, that there must exist an effective link between the person and the state in order that the latter may exercise its right of diplomatic protection on behalf of the former. The Court itself restricted the scope of its Decision by affirming that the acquisition of nationality in a state must be recognised by all other states … subject to the twofold reservation that, in the first place, what is involved is not recognition for all purposes but merely for the purposes of the admissibility of the Application, and, secondly, that what is involved is not recognition by all states but only by Guatemala … But when a person is vested with only one nationality … the theory of effective nationality cannot be applied without the risk of causing confusion. It lacks a sufficiently positive basis to be applied to a nationality which finds support in a state law. There does not in fact exist any criterion of proven effectiveness for disclosing the effectiveness of a bond with a political collectively, and the persons by the thousands who, because of the facility of travel in the modern world, possess the positive legal nationality of a state, but live in foreign states where they are domiciled and where their family and business centre is located, would be exposed to non-recognition, at the international level, of the nationality with which they are undeniably vested by virtue of the laws of their national state, if this doctrine were to be generalised.'

So where there exists a 'genuine' single nationality, the connection by residence or otherwise of the individual with another state is irrelevant.

Position where the individual is stateless – the position of stateless persons was indicated in the *Dickson Car Wheel Company Case: United States of America* v *Mexico* (1931) 4 RIAA 669:

> 'A state ... does not commit an international delinquency in inflicting an injury upon an individual lacking nationality and consequently, no state is empowered to intervene or complain on his behalf either before or after the injury.'

Corporations and their shareholders
Protection of corporations created under the domestic laws of the claimant state – prima facie a corporation has the nationality of the state under the laws of which it is incorporated and in whose territory it has its registered office. Therefore, incorporation may be relied upon by states when pursuing claims against respondent states who have seized corporation property. However, state practice requires something more than mere registration. If a state is to pursue a claim on behalf of a corporation there must be some degree of national control or beneficial ownership of shares in the company concerned.

British state practice is illustrated by the case of *Enrique Cortes and Company* (1896): see *Cheshire and North's Private International Law*, 11th ed, London: Butterworths, 1987, p173 et seq. This company was incorporated in England, but its principal members and all its shareholders were Colombian citizens. The company inquired whether, in case of disorder in Colombia, the company could seek the protection of the British government. The Law Officers after considering the matter reported that in their opinion:

> '... the principle ought not to be recognised that foreigners, by registering themselves here as a limited company, are entitled to claim from Her Majesty's Government the protection accorded to British subjects in foreign countries.'

Application of the Nottebohm 'genuine connection' principle to corporations suggests that the principle of a real or genuine link advanced by the court in the *Nottebohm Case* does apply to corporations. However, this has not been accepted by the ICJ. In *Barcelona Traction, Light and Power Co Ltd Case: Belgium* v *Spain* (1970) ICJ Rep 4 the claim was presented by Belgium on behalf of its nationals who were shareholders in the company incorporated and having its registered office in Canada. The ICJ treated the question whether the company was entitled to Canadian diplomatic protection as being of only indirect relevance. Nevertheless, the Court explained its view that Canada was entitled to exercise diplomatic protection in the following terms:

> 'In allocating corporate entities to states for purposes of diplomatic protection; international law is based, but only to a limited extent, on an analogy with the rules governing the nationality of individuals. The traditional rule attributes the right of diplomatic protection of a corporate entity to the state under the laws of which it is incorporated and in whose territory it has its registered office. These two criteria have been confirmed by long practice and by numerous international instruments. This notwithstanding, further or different links are at times said to be required in order that a right of diplomatic protection should exist. Indeed it has been the practice of some states to give a company incorporated under their law diplomatic protection solely when it has its seat or management or centre of control in their territory, or when a majority or a substantial proportion of the shares has been owned by nationals of the state concerned. Only then, it has been held, does there exist between the corporation and the state in question a genuine connection of the kind familiar from other branches of international law. However, in the particular field of the diplomatic protection of corporate entities, no absolute test of the "genuine connection" has found general acceptance. Such tests as have been applied are of a relative nature, and sometimes links with one state have had to be weighed against those with another. In this connection reference has been made to the *Nottebohm Case*. In fact the Parties made frequent reference to it in the course of the proceedings. However, given both the legal and factual aspects of protection in the present case the Court is of the opinion that there can be no analogy with the issues raised or the decision given in that case.
>
> In the present case, it is not disputed that the company was incorporated in Canada and has its registered office in that country. The incorporation of the company under the law of Canada was an act of free choice. Not only did the founders of the company seek its incorporation under Canadian law but it has remained under that law for a period of over 50 years. It has maintained in Canada its registered office, its accounts and its share registers. Board meetings were held there for many years; it has been listed in the records of the Canadian tax authorities. Thus a close and permanent connection has been established, fortified by the passage of over half a century. This connection is in no way weakened by the fact that the company engaged from the very outset in commercial activities outside Canada, for that was its declared object. Barcelona Tractions links with Canada are thus manifold.'

Thus, the Court rejects the analogy of the *Nottebohm Case* and the 'genuine connection' principle. However, the Court's conclusion on this point may not be regarded as authoritative.

1. Neither Belgium nor Spain contested the Canadian character of the Barcelona Traction Company so the reference to 'genuine connection' was not at issue.
2. The Court does in fact set out the 'manifold' links of the company with Canada.
3. Many jurists do favour the application of the *Nottebohm* principle to the diplomatic protection of limited companies.

The decision in the *Barcelona Traction Case* does, however, preserve the principle that a claim can only have one 'nationality', and thus helps to limit the number of international claims and helps restrict the powers of the large multinational corporations.

The protection of shareholders – generally, a state cannot intervene on behalf of a foreign corporation solely on the basis that some of its nationals are shareholders in the company. The shareholders must rely upon the diplomatic protection available to the corporation itself.

The principles governing the admissibility of claims on behalf of shareholders were clarified by the ICJ in the *Barcelona Traction Case* (above).

The company was established under Canadian law in 1911 in connection with the development of electricity supplies in Spain. In 1948 it was declared bankrupt by a Spanish court. Canada intervened on behalf of the company but later withdrew. At the time 88 per cent of the shares in the company were allegedly owned by Belgian nationals and Belgium brought this claim in respect of the injury to its nationals who were shareholders, resulting from the injury to the company.

Spain objected that since the injury was to the company, not the shareholders, Belgium lacked locus standi to bring the claim.

The Court ruled in favour of the respondent state, Spain, upon the ground that Belgium had no locus standi to espouse before the Court claims of alleged Belgian nationals who were shareholders in the company, inasmuch as the company was incorporated in Canada and was, in an international legal sense, of Canadian nationality. The reasoning relied upon by the Court may be expressed as follows.

1. International law must recognise the general principle of municipal legal systems which provides that an infringement of the rights of a company by outsiders does not involve liability towards the shareholders, even if their interests are detrimentally affected by the infringement. The Court will not look behind the corporate veil.
2. It is a general rule of international law that it is the national state of the company concerned which is entitled to exercise diplomatic protection and seek redress for an international wrong done to the company.
3. A different principle might apply if the wrong were aimed at the direct rights of the shareholders as such, eg their right to attend and vote at general meetings. However, the present case was not concerned with the infringement of the shareholders' direct rights but with the alleged illegal measures taken by Spain against the company.
4. The exclusive entitlement of the national state of the company to exercise diplomatic protection might conceivably, in certain cases, give way to the right of the national state of the shareholders, eg where the company itself had ceased to exist, or the protecting national state of the company lacked capacity to exercise diplomatic protection.

However, in the present case, the company had not ceased to exist as a corporate entity in Canada, nor was the Canadian government incapable of exercising diplomatic protection – it merely chose not to do so.

The Court rejected the argument that for reasons of equity a state should be entitled in certain cases to take up the protection of its nationals who were shareholders in a company, the victim of a breach of international law. The court was afraid that any such alleged equitable justification would open the door to competing claims on the part of different states thereby creating an atmosphere of confusion and insecurity in international economic relations.

The ICJ therefore is reluctant to 'pierce the corporate veil' in order to allow a state, other than the national state of the company, to seek redress for an international wrong done to the company.

In summary, therefore, the Court provided that, as a general rule, the genuine link principle does not apply to companies. However, in three cases the national state of the shareholders will be entitled to assert a claim for diplomatic protection. These three exceptions have been incorporated into the UK Rules Applying to International Claims. Thus, a state may claim on behalf of its nationals as shareholders if:

1. the wrong alleged was directed against the shareholders by reason of their nationality (Rule III, UK Rules);
2. the company has ceased to exist (Rule V, UK Rules);
3. the national state of the company lacks the capacity to bring an international claim (Rule VI, UK Rules).

Exhaustion of local remedies
It is an established principle of international law that a claim brought by a state on behalf of its national will not be admissible before an international tribunal unless the foreign national has exhausted all the legal remedies available to him under the local courts of the defendant state.

For example, Rule VII of the UK Rules on International Claims provides that:

'Her Majesty's Government will not normally take over and formally espouse a claim of a United Kingdom national against another state until all the legal remedies, if any, available to him in the state concerned have been exhausted.'

Therefore, failure to exhaust any local remedies will not constitute a bar to a claim if it is clearly established that in the circumstances of the case an appeal to a higher municipal tribunal would have had no effect. Nor is a claimant against another state required to exhaust justice in that state if there is no justice to exhaust.

Justifications for the principle of exhaustion of local remedies
There are a number of justifications for the above principle: these are as follows.

1. National courts are a more suitable and convenient forum for hearing the claims of individuals and corporations.

2. By residing and operating within the foreign state the individual or corporation has associated himself with the local jurisdiction.
3. It avoids the multiplication of small claims based on diplomatic protection.
4. The local courts are in a better position to adduce the facts of the case and assess the damage caused.
5. The foreign state should be given the opportunity of righting any wrong it has committed and to force its immediate submission to international adjudication would be an interference with its sovereignty.

Situations where principle does not apply

Where there is direct injury to the complainant state itself. The principle applies with regard to claims by a state on behalf of its national. It does not apply to claims by a state in respect of direct injuries to itself. For example, if a state's embassy is damaged there is no obligation upon that state to seek redress in the municipal courts of the foreign state concerned.

In the *Aerial Incident of 27 July 1955 Case* (1960) ICJ Rep 146 an Israeli airliner which had strayed into Bulgarian airspace was shot down by Bulgarian fighter aircraft. Bulgaria argued, inter alia, that the ICJ had no power to hear the action because Israel had failed to exhaust local remedies. Israel contended that as the incident had been a direct inter-state wrong, the local remedies principle was inapplicable. The Israeli agent before the ICJ said he could:

> '... recall no precedent in which a government complaining of actions performed by another government jure imperii has been referred to the courts of the respondent state as a preliminary condition to the obtaining of international satisfaction.'

Where there is no connection between the injured alien and the respondent state. The general principle is that by entering the territory of a foreign state, an individual is presumed to subject himself to the jurisdiction of the local courts. However, it can be argued that where the connection between the injured national and the respondent state is involuntary or purely fortuitous then the local remedies principle should not be applied.

In the *Aerial Incident of 27 July 1955 Case: Israel* v *Bulgaria (Preliminary Objections)* (1959) ICJ Rep 127, for example, Israel argued, inter alia, that there was no link between the victims and the Bulgarian state. Therefore, even assuming the claim could be regarded as being made on behalf of Israeli nationals, there was no need to exhaust local remedies because the connection with Bulgaria was only caused by the illegal act of the Bulgarian authorities in bringing down the plane.

Where the state concerned has already committed a breach of international law. If there has been no breach of international law, but only a breach of local law, then no responsibility arises on the international plane in respect of the breach, unless the individual concerned is denied justice in the local courts.

If the individual is denied justice in the local courts it would seem absurd to require him to seek redress in those same courts. In such a case there may be no justice to exhaust and therefore the principle should not apply.

Where there is no breach of local law. Where there is a breach of international law which does not involve any breach of local law then the principle is inapplicable.

Function of the principle

The function of the principle is to give the respondent state the opportunity, before being subjected to international adjudication, of doing justice in its own way and of having an investigation and adjudication of the issues of law and fact. International relations thus stand to benefit since it prevents a vast number of trivial disputes souring relations between states and the international tribunals from being inundated with cases.

The scope of 'local remedies'

There would seem to be no requirement for the 'local remedies' to be restricted to those remedies of a judicial nature available only through the local courts. The International Law Commission in its 1961 Draft Convention proposed a definition which would include all administrative or judicial remedies or proceedings available under the local law. Thus if a state has an established procedure for remedying the particular injury, the individual suffering such injury must avail himself of that procedure even if it is of a non-judicial form.

In the *Barcelona Traction Case* (above) Judge Bustamente, President of the Court, made reference to Barcelona Traction's failure to appeal against the Spanish Institute of Foreign Exchange's refusal to sanction proposals to deal with the company's overseas bonds payments. He pointed out that in accordance with well established principles, a complaint should have been made to the Minister of Commerce, for:

> '... only a higher authority is able to discern whether a subordinate official has exceeded the limits of a reasonable discretion and ventured into the unlawful domain of arbitrariness or unjust discrimination.'

Thus, it would appear that provided the administrative remedy is based upon some established procedure, then it will constitute a local remedy for the purposes of the exhaustion principle.

The principle does not apply to extra-legal remedies or remedies as of grace. For example, the right to petition the Queen under the Royal Prerogative is an act of grace and not a local remedy which must be exhausted under the principle.

Only effective remedies need be exhausted

Although the local remedies rule is generally strictly applied, it does not mean that it is necessary for the individual to exhaust remedies which, though available in theory, would nevertheless be ineffective or insufficient to redress the injury of which he complains.

For example, there are no local remedies to exhaust where:

1. the local courts are bound by statute or precedent which compels them to reject the claim;
2. the local courts are notoriously corrupt or known to discriminate against foreigners;
3. the wrong has been committed by the legislative itself or by some high official and the local courts refuse to challenge their authority;
4. having lost his claim in the lower court, appeal would be futile because the point at issue is one of fact and the court of appeal may deal only with points of law.

If the conditions within the state are such that the processes available for pursuing local remedies are corrupt or insufficient and unreliable, a foreign national may be excused recourse to such processes.

In the *Robert E Brown Case: United States of America* v *Great Britain* (1923) 6 RIAA 120 Brown, an American citizen, had applied for licences to prospect for gold in South Africa. Under the law of South Africa he was entitled to have the licences granted, but the law was suspended by the Executive Council. He commenced proceedings before the South African courts alleging that this suspension of the law was ultra vires, and obtained judgment that the act of the Executive Council was unconstitutional. The court held that his licence had been wrongfully refused and granted him leave to claim damages.

Before this claim could be heard the Chief Justice was dismissed and a law was introduced directing that the judiciary were to apply resolutions to the Volksraad (lower chamber of Parliament) without referring to their validity under the constitution. The new court refused Brown leave to claim damages by way of motion and held that any claim for such damages must involve a retrial of the case.

The Great Britain/US Arbitral Tribunal rejected a claim of non-exhaustion of local remedies on the ground that under the prevailing circumstances a retrial of the case would be futile. The Tribunal referred to 'the frequently quoted language of an American Secretary of State: "A claimant in a foreign state is not required to exhaust justice in such state when there is no justice to exhaust".' The Tribunal commented that in *Brown's Case*:

> 'All three branches of the Government [of the South African Republic] conspired to ruin his [Brown's] enterprise ... The judiciary, at first recalcitrant, was at length reduced to submission and brought into line with a determined policy of the Executive ...'

In some cases the laws of the respondent state are the basis of the breach of duty. For example, in some cases the injured national may be deprived of any remedy before the local courts as a result of legislation enacted by the offending state. In such cases, if the local courts are bound by that legislation, there can be no local remedies to exhaust.

In the *Norwegian Loans Case: France* v *Norway* (1957) ICJ Rep 9 the French government claimed that a number of international loans issued by Norwegian banks on behalf of the Norwegian state were redeemable by the payment of their gold value and not their original face value. The Norwegian government objected to the Court's jurisdiction, inter alia, on the ground that the bondholders had failed to exhaust local remedies. However, by Norwegian legislation convertibility of Norwegian currency into gold was prohibited. France, therefore, argued that recourse to the Norwegian courts by the bondholders would have been pointless.

Although in the event the Court was not called upon to consider the matter of non-exhaustion of local remedies, Judge Lauterpacht and Judge Read did deal with the issue in their separate opinions.

Lauterpacht's view was that there may have been a remedy under Norwegian law notwithstanding the legislation:

'There has been a tendency in the practice of courts of many states to regard international law, in some way, as forming part of national law or as entering legitimately into the national conception of ordre public. Although the Norwegian Government has admitted that in no case can a Norwegian Court overrule Norwegian legislation on the ground that it is contrary to international law, it has asserted that it is possible that a Norwegian Court may consider international law to form part of the law of the Kingdom to the extent that it ought, if possible, to interpret the Norwegian legislation in question so as not to impute to it the intention or the effect of violating international law.'

Judge Read on the other hand believed that recourse to the local courts under the particular circumstances would be 'obviously futile'. He accepted the French excuse for the failure to institute proceedings before the Norwegian courts. In effect Norway was arguing that the bondholders must exhaust local remedies while at the same time contending that the matter was unquestionably governed by their legislation. In Read's view the local remedies principle had no application where the right of the foreign national had been impaired by the direct intervention of the respondent government or Parliament. Unless Norway could show that it was possible for the bondholders to challenge governmental activities authorised by the legislature in the Norwegian courts, the defence of non-exhaustion of local remedies must fail.

If it is possible for the injured alien to seek redress in the local courts against executive or legislative action on the part of the respondent state, then the exhaustion of local remedies principle will apply.

In the *Interhandel Case: Switzerland* v *United States of America* (1959) ICJ Rep 6 the Swiss government had instituted proceedings before the ICJ against the US. The US government had in 1942 under the provisions of the Trading with the Enemy Act, seized the assets of the General Aniline and Film Company (GAF), which was incorporated in the US. The majority of GAF shares were owned by Interhandel, a Swiss firm, which, in the opinion of the US government was under the control of IG Farben, a German company. The Swiss government contended that Interhandel had severed its ties with IG Farben in 1940, ie before the US entered the war. Therefore, the foreign interest in GAF was Swiss and not German.

In 1946 the Washington Accord was signed between the Allies (Great Britain,

France, and the US) and Switzerland, under which it was agreed to unblock all Swiss assets. However, the US continued to hold the assets of GAF considering them as being German and accordingly they were not covered by the agreement. Between 1948 and 1957 the Swiss Government and Interhandel brought proceedings in the US courts, but when these proved abortive Switzerland made application to the ICJ. However, while the application was being made the Supreme Court of the United states had granted a writ of certiorari and remanded Interhandel's case to the District Court. It was therefore open to Interhandel to avail itself again of the remedies available to it under the Trading with the Enemy Act, and to seek the restitution of its shares by proceedings in the US courts.

The US thereupon objected to the admissibility of the claim on the ground that local remedies had not been exhausted. Switzerland argued that the local remedies principle did not apply, since the failure of the US to comply with the terms of the Washington Accord constituted a direct breach of international law, causing immediate injury to the rights of the applicant state.

The Court rejected this argument, stating that it must:

'... attach decisive importance to the fact that the laws of the United states make available to interested persons who consider that they have been deprived of their rights by measures taken in pursuance of the Trading with the Enemy Act, adequate remedies for the defence of their rights against the Executive.'

Thus, the presumption that where the injury is caused by the activities of the foreign executive or legislature, there may be no remedy available, is rebuttable by the respondent state if, as in the *Interhandel Case*, it can show that its actions may be subject to judicial review in its municipal courts.

The decision of the ICJ in the *Interhandel Case* has, however, come in for a good deal of criticism in that it arguably establishes that an unrealistic test must be satisfied before local remedies will be exhausted. In that case nine years of otherwise futile litigation in the US courts were held to be insufficient to satisfy the local remedies principle.

The ICJ, in a judgment of a chamber of the court in the *ELSI Case* (1989) ICJ Rep 14, reconsidered the application of the principle. In this case, domestic remedies had been pursued by the allegedly injured US companies for a long period of time. Prior to the US adopting the claims, at the international level expert advice was obtained from two Italian lawyers, both of whom confirmed that every domestic remedy avenue had been pursued. In addition, the Italian government had failed to draw attention to the fact that an additional remedy was available under Italian law during protracted pre–litigation negotiations with the US. Against this background the chamber of the Court held that, even though there was a remedy in Italian law that had not been pursued, the claim would be admissible, ie the local remedies principle had been satisfied. The following points emerge from the judgment of the chamber:

1. the onus will be on the state raising the objection of non-exhaustion to adduce the evidence;
2. the local remedies principle will be satisfied if the party has in substance exhausted all available local remedies and has behaved reasonably;
3. whether or not local remedies have been exhausted must be considered in the light of all the circumstances of the case and the principle of good faith.

The process of appeals

Generally local remedies will not be exhausted until the injured party has pursued his claim through the various channels of appeal available to him under the municipal law. Until the highest appellate tribunal determines the issue, the local remedies are not exhausted. However, there is no need to pursue a fruitless course of appeals.

In the *Panevezys-Saldutiskis Railway Co Case: Estonia* v *Lithuania* (1939) PCIJ Rep Ser A/B No 76 the Permanent Court of International Justice said: 'There can be no need to resort to the municipal courts if ... the result must be a repetition of a decision already given'.

In the *Finnish Ships Arbitration: Finland* v *Great Britain* (1934) 3 RIAA 1479 the Arbitrator was asked to decide whether the local remedies principle had been exhausted by Finland in seeking compensation from Great Britain for the hire of Finnish ships requisitioned during the Great War. Finland had sought compensation before the Admiralty Transport Arbitration Board but had been unsuccessful because the Board had found as a fact that, although used during the war by Great Britain, the ships had been requisitioned by or on behalf of Russia and not Great Britain.

The Arbitrator ruled that Finland's failure to appeal to the Court of Appeal did not mean that it had not exhausted local remedies. Such an appeal would have been futile because the Court of Appeal could not have reversed the Board's finding of fact; it could only have considered questions of law.

Where the alien fails to present his claim effectively or pursue it fully there will be no exhaustion of local remedies.

In the *Ambatielos Arbitration: Greece* v *United Kingdom* (1956) 12 RIAA 83 Ambatielos, a Greek national, agreed in 1919 to purchase a number of ships from the British government. The British government had given credit on the sale but had retained a mortgage over the vessels and in due course proceedings were taken to enforce the mortgage. Ambatielos claimed in his defence that the British government had given an undertaking that the vessels would be delivered by specific dates and that he had suffered loss as a result of the late delivery of some of the vessels and sought to cancel the contract of purchase in respect of two of the ships. However, the British government refused to allow the discovery of certain documents relating to the negotiations, under the plea of Crown privilege, and Ambatielos was therefore unable to prove that such an undertaking as to delivery dates had been given.

On appeal to the Court of Appeal Ambatielos asked for leave to call as a witness Major Laing, the British civil servant who had negotiated the contract for the purchase of the ships. The Court held that it could not allow Ambatielos to produce a new witness who could have been called in the court of first instance and leave was therefore refused. Ambatielos did not appeal to the House of Lords. The claim was submitted to a Commission of Arbitration in accordance with the provisions of the Anglo-Greek Treaty of Commerce and Navigation 1886. Before the Tribunal Great Britain invoked the local remedies principle and submitted that the procedural remedies available to Ambatielos in the English courts had not been exhausted. The Greek government contended that in the present case the remedies which English law offered Ambatielos were ineffective and that, accordingly, the principle was not applicable.

The Commission found that the local remedies had not been exhausted:

> 'These ... "local remedies" include not only reference to the courts and tribunals, but also the use of the procedural facilities which municipal law makes available to litigants before such courts and tribunals. It is the whole system of legal protection, as provided by municipal law, which must have been put to the test before a state, as the protector of its nationals, can prosecute the claim on the international plane.
>
> It is clear, however, that (this view) ... cannot be strained too far. Taken literally, it would imply that the fact of having neglected to make use of some means of procedure – even one which is not important to the defence of the action – would suffice to allow a defendant state to claim that local remedies have not been exhausted, and that, therefore, an international action cannot be brought. This would confer on the rule of the prior exhaustion of local remedies a scope which is unacceptable.
>
> In view of the Commission the non-utilisation of certain means of procedure can be accepted as constituting a gap in the exhaustion of local remedies only if the use of these means of procedure were essential to establish the claimant's case before the municipal courts.'

Furthermore, it was not possible for the Greek government to argue that the remedies had been exhausted because a further appeal would have been pointless:

> 'It would be wrong to hold that a party who, by failing to exhaust his opportunities in the court of first instance, has caused an appeal to become futile should be allowed to rely on this fact in order to rid himself of the rule of exhaustion of local remedies.'

Unreasonable delay: extinctive prescription

There is no rule of international law which lays down a time limit within which claims must be presented. Nevertheless, a claim will fail if it is presented after an unreasonable delay by the claimant state. What is reasonable is a question for the tribunal to decide at its discretion.

A claim which is delayed may be denied:

1. where the delay creates difficulty for the defendant state in establishing the facts alleged by the claimant state;

2. where the delay is evidence of acquiescence or waiver on the part of the claimant state.

Waiver of the claim

A claim, once waived by the claimant state, cannot be resurrected. But as the claim belongs to the state and not the injured national, any waiver of the claim by the national in his private capacity does not bind his government.

Improper behaviour by the injured alien

The doctrine of 'clean hands' provides that where the claimant is involved in activities which are illegal, either under municipal or international law, this may bar the claim.

However, the injury caused to such an alien must be proportionate and reasonable in relation to the illegality committed by him.

10.10 Circumstances precluding wrongfulness

The ILC Articles provide for circumstances under which a wrongful act will not give rise to international responsibility. Under the ILC Articles these circumstances preclude wrongfulness and thus provide defences to international claims. Chapter V entitled 'Circumstances Precluding Wrongfulness' specifies the following as defences: consent of an injured state; self-defence; compliance with peremptory norms; countermeasures in respect of an internationally wrongful act; force majeure; distress; and necessity. The circumstances precluding wrongfulness do not authorise or excuse any derogation from a peremptory norm of international law. Consequently, genocide cannot justify counter-genocide and a defence based on necessity cannot excuse the breach of a peremptory norm.

In addition, under art 18 of the ILC Articles a state may avoid international responsibility by pleading coercion to commit a wrongful act, but such an act will nevertheless be a wrongful act for which the coercing state will be held internationally responsible.

Consent

Under the principle volenti non fit injuria, when an injured state consents to an act or conduct, which without that consent will be considered as a wrongful act, the delinquent state cannot be held responsible in international law. For this defence to succeed it is necessary that a valid consent exists and that the delinquent state acts within the scope of the consent. However, a consent given to another state to act in violation of ius cogens, for example to enter its territory and massacre civilians, does not amount to a valid consent.

Countermeasures

The ILC Articles recognise that states are entitled to resort to countermeasures. Countermeasures must not be forcible. Further, non-forcible anticipatory countermeasures are unlawful given that countermeasures constitute a response to an unlawful act. Countermeasures are temporary, reversible steps aimed at inducing the wrongdoing state to comply with its obligations under international law. In the *Case Concerning Gabčikovo-Nagymaros Project: Hungary* v *Slokavia, Merits* (1997) ICJ Rep 7 the ICJ, relying on the Draft Articles of the ILC on State Responsibility, defined the conditions under which a state may resort to countermeasures. The ICJ stated that:

> 'In order to be justifiable, a countermeasure must meet certain conditions ... In the first place it must be taken in response to a previous international wrongful act of another state and must be directed against that state ... Secondly, the injured state must have called upon the state committing the wrongful act to discontinue its wrongful conduct or to make reparation for it ... In the view of the Court, an important consideration is that the effect of a countermeasure must be commensurate with the injury suffered, taking account of the rights in question ... [and] its purpose must be to induce the wrongdoing state to comply with its obligations under international law, and ... the measure must therefore be reversible.'

Self-defence

Self-defence as defined in international law, especially under art 51 of the UN Charter and in customary law, will preclude the wrongfulness of the conduct concerned: see Chapter 16.

Force majeure

Article 23 of the ICL Articles defines force majeure as 'the occurrence of an irresistible force or of an unforeseen event, beyond the control of the state, making it materially impossible in the circumstances to perform the obligation'. However, paragraph 2 of art 23 excludes a defence based on force majeure:

> '(a) when the situation of force majeure is due, either alone or in combination with other factors, to the conduct of the state invoking it; or
> (b) the state has assumed the risk of that situation occurring.'

Force majeure was pleaded by Albania in the *Corfu Channel Case* (1949) ICJ Rep 4. The ICJ rejected the defence on the ground that Albania did not show that it was an absolute impossibility to notify the existence of a minefield in its territorial waters to the UK warships.

In the *Rainbow Warrior Arbitration: New Zealand* v *France* (1987) 26 ILM 1346 the two French members of the French Secret Service, who were apprehended by New Zealand after boarding the *Rainbow Warrior* and placing explosive devices which caused extensive damage to the vessel and also the death of one crew member when they were detonated, were tried under the law of New Zealand and sentenced to ten years' imprisonment. The French government and the government of New Zealand accepted the solution proposed by the UN Secretary-General which consisted of handing over the two agents to the French authorities on the basis that they would be transferred immediately to the French military base on the Island of Hao in French Polynesia and detained there for three years. France, once they were handed over, without the consent of New Zealand and in breach of the above agreement, immediately returned one of them, Major Mafart, to France. The French government justified its decision to repatriate him on urgent medical reasons which, according to France, amounted to force majeure. The Arbitral Tribunal rejected the French defence on the ground that the medical emergency did not amount to 'absolute and material impossibility' which is a necessary requirement for a successful defence based on force majeure.

Necessity

The criteria for such a defence are very stringent under international customary law. They are as follows: there must be exceptional circumstances of extreme urgency, the status quo ante must be re-established as soon as possible and the state concerned must act in good faith.

Article 25 of the ILC Articles defines the conditions for invoking a defence based on necessity. A state is entitled to rely on necessity only if the act in question constitutes the only way for it to safeguard an essential interest against a grave and imminent peril, provided that this does not seriously impair an essential interest of a state or states towards which the obligation exists, or of the international community as a whole. In its commentary the ILC defined the state of necessity as being:

> 'The situation of a state whose sole means of safeguarding an essential interest threatened by a grave and imminent peril is to adopt conduct not in conformity with what is required of it by an international obligation to another state': (1989) Yearbook of the ILC, Vol II, Part 2, 34, para 1.

The commentary emphasised the exceptional nature of this defence.

It is interesting to note the influence of the codification work, not yet completed, on international practice. In the *Case Concerning Gabčikovo-Nagymaros Project: Hungary* v *Slovakia* (1997) ICJ Rep 7 Hungary pleaded necessity when it suspended and abandoned works on a project for a hydro-electric dam which was intended to be built to harness the waters of the River Danube. Hungary alleged that the exploitation of the dam would have grave consequences for the environment. The ICJ relied heavily on the ILC Draft article on necessity. The Court rejected the defence. It stated that Hungary had neither proved the existence of the perils nor that they were imminent. Moreover, at the time of suspension Hungary had available to it other means of responding to these perceived perils.

The defence of necessity was successfully invoked by the United Kingdom when it bombed the *Torrey Canyon*, a ship flying the Liberian flag which was grounded outside British territorial waters, as it represented a threat of an ecological disaster.

Distress

Article 24 of the ILC Articles provides that the situation of distress occurs when 'the author of the act in question has no other reasonable way, in a situation of distress, of saving the author's life or the lives of other persons entrusted to the author's care'. Paragraph 2 of art 24 states that distress cannot be invoked if:

1. the situation of distress is due, either alone or in combination with other factors, to the conduct of the state invoking it; or
2. the act in question is likely to create a comparable or greater peril.

In a situation of distress there is always a choice: to respect an international obligation or to sacrifice one's life or the lives of others who are in one's care. It is generally accepted that an international obligation cannot be observed at the price of human life. Thus, there is no serious alternative for the author. The ILC in its commentary gave an example of the unauthorised entry of an aircraft into foreign territory to save the life of passengers to illustrate the situation of distress.

Compliance with peremptory norms

Article 21 provides that: 'The wrongfulness of an act of a state is precluded if the act is required in the circumstances by a peremptory norm of general international law'.

10.11 Consequences of invoking a circumstance precluding wrongfulness

The exculpatory defences preclude the wrongfulness of an act but not necessarily the responsibility of the perpetrating state. The matter of whether in a situation where a state takes action which causes loss to another state or its nationals, but the action is not unlawful, it will be under an obligation to pay compensation is addressed in art 27 of the ILC Articles. This provision states that 'the invocation of a circumstance precluding wrongfulness ... is without prejudice to ... the question of compensation for any material harm or loss caused by the act in question'.

The exclusion of any right to compensation is certainly justified in circumstances where a state is acting with the consent of the injured state, where it acts in self-defence or takes countermeasures. If an injured state gives its consent and the other state acts within the scope of that consent there is no breach of international law. Consequently, there should be no duty to pay compensation. Also in a situation where a state is taking countermeasures to respond to prior violation of its rights, or where a state exercises its right to self-defence in conformity with international law, any claim to compensation by an injured state should not arise.

However, in a situations of distress or necessity a state has, at least theoretically, a choice between taking an action or breaching an international obligation. There is no reason why in such circumstances a state, which acts for its own benefit, should not bear the cost of its action. Therefore, both distress and necessity may involve a duty to make compensation for the breach of the right of another state.

10.12 Reparation for injury

Article 34 of the ILC Articles sets out the principle that a delinquent state must make full reparation for the injury caused by the commission of the internationally wrongful act. In this respect it is interesting to note that in the *Case Concerning Oil Platforms: Islamic Republic of Iran* v *United States of America* (2003) 42 ILM 1334 the ICJ found that the respondent acted unlawfully but it did not order any reparation, however symbolic, in favour of the claimant. Judge Kooijmans in his Dissenting Opinion was especially critical about this aspect of the Court's judgment. He stated:

'It is, however, unprecedented in the history of both Courts for a claim against a respondent to be rejected while earlier in the same paragraph the respondent is found to have acted unlawfully even though that finding is not – and is not said to be – determinative or even relevant for the dismissal of the claim. This novum can be seen as setting a precedent which in my view is a highly hazardous one since it raises questions about the scope of a judgment of the Court, eg with regard to its res judicata character.'

Reparation may take the form of restitution, compensation or satisfaction, either singly or in combination. Indeed, international law recognises various forms of reparation. The choice of a particular form of reparation varies depending upon the content of the obligation that has been breached and the nature of the injury sustained. In the *Chorzow Factory Case* (1928) PCIJ Rep Ser A No 17, involving a claim by Germany against Poland arising out of the expropriation of a factory, the PCIJ established the essential principle in this area. The Court held that:

'The essential principal contained in the actual notion of an illegal act – a principle which seems to be established by international practice and in particular by the decisions of arbitral tribunals – is that reparation must, as far as possible, wipe out all the consequences of the illegal act and re-establish the situation which would, in all probability, have existed if that act had not been committed. Restitution in kind, or, if this is not possible, payment of a sum corresponding to the value which a restitution in kind would bear; the award, if need be, of damages for loss sustained which would not be covered by restitution in kind or payment in place of it – such are the principles which should serve to determine the amount of compensation due for an act contrary to international law.'

The above principle has been endorsed by the ILC Articles. 'Restitution' is the restoration of the status quo ante, 'compensation' refers to monetary reparation and 'satisfaction' is concerned with reparation not involving material considerations.

Article 39 of the ILC Articles provides that in the determination of reparation the contribution to the injury of the state claiming reparation should be taken into account, in particular any wilful or negligent act or omission of the injured state or any person or entity in relation to whom the injured state seeks reparation. This provision has been criticised by the UK government. It felt that there was no reason why the ILC Articles should emphasise negligence and wilful wrongdoing taking into account that, on the one hand, there are other factors that might be equally worth express mention, given that the provision relates to reparation as a whole and not merely to compensation and, on the other hand, the introduction of a doctrine of contributory tort or negligence as a general principle of state responsibility is inappropriate since a primary rule that has been violated deals with all these aspects itself.

Restitution

Restitution may take the form of 'legal restitution' or restitution in kind or in integrum. Legal restitution is rare, one such example is provided by the *Martini Case* (1930) 2 RIAA 975. It consists of a declaration that an offending treaty, or act of the executive, judiciary or legislature is invalid. Legal restitution can be considered as restitution in integrum or as a kind of satisfaction.

Restitution in kind is the primary remedy at international law. The re-establishment of the status quo ante is, however, in most cases impossible. There have, nevertheless, been circumstances in which courts and tribunals have awarded restitution. In the *Free Zones of Upper Savoy and the District of Gex Case: France* v *Switzerland* (1932) PCIJ Rep Ser A/B No 46 the PCIJ ordered France to withdraw its customs line and to return to the status quo ante regarding the border and customs arrangements between France and Switzerland. Similarly, in the *Temple of Preah Vihear Case: Cambodia* v *Thailand* (1962) ICJ Rep 6 the ICJ ordered Thailand to return to Cambodia religious objects removed unlawfully from the Temple of Preah Vihear.

More controversial has been the question of the power of the court or tribunal to award restitution or specific performance in expropriation cases. The matter was discussed in the Libyan oil nationalisation cases. In *Texaco* v *Libya* (1977) 53 ILR 389 Arbitrator Dupuy, relying on the judgment of the ICJ in the *Chorzow Factory Case*, accepted that restitution was the primary remedy under international law. This aspect of his judgment has, however, come in for severe criticism on the grounds that an order requiring a state to perform its obligations under a concession agreement does not sit easily with the principle of permanent sovereignty over natural resources. It is also unrealistic to assume that an order for restitution will be effective given the circumstances. Certainly, in the *BP* v *Libya* (1974) 53 ILR 297 Arbitrator Lagergren accepted that restitution would not be an appropriate remedy.

The criticisms levelled at the Dupuy approach are reflected in art 35 of the ILC Articles. This provides that restitution will not be available if it is not materially possible or if it would involve 'a burden out of all proportion to the benefit deriving from restitution instead of compensation'.

This provision clearly rejects the Dupuy approach in the *Texaco* case.

Compensation

The most frequent form of reparation is compensation. Article 36 of the ILC Articles provides that compensation should cover any financially assessable damage (damnum emergens) and, if applicable, any loss of profits (lucrum cessans).

Article 38 of the ILC Articles provides important clarifications in respect of interest.

First, it states that interest on any principal sum 'shall be payable when necessary in order to ensure full reparation. The interest rate and mode of calculation shall be set so as to achieve that result.' This provision has been criticised by the UK government, which feels that the payment of interest should not be an optional matter but an obligation imposed on a delinquent state taking into account that it represents the actual loss suffered by the claimant.

Second, art 38(2) specifies that 'Interest runs from the date when the principal sum should have been paid until the date the obligation to pay is fulfilled'.

The ILC Articles, in conformity with the actual state of international law, reject the concept of punitive, vindictive or exemplary damages.

Satisfaction

Article 37 of the ILC Articles defines satisfaction as a remedy for the injury caused by a wrongful act which cannot be made good by restitution or compensation. Paragraph 2 of art 37 states that satisfaction may consist of an acknowledgment of the breach, an expression of regret, a formal apology or another appropriate modality. Indeed, satisfaction usually involves three facets:

1. apology or other acknowledgment of wrongdoing by means of a salute to the flag or payment of indemnity;
2. the punishment of the individual concerned;
3. the taking of measures to prevent recurrence of the harm.

The forms that satisfaction may take are illustrated by the *Borchgrave Case*: *Belgium* v *Spain* (1937) PCIJ Rep Ser A/B No 72. In this case a Belgian national working at the Belgian embassy in Madrid was found dead on the roadside in Spain in 1936. Belgium sought the following reparation in diplomatic proceedings with Spain:

1. an expression of excuses and regrets by the Spanish government;
2. the transfer of the corpse to the port of embarkation with military honours;
3. the payment of an indemnity of one million Belgian francs;
4. the punishment of the guilty.

A declaration by a court or tribunal that a state has acted illegally may itself be sufficient satisfaction in some cases. For example, in the *Corfu Channel Case: UK* v *Albania (Merits)* (1949) ICJ Rep 4 the ICJ declared that the mine-sweeping operation by the British Royal Navy in Albanian territorial waters was a violation of Albanian sovereignty. Albania did not seek damages and the Court held that 'This declaration is in accordance with the request made by Albania through her counsel, and is in itself appropriate satisfaction'.

Article 37(3) of the ILC Articles clearly establishes that satisfaction should not be out of proportion to the injury and should not take a form humiliating to the delinquent state.

11

The Law of Treaties

11.1 Introduction

The expression 'treaty' is used as a generic term to cover a multitude of international agreements and contractual engagements between states. These international agreements are called by various names including treaties, conventions, pacts, declarations, charters, concordats, protocols and covenants. They may be quasi-legislative or purely contractual. They may lay down rules binding upon states concerning new areas into which international law is expanding, or they may codify, clarify and supplement the already existing customary international law on a particular matter.

The Vienna Convention on the Law of Treaties 1969

The law of treaties was codified in the Vienna Convention on the Law of Treaties which came into force on 27 January 1980. By 1990 around 60 states (including the UK), were parties. Although the Convention only applies to treaties made after its entry into force, it is nevertheless important in that most of its provisions attempt to codify the customary law.

11.2 The formalities of a treaty

Article 2(1)(a) of the Vienna Convention on the Law of Treaties defines a treaty for the purposes of the Convention, as:

> '... an international agreement concluded between states in written form and governed by international law, whether embodied in a single instrument or in two or more related instruments, and whatever its particular designation.'

To qualify as a 'treaty' therefore, the agreement must satisfy the following criteria: it should be a written instrument or instruments between two or more parties; those parties must be endowed with international personality; it must be governed by international law; and it should be intended to create legal obligations.

A written instrument between two or more parties

Although the Vienna Convention does not apply to international agreements which are not made in writing, art 3 of the Convention expressly states that the legal force of such non-written agreements shall not be affected by that fact.

Article 3 of the Vienna Convention provides:

> 'The fact that the present Convention does not apply to international agreements concluded between states and other subjects of international law or between such other subjects of international law, or to international agreements not in written form, shall not affect:
> (a) the legal force of such agreements;
> (b) the application to them of any of the rules set forth in the present Convention to which they would be subject under international law independently of the Convention;
> (c) the application of the Convention to the relations of states as between themselves under international agreements to which other subjects of international law are also parties.'

Note, however, that art 102 of the Charter of the United Nations provides:

> '1. Every treaty and every international agreement entered into by any Member of the United Nations after the present Charter comes into force shall as soon as possible be registered with the Secretariat and published by it.
> 2. No party to any such treaty or international agreement which has not been registered in accordance with the provisions of paragraph 1 of this article may invoke that treaty or agreement before any organ of the United Nations.'

This requirement of registration and publication would seem to exclude verbal agreements from the status of 'treaty' as the term is understood and applied by the Charter of the United Nations with particular reference to the ICJ, the principal judicial organ of the UN.

A treaty must be between parties endowed with international personality

The Vienna Convention applies only to those international agreements concluded between states. Other subjects of international law such as international organisations are therefore excluded. The reason for limiting the Convention to treaties entered into between states was the fear that if other agreements were included, the differing rules of international law applicable to such agreements would make the Convention too complicated and delay its drafting.

But again art 3 of the Vienna Convention provides that notwithstanding the exclusion of such 'international agreements concluded between states and other subjects of international law or between such other subjects of international law' from the Convention, this does not affect 'the legal force of such agreements'.

Article 3 of the Vienna Convention therefore recognises that under customary international law entities other than states may have the requisite international personality allowing them to make treaties.

States

Article 6 of the Vienna Convention provides: 'Every state possesses capacity to conclude treaties'.

In this respect the Convention reflects customary international law. According to the International Law Commission commentary, the term 'state' is used in art 6:

> '... with the same meaning as in the Charter of the United Nations, the Statute of the Court, the [Vienna] Convention on Diplomatic Relations; ie it means a state for the purpose of international law.'

Federal states and colonial and similar territories are not within the Convention, but nevertheless they may have treaty-making powers.

Federal states

The Final Draft Articles on the Law of Treaties adopted by the International Law Commission, which served as a basis for discussions at the Vienna Conference (two sessions: 1968 and 1969), include the following paragraph, omitted from the Vienna Convention, regarding federal states: 'states members of a federal union may possess a capacity to conclude treaties if such capacity is admitted by the federal constitution and within the limits there laid down'.

An example of a federal state in which component states have the power to make treaties is the Federal Republic of Germany.

Article 32(3) of the German Constitution provides: 'In so far as the Lander have power to legislate, they may, with the consent of the Federal Government, conclude treaties with foreign states'.

In accordance with this article the Lander of Baden-Wurtemberg and Bavaria are parties with Austria and Switzerland to the Convention for the Protection of Lake Constance against Pollution 1960.

Colonial and other non-self-governing territories

Some colonial and non-self-governing territories have been recognised as having capacity to conclude treaties. For example, Canada, Australia, New Zealand, South Africa and India were invited to take part in the 1919 Paris Peace Conference and became parties to the Treaty of Versailles.

International organisations

The power of an international organisation to enter into a treaty can arise in two ways.

By express grant contained in the constitution of the organisation. For example, arts 57 and 63 of the Charter of the United Nations give the United Nations power to enter into relationship agreements with the various specialised agencies.

Article 43 of the Charter empowers the United Nations to enter into agreements with Member states on the provision of military contingents.

By implication, in order to carry out the duties imposed by the constitution upon the organisation. For example, in the Advisory Opinion on *Reparations for Injuries Suffered in the Service of the United Nations Case* (1949) ICJ Rep 174, it was stated:

> 'Under international law the organisation must be deemed to have those powers which, though not expressly provided for in the Charter, are conferred by necessary implication as being essential to the performance of their duty.'

Limitations on the implied powers

The existence of an implied treaty-making power does not mean that an organisation can conclude any sort of agreement. An organisation cannot act in total disregard of the limitations placed upon it in its constitution. Its treaty-making capacity must be compatible with the letter and spirit of its constitution. As Hackworth J stated in *Reparations for Injuries Suffered in the Service of the United Nations Case* (1949) ICJ Rep 174 at 178:

> 'Powers not expressed cannot freely be implied. Implied powers flow from a grant of express powers, and are limited to those that are "necessary" to the exercise of powers expressly granted.'

If the organisation did exceed its implied powers the act would be ineffective and the treaty void.

Individuals or corporations created under municipal law

Individuals and corporations have never been recognised as having the capacity to make treaties, whether with states, other individuals or with other international persons with treaty-making capacity. It is possible for a state to enter into a contract with an individual or a corporation, but such an agreement will not have the status of a treaty under international law.

In the *Anglo-Iranian Oil Company Case* (1952) ICJ Rep 93 the UK alleged that the 1933 concessionary agreement between the Iranian government and the Anglo-Iranian Oil Company was in the nature of an international agreement. The UK argument was founded upon the fact that the concession had been negotiated in order to settle a dispute between the UK and Iran which had been before the Council of the League of Nations and therefore the UK had played a part in its negotiation although it was not itself a party to the actual final agreement.

The Court held that the background against which the agreement was negotiated could not give the concession the international character suggested by the UK. The UK was not a party. It was therefore nothing more than a concessionary contract between a government and a foreign corporation.

The agreement must be governed by international law

The requirement that an agreement must be governed by international law represents a significant innovation compared to the position under customary international law. Under customary international law, international courts and commissions do not have jurisdiction over all cases concerning claims that a treaty is invalid, but only over those cases where the parties agree to submit the matter to such a court or commission.

Simply because two entities endowed with international personality and possessing treaty-making capacity enter into an agreement, it does not follow that the agreement is necessarily a treaty. Certain inter-state agreements can be subject to municipal law, either expressly or by implication.

For example, during the period 1966 to 1968 Denmark entered into a series of loan agreements with other states (eg Malawi) which stipulated that, except as otherwise provided therein, 'the Agreement and all rights and obligations deriving from it shall be governed by Danish law'.

There would seem to be no reason why an agreement must be governed exclusively by either international law or by municipal law. Many agreements between states are of a hybrid nature and as such are binding on the international plane as well as being directly governed by municipal law.

The International Law Commission Fourth Special Rapporteur stated in his First Report (1962):

> '... the Commission felt in 1959 that the element of subjection to international law is so essential a part of an international agreement that it should be expressly mentioned in the definition. There may be agreements between states, such as agreements for the acquisition of premises for diplomatic missions or for some purely commercial transaction, the incidents of which are regulated by the local law of one of the parties or by a private law system determined by reference to conflict of law principles. Whether in such cases the two states are internationally accountable to each other at all may be a nice question; but even if that were held to be so, it would not follow that the basis of their international accountability was a treaty obligation. At any rate, the Commission was clear that it ought

to confine the notion of an 'international agreement' for the purposes of the law of treaties to one, the whole formation and execution of which (as well as the obligation to execute) is governed by international law': Sir Humphrey Waldock (1962) 2 Yearbook of the International Law Commission 32.

The agreement should create a legal obligation

The intention to create legal relations is not mentioned in the Vienna Convention.

The International Law Commission's Rapporteur stated that 'insofar as this [requirement] may be relevant in any case, the element of intention is embraced in the phrase "governed by international law"'.

There are, however, practical reasons for excluding any specific reference to intention. States may wish to reach an agreement as to political intent without going to the extent of making it legally enforceable. Therefore, what may appear to be a treaty may in fact be devoid of any legal content. This is particularly true of the so-called 'joint declaration' by states, examples being the Atlantic Treaty of 1941 and the Cairo Declaration of 1943. Such declarations are statements of 'common principles' or 'common purpose' imposing no legal obligation upon the parties to pursue those policies.

Similarly, the Final Act of the Helsinki Conference on Security and Co-operation in Europe 1975 was stated to be: 'not eligible for registration under art 102 of the Charter of the United Nations' and the general understanding expressed at the conference was that the Act would not be binding in law.

However, such agreements, even if not creating rights and obligations directly, may provide the basis for new rights and obligations in the future. So that today, for instance, it is of little practical significance that the Universal Declaration of Human Rights adopted by the General Assembly in 1948 was agreed to by member states only on the understanding that it did not create binding obligations upon them.

11.3 Unilateral acts

Acts and conduct by governments, although not intended to formulate agreements may nevertheless result in legal effect.

Unilateral declarations

A state may accept obligations vis-à-vis other states by the making of a public declaration expressing a clear intention on its behalf.

In the *Legal Status of Eastern Greenland Case: Norway* v *Denmark* (1933) PCIJ Rep Ser A/B No 53 the Danish government notified the Norwegian government through the Danish minister in Norway that Denmark would not raise objections to Norway's claim to Spitzbergen. The intention was to obtain a reciprocal undertaking from the Norwegian government with respect to Denmark's claim to Greenland.

The Danish government stated that it was 'confident' that the Norwegian government 'would not make any difficulties in the settlement of this question'. The Norwegian Foreign Minister replied to the effect that his government would make no such difficulties. The Court held that even if this declaration by the Foreign Minister could not be considered as recognition of Denmark's claim to Greenland, it nevertheless created an obligation binding upon Norway to refrain from contesting Danish sovereignty over Greenland.

The Court stated:

> 'The Court considers it beyond all dispute that a reply of this nature given by the Minister of Foreign Affairs on behalf of his government in response to a request by the diplomatic representative of a foreign power, in regard to a question falling within his province, is binding upon the country to which the Minister belongs.'

Juridical nature of the declaration

The juridical nature of unilateral declarations was considered by the ICJ in the *Nuclear Tests Cases: Australia* v *France; New Zealand* v *France* (1974) ICJ Rep 253, 457.

Australia and New Zealand had sought a decision of the Court that the French testing of nuclear weapons in the atmosphere was contrary to international law. The French government refused to comply with the Court's interim order requiring it to refrain from commencing the tests until the Court reached a decision in the case.

However, in a series of public pronouncements, members of the French government had stated that France was going to commence underground testing in the following year and at a press conference the President of the Republic stated that he had 'made it clear that this round of atmospheric tests would be the last'.

The Court concluded that as these pronouncements were binding upon France the applicants had achieved their objective and therefore the dispute between the parties no longer existed. The Court said it had 'no doubt' that declarations made by way of unilateral acts, concerning legal or factual situations, may have the effect of creating legal obligations.

The criteria for such an obligation are:

1. the intention of the state making the declaration that it should be bound according to its terms; and
2. that the undertaking be given publicly. 'No subsequent acceptance of the declaration, nor even any reply or reaction from other states, is required for the declaration to take effect.'

When, as in the *Nuclear Tests Cases*, the declaration is not directed to a specific state or states but is merely expressed generally the question as to whether there is an intention to be legally bound will require very careful consideration.

In the *North Sea Continental Shelf Cases* (1969) ICJ Rep 3 the ICJ stated that the unilateral assumption of the obligations of a convention by conduct was 'not lightly to be presumed' and that 'a very consistent course of conduct' was required in such cases.

11.4 The making of treaties

Negotiation

This is carried out by the accredited representatives of the state in question. Article 7 provides that the representative of the state will be someone equipped with an instrument of 'full powers' or if it appears from the normal practice of the state that the person concerned has such powers. Article 7(2) of the Vienna Convention then indicates three categories of person who are deemed to have 'full powers':

1. Heads of State, heads of government and ministers of foreign affairs;
2. heads of diplomatic missions, ie ambassadors to the state concerned;
3. representatives accredited to international conferences or organisations.

Adoption of the text of a treaty

The adoption of the text is the first stage of the conclusion of a treaty.

Article 9 of the Vienna Convention provides:

'1. The adoption of the text of a treaty takes place by the consent of all the states participating in its drawing up except as provided in paragraph 2.
2. The adoption of the text of a treaty at an international conference takes place by the vote of two-thirds of the states present and voting, unless by the same majority they shall decide to apply a different rule.'

Therefore, consent remains the general rule for bilateral treaties and for those treaties drawn up between few states. But art 9(2) recognises that it would be unrealistic to demand unanimity as the general rule for the adoption of treaties drawn up at conferences or within organisations, where the widest possible measure of agreement between the participants is desirable.

The adoption of the text does not by itself create any obligations.

Authentication of the treaty

The authentication of the text of the treaty in the form which the parties may later ratify may be done in a number of ways. The method of authentication to be adopted is a matter for the parties themselves to agree, but the two usual methods are: signing and initialling. The text may, however, be authenticated in other ways, eg by incorporating the text in the final act of the conference.

Consent to be bound

Article 11 of the Vienna Convention provides: 'The consent of a state to be bound by a treaty may be expressed by signature, exchange of instruments constituting a treaty, ratification, acceptance, approval or accession; or by any other means if so agreed'.

The traditional methods of expressing consent to a treaty are signature, ratification and accession.

Signature
The legal effects of signature are as follows.

1. The signing of a treaty may represent simply an authentication of its text.
2. Where such a signature is subject to ratification, acceptance or approval, signature does not establish consent to be bound.

   In the case of a treaty which is only to become binding upon ratification, acceptance or approval there is some uncertainty as to the relationship of the parties to the instrument before the appropriate step is taken. Such a treaty, unless declaratory of customary law, will not be enforceable against a party until that step is taken.

   In the context of the *North Sea Continental Shelf Cases* (above) the Federal Republic of Germany had been a signatory to the Geneva Convention on the Continental Shelf 1958, but had not ratified it. The Court held that art 6 of that Convention was not binding on the Federal Republic because its signature had only been 'a preliminary step: it did not ratify the Convention, is not a party to it and therefore cannot be contractually bound by its provisions'.

   However, under art 18 of the Convention, the act of signing the treaty creates an obligation of good faith on the part of the signatory: to refrain from acts calculated to frustrate the objects of the treaty; and to submit the treaty to the appropriate constitutional machinery for approval.

   Signature does not, however, create an obligation to ratify.
3. Where a treaty is not subject to ratification, acceptance or approval, signature will signify consent to be bound.

   In such cases guidance is provided by art 12(1) of the Vienna Convention which provides:

   > 'The consent of a state to be bound by a treaty is expressed by the signature of its representative when:
   > (a) the treaty provides that signature shall have that effect;
   > (b) it is otherwise established that the negotiating states were agreed that signature should have that effect; or
   > (c) the intention of the state to give that effect to the signature appears from the full powers of its representative or was expressed during the negotiations.'

Ratification
Meaning of ratification. Ratification is the formal act whereby one state declares its acceptance of the terms of the treaty and undertakes to observe them. Ratification is used to describe two distinct procedural acts, one municipal and one international.

1. *Ratification in municipal law.* In the municipal law sense ratification may be the formal act of the appropriate organ of the state and may be called ratification in

the constitutional sense. For example, according to English law, ratification is effected in the name of the Crown.

2. *Ratification in international law.* In the international law sense ratification is the procedure which brings a treaty into force, ie formal exchange or deposit of the instrument of ratification. It is not concerned with the question as to whether a state has complied with the requirements of its constitutional law.

Reasons why ratification may be required. Despite the fact that a treaty may be made effective by signature alone in many cases states still insist upon formal ratification. There are several reasons for this.

1. Historically the subsequent ratification by the sovereign prevented diplomats from exceeding their instructions and confirmed the power of the representative to negotiate the treaty.
2. The delay between signature and ratification allows the sovereign time to reconsider the matter and allows time for expression of public opinion on the matter.
3. Consent of the legislature may be required for ratification in accordance with the state municipal law.

Ratification under the Vienna Convention. Article 14(1) of the Vienna Convention provides:

> 'The consent of a state to be bound by a treaty is expressed by ratification when:
> (a) the treaty provides for such consent to be expressed by ratification;
> (b) it is otherwise established that the negotiating states were agreed that ratification should be required;
> (c) the representatives of the state has signed the treaty subject to ratification; or
> (d) the intention of the state to sign the treaty subject to ratification appears from the full powers of its representative or was expressed during the negotiations.'

Thus, if a treaty should contain no express provision on the subject of ratification art 14 will regulate the matter by reference to the intention of the parties.

Ratification by performance. Performance of a treaty may constitute tacit ratification. If a state successfully claims rights under an unratified treaty it will be estopped from alleging that it is not bound by the treaty.

Accession

Accession or adherence or adhesion occurs when a state which did not sign a treaty formally accepts its provisions. Accession may occur before or after the treaty has entered into force. It is only possible if it is provided for in the treaty, or if all the parties to the treaty agree that the acceding state should be allowed to accede. Accession, therefore, has the same effect as signature and ratification combined.

Reservations

A state may be willing to accept most provisions of a treaty, but it may, for various reasons, wish to object to other provisions of the treaty.

Definition of a reservation
A reservation is defined in art 2(1)(d) of the Vienna Convention as:

> '... a unilateral statement, however phrased or named, made by a state, when signing, ratifying, accepting, approving or acceding to a treaty, whereby it purports to exclude or to modify the legal effect of certain provisions of the treaty in their application to that state.'

The effect of such a reservation depends upon whether it is accepted or rejected by the other states concerned.

Traditional view
The traditional view was that reservations were valid only if the treaty concerned permitted reservations and if all the other parties to the treaty accepted the reservation. In 1927 for instance, the League of Nations adopted the following approach to reservations with regard to multilateral treaties:

> 'In order that any reservation whatever may be validly made in regard to a clause of the treaty, it is essential that this reservation should be accepted by all the other contracting parties, as would have been the case if it had been put forward in the course of the negotiations. If not, the reservation, like the signature to which it is attached, is null and void.'

Limitation of the traditional approach
In the case of a bilateral treaty or a treaty involving few parties no real difficulty arose in deciding whether a reservation had been accepted by the other party. However, the increasing numbers of multilateral treaties made the situation more complicated, and particularly with regard to those conventions drafted through the auspices of the United Nations it was soon apparent that this traditional approach would have to change.

Reservations to the Convention on the Prevention and the Punishment of the Crime of Genocide (1951) ICJ Rep 15
Following the adoption of the Convention on the Prevention and Punishment of the Crime of Genocide by the General Assembly of the United Nations in 1948 a conflict of opinion arose on the admissibility of reservations to the Convention. The Convention contains no reservations clause and so questions as to the effects of the reservations were submitted to the ICJ for an advisory opinion.

The Court held:

> '... insofar as concerns the Convention on the Prevention and Punishment of the Crime of Genocide, in the event of a state ratifying or acceding to the Convention subject to a reservation made either on ratification or on accession, or on signature followed by ratification,

On Question I:

that a state which has made and maintained a reservation which has been objected to by one or more of the parties to the Convention but not by others, can be regarded as being a party to the Convention if the reservation is compatible with the object and purpose of the Convention; otherwise, that state cannot be regarded as being a party to the Convention.

On Question II:

(a) that if a party to the Convention objects to a reservation which it considers to be incompatible with the object and purpose of the Convention, it can in fact consider that the reserving state is not a party to the Convention;

(b) that if, on the other hand, a party accepts the reservation as being compatible with the object and purpose of the Convention, it can in fact consider that the reserving state is a party to the Convention.

On Question III:

(a) that an objection to a reservation made by a signatory state which has not yet ratified the Convention can have the legal effect indicated in the reply to Question I only upon ratification. Until that moment it merely serves as a notice to the other state of the eventual attitude of the signatory state;

(b) that an objection to a reservation made by a state which is entitled to sign or accede but which has not yet done so, is without legal effect.'

The Advisory Opinion therefore laid the foundations for a more flexible approach to the problem of reservations to multilateral treaties. However, the classification of reservations into those that are 'compatible' and those that are 'incompatible' with the 'object and purpose' of a Convention was rejected by the International Law Commission who considered the test too subjective and preferred the traditional rule of unanimous consent.

Present approach of the United Nations
Faced with this conflict of opinion between the traditional view and the view of the Court as expressed in the *Genocide Case*, the General Assembly of the United Nations in 1952 requested the Secretary General to follow the ICJ's Advisory Opinion in the *Genocide Case*. The Secretary-General as depositary for the Genocide Convention and, as depositary of future multilateral conventions, was asked to continue to act as depositary in connection with the deposit of documents containing reservations or objections, without passing upon the legal effect of such documents; and to communicate the text of such documents relating to reservations or objectives to all states concerned, leaving it to each state to draw legal consequences from such communications.

In 1959 this directive was extended to cover all conventions concluded under the auspices of the United Nations, unless they contain provisions to the contrary.

Position under the Vienna Convention
Articles 19–21 of the Vienna Convention follow the principles laid down by the Court in the *Genocide Case* but do, however, make some concessions to the

traditional rule by recognising that every reservation is incompatible with certain types of treaty unless accepted unanimously.

Permissible and impermissible reservations

The Vienna Convention distinguishes between 'permissible' and 'impermissible' reservations. This distinction derives from the will of the parties in that they may either prohibit certain reservations or expressly authorise certain reservations.

Freedom to formulate the reservation

Article 19 of the Vienna Convention provides as follows:

'A state may, when signing, ratifying, accepting approving or acceding to a treaty, formulate a reservation unless:
(a) the reservation is prohibited by the treaty;
(b) the treaty provides that only specified reservations, which do not include the reservation in question, may be made; or
(c) in cases not falling under sub-paragraphs (a) and (b), the reservation is incompatible with the object and purpose of the treaty.'

Acceptance of and objection to reservations other than those expressly authorised by a treaty

Article 20 of the Vienna Convention provides as follows:

'1. A reservation expressly authorised by a treaty does not require any subsequent acceptance by the other contracting states unless the treaty so provides.
2. When it appears from the limited number of the negotiating states and the object and purpose of a treaty that the application of the treaty in its entirety between all the parties is an essential condition of the consent of each one to be bound by the treaty, a reservation requires acceptance by all the parties.
3. When a treaty is a constituent instrument of an international organisation and unless it otherwise provides, a reservation requires the acceptance of the competent organ of that organisation.
4. In cases not falling under the preceding paragraphs and unless the treaty otherwise provides:
(a) acceptance by another contracting state of a reservation constitutes the reserving state a party to the treaty in relation to that other state if or when the treaty is in force for those states;
(b) an objection by another contracting state to a reservation does not preclude the entry into force of the treaty as between the objecting and reserving states unless a contrary intention is definitely expressed by the objecting state;
(c) an act expressing a state's consent to be bound by the treaty and containing a reservation is effective as soon as at least one other contracting state has accepted the reservation.
5. For the purpose of paragraphs (2) and (4) and unless the treaty otherwise provides, a reservation is considered to have been accepted by a state if it shall have raised no objection to the reservation by the end of a period of twelve months after it was notified of the reservation or by the date on which it expressed its consent to be bound by the treaty, whichever is later.'

The beneficial results of this more flexible approach are obvious. In its commentary the International Law Commission stated:

> 'The majority of reservations relate to a particular point which a particular state for one reason or another finds difficult to accept, and the effect of the reservation on the general integrity of the treaty is often minimal; and the same is true even if the reservation in question relates to a comparatively important provision of the treaty, so long as the reservation is not made by more than a few states. In short, the integrity of the treaty would only be materially affected if a reservation of a somewhat substantial kind were to be formulated by a number of states. This might no doubt, happen; but even then the treaty itself would remain the master agreement between the other participating states. What is essential to ensure both the effectiveness and the integrity of the treaty is that a sufficient number of states should become parties to it, accepting the great bulk of its provisions ... But when today the number of the negotiating states may be upwards of one hundred states with very diverse cultural, economic and political conditions, it seems necessary to assume that the power to make reservations without the risk of being totally excluded by the objection of one or even a few states may be a factor in promoting a more general acceptance of multilateral treaties.'

Interpretative declarations

Some states have adopted the practice of classifying as reservations declarations which are no more than statements as to their understanding or interpretation of a particular treaty provision.

The International Law Commission has commented:

> 'States ... not infrequently make declarations as to their understanding of some matter or as to their interpretation of a particular provision. Such a declaration may be a mere clarification of the state's position or it may amount to a reservation, according as to whether it does or does not vary or exclude the application of the terms of the treaty as adopted.'

The test is the effect the statement purports to have, and it turns upon whether the statement seeks to exclude or modify the legal effect of the provisions of the treaty.

The point is illustrated by the USSR's reservation to art 11(1) of the Vienna Convention on Diplomatic Relations 1961 that 'any difference of opinion regarding the size of a diplomatic mission should be settled by agreement between the sending state and the receiving state'.

Given that art 11 allowed the receiving state the sole power to limit the size of a mission in the absence of agreement, a number of states objected to this reservation on the ground that it did not 'modify any rights or obligations'. In other words, it was not a true reservation.

Effect of such a declaration

It has become increasingly common for a state to couch a unilateral statement in the language of an interpretative declaration and announce that it is only prepared to enter into the treaty on the basis of its interpretation being accepted. Such an approach causes a dilemma for the other parties to the treaty. If the other states accept the statement as a reservation and therefore as being impermissible this may lead to one of two courses: disregarding the 'reservation' as a nullity; or rejecting the treaty relations entirely.

The better view would be to accept the declaring state's characterisation, but refuse to accept the interpretation thus forcing the issue to some form of independent adjudication as a matter of treaty interpretation.

If a statement is determined to be an interpretative declaration although some parties may accept it and others not, there is no question of non-acceptance as if it were an objection for purposes of arts 20 and 21, so as to exclude the affected provision or even exclude the treaty from entering into force between the reserving state and the objecting state.

A dispute over an interpretative declaration goes to interpretation of the treaty and no more. The only problem arises when there is a dispute as to whether the expression is a true reservation or an interpretative declaration. This problem can be disposed of by recourse to a recognised judicial tribunal.

The issue arose for consideration in the *UK/France Continental Shelf Arbitration* (1977) 54 ILR 6 where France argued that a statement it had made at the time of the Geneva Convention on the Continental Shelf 1958 was in fact a reservation. The UK argued, in contrast, that it was an interpretative declaration and that it, therefore, had no binding force. The tribunal, however, held that it was a reservation as it expressed a condition to the French acceptance of the treaty obligations. Similarly, in the recent decision in *Belilos* v *Switzerland* (1988) 10 EHRR 466 before the European Court of Human Rights, the question arose as to whether a Swiss statement was an interpretative declaration or a reservation. The Court held that the character of the statement would not depend on how it was described. If the statement purported to exclude or vary the legal effect of the treaty it would be a reservation. In the case in issue the Court held that the statement did constitute a reservation but that it was an unpermissible reservation and that, as a result, it had no legal effect.

Entry into force

Where the treaty does not specify a date, there is a presumption that the treaty is intended to enter into force as soon as all the negotiating states have expressed their consent to be bound by it.

In the case of multilateral treaties negotiated by many states it is very unlikely that they will all proceed to ratify it. In such a case the treaty usually provides that it shall enter into force when it has been ratified by a specified number of states. When the minimum number of ratifications is reached the treaty enters into force between those states which have ratified it.

Registration

Article 102 of the Charter of the United Nations provides as follows:

> '1. Every treaty and every international agreement entered into by any Member of the United Nations after the present Charter comes into force shall as soon as possible be registered with the Secretariat and published by it.
>
> 2. No party to any such treaty or international agreement which has not been registered in accordance with the provision of paragraph (1) of this article may invoke that treaty or engagement before any organ of the United Nations.'

Article 102 was intended to prevent states from entering into secret agreements without the knowledge of their nationals, and without the knowledge of other states, whose interests might be affected by such agreements.

11.5 Validity of treaties

Article 42(1) of the Vienna Convention provides that 'The validity of a treaty or of the consent of a state to be bound by a treaty may be impeached only through the application of the present Convention'.

This is to prevent a state from attempting to evade an inconvenient treaty obligation by alleging spurious grounds of invalidity.

Non-compliance with provisions of municipal law

Many states have provisions in their constitutions which prevent their government from entering into treaties, or into certain types of treaty, without the consent of the legislature or some organ of the legislature.

Effect of non-compliance with municipal law

What is the position if a competent representative, ie Head of State, foreign secretary, etc disregards the requirements of his state's constitutional law when entering into a treaty? Is the treaty valid or not?

The extent to which such constitutional limitations on the treaty-making power can be invoked on the international plane is a matter of controversy and the following views have been put forward:

1. the treaty is void if there is a failure to comply with the requirements of the state's constitutional law;
2. the treaty is only void if the constitutional rule in question is 'notorious', ie a well-known constitutional limitation;
3. the treaty is valid irrespective of non-compliance with the constitutional law of the state;
4. the treaty is valid except where one party to the treaty knew that the other party was acting in breach of a constitutional requirement.

An additional view, and the one favoured by most states, is reflected in art 46 of the Vienna Convention, which provides:

'1. A state may not invoke the fact that its consent to be bound by a treaty has been expressed in violation of a provision of its internal law regarding competence to conclude treaties as invalidating its consent unless that violation was manifest and concerned a rule of its internal law of fundamental importance.

2. A violation is manifest if it would be objectively evident to any state conducting itself in the matter in accordance with normal practice and in good faith.'

Treaties entered into by a representative who lacks authority

Who is a representative?

Article 7(1) of the Vienna Convention provides:

'A person is considered as representing a state for the purpose of ... expressing the consent of the state to be bound by a treaty if: he produces appropriate full powers; or it appears from the practice of the states concerned or from other circumstances that their intention was to consider that person as representing the state for such purposes and to dispense with full powers.'

Article 7(2) of the Vienna Convention provides:

'In virtue of their functions and without having to produce full powers, the following are considered as representing their state: Heads of State, heads of government and ministers for foreign affairs ... heads of diplomatic missions ... representatives accredited by states.'

Article 8 of the Vienna Convention provides:

'An act relating to the conclusion of a treaty performed by a person who cannot be considered under art 7 as authorised to represent a state for that purpose is without legal effect unless afterwards confirmed by that state.'

Specific restrictions on authority

If the authority of a representative to express the consent of his state to be bound by a particular treaty has been made subject to a specific restriction, then if he fails to observe the restriction what is the position?

Article 47 of the Vienna Convention provides:

'If the authority of a representative to express the consent of a state to be bound by a particular treaty has been made subject to a specific restriction, his omission to observe that restriction may not be invoked as invalidating the consent expressed by him unless the restriction was notified to the other negotiating states prior to his expressing such consent.'

Corruption of a state representative

Article 50 of the Vienna Convention provides:

'If the expression of a state's consent to be bound by a treaty has been procured through the corruption of its representative directly or indirectly by another negotiating state, the state may invoke such corruption as invalidating its consent to be bound by the treaty.'

The 'corruption' must be a 'substantial influence'. A small courtesy or favour shown to a representative will be insufficient.

Error

Article 48 of the Vienna Convention provides:

> '1. A state may invoke an error in a treaty as invalidating its consent to be bound by the treaty if the error relates to a fact or situation which was assumed by that state to exist at the time when the treaty was concluded and formed an essential basis of its consent to be bound by the treaty.
> 2. Paragraph (1) shall not apply if the state in question contributed by its own conduct to the error or if the circumstances were such as to put that state on notice of a possible error.
> 3. An error relating only to the wording of the text or a treaty does not affect its validity.'

Thus, only if the error is essential or fundamental to the obligations that a state believed it had undertaken will it be a reason for invalidating the treaty.

Article 48 is reflective of current law. As the International Law Commission pointed out, in practice most alleged errors 'concern geographical errors, mostly errors on maps'.

In the *Temple of Preah Vihear Case* (1962) ICJ Rep 6 the ICJ was asked to rule that Cambodia and not Thailand had sovereignty over the Temple of Preah Vihear. In 1904 the boundary between Cambodia (a French protectorate) and Thailand (then Siam) was determined by treaty between France and Siam. The treaty stated that it was to follow the watershed line and surveys were conducted by experts on the basis of which a map was prepared. The map placed the Temple in Cambodia and it was this map upon which Cambodia relied for its claim. Thailand argued, inter alia, that the map embodied a material error in that it did not follow the watershed line as required by the treaty. This was argued despite the fact that the map had been received and accepted by the Siamese. The Court rejected Thailand's arguments as follows:

> 'It is an established rule of law that the plea of error cannot be allowed as an element vitiating consent if the party advancing it contributed by its own conduct to the error, or could have avoided it, or if the circumstances were such as to put that party on notice of a possible error. The Court considers that the character and qualifications of the persons who saw the ... map on the Siamese side would alone make it difficult for Thailand to plead error in law.'

Fraud

Article 49 of the Vienna Convention provides:

> 'If a state has been induced to conclude a treaty by the fraudulent conduct of another negotiating state, the state may invoke the fraud as invalidating its consent to be bound by the treaty.'

Coercion of a state's representatives

Article 51 of the Vienna Convention provides:

> 'The expression of a state's consent to be bound by a treaty which has been procured by the coercion of its representative through acts or threats directed against him shall be without any legal effect.'

Such coercion may include, for example, blackmailing threats or threats against the representative's family. Such coercion must be directed at the representative personally and not at coercion of him through a threat of action against his state.

Coercion of a state

The traditional doctrine prior to the Covenant of the League of Nations was that the validity of a treaty was not affected by the fact that it had been brought about by the threat of or the use of force. However, art 2(4) of the Charter of the United Nations which prohibits the threat or use of force, together with other developments, now justifies the conclusion that a treaty procured by such coercion shall be void.

Article 52 of the Vienna Convention provides:

> 'A treaty is void if its conclusion has been procured by the threat or use of force in violation of the principles of international law embodied in the Charter of the United Nations.'

This modern rule against the use of force does not operate retroactively. If a treaty was procured by force before the use of force was made illegal the validity of the treaty is not affected by this subsequent change in the law.

Force, in the context of art 52, does not include 'economic and political' pressure. An amendment defining force to include these matters was withdrawn.

Unequal treaties

Soviet writers have propounded the doctrine of 'equal treaties', according to which treaties concluded in circumstances where there is inequality of the contracting parties are not legally binding:

> 'The principle that international treaties must be observed does not extend to treaties which are imposed by force, and which are unequal in character ...
>
> Equal treaties are treaties concluded on the basis of the equality of the parties; unequal treaties are those which do not fulfil this elementary requirement. Unequal treaties are not legally binding.'

Examples of such treaties are the Munich Agreement 1938 and the Anglo-Egyptian Treaty of Alliance 1936.

Western jurists oppose the doctrine on the ground of its vagueness but it is attracting considerable support especially from the newly independent states.

However, the International Court rejected the legality of such a principle. In *Case Concerning the Territorial Dispute: Libyan Arab Jamahiriya* v *Chad* (1994) ICJ Rep 6 Libya argued that a treaty negotiated in 1955 between itself and France, although valid, should be interpreted favourably towards Libya because, at the time of negotiation, Libya lacked experience in the negotiation of international agreements especially compared to the experience of the French negotiators. The Court refused to recognise this factor as a justification for interpreting the treaty in favour of Libya and hence the doctrine of unequal treaties appears to have lost its relevance.

Conflict with a peremptory norm of general international law – ius cogens

Article 53 of the Vienna Convention deals with the topic of conflict between the rules of ius cogens and the provisions of a treaty. It provides:

> 'A treaty is void if, at the time of its conclusion, it conflicts with a peremptory norm of general international law. For the purposes of the present Convention, a peremptory norm of general international law is a norm accepted and recognised by the international community of states as a whole as a norm from which no derogation is permitted and which can be modified only by a subsequent norm of general international law having the same character.'

Article 64 of the Vienna Convention further provides:

> 'If a new peremptory norm of general international law emerges, any existing treaty which is in conflict with that norm becomes void and terminates.'

(On ius cogens: see Chapter 2, section 2.11.)

11.6 Application of treaties

Territorial application

Article 29 of the Vienna Convention provides:

> 'Unless a different intention appears from the treaty or is otherwise established, a treaty is binding upon each party in respect of its entire territory.'

In the absence of any territorial clause or other indication of a contrary intention, a treaty is presumed to apply to all the territories for which the contracting states are internationally responsible. So treaties made by the UK automatically extend to its overseas territories unless the treaty indicates otherwise.

Inconsistent treaties

Where a party to a treaty subsequently enters into another treaty with overlapping provisions then the position is regulated by art 30 of the Vienna Convention which provides as follows:

'1. Subject to art 103 of the Charter of the United Nations, the rights and obligations of states parties to successive treaties relating to the same subject matter shall be determined in accordance with the following paragraphs.

2. When a treaty specifies that it is subject to, or that it is not to be considered as incompatible with, an earlier or later treaty, the provisions of that other treaty prevail.

3. When all the parties to the earlier treaty are parties also to the later treaty but the earlier treaty is not terminated or suspended in operation under art 59, the earlier treaty applies only to the extent that its provisions are compatible with those of the later treaty.

4. When the parties to the later treaty do not include all the parties to the earlier one:

(a) as between states parties to both treaties the same rule applies as in paragraph (3).

(b) as between a state party to both treaties and a state party to only one of the treaties, the treaty to which both states are parties governs their mutual rights and obligations.

5. Paragraph (4) is without prejudice to art 41, or to any question of the termination or suspension of the operation of a treaty under art 60 or to any question of responsibility which may arise for a state from the conclusion or application of a treaty the provisions of which are incompatible with its obligations towards another state under another treaty.'

Third states

The general rule

The general rule is that a treaty applies only between the parties to it, and this principle is a corollary of the principle of consent and the sovereignty and independence of states.

Article 34 of the Vienna Convention provides: 'A treaty does not create either obligations or rights for a third state without its consent'.

This general rule is known by the maxim pacta tertiis nec nocent nec prosunt and art 34 undoubtedly reflects customary international law in this respect.

Exceptions to the general rule

Whether such exceptions exist is a matter of controversy. The International Law Commission was of firm opinion that a treaty cannot of itself create obligations for non-parties.

Article 35 of the Vienna Convention provides:

'An obligation arises for a third state from a provision of a treaty if the parties to the treaty intend the provision to be the means of establishing the obligation and the third state expressly accepts that obligation in writing.'

The International Law Commission commenting upon this provision acknowledged that the requirements in it are so strict that when they are met:

'... there is, in effect, a second collateral agreement between the parties to the treaty, on the one hand and the third state on the other; and that the juridical basis of the latters obligation is not the treaty itself but the collateral agreement.'

However, two exceptions to the general rule have been recognised.

1. A treaty may become binding on non-parties if it becomes a part of international

customary law. An example is the 1907 Hague Convention on the rules of land warfare which now reflect customary international law and therefore have application to states generally.

2. A treaty may provide for sanctions to be imposed on aggressor states which violate the law.

In this respect the effect of art 2(6) of the Charter of the United Nations must be noted. Article 2(6) provides:

'The Organisation shall ensure that states which are not Members of the United Nations act in accordance with these Principles so far as may be necessary for the maintenance of international peace and security.'

One view is that this provision creates duties and liabilities for non-members of the Organisation to impose sanctions under the enforcement provisions of the Charter.

However, it can be argued that the only justification for such an interpretation would be that the principles set out in art 2 of the Charter of the United Nations reflect customary international law.

Can a treaty confer rights on a third party?

Some treaties contain provisions in favour of specified third states or in respect of states generally. Examples of such third party rights are contained for instance in the treaty provisions guaranteeing freedom of passage for ships through the Suez and Kiel Canals. For example, in the Convention Respecting Free Navigation of the Suez Canal 1888 art 1 provides: 'The Suez Maritime Canal shall always be free and open, in time of war as in time of peace, to every vessel of commerce or of war, without distinction of flag'.

When, if at all, does such a right conferred upon a third state become established and enforceable by it?

Two opposing views have been expressed on this point:

1. the accepted view is that the third state may only claim the benefit if it assents, either expressly or impliedly, to the creation of the right;
2. the right created in favour of the third party is not conditional upon any express act of acceptance by the third party.

The International Law Commission adopted the view that in practice the effects of the two opposing views would be substantially the same. The matter was given effect in art 36 of the Vienna Convention which provides:

'1. A right arises for a third state from a provision of a treaty if the parties to the treaty intend the provision to accord that right either to the third state, or to a group of states to which it belongs, or to all states, and the third state assents thereto. Its assent shall be presumed so long as the contrary is not indicated, unless the treaty otherwise provides.

2. A state exercising a right in accordance with paragraph (1) shall comply with the conditions for its exercise provided for in the treaty or established in conformity with the treaty.'

So this article creates a presumption of assent on the part of the third state.

Revocation and modification of third party rights
Article 37 of the Vienna Convention provides:

'1. When an obligation has arisen for a third state in conformity with art 35, the obligation may be revoked or modified only with the consent of the parties to the treaty and of the third state, unless it is established that they had otherwise agreed.
2. When a right has arisen for a third state in conformity with art 36, the right may not be revoked or modified by the parties if it is established that the right was intended not to be revocable or subject to modification without the consent of the third state.'

11.7 Amendment and modification of treaties

Amendment

The normal method of amending a treaty is by the unanimous agreement of the parties and art 39 of the Vienna Convention provides that: 'A treaty may be amended by agreement between the parties'.

If all the parties agree to the amendment no difficulty arises. But in a large multilateral convention it may not be possible to obtain unanimous agreement to a proposed amendment.

Many treaties contain provisions for an amendment procedure
For example, art 109 of the Charter of the United Nations provides for the holding of a General Conference of Member states 'for the purpose of reviewing the present Charter'.

Other multilateral treaties provide for possible revision at the end of specified periods. For example, art 312 of the UN Convention on the Law of the Sea 1982 provides that any party, after the expiry of ten years from the entry into force of the Convention, may request the revision of the Convention by a notification in writing to the United Nations Secretary General.

Cases where the treaty contains no reference to amendment
In these cases art 40 of the Vienna Convention provides as follows:

'1. Unless the treaty otherwise provides, the amendment of multilateral treaties shall be governed by the following paragraphs.
2. Any proposal to amend a multilateral treaty as between all the parties must be notified to all the contracting states, each one of which shall have the right to take part in:
(a) the decision as to the action to be taken in regard to such proposals;
(b) the negotiation and conclusion of any agreement for the amendment of the treaty.

3. Every state entitled to become a party to the treaty shall also be entitled to become a party to the treaty as amended.

4. The amending agreement does not bind any state already a party to the treaty which does not become a party to the amending agreement; art 30, paragraph (4(b)) applies in relation to such state.

5. Any state which becomes a party to the treaty after the entry into force of the amending agreement shall, failing an expression of a different intention by that state:

(a) be considered as a party to the treaty as amended; and

(b) be considered as a party to the unamended treaty in relation to any party to the treaty not bound by the amending agreement.'

Effects of amendment

In general, therefore, an amendment will only bind parties that have agreed to it and if one state has agreed to the amendment and another state has not, then the terms of the original treaty will remain operative between them.

'Legislative' amendment

In some cases a state may consent in advance to accept amendments agreed upon by a majority of the parties to the treaty. The obvious case is when the original treaty provides for its amendments to have effect if supported by a specified majority of contracting states.

For example, art 108 of the Charter of the United Nations provides:

'Amendments to the present Charter shall come into force for all members of the United Nations when they have been adopted by a vote of two-thirds of the Members of the General Assembly and ratified in accordance with their respective constitutional processes by two-thirds of the members of the United Nations, including all the permanent members of the Security Council.'

Modification

This occurs where a number of parties to the treaty formally agree to modify the effects of the treaty amongst themselves, while continuing to be bound by the treaty in their relations with the other parties.

This matter is covered by art 41 of the Vienna Convention:

'1. Two or more of the parties to a multilateral treaty may conclude an agreement to modify the treaty as between themselves alone if:

(a) the possibility of such a modification is provided for by the treaty; or

(b) the modification in question is not prohibited by the treaty and

(i) does not affect the enjoyment by the other parties of their rights under the treaty or the performance of their obligations;

(ii) does not relate to a provision, derogation from which is incompatible with the effective execution of the object and purpose of the treaty as a whole.

2. Unless in a case falling under paragraph (1(a)) the treaty otherwise provides, the parties in question shall notify the other parties of their intention to conclude the agreement and of the modification to the treaty for which it provides.'

Modification by subsequent practice

A consistent practice, if it establishes common consent of the parties to be bound by a different rule from that laid down in the treaty, will have the effect of modifying the treaty. The following is an illustration of the process in operation.

The Italian Peace Treaty of 1947 was signed and ratified by nearly 20 states. It provided for the setting up of a Free Territory of Trieste, but this proved impracticable owing to disagreements between the Great Powers. It was subsequently agreed by four of the signatories that Italy and Yugoslavia should each administer half the territory. This agreement was acted upon by Yugoslavia and Italy and was not objected to by the other states. Thus, the terms of the original Peace Treaty were modified by subsequent practice.

11.8 Interpretation of treaties

The Vienna Convention states the general rules as follows in art 31:

'1. A treaty shall be interpreted in good faith in accordance with the ordinary meaning to be given to the terms of the treaty in their context and in the light of its object and purpose.
2. The context for the purpose of the interpretation of a treaty shall comprise, in addition to the text, including its preamble and annexes:
(a) any agreement relating to the treaty which was made between all the parties in connection with the conclusion of the treaty;
(b) any instrument which was made by one or more parties in connection with the conclusion of the treaty and accepted by the other parties as an instrument related to the treaty.
3. There shall be taken into account, together with the context:
(a) any subsequent agreement between the parties regarding the interpretation of the treaty or the application of its provisions;
(b) any subsequent practice in the application of the treaty which establishes the agreement of the parties regarding its interpretation;
(c) any relevant rules of international law applicable in the relations between the parties.
4. A special meaning shall be given to a term if it is established that the parties so intended.'

Article 32 of the Vienna Convention further provides:

'Recourse may be had to supplementary means of interpretation, including the preparatory work of the treaty and the circumstances of its conclusion, in order to confirm the meaning resulting from the application of art 31, or to determine the meaning when the interpretation according to art 31:
(a) leaves the meaning ambiguous or obscure; or
(b) leads to a result which is manifestly absurd or unreasonable.'

The Vienna Convention lays emphasis on a textual approach to interpretation. The words used should be given their natural and ordinary meaning. If the words used are clear and unambiguous then an international tribunal must give effect to the treaty in the sense required by the clear and unambiguous wording, unless some valid ground can be shown for interpreting the provision otherwise.

In the *Competence of the General Assembly for the Admission of a State to the United Nations Case* (1950) ICJ Rep 4 the ICJ stated the position as follows:

> 'The Court considers it necessary to say that the first duty of a tribunal which is called upon to interpret and apply the provisions of a treaty, is to endeavour to give effect to them in their natural and ordinary meaning in the context in which they occur. If the relevant words in their natural and ordinary meaning make sense in their context, that is an end of the matter ... When the Court can give effect to a provision of a treaty by giving to the words used in it their natural and ordinary meaning, it may not interpret the words seeking to give them some other meaning.'

The textural approach includes the following principles:

1. the words used should be given their ordinary and natural meaning;
2. the words must be interpreted in the context of the treaty as a whole;
3. the natural and ordinary meaning must be unambiguous;
4. the ordinary and natural meaning must not lead to an absurd or unreasonable result.

In addition to the textual approach, attention must also be drawn to the 'objects and purposes' test, otherwise known as the principle of effectiveness. In the *Interpretation of Peace Treaties with Bulgaria, Hungary and Romania (Second Phase)* (1950) ICJ Rep 221 the Court interpreted the effectiveness principle narrowly, holding that the duty of the Court was to interpret treaties, not to revise them. In the *International Status of South West Africa* (1950) ICJ Rep 128, however, the Court's opinion that the UN trusteeship system had succeeded the mandate system under the League of Nations was, arguably, based on the notion of effectiveness as there was no clear indication of this in the Charter. Of interest, also, is the strong emphasis in favour of effectiveness adopted by the European Court of Justice in its interpretation and application of the Treaty of Rome: see, for example, *Van Gend en Loos* [1963] ECR 1.

11.9 Termination of treaties

The rule, pacta sunt servanda, is the fundamental principle of the law of treaties and is expressed in art 26 of the Vienna Convention: 'Every treaty in force is binding upon the parties to it and must be performed by them in good faith'.

A state cannot release itself from its treaty obligations whenever it feels like it. If it could, treaties would become worthless. However, few treaties last for ever, and in order to prevent the law from becoming too rigid some provision is made for the termination of treaties. But in so doing, the law regarding the termination of treaties tries to steer a middle course between the two extremes of rigidity and insecurity.

Article 42(2) of the Vienna Convention in seeking to protect the security of legal relations provides:

'The termination of a treaty, its denunciation or the withdrawal of a party, may take place only as a result of the application of the provisions of the treaty or of the present Convention. The same rule applies to suspension of the operation of a treaty.'

Termination in accordance with the terms of the treaty

Article 54(a) provides that the termination of a treaty or the withdrawal of a party may take place 'in conformity with the provisions of the treaty'.

The following are examples of the most frequently used provisions for the termination of or for the withdrawal from treaty obligations.

1. The treaty may be for a specified period.
2. The treaty may be for a minimum period with a right to withdraw at the expiry of that period.
3. The treaty may be for a specific purpose and terminate on completion of that purpose.
4. The treaty may allow withdrawal at any time.
5. The treaty may allow withdrawal in special circumstances.

Termination by agreement

Article 54(b) of the Vienna Convention provides that the termination of a treaty or withdrawal of a party may take place 'at any time by consent of all the parties after consultation with the other contracting states'.

Implied right of denunciation or withdrawal

The agreement of the parties to terminate the treaty may be implied. In this respect art 56 of the Vienna Convention provides:

'1. A treaty which contains no provision regarding its termination and which does not provide for denunciation or withdrawal is not subject to denunciation or withdrawal unless:
(a) it is established that the parties intended to admit the possibility of denunciation or withdrawal; or
(b) a right of denunciation or withdrawal may be implied by the nature of the treaty.
2. A party shall give not less than twelve months notice of its intention to denounce or withdraw from a treaty under paragraph (1).'

A right of denunciation or withdrawal may therefore be implied in certain types of treaties because of their very nature, for example, treaties of alliance and commercial treaties.

But under art 56 a right to denunciation or withdrawal can never be implied if the treaty contains an express provision regarding denunciation, withdrawal or termination.

Implied termination where the parties enter into a similar treaty on the same subject matter

Article 59 of the Vienna Convention provides:

'1. A treaty shall be considered as terminated if all the parties to it conclude a later treaty relating to the same subject matter and:
(a) it appears from the later treaty or is otherwise established that the parties intended that the matter should be governed by that treaty; or
(b) the provisions of the later treaty are so far incompatible with those of the earlier one that the two treaties are not capable of being applied at the same time.
2. The earlier treaty shall be considered as only suspended in operation if it appears from the later treaty or is otherwise established that such was the intention of the parties.'

Therefore, it is apparent from art 59 that in the case of multilateral treaties implied termination is less readily established.

Reduction of the parties to a multilateral treaty below the number necessary for its entry into force

If the parties to a multilateral treaty state that it should only enter into force once a certain number of states have ratified it, there is no reason, in the absence of a specific provision to the contrary, why the treaty should terminate if, subsequently, the number of parties falls below the number necessary to bring the treaty into force.

This general rule is laid down in art 55 of the Vienna Convention:

'Unless the treaty otherwise provides, a multilateral treaty does not terminate by reason only of the fact that the number of the parties falls below the number necessary for its entry into force.'

Material breach of the treaty

It is recognised that the material breach of a treaty by one party entitles the other party or parties to the treaty to invoke the breach as a ground of termination or suspension.

Article 60(1) of the Vienna Convention provides:

'A material breach of a bilateral treaty by one of the parties entitles the other to invoke the breach as a ground for terminating the treaty or suspending its operation in whole or in part.'

This right of termination or suspension has become accepted as being the main sanction for securing the observance of treaties.

However, the problem has become more complex in the case of breach of a multilateral treaty. There are two aspects to such treaties: the rights of the parties to the treaty as a group, and the rights of the individual states towards the breach.

In this respect art 60(2) of the Vienna Convention provides:

'A material breach of a multilateral treaty by one of the parties entitles:
(a) the other parties by unanimous agreement to suspend the operation of the treaty in whole or in part or to terminate it either;
(i) in the relations between themselves and the defaulting state, or
(ii) as between all parties;
(b) a party specially affected by the breach to invoke it as a ground for suspending the operation of the treaty in whole or in part in the relations between itself and the defaulting state;
(c) any party other than the defaulting state to invoke the breach as a ground for suspending the operation of the treaty in whole or in part with respect to itself if the treaty is of such a character that a material breach of its provisions by one party radically changes the position of every party with respect to the further performance of its obligations under the treaty.'

Article 60(2)(c) applies in respect of those treaties where a breach by one party tends to undermine the whole regime of the treaty as between all the parties, the best example being disarmament treaties.

The breach must be 'material'
Article 60(3) of the Vienna Convention provides:

'A material breach of a treaty, for the purposes of this article, consists in: a repudiation of the treaty not sanctioned by the present Convention; or the violation of a provision essential to the accomplishment of the object or purpose of the treaty.'

Such a breach does not automatically terminate the treaty; it merely gives the injured party or parties an option to terminate or suspend the treaty. Article 45 of the Vienna Convention provides that an injured party will lose this right to exercise the option:

'… if after becoming aware of the facts: it shall have expressly agreed that the treaty … remains in force or continues in operation, as the case may be; or it must by reason of its conduct be considered as having acquiesced … in its [the treaty] maintenance in force or in operation, as the case may be.'

Breaches giving no right of termination or suspension
Article 60(5) of the Vienna Convention provides:

'Paragraphs 1 to 3 [of art 60] do not apply to provisions relating to the protection of the human person contained in treaties of a humanitarian character, in particular to provisions prohibiting any form of reprisals against persons protected by such treaties.'

The provisions contained in the Geneva Convention IV 1949 prohibiting reprisals against the persons protected by that Convention would accordingly prevent suspension or termination of that Convention.

Supervening impossibility of performance

There may be circumstances in which a treaty is literally impossible to perform by one of the contracting parties. The International Law Commission gave examples of the submergence of an island, the drying up of a river or the destruction of a dam, indispensable for the execution of a treaty. Article 61 therefore provides:

'1. A party may invoke the impossibility of performing a treaty as a ground for terminating or withdrawing from it if the impossibility results from the permanent disappearance or destruction of an object indispensable for the execution of the treaty. If the impossibility is temporary, it may be invoked only as a ground for suspending the operation of the treaty.

2. Impossibility of performance may not be invoked by a party as a ground for terminating, withdrawing from or suspending the operation of a treaty if the impossibility is the result of a breach by that party either of an obligation under the treaty or of any other international obligation owed to any other party to the treaty.'

Such impossibility of performance does not automatically terminate the treaty, but merely gives a party an option to terminate.

Fundamental change of circumstances

A party is not bound to perform a treaty if there has been a fundamental change of circumstances since the treaty was concluded.

The Vienna Convention in art 62 confines this rule within very narrow limits by providing:

'1. A fundamental change of circumstances which has occurred with regard to those existing at the time of the conclusion of a treaty, and which was not foreseen by the parties, may not be invoked as a ground for terminating or withdrawing from the treaty unless:

(a) the existence of those circumstances constituted an essential basis of the consent of the parties to be bound by the treaty; and

(b) the effect of the change is radically to transform the extent of obligations still to be performed under the treaty.

2. A fundamental change of circumstances may not be invoked as a ground for terminating or withdrawing from the treaty:

(a) if the treaty established a boundary; or

(b) if the fundamental change is the result of a breach by the party invoking it either of an obligation under the treaty or of any other international obligation owed to any other party to the treaty.

3. If, under the foregoing paragraphs, a party may invoke a fundamental change of circumstances as a ground for terminating or withdrawing from a treaty, it may also invoke the change as a ground for suspending the operation of the treaty.'

This article reflects the doctrine of rebus sic stantibus (things remaining as they are). Some writers base this principle on the fictional rule that every treaty contains an implied term that it shall only remain in force so long as circumstances remain the same. Although state practice supports the principle many jurists dislike the doctrine and prefer to confine its scope within very narrow limits. They see the doctrine as a considerable threat to the security of treaties and the International Law

Commission considered the fiction to be undesirable in that it increases the risk of subjective interpretation and abuse.

Article 62(2)(a) excludes treaties fixing boundaries from the operation of the principle in order to avoid threats to the peace.

In the *Fisheries Jurisdiction Case: United Kingdom* v *Iceland* (1973) ICJ Rep 3 the ICJ said that art 62 'may in many respects be considered as a codification of existing customary law on the subject' but held that the dangers to Icelandic interests resulting from new fishing techniques 'cannot constitute a fundamental change with respect to the lapse or subsistence' of the jurisdictional clause in a bilateral agreement.

New peremptory norm of general international law (ius cogens)

Article 64 of the Vienna Convention provides:

> 'If a new peremptory norm of general international law emerges, any existing treaty which is in conflict with that norm becomes void and terminates.'

But this does not have retroactive effects on the validity of the treaty.

War and armed conflict

In the past war was regarded as ending all treaties between belligerent states. However, today few belligerent states will admit to being in a state of war and hostilities short of war do not automatically terminate a treaty. Therefore some treaties may be suspended, others may terminate on the grounds of impossibility or fundamental change of circumstances but others will remain binding, eg the Charter of the United Nations and the 1949 Geneva Conventions. Also many multilateral treaties will today include neutral states as well as belligerents among their parties.

The Vienna Convention does not specifically deal with the effects of war on treaties.

11.10 Settlement of disputes

Articles 65–68 of the Vienna Convention provide for the situation where a state:

> '... invokes either a defect in its consent to be bound by a treaty or a ground for impeaching the validity of a treaty, terminating it, withdrawing from it or suspending its operation.'

Article 65(1) provides that the state must notify the other parties of the 'measure proposed to be taken with respect to the treaty and the reasons therefore'.

Article 65(2) provides that the notification should specify a period within which the other parties should raise objections and this period 'except in cases of special urgency, shall not be less than three months after the receipt of the notification'.

Article 65(3) provides that if an objection is raised the state making the notification and the other party or parties objecting 'shall seek a solution' in accordance with art 33 of the Charter of the United Nations: viz 'negotiation, equity, mediation, conciliation, arbitration, judicial settlement, resort to regional agencies or arrangements, or other peaceful means of their own choice'.

If no solution has been reached by the means specified in art 65(3) 'within a period of 12 months following the date on which the objection was raised' art 66 confers jurisdiction on the ICJ over disputes arising from art 53 (ius cogens) and confers jurisdiction over other disputes on a special conciliation commission set up under an annex to the Convention.

These rules represent a significant innovation compared to the position under customary international law. Under customary international law, international courts and commissions do not have jurisdiction over all cases concerning claims that a treaty is invalid, but only over those cases where the parties agree to submit the matter to such a court or commission.

11.11 Treaties by international organisations

The Vienna Convention on the Law of Treaties between States and International Organisations or between International Organisations 1986 regulates the procedures for negotiating treaties between states and international organisations and among international organisations themselves. For the most part, the 1986 Convention repeats the rights and duties contained in the Vienna Convention on the Law of Treaties 1969, relating to matters such as the formalities and negotiating procedures for making treaties, validity, the application of treaties, the amendment and modification of treaties, interpretation and termination.

The capacity of international organisations to enter treaties is governed by art 6 which provides that 'the capacity of an international organisation to conclude a treaty is governed by the rules of that organisation'.

An international organisation that is a party to a treaty is prohibited from invoking the terms of its constitution or internal rules as a justification for failing to perform its obligations under an international agreement. Nor can an agreement entered into by an international organisation establish rights for third states in the absence of the consent of such a third state. International organisations express their consent to be bound by the terms of a treaty through agents who have been delegated authority to enter into such commitments by the internal rules and procedures of the organisation.

12

The International Protection of Human Rights

12.1 Introduction

12.2 The International Bill of Human Rights

12.3 Other international conventions

12.4 The UN human rights machinery

12.5 Regional protection of human rights

12.6 Customary international human rights and ius cogens

12.7 General conclusions

12.1 Introduction

International law from its inception has been concerned with the protection of human beings against acts of barbarism. These considerations can be found in the writing of the fathers of international law: Francisco de Vittoria, Francisco Suarez and Bartholomy de Las Casas. In the seventeenth and eighteenth centuries Hugo Grotius, Samuel von Pufendorf and Jean Jacques Burlamagui contributed to the development of the concept of human rights considering them as rights, which are inherent to human beings. This philosophy was reflected in the French Declaration of the Rights of Man and the Citizen 1789, in particular its art 2 which states that:

'The aim of all political association is the conservation of the natural and inalienable rights of man. These rights are: liberty, property, security and resistance to oppression.'

The basic principle of the French Declaration was that all men are born and remain free and equal in their rights. In particular the Declaration referred to civil and political rights such as equality before the law, freedom from arrest except in conformity with the law, the presumption of innocence, protection against retroactivity of the law, freedom of expression and the freedom to do anything which is not harmful to others.

One of the first national instruments guaranteeing some rights to individuals was the English Magna Carta 1215 which recognised that the citizen should enjoy freedom from imprisonment, from the dispossession of his property and from prosecution or exile unless justified 'by the lawful judgment of his peers or by the law of the land'. Magna Carta also contained a primitive formulation of the right to fair trial. The ideas expressed in the Magna Carta were further developed by the colonists in North America when they fought for independence. They considered that the Americans 'were free people claiming their rights as derived from the laws of nature and not as the gift of their Chief Magistrate'. The Declaration of Independence 1776 drafted by Jefferson emphasised that human beings have natural rights, in particular:

> 'We hold these truths to be self-evident, that all men are created equal, that they are endowed by their Creator with certain unalienable rights, that among these are life, liberty and the pursuit of happiness.'

The first attempt at international level to protect human rights concerned the abolition of slavery which was legal under national laws at the end of eighteenth century. In the nineteenth century a number of international conventions outlawed slavery, the most important being the Anti-Slavery Act 1890 to which 18 states became contracting parties. The international efforts to abolish slavery culminated with the adoption, under the auspices of the League of Nations, of the Convention on the Abolition of Slavery and the Slave Trade 1926.

Another important development which took place in the nineteenth century was the gradual protection of human beings involved in armed conflicts through the advancement of international humanitarian law. This area is dealt with in Chapter 18.

During the nineteenth century some human rights were enshrined in national constitutions, but the number of democratic countries was so limited, even in Europe, that the idea of international protection of human rights did not have any place in international law. To the contrary, international law recognised that the treatment of nationals was a matter within the exclusive domestic jurisdiction of a state. Aliens were required to be treated according to a certain minimum standard. If they were nationals of another state this standard was respected on the basis of reciprocity rather than any obligation to aliens themselves. Consequently, international law made no provision for refugees and stateless, or displaced, persons. Only states were subjects of international law. Individuals had no enforceable rights in international law.

Following World War I some progress was made towards the establishment of international protection of human rights in the sense that certain rights and certain categories of persons were recognised as being of concern to the international community. In the period between World War I and World War II no attempt was made to protect human rights generally. The Peace Treaties of 1919 creating new states after the dissolution of the Austrio-Hungarian Empire, the collapse of the Ottoman Empire and the defeat of Germany were redrawing the frontiers in Europe.

It was not always possible to respect the principle of nationality whilst creating new states and changing the frontiers of existing states. For that reason it was necessary to introduce mechanisms protecting minorities. These took three forms:

1. special treaties on minorities were signed between the Allied powers and the following newly created states, ie Poland (Versailles 1919), Czechoslovakia and Yugoslavia (St Germaine-en-Laye 1919), Romania (Trianon 1920) and Greece (Sevres 1920);
2. chapters on the protection of minorities were included in the peace treaties with the ex-enemy states, ie Austria (St Germaine-en-Laye 1919), Bulgaria (Neuilly 1919) Hungary (Trianon 1920) and Turkey (Lausanne 1923);
3. admission to the newly created League of Nations was made conditional upon a declaration before the Council ensuring the protection of rights of minorities living within the territory of a candidate state (Finland in 1921, Albania in 1921, Lithuania in 1922, Latvia in 1923, Estonia in 1923 and Iraq in 1932).

The above arrangements were intended to ensure that minorities were not discriminated against and that they were entitled to freedom of religion, freedom to use their own language, together with the right to protect their cultural identity including the right to maintain educational establishments. The League of Nations was to supervise the system of protection of minorities.

Other initiatives towards the international protection of human rights under the auspices of the League of Nations included: the creation of the mandate system in respect of colonies belonging to the ex-enemy states; the supervision of prohibition of traffic in women and children; the supervision of prohibition of traffic in dangerous drugs; and the establishment of first arrangements for the international protection of refugees.

Also the International Labour Organisation which was established as a part of the Treaty of Versailles 1919 initiated the protection of workers through international conventions.

Genocide, atrocities and suffering inflicted upon millions of human beings by the Nazi and totalitarian regimes in the 1930s and 1940s gave a new impetus to those demanding international recognition and enforcement of fundamental human rights and freedoms. As a result, the concept of the protection of human rights has been internalised and universalised after World War II. According to Henkin 'universalisation' means general acceptance of human rights by national governments, whilst 'internationalisation' refers to the recognition that the 'treatment of citizens in one country has become the business of other countries': 'Internationalisation of Human Rights, Human Rights: A Symposium', Columbia University, *Proceedings of the General Education Seminar*, 6, No 1 (1977) 5–16.

Since the end of World War II an impressive number of legal rules – conventional and customary, universal and regional – has been created to ensure the protection of human rights at both international and regional levels. The demise of the Soviet Union has had an important impact, not only on the structure of the international community and the functioning of international organisations but also on the development of human rights. The international community is now directly involved in situations of grave violations of human rights. As the Secretary-General of the UN emphasised at the opening of the World Conference on Human Rights held in Vienna in June 1993 the language of human rights has become universal. Therefore, human rights have the same meaning for all people around the world. The international community has reaffirmed many times the universality, indivisibility, interdependence and interelateness of all human rights, whether civil, political, economic, social or cultural. Every person is entitled to them by virtue of being a human being. Humans have inalienable rights, irrespective of whether they exercises them individually or collectively. They live in both material and spiritual worlds. That is why economic, social and cultural rights are as fundamental to their welfare as civil and political rights. The fact that violations of human rights continue to take place demonstrates that the attempts to provide international protection are not as effective as they ought to be and that a great deal remains to be done to improve existing international procedures.

This chapter will focus on the most important documents in respect of the international protection of human rights, that is the International Bill of Human Rights, which consists of the Universal Declaration of Human Rights, the International Covenant on Civil and Political Rights and its two Optional Protocols, and the International Covenant on Economic, Social and Cultural Rights. Other important international conventions and new trends in the development of human rights law will also be examined. Special emphasis will be put on the European Convention on Human Rights as the most effective and sophisticated regional arrangement intended to protect human rights.

12.2 The International Bill of Human Rights

The draftsmen of the Charter of the United Nations included among its provisions the foundations for the international protection of human rights. At the 1945 San Francisco Conference a proposal was submitted to insert a 'Declaration on the Essential Rights of Man' into the Charter. It was rejected on the ground that more time was required in order to elaborate that idea. Nevertheless, the Charter contains many provisions on human rights. In the preamble to the Charter, the Peoples of the United Nations reaffirm their:

> '... faith in fundamental human rights, in the dignity and worth of the human person, in the equal rights of men and women ...'

Article 1(3) of the Charter enumerates among the purposes and principles of the United Nations the promotion of and respect for human rights and for fundamental freedoms for all 'without distinction as to race, sex, language and religion'.

The most important provisions are contained in arts 55 and 56 of the Charter. Article 55 states that:

'With a view to the creation of conditions of stability and well-being which are necessary for peaceful and friendly relations among nations based on respect for the principle of equal rights and self-determination of peoples, the United Nations shall promote ...
(c) universal respect for, and observance of, human rights and fundamental freedoms for all without distinction as to race, sex and language or religion.'

Under art 56 of the Charter:

'All members pledge themselves to take joint and separate action in co-operation with the Organisation for the achievement of the purposes set forth in art 55.'

The Charter assigns important responsibility for discharging the functions contained in arts 55 and 56 to various organs of the UN. The General Assembly (art 60) and the Trusteeship Council (art 76) are charged with the promotion of human rights within the general framework of their obligations and the Economic and Social Council, under art 68, 'shall set up commissions in economic and social fields and for the promotion of human rights'.

At the recommendation of the Preparatory Commission of the United Nations the Economic and Social Council established, in 1946, the Commission on Human Rights for the promotion of human rights as provided for in art 68.

However, the fundamental human rights which the members of the UN have to respect are not defined by the Charter, apart from the right to non-discrimination ('without distinction as to race, sex, language or religion'). This is the only human right which explicitly derives from the Charter. In the Advisory Opinion on the *Legal Consequences for States of the Continued Presence of South Africa in Namibia (South West Africa) Notwithstanding Security Council Reolution 276 (1970)* (1971) ICJ Rep 16 the ICJ confirmed that:

'... to establish ... and to enforce distinction, exclusion, restrictions and limitations exclusively based on grounds of race, colour, descent or national or ethnic origin which constitute a denial of fundamental human rights is a flagrant violation of the purposes and principles of the Charter.'

The Universal Declaration of Human Rights (UDHR)

The language of the Charter with regard to human rights is vague and general. In order to define the fundamental human rights and to provide specific standards for the guidance of the international community the General Assembly at its first session in 1946, after examining a draft Declaration on Fundamental Human Rights and Freedoms, decided to forward it to the Economic and Social Council 'for reference to the Commission on Human Rights for consideration ... in its preparation of an international bill of rights': Resolution 43 (I). The Commission, at its first session held in 1947, decided to prepare a preliminary draft of an International Bill of Human Rights and set up a Drafting Committee. During its second session held in December 1947 the Commission, after examining the proposal from the Drafting Committee, decided that the term 'International Bill of Human Rights' would be applied to the series of documents under preparation by three working groups, one on the declaration, one on the convention (which was later called 'covenant') and one on implementation. The declaration was submitted to the General Assembly meeting in Paris. On 10 December 1948 the General Assembly adopted the Universal Declaration of Human Rights: Resolution 217A (III). Forty-eight states voted in favour, none against, and eight abstained (inter alia, the Soviet Union and its allies on the ground that the economic and social rights were not sufficiently developed, and South Africa argued that social and economic rights were within the domestic jurisdiction of a state).

The Declaration consists of six preambles and 30 articles. Its arts 1 and 2 state that all human beings 'are born equal in dignity and rights' and are 'entitled to enjoy rights and freedoms set forth in the Declaration without any discrimination based on race, sex, language, religion, political or other opinion, national or social origin, property, birth or any other status'.

The Declaration sets out a wide range of human rights and freedoms to be protected, ranging from traditional civil and political rights to economic, social and cultural rights. Articles 3–21 refer to civil and political rights being:

1. the right to life, liberty and security;
2. freedom from slavery, servitude, torture or cruel, inhuman or degrading treatment or punishment;
3. the right to recognition as a person before the law, the right to judicial remedy, freedom from arbitrary arrest, detention or exile, the right to a fair trial and a public hearing by an independent and impartial tribunal, the right to be presumed innocent until proven guilty;
4. freedom from arbitrary interference with privacy, family, home or correspondence; and freedom from attacks upon honour and reputation;
5. freedom of movement, the right to seek asylum, the right to a nationality;
6. the right to marry and to found a family, the right to own property;
7. freedom of thought, conscience and religion, freedom of opinion and expression;
8. the right to peaceful assembly and association;
9. the right to take part in government and the right to equal access to public services.

Articles 22–27 define the economic, social and cultural rights, including the rights, to: work, social security, equal pay, join trade unions, rest and leisure, an adequate standard of living, education, and the right to participate in the cultural life of the community.

Articles 28–30 recognise that everyone is entitled to a social and international order in which the human rights set forth in the Declaration may be fully realised and emphasise that each person has duties to the community in which he lives. Article 29(2) states that:

'In the exercise of his rights and freedoms, everyone shall be subject only to such limitations as are determined by law solely for the purpose of securing due recognition and respect for the rights and freedoms of others and of meeting the just requirements of morality, public order and the general welfare in a democratic society.'

In its Preamble, the Declaration defines:

'... a common standard of achievement for all peoples and nations, to the end that every individual and every organ of society, keeping this Declaration constantly in mind, shall strive by teaching and education to promote respect for these rights and freedoms and by progressive measures, national and international, to secure their universal and effective recognition and observance, both among the peoples of Member States themselves and among the peoples of territories under their jurisdiction.'

The Declaration has no binding legal force. Therefore it does not impose any immediate duty upon member states to implement its provisions. However, it has had considerable impact on the development of human rights: it has been partially incorporated into many national constitutions (including those of the Soviet Union and China), has served as a basis for national legislation, has been referred to in court opinions and decisions and deliberations of the UN and has constituted a source of inspiration for many internationally binding treaties. Even the Soviet bloc, despite their abstention at the time of its adoption in 1948, acknowledged the Declaration in the 1975 Helsinki Accord by stating that:

'In the field of human rights and fundamental freedoms, the participating states will act in conformity with the purposes and principles of the Charter of the United Nations and with the Universal Declaration on Human Rights.'

With the passing of time, many provisions of the Declaration have acquired the status of customary rules. The Declaration itself was unanimously proclaimed by the International Conference on Human Rights held in Teheran in 1968 as representing 'a common understanding of the peoples of the world concerning the inalienable and inviolable rights of all members of the human family and constitutes an obligation for the members of the international community'.

The Declaration constitutes an authoritative interpretation of the Charter obligations and provides a comprehensive list of human rights and freedoms to be protected. It represents a consensus of the international community regarding human rights which each of its members must respect, promote and observe.

The 1966 International Covenants on Human Rights

In order to translate the UDHR into binding instruments the General Assembly (GA) requested the Commission on Human Rights, on the same day it adopted the Universal Declaration, to prepare, as a matter of priority, a draft covenant on human rights, together with draft measures for its implementation. During the preparatory work the GA decided that the covenant should also include economic, social and cultural rights, considering them interconnected with, and interdependent on, civil and political rights. Practical reasons led the GA in 1951/1952 to request the Commission on Human Rights to prepare two covenants with as many similar provisions as possible, one on civil and political rights and the other on economic, social and cultural rights: Resolution 543 (VI).

On 16 December 1966 the GA adopted the International Covenant on Economic, Social and Cultural Rights (ICESCR) and the International Covenant on Civil and Political Rights (ICCPR) (Resolution 2200A (XXI)), together with the Optional Protocol to the ICCPR which provides for a mechanism for dealing with communications from individuals claiming to be victims of violations of the rights set out in the Covenant.

The differences between the UDHR and the Covenants are:

1. the Covenants are more precise, providing detailed guidelines for the conduct of governments, specific legal protection for individuals, and detailing instances in which public order, safety, health, morals etc can be invoked to limit individual rights;
2. the Covenants contain various measures of implementation, in some cases recognising the right of individuals to seek redress of their grievances on the international plane;
3. the Covenants were not adopted by the GA but were subject to ratification.

Although the Covenants are treaties binding only those who ratify them, they also constitute the codification of human rights, and consequently some of them reflect customary international law.

The preambles and articles 1, 3 and 5 of the two Covenants are almost identical. The preambles refer to the obligation of states under the UN Charter to promote human rights and they confirm the connection between, on the one hand, civil and political rights and, on the other hand, economic, social and cultural rights, in the achievement of the ideals set out in the Universal Declaration of Human Rights.

Article 1 of both Covenants states that all people have the right to self-determination, art 3 refers to the equality between men and women in the enjoyment of human rights and enjoins states to take steps to implement that equality, and art 5 provides for safeguards against limitation of the rights and fundamental freedoms set forth in the Covenants. In this respect, the ICCPR provides that certain rights can never be suspended or limited, even in emergency situations. These rights and freedoms are: right to life, freedom from torture, freedom from enslavement or servitude, freedom from imprisonment for debt, freedom from retroactive penal laws, right to recognition as a person before the law, and freedom of thought, conscience and religion. Under the ICCPR in an emergency threatening the life of the nation the limitations are confined 'to the extent strictly required by the exigencies of the situation' and must never be discriminatory on the ground of race, colour, sex, language, religion or social origin: art 4. Any such limitations or suspension must be notified to the United Nations.

The difference between the Covenants is that the ICCPR is immediately applicable upon ratification, whilst contracting states to the ICESCR are obliged to ensure 'progressively' the full enjoyment of the rights recognised under it.

The International Covenant on Economic, Social and Cultural Rights (ICESCR) and its implementation
The ICESCR entered into force on 3 January 1976. As of 1 October 2004 it had been ratified by 150 states. The Covenant covers three categories of rights:

1. the right to work and to the enjoyment of just and favourable conditions of work, including the right to form and join trade unions;
2. the right to social protection, to an adequate standard of living and to the enjoyment of the highest attainable standard of physical and mental health;
3. the right to education and to participation in cultural life.

Under the Covenant itself the contracting parties are obliged to send periodic reports to the UN Economic and Social Council (ECOSOC) on progress in implementation of its provisions. In order to fulfil this task in 1978 ECOSOC set up a sessional working group of 15 members to meet annually and to report to it. The group was not successful and in 1985 ECOSOC decided to establish a new Committee on Economic, Social and Cultural Rights made up of 18 independent experts to study reports from contracting states and discuss them with the governments concerned. The Committee is not autonomous and is accountable to ECOSOC. The Committee may make recommendations to ECOSOC based on annual reports but has no power to hear individual petitions or inter-state complaints.

The International Covenant on Civil and Political Rights (ICCPR) and its implementation
The ICCPR and its First Optional Protocol entered into force on 23 March 1976. As at 1 October 2004 the ICCPR had been ratified by 153 states and its First Optional Protocol by 104 states. The Second Optional Protocol to the ICCPR which deals with the abolition of the death penalty was adopted by the GA on 15 December 1989 (Resolution 44/128) and entered into force on 11 July 1991. As at 1 October 2004 it had been ratified by 51 states.

The ICCPR is generally based upon the European Convention on Human Rights. Its articles 6–27 promote and protect the following rights and fundamental freedoms: right to life (art 6), freedom from torture or cruel, inhuman or degrading treatment or punishment (art 7), freedom from slavery and servitude and forced or compulsory labour (art 8); freedom from arbitrary arrest or detention (art 9); right to human treatment for all persons deprived of their liberty (art 10); freedom from imprisonment on the ground of inability to fulfil contractual obligations (art 11); freedom to choose residence (art 12); limitations on expulsion of aliens lawfully admitted to the territory of a contracting state (art 13); right to fair trial (art 14); freedom from the retroactive application of criminal law (art 15); right to recognition as a person before the law (art 16); freedom from arbitrary interference with privacy and freedom from attacks on honour and reputation (art 17); freedom of thought, conscience and religion (art 18); freedom of opinion and expression (art 19); freedom from war propaganda, and the advocating of racial or religious hatred (art 20); right to peaceful assembly (art 22); right to family life and right to equality between spouses in respect of their rights and responsibilities as to marriage, during marriage and at its dissolution (art 23); right of children to be protected (art 24); right to participate in public affairs and elections (art 25); right for all persons to be regarded as equal before the law and entitlement to equal protection of the law (art 26); protection of the rights of minorities in the territories of contracting states (art 27).

Article 28 of the ICCPR provides for the establishment of a Human Rights Committee responsible for the supervision of the implementation of its provisions.

In respect of the implementation of the ICCPR three procedures are used.

Reports. Contracting states are required to submit reports on measures taken to implement the Covenant to the 18 members Human Rights Committee. This Committee is elected by the contracting parties for a four-year term on the basis of equitable geographical representation and with due consideration to an adequate representation of the different forms of civilisation and of principal legal systems. A Contracting party has to provide a report within a year of the ratification of the ICCPR, and subsequent reports are required every five years. The Commission discusses reports with the state concerned in a constructive way.

By virtue of art 40 of the ICCPR the Committee is empowered to make 'general comments as it may deem appropriate'. Since 1980 such comments are permitted provided that:

1. they promote co-operation between states in the implementation of the Covenant;
2. summarise the experience of the Committee in examining the states' reports;
3. draw the attention of the contracting states to matters relating to the improvement of the reporting procedures and the implementation of the Covenant.

Comments are adopted by consensus and are of a general character. Therefore, they are not controversial.

Inter-state complaints. Under art 42 of the Covenant the Committee is entitled to hear inter-state complaints providing that both states are contracting parties to the Covenant and have made a declaration recognising its competence.

Individual complaints under the Optional Protocols to the ICCPR. Under the First Optional Protocol, a contracting party to both the Protocol and the ICCPR recognises the competence of the Human Rights Committee to receive and consider individual communications alleging violations of the ICCPR by that party. An individual must exhaust all available domestic remedies before submitting a written communication to the Committee which decides on its admissibility. If a communication is considered as admissible it is forwarded to the state concerned which must within six months submit written explanations or statements relating to the alleged violation of the Convention and, if appropriate, indicate the measures it intends to apply to remedy the violation.

On the basis of information submitted by the individual and the state in question the Committee, at a closed meeting, considers the matter and then forwards its opinion to the state concerned and to the individual: art 5. Therefore, unlike the European Convention on Human Rights (ECHR), there is no judicial determination of the issue. The machinery for enforcement is thus much weaker than under the ECHR.

The Second Optional Protocol provides for the abolition of the death penalty in the territory of a contracting state. Its art 1 states that no one within the jurisdiction of a contracting party may be executed. Article 3 requires that a contracting party submits reports to the Human Rights Committee on measures taken to implement the Protocol. Under art 5 of the Second Optional Protocol the Human Rights Committee is entitled to receive and consider an individual communication if a contracting party to the First Optional Protocol has not made a statement to the contrary at the moment of ratification or accession.

12.3 Other international conventions

There is an impressive number of international instruments in the field of human rights inspired by the Universal Declaration of Human Rights and aimed at expanding and supplementing the provisions of the 1966 Covenants. Among the most important are as follows.

Convention on the Prevention and Punishment of the Crime of Genocide 1948

This is discussed in Chapter 18.

Geneva Convention Regarding to the Status of Refugees 1951, as supplemented by the Hague Protocol Regarding to the Status of Refugees 1967

This is discussed in Chapter 13.

Convention Relating to the Status of Stateless Persons 1953 and the Convention on the Reduction of Statelessness 1961

This is discused in Chapter 13.

International Convention on the Elimination of All Forms of Racial Discrimination 1966

The Committee on the Elimination of Racial Discrimination (CERD) was set up under the Convention with the task of monitoring its implementation, in particular to consider reports from contracting states, to process inter-state complaints (to date no such complaint has been received by CERD) and, if authorised, petitions from individuals who claim to be victims of violations of the Convention by a contracting state.

The Convention entered into force in 1969. As of 1 October 2004 it had been ratified by 169 states, 30 of whom had made a declaration recognising the competence of CERD to receive individual complaints. Individual petitioners must exhaust all domestic remedies before petitioning CERD. Individual complaints are brought to the attention of a state in question. However, CERD cannot disclose, without the consent of that state, the identity of the individual or group claiming a violation. The state concerned is required to provide its explanations and may suggest a remedy. Then the matter is debated by CERD which may make suggestions and recommendations to both the petitioner and the state concerned. CERD has played an important role in respect of trust and non-self governing territories as it is empowered to receive petitions on matters of racial discrimination by any of the populations concerned irrespective of whether or not the administering power is a contracting party to the Convention. CERD examines the complaint and makes a report with recommendations to the General Assembly (GA).

The GA in its Resolution 48/91 of 20 December 1993 proclaimed the Third Decade to Combat Racism and Racial Discrimination beginning in 1993, and adopted the Programme of Action for the Decade. The objectives of the first two Decades have not been achieved. Racism and racial discrimination are very much present worldwide. Within the programme for the Third Decade the GA proclaimed Year 2001 as the International Year of Mobilisation against Racism, Racial Discrimination, Xenophobia and Related Intolerance. The activities implemented within the framework of the International Year were directed towards the preparation of the World Conference against Racism, Racial Discrimination, Xenophobia and Related Intolerance which took place in Durban, South Africa from 31 August to 7 September 2001. The High Commissioner for Human Rights invited eminent political leaders and intellectuals to form the Eminent Persons Group, under the patronage of Nelson Mandela and including Michail Gorbachev, Jimmy Carter and Nobel Prize laureates Elie Wiesel and Roberta Menchu, to provide inspiration and leadership at the World Conference.

The Durban conference was the third of the World Conferences Against Racism. The two previous ones, held in Geneva in 1978 and in 1983, made little contribution to the elimination of racism and racial discrimination. The Durban conference was a difficult meeting. The US and Israel left the Conference before its end as a sign of discontent and dissatisfaction with the proceedings. Both countries urged other participants to withdraw from the Conference. Fortunately none followed. The Conference achieved an agreement on a Declaration (121 paragraphs) and a Programme of Action (222 paragraphs). These documents recognise that much is to be done to eradicate racism and racial discrimination. The success of the Durban Conference will depend upon whether or not the international community takes concrete steps to implement the Programme of Action.

The International Bill of Rights for Women

The International Bill of Rights for Women comprises the Convention on the Elimination of All Forms of Discrimination against Women 1979, which, as at 20 October 2004 had been ratified by 179 states, and the 1999 New York Optional Protocol to the Convention which, as at 20 October 2004, was in force in 67 states. Under the Convention the Committee on the Elimination of Discrimination against Women was set up to supervise its implementation and receive reports from contracting states. Under the Optional Protocol individuals who claim to be victims of violations of their rights under the Convention can complain against the state concerned to the Committee, provided that all domestic remedies have been exhausted and that the state concerned is a contracting party to both the Convention and the Protocol. Under the Protocol the Committee on the Elimination of Discrimination against Women is entitled to make inquiries into serious or systematic violations of the Convention in a state which has ratified both instruments, provided that such state did not opt out of the inquiry procedure.

The International Bill of Rights for Women was prepared by the Commission on the Status of Women created in 1946 by ECOSOC. The Commission is responsible for advancing the status of women around the world. It is made up of representatives of 45 member states representing the major legal systems and reflecting the geographical distribution of UN membership. The Commission, apart from initiating and drafting the above Bill of Rights for Women and other instruments intended to improve the status of women, is empowered to make recommendations and reports to ECOSOC on the promotion of the rights of women in political, economic, social and educational fields and in respect of urgent problems requiring immediate attention in the field of women's rights, with a view to implementing the principle of equality between men and women. The Commission drafts proposals for the implementation of its recommendations.

It was also the Commission on the Status of Women that initiated the work on the Optional Protocol. The Commission was dissatisfied with the pace of implementation of the Nairobi Forward-looking Strategies for the Advancement of Women to the Year 2000 produced by the Third World Conference on Women. In 1995, at the Fourth World Conference on Women held in Beijing, the Commission decided to press for the establishment of an individual complaints procedure to the Committee on the Elimination of Discrimination against Women in respect of violations of the Convention by a contracting state.

The Fourth World Conference on Women, apart from approving the initiative of the Commission, adopted the Beijing Declaration and the Platform for Action (the Beijing Platform for Action, or BpfA) which identified 12 critical areas of concern and outlined a series of concrete actions that governments, the international community and civil society should take to overcome obstacles to the advancement of women's rights. Among the areas of concern are:

1. the increase and persistent burden of poverty on women;
2. unequal access for women to education, health care services, political and economic life, employment, and in particular in respect of the sharing of power and decision-making at all levels;
3. the lack of interest and commitment on the part of governments to recognise women's rights and their contribution to society and to promote the advancement of women.

In 2000 the UN GA Special Session 'Women 2000: Gender Equality, Development and Peace for the 21st Century' (this was called the 'Beijing +5': the Review and Appraisal of the Beijing Declaration and Platform for Action five years after the Beijing Fourth World Conference on Women) reviewed progress achieved since the Beijing Conference and put forward proposals for new actions aimed at the implementation of the Nairobi Forward-looking Strategies for the Advancement of Women (adopted in 1985) and the BpfA (adopted in 1995). The Beijing +5 Outcome Document emphasises the importance and necessity of eradicating harmful traditional practices such as female genital mutilation, forced marriages, etc. Further, the document calls upon governments to eliminate gender discriminatory legislation by 2005 and to ensure greater access to affordable treatment and care for women and girls living with HIV or AIDS. The Commission on the Status of Women is in the process of preparing a global review and assessment of all the above action plans (Nairobi (1985), BpfA (1995), Beijing +5 (2000)) with a view to presenting its recommendations at its forty-ninth session in March 2005 (this was called the 'Beijing +10': the Review and Appraisal of the Beijing Declaration and Platform for Action ten years after the Beijing Fourth World Conference on Women).

The International Bill of Rights of the Child

The International Bill of Rights of the Child consists of the New York Convention on the Rights of the Child 1989 which has been ratified by 192 states (as at 1 October 2004) and its two optional protocols: the 2000 New York Optional Protocol on the Involvement of Children in Armed Conflicts and the 2000 New York Optional Protocol on the Sale of Children, Child Prostitution and Child Pornography. Both Protocols are in force: the first has been ratified by 82 states and the second has obtained 83 ratifications.

The 1989 Convention is not very ambitious. Whilst it sets out a minimum standard of treatment of children in contracting states it leaves these states the discretion as to the manner in which its provisions are to be implemented. The Convention is based on four principles: the principle of non-discrimination, including equality of opportunity between boys and girls the principle that a contracting state must, when taking any measures affecting children, act in their best interests; the principle that children's opinions should, with due regard to their age and maturity, be taken into consideration in all matters affecting them; and the principle that children have the right to life, survival and development which a contracting state must ensure 'to the maximum extent possible'. Under the Convention the Committee on the Rights of Child was set up in 1991 with a task of receiving reports from contracting states on the implementation of the Convention. However there is no procedure for individual petitions under the Convention, although the Committee may request a contracting state to forward additional information relevant to the implementation of the Convention if it is seriously concerned with the situation of children in that state. In 1992 the Committee initiated a study leading to the adoption of two Optional Protocols to the Convention.

Under the First Optional Protocol on the Involvement of Children in Armed Conflicts contracting states are required to take all necessary measures to ensure that children under the age of 18 are not directly participating in hostilities, that any compulsory recruitment is fixed above the age of 18, and that the minimum age for voluntary recruitment is above the current international standard of 15. Contracting states are also required to take all measures to prevent non-governmental groups from using and recruiting children under the age of 18.

Under the Second Optional Protocol the contracting states are required to criminalise the sale of children, child prostitution and child pornography.

The Chairman of the UN Commission on Human Rights stated that the effective implementation of these Protocols 'should greatly contribute to seeing children take up books not arms, seeing them in school not in brothels': at the closing of the 56th session of the Commission on 28 April 2000.

Child labour is another issue of great importance to the UN.

The Convention against Torture and Other Cruel Inhuman or Degrading Treatment or Punishment 1984

The Convention requires a contracting state to prevent and punish acts of torture, cruel, inhuman or degrading treatment committed within its territory, at the instigation of, or with the consent or acquiescence of, a public official or other person acting in an official capacity. It also states that a contracting state must not expel, return or extradite a person to a state where a person might be tortured. The act of torture is made an extraditable offence under the Convention. When an alleged offender is within the territory of a contracting state the principle 'out punire out dedire' applies, that is if such a person is not extradited, national courts have jurisdiction over offences.

The Committee against Torture was established under the Convention. It started work in 1987. Its main task is to supervise the implementation of the Convention in contracting states. It is charged with examining periodic reports submitted by each of the contracting states and on the basis of such examination to adopt recommendations in respect of the state concerned. It has an inter-state complaint competence under art 21 of the Convention and may hear individual petitions under art 22 providing that the state concerned has recognised the Committee's competence in respect of such complaints. As at 20 October 2004, 138 states had ratified the Convention and 44 had recognised the Committee's competence. The Committee is also empowered to conduct investigations if it has evidence that torture is being practised in the territory of a contracting state. The investigation, including on site visits, is confidential and carried out in co-operation with the state concerned. The Committee discusses its findings with the state concerned. However, the Committee after consultation with the state concerned may decide to publicise the result of its investigation in its annual report.

On 18 December 2002 the GA approved an Optional Protocol to the Convention against Torture. As of 1 October 2004 the Protocol had obtained only five ratifications. It will enter into force on the thirtieth day after the date of deposit of the twentieth instrument of ratification or accession. The Protocol establishes procedures for systematic visits by independent international and national bodies to 'places where people are deprived of their liberty' to ensure that these people are not tortured or submitted to cruel, inhuman and degrading treatment or punishment. The Optional Protocol provides for enforcement mechanisms at international and national levels. Within the existing Committee against Torture a new body will be established, a Sub-committee on Prevention of Torture and Other Cruel, Inhuman and Degrading Treatment or Punishment, to supervise practical arrangements regarding the visits. At national level, a contracting party will be required to set up one or several domestic 'visiting bodies' to detention places. The Protocol provides an exception to such visits based on 'urgent and compelling grounds of national defence, public safety, natural disasters or serious disorder in the place to be visited which temporarily prevent the carrying out of such visits'. However, a state of emergency cannot be relied upon by a contracting party to object to a visit.

The protection of rights of indigenous people

This is discussed in Chapter 14.

The Convention on the Suppression and Punishment of the Crime of Apartheid 1973

This Convention is discussed in Chapter 19.

New developments in human rights

Human rights are constantly evolving. New rights are emerging with the development of the international community. In this respect two new developments are worth mentioning: the consolidation of right to democracy and the efforts of the UN to protect defenders of human rights.

The right to democracy

The human rights treaty system is of utmost importance, but the main responsibility for the effective protection of human rights lies with a state. Only democratic and accountable governments can promote and protect human rights. In 1988 the GA adopted the first resolution aimed at promoting democracy entitled 'Enhancing the Effectiveness of the Principle of Periodic and Genuine Elections' and called upon the UN Commission on Human Rights to find the appropriate means and methods of implementing the above resolution. Since 1988 the GA has adopted at least one resolution annually dealing with some aspect of democracy whilst the UN Commission on Human Rights, in a series of resolutions, has focused on the promotion and consolidation of the right to democracy from the perspective of the enjoyment of human rights. Three resolutions of the UN Commission are particularly important.

1. Resolution 2000/47 which urges states to strengthen democracy through the development of an independent judiciary, an effective and accountable civil service and free and fair electoral systems.
2. Resolution 2001/37 which focuses on the link between democracy and sustainable human development and the realisation of all human rights, including the right to development.
3. Resolution 2001/41 which places emphasis on stimulating dialogue among states on measures to promote and consolidate democracy. In particular it endorses the UN Secretary-General's recommendations for the development by the UN of an integrated democracy assistance programme consisting, inter alia, of sharing information, expertise and best practices in promoting and consolidating democracy between states.

The right to democracy has also been discussed outside the UN structure. International Conferences such as the World Conference on Human Rights and the International Conference on New and Restored Democracies have contributed to the debate on the interdependency of human rights and democracy.

The protection of defenders

The work of individuals and NGOs both at international and national levels remains crucial to the implementation of human rights. Often, such persons, whether individually or as members of non-governmental organisations and groups are threatened, harassed, imprisoned and even executed by the national authorities.

Their role and the necessity to protect them has been recognised by the international community. On 9 December 1998 the GA adopted the Declaration on the Rights and Responsibilities of Individuals, Groups and Organs of Society to Promote and Protect Universally Recognised Rights and Fundamental Freedoms: Resolution 53/144. In order to implement the Declaration the Secretary-General prepared a report (E/CN4/2000/95) which was discussed by the UN Commission on Human Rights at its 56th session. The deliberations resulted in the adoption of Resolution 2000/61 in which the Commission requested the Secretary-General to appoint a special representative for a period of three years who will report on the situation of human rights' defenders and on possible ways to reinforce their protection. In particular, the person appointed will examine situations such as those mentioned above, respond to them and attempt to establish a dialogue with the governments concerned. On 18 August 2000, the first Special Representative of the UN Secretary-General on Human Rights Defenders was appointed.

The extent of the work of the United Nations, including its specialised bodies and agencies such as the International Labour Organisation (ILO), the United Nations Children Fund (UNICEF), the World Health Organisation (WHO), the United Nations Educational, Scientific and Cultural Organisation (UNESCO), the United Nations Development Plan (UNDP), the Office of the United Nations High Commissioners for Refugees (UNCHR) etc, in the codification, development and promotion of human rights is beyond the scope of this publication.

12.4 The UN human rights machinery

The UN human rights machinery consists of three categories of institutions:

1. bodies which have been established directly on the basis of the UN Charter, such as the General Assembly, the Security Council, the Economic and Social Council and the Commission on Human Rights;
2. bodies which have been established indirectly by the UN Charter, that is whose creation was authorised by one of the bodies belonging to the first category, eg the Sub-Commission on the Promotion of Human Rights, the Commission on the Status of Women, the Office of High Commissioner for Human Rights, etc;
3. bodies which have been established on the basis of international treaties, for example the Human Rights Committee under the ICCPR, the Committee against Torture, the Committee on the Elimination of All Forms of Racial Discrimination, etc. The most important have already been examined in this chapter.

In assessing the UN human rights machinery two bodies – the Commission on Human Rights and the Office of the High Commissioner for Human Rights (OHCHR) – merit special attention in the light of their contribution to the development and enforcement of human rights.

The UN Commission on Human Rights

The Commission is made up of 53 representatives of member states of the UN who are selected for a three-year term by ECOSOC on the basis of equitable geographic distribution. The Commission meets for six weeks each year in Geneva but has been authorised by ECOSOC to meet exceptionally between its regular session to deal with urgent and acute human rights situations. As already mentioned the Commission was created in 1946 as a subsidiary organ of ECOSOC in order to draft the International Bill on Human Rights. Since then not only have the competences of the Commission greatly extended but its priorities have also changed.

In the first 20 years of its existence the Commission focused on preparing an impressive number of international instruments and thus translating the rights proclaimed in the Universal Declaration into binding provisions. This standard-setting period of the Commission culminated with the adoption of the 1966 International Covenants, although it has never ended as the Commission is always active in this area.

In 1967 the Commission was authorised by ECOSOC under Resolution 1235 to hold an annual public debate on gross human rights violations and to decide to examine situations which 'reveal a consistent pattern of violations of human rights' and to report, with recommendations, to ECOSOC. The procedure under Resolution 1235 has evolved. Now it takes two forms.

1. During the Commission's annual session a public debate takes place allowing representatives of governments and NGOs to identify human rights situations that they consider should merit the Commission's attention.
2. The Commission examines, and investigates, particular situations (or individual cases) by means of extra-conventional procedures: by the appointment of special rapporteurs, representatives, experts and the setting-up of working groups. Under these procedures the situation in a specific country (known as country mechanism) or on a major situation of human rights violations worldwide (known as thematic mechanism) is examined, supervised and publicly reported. If the Commission decides that there are violations of human rights it may take a number of measures, ranging from expressing its concern, without any formal condemnation, via offering the state concerned 'advisory services', to requesting the Security Council to take up the matter with a view to considering the imposition of sanctions and other coercive measures.

In 1970 ECOSOC adopted Resolution 1503 under which the Commission's Sub-Commission on Prevention of Discrimination and Protection of Minorities (in 1999 ECOSOC changed the name of the Sub-Commission, now it is called the Sub-Commission on the Promotion and Protection of Human Rights) is charged with the examination of individual petitions. If such an examination reveals that there is 'a consistent pattern of gross and reliably attested violations of human rights' the Sub-Commission refers to the Commission which decides whether or not further action is required. If so, the Commission prepares a report and recommendations for ECOSOC or may set up an ad hoc committee to investigate the situation. However, the second option requires the express consent of the government concerned. Under the 1503 procedure on average 50,000 petitions are received each year. All steps in the initial procedure are confidential. Since 1978, however, the chairman of the Commission has announced the names of the countries who have been under consideration during the year. Between 1972 and 1999, 75 states were investigated under the procedure. The 1503 procedure is time-consuming. Some amendments to the procedure were made by Resolution 2000/3 of 16 June 2000 by ECOSOC which should accelerate the examination of complaints. The criteria for admissibility of individual complaints are very stringent:

1. the domestic remedies must be exhausted unless the applicant can demonstrate that the solution at national level would be ineffective or take an unreasonable length of time;
2. applicants must be victims of violations or have direct, reliable knowledge of violations;
3. the application must contain the facts, state its purpose and indicate the rights that have been violated. As a rule applications containing abusive language or insulting remarks about the state concerned are rejected;
4. politically motivated applications or those which run counter to the principles of the UN Charter are rejected;
5. the applicant must have a prima facie case and the replies sent by the state concerned must convince the Commission that there is a consistent pattern of gross and reliably attested violations of human rights.

During the 1970s and 1980s the main concern of the Commission was the monitoring, through numerous procedures and mechanisms, of compliance by states with the law on human rights.

Since 1990 the priority of the Commission has been to provide advisory and technical assistance to member states in the field of human rights and to focus on social, economic and cultural rights, including the right to development and to an adequate standard of living. This matter was very much on the Commission's agenda at its 57th session held in March and April 2001. In this respect the Commission adopted a number of resolutions, inter alia, Resolution 2001/31 on human rights and extreme poverty in which the Commission reaffirmed that poverty and exclusion from society constitute a violation of human dignity and urged the international community and national governments to take all possible measures to eradicate both.

The Office of the High Commissioner for Human Rights

The Vienna Declaration and Programme of Action 1993 adopted by 171 states at the World Conference on Human Rights called for the strengthening and harmonising of the monitoring of the implementation of human rights under the UN system. To this effect, among other concrete actions, the proposal for the establishment of the Office of the High Commissioner for Human Rights was put forward. The General Assembly created such a post on 20 December 1993 (Resolution 48/141) and enumerated the main tasks of the High Commissioner as being:

1. to promote and protect the enjoyment of all human rights, including the right to development;
2. to provide all forms of assistance (including financial and technical aspects) in the field of human rights at the request of a state;
3. to stimulate and to co-ordinate action on human rights within the UN system and at international level.

Another important task of the High Commissioner is to prevent and to respond to serious violations of human rights throughout the world. The High Commissioner is appointed by the Secretary-General with the approval of the GA for a period of four years, renewable for a further four years. The High Commissioner is in charge of all UN human rights activities. He acts under the direction and authority of the Secretary-General, and within the framework of the overall competence, authority and decisions of the GA, ECOSOC and the Commission on Human Rights.

The mandate of the first High Commissioner commenced on 5 April 1994. Since then the OHCHR has become widely known and respected. It has developed many initiatives to fulfil its task, including the establishment of field offices and operations which provide advice, training and assistance to governments and, if required, supervise the observance of human rights in particularly sensitive places or work with local NGOs.

12.5 Regional protection of human rights

There are a number of arrangements aimed at protecting human rights within a specific region. Human rights initiatives in the Americas, Africa, Asia and Europe are examined below. Among regional arrangements the European system of protection of human rights is the best in terms of effectiveness and maturity.

The inter-American human rights system

The inter-American human rights system is based on the Charter of the Organisation of American States (OAS), the American Declaration of the Rights and Duties of Man adopted in Bogota, Colombia in 1948 and the Inter-American Convention on Human Rights 1969. There are two bodies in charge of the enforcement of human rights in the Americas: the Inter-American Commission of Human Rights with its headquarters in Washington, DC, and the Inter-American Court of Human Rights which is located in San José, Costa Rica.

In May 1948 the ninth Inter-American Conference set up the Organisation of American States (OAS). Its Charter contains two provisions relating to human rights: art 5, which provides that 'American states proclaim the fundamental rights of the individual without distinction as to race, nationality, creed and or sex' and art 16, which requires that a member state respects the rights of the individual and the principle of universal morality. These provisions were inspired by the UN Charter and constitute statements of moral principles rather than conferring any specific rights on individuals. The same Conference adopted the American Declaration of the Rights and Duties of Man, another document which has no binding force. The Declaration specifies civil and political rights and the duties include which individual's duty to obey the law and a general duty to conduct one's self in a way that serves the immediate community and the nation.

In 1959 the OAS established the Inter-American Commission on Human Rights (IACHR) as its autonomous organ. The main task of the Commission is to ensure the respect of human rights and to serve as a consultative body in this area for the OAS. For the first time the IACHR conducted an investigation into violations of human rights in Cuba in 1959. When the government of Fidel Castro did not allow the Commission to visit Cuba the Commission carried out investigations in Florida, where it interviewed Cuban refugees. The result of the Commission's investigation was the expulsion of Cuba from the OAS. Unfortunately, during the following two decades, the OAS did not impose any sanctions on its member states when military dictatorships took over democratic governments in most Latin American countries and subsequently gross and systematic violations of human rights occurred in these countries.

From 1961 the IACHR carried out on site visits to verify the human rights situations in specific countries. In 1965 the IACHR was authorised by the OAS to examine complaints concerning alleged violations of human rights in member states of the OAS. However, its powers were limited: first, in the light of its limited resources it investigated general situations of human rights in each member state rather than individual cases; and, second, it had no teeth as no sanction could be imposed on a state in breach of human rights. The best it could do, as a weak substitute for some form of sanction, was to make a declaration that a member state had violated the American Declaration of the Rights and Duties of Man. Consequently, before the entry into force of the Inter-American Convention on Human Rights 1969, as Medina said:

> '... the Commission was the sole guarantor of human rights in a continent plagued with gross, systematic violations, and the Commission was part of an international organisation for which human rights were definitely not the first priority, and these facts made an imprint on the way the Commission looked upon its task ... Apparently, the Commission viewed itself more as an international organ with a highly political task to perform than as a technical body whose main task was to participate in the first phase of quasi-judicial supervision of the observance of human rights. The Commission's past made it ill-prepared to efficiently utilise the additional powers the [American] Convention

subsequently granted it': 'The Inter-American Commission on Human Rights and the Inter-American Court of Human Rights: Reflections on a Joint Venture' (1990) 12 Hum Rts Q 441.

The Inter-American Convention on Human Rights was signed on 22 November 1969 at San José, Costa Rica. It entered into force in 1978 and has been ratified by 24 counties of the Americas. Trinidad and Tobago which had been a state party denounced the American Convention on 26 May 1998, effective on 26 May 1999. The Convention contains 82 articles which cover civil and political rights and a general provision (art 26) referring to economic, social and cultural rights. The 1988 Additional Protocol to the Inter-American Convention on Human Rights in the Area of Economic, Social and Cultural Rights (known as the San Salvador Protocol), similar in terms to the International Covenant on Economic, Social and Cultural Rights 1966, defined these rights. The Protocol entered into force in 1999 and has been ratified by 11 contracting parties. Consequently, very little has been achieved in the Americas in respect of economic, social and cultural rights.

In 1990 the OAS adopted an Additional Protocol to the Convention Relating to the Abolition of the Death Penalty, which entered into force on 28 August 1991.

Under the Convention two bodies have been set up to enforce its provisions: the pre-existing Inter-American Commission on Human Rights and the new Inter-American Court of Human Rights.

The Inter-American Commission on Human Rights

The Commission has retained its status and functions under the OAS and acquired new functions under the American Convention. These functions are to:

1. monitor the general human rights situations in the member state and publish special reports when appropriate;
2. conduct on-site visits and investigations in respect of specific situations. After examining the situation the Commission will publish a report and send it to the OAS;
3. promote human rights in the Americas by organising seminars, conferences, etc;
4. recommend to the member states of the OAS the adoption of measures aimed at improving the protection of human rights in the Americas;
5. request the state concerned to adopt 'precautionary measures' or if that state refuses, to ask the Court to order 'provisional measures' (these steps can only be taken in urgent cases when there is a risk that serious and irreparable damage will occur to human rights);
6. request an advisory opinion from the Court on the interpretation of the American Convention;
7. submit cases before the Inter-American Court;
8. receive and examine individual petitions alleging violations of the Convention.

The Commission is competent to deal with individual cases where one of the member states of the OAS is accused of human rights violations. In cases against a contracting state to the Convention the Commission processes the case under that Convention. For other states the Commission applies the American Declaration. The petitioner must have exhausted remedies available under domestic law, or must demonstrate that he has tried to exhaust domestic remedies but failed because either domestic remedies are inadequate or were denied, or there has been undue delay in the decision on those remedies. The petition must be lodged within six months after the final decision in the domestic proceedings or within a reasonable time when domestic remedies have not been exhausted.

The Commission decides on both the admissibility and the merits. If a case is admissible the Commission forwards the relevant part of the petition to the government concerned with a request for relevant information. Each party is asked to comment on the reply of the other party. At this stage the Commission may carry out its own investigations including on-site visits. The Commission may also decide to have a hearing in the presence of both parties and ask them to submit their legal and factual arguments. The Commission will try to reach a friendly settlement.

When the Commission fails to settle a case and decides that it has sufficient information it prepares a report, including its conclusions and recommendations, which is forwarded to the state concerned. The report is confidential and the Commission gives the state concerned a fixed period of time to resolve the matter and to comply with its recommendations.

After the expiry of that time limit the Commission has two options: first, it may prepare a second report, similar to the first report, and give the state concerned an additional fixed period to comply with its recommendations. If a state fails to do so, the Commission may publish the report, although under the Convention this option is at the discretion of the Commission. Second, the Commission may decide to bring proceedings against the defaulting state before the Inter-American Court.

Inter-American Court of Human Rights

The Inter-American Court of Human Rights was inaugurated on 3 September 1979. Its main task is to apply and to interpret the American Convention. The Court has contentious and advisory jurisdiction. In respect of contentious jurisdiction it determines cases brought by contracting states to the Convention and by the Commission and may order provisional measures in urgent cases involving danger to persons, even when a case has not yet been submitted to it. However, the contentious jurisdiction of the Court is very limited. Only contracting states and the Commission may commence proceedings. Individuals have no direct access to the Court, even if a contracting state is willing to waive the requirements of exhausting domestic remedies against it in national courts and before the Commission: *Re Viviana Gallardo* (1981) 20 ILM 1424, decision of 13 November 1981. Furthermore, both inter-state and individual cases can be determined by the Court only if a contracting state allows it to do so by making a general declaration to this effect, although the contracting state which has not made such a declaration may authorise the Court to exercise its jurisdiction in a specific case. Out of 24 contracting states to the Convention nine have accepted the general competence of the Court in inter-state cases, and 21 in cases concerning individual applications. For these above states the judgments of the Court are binding. However, there is no way to force a contracting state to comply with the judgment.

In its advisory capacity the Court is empowered to give opinions on the interpretation of the American Convention and other treaties relating to the protection of human rights at the request of member states and organs of the OAS. Also, a member state may ask the Court to give its opinion on the compatibility of its internal laws with the American Convention and other international instruments in the field of human rights.

The inter-American system of the protection of human rights is very disappointing for a number of reasons; the most important are highlighted below.

1. It did not fulfil its mission when most Latin American countries were under military dictatorships. With the entry into force of the Inter-American Convention in 1978 the Inter-American Commission had a legal foundation to act and therefore, at least, to attempt to prevent several decades of human rights violations in Latin America. The Convention requires that contracting states respect human rights and 'ensure' the free and full exercise of these rights. The Commission did nothing. Furthermore, the US and many other countries of the region, have never ratified the Convention on the ground that they could not determine the extent of their commitment under the 'full and free exercise of human rights' provision of the convention. The US, which should have been the leading light in the implementation and the enforcement of the Convention has never been interested in ensuring its effectiveness.
2. The enforcement mechanisms are complex and ineffective.
3. The inter-American system has never lived up to its potential.

Africa

The Charter of the Organisation of African Unity 1963 contains some references to the protection of human rights. Like other documents of this type the Charter's provisions are moral rights which await implementation. This was done by the African Charter on Human and Peoples' Rights adopted by the OAU in 1981 in Nairobi which entered into force on 21 October 1986. At the time of writing it is in force in 53 African states. The Charter proclaims various rights, including collective human rights. Its art 22 recognises the right to development. However, it also emphasises duties of individuals, such as the duty to preserve family, society, the state and the OAU. As Nigeria's Professor Umozurike said:

> '[The] concept of duties stressed in the Charter is quite likely to be abused by a few regimes on the continent, if the recent past can be any guide to future developments. Such governments will emphasise the duties of individuals to their states but will play

down the rights and legitimate expectations': 'The African Charter on Human and Peoples' Rights' (1983) 77 AJIL 911.

The guardian of the Charter is the African Commission of Human Rights and Peoples made up of 11 independent members. Its role is to interpret the Charter, to promote human rights and to assess the situations of violations, including inter-state and individual complaints. However, the Commission has no teeth, it may only examine situations, make reports and make recommendations. It has no enforcement powers. The only sanction against a state in breach of human rights is the publication of a report.

In 1998 the OAU adopted a Protocol to the Charter establishing an African court to 'complement and reinforce the functions' of the Commission. The Protocol entered into force on 25 January 2004, after receiving the 15 required ratifications. The African Court on Human and Peoples' Rights is therefore in the process of being established.

The African regional arrangement is still not very effective, taking into account that member states have rarely, if ever, taken any action to condemn even the most serious violations of human rights. In 1997 the Commission received 200 complaints and rendered 21 decisions which constitutes a significant increase considering that from its inception to 1992 it received 76 communications and did not render any decision on merits: Ch Odinkalu, 'The Individual Complaints Procedures of the African Commission on Human and Peoples' Rights: A Preliminary Assessment' (1998) 8 Transnat'l & Contemp Probs 359.

Asia

There have been some attempts towards the establishment of a regional arrangement designed to ensure the protection of human rights in Asia. Since 1982 Asian countries have been participating in a number of workshops organised by the UN with a view to preparing such an arrangement.

It seems that the Asian perspective on human rights (which emphasises that human rights are meaningless when people do not have the basic necessities of life and therefore poor and underdeveloped countries cannot afford to confer basic rights on its nationals until they reach a certain standard of development) belongs to the past. Poverty cannot justify torture or imprisonment without due process of law. This was clearly recognised in the 1993 Vienna Declaration by almost all countries of the world. The conclusions of the 2001 Kuala Lumpur Workshop state that:

'... while the significance of the national and regional particularities and various historical, cultural and religious backgrounds must be borne in mind, it is the duty of states, regardless of their political, economic and cultural systems to promote and protect all human rights and fundamental freedoms': www.unhcr.ch/html/menu6/kualalumpurconc.htm.

It is important to note that there is a growing number of NGOs in Asia which are very active in the field of human rights. One of the most important is the Asian

Human Rights Commission (AHRC) established in 1986 by a prominent group of jurists and human rights defenders. Its main objective is to promote greater awareness of human rights in Asia, to investigate human rights abuses and to mobilise Asian and international public opinion to obtain relief and redress for the victims of human rights abuses. Under its auspices, and together with over 200 NGOs, it prepared the Asian Human Rights Charter which was formally proclaimed on 17 May 1998 in Kwangju in South Korea at the international conference commemorating the Kwangju uprising. The Charter enshrines civil, political, economic, social and cultural rights. It states that the peoples of Asia realise the connection between their poverty and political powerlessness and the denial to them of basic human rights, and that they 'believe that political and economic systems have to operate within a framework of human rights and freedoms to ensure economic justice, political participation and accountability, and social peace'.

Europe

The main element of the European system for the protection of human rights is the European Convention for the Protection of Human Rights and Fundamental Freedoms 1950 (ECHR), together with its enforcement mechanisms. In addition, both the Council of Europe and the European Union (EU) are stout defenders and promoters of human rights. In respect of the EU its competences, both internal and external, relate to many aspects of human rights.

The Council of Europe
The Council of Europe, which has its headquarters in Strasbourg in the Palais de l'Europe, is one of the most efficient and competent inter-governmental organisations in Europe. The Statute of the Council of Europe was signed in London on 5 May 1949. At its inception it had only ten members. Since the collapse of the Soviet Union and the admission of new members from central and eastern European states, including Russia, the Council of Europe encompasses almost the entire continent, and as at 19 November 2004 had claimed a membership of 46 states, including 21 central and eastern European states. Only democratic countries which ensure the protection of human rights may become members of the Council of Europe.

The main objectives of the Council of Europe are: the promotion of European unity by proposing and encouraging common European action in economic, social, legal and administrative matters; the protection of human rights, fundamental freedoms and pluralist democracies; and the development of a European cultural identity. Since the end of the Soviet regime the Council of Europe within its 'oriental' policy provides assistance to central and eastern European countries with their political, legislative and constitutional reforms (eg the Demo-droit and Themis programmes). In addition, it supervises the protection of human rights in post-communist democracies.

Under the auspices of the Council of Europe, approximately 196 conventions, agreements and protocols have been established, the majority of them are in force in member states, and hundreds of recommendations have been adopted in the light of which member states subsequently harmonise and modernise their own legislation.

The greatest achievement of the Council is undoubtedly the adoption of the ECHR based on art 3 of the Statute of the Council of Europe under which a member state 'must accept the principles of the rule of law and of the enjoyment by all persons within its jurisdiction of human rights and fundamental freedoms'.

Other important conventions prepared by the Council of Europe which complement and extend the protection of human rights in Europe include the following.

1. The European Social Charter 1961 and its 1988 Additional Protocol promote social rights and supervise their implementation in contracting states. The 1988 Protocol extends the rights granted under the 1961 Charter but it constitutes a legally independent instrument which has been ratified by 12 contracting states (as at 19 November 2004).

   The Social Charter covers rights relating to conditions of employment and to social cohesion. At the time of writing 27 states have ratified the Social Charter. The implementation of the Charter is monitored by the Committee of Independent Experts which regularly receives reports from contracting states and assesses them. On the basis of these assessments the Committee of Ministers issues recommendations to governments concerned, requiring them to change their legislation or practice in conformity with the Charter.

   Under the 1995 Additional Protocol to the Charter a system of collective complaints was adopted which allows certain workers' and employers' organisations and non-governmental organisations to submit complaints against a contracting state for alleged violations of the Charter to the Committee of Independent Experts. The 1995 Protocol is in force in 11 contracting states (as at 19 November 2004).

   The 1961 Charter was revised in order to respond to new developments. The revised Charter entered into force in 1 July 1999 and has been ratified by 15 states. It contains new provisions ensuring protection against poverty and social exclusion, the right to decent housing, the right to protection in cases of termination of employment etc. The revised Charter will eventually replace the initial Charter. For the time being relevant provisions of the initial Charter are replaced by corresponding provisions of the 1999 Charter for a contracting state that has ratified both of them.

   Another important instrument protecting social rights is the European Code of Social Security 1971 and its Protocol which ensure a minimum level of protection in this area. The Code was revised in 1990 but its revised version has not yet come into force. Also the protection of migrant workers and their families has been of concern to the Council of Europe which has adopted, inter alia, the European Convention on Social Security 1972, the European Convention on

Social and Medical Assistance 1953, the European Convention on the Legal Status of Migrant Workers 1977, etc.

2. The Framework Convention for the Protection of National Minorities which was adopted by the Council of Europe in 1994 and opened for signature on 1 February 1995. It entered into force on 1 February 1998 and at the time of writing has been ratified by 35 states. Being a Framework Convention it contains mostly programme-type provisions setting out objectives which contracting states undertake to achieve, but leaves the choice of measures which are necessary to achieve these objectives to a contracting state. Consequently, these provisions are not directly applicable. The protection of national minorities is envisaged through protection of the rights of individuals belonging to such a minority and not as a collective right, although the exercise of these rights may be on an individual or collective basis. The Convention enshrines the principle of equality and non-discrimination in respect of individuals belonging to a minority and deals with such issues as the use of minority language, recognition of names, education, prohibition of forced assimilation, protection and development of culture and national identity. The Convention set up a monitoring system. A contracting state must, within one year of its ratification, and then every five years, submit a report on the measures taken in order to implement the Convention. The Committee of Ministers, assisted by an advisory committee of independent experts, assesses these reports and determines whether a contracting state has complied with its obligations or whether there is a necessity to adopt recommendations in respect that state.

3. The European Convention for the Prevention of Torture and Inhuman or Degrading Treatment or Punishment. The Convention was adopted in 1987 and came into force in 1989. As at 19 November 2004 it was in force in 45 contracting states. The Convention's originality lies in its system of supervision. The Committee set up under the Convention is entitled to visit, periodically or on an ad hoc basis, places of detention to interview the detainees in private and to ask any person, including non-governmental organisations, for relevant information. After a visit the Committee prepares a report which is sent to the contracting state concerned. The report may request further information and may contain recommendations and comments. The state concerned must give an interim response to the report within six months and a full reply within 12 months. The report and replies are confidential, although it is now widely accepted practice for a state to agree to make them public. If a state fails to co-operate, the Committee may decide to make a public statement.

4. The Committee of Ministers during its 104th session held on 6 and 7 May 1999 in Budapest adopted a resolution establishing the Office of the Council of Europe Commissioner for Human Rights responsible for promoting and ensuring effective respect and full enjoyment of human rights in all member states of the Council. Its function is very similar to the UN High Commissioner for Human Rights but confined to member states of the Council of Europe.

The European Convention on Human Rights and its Protocols 11 and 14

The ECHR was opened for signatures on 4 November 1950 and entered into force in September 1953. Since then 12 Protocols have been adopted adding further rights and liberties to those guaranteed by the Convention or modifying the control mechanism established by the ECHR. As at 19 November 2004, 45 European states were contracting parties to the ECHR. The ECHR, together with its Protocols and procedures for enforcement, constitutes the first and the most efficient regional arrangement for the protection of human rights. Rights protected under the Convention are both civil and political rights. The originality of the ECHR lies in its unique enforcement machinery which has become even more efficient as a result of the entry into force of Protocol 11 on 1 November 1998.

Protocol 11 does not create new human rights nor advance the ones that already exist. It consolidates the whole system of European protection of human rights by enhancing the machinery for their enforcement. For that reason there are no changes to arts 1–18 of the ECHR concerning substantive rights. However, Protocol 11 adds titles to those articles:

Article 2 is now entitled the 'Right to Life'
Article 3 is now entitled the 'Prohibition of Torture'
Article 4 is now entitled the 'Prohibition of Slavery and Forced Labour'
Article 5 is now entitled the 'Right to Liberty and Security'
Article 6 is now entitled the 'Right to a Fair Trial'
Article 7 is now entitled the 'Right to No Punishment without Law'
Article 8 is now entitled the 'Right to Respect for Private and Family Life'
Article 9 is now entitled the 'Freedom of Thought, Conscience and Religion'
Article 10 is now entitled the 'Freedom of Expression'
Article 11 is now entitled the 'Freedom of Assembly and Association'
Article 12 is now entitled the 'Right to Marry'
Article 13 is now entitled the 'Right to an Effective Remedy'
Article 14 is now entitled the 'Prohibition of Discrimination'

Under art 1 contracting states are obliged to secure to everyone within their jurisdiction the rights and freedoms contained in the ECHR.

Article 15 of the ECHR provides that in a time of war or other emergencies threatening the life of the nation a contracting state is allowed to take measures derogating from its obligations to the 'extent strictly required by the exigencies of the situation, provided that such measures are not inconsistent with its other obligations under international law'. Furthermore, no derogations are permitted from art 2, apart from deaths resulting from lawful acts of war, or from arts 3, 4(1) and 7. A contracting state must inform the Secretary of the Council of Europe of the emergency measures taken as well as of their termination.

New headings are also given to Protocols 1, 4, 6 and 7. The changes make it easier to understand the Convention and its Protocols.

A very limited number of applications is examined on the merits by the

European Court of Human Rights. Between 1 January 2000 and 31 December 2000 the Court delivered 695 judgments, 6,769 applications were struck out or declared inadmissible and 1,082 were declared admissible. In 2003 the Court delivered 703 judgments, 17,270 applications were rejected and 753 applications were declared admissible.

The main reason for the creation of Protocol 11 was the increasing number of applications made to the Commission: in 1981 there were 404 applications, in 1993 there were 2,037 and in 1997 the figure had reached 4,750. Also in 1997 the Commission had 12,000 unregistered or provisional files for investigation. This resulted in the increased workload of the Court: in 1981 the Commission transferred seven cases to the Court, in 1997 the number was 119. Other factors which contributed to substantial changes in the enforcement mechanisms under the ECHR were: the fact that the Court and the Commission did not work on a full-time basis; the increased understanding of the Convention, resulting in more sophisticated claims being brought before the Commission and the Court; and the increasing number of contracting parties to the ECHR. All these factors resulted in considerable delays in dealing with cases (up to five years). Taking into account that justice delayed is justice denied it was necessary to remedy the situation.

Protocol 11
The main changes introduced by Protocol 11 are as follows.

In respect of the bodies entrusted with the enforcement of the ECHR. Prior to entry into force of Protocol 11 there were three bodies charged with this task.

1. The *European Commission of Human Rights.* This was made up of one representative from each contracting state who served in an individual capacity. All applications, whether made by contracting states or individuals, were submitted to the Commission. The main role of the Commission was to filter out applications and to attempt to reach a friendly settlement between the parties. Once the Commission decided that an application was admissible, and provided no friendly settlement was possible, it was the task of the Commission to give its opinion on the merits of the case if it did not intend to refer it for a final judgment to the Court or the Committee of Ministers.

   The Commission was a part time body which usually sat for about 14 weeks a year.

   Protocol 11 abolished the Commission. As a result there is no longer an administrative barrier between the individual and the Court.

2. The *European Court of Human Rights.* Under Protocol 11 the Court has become a full-time institution. The number of judges is the same as the number of contracting states. The Protocol allows judges to share the same nationality which was not permitted under old rules. The criteria for the office of judges set out in Protocol 11 are as before: a judge sits in his individual capacity and does not represent any state, he must hold a high moral standing, have relevant

qualifications in his own country for holding a position of high office, and must act with total impartiality and independence. Judges are nominated by a contracting state and not by the Council of Ministers (old rules). The term of office has been shortened by Protocol 11. Judges are now elected for six years. After three years one half of the elected judges is replaced. Consequently, the term of office of one half of the judges elected at the first election will expire after three years. A system for dismissal of judges has been introduced by Protocol 11. If two-thirds of the judges other than the judge in question consider that a judge has failed to maintain conditions required for being a judge he will be removed.

Protocol 11 changed the organisation of the Court. Under the old rules the Court sat in Chambers composed of seven judges. The names of the particular judges for any chamber were chosen by lot by the President before the opening of the case. The Court sat for about 80–90 days a year. Its decisions were taken by a majority vote and its hearings were public.

Under Protocol 11 the Court consists of Committees of three judges, Chambers of seven judges and of a Grand Chamber of 17 judges. Under the Rules of the Court, the Court is divided into four sections, whose composition is fixed for three years. A Committee is established within each section for a 12-month period and is in charge of examining applications and deciding on their admissibility. Chambers are constituted within each section on the basis of rotation. The Grand Chamber is constituted for three years. Its ex officio members are the President, Vice-President and section presidents.

3. The *Committee of Ministers.* The Committee of Ministers was set up by the Council of Europe and not under the ECHR. Its composition and functions are governed by the Statute of the Council of Europe: arts 13–21. The Committee is made up of one representative from the government of each member state of the Council of Europe usually, the minister for foreign affairs. The Committee is a political body but prior to the entry into force of Protocol 11 it had exercised two functions: judicial or quasi-judicial and supervisory.

As a judicial body, when the Commission failed to secure a friendly settlement of a dispute and decided not to transfer the case to the Court, on the basis of a report forwarded by the Commission the Committee was required to decide whether or not a violation of the ECHR had taken place If the Committee decided that there had been a violation of human rights it had power to order the government concerned to take remedial measures within a prescribed time limit. If the government concerned failed to remedy the violation the Committee was required to take further action and if necessary to publish a report of the Commission. This sanction was quite powerful, taking into account that no democratic government would like to be publicly criticised by an independent and impartial body for its violation of human rights. Also under art 8 of the Statute of the Council of Europe the Committee is empowered to expel any contracting state for violation of art 3 of the Statute which requires respect for the rule of law and protection of human rights.

Under Protocol 11 the quasi-judicial function is no longer exercised by the Committee of Ministers. However, the Committee will still exercise its second function consisting of supervising compliance with a judgment. Consequently, the Committee is to verify whether or not satisfactory remedial measures have been taken by the contracting state concerned.

In respect of complaints. There are two categories of applicants under the ECHR: contracting states and individuals.

In respect of inter-state complaints, under Protocol 11 no changes have been introduced. Any contracting state is entitled to submit an application in respect of any alleged violations of the ECHR by another contracting state. The violations may be against any person, not necessarily a national of the complaining state. Also an application regarding an abstract situation, for example incompatibility of a state's legislation or administrative practices with the ECHR is admissible. Inter-state applications have not proved to play an important role in the protection of human rights. Contracting states prefer not to get involved in a situation which is not of any direct concern to them (although there have been some exceptions: two complaints brought by Denmark, Norway and Sweden against Greece in 1969 concerning the violations of human rights in Greece following the coup d'etat in April 1967 and the case brought by Denmark, France, The Netherlands, Norway and Sweden against Turkey in 1982 relating to the situation in that country under the military regime).

A very important innovation has been introduced by Protocol 11 with regard to individual applications. Under the old rules individual applications were admissible only against contracting states which had made a declaration that they recognised the competence of the Commission to receive such applications. Under Protocol 11 the right of individual petition is unfettered.

In respect of the procedure before the Court. Under Protocol 11 the procedure is judicial in its entirety.

1. *Admissibility procedure.*
   When an application is lodged with the Court it is assigned to a Section whose President designates a rapporteur who, after initial scrutiny, decides whether the application is to be considered before a three-member Committee or by a Chamber. The conditions of admissibility have not changed under Protocol 11: there must be a prima facie violation of one or more of the provisions of the ECHR, the available domestic remedies must be exhausted, and the application must be lodged within six months of the final decision of the highest domestic court or authority.

   The possibility for the rapporteur to refer the application directly to the

Chamber is intended to shorten the duration of proceedings. Under the old framework, an applicant had to wait until the Commission failed to achieve a friendly settlement before forwarding the case to the Court or the Committee of Ministers. Under Protocol 11 an application may be considered directly by the Chamber.

If the rapporteur decides that the application should be examined by a three-member Committee, the Committee determines its admissibility in the light of the criteria set out in art 35 of the Protocol. An application will be rejected if: it is anonymous, if it is similar to a case already decided by the Court or has already been submitted to another procedure or international investigation or settlement, if it constitutes an abuse of the right of complaint (for example it is brought for political propaganda purposes), and if it concerns matters falling outside the scope of the ECHR. The three-member Committee declares, by unanimous vote, about the admissibility of the application. If it is considered as being admissible the application is then examined by a Chamber.

A Chamber will consider applications on both admissibility and merits. It deals with applications referred to it by the Committee, by the rapporteur or submitted by a contracting state. The Chamber may decide to relinquish jurisdiction in favour of a Grand Chamber where the case raises serious questions affecting the interpretation of the Convention. Such relinquishment is mandatory if there is a possibility of conflict with a previous judgment, unless one of the parties objects within one month of notification of the intention to relinquish.

2. *Procedure on the merits.*

Chambers decide cases by a majority vote, and judges are allowed to give separate dissenting or concurrent judgments. Under Protocol 11 an appeal procedure has been introduced. Within three months of the judgment of a Chamber, any party may ask for a referral to a Grand Chamber. A panel of five judges, comprising the President of the Court, the Section Presidents, apart from the President of the section which dealt with the case, and a judge selected by rotation who was not member of the original Chamber, decides whether or not to allow an appeal to be made. The panel must be convinced that the 'case raises a serious question affecting the interpretation or application of the Convention or the protocols ... or a serious issue of general importance': art 43(2). Therefore, an appeal will only be allowed to occur in exceptional circumstances. If the request to appeal is granted the Grand Chamber will examine the merits of the case and, by a majority vote, give a final judgment. A final judgment is binding on the respondent state concerned and its execution is supervised, as under the old framework, by the Committee of Ministers.

3. *Advisory opinions.*

Among other important innovations introduced by Protocol 11 is the possibility for the Committee of Ministers to request advisory opinions from the Court on the interpretation of the ECHR and its Protocols. An advisory opinion is given by the Grand Chamber by a majority vote. Judges are allowed to submit a separate opinion or a bare statement of dissent.

The system introduced by Protocol 11 is not perfect but for the following reasons it is certainly far more fair for individuals than it was previously: they have direct and automatic access to the Court, their applications are determined by the judicial process, they can request an appeal, their applications should be dealt with more speedily and more cheaply as the Court is now sitting on a full time basis, the acceptance of the judgment is now compulsory for all contracting states, and the renewal of half of the judges every three years will ensure greater independence of judges and provide new input.

Protocol 11 has maintained some important and useful features of the old framework: a friendly settlement is encouraged and is possible at any stage of proceedings before the Court. As under the old framework the Court is empowered to award 'just compensation' to victims of violations of human rights.

Protocol 14

Notwithstanding the entry into force of Protocol 11, the European Court of Human Rights can hardly deal with the increasing number of applications. During the three years which followed the entry into force of Protocol 11, the number of applications rose from 5,979 in 1998 to 13,858 in 2002, representing an increase of approximately 130 per cent. For that reason the Ministerial Conference on Human Rights held in Rome on 3 and 4 November 2002, organised to celebrate the fiftieth anniversary of the opening of the Convention for signature, decided to initiate a process of further reform of the Convention. Subsequently a Steering Committee for Human Rights was established to draw up proposals relating to measures that could be implemented without delay and to possible amendments to the Convention. In April 2004 the Steering Committee submitted its final report, containing a draft amending Protocol to the Convention, to the Committee of Ministers. The draft Protocol was adopted by the Committee of Ministers at the ministerial session held on 12 and 13 May 2004. In a declaration adopted at the same session on 'Ensuring the Effectiveness of the Implementation of the European Convention on Human Rights at National and European Levels' member states committed themselves to ratify Protocol 14 within two years. Protocol 14 was opened for signature on 13 May 2004. It will enter into force when ratified by all contracting parties to the Convention. As of 4 November 2004 it had achieved five ratifications.

The changes introduced by Protocol 14 are aimed at ensuring greater effectiveness and flexibility in terms of the functioning of the control system under the Convention rather than changing its existing structure. The main changes are outlined below.

1. *Reinforcement of the Court's filtering capacity.* A committee of three judges which at present decides on the admissibility or otherwise of applications will be

replaced by a single judge assisted by non-judicial rapporteurs who will be part of the Registry.

2. *Repetitive cases.* A new simplified procedure will be introduced to deal with cases which arise from the same structural defect at national level. The committee of three judges (instead of the seven-judge Chamber under Protocol 11) will be competent to rule on both the admissibility and the merits of an application.

3. *New admissibility criterion.* A new admissibility criterion has been added to the existing admissibility requirements. An application will be rejected when an applicant has not suffered any significant disadvantage as a result of any violation of his rights. This is subject to the satisfaction of either of two safeguards. The first is that his case does not otherwise require an examination on the merits by the Court. The second is that he, even when his complaint is of a trivial nature, is not left without any judicial remedy. The second safeguard ensures that every case receives a judicial examination either at national level or at European level.

4. *Compliance with judgments of the European Court of Human Rights.* In order to ensure compliance with judgments delivered by the Court, the Committee of Ministers may decide, by a two-thirds majority, to bring proceedings before the Grand Chamber against a contracting party which, after having been given an appropriate notice, refuses to comply with the final judgment of the Court rendered against it. The Court will have jurisdiction to declare the failure of such a contracting party to fulfil its obligations under art 46(1) of the ECHR.

5. *Interpretation of judgments.* In some circumstances the Committee of Ministers will be able to request the Court to give an interpretation of a judgment.

6. *Terms of office of judges.* The term of office for judges will be increased to nine years. However, contrary to the present position, they will not be eligible for re-election.

The European Union

In the EU the protection of human rights has acquired two dimensions. First, many issues relating to human rights arise under the EU internal and external competences. This is especially the case in the area of gender discrimination and social policy where the protection conferred by EC law upon EU citizens goes far beyond that which the national law of most member states has been ready to offer. The second dimension is that human rights are envisaged in a broad context in respect of all EU policies as being part of the general principles of EC law.

At their inception the Communities focused on economic objectives. This fact, and the existence of the European Convention on Human Rights, explain why human rights have been relatively neglected. Nevertheless, the European Court of Justice (ECJ) was confronted with fundamental human rights issues from the beginning. The question of the fundamental rights which first arose before the ECJ concerned the alleged contradictions between obligations imposed by the High Authority of the European Coal and Steel Community (CS) and the rights which were granted to undertakings under their national constitutional law. The rights and freedoms contained in national constitutions were superior to any other sources of law and their observance was imposed on any public authorities of member states in their dealings with the public. However, it was impossible to permit national constitutional laws to prevail over Community law without compromising its uniform application throughout the Community, but the founding Treaties neither contained any reference to fundamental human rights nor imposed on EC institutions any requirement to observe these rights. It was the task of the ECJ to find a solution to this legal impasse. For the first time in *Stork* v *High Authority* Case 1/59 [1959] ECR 17 the ECJ refused to allow the examination of Community law in terms of its compliance with fundamental human rights and freedoms contained in national constitutions on the ground that this approach would challenge the supremacy of Community law. The criticism expressed by member states, and especially the German Constitutional Court, led the ECJ to adjust its position in an obiter statement in *Stauder* v *City of Ulm* Case 29/69 [1969] ECR 419, in which it held that fundamental human rights constituted general principles of Community law and as such were protected by the ECJ. This position was further elaborated in *Internationale Handelsgesellschaft GmbH* Case 11/70 [1970] ECR 1125 when the Court emphasised that:

> 'The protection of such rights, whilst inspired by the constitutional traditions common to the member states, must be ensured within the framework of the structure and objectives of the Community.'

This solution was criticised by the member states. In order to increase the protection of fundamental human rights, the ECJ decided to make reference to international conventions in this area, especially to the ECHR to which all member states are contracting parties. In *Nold KG* v *Commission* Case 4/73 [1974] ECR 491 the ECJ held that 'international treaties for the protection of human rights on which the member states have collaborated or of which they are signatories, can supply guidelines which should be followed within the framework of Community law'.

Nevertheless, the ECJ highlighted that these rights are not absolute and 'far from constituting unfettered prerogatives, [they] must be viewed in the light of the social function', and thus it is legitimate that 'these rights should, if necessary, be subject to certain limits justified by the overall objectives pursued by the Community, on condition that the substance of these rights is left untouched'.

Subsequently the ECJ has recognised, inter alia, the following rights.

1. The right to equal treatment including non-discrimination based on gender: *Defrenne* Case 149/77 [1978] ECR 1365.
2. The right to exercise economic and professional activities, although this may be legitimately restricted in the light of the social function of the protected activity: *Nold KG* Case 4/73 [1974] ECR 491; *Hauer* Case 44/79 [1979] ECR 3727; *Keller* Case 234/85 [1986] ECR 2897; *Neu EA* Cases C–90 and 91/90 [1991] ECR I–3617.

3. The right to private and family life, domicile and correspondence as set out in art 8 of the ECHR, but this does not exclude the interference of public authorities under the conditions defined by law and necessary to ensure public security and the economic welfare of a country or actions exercising the enforcement powers of the Commission in competition matters: *National Panasonic* Case 136/79 [1980] ECR 2033; *X* v *Commission* Case C–404/92P [1994] ECR I–4737; *Piera Scaramuzza* v *Commission* Case C–76/93P [1994] ECR I–5173.

4. The right to property (*Hauer* Case 44/79 [1979] ECR 3727) but commercial interests in which the risk factor is inherent to its substance are not protected: *Valsabbia* Case 154/78 [1980] ECR 907.

5. The right to medical secrecy: *Commission* v *Germany* Case C–62/90 [1992] ECR I–2575.

6. The right of association: *Union Syndicale* Case 175/73 [1974] ECR 917.

7. The right to free speech: *Elliniki* Case C–200/89 [1991] ECR I–2925; *TV 10 SA* Case C–23/93 [1994] ECR I–4795.

8. The right to religious freedom: *Prais* Case 130/75 [1976] ECR 1589.

9. The principle of non-retroactivity of penal measures: *Kent Kirk* Case 63/83 [1984] ECR 2689.

10. The principle 'nulla poena sine lege': *Berner Allemeine* Case C–328/89 [1991] ECR I–3431.

Procedural rights – such as the right to defence, access to the court, fair hearing, etc – protected under the ECHR have also been recognised by the ECJ. In addition, in *Wachauf* Case 5/88 [1989] ECR 2609 the ECJ held that the protection of fundamental human rights is not only imposed on EC institutions, especially while they adopt binding measures, but also on the member states in their application of such measures. Thus, national authorities in applying EC law must ensure 'as far as possible' that human rights are protected.

The importance of fundamental human rights prompted the Council, the Commission and the European Parliament to sign a Joint Declaration on 5 April 1977 which expressed their attachment to the protection of human rights. Although the Declaration was solely a political statement, it initiated a new approach, that is the need for the Community to incorporate the European Convention on Human Rights into Community law. This initiative was blocked by the member states at the Maastricht Conference and finally in *Opinion 2/94* [1996] ECR I–1759 the ECJ held that the EC had no competence to accede to the ECHR without revising the EC Treaty.

For the first time the provisions relating to human rights were incorporated into EU law by the Treaty on European Union 1992. These were: art F(2) (now art 6(2) EU) which envisaged fundamental human rights in the context of the European Union and in particular as general principles of Community law; and art K.2 (now art 30 EU) which provided that matters of common interest in co-operation in the fields of justice and home affairs shall be dealt with in accordance with the requirements of the ECHR and the 1951 Refugee Convention.

The Treaty of Amsterdam 1997 reinforces the EU commitment to the protection of human rights. The principles of liberty, democracy, respect for human rights and fundamental freedoms and the rule of law on which the EU is founded have been recognised as conditions for admission of new members.

Article 7 EU deals with 'serious and persistent violation' of human rights by a member state. This provision states that Council, meeting in the composition of the Heads of State or government and acting by unanimity (the defaulting member state is excluded) on a proposal by one-third of the member states or by the Commission and after obtaining the assent from the European Parliament, may determine the existence of a violation of fundamental freedoms and then, acting by a qualified majority, may decide to suspend certain rights of the defaulting member state, including the suspension of its voting rights in the Council. However, in applying the provision the Council must take into account the possible consequences of such a suspension on the rights and obligations of natural and legal persons.

For the first time the EU imposed diplomatic sanctions against Austria in February 2000 to express its condemnation of the entrance of Joerg Haider, a leader of the extreme right Austrian Freedom Party known for his racist and xenophobic policies, into the Austrian government. The sanctions consisted of freezing bilateral relations between Austria and the 14 other member states and the suspension of all contacts at an inter-governmental level between Austria and the EU.

Article 6 EU reaffirms the principle of respect for human rights and fundamental freedoms. It also states that the EU 'shall provide itself with the means necessary to attain its objectives and carry through its policies' set out in this provision. In respect of human rights the substantive action of the EU was initiated by the Cologne European Council held in June 1999 which decided to draw up a charter of the basic human rights of EU citizens by December 2000. The Tampere Summit held in October 1999 reached an agreeement on the composition, method of work and practical arrangements for the Convention, the body entrusted with this task. The Convention was made up of 62 members: 15 personal representatives of the Heads of State or government, 16 members of the European Parliament and 30 members of national parliaments. The Convention commenced its work in November 1999, electing as its chairman the former president of the Federal Republic of Germany, Roman Herzog. It completed its work on 20 October 2000 and sent its draft Charter to the European Council.

The Nice European Council held on 7, 8 and 9 December 2000, which concluded the Intergovernmental Conference on the Reform of European Institutions (IGC), adopted a declaration on the Charter of the Fundamental Human Rights of the European Union and welcomed the proclamation made jointly by the Council, the European Parliament and the Commission of the Charter but decided that it would examine the matter of its binding force later. As matters stand at the time of writing, the Charter is not binding but many member states wish the

Charter to be incorporated into the treaties. The Charter, even as a non-binding document, has some impact on EU law: the three institutions which proclaimed the Charter have committed themselves to respect it and the Court of Justice of the European Communities takes it into consideration when deciding cases.

The Charter contains 50 articles. Its main purpose is to make fundamental rights and freedoms more visible, more explicit and more familiar to EU citizens. The Charter expresses the fundamental human values shared by all member states. The Charter, contrary to the European Convention on Human Rights, contains not only civil and political but also economic, social and societal rights. The Charter of Fundamental Rights was published in the OJ: OJ C364 (2000).

The Nice European Council agreed on amendments to the Treaty of Amsterdam 1997 by the new Treaty of Nice. In respect of the protection of human rights the Nice Treaty has introduced a new mechanism aimed at preventing infringements of human rights by member states which substantially amends art 7 EU. A new provision added to art 7 EU specifies that the Council, acting by a majority of four-fifths of its members, after receiving the assent of the European Parliament and having heard the member state concerned, may decide that there is a clear risk of a serious breach by a member state of fundamental human rights and freedoms. The Council may send appropriate recommendations to that state. The new procedure may be commenced at the initiative of one-third of the member states, the Commission or the European Parliament.

The Treaty of Nice entered into force on 1 February 2003. The issue of the Charter of Fundamental Rights of the European Union was further considered by a Convention set up to draft the EU constitution which started its work in February 2002. On 29 October 2004, the Heads of State or government of 25 member states and the three candidate states signed the Treaty establishing a Constitution for the EU. The Constitution incorporated the Charter as its Part II. The new Treaty can only enter into force if ratified by all member states. The Treaty Establishing the EU Constitution has set the date for its entry into force as at 1 November 2006.

12.6 Customary international human rights and ius cogens

There is an ongoing debate whether human rights in their entirety or only some of them form part of customary international law. Have all the provisions of the Universal Declaration of Human Rights achieved the status of cutomary law? In other words, has the Universal Declaration imposed a wide range of obligations in the field of human rights independently of specific treaties? It is uncontested that the Universal Declaration has been used on numerous occasions to intepret human rights obligations arising out the the UN Charter. Furthermore, the General Asssembly has always emphasisied in its declarations and resolutions the binding nature of the Universal Declaration. For example, the GA Resolution 1514 (XV), the Declaration on the Granting of Independence to Colonial Countries and Peoples

1960 states that: 'All states shall observe faithfully and strictly the provisions of ... the Declaration of Human Rights'. A very similar statement can be found in the Declaration on Elimination of All Forms of Racial Discrimination 1963. Also in its resolutions the Security Council has referred to the binding nature of the Universal Declaration, eg its resolutions condemning apartheid. Additionally, member states have made statements expressly acknowlegding the binding force of the Universal Declaration, inter alia, in the Final Act of the Helsinki Conference on Security and Co-operation in Europe 1975 and, in the 1993 Vienna Declaration. The argument that states cannot, on some ocassions, accept the binding force of the Declaration, and on others reject it is very convincing. The Commission on Human Rights' Special Rapporteur on the situation in Iran, Mr Galindo Pohl, had no hesisitaions in affirming that: 'The rights and freedoms set out in the Universal Declaration have become international customary law through state practice and opinio juris'. The Commission accepted his report without any debate on the matter of binding force of the Universal Declaration': UN Doc E/CN4/1987/SR56/Add 1 paras 10–37.

For the organs of the UN the binding nature of the Universal Declaration is evident. However, state practice does not confirm that view. Human rights violations are still widespread and generally tolerated by the international community. This negative attitute, however, is confined to the minority of states.

What emerges from state practice is that some rights set out in the Universal Declaration are widely recognised by member states and their violation by a state is strongly condemned by the international community (eg genocide and torture), while the violations of other rights do not provoke such a reaction (eg equality between men and women and right to nationality).

The question arises how to indentify human rights which have satisfied the requirement of custom. In this respect the Restatement (Third) of the Foreign Relations Law of the United States, prepared by the American Law Institute, identifies (in para 702) the following acts as violations of international law, if practised, encouraged, or condoned as a matter of state policy:

1. genocide;
2. slavery or slave trade;
3. the murder or causing the dissaperance of individuals;
4. the torture or other cruel, inhuman, or degrading treatment or punishment;
5. prolonged arbitrary detention;
6. systematic racial discrimination; and
7. a consistent pattern of gross violations of internationally recognised human rights.

In the commentary to the the last-mentioned violation the Restatement refers to: systematic harassment, invasions of the privacy of the home, arbitrary arrest and detention even if not prolonged, grossly disproportinate punishment, denial of fair trial, freedom to leave the country or return to one's own country, freedom of conscience and religion, personality before the law, basic privacy such as the right to marry and raise a family, racial or individual religiuos dicrimination, and mass uprooting of part of the population.

Many authors have proposed lists of customary international human rights, and generally speaking these lists conform to the Restatement. It is probably safe to say that the rights set out in the Restatement have acquired the status of customary international law.

There is a growing opinion that some human rights are part of ius cogens. It is very difficult to establish a list of rights which can be classified as ius cogens taking into account the controversy surrounding the topic. The UN Commission on Human Rights has always considered that the prohibition of genocide and slavery are ius cogens. The prohibition of torture ought also to be recognised as ius cogens. In *Furundzija* IT–95–17/1 'Lasva Valley' (1999) 38 ILM 317 the International Criminal Tribunal for the Former Yugoslavia held that the prohibition of torture is regarded as ius cogens. In the *Pinochet* judgment the House of Lords confirmed that the prohibition of torture prevails over rules relating to state immunity. However, recent judgments of the International Court of Justice, the European Court of Human Rights and national courts refuse to give the prohibition of torture the status of ius cogens, so that it would override the principle of state immunity: see Chapter 9.

12.7 General conclusions

Efforts made by the international community to ensure the protection of human rights are certainly encouraging but they must be assessed in the light of what many nations are actually doing. The respect for human rights can not be confined to mere declarations. So far as the UN system is concerned its effectiveness in the enforcement of human rights is still weak for many resons, the most important being:

1. it is not mandatory, therefore there are many states unwilling to submit themselves to any external scrutiny;
2. there is no judicial mechanism within the UN to deal with individual complaints;
3. the reporting and monitoring system is still based on confidentiality;
4. the Security Council has not taken any consistent and firm stand in respect of states violating basic human rights. The principle of non-interference in domestic matters, and the political assessment of human rights situations, often prevail.

At the regional level (apart from Europe where the protection of human rights is well advanced) there is a very large credibility gap between promises, which are easy to make, and performance which either seems to be very hard to effect or in respect of which there is not the will to carry through.

13

Nationality, Statelessness, Refugees and Internally Displaced Persons

13.1 Introduction

13.2 Nationality

13.3 Statelessness

13.4 Refugees

13.5 Regional arrangements

13.6 Internally displaced persons

13.1 Introduction

There is no universally accepted definition of nationality, although there is a general agreement that nationality constitutes a legal bond creating reciprocal rights and obligations between an individual and a state. In the 1929 Draft Convention prepared by the Harvard Law School nationality is defined as 'the status of a natural person who is attached to a particular state by the tie of allegiance': art 1 on Nationality, Responsibility of States, Territorial Waters, Spec Supp to (1929) 23 AJIL 22.

Municipal law determines the rights and privileges enjoyed by nationals and at the same time imposes some duties upon them. For an individual there is no greater right or privilege than nationality and the distinction between nationals and non-nationals is of the utmost importance when it comes to the enjoyment of political, civil, social and cultural rights and the right to enter and remain permanently within the territory of a home state. Nationality is also relevant in a number of situations, eg in a time of war an enemy status is determined on the basis of nationality of the person concerned, or a state may exercise jurisdiction in criminal or other matters over its nationals for events which take place abroad or, conversely, over foreigners who have injured its nationals. Being a national of a particular state may involve fulfilment of certain obligations, such as conscription. Also, a state may tax its nationals upon income earned anywhere in the world.

At international level, a state is expected to ensure diplomatic protection of its nationals and their property abroad and it is entitled, as a general rule and in the absence of a specific treaty (or a resolution of the Security Council as occurred in the *Lockerbie* case), to refuse the extradition of its own nationals.

In the *Nottebohm Case* (1955) ICJ Rep 4 the International Court of Justice introduced the concept of 'effective nationality' requiring that for the granting of nationality to be recognised by other states the existence of a genuine link between an individual and the state granting naturalisation is necessary. The ICJ confirmed, on the one hand, that the matter of nationality is within the exclusive competence of a state and, on the other hand, held that other states are entitled to challenge the grant of nationality unless there is a genuine connection between the individual concerned and the state conferring its nationality upon him.

In the context of the *Nottebohm Case* it is important to emphasise that the Court was particularly influenced by two factors, first by a letter from the German Foreign Office of 4 July 1939 stating that German interests may require that some of its citizens may acquire foreign nationality and for that reason their request for denationalisation as well as subsequent renaturalisation should be facilitated and looked upon favourably. Second, Nottebohm was an active member of the Nazi party and as such was on the British and the US blacklist.

It seems that the judgment of the ICJ in the *Nottebohm Case* concerned exceptional circumstances. The concept of 'effective nationality' has been called into question by both state practice and subsequent decisions of international courts and tribunals. For any state to have its naturalisation process challenged by another state is an unwelcome interference in its internal affairs entailing a judgment of another state on its domestic legislation in the matter which, being a manifestation of national sovereignty, is jealousy guarded by a state.

Nationality is of vital importance to any natural person as it provides an essential element of stability to his personal and societal life. However, some individuals do not possess any nationality. They are stateless persons. Some others, instead of being protected by their own state, are persecuted by it. Often they have to flee their own country and seek refuge in another country. Sometimes, they are stripped of their nationality by their home state. They are, simultaneously, refugees and stateless persons. There is also a growing number of people who are refused any protection by their own state and are forced to abandon their home but remain within the national territory. They are known as internally displaced people.

This chapter will examine the concept of nationality and the manner in which international law protects those who are refused any protection, or are even persecuted by their state of origin.

13.2 Nationality

Classic international law considered nationality as one of the fundamental prerogatives of a sovereign state. As a result each state was entitled to determine for itself who were its nationals.

The PCIJ in its Advisory Opinion of 7 February 1923 concerning *Nationality Decrees* in *Tunis and Morocco* held that:

'The question whether a certain matter is or is not solely within the jurisdiction of a state is an essentially relative question: it depends upon the development of international relations. Thus, in the present state of international law, questions of nationality are, in the opinion of the Court, in principle within this reserved domain': (1923) Ser B No 4, 23.

In this case the PCIJ decided that any limitation upon municipal laws on nationality depends upon the development of international law. Thus, the right of each state to decide on the acquisition or withdrawal of nationality was not unfettered but subject to changes occurring in international relations as reflected in the rules of international law.

With the development of international human rights many felt that a state's freedom to arbitrarily determine the conditions of its nationality should be restricted by international law. Deprivation of nationality should be conditional upon the simultaneous acquisition of another nationality. This idea has been reflected in many international instruments, the most important being art 15 of the Universal Declaration of Human Rights (UDHR) which recognises the right to nationality. Article 15 of the UDHR provides that 'everyone has the right to a nationality' and that 'no one shall be arbitrarily deprived of his nationality nor denied the right to change his nationality'.

Article 15 contains three different categories of rights concerning nationality: the right to have a nationality, the right to retain that nationality and the right to change it. The idea behind art 15 was stated by Mrs Roosevelt during the debates of the Third Commission which was in charge of preparing the UDHR. She said that art 15 'was designed to make clear first, that individuals should not be subjected to action such as was taken during the Nazi regime in Germany when thousands had been stripped of their nationality by arbitrary government action, and secondly, that no one should be forced to keep a nationality which he did not want and that he should not therefore be denied the right to change his nationality': 3 UN GAOR C3 (123s mg) 352 (1948), A/C3/SR 123.

Article 15 is vague and imprecise. It neither specifies which state is obliged to grant nationality upon an individual who has no nationality nor does it contai an absolute prohibition of deprivation of nationality as it refers to the concept of arbitrariness. Other international instruments which subsequently transposed the UDHR into binding legal instruments have imposed limitations on a state's freedom in the matter of nationality. The UN Convention on the Reduction of Statelessness 1961, which is examined below, does not confer a general right of individuals to possess a nationality. The International Covenant on Civil and Political Rights 1966 in its art 24(1) recognises that children have the right to nationality but does not mention adults. The only internationally binding instrument which expressly proclaims the right to nationality is art 20 of the Inter-American Convention on Human Rights which states:

'1. Every person has the right to a nationality.
2. Every person has the right to the nationality of the state in whose territory he was born if he does not have the right to any other nationality.
3. No one shall be arbitrarily deprived of his nationality or of the right to change it.'

In *Amendments to the Naturalisation Provisions of the Constitution of Costa Rica* (1984) 5 HRLJ 161 the Inter-American Court on Human Rights was requested to rule upon the compatibility of certain proposed amendments to the Costa Rica constitution with art 20 of the Convention. The Court did not hesitate to state that:

'It is generally accepted today that nationality is an inherent right of all human beings. Not only is nationality the basic requirement for the exercise of political rights, it also has an important bearing on the individual's legal capacity.'

The Court decided that international law imposes limitations on powers enjoyed by a state in the domain of nationality as such powers are circumscribed by their obligations to ensure full protection of human rights.

Parallel questions remain as to whether international law, first, leaves a state complete and unrestricted freedom to determine who are its nationals and, second, whether the right to a nationality is a human right? The answers are not easy. On the one hand, international law through various international instruments, including the Universal Declaration of Human Rights, affirms that the right to nationality is an inherent human right; on the other hand, this is probably one of the weakest human rights whose development has been constantly stifled by states extremely reluctant to allow any limitation on, or supervision of, international law over the matter which constitutes one of the main prerogatives of a sovereign state. It is probably safe to say that there is a growing trend in international law to recognise the right to nationality as a human right.

The development of the international law of nationality is still largely state-oriented and dominated by state interests.

In the context of nationality it is interesting to mention the concept of EU citizenship.

EU citizenship is based on nationality of a member state. Article 17(1) EC states that 'Every person holding the nationality of a member state shall be a citizen of the Union. Citizenship of the Union shall complement and not replace national citizenship.' This point is enhanced in the Declaration on Nationality of a Member State 1992 attached to the Treaty on European Union 1992 which provides that:

'... wherever in the Treaty establishing the European Community reference is made to nationals of the member state, the question whether an individual possesses the nationality of a member state shall be settled solely by reference to the national law of the member state concerned.'

The requirement of nationality of a member state as a prerequisite of EU citizenship means that nationals of third countries, refugees and stateless persons legally residing in a member state do not acquire any rights under art 17 EC. In practice around 9 million people residing legally in the EU are excluded from benefiting from EU citizenship, although they contribute to the prosperity of the EU and are treated in member states on an equal footing with nationals.

13.3 Statelessness

Statelessness as a social phenomenon has always existed and one might even consider Adam and Eve as the first stateless persons since they were expelled from Paradise which had until then been their homeland and God, in order to punish them, had withdrawn his protection. The history of mankind is in a certain sense the history of statelessness. However, from a legal point of view, the Pericles' Citizenship Law of 451–500 BC, the first known legislation regulating citizenship, created a distinction between nationals and non-nationals. An individual could claim the citizenship of Athens only if his father had been a citizen of the city: C Patterson, *Pericles' Citizenship Law of 451–500 BC*, 1981, p8. Nationality in the modern meaning appeared at the time of the French Revolution and was closely connected with the emergence of the nation state.

The phenomenon of statelessness emerged with a particular acuity after World War II but has, by no means, been eradicated. The exact number of stateless persons is difficult to determine. Apart from nomads and gypsies who, because of their way of life, are usually stateless and those who are born stateless as a result of inconsistencies and divergences of municipal laws on nationality, today the situation of statelessness occurs in particular in the following circumstances.

1. In Kuwait, where up to 250,000 Bidoons (this term in Arabic means 'without nationality') who for generations lived in Kuwait were expelled after the Gulf War for alleged collaboration with Iraqi forces. The same treatment was applied to the Palestinians working in Kuwait before the Iraqi invasion. These people are now scattered over many countries in the Persian Gulf.
2. In Syria, where up to 200,000 Kurds were made stateless as a result of a 1962 census, on the basis of which they were refused Syrian nationality as being allegedly illegal immigrants from Turkey.
3. In Myanmar, where up to two million of the Rohingya people, a Moslem minority living in Western Myanmar, were denied citizenship. A small number of them now live in refugee camps in Bangladesh.
4. In Zaire, where up to 800,000 Banyarwanda and Banyamulenge people living in Eastern Zaire were refused recognition as citizens of Zaire.
5. In Cambodia, where up to 500,000 ethnic Vietnamese are awaiting the decision of the Cambodia legislature as to their nationality.
6. In Bhutan, where up to 120,000 living in Southern Bhutan, but speaking Nepali, were denied citizenship. Currently, they live in Nepal and India.

The phenomenon of statelessness is not confined to less developed countries. In

Europe thousands of people have become stateless as a result of the disintegration of the USSR, Yugoslavia and the separation of Slovakia from the Czech Republic.

Pittius vividly depicted the situation of stateless persons in the following terms:

> 'In the case of statelessness, an unfortunate individual is placed in the unenviable position of being without any country at all … such an ill-fated person will discover to his consternation that the frontiers of all civilised states are closed upon him, he is a tertium quid whose home is presumably somewhere between all other countries. If dual nationality is a unfortunate predicament, statelessness is a calamity': E F Pittius and W Van Gey, *Nationality within the British Commonwealth of Nations* (1930), pp132–133.

Indeed, according to the classic view of nationality the legal position of stateless persons was precarious.

First, an individual was not a direct subject of international law. As a result, his state of nationality provided necessary protection for his person and interests at international level.

Second, there was no distinction between refugees (who were often stripped of nationality by their state of origin or de facto unprotected by any state) and stateless persons. Indeed, it is difficult to identify one from another since both produce similar legal effects. This is the main reason why statelessness for centuries and even today, to a certain extent, has been linked with the issue of refugees. The situations are by no means similar. The confusion arose because often refugees are deprived of their nationality by the country of origin. They are, simultaneously, stateless persons and refugees. Furthermore, the first international instrument (intended to ensure international protection for Russians who fled the 1917 Bolshevik revolution) did not deal with refugees and stateless persons separately because, by virtue of the Decree of the Council of Commissioners of People of 28 October 1921, all Russians outside the Soviet Union who refused to return were stripped of their nationality. Subsequently, all international arrangements adopted under the auspices of the League of Nations made no distinction between refugees and stateless persons. They were based on a case-by-case approach, consisting of extending the existing rules to new waves of refugees fleeing persecution at home. Therefore, the League of Nations never envisaged statelessness as a separate issue. After World War II international law ceased its empirical approach towards refugees and subsequently it has become clear that statelessness must be dealt with separately, taking into account that statelessness, contrary to the issues of refugees, has no political dimension.

Statelessness has its origin in the insufficiencies and divergences of municipal laws on nationality and occurs when no state is willing to grant its nationality to certain categories of persons either at birth (absolute statelessness) or subsequent to birth (relative statelessness).

The acquisition of nationality by birth is based on two principles:

1. ius soli – according to which a child born in the territory of a state becomes automatically a national irrespective of the nationality of his parents;
2. ius sanguinis – under which nationality derives from parentage and thus a newborn acquires the parent's nationality regardless of the place of birth.

The sole application of one of the above principles can lead to statelessness, if, for example, a child is born in the territory of a state which grants its nationality on ius sanguinis and his parents are nationals of a state whose nationality is based on ius soli.

A comprehensive comparative study of 38 municipal legislations in the area of nationality carried out by the Canadian Center for Immigration Studies found that 13 states including Canada, Mexico, Brazil and Spain were applying the principle of ius soli, and 25 imposed an additional requirement that at least one parent be a citizen of the country (six out of the 25 specified which parent, a father or a mother, was to provide a link). Other states (eg Germany) based the acquisition of nationality by birth solely on the principle of ius sanguinis: (1996) 3 Migration Law 6.

With regard to relative statelessness, it has many causes: denationalisation by a voluntary act of a national or by an act of the state, changes of sovereignty over territory, changes of marital status by marriage or divorce, an extended stay abroad, etc.

The problem of statelessness has been tackled by the international community from two perspectives: first, international protection was granted to stateless persons by the Geneva Convention Relating to the Status of Stateless Persons 1954; and, second, reduction was provided for by the Convention on the Reduction of Statelessness 1961.

The Geneva Convention Relating to the Status of Stateless Persons 1954

The Geneva Convention relating to the Status of Stateless Persons 1954 did, for the first time, recognise statelessness as an autonomous concept. It entered into force in 1960 and as at 1 October 2004 had been ratified by 57 states.

Article 1 of the 1954 Convention defines a stateless person as 'a person who is not considered as a national by any state under the operation of its law'.

Under art 1(2)(iii) the following persons will be refused recognition as stateless persons:

1. those who have committed a crime against peace, a war crime or a crime against humanity;
2. those who have committed a serious non-political crime outside the country of their residence prior to their admission to that country;
3. those who have been guilty of acts contrary to the purposes and principles of the United Nations.

The 1954 Convention is not very generous. It is based on a minimum treatment, that is stateless persons should be treated as favourably as aliens in general. Treatment as if a national applies only in very limited areas such as access to the courts, access to social security and labour law, access to primary education, and protection of intellectual property rights.

The 1954 Convention provides that naturalisation of stateless persons is to be made as easy as possible but does not specify any timetable.

The reduction of statelessness

The possibility of the elimination of, or at least the reduction of, statelessness was examined, for the first time, by the 1930 Hague Codification Conference held under the auspices of the League of Nations. The Hague Conference adopted:

1. the Convention on Certain Questions Relating to the Conflict of Nationality Laws 1930;
2. a Protocol Relating to a Certain Case of Statelessness;
3. a Special Protocol Concerning Statelessness.

Article 15 of the above Convention states that a child born to stateless parents or parents of unknown nationality may acquire the nationality of the state where he is born. However, this provision contains a limitation as it allows the state concerned to determine the condition of acquisition of its nationality. The Protocol is more compelling as it obliges a contracting state to grant nationality to such a child if his mother is a national of that state. The Convention is silent on the most important problem of denaturalisation or deprivation of nationality, which is the main cause of statelessness. The Special Protocol is concerned with the readmission of nationals who have been deprived of their nationality after entering another state. The Convention and the Protocol entered into force on 1 July 1937. The Convention has been ratified by 20 states and the Protocol by 21 states. The Special Protocol has never entered into force. This first attempt at the reduction of statelessness was disappointing; nevertheless it recognised that nationality was of concern to the international community and thus has paved the way for further developments.

The Convention on the Reduction of Statelessness 1961 entered into force in 1975 and the number of its ratifications is very limited: as at 1 October 2004 it was in force in 29 states.

The 1961 Convention provides for the establishment of a UN body entrusted with the supervision of its application, in particular to deal with claims based on the Convention. This body has never materialised. The United Nations High Commission for Refugees, by virtue of a mandate by the UN General Assembly, assumes the responsibility for stateless persons but does not exercise the functions which were assigned to the body envisioned by the 1961 Convention.

The 1961 Convention sets out a general rule in art 1 that a contracting state shall grant its nationality to a person born in its territory who would otherwise be stateless. However, this rule is subject to may exceptions: states may refuse an application submitted after the applicant's 21st birthday, or if the applicant has not lived in the state's territory for five years prior to the submission of the application, or if the applicant has at some time possessed another state's nationality or if the applicant has been convicted for committing certain criminal offences.

With regard to depravation of nationality, art 8, which attacks the main source of statelessness, provides that a contracting state shall not deprive a person of its nationality if such deprivation would render him stateless. This provision is, once again, subject to qualifications, and deprivation would be permitted if the person concerned, whether naturalised or a national by birth, has conducted himself in a manner seriously prejudicial to the vital interests of the state. Naturalised persons may also be rendered stateless by withdrawal of nationality due to prolonged residence abroad, or in the situation where nationality was obtained by misrepresentation or fraud, or where a naturalised person renders services to another state, receives emoluments from another state, makes an oath or declaration of allegiance to another state, etc.

The 1961 Convention is not very ambitious. Notwithstanding this, it has obtained a small number of ratifications which demonstrates that the matter of nationality is still jealously guarded by states that are very reluctant to forgo sovereignty in this area.

Among other international instruments dealing with the reduction of statelessness it is important to mention the following.

1. The Convention on the Nationality of Married Women 1957 and the Convention on the Elimination of All Forms of Discrimination against Women 1979, both requiring that the change of the personal status of a woman should not result in statelessness and thus such change should be conditional upon possession or acquisition of another nationality.
2. The Convention on the Rights of the Child 1989 intends to ensure that children have the right to be registered and to acquire a nationality from birth.
3. The European Convention on Nationality adopted by the Council of Europe on 15 May 1997 which entered into force on 1 March 2000. As at 24 November 2004 it had been ratified by 12 states. The 1997 European Convention is aimed at reducing the instances of statelessness but not at eliminating statelessness. Furthermore, it does not establish any enforcement mechanisms.
4. The European Convention on the Adoption of Children. Its art 11(2) provides that a loss of nationality which could result from an adoption shall be conditional upon possession or acquisition of another nationality. The Convention entered into force on 26 April 1968. As at 24 November 2004 it had been ratified by 18 states.

The issue of eliminating statelessness has been given a new impetus since 2001 when the UN General Assembly adopted Resolution 50/152 (2001) extending the mandate of the United Nations High Commissioner for Refugees (UNHCR) to provide protection for stateless persons and requesting the UNHCR to report biannually on its activities in the field of statelessness. In the Report submitted in June 2003 the UNHCR summarised its main activities in this area as consisting of:

1. conducting a survey on the steps taken by states to reduce statelessness and to

protect stateless persons within the framework of the implementation of the Agenda for Protection;

2. providing technical and advisory services: in this respect the UNHCR assisted more than 60 states in drafting new nationality laws and amendments to laws with a view to eliminating statelessness;

3. promoting the existing UN Conventions on Statelessness: between 2001 to 2003 the UNHCR achieved two more accessions to the 1953 Convention relating to the Status of Stateless Persons and three more accessions to the 1961 Convention on the Reduction of Statelessness;

4. co-operating with other international organisations interested in the issue such as the Council of Europe, the Organisation for Security and Co-operation in Europe (OSCE), the Organisation of African Unity, the European Union, etc;

5. providing training and briefing sessions on statelessness to interested governments and groups of states.

The UNHCR's main actions for the future in the field of statelessness will be to identify the main problems outlined by states under the survey mentioned above and to address them accordingly, whilst continuing its previous work on the prevention and reduction of statelessness.

13.4 Refugees

In the aftermath of the 1917 Bolshevik revolution approximately 800,000 Russian refugees were scattered around Europe. They found themselves without financial resources, without a place to live, without medication and without legal protection of any state. By virtue of the Decree of 20 December 1921 issued by the Council of Commissioners of People, all Russians living abroad who refused to return to the Soviet Union were stripped of their nationality. They became stateless persons and refugees at the same time. The Director of the Russian Red Cross forwarded a letter to the Council of the League of Nations asking for economic and legal assistance for Russian refugees. This was supported by the International Committee of the Red Cross (ICRC), which, after an international conference gathering together various international organisations, asked the Council of the League of Nations to find a solution at international level to the problem caused by the Russian refugees.

On 27 June 1921 the Council of the League of Nations created the Office of the High Commissioner for Russian Refugees and entrusted it with the triple task of providing humanitarian assistance, facilitating their repatriation to Russia and co-ordinating, under the auspices of the League of Nations, all efforts which had already been made. Dr Frdtjof Nansen, a scientist and a leading Arctic explorer, was appointed to the office which he carried out gratuitously from 1921 until his death in 1930. Dr Nansen, who had personal contacts with the Soviet government as he was one of the organisers of the repatriation of half a million prisoners of war from

26 countries mostly from south-eastern Europe and the USSR, tried to negotiate with the Soviet government to accept the refugees. This solution proved unworkable. As a result it was necessary to settle the Russian refugees in other European countries and to regulate their stay there. The matter of identity papers and conditions of acceptance in other countries became urgent. The proposal of Dr Nansen which consisted of issuing provisional passports was rejected. Instead, a special conference gathering together 16 governments held in Geneva in 1922 decided to create a certificate of identity for the Russian refugees. This arrangement was adopted by 53 states and constitutes the establishment of the 'Nansen passport'. A contracting state was free to determine the conditions of residence in its territory for a bearer of the Nansen passport. Moreover, only the state of delivery was authorised to issue and to renew the passport and, after leaving, its holder had no right to return without a special authorisation.

The protection provided for the Russian refugees was gradually extended to other groups: Assyrians, Turks, Armenians, Spaniards and Austrian and German Jews. Each wave of refugees was treated separately and special arrangements, similar to those made for the Russian refugees, were concluded for each.

After World War II the number of refugees, stateless persons and displaced persons reached 21 million. In 1948 the United Nations set up a new body being the International Refugee Organisation (IRO), which replaced the United Nations Relief and Rehabilitation Agency (UNRRA), to deal with the problem. Its main objective was to repatriate refugees. The Cold War made it impossible. Those who had 'valid objections' including 'persecution, or fear of persecution because of race, religion, nationality or political opinion' had to be resettled. The IRO, from its creation until the termination of its mandate in 1951, helped to resettle over one million refugees, repatriated 73, 000 and made arrangements for 410,000 internally displaced persons. On 3 December 1949 the General Assembly adopted Resolution 319A (IV), creating the UN High Commission for Refugees (UNHCR) as a subsidiary organ of the GA, initially for a period of three years. Since then the mandate of the UNHCR has been extended many times. The UNHCR has its seat in Geneva and has offices in 120 countries. As at 1 January 2004 the UNHCR was concerned with 17.084 million people. The main tasks of the UNHCR are:

1. to provide international protection for refugees;
2. to seek permanent solutions for the problems of refugees;
3. to co-ordinate international action in favour of refugees;
4. to promote the conclusion and ratification of international conventions for the protection of refugees and to supervise their application.

The UNHCR in fulfilling its mandate has helped millions of refugees and asylum-seekers by providing international protection and by assisting refugees to restart their lives, either through voluntary repatriation to their home country or resettlement in new countries. In addition, the UNHCR is assisting internally displaced persons in all possible ways. For example, it provided material assistance in Bosnia-Herzegovina and for the Kurds in Northern Iraq. In Sarajevo the UNHCR initiated the longest humanitarian airlift ever to supply food and medications to its inhabitants. In 1990 it airlifted 43,000 Namibian refugees back to their country shortly before independence and in 1966 during the Great Lakes crisis flew 60,000 refugees from Congo to Rwanda.

The Geneva Convention Regarding the Status of Refugees 1951

After World War II it became necessary to regulate the situation of refugees at international level. Under the auspices of the UN an International Conference was convened in Geneva in 1951 which produced the most important international instrument relating to the protection of refugees: the Geneva Convention Regarding the Status of Refugees 1951. As at 1 October 2004 the 1951 Geneva Convention had been ratified by 145 states.

The Convention defines a refugee in its art 1 as any person who:

'... as a result of events occurring before 1 January 1951 and owing to well-founded fear of being persecuted for reasons of race, religion, nationality, membership of a particular social group or political opinion, is outside the country of his nationality and is unable, or owing to such fear, is unwilling, to avail himself of the protection of that country; or who, not having a nationality and being outside the country of his former habitual residence as a result of such events, is unable or, owing to such fear, is unwilling to return to it.'

The Executive Committee of the UNHCR, comprising representatives from 50 states, adopted non-binding policy guidelines to assist national authorities in the determination of persons eligible for the status of 'refugee' within the meaning of the 1951 Convention. Also the UNHCR's *Handbook on Procedures and Criteria for Determining Refugee Status* is considered as an authoritative interpretation of the 1951 Convention. Normally, the determination of whether a person can claim refugee status is made on a case-by-case basis. However, in the event of mass exodus resulting from widespread violations of human rights aimed at a particular sector of the population, a 'group determination' may be applied. Each member of the group is considered as a refugee in the absence of evidence to the contrary.

The above definition of a refugee clearly establishes five grounds of persecution: race, religion, nationality, membership of a particular group and political opinions. Consequently, not only political persecution (and therefore those who are persecuted because they fight for freedom) but also others may be eligible for refugee status. Thus, the definition is sufficiently flexible to encompass new types of refugee as they have emerged over the years. For example, in France, Canada and the United states it has been officially recognised that genital mutilation of women traditionally practised in some African countries constitutes a form of persecution and that women who fear genital mutilation in their countries may be recognised as refugees under the 1951 Convention. Also a woman who refuses to wear restrictive clothing, who is forced into an arranged marriage or who is deprived from leading an independent life because of religious or other restrictions, has a legitimate claim to refugee status. However, the 1951 Convention is clear that war criminals are excluded from the benefit of the protection.

The determination of who is entitled to refugee status is left to the contracting states. The UNHCR can provide advice and assistance to both contracting and non-contracting parties to the 1951 Convention. However, in some cases the UNHCR may determine that a person is entitled to refugee status.

The 1951 Convention establishes a minimum standard treatment for refugees in a contracting state and sets out the basic rights to which they are entitled. In some areas they are treated in the same manner as nationals, ie in relation to wage-earning employment and social security, protection of industrial and intellectual property, access to justice (including an exemption from cautio judicatum solvi), access to primary education, access to public relief and assistance, and fiscal charges. In some areas treatment as favourable as possible but not less favourable than that accorded to foreigners in general should apply to them, ie in connection with the acquisition of immovable and movable property, the exercise of any liberal profession, establishment as self-employed, housing, access to education other than primary education, and freedom of movement. In some areas a contracting state should accord to refugees the most favourable treatment applicable to nationals of a foreign country in the same circumstances, ie in respect of the right of association and the right to belong to a trade union.

A person recognised as a refugee under the 1951 Convention has a right to identity papers and to travel documents.

One of the most important provisions of the 1951 Convention is art 33(1), which prohibits expulsion or forcible return ('refouler') of a refugee to any country where he is likely to be persecuted or tortured. The non-refoulment principle refers to the situation where a person is discovered to have illegally entered the territory of a state and is being summarily re-conducted to the frontier, or a person is in the possession of a visa or other papers allowing him to enter the territory but is refused admission to the territory. Therefore, refoulment is quite distinct from expulsion or deportation which concern the situation where a person has been lawfully admitted to the national territory but is required to leave it or to be forcibly removed from it. Article 33(1) is of vital importance for refugees within the meaning of art 1 of the 1951 Convention but ever more so to asylum-seekers. This provisions ensures that at the stage when a refugee has not been officially recognised by a contracting state as such, he is entitled to effective international protection.

Article 33(1) is reinforced by art 3 of the 1984 Torture Convention which expressly provides that:

'No state shall expel, return ("refouler") or extradite a person to another state where there are substantial grounds for believing that he would be in danger of being subjected to torture.'

In the European context, art 3 of the ECHR, which prohibits torture or inhuman or degrading treatment or punishment, provides wide and flexible protection for refugees and asylum-seekers. This provision can be invoked before national courts and before the European Court of Human Rights. Article 3 of the ECHR is formulated in absolute and unqualified terms and applies to any person within the jurisdiction of a contracting state irrespective of whether or not he is a national of that state and irrespective of his past conduct. For example, in *Soering* v *United Kingdom* (1989) 11 EHRR 439 the applicant was a German national accused of murdering his girlfriend's parents in Virginia in the US. If extradited he would have faced the death penalty. The UK was prevented from extraditing him to the US on the ground that if extradited there was a real risk that he would be subjected to inhuman punishment, not because of the imposition of the death penalty in the state of Virginia but because of the so-called 'death row phenomenon' whereby a person, before being executed, is detained in a Virginian prison for on average six to eight years, under stringent security regime and in the knowledge that he would be executed. In *Chahal* v *United Kingdom* (1997) 23 EHRR 413 the Court decided that Mr Chahal, who was considered as posing a risk to national security as he was involved in terrorist activities in India, could not be deported to India by the UK authorities by virtue of art 3 of the ECHR. Article 3 provides more extensive protection to refugees and asylum-seekers than art 33 of the 1951 Geneva Convention which removes the benefit of art 33(1) in the situation where a contracting state has reasonable grounds to believe that a refugee represents a danger to national security or, having been convicted by a final judgment of a particularly serious crime, constitutes a danger to the community of that state.

The 1967 Protocol

The 1951 Geneva Convention contains a temporal restriction. This was due to the fact that at the time of the adoption of the 1951 Geneva Convention it was believed that the refugee crisis was a temporal phenomenon resulting from World War II and confined to Europe. In addition, contracting states were given an option to limit the geographical application of the 1951 Convention to Europe. This optimistic view has been challenged by waves of refugees arriving in the late 1950s and 1960s from other parts of the world, in particular from Africa. A Protocol adopted in 1967 lifted both the temporal and the geographical limitations on the application of the 1951 Convention which has since become of universal scope.

Assessment

The 1951 Geneva Convention has been criticised for not being able to deal with the increasing number of asylum-seekers and the increase in people-smuggling networks which involve increasing costs for contracting states in processing asylum applications. These activities create the perception that all asylum-seekers are 'bogus'. In this respect it is important to note that the increase is due to three major wars in Europe during the last decade and that it is exactly the objective of the 1951

Convention: to separate those who genuinely need international protection, because they have been persecuted, tortured or otherwise abused or have a real fear of being killed or subjected to inhumane treatment in their home country, from those who are looking for a better life in rich countries. As Erika Feller, UNHCR's Director of International Protection stated: 'The Convention was never intended to sort out all the world's migration problems. The trouble is, with virtually no other migration path open from poor countries to rich ones, the Convention has been subjected to pressures which should be catered for by alternative migration management tools': www.unhcr.ch/news/pr/pr010726.htm.

In respect of the UK, Professor G S Goodwin-Gill, a leading authority on international refugee law, stated that there is nothing wrong with the 1951 Convention, the problem that many countries experience, including the UK, is the systematic inefficiency of their systems of processing asylum requests: 'Asylum: Myths and Reality' *The Guardian*, 19 August 2001.

In 2001 the 1951 Geneva Convention celebrated its 50th anniversary. It has saved many lives and ensured international protection for those who needed it most.

13.5 Regional arrangements

Regional arrangements complement the 1951 Geneva Convention and the 1967 Protocol, which remain the main international instruments in this area, by taking into account the specificity of the refugees problems in a particular region of the world.

Africa

On 10 September 1969, under the auspices of the Organisation of African Unity, the Convention on Refugee Problems in Africa was concluded with a view to regulating the problem of refugees from an African perspective. The 1969 Convention extends the definition of a refugee taking into account the peculiarity of the refugee situation in Africa. Its art 1 states that the term 'refugee' applies not only to a person who has 'well-founded fear of persecution' but also to every person who, 'owing to external aggression, occupation, foreign domination or events seriously disturbing public order in either part or the whole of his country of origin or nationality, is compelled to leave his place of habitual residence in order to seek refuge in another place outside his country of origin or nationality.'

South America

Latin American countries have expanded the definition of a refugee under the Cartagena Declaration on Refugees 1984. The Declaration defines refugees as those who 'have fled their country because their lives, safety or freedom have been threatened by generalised violence, foreign aggression, internal conflicts, massive violation of human rights or other circumstances which have seriously disturbed public order'. To date, ten Latin American countries have incorporated the definition of 'a refugee' provided in that Declaration into their national legislation whilst three apply the definition in practice. In order to commemorate the 20th anniversary of the Cartagena Declaration 18 Latin American countries organised a two-day event hosted by the government of Mexico on 16–17 November 2004. At the end of the commemoration the participating states issued a declaration reaffirming their commitment to the protection of asylum-seekers and refugees and adopted a plan of action aimed at improving the existing refugee protection throughout the region and responding to the humanitarian situation of Colombians in need of protection.

Traditionally, South American countries have been particularly interested in the development of regional rules on political asylum and on diplomatic asylum. The Montevideo Treaty 1889 was the first regional arrangements introducing the concept of political asylum. The Caracas Convention on Territorial Asylum 1954 reiterates previous arrangements in this area.

Europe

In Europe the Council of Europe and the European Union have introduced a number of specific arrangements concerning refugees and asylum-seekers.

The Council of Europe

The Council of Europe has been very active in improving the protection and treatment granted to asylum-seekers and refugees. The most important instruments adopted by the Council of Europe are:

1. the European Agreement on the Abolition of Visas for Refugees 1969;
2. Resolution 14 (1967) on Asylum to Persons in Danger of Prosecution;
3. the European Agreement on Transfer of Responsibility for Refugees 1981;
4. Recommendation on the Harmonisation of National Procedures Relating to Asylum (1981);
5. Recommendation on the Protection of Persons Satisfying the Criteria in the Geneva Convention Who Are Not Formally Refugees (1984);
6. Recommendation on the Right of Asylum (1994);
7. Recommendation on the Situation of Asylum-Seekers Whose Applications Have Been Rejected (1994);
8. Recommendation on Refugees and Asylum-Seekers in Central and Eastern Europe (1995);
9. Recommendation on the Training of Officials Receiving Asylum-Seekers at Border Points (1996);

10. Recommendation on the Protection and Reinforcement of the Human Rights of Refugees and Asylum-Seekers in Europe (1997);
11. Recommendation on the Situation of Refugee Women in Europe (1998).

In the light of the restrictive policies and practices of its member states the Council of Europe adopted Recommendation 1440 (2000) on Restrictions on Asylum in the Member States of the Council of Europe and the European Union which identifies the main restrictive practices in immigration and asylum policies of its member states and urges Member States to revise their national policies to conform with the 1951 Geneva Convention. The Recommendation also urges the member states to take into consideration when dealing with asylum applications that:

1. persecution may also originate from entities with have no link to the state and over which the state has no control;
2. war and violence may be used as instruments of persecution, in particular in respect of specific groups on account of their ethnicity or other characteristics;
3. asylum-seekers should not be required to prove that they have exhausted all possibilities of reaching safety in some areas within their own country before seeking international protection;
4. women seeking asylum should be allowed to apply separately from their spouses or companions in consideration of their specific needs and motivations.

The European Union
All member states of the EU are contracting parties to the 1951 Geneva Convention.
Co-operation between member states in asylum and immigration matters has a long history although it has been based mostly on ad hoc arrangements. The first arrangement in this area, the Schengen Agreement, was concluded outside the framework of the EU but was incorporated into its structure by the Treaty of Amsterdam 1997.

The Schengen system
The agreement between France and Germany in July 1984 in Saarbrucken on the elimination of frontier controls between the two countries, which was intended as a way of strengthening Franco-German relations, gave birth to the Schengen system. The Benelux countries had already abolished border checks for their nationals. They decided to join the Franco-German project. It resulted in the adoption of the Schengen Convention on the Gradual Abolition of Checks at Common Borders. On 14 June 1985 the Schengen I agreement was signed between the Benelux countries and France and Germany. It provided that border controls should be abolished on 1 January 1990 between territories of the contracting parties. In order to achieve this objective, working groups were established to draw up necessary measures on the relaxation of border controls, such as the introduction of mixed checks at the borders, visual checks on EC nationals (green stickers in the front windows of cars) and co-ordination of measures strengthening the control of external borders to keep

out undesirables by harmonising visa controls, asylum and deportation policies. Also issues relevant to internal security, such as harmonisation of firearms and ammunition laws, police co-operation in combatting illegal trade in drugs and serious international crimes were addressed. Their work culminated in the adoption of the Schengen Implementing Convention on 19 June 1990 (Schengen II) between the same five contracting states. This Convention entered into force on 1 September 1993. The Amsterdam Summit of June 1997 decided to incorporate the Schengen system into the revised Treaty on European Union.

In the relationship between the Schengen group and the EC, the Commission had the status of observer at the Schengen meetings. The Schengen system was subordinated to EC law through the compatibility requirement established in art 134 of Schengen II, which states that the Schengen provisions shall only apply if they are compatible with EC law. For that reason it was quite easy to incorporate the Schengen system into the Treaty of Amsterdam 1997.

The main features of the Schengen II is that it abolishes the internal borders of the signatory states and creates a single external border where immigration checks for the Schengen territory are carried out in accordance with a single set of rules. Furthermore, if a non-EC national is considered to be unlawfully in one Schengen country, he is deemed to be illegally in all and will be expelled from the Schengen territory. Also, it introduces tight controls on non-EC nationals entering the Schengen territory aimed at eliminating illegal immigration and strengthens the co-operation between police and immigration authorises. Finally, it sets up a system for the computerised exchange of information known as the Schengen Information System (SIS), located in Strasbourg, which contains information on policing, crime and immigration including arrest warrants, missing persons, stolen documents and goods, etc. At its head is the SIRENE system (Supplementary Information Request at the National Entries), a communication system used in urgent situations where a contracting state needs specific information. It is a central contact point for each Schengen country. Requests for information through the SIS are verified and legally validated.

Thirteen member states are contracting parties to the Schengen II and since 19 December 1999 Norway and Iceland have been associated with the Schengen II (they have no voting rights but participate on the Schengen Executive Council). The protocol attached to the Treaty of Amsterdam provided for incorporating the Schengen II agreement into the EU framework. In order to do so, the Council which replaced the Executive Committee set up under the Schengen Agreement, took a number of decisions. On 1 May 1999 it established a procedure incorporating the Schengen Secretariat into the General Secretariat of the Council: OJ L119 (1999). The elements of the Schengen II which should be incorporated into the EC Treaty (the Schengen acquis) were defined by the Council Decision adopted on 20 May 1999: OJ L176 (1999).

Not all member states of the EU participate in the Schengen II. The legal position of dissenting member states – Ireland, the UK and Denmark – is regulated by protocols annexed to the Treaty of Amsterdam. The UK and Ireland may join the Schengen II provided the Council of the 13 participating member states decides unanimously to accept them, while Denmark is given an option to adopt the Schengen principles. If the UK and Ireland decide to participate in the adoption of measures based on the Schengen acquis they may do so by notifying the Presidency within a reasonable time. In March 1999 the UK asked to participate in some aspects of Schengen, namely police and legal co-operation in criminal matters, the fight against drugs and the SIS. The Commission gave a favourable opinion on 21 July 1999.

The Treaty on European Union 1992 (TEU)

The Treaty on European Union 1992 (also known as the Maastricht Treaty) included immigration and asylum matters within the competences of the EU. They were covered by the so-called Pillar III of the TEU devoted to co-operation in justice and home affairs. The framework of co-operation was based on an intergovernmental decision-making procedure with marginal contributions from the Community institutions. Pillar III consisted of determination of nine areas listed in Art K.1 of the TEU (now art 29 EU) which were considered as 'matters of common interests' to the member states, inter alia, asylum and immigration policy. Until the TEU these issues were mostly left to the member states. The EC decided not to deal with immigration and asylum because this had already been done by the Schengen group, and the Ad Hoc Group on Immigration. Some governments, the UK in particular, considered that these matters were within their exclusive competences and refused to surrender their sovereign rights in border checks even for travellers from the EC, not trusting continental immigration authorities to keep illegal immigrants outside the UK.

The main instrument adopted under the TEU in the area of asylum is the Dublin Convention, which is considered below.

The Dublin Convention

The Convention Determining the State Responsible for Examining Applications for Asylum Lodged in One of the Member States of the European Communities was signed on 15 June 1990 in Dublin. It entered into force on 1 September 1997. The main objective of the Convention is to prevent an asylum-seeker from making multiple applications and from selecting the country of asylum. As a result, if his application is refused in one country, the application is considered as refused by all other member states. It also acknowledged the first 'safe' country principle. If an asylum-seeker on his way from a country where he was persecuted went through a host third country, that is a country which is considered safe or where he could have applied for asylum, his application in the EC would be deemed unlawful and he would be returned to the host country.

The Convention determines the member state which should deal with an asylum application, that is, the one which granted him a visa or allowed him illegal entry into the Community unless he has a close family – only husband or wife or parents or children – with refugee status in an EC country. In that case the state of residence of his close family will deal with his application. The receiving state notifies the responsible state of the presence of an asylum-seeker and sends the asylum-seeker to that state. Under the Dublin Convention the entire Union is treated as one country for the purposes of an asylum application.

Under art 18 of the Dublin Convention a Committee responsible for its implementation was set up. So far the Committee has taken only a few decisions, inter alia, Decision 2/97 setting up the rules of procedure (OJ L281 (1997)) and Decision 1/98 of 30 June 1999 (OJ L196 (1998)) clarifying important issues in respect of the implementation of the Convention, such as the exchange of fingerprint data between member states, the exchange of information on ways and means asylum-seekers enter the European Union and the establishment of close working relationships between officials of member states carrying out functions in relation to the Convention. The decisions of the Committee are of vital importance for the national authorities of the member states responsible for the examination of applications for political asylum.

Another important decision – Decision 1/2000 – was adopted on 31 October 2000 in respect of the transfer of responsibility for family members in accordance with arts 3(4) and 9 of the Dublin Convention (OJ L281 (2000)) which entered into force on 7 November 2000.

Decision 1/2000 is aimed at ensuring effective and harmonised implementation of arts 3(4) and 9 of the Dublin Convention in respect of family reunification or of maintenance of the family group. Articles 3(4) and 9 provide that a contracting party may examine an application for asylum for humanitarian reasons, namely family or cultural considerations, even though it is not responsible for such examination under the criteria defined in the Dublin Convention. By virtue of art 9 of the Dublin Convention the state examining an application for asylum with the consent of the applicant may ask the state responsible for such examination to transfer this responsibility to it. Decision 1/2000 brings important clarification in this area.

First, it defines the meaning of 'family members'. Article 1(1) of the Decision provides that family members include the spouse of an applicant, his unmarried child under the age of 18, and his father or mother if the applicant is a minor under 18 years old and unmarried. However, art 1(2) broadens the notion of family members as it includes other close relatives of an applicant, namely persons who were living together with the applicant as a family unit before they left their country of origin and where there was a relationship of dependency between them.

Second, art 2 of the Decision sets out conditions for family reunification and for maintenance of a family group. This provision does not impose any obligation on a contracting party to depart from the criteria laid down in the Dublin Convention in respect of responsibility for dealing with applications for asylum in relation to the applicant's family. It is for a contracting party in the light of the particular circumstances of each case to decide whether or not to take such responsibility for humanitarian reasons. The Decision, nevertheless, provides a non-exhaustive list of factors which a contracting party should take into consideration, including the fact that family members lived in the same household before leaving their country of origin and the reasons which led to divided responsibility for family members or a separation of the family.

Article 2(2) specifies that families should normally be reunited:

1. where a family member is a minor under 18 and would otherwise be unaccompanied in a member state;
2. a family member is dependent on support on account of pregnancy, serious illness, serious handicap or old age.

Third, art 5 of the Decision provides for co-operation between contracting parties in cases of shared responsibility where asylum proceedings are conducted by family members in different member states. In this respect, contracting parties should exchange information at the earliest opportunity and notify each other without delay of the completion of the respective asylum proceedings.

The Amsterdam Treaty 1997

One of the main objectives of the Amsterdam Treaty is the progressive establishment of an area of freedom, security and justice. It has as a main constituent the abolition of border controls between member states in order to ensure the free movement of persons. Under art 62 EC the Council, acting by unanimity, has five years from the entry into force of the Treaty of Amsterdam to eliminate internal border controls and in particular:

1. to introduce measures removing border controls for persons within the EU whether or not EC nationals;
2. to set out common rules for the crossing of external borders by non-EC nationals;
3. to establish conditions for the issue of visas for non-EC nationals to enter and stay up to three months within the territory of a member state;
4. to prepare a list of countries whose nationals are exempted from the visa requirements (Council Regulation 574/1999 of 12 March 1999 has determined the third countries whose nationals must be in possession of visas when crossing the external borders of the member states: OJ L72 (1999)).

The free movement of persons is to be mainly achieved by the incorporation of the Schengen acquis into the framework of Community law as it covers the main arrangements concerning the common treatment of non-EC nationals and a system of common control at external borders.

Immigration and asylum is covered by art 63 EC. It concerns:

1. the determination of a member state responsible for dealing with an application for political asylum;

2. the establishment of minimum standards in relation to qualification for, and grant of, asylum;
3. the establishment of minimum standards for temporary protection of displaced persons from third countries who are unable to return to their home country;
4. the adoption of common rules on immigration policy, including such issues as the conditions of granting long-term visas and residence permits for non-EC nationals as well as facilitating non-EC nationals legally residing in one member state to establish themselves in another member state.

Under art 64 EC the Council is entitled to adopt measures combatting illegal immigration and to introduce temporary measures to deal with emergency situations involving a sudden inflow of non-EC nationals seeking protection from outbreak of violence or persecution in their country of origin.

It is interesting to note that a Protocol on Asylum for Nationals of the Member States of the EU has been annexed to the EC Treaty. It contains one article which provides that taking into account the respect for fundamental human rights in the member states, they should, for all legal and practical purposes regarding asylum applications, consider each other as safe countries of origin. They are permitted, nevertheless, to examine applications for political asylum submitted by nationals of other member states, although in such an event the application should be dealt with on the basis of the presumption that it is manifestly unfounded. The main objective of the Protocol is to ensure that terrorist suspects will not take advantage of asylum procedures in another member state in order to avoid extradition.

Post-Amsterdam developments
The Dublin Convention has been strongly criticised, inter alia, for creating 'fortress Europe', that is, asylum-seekers suffer great difficulties and privations in their attempts to obtain sanctuary in EC and EFTA countries. Even if they cross the external frontiers, almost all EU countries have introduced new stringent laws on asylum, accelerated procedures for 'manifestly unfounded' applications without appeal, and detention for those that cannot prove their identity. Additionally, compulsory fingerprinting and detention in prisons and special centres is imposed. Further, measures, such as carriers being liable for bringing a person without proper documents into the territory of a member state or the examination of asylum requests at the border, mean that in effect border guards and stewardesses decide whether a person is entitled to obtain refugee status!

The Tampere European Council (15–16 October 1999) was exclusively devoted to the protection of human rights. One of the main issues was the creation of a common asylum and immigration policy in the light of the criticism expressed by NGOs and the UNHCR regarding the EU policy which, instead of harmonising the measures, has mostly focused on restricting access to the EU of refugees. The Tampere Council adopted short- and long-term objectives for the EU in the establishment of 'A Common European Asylum System, based on the full and inclusive application of the Geneva [Refugee] Convention'. The short-term objectives (the Tampere Programme) consist of establishing:

1. workable criteria for determining the state responsible for deciding an asylum claim (the Dublin Convention);
2. common standards for a fair and efficient asylum procedure;
3. common minimum reception standards for asylum-seekers, rules on recognition and content of refugee status; and
4. rules on subsidiary forms of protection for those not meeting the refugee definition but who still require protection.

The target date for the achievement of these objectives was set at May 2004.

The long-term objectives refer to the establishment of a 'common asylum procedure and a uniform status for those who are granted asylum' (the Hague Programme).

The Tampere Programme (expired in June 2004)

Progress in the achievement of the objectives set out in the Tampere Programme was, initially, slow. A new impetus was given to a common asylum policy by the Seville European Council held in June 2002. The Seville Council decided to speed up new legislation on EU proposals for legal immigration and asylum. A deadline in 2003 was set for the adoption of measures which were necessary to complete the Tampere Programme. In November 2004 only one measure was outstanding, an EU Directive on the Asylum Procedures. In this respect the European Summit, held in November 2004, urged the Council of the European Union to adopt the remaining Directive without delay. Also member states were called upon to fully implement all measures adopted within the Tampere Programme.

The most important secondary legislation adopted in order to implement the Tampere Programme is as follows.

Council Decision 2000/596/EC of 28 September 2000 establishing a European Refugee Fund: OJ L252 6/10/2000/1

This important step in the protection of refugees at Community level was taken by Council Decision 2000/596/EC establishing a European Refugee Fund (ERF) operating from 1 January 2000 to 31 December 2004. The Fund amounts to 216 million euros. The Fund has been set up to support and encourage the efforts by the member states in receiving, and bearing the consequences of receiving, refugees and displaced persons. Based on the principle of solidarity between member states, funds are allocated proportionally to the burden each member state bears in respect of receiving refugees and displaced persons.

Three categories of action are supported by the Fund.

1. Relating to conditions for reception, such as providing appropriate accommodation and financial assistance, health care, social assistance and help

with administrative and judicial formalities. This also includes the provision of fair and effective asylum procedures.

2. Relating to integration of such persons when their stay in a member state is of a lasting and stable nature, in particular by providing social assistance in areas such as housing and by allowing them to participate in various education and vocational programmes with a view to preparing them for employment.

3. Relating to the repatriation of refugees and displaced persons, if they so wish. The action may concern information and advice about voluntary return programmes and the situation in the country of origin.

In addition to the above action categories, the Fund is also used to finance emergency measures aimed at assisting one or more or all member states in the event of a sudden influx of refugees and displaced persons, or to help to evacuate such persons from a third country at the request of international organisations. However, emergency measures financed from the Fund are limited to a period of six months and must not exceed 80 per cent of the cost of each measure.

Further, at the proposal of the Commission up to 5 per cent of the Fund's available resources may be used to finance innovatory actions or actions of interest to the Community as a whole. Such actions may be fully financed by the Fund.

The member states implement actions supported by the Fund and are responsible in the first instance for the financial control, whilst the European Commission verifies whether the member states comply with their obligations.

Decision 2000/596/EC applies to the UK and Ireland by virtue of the notifications which those countries have communicated pursuant to art 3 of the Protocol on the position of the UK and Ireland which is attached to the TEU and to the Treaty Establishing the European Community. However, the decision is not applicable to Denmark.

In 2004, the EU adopted a new European Refugee Fund for the period 2005–2010, based on the principles set out in Decision 2000/596/EC.

Directive 2003/9/EC of 27 January laying down minimum standards for the reception of asylum-seekers

The Directive aims to improve the reception conditions for asylum seekers during the period when their application is being examined by setting out minimum standards on the reception of asylum applicants. The adoption of the above Directive was necessary, taking into account that asylum seekers under the Dublin Convention are prevented from making multiple applications and from selecting the country of asylum.

The Directive provides for certain minimum standards in respect of issues of information, documentation, freedom of movement, healthcare, accommodation, access to the labour market and to vocational training. It also contains provisions applicable to persons with special needs, unaccompanied children and victims of torture. The original proposal for a Council Directive was submitted by the

European Commission in April 2001: COM (2001) 181 final. The European Commission was particularly concerned about applicants with special needs and those who are detained. The final version was considerably amended by the member states in that it waters down the standards originally proposed by the European Commission. The following should therefore be noted.

1. Contrary to the European Commission proposal the Directive does not affect the freedom that member states enjoy in respect of restrictions imposed on the free movement of an asylum-seeker within the national territory of a member state which deals with his application. In this respect the European Commission proposal sets out a list of grounds allowing member states to limit the movement of asylum-seekers within the national territory. The Council decided not to include the list in the Directive. Further, the Directive introduces the list of grounds that allow member states to impose a specific place of residence upon asylum-seekers and allows member states to refer to national law to identify the situations in which an asylum-seeker may be detained.

2. The Directive has reduced the notion of family members to that of the spouse or the unmarried partner of the applicant (only in the situation where the member state concerned treats unmarried couples in a way comparable to married couples under its immigration law) and the minor children. With regards to other members of the family the issue of whether or not the Directive will cover them is left to be determined by reference to national law of the member state concerned.

3. The dignified standard of reception in the member state concerned which the European Commission strived to introduce has been considerably challenged in the Directive. The Commission proposed 'a standard of living adequate for the health and the wellbeing of applicants … as well as the protection of their fundamental rights'. The Directive reduced this to 'a standard of living adequate for the health and to enable the subsistence of the applicants'. Further, under the Directive, a member state may refuse reception conditions in cases where an asylum-seeker has failed to make the application as soon as reasonably practicable after arrival in the member state.

4. The Directive leaves member states a wide measure of discretion in the implementation of certain crucial provisions, such as access to employment and access to social benefits. Each member state is free to determine whether or not an applicant will be allowed to work during the examination of his application, even if such examination is delayed longer than one year for reasons unconnected with the applicant. Also access to social benefits – such as health care, housing, education for children – may be refused to applicants who have failed to apply for asylum as soon as possible after their arrival in the member state.

Council Regulation 343/2003 of 18 February 2003 (Dublin II Regulation) establishing the criteria and mechanisms for determining the member state responsible for examining an asylum application lodged in one of the member states by a third-country national: OJ L050, 25/02/2003/1
This Regulation introduces only minor changes to the Dublin Convention. The responsibility based on irregular entry over the external border and that deriving from an irregular stay on the territory of a member state is limited to a period of 12 months after the date on which the irregular border crossing took place. After that period, if it is impossible to determine the state of entry, the state responsible for dealing with an application will be the state in which the applicant has been residing illegally for more than five months. Irregular entry is not the main criterion in respect of the determination of a member state responsible for dealing with an asylum application. Indeed, under the Regulation the criteria used to determine the member state responsible for examining an asylum application has not changed. The hierarchy of criteria assigns responsibility in the following order:

1. the member state in which a family member of the applicant is already residing as a refugee;
2. the member state which issued a residence permit to the applicant;
3. the member state which granted him a visa.

The member state responsible for examining the asylum application has a duty to admit the applicant to its territory, to process his application and to readmit him in the situation where the applicant has travelled to another member state without authorisation of the receiving member state.

The European Automated Fingerprint Identification System (AFIS)
On 15 January 2003 EURODAC, a system which registers, for comparison purposes, the fingerprints of asylum-seekers and certain categories of illegal immigrants, became operational in all member states of the EU (except in Denmark) and in Norway and Iceland (see Regulation 2725/2000 [2000] OJ L316/1). Under the system, participating states take the fingerprints of all fingers of every asylum-seeker over the age of 14 and send them to a central unit located with the European Commission where they are stored. EURODAC's main objective is to establish whether or not an asylum-seeker's fingerprints have already been recorded and, if so, he will be sent to the country where his fingerprints were originally recorded.

The Hague Programme
A multi-annual programme called 'the Hague Programme' was agreed by the European Summit held on 4–5 November 2004. It concerns all policies relating to the creation of the area of freedom, security and justice, including the external aspects, inter alia, asylum and immigration. The European Commission has been given one year to prepare proposals for concrete action and a timetable for their adoption and implementation. Further, the European Commission is required to

present a study on the legal and practical implications of joint processing of asylum applications within the EU. The UNHCR welcomed this new development in the EU, emphasising that this will eliminate the existing discrepancies in the granting of asylum by member states: for example, by September 2004, 50 per cent of Chechen asylum-seekers in most EU countries had been granted the status of refugee whilst in the Slovak Republic, out of 1,081 applications only two had been decided in favour of the claimants (see the official website of the UNHCR). In its conclusion the 2004 European Summit emphasised that the Common European Asylum System would be based on the full and inclusive application of the 1951 Geneva Convention on the Status of Refugees and other relevant Treaties. The Hague Programme is very ambitious. It aims to create a high quality asylum system common to all member states by 2010.

13.6 Internally displaced persons

The Special Representative of the UN Secretary-General for Internally Displaced Persons estimates that there are between 20 and 25 million internally displaced persons (IDPs) worldwide. Other estimates are more optimistic. According to UNHCR there are about six million of them. Whatever the number, it is uncontested that millions of people can rely neither on the protection of their governments nor on the protection of the international community.

Displaced people can be defined as those who are forced to leave their home to flee persecution, armed conflicts or human rights abuses but for whatever reasons are still within the territory of their own country. There are no specific international instruments relating to the protection of internally displaced people. As any human beings they are protected by international human rights and humanitarian law but taking into account their situation at home instead of being protected by their governments they are victims of persecution and abuses. Moreover, the application and enforcement of humanitarian law in internal conflicts has always been very problematic.

The response of the international community to the plight of IDPs is very weak. The International Committee of the Red Cross has for decades provided general humanitarian assistance to IDPs. UNHCR is also involved in helping the IDPs but it can only act at the request of the UN Secretary-General, or a competent principal organ of the UN, after obtaining the consent of the state concerned.

At the international level, there are only non-binding instruments dealing with the situation of IDPs. Examples include:

1. the Guiding Principles on Internal Displacement, a study presented by the Representative of the Secretary-General on Internally Displaced Persons which restates the existing law and considers it as providing a broad protection to such persons and also addresses certain grey areas and gaps in their protection;

2. a Handbook on Internal Displacement;
3. a Guidance Note on a Durable Solution for Displaced Persons prepared by the UN Development Group.

The Darfur crisis illustrates the precarious situation of IDPs. In Darfur, the western region of Sudan, since 2003 the government of Sudan has been using regular armed forces and a government-sponsored militia known as the Janjaweed, to kill, rape and otherwise ill-treat the Fur, Masalit and Zaghawa ethnic groups who are suspected of supporting two rebel groups, the Sudan Liberation Army and the Justice and Equality Movement, both of which oppose the government.

In September 2004 the US Secretary of State, Colin Powell, on the basis of a US inquiry into the situation in Darfur and other reports, concluded that genocide had been committed in Darfur for which the government of Sudan should be held responsible. Although the UN Security Council has been urged by the international community to authorise an international action to protect civilians in Darfur, at the time of writing no authorisation under art 42 of the UN Charter has been given. On 11 November 2004 the UNHCR was forced to withdraw its international staff from Darfur because the Sudanese government prevented them from carrying out vital protection for thousands of IDPs.

As of October 2004, an estimated 1.45 million people had been internally displaced within Darfur and an additional 200,000 had found refuge in neighbouring Chad. An estimated 70,000 people have died since the beginning of the conflict in 2003.

14

Self-Determination of Peoples

14.1 Introduction

14.2 The historical background

14.3 Decolonisation

14.4 The limits of the right to self-determination in the colonial context

14.5 The extension of the right to self-determination to people living under racist regimes and foreign domination

14.6 The right to self-determination as a human right

14.7 Self-determination in the post-Cold War era

14.8 Conclusion

14.1 Introduction

In some guises the concept of self-determination exists in a clearly defined form; in others it is ambiguous and uncertain. It has throughout history meant different things to different people and continues to do so today. It was invoked by the founding fathers of the United States, the French revolutionaries, Lenin and Wilson during World War I, Gandhi and Nkrumah in the period of decolonisation, and is today relied upon by various groups such as the KLA, ETA, the IRA, Polisario, and by many minorities that are seeking to secede from existing states. The right to self-determination has both justified the establishment of new states and at a later time justified the disintegration of those self-same states. Because its application undermines the sovereignty and territorial integrity of states it challenges the stability of the international community.

There are two basic theories on self-determination.

1. One links the concept with the existence of a state-decision procedure which allows peoples to participate in the conduct of their common affairs within a state. According to this theory a nation, being an artificial community, is composed of individuals linked by the existence of such a state-decision procedure. A nation identifies with a state. The presence and proper functioning

of a decision-making procedure constitutes the essence of the right to self-determination.

2. The other is more romantic. It emphasises the importance of nationhood as the common identification of the people or the nation and minimises the role of statehood. Nationhood is much more than a decision-making procedure.

There is a conflict between the two theories which international law has, to date, failed to resolve. Koskenniemi has described this conflict as follows:

> 'National self-determination, has an ambiguous relationship with statehood as the basis of the international legal order. On the one hand, it supports statehood by providing an explanation for why we should honour existing de facto boundaries and the acts of the state's power-holders as something other than gunman's orders. On the other hand, it explains that statehood per se, embodies no particular virtue and that even as it is useful as a presumption about the authority of a particular territorial rule, that presumption may be overruled or its consequences modified in favour of a group or unit finding itself excluded from those positions of authority in which the sustenance of the rule is determined': 'National Self-determination Today: Problems of Legal Theory and Practice' (1994) 43 ICLQ 248.

In the context of decolonisation international law has recognised the right of self-determination. Whether or not, and to what extent, the right to self-determination applies in circumstances other than decolonisation is subject to controversy.

In this chapter the right to self-determination is examined from a historical perspective, its content is analysed in the context of decolonisation and, finally, its relevance and application in the post Cold-War era is explored.

14.2 The historical background

For the first time the right of people to self-determination was invoked by two revolutionary movements that succeeded in their aspirations. The American War of Independence and the French Revolution both legitimated new governments on the basis of defending the unalienable right of people to organise their own government which, in turn, established on the basis of peoples' consent, was accountable to them. The French National Assembly stated on 17 November 1792 that:

> 'In the name of the French people, the National Assembly declares that it will give help and support to all peoples wanting to recall their freedom. Therefore, the Assembly considers the French authorities responsible to give orders to grant all means of assistance to those people, to protect and compensate the citizens who might be injured during their fight for the cause of liberty': J E S Hayward, *After the French Revolution: Six Critics of Democracy and Nationalism* (1991).

The concept of self-determination played an important role in the formation of European nations in the nineteenth century. Colonisation was legitimated by international law. The Treaty of Berlin of 28 February 1885 excluded the universal scope of application of self-determination by denying it to colonial people. Only Western people were entitled to rely on the concept of self-determination. This was confirmed by the Treaty of Versailles 1919. President Wilson, considered as the father of modern self-determination, in his Fourteen Points Address to the US Congress on 8 January 1918 refused to give this concept an absolute and universal scope. He referred to the right to democracy in the context of oppressed minorities and ethnic nationalities rather than to their right to statehood. On the one hand, he advocated that national aspirations should be given 'the utmost satisfaction'; on the other hand, he emphasised that this should be done 'without introducing new or perpetuating old elements of discord and antagonism': Whelan 'Wilsonian Self-Determination and the Versailles Settlement' (1994) 43 ICLQ 102. The Wilsonian perception of self-determination was reflected in the Treaty of Versailles 1919 which:

1. granted to identifiable people statehood;
2. provided that disputed areas should be settled on the basis of plebiscites; and
3. set up a system of protection for ethnic minorities too small to be accorded statehood. The system of protection of minorities was supervised by the Council of the League of Nations.

Colonial people were denied any right to self-determination. The colonies of the defeated powers not yet ready for self-government were allocated to the Allied powers under the mandate system. The tutelage of 'advanced nations' in respect of such territories was to be exercised under the principle that 'the well-being and development of such people form a sacred trust of civilisation'. The Council of the League of Nations was responsible for supervising the mandate system. The terms of each mandate were agreed between the Council and each mandatory.

The territories under mandate were divided into three categories.

1. *Mandate A*. Territories which were nearly ready for self-government. They were the former Turkish territories, Lebanon and Syria which were placed under French mandate, and Iraq, Palestine and Trans-Jordan which were allocated to the British. All of the Mandate A territories became sovereign states between 1932 and 1947.
2. *Mandate B*. Territories in central Africa which belonged to Germany before World War I. They were considered by the Council as being further away from the attainment of self-government than Mandate A territories. Mandate B territories consisted of Cameroons and Togoland which were divided into two territories, one governed by France and one by the UK, and Tanganyika which was assigned to Belgium.
3. *Mandate C*. Territories which were considered by the Council as being incapable of self-government in the then foreseeable future. Mandatories were allowed to govern Mandate C territories as an integral part of their own territory because of the small population of Mandate C territories or of their contiguity to the mandatory's territory. Mandate C territories were: the former German colonies of

South West Africa which were placed under the tutelage of South Africa; the Marianas, Caroline and Marshall Islands which were allocated to Japan; and New Guinea and Nauru which were placed under the mandate of Australia.

All Mandate B and C territories except South West Africa became trust territories under the UN trusteeship system.

The principle of self-determination was examined by the Council of the League of Nations in the *Åaland Islands Case* (1920) LNOJ Spec Supp No 3, 3. The Åaland Islands were ceded by Sweden to Russia in 1809. When Finland became independent from Russia in 1917, the inhabitants of the Åaland Islands, 92 per cent of whom were of Swedish origin, requested Sweden to support their claim to return to Swedish jurisdiction. Finland refused to hold a plebiscite and claimed that the matter was within its exclusive domestic jurisdiction. Under art 15 of the Covenant of the League of Nations 1919 disputes between members of the League were to be brought before the Council in certain circumstances and the Council could hear the facts and make recommendations. Disputes within the domestic jurisdiction of a party to the dispute were excluded from the scope of art 15. In respect of the dispute concerning the Åaland Islands the Council set up a Commission of Jurists charged with the preparation of an advisory opinion on whether or not the matter was within the scope of art 15. The Commission of Jurists decided that the dispute was outside the exclusive domestic jurisdiction of Finland because, first, the government of Finland was not sufficiently established and, second, the dispute between Sweden and Finland did not concern 'a definitive established political situation depending exclusively upon the territorial sovereignty of a state'.

Following the Report of the Commission of Jurists the Council established a second body, a Commission of Rapporteurs, to examine the matter. The Commission of Rapporteurs, as did the Commission of Jurists beforehand, confirmed that self-determination of people was not a general rule of international law, but concluded that although the dispute was, in principle, within the domestic jurisdiction of Finland, it was also within the competence of the Council because 'it had acquired such considerable international importance that it was necessary to submit it to the high authority which the League of Nations represents in the eyes of the world'.

The Commission of Rapporteurs clearly stated that a minority living within the territory of a state had no right to separate itself from a state or to declare its independence. It emphasised that:

'To concede to minorities, either of language or religion, or to any fraction of population the right of withdrawing from the community to which they belong, because it is their wish or their good pleasure, would be to destroy order and stability within states and to inaugurate anarchy in international life': *Report of the Commission of Rapporteurs*, 16 April 1921, League of Nations, 28.

Both Commissions agreed that minorities should be protected within the existing territorial entities. The secession of a minority from a state was approved by the

Rapporteurs (but not by the International Commission of Jurists) only in exceptional circumstances and as a remedy of last resort when a state was refusing to grant a minimum of guarantees to a particular minority. This was not the case in the Åalands dispute as Finland was willing to grant the Åaland islanders satisfactory guarantees to protect their cultural autonomy. Consequently, the Council of the League of Nations granted the inhabitants of the Åaland Islands the right to be protected as a minority instead of the right to rule themselves.

The transformation of self-determination from a political concept into a legal rule was envisaged by the Atlantic Treaty 1941 signed between Churchill and Roosevelt. They agreed that self-determination would become a basic right upon the termination of World War II. This was achieved under the UN Charter. Its arts 1(2), 55 and 73 and Chapter XII recognise the right to self-determination. Article 1(2) of the UN Charter states that one of the purposes of the UN is 'to develop friendly relations among nations based on respect for the principle of equal rights and self-determination of peoples'. Similar terms are used in art 55 of the Charter. However, the meaning of self-determination under the UN Charter is unclear: the right to self-determination is mentioned indirectly in the context of friendly relations among nations. This gave rise to various interpretations of the principle of self-determination, the most likely being that arts 1(2) and 55 of the UN Charter refer to the rights of the peoples of one state to be protected from interference by other states or governments and thus both provisions emphasise the equal rights of states, rather than the right of dependent peoples to be independent (R Higgins, *Problems and Process: International Law and How We Use it*, Oxford: Clarendon Press, 1995, p112). In addition, the Charter limits the scope of art 1(2) in so far as it applies to colonial relations under the trusteeship system and to non–self-governing territories.

The international trusteeship system

Chapter XII of the UN Charter sets up the international trusteeship system under which the Trusteeship Council, one of the main organs of the United Nations, is charged with the task of supervising and administering trust territories placed under the system. The trusteeship system was intended to promote the welfare of the native inhabitants, to advance them toward self-government, to further peace and security and to encourage respect for human rights and for fundamental freedoms.

The trust territories consist of the following.

1. Territories held under mandates established by the League of Nations apart from South West Africa which remained under mandate until it achieved independence as Namibia in 1990.
2. Territories detached from enemy states after World War II. This included Pacific islands over which the United states was granted a strategic trusteeship and Italian Somaliland which was assigned by the General Assembly to Italy as trustee for the period of ten years starting in 1950. In 1960 Italian Somaliland together with former British Somaliland became Somalia.

3. Territories voluntarily placed under the system by states responsible for their administration. No colonial power volunteered to place any of its territories under the supervision and administration of the United Nations. Thus, in fact, the trust territories encompassed only the two above-mentioned categories.

The Trusteeship Council is placed under the authority of the General Assembly in respect of trust territories and under the authority of the Security Council in respect of 'strategic trusteeship' territories. The Council is made up of the five permanent members of the Security Council.

In order to fulfil its tasks the Trusteeship Council is authorised to examine and discuss annual reports from the administering authorities, in consultation with the administering authorities to examine petitions from individuals and groups, and to conduct visiting missions to verify the manner in which trust territories are administered, in particular to compare the reports from the administering authority with the actual conditions within the territory.

Eleven territories administered by seven member states were placed under the system. They were: Togoland (UK) which united with the Gold Coast to become Ghana in 1957; Togoland (France) which become Togo in 1960; Cameroons (France) which become the Republic of Cameroon in 1960; Cameroons (UK) the northern part of which joined Nigeria in 1961, whilst the southern part joined the Republic of Cameroon in the same year; Somaliland (Italy) which become Somalia in 1960; Tanganyika (UK) which become independent in 1961 and joined with Zanzibar in 1964 to become the United Republic of Tanzania; Western Samoa (New Zealand) which become Samoa in 1976; Nauru (Australia) which become independent in 1968; Ruanda-Urindi (Belgium) which become the states of Rwanda and Burundi in 1962; New Guinea (Australia) which become independent as Papua New Guinea in 1975. The Pacific Islands Territory obtained commonwealth status as the Northern Mariana Islands and part of them, the Marshall Islands and the Federation of States of Micronesia, signed the Compact of Free Association with the US in 1986. The last trust territory under the supervision of the Trusteeship Council, Palau, exercised freely its right to self-determination in a series of plebiscites and decided to become associated with the United States. The resultant Compact of Free Association between the US (an Administering Authority) and the Government of Palau entered into force on 1 October 1994.

The Trusteeship Council suspended its operation on 1 November 1994. The Trusteeship Council by a resolution adopted on 25 May 1994 decided to meet 'only on an extraordinary basis, as the need arose'.

Non-self-governing territories

Chapter XI of the UN Charter entitled 'Declaration Regarding Non-Self-Governing Territories' provides fundamental guarantees for subjected peoples who have not yet attained a full measure of self-government. Non-self-governing territories are outside the trusteeship system. Chapter XI neither imposes any legal obligations on the administering powers nor contains any enforcement mechanism. Under art 73 administering powers recognise the principle that 'the interest of the inhabitants of these territories are paramount' and accept 'as a sacred trust the obligation to promote to the utmost … the well-being of the inhabitants of these territories'. In order to fulfil this obligation the administering powers promised:

1. to ensure political, economic, social and educational advancement of these people and their just treatment;
2. to develop self-government and free political institutions in these territories not necessarily leading to independence; and
3. to transmit regularly to the Secretary-General statistical and technical reports concerning economic, social and educational conditions in these territories.

The reports were intended for information purposes only and no provision was made for their further use. Also the reports did not contain any political data. In 1946 the colonial powers submitted a list of 74 territories on which they were willing to transmit reports. However, with time, many colonial powers decided not to submit reports, arguing that the change of status of some of the non-self-governing territories extinguished their obligation to forward information. The UK decided not to report on any matters on which local autonomy had been granted, France considered that her overseas territories, being a part of the French Union, were outside the scope of art 73, and Portugal and Spain when they joined the UN in 1955 claimed that their overseas territories formed an integral part of their national territories. Many colonial powers claimed that they had an exclusive right to determine the status of territories under their jurisdiction. The system set up by art 73 lacked teeth as the administering powers were entitled to decide unilaterally what territories were non-self-governing and to cease their obligation of submitting reports to the General Assembly at any time. The matter of the international accountability of the administering powers for their administration of dependent territories was of considerable concern to the General Assembly which had sought to exercise some measure of control in deciding whether to accept the cessation of information. However, the General Assembly had no enforcing powers and could use only persuasion and adverse publicity in respect of the defaulting states. In some cases the termination of reports on non-self-governing territories was accepted by the General Assembly (Puerto Rico, Greenland, Alaska, Hawaii), but in most cases the matter was decided unilaterally by the administering power!

At the time of writing there are 16 non-self-governing territories: American Samoa, Anguilla, Bermuda, British Virgin Islands, Cayman Islands, Falkland Islands, Gibraltar, Guam, Montserrat, New Caledonia, Pitcairn, St Helena, Tokelau, Turks and Caicos Islands, United States Virgin Islands and Western Sahara. The current administering powers are France, New Zealand, the UK and the US. In 2002 East Timor became an independent state following two-and-a-half years of UN transitional administration. The official name of East Timor is now Timor-Leste.

With the growing anti-colonial movement the principles contained in art 73 of the UN Charter were invoked to support the immediate granting of self-government and independence to all colonial people.

14.3 Decolonisation

The list of non-European countries which have never been colonies is very short. It comprises: Thailand, Iran, Turkey, Liberia, Afghanistan and Japan. In the nineteenth China was a semi-colony, with European empires' 'spheres of influence' set up along its coast. At the beginning of the twenty-first century there were no European colonial powers. First to declare their independence were the 13 colonies of the UK in North America which in 1776 became the United States of America. In the early nineteenth century Spain and Portugal lost its colonies in South America.

The substantial decolonisation occurred after World War II, although from 1930 onwards nationalist movements in European colonial empires, especially in Asia, were growing in power. However, they were not strong enough to achieve independence. World War II was the catalyst for the realisation of the aspirations of colonial peoples for a number of reasons.

1. The pattern of control over colonies was interrupted.
2. European colonial empires, in order to ensure the support of their colonies, promised them various degrees of autonomy after the end of World War II.
3. European colonial empires were weakened or destroyed by the war. They no longer had resources to control their colonies.
4. Many colonies were occupied by Japan. After Japan's withdrawal nationalist movements took advantage of the power vacuum so created. Civil wars erupted in China, Burma, Korea and Indochina. Anti-colonial movements, often inspired by communist ideology, fought hard for independence.

The first wave of decolonisation was confined to Asia. Newly independent states were committed to destroying the colonial system. In 1955 at the Conference of Bandoeng they clearly expressed in the final communication that colonialism in all its manifestations was an evil which must be immediately terminated. The fight against colonial domination was supported by the Soviet Union and the US. After the death of Stalin in 1953 the colonies were offered 'friendship treaties', military advice, trade credits and measures of general support to liberate them from colonial domination. The United States has never forgotten that it was the first colony to achieve independence. Furthermore, the US had a clear conscience as in 1948 the only colony of the US, the Philippines, became independent.

The second wave of decolonisation took place in Africa in the late 1950s and early 1960s. The year 1960 was a turning point in decolonisation. With a growing number of new independent states and their admission to the UN they became the majority in the General Assembly. In this context on 14 December 1960 the GA adopted Resolution 1514 (XV) on the Declaration on the Granting of Independence to Colonial Countries and Peoples by a vote of 89 for, none against and nine abstentions (the abstentions being: Portugal, Spain, South Africa, the UK, the US, Australia, Belgium, the Dominican Republic and France). The Declaration constitutes the foundation in international law of the right to self-determination. It calls for immediate emancipation of colonial people 'without any condition or reservation in order to allow them to enjoy full independence' and irrespective of the stage of their political, economic social or educational development. The Declaration calls into question the system set out in the UN Charter in Chapters XI and XII consisting of progressive accession to independence of colonial people under the supervision of administering powers.

The main provisions of the 1960 Declaration state that:

1. the subjugation, domination and exploitation of people constitutes a denial of human rights contrary to the principles of the UN Charter;
2. all people have a right to self-determination;
3. the inadequacy of political, economic, social or educational preparedness should not serve as a pretext for delaying independence;
4. any repressive measures or any armed action directed against dependent people should cease;
5. non-self-governing territories should be granted immediately all necessary powers to achieve complete independence and freedom;
6. any attempt to disrupt partially or totally the territorial integrity of a state is incompatible with the principles and purposes of the UN;
7. all states must observe the Charter, the Universal Declaration of Human Rights, the present Declaration and the principle of non-intervention in the internal affairs of another state.

Exceptional importance has been conferred to the 1960 Declaration. Its scope of application was further defined by subsequent resolutions, in particular Resolution 1541 (XV) which defines the concept of 'full measure of self-government'. It provides that self-determination may be exercised by the people concerned, through voting in free and fair elections, in three ways:

1. they may decide to constitute themselves as a sovereign independent state;
2. they may decide to associate freely with an independent state;
3. they may integrate with an independent state already in existence.

In order to transform Resolution 1514 into an instrument for action in 1961 the GA set up the Special Committee on the Situation with Regard to the Implementation of the Declaration on the Granting of Independence to Colonial Countries and People which in 1962 became the Special Committee of Twenty-Four. Its task is to examine the application of the 1960 Declaration and to make recommendations on its implementation. The Committee meets annually, hears reports from appointed and elected representatives of the territories and petitioners and decides on visiting missions to the territories. During the International Decade for the Eradication of Colonialism (1990–2000) the Committee was very active in making proposals and carrying out actions, previously approved by the GA, relevant to the objective of the Decade.

The right to self-determination in the colonial context has been recognised as one of the fundamental principles of international law, equal in importance to the principle of the prohibition of aggression or the principle of peaceful settlement of disputes. Resolution 2625 (XXV) entitled 'Declaration on Principles of International Law Concerning Friendly Relations and Co-operation among States in Accordance with the Charter of the UN', which is regarded as interpreting and clarifying the UN Charter taking into account that it was adopted by consensus (passed by the GA without a vote), provides that every state has a duty 'to bring a speedy end to colonialism having regard to the freely expressed will of the peoples concerned'.

The International Court of Justice discussed the right to self-determination in the *Legal Consequences for States of the Continued Presence of South Africa in Namibia (South West Africa) Notwithstanding Security Council Resolution 276 (1970)* (1971) ICJ Rep 16 and the *Western Sahara Case* (1975) ICJ Rep 12 Advisory Opinions. In respect of Namibia the Court held that 'the subsequent development of international law in regard to non-self-governing territories as enshrined in the Charter of the United Nations made the principle of self-determination applicable to all of them': (1971) ICJ Rep 16 at 52. In the *Western Sahara* the Court stated that:

> 'In the domain to which the present proceedings relate [the application of the principle of self-determination to non-self-governing territories], the last 50 years ... have brought important developments. These developments leave little doubt that the ultimate objective of the sacred trust was the self-determination and independence of the people concerned. In this domain, as elsewhere, the corpus iuris gentium has been considerably enriched, and this the Court, if it is faithfully to discharge its functions, may not ignore': (1975) ICJ Rep 12 at 31.

In the *East Timor Case: Portugal v Australia* (1995) ICJ Rep 90 the ICJ emphasised that the right of peoples to self-determination was 'one of the essential principles of contemporary international law'. In the *Advisory Opinion on the Legal Consequences of the Construction of a Wall in the Occupied Palestinian Territory* (2004) 43 ILM 1009 the ICJ emphasised that the right of the Palestinian people to self-determination has acquired an erga omnes character.

14.4 The limits of the right to self-determination in the colonial context

The right to self-determination is given to people integrated into an existing state. This entails that when the people concerned exercise their right to self-determination they challenge the national unity and territorial integrity of that state. Consequently, there is a conflict between, on the one hand, state sovereignty which authorises a state to ensure national unity and territorial integrity and imposes on other states the obligation of non-intervention and, on the other hand, the aspirations of colonial people to freely determine their destiny. This contradiction is present in paragraph 6 of Resolution 1514 (XV), the intention of which is to preserve the identity of colonial states when dependent people attempt to attain independence. It provides that:

> 'Any attempt aimed at partial or total disruption of the national unity and territorial integrity of a country is incompatible with the purposes and principles of the Charter of the United Nations.'

The territorial integrity clause was intended to prevent colonial powers from retaining some parts of a colony. This clause was invoked in respect of the Island of Mayotte which had remained French when Comores attained independence. It also means that Resolution 1514 does not consider that decolonisation affects the territorial integrity of the colonial power, although it does affect 'the national and territorial integrity of a state'. This clause is very important since self-determination without the counter-balancing force of territorial integrity would run the risk of anarchy: L Brilmeyer, 'Secession and Self-Determination: A Territorial Interpretation' (1991) 16 YIL 177–202. Resolution 2625 (XXV) emphasises this interpretation by stating that:

> 'Nothing in the foregoing paragraphs shall be construed as authorising or encouraging any action which would dismember or impair, totally or partially, the territorial integrity or political unity of sovereign and independent states conducting themselves in compliance with the principle of equal rights and self-determination as described above and thus possessed of a government representing the whole people belonging to the territory without distinction as to race, creed or colour.'

This entails that colonial frontiers must be respected even though they were artificially drawn by the colonial powers without any consideration as to ethnic or historical tradition of peoples living there. The African leaders in the Cairo Declaration 1964 confirmed their adherence to this principle and Judge Djibo in the *Case Concerning the Frontier Dispute: Burkina Fasi* v *Republic of Mali* (1986) ICJ Rep 554 at 567 explained that the African people consented, through the Cairo Declaration, to the maintenance of colonial boundaries because this was an essential requirement for stability necessary to develop and consolidate their independence.

14.5 The extension of the right to self-determination to people living under racist regimes and foreign domination

In the period between the end of decolonisation and the end of the Cold War the international community rarely agreed to recognise the application of the right of self-determination outside the context of decolonisation. However, in some situations the right of self-determination was extended to people other than colonial people.

This occurred in respect of black peoples living in South Africa under the system of racial separation called apartheid (apartness) and to the people living in occupied territories such as the Palestinians or inhabitants of Afghanistan after the Russian invasion in 1979.

South Africa

Black people living in South Africa were in 'a psychologically colonial' situation. In 1652 the Dutch East India Company set up a 'refreshment station' at the Cape of Good Hope. This was the beginning of South Africa as a Dutch colony. With time, Dutch farmers known as Boers moved inland taking whatever land they wanted and subjugating the natives. During the Napoleonic wars the British took the Cape and the province of Natal. This incited Boers, who hated the British presence, to establish two small republics, the Transvaal and Orange Free state. When the British started to fight the Boers in 1899 in order to get hold of their land rich in gold and diamonds the Boers fought back with such determination and desperation that the British, in order to win the war, resorted to such extreme measures as putting Boer families into 'concentration camps', where some 26,000 died from typhoid. In 1902 the Boers capitulated, however, their descendants (Afrikaners) won control of the political system in South Africa. Afrikaners consider themselves as colonised by the British and not as colonialists.

In 1948 the Afrikaners, who constituted 60 per cent of the white population, won the elections and started to introduce apartheid, a system of strict racial segregation and discrimination reinforced by 'influx control' under which black people were kept out of cities. Black people had no rights whatsoever, any protest was illegal and consequently severely punished. Deprived of any form of democratic participation they turned to violence. The African National Congress (ANC) which was founded in 1912 tried for many years to fight apartheid by peaceful means. After the Sharpeville incident in 1960 when the police panicked and opened fire on peaceful black protesters killing 69 of them, the ANC under the leadership of Nelson Mandela turned to violence. The ANC was banned and Nelson Mandela was tried and condemned to life imprisonment. The ANC went underground and continued the fight.

The General Assembly adopted many resolutions supporting the fight of 'oppressed people of South Africa' by all possible and appropriate measures, including the use of armed force against the racist, minority and illegitimate regime of apartheid. The right to self-determination was conferred on the people of South Africa in its entirety (eg Resolution 33/183 of 24 January 1979). Consequently, the right to self-determination entailed the suppression of the racist regime and the establishment of a democratic government, but not the right to secession.

Due to many considerations, mainly the political wisdom and vision of President F W de Klerk who replaced P W Botha in 1989, Nelson Mandela and other ANC activists were released from prison in 1990. Also the South African Parliament repealed the apartheid laws. As a result of negotiations between blacks and whites the first free election, based on the principle of one-person-one vote, took place in 1994. In the new multiracial and multi-party parliament the ANC won a majority. Nelson Mandela was elected President of South Africa.

The Palestinians

During World War I the British, in order to gain allies, made promises to the Arabs (The McMahon Letters to Hussein the Sheriff of Mecca and Medina (1915–1916)) and to the Jews (the Balfour Declaration of 1917) to support their claims for independence. After World War I the League of Nations granted the UK mandate over Palestine. In order to honour the Balfour Declaration promising the Jews a homeland in Palestine the British allowed about 10,000 Jews to enter Palestine annually from 1919 to 1931. To respect their commitment to the Arabs in 1921 the British split off Transjordan from Palestine and gave it to one of Hussein's sons. This become, in 1948, the Kingdom of Jordan.

The influx to Palestine of Jewish settlers from Europe angered the Arabs and in 1936 a virtual war broke out between them. The UK knew that war was approaching in Europe. In order to calm the Arabs, and to gain their support in this strategically important area rich in petroleum, the UK issued a White Paper in 1939 restricting the Jewish immigration (at a time when Jews from Europe desperately needed a refuge). In a situation of utmost frustration for the Jews, who claimed that 'The Nazis kill us, and the British won't let us live', they turned to terrorism. After World War II the international community discovered the real extent of the Nazi's crimes against the Jewish people, some six million having been exterminated. The Jewish survivors wanted to live in Palestine and the Zionist movement, founded in the 1930s, wanted an independent state. The British became targets of terrorist attacks. The UK in the light of her limited resources and her untenable situation in Palestine decided in 1947 to ask the United Nations for a solution to the problem.

The UN Commission recommended the partition of Palestine into Jewish and Arab areas, with Jerusalem as a corpus separatum, a neutral city under international trusteeship. The GA in Resolution 18 (II) (adopted by 33 votes to 13 with 10 abstentions) approved the recommendation. The GA provided for the Trusteeship Council to draft a statute for the city of Jerusalem and for the UN Palestine Commission to implement the recommendations of the GA. The Jews accepted the Partition Resolution but the Arabs rejected it. In the meantime the British fixed the end of their mandate for Palestine on 15 May 1948.

On 14 May 1948 David Ben-Gurion proclaimed the establishment of the state of Israel. The US immediately recognised Israel. The next day five Arab armies – Egypt, Syria, Iraq, Jordan and Lebanon – invaded Israel. All but the Jordanians, who controlled the West Bank and the eastern part of Jerusalem including the old city, were beaten by Israel. A Truce Commission for Palestine was established by the Security Council. Finally, a truce was agreed under which Israel held 80 per cent of the Palestine mandate; some 700,000 Palestinians left the territory occupied by Israel and fled to refugee's camps in the Gaza Strip and the West Bank.

The Suez Crisis of 1956 worsened Arab-Israeli relations but brought no changes in the situation of Palestinians. Next came the Six Day War (which started on 5 of June 1967) during which Israel destroyed the Egyptian army and reached the Suez Canal by 6 of June 1967, took the Old City of Jerusalem and the West Bank from Jordan, and the Golan Heights from Syria. All was achieved in six days. The three Arab states lost 14,000 soldiers, Israel lost 700. The victory was not as brilliant as it looked. In the territory seized by Israel, being the West Bank and the Gaza Strip, lived 1.3 million Palestinians, most of them refugees from the 1948–49 war. The Security Council adopted Resolution 242 calling for the withdrawal of Israeli forces from occupied territories and for Arabs to accept the existence of Israel on peaceful terms and for the settlement of the refugee problem. The occupation of the territories gained during the Six Day War was one of the main factors in the rise of Palestinian nationalism.

The Arabs living in Palestine started to forge their national identity as a result of the Jewish influx to Palestine, the war in 1948–49 and, especially, the Six Day War. With the occupation of the West Bank and the Gaza Strip Palestinians realised that there was no Arab state to protect them, that they had no status in territories occupied by Israel, that they had no home or country ready to accept them and that they had no peaceful way to change their life, as any display of Palestinian nationalism in Israel was illegal. Palestinians had become like Jews before the establishment of Israel – dispersed, homeless and unwanted people. The Palestinians started to fight back. The largest and most moderate of many Palestinian organisations is the Palestinian Liberation Organisation (PLO) founded in Egypt in 1964. It has become the main representative of the Palestinian people under the leadership of Yassir Arafat who, with time, put more emphasis on diplomacy and on the creation of, at a minimum, a Palestinian state on the West Bank and the Gaza Strip than on the eradication of Israel.

The next development in Israeli-Arab relations was the 1973 war called by the Israelis the Yom Kippur and by Arabs the Ramadan or October War. It started as a surprise attack by Syria and Egypt against Israel. Israel, initially unprepared, fought hard on the Golan Heights against Syria and in the Sinai against Egypt. What was important was the psychological impact of Egypt's initial military success. It allowed Egyptian President Anwar Sadat to accept the Israeli invitation to face-to-face talks with the then Prime Minister of Israel, Menachem Begin. Sadat came to Jerusalem as an equal, not as a loser. The talks led to the Camp David Accords of 1978 and the Egypt-Israel Peace Treaty of 1979. As a result of the Camp David Accords Sadat got the Sinai back for Egypt and more US aid, whilst Begin got the opportunity to destroy the unity of the Arab world (Egypt was expelled from the Arab bloc) and more aid from the US. The Accords were accompanied, inter alia, by the Framework for Peace in the Middle East providing for an 'elected self-governing authority in the West Bank and Gaza'. The Palestinians and other Arab states refused to participate in the Camp David Accords. There was no political will on the part of Israel to grant any autonomy to the Palestinians. To the contrary, land seizures for new Israeli settlements on the West Bank increased. In 1981 Moslem fundamentalists assassinated Sadat considering him as a traitor. In 1982 Israel invaded Lebanon to help Lebanese Christians to unify but its fundamental objective was to destroy the PLO bases in southern Lebanon from which PLO fighters were shelling Israeli settlements and other targets in northern Israel. The Christians did not fight, although they massacred Palestinians in the Sabra and Shatilla camps. The Palestinians were evacuated from Beirut by international peacekeeping forces and Arafat set up his bases in Tunis. Israel eventually withdrew from southern Lebanon, although it kept a nine-mile-wide security zone. In 1987 the Palestinians in the occupied territories, fed up with no progress towards the solution of the conflict, started an uprising (the intifada) against Israel. At that stage Israel started to realise the extent of the problem. It had two million Palestinians under its jurisdiction. Refusal of any rights for them was not a realistic option in the long run. Their integration into Israel entailing granting them Israeli citizenship would, given the high birthrate of Palestinians, change a Jewish Israel into an Arab Israel within the foreseeable future. On the Palestinian side Arafat was in favour of negotiations and diplomacy. In 1988 he accepted Israel's right to exist and renounced terrorism. These two points were a precondition for the recognition of the PLO by the US. In the summer of 1988 Jordan formally renounced its claims to the West Bank. The collapse of the Soviet Union, a traditional political and military ally of the Arabs, and the Bush (senior) administration's firm commitment to cut off financial support for Israel until it agreed to negotiate with the Palestinians and other factors, led to the Madrid Conference where, in October 1991, the Palestinians and the Israelis met face-to-face and agreed on a framework for peace negotiations. However, there was no progress in negotiations.

Unknown to anyone, secret negotiations began in Oslo under the mediation of the Norwegian Foreign Minister. In August 1993 Israel and the PLO announced that they had reached an agreement. The Declaration of Principles was formally signed on 13 September 1993 on the White House lawn in the presence of US President Bill Clinton. The Declaration and the following Agreements provide for the gradual transfer of power to Palestinians in the West Bank and the Gaza Strip, and 'permanent status' negotiations on the most controversial issues namely, Jerusalem, final borders, Jewish settlements, the return of Palestinian refugees and security arrangements.

The failure to implement the Oslo Accords and the failure in March 2000 to achieve the Sharm ash Sheik Accords (inter alia, the Palestinians refused to renounce the right of Palestinian refugees to return to the Occupied Palestinian Territory) prepared the ground for the Second Intifada (B Morris, *The Birth of the Palestinian Refugee Problem 1947–1949*, Cambridge, 2001, p627).

The spark that triggered it was a visit to the Al Aqsa mosque by Ariel Sharon, who in the company of dozens of policemen strolled into the compound. This was a highly provocative and deliberate act (Confirmed by UN Security Council Resolution 1322 (2000)).

Following the beginning of the Second Intifada, Israel started to build a 720 kilometres long wall in the region of the boundary between Israel and Palestine. The 'wall' has an average width of 50–70 metres. The wall does not follow the Green Line which marks the de facto boundary between Israel and Palestine fixed by the general armistice agreement of 3 April 1949 between Israel and Jordan. It deviates in certain places to bring 'within' the wall: illegal Israeli settlements; fertile Palestinian land; and some of the most important water wells in the region. In some places, the wall has been built on land requisitioned by the state of Israel. When completed approximately 16.6 per cent of the area comprised by the West Bank and East Jerusalem will lie between the wall and the Green Line. This 16.6 per cent of the said area, inhabited by 17,000 Palestinians in the West Bank and 220,000 in East Jerusalem, will be 'encircled'. According to the Report of Special Rapporteur John Dugard of the UN's Commission on Human Rights: 'Palestinians living between the wall and the Green Line will be effectively cut off from their farmlands and workplaces, schools, health clinics and other social services'. For example, the entire city of Qalqiliya has been completely surrounded by the wall. Some 600 shops and businesses in the city have reportedly closed. As Professor Dugard commented the construction of the wall is likely to create 'a new generation of refugees or internally displaced persons'. The wall will, once completed, in addition to those Palestinians living in the West Bank and East Jerusalem, affect another 160,000 Palestinians who will live in enclaves. The beneficiaries of the construction of the wall will be 320,000 Israeli settlers, whose homes (including those of the approximately 178,000 living in occupied East Jerusalem) will in effect, be incorporated into Israel.

The main justification submitted by Israel for building the wall was based on self-defence. Israel claimed that it had the right and duty to protect its people against terrorist attacks, in particular to prevent suicide bombers penetrating into Israeli territory from the West Bank. According to the Palestinians the construction of the wall constituted an attempt by Israel to fix borders unilaterally ahead of any future settlement between Israeli and the Palestine peoples and is used as an excuse to annex territory wrongfully.

The UN Security Council, unlike the UN General Assembly, did not condemn the building of the wall by Israel. This resulted from the fact that the USA vetoed the Palestinian drafted resolution submitted to the UN Security Council on 9 October 2003 seeking to ban Israel from extending the wall deep into the West Bank. The veto allegedly was based on the ground that Israel had the right to defend itself against suicide bombings.

In those circumstances on 8 December 2003 the UN General Assembly requested the ICJ to 'urgently render an advisory opinion' on the following question:

'What are the legal consequences arising from the construction of the wall being built by Israel, the Occupying Power, in the Occupied Palestinian Territory, including in and around East Jerusalem, as described in the report of the Secretary-General, considering the rules and principles of international law, including the Fourth Geneva Convention of 1949, and the relevant Security Council and General Assembly resolutions?'

The General Assembly decided to make such a request because, first, the UN Security Council was unable to take necessary measures due to the veto of the USA, and second, Israel had refused to comply with Resolution 10/13 of 21 October 2003 adopted at the Tenth Emergency Session of the General Assembly which demanded that Israel 'stop and reverse the construction of the wall in the Occupied Palestinian Territory'.

On 9 July 2004 the ICJ delivered the Advisory Opinion. The ICJ ruled that:

1. Israel was in breach of international law and requested Israel to dismantle the wall immediately and make reparation for any damage caused;
2. Israel could not rely on the concept of self-defence in order to justify the building of the wall as a measure taken in order to fight terrorist attacks;
3. the IV Geneva Convention and international human rights treaties such as the International Covenant on Civil and Political Rights (ICCPR), the International Covenant on Economic, Social and Cultural Rights (ICESCR) and the UN Convention on the Rights of the Child applied to the Occupied Palestinian Territory.

The Advisory Opinion constitutes confirmation from the Court that Israel has violated a large number of international conventions and completely ignored a multitude of legally binding UN Resolutions. In the Advisory Opinion the ICJ firmly confirmed the right of the Palestinian people to self-determination. Indeed, the General Assembly has passed an impressive number of resolutions (starting with Resolution 3236 (XXIX) of November 1974) confirming the inalienable right of the Palestinian people to self-determination, the right to national independence and the right to return to their homes and property. In 1975 the GA, frustrated by the lack of progress in the implementation of Resolution 3236, set up the Committee on the Exercise of the Inalienable Rights of the Palestinian People. Its main task is to recommend to the GA a programme of action for the achievement of the Palestinian peoples' rights to self-determination. Also, the UN Commission on Human Rights on 6 April 2001 adopted by a roll-call vote for a resolution reaffirming the 'inalienable, permanent and unqualified right' of the Palestinian people to self-determination, including their right to establish a sovereign and independent Palestinian state (48 in favour and two against (the US and Guatemala) with two abstentions).

In the Advisory Opinion the ICJ determined the legal consequences for Israel, for other states and for the United Nations deriving from the violations by Israel of international law, and determined the impact of the construction of the wall on the right of the Palestinian people to self-determination.

In this respect, the ICJ observed that Israel, by constructing the wall, de facto annexed territories over which the Palestinian people are entitled to exercise their right to self-determination. Israel submitted assurances that the wall constituted a temporary measure and that Israel was ready to adjust and dismantle the wall if so required by a political settlement, and that with the termination of the terrorist attacks launched from the West Bank the wall would no longer be necessary. The Court stated that the construction of the wall amounted to de facto annexation of those territories and as such was in breach of customary international law prohibiting the acquisition of territory by the use of force. This prohibition is enshrined in the 1928 Kellog-Briand Pact and in art 2(4) of the UN Charter. Further, the Declaration of Principles of International Law Concerning Friendly Relations and Co-operation Among States in Accordance with the UN Charter (GA Resolution 2625 (XXV) of 24 October 1970) states that: 'the territory of a state shall not be the object of acquisition by another state resulting from the threat or use of force. No territorial acquisition resulting from the threat or use of force shall be recognised as legal.' Also, the Oslo Accords provide that the status of the West Bank and Gaza shall not be changed pending the outcome of permanent status negotiations and that protected persons under art 47 of the IV Geneva Convention should not be deprived of the benefits of the territory 'by an annexation … of the occupied territory'.

The Court noted that the route of the wall includes some 80 per cent of the Jewish settlers living in the Occupied Territories (including Jerusalem). The establishment of Jewish settlements, the ICJ emphasised, was in breach of international law, in particular art 49(6) of the IV Geneva Convention, and in breach of binding UN Security Council Resolutions. The Court considered that the construction of the wall and its associated regime created a 'fait accompli' given that this temporary situation could easily become permanent. The ICJ ruled that the construction of the wall in conjunction with the measures taken previously by Israel, namely the establishment of Jewish settlements in the Occupied Territories, severely impeded the exercise by the Palestinian people of their right to self-determination, being a right which had been recognised by the international community and by Israel itself. Consequently, Israel was in breach of the obligation to respect the right of the Palestinian people to self-determination.

The ICJ specified the legal consequences for Israel, for other States and for the United Nations arising from the violation by Israel of international law.

Legal consequences for Israel
With regard to Israel the ICJ noted that any breach of international law triggered the responsibility of the culprit state under international law. The ICJ noted the following points.

1. Israel is obliged to comply with the obligation to respect the right of the Palestinian people to self-determination and its obligations under international humanitarian law and human rights law.

2. Israel must ensure freedom of access to the Holy places that came under its control subsequent to the 1967 war.
3. Israel must put an end to the violations of its international obligations relating to the construction of the wall in the Occupied Territory.
4. Israel must immediately cease the works of construction of the wall being built in the Occupied Territories, including in and around East Jerusalem, and must dismantle the existing parts of the wall.
5. Israel must repeal all legislative and regulatory measures adopted with a view to the wall's construction, and to the establishment of the associated regime except insofar as those acts provide for compensation for the Palestinian population.
6. Israel must make reparation for the damage caused to all natural and legal persons concerned in accordance with the principle of international law as explained in *Chorzow Factory Case (Indemnity) (Merits): Germany* v *Poland* (1928) PCIJ Rep Series A No 17, that is, that reparation must, as far as possible, wipe out all the consequences of the illegal act and re-establish the situation which would, in all probability, have existed if that act had not been committed. Consequently, Israel must return the land and other immovable property seised or, if such restitution is materially impossible, compensate the persons concerned for the damage suffered.
7. Israel must compensate any natural or legal person having suffered any form of material damage resulting from the construction of the wall.

Legal consequences for states other than Israel
The ICJ noted that the obligations violated by Israel include certain erga omnes obligations such as the right of the Palestinian people to self-determination, and some intransgressible principles of customary humanitarian law. The erga omnes character of the above obligations requires that no states must recognise the illegal situation created by the construction of the wall in the Occupied Territory, and that all states must abstain from rendering any aid or assistance in maintaining the situation resulting from such construction and must bring to an end any impediment resulting from the construction of the wall to the exercise by the Palestinian people of their right to self-determination.

Legal consequences for the United Nations
The ICJ considered that the UN, in particular the UN Security Council and the UN General Assembly, should decide what further action is required in order to bring to an end the illegal situation created by the construction of the wall and the associated regime in the light of the present Advisory Opinion. The ICJ urged the United Nations as a whole to 'redouble its efforts to bring the Israeli-Palestinian conflict, which continues to pose a threat to international peace and security, to a speedy conclusion, thereby establishing a just and lasting peace in the region'.

The GA fully endorsed the Advisory Opinion at its Tenth Special Emergency Session held on 20 July 2004 by adopting Resolution 10/18 (150 votes in favour, six

352 Self-Determination of Peoples

votes against and ten abstentions) which demanded that Israel and all states comply with the legal obligations specified in the Opinion, requested the UN Secretary-General to set up a register of all damage caused to all natural and legal persons resulting from the construction of the wall in the Occupied Territory and reaffirmed the right and duty of all states to take necessary actions in accordance with international law to counter deadly acts of violence against the civilian population. The GA had also reserved the right to reconvene to consider further actions in the case of non-compliance with the above Opinion. Further actions may include non-binding sanctions.

At the time of writing the situation in this region is tense. On the Palestinian side, the recent death of Yassir Arafat has created a political vacuum. In the weeks and months ahead the Palestinians will have to decide on their new leadership and consequently on the terms on which they want to reach a settlement with Israel. On the Israeli side, on 26 October 2004 the Knesset (the Israeli Parliament) voted in favour of an Israeli withdrawal (including the removal of its settlers) from the Gaza Strip and part of the northern West Bank.

As to the Arab countries, their involvement in the troubled peace process has increased since the October 2000 Arab Summit in Cairo. In March 2002, the Arab Summit in Beirut agreed the first collective Arab peace initiative, sponsored by Saudi Arabia, offering Israel the normalisation of relations with all Arab States provided Israel withdrew from all land occupied since the 1967 War. This initiative was ignored by the Israeli Prime Minister Ariel Sharon who has been pursuing his own plan consisting of withdrawing in 2005 from the Gaza Strip whilst consolidating Jewish settlements in the West Bank. As to the commitment of the US administration to the peace process, the US President, following his successful re-election, stated that he intended to use his second term in office to achieve the creation of an independent Palestinian state by 2008.

All parties concerned consider the Israeli withdrawal from the Gaza Strip by 2005 as a first step that opens negotiations between Palestinians and Israeli on a permanent peace settlement.

14.6 The right to self-determination as a human right

International law recognises that the right to self-determination constitutes a fundamental human right and applies to all people. It is probably unfortunate that the principle of self-determination was, at its inception, so closely linked with the issue of decolonisation. Even Resolution 1514 states that any people being subject to 'subjugation, domination or exploitation' have an inherent right to self-determination. Nevertheless, the context in which the Resolution was adopted strongly suggests that its addressees were primarily people living under colonial rule.

The right to self-determination as a right granted to all people was clearly set out in the Covenant on Civil and Political Rights 1966 and the Covenant on Economic,

Social and Cultural Rights 1966. Both instruments contain an identical art 1 which provides that 'all people have the right to self-determination. By virtue of that right they freely determine their political status and freely pursue their economic, social and cultural development.' Contracting states to these instruments 'shall respect the realisation of the right of self-determination and shall respect that right in conformity with the provisions of the Charter of the United Nations'. The UN Commission on Human Rights has always interpreted art 1 literally, so confirming the right of all people to self-determination.

Among other international instruments which confirm that self-determination is not restricted to colonial people, people subjected to a racist regime, or foreign or alien domination are: the Helsinki Final Act 1975 and the African Charter on Human and Peoples' Rights 1981 (art 20).

Despite the clearly recognised fundamental human right referred to above the reality is that in circumstances where a people wishes to secede from a state of which they form part (and this is almost the only circumstance in which the right has any relevance) the international community has been extremely reluctant to recognise or support the alleged right. The right to self-determination has been rejected in favour of the territorial integrity of a state. The Declaration on Principles of International Law 1970 clearly subjugates the right of self-determination to the principle of territorial integrity! Furthermore, the main purpose of the UN, which is the maintenance of international peace and stability, has imposed important restrictions on the content of the right to self-determination taking into account that the exercise of the right of self-determination would entail disintegration of existing states and fragmentation of newly created states. In this context, neither the UN nor the Organisation of African states recognised any right to self-determination of the Ibo Community in Biafra fighting in 1988 to break away from Nigeria. The UN made no statement in respect of the secession of East Pakistan from the state of Pakistan although there were allegations of genocide by the Pakistani army committed on the Banglas. However, once an independent state of Bangladesh was created and consolidated it was recognised by the UN.

The position of the UN was summarised by U Thant, its former Secretary-General, in 1970 when he said that:

'As far as the question of secession of a particular section of a member state is concerned, the United Nations attitude is unequivocal. As an international organisation, the United Nations has never accepted and does not accept and I do not believe it will ever accept, a principle of secession of a part of a member state': *UN Monthly Chronicle*, No 2 (1970) 36.

14.7 Self-determination in the post-Cold War era

The right to self-determination has acquired a new dimension in the post-Cold War era due to many factors, the most important being the collapse of the Soviet Union.

People of eastern European countries living under the hegemony of the Soviet Union since the end of World War II took advantage of the changing situation and speedily dismantled 'socialism' proving how little legitimacy these regimes enjoyed in their eyes. With the end of the Cold War new problems emerged. Old states ceased to exist and have been replaced by new states created on the territory of an old state, and minority groups living within old or newly created states started to demand political rights ranging from internal autonomy to a right to secession. In these circumstances claims of indigenous people to self-determination have gained a new momentum. The complexity of these issues has emphasised the controversies surrounding the right to self-determination.

It seems that each situation is different, although some general principles can be applied to all of them. They are examined below.

Dissolution of a state and self-determination

International law recognises the right to dissolve a state in a peaceful way and to create new states on the territory of the former state. The agreement of all concerned parties is at the centre of this principle. The Final Act of the Helsinki Conference on Security and Co-operation in Europe (CSCE) of 1 August 1975 in its Principle III states that changes of frontiers in Europe are allowed provided they are peaceful and have the consent of the parties involved. This principle was applied when the Soviet Union was replaced by 15 new independent states, 11 of which become loosely associated with Russia within the Commonwealth of Independent states (CIS). Lithuania, Latvia, Georgia and Estonia, which were incorporated into the Soviet Union in the 1940s, refused any form of association with Russia. This was not challenged by Russia. Similarly, in the case of Czechoslovakia a referendum was held which led to the so-called Velvet Divorce between the Czech and the Slovak Republics. The Union between them was dissolved and they become independent states.

International law does not consider that the right to dissolve a state by force and to create new states on the territory of the former state is an internal matter of the state concerned. This is a matter of international law to which the principle of self-determination applies. A good example relates to the breaking up of the former Yugoslavia. The international community has always maintained the view that the right to self-determination was granted to inhabitants of each republic as a whole and not to each minority grouping living within a particular republic.

Uti possedetis and self-determination

The concept of self-determination has been greatly influenced by the doctrine of uti possedetis (Shaw (1996) 67 BYIL) which derives from Roman law and which was applied in the context of the decolonisation of Latin America in the nineteenth century. According to the doctrine, when Spain was leaving its Latin American territories the boundaries left behind were to be respected and could not be changed under any circumstances. This rule has become recognised in customary law and was applied in the context of later decolonisations. In the *Case Concerning the Frontier Dispute: Burkina Faso* v *Republic of Mali* (1986) ICJ Rep 554 at 565 the ICJ stated that the doctrine of uti possedetis:

'... is a general principle, which is logically connected with the phenomenon of the obtaining of independence, whenever it occurs. Its obvious purpose is to prevent the independence and stability of states being endangered by fratricidal struggles provoked by the challenging of frontiers following the withdrawal of the administering power.'

In 1991 the Badinter Arbitration Committee which was charged by the EC with preparing guidelines on the recognition of new states emphasised the importance of uti possedetis by stating that:

'... it is well established that, whatever the circumstances, the right to self-determination must not involve changes to existing frontiers at the time of independence [uti possedetis juris] except where the states concerned agree otherwise': (1991) 92 LLR 168.

In practice, existing frontiers were challenged in the case of the former Yugoslavia except in respect of the border between Slovenia and Croatia. However, the international community has, so far, never recognised the changing of pre-existing frontiers between the republics without the consent of all parties involved.

The Commonwealth of Independent States (CIS) which emerged after the break-up of the Soviet Union, upheld the principle of uti possedetis. The Charter of the CIS signed at Minsk on 8 December 1991 provides that 'the High Contracting Parties acknowledge and respect each other's territorial integrity and the inviolability of existing borders within the Commonwealth'. This was further confirmed by the Alma Ata Declaration of 21 December 1991.

In assessing the principle of uti possedetis it can be said that it is not a rule of ius cogens taking into account that interested parties by mutual agreement are allowed to depart from it. This was confirmed by the ICJ in *Case Concerning Land, Island and Maritime Frontier Dispute: El Salavador* v *Honduras, Nicaragua Intervening* (1992) ICJ Rep 92 at 408 in which the ICJ confirmed that the parties involved were allowed to modify the existing frontiers through an exchange of territory. In this respect the Court stated that 'it was obviously open to those states to vary the boundaries between them by agreement'. Consequently, existing boundaries are not immutable and may be changed but the consent of all parties concerned is required.

'People' and self-determination

International law does not determine who are the 'people' entitled to exercise their right to self-determination. Consequently, as Ms Lâm put it, 'the meanings of both "self-determination" and "people" remain contentious, and fluctuate with the UN practice': 'Making Room for Peoples at the United Nations: Thoughts Provoked by

Indigenous Claims to Self-Determination' (1992) 25 Cornell Int LJ 615–616. For that reason often states use the term 'minorities' instead of 'people' when they refer to certain groups in order to emphasise that such groups have no claims to self-determination. It results from the relevant international instruments and from the state practice that by 'all people' international law refers to all the people of a given territory. In this context only two categories of people would be able to claim the right to self-determination: people living in territories subjugated in violation of international law and people living in a state that violates the basic human rights of its citizens and in extreme cases commits the crime of genocide against them. In both cases they will be entitled to fight against such a government. It is clearly stated in the third preamble to the Universal Declaration of Human Rights 1948 that: 'Whereas it is essential, if a man is not to be compelled to have recourse, as a last resort, to rebellion against tyranny and oppression, that human rights should be protected by the rule of law.' In the second case no territorial changes are involved.

The Supreme Court of Canada in *Re Secession of Quebec* [1998] 2 SCR 217 disagreed with the above definition of 'people'. It stated that:

> 'It is clear that "a people" may include only a portion of the population of an existing state. The right to self-determination has developed largely as a human right, and is generally used in documents that simultaneously contain reference to "nation" and "state". The juxtaposition of these terms is indicative that the reference to "people" does not necessarily mean the entirety of a state's population ...'

In such a situation the problem remains: who are the beneficiaries of the right to self-determination?

Minorities and self-determination

International law refuses to grant minority groups living within a state the right to secession but ensures that their rights as minorities are respected. The obvious problem is that if one group is granted a right to break away from an existing state, unless such a group lives within a well defined territory and is almost 100 per cent homogenous other minorities may be forcibly included in the prospective new state's seceding territory unless that intended new state will give the same rights to its minorities. A refusal would prove that a new state applies a 'racist double standard', while the granting of such a right would lead to the creation of thousands of new states. The problem has been illustrated in respect of Quebec. Aboriginal people living in Quebec challenged the right of Quebec to secede. They argued that in the province of Quebec there are more than one distinct Quebecois 'people' taking into account that there are many distinct Aboriginal peoples living in Quebec. Their claim to self-determination is much stronger than that of other peoples in Quebec. Furthermore, the cost of an 'ethnic divorce' has been well illustrated in the case of Yugoslavia, Rwanda and Sri Lanka. Even the velvet separation between the Czechs and the Slovaks had its drawbacks since recent analysis shows the decline of Slovakia's economy and the growing authoritarianism of its government.

As stated above international law does not prohibit secession. Therefore, it is always possible for a state to allow a minority to determine freely its destiny including the right to secession.

It has been stated that different treatment should be applied to oppressed minorities from that applied to minorities living in a democratic state. So far, state practice has not confirmed the above statement. In this respect in is interesting to compare the situation of Quebec and Kosovo.

Quebec

Quebec nationalism and its quest for independence has led, so far, to two referenda: in 1980 and in 1995. The final objective of the nationalist movement is to separate Quebec completely from the Canadian Federation and to create an independent state. A majority in favour of independence in the referendum would give legitimacy to Quebec's claim. In both referenda the majority of residents of Quebec said 'No'. However, in the 1995 referendum the nationalist movement was very close to victory. It failed by just over 1 per cent of the vote (the 'No' vote was 50.58 per cent, the 'yes' vote 49.42 per cent). The government of Quebec has not given up its objective. It has expressed the firm intention of conducting yet another referendum in the near future. The spectre of a unilateral declaration of independence by Quebec and its implications prompted the Federal government to refer three questions to the Supreme Court of Canada regarding the legality under both the Canadian constitution and international law of such a declaration: *Re Secession of Quebec* [1998] 2 SCR 217. The Supreme Court answered that unilateral secession was illegal under both. The second question is of particular interest as it was formulated in the following manner:

> 'Does international law give the National Assembly, legislature or government of Quebec the right to effect the secession of Quebec from Canada unilaterally? In this regard, is there a right to self-determination under international law that would give the National Assembly, legislature or government of Quebec the right to effect the secession of Quebec from Canada unilaterally?'

The Supreme Court of Canada answered that international law 'does not specifically grant component parts of sovereign states the legal right to secede unilaterally from their "parent" state'. It emphasised that the protection of territorial integrity prevails over the right to external self-determination since 'A state whose government represents the whole of the people or peoples resident within its territory, on a basis of equality and without discrimination, and respects the principles of self-determination in its own internal arrangements, is entitled to the protection under international law of its territorial integrity'. The Supreme Court of Canada concluded that:

> 'In summary, the international law right to self-determination only generates, at best, a right to external self-determination in situations of former colonies; where a people is oppressed ... or where a definable group is denied meaningful access to government to pursue their political, economic, social and cultural development ... Such exceptional circumstances are manifestly inapplicable to Quebec under existing conditions.'

It is regrettable that the Supreme Court of Canada did not attempt to analyse the evolving nature of self-determination, especially in the light of developments in the former Soviet Union and the former Yugoslav Federation.

Kosovo

The case of Kosovo is very special. Albanian Kosovars were victims of an oppressive regime to such an extent that NATO decided to intervene militarily on their behalf. At the time of writing the political future of Kosovo is uncertain. The Constitutional Framework for Provisional Self-Government in Kosovo was signed by the head of the UN Interim Administration Mission in Kosovo (UNMIK) on 15 May 2001. It provides for new provisional institutions, including a legislative assembly, and contains guarantees to protect the rights and interests of all of Kosovo's communities. The return to normal, however, has not been swift. In November 2004 the ethnically divided province was still under the administration of the UNMIK (despite elections being held in November 2001 and in October 2004) and the presence of the UNMIK or other similar multinational force (eg NATO) will be required in the future to keep peace in the province and to help the province's government in establishing a stable, multi-ethnic society.

The international community has never recognised the right of Albanian Kosovars to secede from Yugoslavia. Their right to internal self-determination is now ensured under the Constitutional Framework.

It is submitted that the right to self-determination and the recognition of a new state which has been established as a result of people exercising that right in the context of secession from another state are two different matters. The recognition of a state involves a political decision of other states which legitimises and validates, post factum, the successful exercise of the right to self-determination of a particular group of people. On the one hand, international law does not authorise secession and, on the other hand, it will, sooner or later, recognise the creation of a new state once it has been made effective. Therefore, recognition, essentially political in content, provides retroactive legitimacy to the act of self-determination. Consequently, a claim to secession, not justified on any coherent theory of self-determination, will not preclude or prevent subsequent recognition by the international community of a new state, although the legality of the steps leading to its creation will be assessed by other states and will facilitate or hinder of recognition. This point has been well illustrated by the secession of East Pakistan in 1972 from Pakistan to form Bangladesh, the recognition of the Baltic states based on a legitimate rectification of their unlawful annexation by the Soviet Union in the

1940s and the recognition of the new states emerging after the break up of the former Yugoslavia.

Divided states and self-determination

International law recognises the right of divided states to unite. The best example is provided by Germany. The Preamble to the Treaty on the Final Settlement with Respect to Germany 1990 stated that:

> 'German people, freely exercising their right of self-determination, have expressed their will to bring about the unity of Germany as a state': R McCorquodale, 'Self-Determination: A Human Rights Approach' (1994) 43 ICLQ 861.

Indigenous people and self-determination

Indigenous people and the right to self-determination constitutes a matter apart! There are an estimated 300 million indigenous people living across the world.

Indigenous people are the most entitled to be considered as 'people' in the context of self-determination. Even the way we refer to them as 'people' with the 'indigenous' in front suggests that they should be considered as a special category of colonial people and therefore benefit from the right to self-determination as envisaged in Resolution 1514. International law, however, did not include them in the decolonisation movement, although they have been the longest victims of colonisation. Indigenous people have always considered themselves as equals within the international community.

The concept of terra nullius which was used to justify the claims of the Europeans to the title to land in territories which, at the time of discovery and subsequent colonisation or first settlement, were inhabited by indigenous people was first contested by Francisco de Vittoria, a Spanish Dominican and a professor of theology at the University of Salamanca in the sixteenth century. He argued that indigenous people enjoyed intrinsic sovereignty and consequently were entitled to negotiate with the European nations on equal terms and to enter into international agreements. De Vittorio's justification for the European conquest of the Americas was based on the inferiority of indigenous civilisations. Indigenous people were more often than not formally recognised by colonial powers which at first entered into commerce or friendship treaties with local populations but subsequently denied them any rights. In North America during the time when England, France and Spain were fighting each other in order to conquer the continent these states often entered into international agreements with Indian tribes and treated them as sovereign and independent nations. With the end of the intra-European rivalry and the subsequent withdrawal of European powers from the US (cession of Louisiana by France in 1803, Florida by Spain in 1819) the federal government no longer needed Indian tribes. They were dealt with by force of arms.

Nowadays the concept of terra nullius is regarded as particularly inappropriate and unjust. It has been criticized by ICJ and national courts: *Mabo* v *Queensland* (1992) 66 ALJR 408. In the *Western Sahara Case* the ICJ stated that:

> '[A] determination that Western Sahara was a "terra nullius" at the time of colonisation by Spain would be possible only if it were established that at that time the territory belonged to no one in the sense that it was open to acquisition through the legal process of "occupation"': (1975) ICJ Rep 12 at 56.

The International Labour Organisation was the first to show any interest in indigenous people. Its Convention 107 of 1957 on Living and Working Conditions of Indigenous Populations defines indigenous people as the original inhabitants of lands subjugated by colonial powers. Convention 107 focused on the integration of indigenous people and prohibition of discrimination. For that reason in the 1970s, with a new understanding of the right of self-determination and in the light of the Declaration on Friendly Relations 1970, the Convention needed a major revision. The ILO decided to revise Convention 107 in 1986 and to invite the NGOs of indigenous people to participate in the revision process which ended in 1989 with the adoption of Convention 169 (128 votes to one, with 49 abstentions). Convention 169 has been strongly criticised by indigenous people for both their limited participation in its preparation and the actual content. Nevertheless, Convention 169 has made an important contribution to the recognition of the rights of indigenous people. It replaces the term 'populations' used by Convention 107 by the term 'people'. This bold approach was subject to extensive debate because the recognition of those who are indigenous as 'people' entails far-reaching consequences in international law, namely 'people' are entitled to choose for themselves a form of political organisation that they consider appropriate for their development and their choice may be independence as a state, association with other groups into a federal state, or autonomy or assimilation into a unitary state. Many states were frightened that indigenous people would assert their right to self-determination by a way of secession. For that reason para 3 was added to art 1 of Convention 169 which provides that 'the use of the term "people" in this Convention shall not be construed as having any implications as regards the rights which may attach to the term under international law'. Nevertheless, Convention 169 constitutes an important step in the recognition of rights of indigenous people. It provides that 'irrespective of their legal status indigenous people should retain some or all of their own social, economic, cultural and political institutions'. It also encourages the contracting states to apply the participatory approach in respect of any development projects or matters that affect indigenous people. Convention 169 was designed to ensure a minimum standard 'to establish a floor under the rights of indigenous and tribal peoples and, in particular, to establish a basis for government conduct in relation to them'. In this respect, Convention 169 has achieved its objective. Furthermore, through the ILO supervising mechanisms its implementation in contracting states is closely monitored by the ILO. The ILO is very much involved in improving the situation of indigenous people through technical assistance programmes consisting, inter alia, of assisting states in drafting legislation for the indigenous people (eg Russia) and in setting up institutional frameworks intended to solve the problems faced by indigenous communities living in a particular state (eg Guatemala).

In the 1970s indigenous people started to organise themselves and fight for their rights. They wanted to raise international awareness of problems faced by indigenous people. They fully achieved their objective. Their situation has attracted the attention of the international community. At the Earth Summit in 1992 states acknowledged the need to recognise indigenous peoples' values, territories and traditions and their special relation with the earth in terms of their ecological knowledge and agricultural systems. In 1993 the General Assembly adopted Resolution 48/163 proclaiming the International Decade of the World's Indigenous People (1995–2004) which was launched on 8 December 1994. The main objective of the Decade was to promote new partnership between indigenous people and states and between indigenous people and the United Nations, to alleviate the plight of indigenous people and to intensify efforts to respond to their legitimate demands and needs in such areas as human rights, environment, development, education and health. To date, the main achievements of the International Decade are twofold.

First, the issue of the indigenous people has been put on the United Nations agenda. On the basis of the 1974 study prepared by the UN Sub-Commission on the Prevention of Discrimination and Protection of Minorities, the UN in 1982 set up a Working Group on Indigenous Populations. Under its auspices two important Drafts were prepared: the Draft Declaration of the Rights of Indigenous People 1993, which is now under review by an ad hoc working group of the UN Commission on Human Rights, and the Draft Principles and Guidelines on the Protection of the Heritage of Indigenous People 1996 which, after being revised by a United Nations seminar in February/March 2000, has been transmitted for further action to the Commission on Human Rights.

One may wonder why the 1993 Declaration has not yet been adopted taking into account that it will have no binding force. The answer is that the Declaration will constitute a moral victory for indigenous people. It will acknowledge their rights and will provide for the manner in which governments should implement those rights. The most controversial is art 3 of the Draft which states that:

'Indigenous people have the right of self-determination. By virtue of that right they freely determine their political status and freely pursue their economic, social and cultural development.'

The governments concerned fear that the recognition of the right to self-determination will entail secession by indigenous people. They have suggested that the formula of self-determination should be replaced by self-management and that the aspiration of indigenous people for self-determination should be realised without challenging the territorial integrity of the existing states, that is it should take the form of greater autonomy or self-government for indigenous people.

Furthermore, many governments are submitting that the Declaration on Friendly Relations 1970 provides that the alternatives for the exercise of the right to self-determination include 'any other' political status freely determined by the people concerned. Thus, it would be appropriate to consider autonomy arrangements as 'any other political status' determined by the people. Indigenous people argue that their right to self-determination cannot be qualified.

Another important new development is the creation of a subsidiary permanent organ of the UN Economic and Social Council, a 'Permanent Forum on Indigenous Issues'. By Resolution ECOSOC 2000/22, adopted by consensus by the UN Economic and Social Council on 28 July 2000, the new Permanent Forum formally integrates indigenous people through their representatives into the structure of the United Nations. The Forum is made up of eight members nominated by governments and elected by the Council and eight members appointed by the President of the Council following broad consultations with indigenous organisations and groups. Thus, for the first time, the representatives of states and non-states have been given parity in a permanent representative body of the United Nations organisation proper. Populations may participate in the Forum as observers. According to Resolution 2000/22 the Permanent Forum 'shall serve as an advisory body to the Council with a mandate to discuss indigenous issues within the mandate of the Council relating to economic and social development, culture, the environment, education, health and human rights'. The Forum 'shall hold an annual session of ten working days at the United Nations Office at Geneva or at the United Nations Headquarters or at such other place as the Permanent Forum may decide in accordance with the existing financial rules and regulations of the United Nations'. The first session of the Permanent Forum was held at the UN headquarters from 13–24 May 2002 and, as an inaugural session, was mainly concerned with procedural issues. The second session held from 12–23 May 2003 discussed the issues relating to 'Indigenous Children and Youth'. All recommendations of the Second Session were acknowledged by the UN Economic and Social Council.

The creation of the Permanent Forum did not challenge the existence of the UN Working Group on Indigenous Populations. To the contrary, it has rationalised UN activities in respect of indigenous peoples. Currently, there are three bodies within the UN system to deal with indigenous issues.

1. The Permanent Forum. Its main functions are: to provide expert advice and recommendations on indigenous issues to the UN Economic and Social Council; to raise awareness and promote the integration and co-ordination of activities concerning indigenous issues within the UN system; and to prepare and disseminate information on indigenous issues.
2. The UN Working Group on Indigenous Populations. Its main task is to monitor the respect afforded to the human rights of indigenous people and to develop normative standards aimed at improving the situation of these people.
3. A Special Rapporteur on the Situation of Human Rights and Fundamental

Freedoms of Indigenous People. A Special Rapporteur investigates allegations of systematic abuses and atrocities against indigenous people through fieldwork, direct communications with governments and local indigenous groups.

Many initiatives have been taken to improve the lives of indigenous people through the UN Development Programme (UNDP), UNESCO, the United Nations International Fund for Agricultural Development (IFAD), etc. The World Bank has made a commitment not to assist development projects which infringe indigenous peoples' traditional territories unless adequate safeguards are provided, such as, for example, the demarcation and protection of indigenous lands.

Second, within the partnership between indigenous people and states there is a growing trend towards the recognition of the rights and aspirations of indigenous people. Many countries have acknowledged the right of their indigenous people to self-government: Sweden and Finland have established a Parliament for their Saami indigenous people; the Australian Parliament enacted the Native Title Act 1993 which recognises that Australia was not terra nullius when the British first arrived in the late eighteenth century. In Colombia, Bolivia and Argentina new laws were enacted protecting and promoting the rights of indigenous people. In many countries including the US the emphasis is more on economic and social development of indigenous people than on political autonomy.

An interesting development took place in Canada. As a result of two agreements – the Nunavut political accord and the Nunavut land claim agreements concluded between the federal government of Canada and Nunavut people (82 per cent of them are Inuit) – the Canadian Northwest Territories were divided in order to create a new Canadian territory – Nunavut. This self-governing territory has 27,500 inhabitants and occupies an area of 1,994,000 sq km which constitutes 20 per cent of Canada (approximately four times the territory of Sweden). For the first time the Nunavut people elected their own legislative assembly in February 1999 and on 1 April 1999 Nunavut's elected government assumed responsibility for governing the new territory. The arrangement between Canada and the Nunavut people respects the form of self-government chosen by Nunavut's people while ensuring the territorial integrity of Canada.

The UN Economic and Social Council at its 48th and 49th meetings recommended to the GA that it declare a second International Decade of the world's indigenous peoples after the conclusion of the current International Decade of the World's Indigenous people in December 2004. The Secretary-General submitted to the UN Economic and Social Council a preliminary review by the Co-ordinator of the International Decade of the World's Indigenous People on the activities of the UN in relation to the Decade. The report notes that although some progress had been made in advancing the rights of indigenous people, including important institutional developments within the framework of the Decade, they, in many countries, continue to be among the poorest and most marginalised people.

14.8 Conclusion

The right to self-determination has been declared as a fundamental human right by all important human rights instruments, including the Universal Declaration of Human Rights. Self-determination is regarded as the right of all peoples to control their destiny, to choose their political status and to make decisions about their own development. However, international law is still unclear as to the exact meaning and scope of application of the right to self-determination. Only in the context of decolonisation, provided one is not too precise about the definition of 'decolonisation', is self-determination clearly recognised as a legal right. In other cases political considerations determine which 'oppressed' people gain sufficient acceptance and support to merit their being recognised as having the right to self-determination. This recognition has most often been expressed by UN resolutions which 'grant' to certain oppressed groups the status as peoples possessing legitimate aspirations of self-determination. Left unanswered is the question of the legal competence of the UN to grant this recognition in the first place.

It is probably safe to say that the content and the understanding of the right to self-determination has evolved as a result of the end of the Cold War. Some authors have argued that state practice started to recognised a more expansive right to secede in the light of the cases of Bangladesh, the Baltic republics, Slovenia, Croatia, Bosnia-Herzegovina, Eritrea, and the velvet divorce between Slovakia and the Czech Republic. Nevertheless, each case is different and it is impossible to deduce any clear rules from the above cases. The Supreme Court of Canada in its decision concerning secession of Quebec from Canada did not hesitate to state that international law recognises no right of a political sub-unit to secede as long as the government of the state 'represents the whole of the people or peoples resident within its territory, on a basis of equality and without discrimination' and the state 'respects the principles of self-determination in its own internal arrangements': (1998) 2 SCR 217 para 130. Furthermore, the case of Kosovo demonstrates that even if a government violates the fundamental human rights of its oppressed minority the international community is not prepared to recognise the right of that minority to secede from such a state.

The new perception of the right to self-determination is probably the most evident in respect of indigenous people. The Draft Declaration on the Rights of Indigenous People 1993 expressly recognises their right to self-determination and their right to their lands, territories and resources. They are no longer considered as conquered ethnic minorities. National self-government arrangements and the Draft Declaration on the Rights of Indigenous People demonstrate that there is, at both national and international levels, a tendency towards the recognition of the right to self-determination of indigenous peoples. At the time of writing autonomy and self-government are the principal means through which their right is exercised, but if these options are not acceptable to them, for whatever reason, they should be entitled to full independence.

It is interesting to note that the first International Conference on 'The Right to Self-Determination and the United Nations' held in Geneva in August 2000 unanimously adopted a number of resolutions intended to clarify the content and scope of application of the right to self-determination and to establish new UN mechanisms related to self-determination. The Conference discussed the self-determination needs and aspirations of indigenous people, minorities and nations including the Kashmiris, native Americans, African Americans, Irish, Tamils, Saamis, Dalits of India, Canadian First Nations, Khmer Krom of Vietnam, Chechens, Mon of Burma, Puerto Ricans etc. The Resolutions called for:

1. the establishment of an Office of the High Commissioner for Self-Determination;
2. the establishment of a Self-Determination Commission made up of representatives of United Nations member states.

It also reaffirmed the importance of the right to self-determination and condemned all violations of this right, and invited the UN to set up a process under which individual cases may be comprehensively discussed at an international forum and appropriate resolutions adopted accordingly.

15

Peaceful Settlement of Disputes between States

15.1 Introduction

15.2 Diplomatic means of dispute settlement between states

15.3 Arbitration

15.4 Judicial settlement of inter-state disputes

15.5 Contentious jurisdiction of the International Court of Justice

15.7 The advisory jurisdiction of the International Court of Justice

15.7 Assessment of the International Court of Justice

15.1 Introduction

The principle of peaceful settlement of disputes is enshrined in art 2 of the UN Charter which provides that in the pursuit of the fundamental objectives of the UN, namely the maintenance of peace and security, its member states are bound to settle their international disputes by peaceful means in such a manner as not to endanger international peace, security and justice. This obligation is reinforced in art 33(1) of the UN Charter which provides that:

> 'The parties to any dispute, the continuance of which is likely to endanger the maintenance of international peace and security, shall, first of all, seek a solution by negotiation, enquiry, mediation, conciliation, arbitration, judicial settlement, resort to regional agencies or arrangements, or other peaceful means of their own choice.'

Article 33 leaves the parties free to choose the means which they consider as the most appropriate to the circumstances and the nature of their dispute. However, if the parties fail to make any meaningful attempt to resolve a dispute which threatens international peace and security then, under art 33, the Security Council may call upon the parties to settle the dispute without specifying what means to use. However, it may recommend a particular means of settlement, it may recommend the actual terms of settlement, it may investigate the dispute and it may set up machinery for settlement.

The principle of peaceful settlement of international disputes has been reaffirmed by numerous declarations and resolutions of the UN General Assembly, in particular: Resolution 2625 (XXV) which extends the obligation of peaceful settlement of international disputes to all states and not only to the member states of the UN; and the Manila Declaration on the Peaceful Settlement of International Disputes 1982 which imposes on states the obligation to seek in good faith and a spirit of co-operation an early and equitable settlement of their disputes. In 1988 the General Assembly adopted the Declaration on the Prevention and Removal of Disputes and Situations Which May Threaten International Peace and Security and on the Role of the UN in This Field, which emphasises the need for the ICJ to play a greater role in the settlement of international disputes and recommends the adoption of a universal convention on peaceful settlement of disputes. The principle of peaceful settlement of international disputes has been recognised by the ICJ in the *Nicaragua Case: Nicaragua v US (Merits)* (1986) ICJ Rep 14 as having the status of customary law. Moreover, the traditional approach to the settlement of international disputes, consisting of leaving to the parties a free choice between various peaceful means in order to select the most appropriate to the circumstances and the nature of a dispute, has been considerably altered in favour of compulsory recourse to a specific procedure provided for by an increasing number of multilateral treaties.

Today, the principle of peaceful settlement of international disputes is universally recognised and has become what Léon Bourgeois dreamt of when he said that 'the obligation of settling international conflicts by pacific means is the first law of human society'. (Bourgeois was a French politician and statesman, and an ardent promoter of the League of Nations. He was awarded the Nobel Prize for Peace in 1920. He represented France at the First Hague Peace Conference of 1899 where he advocated international co-operation among nations.) The path towards its recognition was long and bristling with difficulties. Indeed, before the views of humanity on war and peace became more sophisticated the main method of resolving disputes was war. From the historical perspective two approaches have developed in the search for the peaceful settlement of disputes.

The first consisted of settling of international disputes through the channels of diplomacy. Within this, various forms of negotiation, mediation and conciliation have been developed in response to the need to resolve international conflicts in the context of the gradual expansion of an international legal order.

The second method of settling international disputes, through judicial process, in particular by arbitral tribunals and international courts, being more complex and controversial, took longer to attain recognition. Alongside state practice efforts were made by pacifists, anti-war movements and idealists to ban the use of force in international relations. It was towards the end of the nineteenth and the beginning of the twentieth century, at the two Hague Peace Conferences of 1899 and 1907, that restrictions on the use of force and the necessity for the peaceful settlement of international disputes were effectively linked. The Hague Conferences laid down the foundations of the World Court by adopting numerous conventions and various institutions that have since been operating on the premises of the Peace Palace in the Hague, such as the the Permanent Court of International Justice (PCIJ) and its successor the International Court of Justice (ICJ), the Permanent Court of Arbitration (PCA), the Hague Academy of International Law and the Law Library, one of the most comprehensive in the world.

In this chapter both diplomatic and judicial means as well as arbitration will be examined.

15.2 Diplomatic means of dispute settlement between states

Diplomatic means of settlement of international disputes tend to facilitate an agreement between the parties as, in contrast to legal means, they are not binding on the parties and place less emphasis on their formal position under the law. Such methods include negotiation, good offices, enquiry and conciliation. Diplomatic means are flexible. The parties to a dispute exercise full control over these procedures.

Negotiation

Negotiation is the most frequently and probably the only universally accepted means of dispute settlement. It is also the normal method of diplomatic interchange and as such in certain cases negotiation constitutes a necessary first step before the parties decide to use other procedures in order to resolve their dispute. Moreover, often, international treaties include clauses providing for negotiation as a prerequisite to other forms of settlement. Negotiation is more than mere deliberation and thus may lead to an agreed solution. Negotiation may be bilateral or multilateral, in which case it often takes the form of conferences. The value of negotiation as a method of settlement of international disputes has been acknowledged by both the PCIJ and the ICJ: *Free Zones of Upper Savoy and the District of Gex Case* (1932) PCIJ Rep Ser A/B No 46; *North Sea Continental Shelf Cases: Federal Republic of Germany* v *The Netherlands* (1969) ICJ Rep 3. The main drawback of negotiation is that no third neutral party is involved in the settlement of a dispute. For that reason when a party denies the existence of a dispute or refuses to conduct meaningful negotiations other means of dispute settlement must be used.

Good offices and mediation

Good offices involves the participation of a third party, whether a state, an individual or a body, offering assistance to prevent further deterioration of the dispute. An offer of good offices is subject to acceptance by the parties to a dispute. The impartiality of a third party is of the essence as confidence in its reliability constitutes a necessary condition of establishing contact between the parties in dispute. The main role of a third party is to provide a channel of communication thus facilitating the establishment of dialogue between the parties. The third party does not participate in the actual settlement of a dispute. However, if the third party becomes actively involved and starts to make proposals for the solution of a dispute he no longer exercises the function of 'good offices' but becomes a mediator. The transformation of good offices into mediation occurs very often in practice, taking into account the acceptance of a third party by the parties to a controversy. Mediation therefore is an extension of good offices. The main difference is that a mediator submits his recommendations and advice which are not, however, binding on the parties. Good offices are based on customary international law and has been included in many international agreements, such as the Hague Convention I for the Pacific Settlement of International Disputes 1907, the UN Charter, the Bogotá Pact 1948 and the Vienna Convention on Diplomatic Relations 1961. UN Secretary-Generals have often been asked to render good offices. For example, since becoming UN Secretary-General Mr Annan has provided good offices in a range of situations, including Cyprus, East Timor, Iraq, Libya, Nigeria and West Sahara.

Successful mediation was carried out by Germany during the 1878 Berlin Congress, by the Soviet Union during the 1966 Indo–Pakistan conflict, by the US in the 1978 peace talks between Egypt and Israel, by the UN Secretary-General in 1988 in respect of the termination of war between Iran and Iraq, etc.

Most conflicts in the post-Cold War era involved numerous attempts to use mediation to achieve peace.

Inquiry

Inquiry involves third-party investigation of facts surrounding the dispute and as such is normally of a technical character. Many conventions adopted by the 1899 and 1907 Hague Peace Conferences expressly refer to the establishment of an international commission of inquiry in order to 'elucidate through an impartial and conscientious examination the question of facts' and thus to facilitate the settlement of disputes. The Treaties of Bryan (the name of the US Secretary of State who initiated them) concluded between the US and various states in 1913–1914 set up a permanent commission of inquiry under which contracting states in the case of a dispute were bound to wait for a report from such a Commission before starting war. The involvement of a third party, although customary, is not imperative. Many international treaties provide for the establishment of permanent commissions of inquiry, fact-finding or investigation, in particular, conventions relating to the protection of human rights. Normally, at the conclusion of an inquiry a report containing the factual findings is submitted to the parties, which may also contain non-binding recommendations. Inquiry requires that the parties involved in a dispute provide their assistance and co-operation during the investigation which often involves the examination of witnesses and on-site visits.

Conciliation

Conciliation is a quasi-judicial procedure. It occurs by agreement between the parties, whereby a third party is appointed to investigate the dispute and to suggest terms for a settlement. The parties, are not, however, bound by these recommendations. A third party entrusted with conciliation examines all aspects of the dispute. In this respect conciliation exceeds the inquiry procedure as not only the facts of the dispute are established but also the dispute in its entirety is subject to examination. The third party attempts to suggest a solution acceptable to the parties involved in the controversy. Pragmatism rather than legal considerations governs conciliation proceedings. Conciliation is a flexible method of settlement of disputes which leaves the parties free to reject the proposed solution, to accept it or to consider it as a source of inspiration for the future resolution of a dispute. In respect of cases of a politically delicate nature, and of non-justiciable disputes, conciliation has been used frequently. Numerous conventions concluded under the auspices of the League of Nations provide for the establishment of commissions of conciliation. Modern multilateral treaties often provide for compulsory conciliation which is a more popular alternative to binding procedures for two reasons: first, it satisfies states which wish to have some pre-established mechanism of settling disputes that may arise under a particular treaty; second, it is acceptable to states which do not wish to have imposed upon them any legally binding solution to a future dispute. An example of compulsory conciliation is provided by the Vienna Convention on the Law of Treaties 1969 in respect of disputes concerning any provision on the invalidity of treaties except those on ius cogens.

15.3 Arbitration

Arbitration between states is a different form of arbitration from that often used in the settlement of civil disputes, and from the concept of mixed arbitral tribunals dealing with claims by natural or legal persons. The Convention for the Pacific Settlement of International Disputes 1899 states that: 'International arbitration has for its object the settlement of disputes between states by judges of their own choice and on the basis of respect for law. Recourse to arbitration implies an engagement to submit in good faith to the award.' The International Law Commission defined arbitration as 'a procedure for the settlement of disputes between states by a binding award on the basis of law as a result of an undertaking voluntarily accepted'.

The importance of arbitration justifies a short summary of its history, followed by the examination of various legal aspects of arbitration including the effect of the arbitral award.

History of arbitration

Arbitration was first used by the ancient Greek city-states to settle their disputes. Although during the Middle Ages arbitration found some favour in respect of disputes between Italian city states, the Swiss Cantons and the Hanseatic League, its use declined with the rise of independent sovereign states. Modern arbitration dates from the establishment of three mixed claims commissions under the Jay Treaty of 1774 between Great Britain and the US to settle highly controversial matters after the War of Independence which had not been settled by diplomacy. Both nations appointed an equal number of British and American nationals to serve on an arbitral commission. The Jay Arbitration was very successful and stimulated international interest in arbitration as a dispute-resolution mechanism. This also encouraged the US to conclude similar arbitration treaties with young South American states very interested in introducing arbitration to settle regional disputes, as exemplified by the General, Permanent and Absolute Arbitration Treaty between Colombia and Chile 1880. Further development of arbitration was prompted by the conclusion of the Treaty of Washington 1871 between Great Britain and the US which defined the rights and duties of neutral states. Under the Treaty the famous *Alabama Case (Alabama Claims Arbitration* (1872) Moore, 1 Int Arb 495) was settled in which the US accused Great Britain of infringing customary rules on neutrality by helping the southern states during the US Civil War. The ship *Alabama* was built in British shipyards and with the help of the British destroyed some 70 ships of the Union before being sunk. When the arbitral tribunal ordered Great Britain to pay compensation she complied. The *Alabama Case* contributed to the popularity of arbitration and initiated the practice of inserting arbitration clauses into international treaties. It also clarified certain matters relating to neutrality and the composition and competence of arbitral tribunals.

During the nineteenth century many arbitration tribunals were established on an ad hoc basis to settle a particular dispute or to deal with pecuniary claims for compensation for injury to aliens who could not obtain justice in foreign courts. An example is the 1868 Convention between the US and Mexico which established a mixed arbitral commission to deal with claims of nationals of each country arising from the US Civil War.

Arbitration was further developed by the 1899 Hague Peace Conference which adopted a Convention for the Pacific Settlement of International Disputes (revised at the Second Hague Conference in 1907) providing for the establishment of the Permanent Court of Arbitration (PCA) which materialised in 1900. The name given to this institution is highly misleading as it is neither a court nor an arbitration tribunal nor does it involve any permanency. The PCA can be described as 'a permanent arbitration service' as it consists of a list of individuals who declare themselves available, for a renewable term of six years, to serve as arbitrators in the case of a dispute. The contracting states submit a list of up to four potential arbitrators who may be their nationals or may be foreigners selected on the basis of their expertise and the highest moral reputation. At the time of writing the PCA is made up of approximately 260 members elected by 85 contracting parties to the 1899 and 1907 Hague Conventions.

When a dispute is submitted to the PCA an ad hoc arbitral tribunal is established comprising the candidates from the list or in some cases outside the list. Three different systems have been used with regard to the composition of an arbitral tribunal. It may consist of a single arbitrator (eg Asser in the *Island of Palmas Arbitration: The Netherlands* v *US* (1928) 2 RIAA 829) or a panel of three or five arbitrators. Parties to a dispute must agree on a single arbitrator, or if they decide to have a panel of three arbitrators, each nominates one arbitrator, and the two who are nominated select the third. If there are to be five arbitrators, each party nominates two and the four who are nominated select a fifth who is the head of arbitration. If no agreement is reached the missing arbitrator will be selected by drawing lots from the list.

The International Bureau which compiles a list of arbitrators is the only permanent feature of the PCA. It is also empowered to function as a registry for Commissions of Inquiry. Such Commissions have been established on four occasions (in 1904, 1912, 1921 and in 1961). In 1937 the Bureau was authorised by the Administrative Council to set up Conciliation Commissions. Such commissions have been set up on three occasions, in 1937, 1954 and 1965.

The executive body of the PCA, its Administrative Council, supervises the work of the International Bureau and is in charge of all administrative tasks, such as budgetary matters and the preparation of an annual report on the activities of the PCA for the contracting parties, although on some occasions it has taken important decisions, for example concerning the revision of the PCA's rules of procedure. The Council is chaired by the Foreign Minister of The Netherlands, being the person who is the depository of the Hague Conventions, and comprises diplomatic representatives of the contracting states.

The importance of the PCA has declined with the establishment of the Permanent Court of International Justice and its successor the International Court of Justice. Twenty-three cases were arbitrated between 1902 and 1939, and only four after World War II. As can be seen the PCA was at its most successful during the period up to the beginning of World War I. Its most significant awards were given in the *Muscat Dhows* ((1905) 1 Scott 95), the *North Atlantic Fisheries Arbitration* ((1910) 11 RIAA 167), *Savarkar* ((1911) 1 Scott 276) and the *Island of Palmas Arbitration* (above). Since 1959 the PCA, in its search for revitalisation, has introduced many initiatives, such as offering its services for arbitrations between states and individuals or corporations, concluding in 1968 a co-operation agreement with the International Centre for the Settlement of Investment Disputes, revising its rules of procedure etc. Also the PCA actively co-operates with the UN and has been given the status of a Permanent Observer at the UN General Assembly in 1993: 13 UN Doc A/48.49 (1993).

Whether the under-utilisation of the PCA is due to external factors, ie contracting states are reluctant to use arbitration, or internal reasons, ie the procedures and principles underlining its functioning, the fact remains that the PCA is not the most successful institution in the settlement of international disputes.

Despite the lack of success of the PCA, arbitration is still used by states in the settlement of their disputes. The recourse to arbitration is based on the consent of the parties to a dispute and may result from a number of factors.

1. Arbitration clauses inserted into a treaty which require that if a dispute arises between the contracting parties in respect of the interpretation or application of that treaty they will be bound to submit it to arbitration.
2. Compromis which is a formal agreement, after the dispute has occurred, to submit the dispute to arbitration. Compromis will normally stipulate the terms under which the tribunal will function, its composition, competences and the law applicable to the dispute. Although the parties are free to organise the procedure at their convenience, often they refer to the rules of procedure set out in the 1899 Hague Convention (as revised in 1907) rather than the 1955 Model Rules drafted by the International Law Commission and recommended for use by member states by the General Assembly in 1958. The reason is that the procedure under the 1899 Hague Convention, unlike the 1955 Model Rules, ensures that the parties enjoy the largest possible autonomy.
3. The treaty of arbitration. Arbitration as a method of settlement of international disputes is provided for in numerous treaties, including the Geneva General Act for the Settlement of Disputes 1928 adopted by the League of Nations and reinvigorated by the General Assembly in 1949, the Washington Treaty of Inter-American Arbitration 1929, the American Treaty on Pacific Settlement of Disputes 1948 and the European Convention for the Peaceful Settlement of Disputes 1957 elaborated under the auspices of the Council of Europe. Unfortunately these treaties are for various reasons – eg lack of sufficient number of ratifications, important reservations inserted by contracting parties, etc – of little practical importance.

The most significant ad hoc arbitration settlements which have taken place since World War II are: the *Rann of Kutch Arbitration* (1968) 50 ILR 2 between India and Pakistan, the *Delimitation of the Continental Shelf Case* (1978) 54 ILR 6 between the UK and France and the *Beagle Channel Case* (1977) 52 ILR 93 between Argentina and Chile which was first submitted for arbitration to the Queen of England by virtue of a treaty signed by the parties in 1902 (the actual tribunal consisted of five judges of the ICJ). When Argentina rejected the award both parties agreed to papal mediation leading to an agreement on the Pope's arbitration which was subsequently complied with by the parties in 1984.

The main features of arbitration

1. The selection of the arbitrator is made by the parties themselves or by means of a mechanism agreed between the parties, thus distinguishing arbitration from judicial settlement. The amount of freedom that the parties enjoy as to the appointment of the arbitrator may challenge the arbitration agreement if one of the parties resiles from its obligation to arbitrate by deliberately failing to appoint its own member or members of the arbitral tribunal. This occurred in respect of the 1947 Allies' peace treaties with the former enemy states of Bulgaria, Hungary and Romania. These treaties contain a clause relating to the protection of human rights. In the first years of the Cold War the Allied states accused the former enemy states of the violation of that clause. The treaties required the establishment of an arbitration commission in the event of a dispute. The former enemy states deliberately failed to appoint members of the arbitral commission, thereby rendering the arbitral provision of the treaties inoperative. The General Assembly asked the ICJ for an advisory opinion on the matter. The ICJ held that the governments of Bulgaria, Hungary and Romania were obliged to appoint arbitrators although upon their failure to do so the Secretary-General of the UN was not authorised to appoint arbitrators on their behalf: Advisory Opinion on the *Interpretation of Peace Treaties with Bulgaria, Hungary and Romania* (1950) ICJ Rep 65. To avoid this problem provisions have been adopted in arbitration treaties to provide for the appointment of arbitrators where one of the parties to the dispute fails to co-operate. For example, art 21 of the European Convention for the Peaceful Settlement of Disputes 1957 provides:

   > 'If the nomination of the members of the Arbitral Tribunal is not made within a period of three months from the date on which one of the parties requested the other party to constitute an Arbitral Tribunal, the task of making the necessary nomination shall be entrusted to the Government of a third state chosen by agreement between the parties, or failing agreement within three months, to the President of the International Court of Justice. Should the latter be a national of one of the parties to the dispute, this task shall be entrusted to the Vice-President of the Court, or to the next senior judge of the Court who is not a national of the parties.'

2. Arbitration tribunals are usually created to deal with a particular dispute or class of disputes. Arbitration is an especially convenient method of settling large numbers of outstanding claims between two states. For example, a number of claims between the US and Italy arising from World War II were settled in accordance with the arbitral provisions laid down in the Italian Peace Treaty 1947. Another example is provided by the Iran-US Claims Tribunal which dealt with economic claims of individuals and businesses harmed by the hostage crisis between these two countries.

3. The arbitration tribunal may consist of a single arbitrator or be a collegiate body, comprising two or more arbitrators appointed in equal numbers by each of the parties separately, plus an umpire appointed jointly by the parties or by the

arbitrators appointed by them. Heads of State or judges from neutral countries are the most likely candidates to be a sole arbitrator. In 1931 the King of Italy was appointed as a sole arbitrator in the *Clipperton Island Arbitration* (1932) 26 AJIL 390 between France and Mexico, and in the *Tinoco Arbitration* (1923) 1 RIAA 369 between Great Britain and Costa Rica Chief Justice Taft of the US Supreme Court acted as a sole arbitrator. An arbitral tribunal as a collective body may take two forms: a joint commission or a mixed commission. A joint commission consists of an equal number of arbitrators nominated by each party. In such a case arbitrators represent the state that has appointed them. The main disadvantage of a joint commission is that often it not able a reach any kind of agreement. In order to avoid stalemate the second form of arbitration is the most frequently used: a mixed commission. The appointment of an odd number of arbitrators, which do not necessarily represent the parties, and neutral arbitrators increases the likelihood of successful arbitration. In the *Alabama Claims Arbitration* (above) the UK and the US each appointed an arbitrator (ie two out of five). The two arbitrators then decided to ask Brazil, Italy and Switzerland to appoint one arbitrator each.

4. The law applicable to arbitration between two states is usually international law, in particular, the general principles of international law. Article 37 of the Hague Convention 1899 provides that the object of arbitration is the settlement of disputes 'on the basis of respect for law'. However, the parties are free to specify in the compromis the law applicable to their dispute and may decide to apply the principles of equity or justice or ask the arbitrators to find an equitable solution to their dispute. This is especially appropriate in respect of disputes of a political rather than legal nature.

The effect of the arbitral award

Normally arbitration between states is intended to be final and the award binding as a final settlement of a dispute: art 81 of the Hague Convention 1899. The general principle is that the decision of the arbitral tribunal should not be disturbed except in the event of a manifest error of law or fact, irregularity in the appointment of arbitrators, or an essential procedural error.

Appeal of an arbitral award to the ICJ by a dissatisfied state has been permitted in the *Maritime Delimitation between Guinea-Bissau and Senegal: Guinea-Bissau* v *Senegal* (1992) 31 ILM 32. The ICJ in its decision clarified a number of points concerning the grounds on which such appeals may be made. There appear to be three separate grounds on which an appeal against an arbitral award will be accepted.

1. Excess de pouvoir – if an arbitral body exceeds its competence, its decision is null and void. Arbitrators have only such powers as the parties have conferred upon them.

2. Failure to reach a decision by a true majority – if the vote passing the decision of the tribunal does not amount to a true majority the decision cannot be given legal effect.
3. Insufficiency of reasoning – the decision of the arbitral tribunal must be supported by adequate legal arguments. However, a statement of reasoning, although relatively brief and succinct, if clear and precise, does not amount to an insufficiency of reasoning.

If an arbitral decision is overturned on appeal, the award is null and without binding force on the parties concerned. In some cases the issue of nullity will itself be referred to further arbitration. However, there is always a possibility for the parties to ask the arbitral tribunal to interpret the award.

15.4 Judicial settlement of inter-state disputes

Two stages can be distinguished in the development of the judicial settlement of inter-state disputes. The first is associated with the Permanent Court of International Justice (PCIJ). The second with its successor the International Court of Justice (ICJ).

Article 14 of the Covenant of the League of Nations provided for the establishment of the PCIJ. In 1920 the Council of the League of Nations set up the Commission of Jurists which was entrusted with the preparation of a draft Statute of the Court. The draft, which was unanimously approved by the Council and the Assembly of the League, was contained in the so-called Protocol of Signature which was opened for signature as a separate international convention on 17 December 1920. On 1 September 1921 it entered into force having obtained 22 ratifications. The PCIJ held its opening ceremony on 15 February 1922 at its seat at the Peace Palace in The Hague. The PCIJ held its last public sitting on 4 December 1939 when it dealt with the request for interim measures in the *Electricity Company of Sofia Case* (1939) PCIJ Rep Ser A/B No 79. Before the German invasion of The Netherlands, in early May 1940, the PCIJ moved from The Hague to Geneva. All judges of the PCIJ resigned on 30 January 1946 and the PCIJ was dissolved by a Resolution of the UN General Assembly on 18 April 1946, on the same day the International Court of Justice (ICJ) was inaugurated.

Between 1922 and 1940 the PCIJ was seised of 66 cases and 28 requests for advisory opinions. Twelve cases were settled out of court. Altogether the PCIJ rendered 32 judgments and 27 advisory opinions. Despite many criticisms addressed to the PCIJ it was the first permanent court available to all states of the world. It also considerably contributed to the development of international law. As Rosenne said:

'From its experimental beginnings it established the point that a permanent international judicial organ integrated with the political organisation of the international community is both feasible and necessary, even without going so far as to be accompanied by any true compulsory jurisdiction ... The experience of the Permanent Court, its dispassionate and unhurried consideration of issues brought before it, the high standard of personal integrity and professional competence, and worldly wisdom, of its members, the fact that the judicial pronouncements were endowed with strong moral authority in addition to their formal finality, provided the foundations for the reconstructed system of international adjudication after the dust of the Second World War had started to settle': *Law and Practice of the International Court*, Leyden: Sithoff, 1965, pp13–14.

Two factors greatly undermined the work of the PCIJ. First, the PCIJ was not an organ of the League of Nations. Second, although its Statute was ratified by 48 states the leading powers – the US and the Soviet Union – had never become contracting parties. The US signed the Protocol but the US Senate failed to ratify it on two occasions, first when it rejected the Paris Peace Treaties in 1920 and again in January 1935, despite the fact that both the 1920 Protocol and its 1929 revised version were signed by the US in 1929. The Soviet Union became a member of the League of Nations in 1934 but never ratified the Statute of the PCIJ and never participated in any litigation. Finally, the outbreak of World War II destroyed the potential effectiveness of the PCIJ.

During World War II the need for an international court of justice was never challenged. However, the idea of reorganisation of the international judicial system was present in many places, including the following.

1. Washington: the announcement concerning the willingness of the US to establish such a court after the war was made by US Secretary of State Hull in July 1942.
2. South America: the foreign ministers of the South American republics requested in January 1942 the Inter-American Judicial Committee to prepare recommendations in this respect.
3. Moscow: the proposal of Krylev.
4. London: the invitation of the British government addressed to the government of the US in October 1941 to discuss the future of the PCIJ.

The British offer was declined but this initiative was resumed in 1943 when representatives of ten governments in exile in the UK met in London to discuss the matter and subsequently set up the Informal Inter-Allied Committee of Experts chaired by Sir William Malkin, which in 1944 presented a report on the future of the International Court. The report made three recommendations: first, the Statute of the PCIJ was considered to be highly appropriate for any future court; second, it recommended that political matters should be excluded from the jurisdiction of a future court; and, third, it stated that the advisory jurisdiction should be retained by a future court. The matter whether or not the PCIJ should be reactivated was not examined. The report served as a source of discussion at the Dumbarton Oaks Conference in August–September 1944 when the establishment of the UN was at issue. The Conference decided to link the new court with the UN and retain the Statute of the PCIJ, but the most controversial matters – such as whether or not a new court should be established, its compulsory jurisdiction and the number of judges – were left to the examination of a newly set up Committee of Jurists. The Washington Committee of Jurists, which was made up of representatives of 44 nations invited by the US government to meet in April in Washington, prepared its recommendations relating to the Statute of the Court (in fact minor technical amendments were made to the Statute of the PCIJ) but still could not resolve the main issues. The San Francisco Conference which took place in April–June 1945 and was in charge of preparing the Charter of the UN, decided to establish a new court as a component part of the UN, its judicial body. Chapter XIV of the UN Charter deals with the new court, the International Court of Justice (arts 92–96), to which the Statute of the Court is annexed. On 26 June 1945 the Charter of the UN was adopted, together with the Statute of the ICJ, by 51 states and entered into force on 24 October 1945.

The provisions of the UN Charter relating to the ICJ

The UN Charter forged a direct link between the ICJ and the UN. The Court, under the Charter, is one of the six principal organs of the UN. Under art 93(1) of the UN Charter all members of the UN are automatically contracting parties to the Statute of the ICJ. Non-members of the UN may also become parties to the Statute of the ICJ but a special procedure is applied to them. Under art 94(1) of the Charter each member of the UN is obliged to comply with the decision of the ICJ. Article 94(2) provides that if a party to a dispute fails to comply with a judgment the other party may have recourse to the Security Council which may make recommendations or take enforcement measures to give effect to the judgment. On a number of occasions states have refused to comply with the judgment of the ICJ as exemplified in the *Legal Consequences for States of the Continued Presence of South Africa in Namibia (South West Africa) Notwithstanding Security Council Resolution 276 (1970)* (1971) ICJ Rep 16, where South Africa refused to withdraw from Namibia, or *Military and Paramilitary Activities in and against Nicaragua (Jurisdiction)* (1984) ICJ Rep 392 and *(Merits)* (1986) ICJ Rep 14, where the US challenged the jurisdiction of the ICJ in respect of allegations made by Nicaragua concerning the mining of its harbours by the US Central Intelligence Agency. When the ICJ asserted its jurisdiction the US refused to defend the case and subsequently refused to recognise the judgment given against it.

The Security Council has a limited experience in respect of enforcing compliance with a judgment rendered by the ICJ. In 1971 when South Africa failed to comply the Security Council ordered South Africa to comply and ordered other states to abstain from dealing with South Africa. Although subsequently South Africa agreed to co-operate with the UN, it maintained its presence in Namibia until 1990! In the *Nicaragua Case*, when Nicaragua asked the Security Council for the enforcement of the judgment against the US, the US vetoed the Nicaraguan application.

The functions of the ICJ

The main function of the ICJ is to decide cases on the basis of the law as it stands at the time of the decision. Judge Lachs said in *Case Concerning Questions of Interpretation and Application of the 1971 Montreal Convention Arising from the Aerial Incident at Lockerbie: Libyan Arab Jamahiriya* v *United Kingdom (Provisional Measures)* (1992) ICJ Rep 3 that the Court is the guardian of legality of the international community as a whole within and without the UN. The ICJ is competent to decide only legal disputes. The fact that such disputes very often involve political issues, and on a number of occasions have been the subject of consideration before political organs of the UN or international organisations, does not deprive the ICJ of its jurisdiction. There is no definition of a legal dispute but the Court has developed its own approach as to what should be considered as a legal dispute. In the *Mavromattis Palestine Concessions Case* (1924) PCIJ Rep Ser A No 2, 12 the PCIJ stated that a dispute is a disagreement over a point of law or fact, a conflict of legal views or of interests between two persons. The ICJ, in a number of cases, emphasised that a legal dispute arises when the respondent state before the ICJ denies the allegations of the claimant state. In the *East Timor Case: Portugal* v *Australia* (1995) ICJ Rep 90 the ICJ stated that 'Portugal has rightly or wrongly formulated complaints of fact and law against Australia, which the latter has denied, by virtue of this denial there is a legal dispute'. Similarly, in the *Case Concerning the Application of the Convention on the Prevention and Punishment of the Crime of Genocide: Bosnia and Herzegovina* v *Yugoslavia (Preliminary Objections)* (1996) ICJ Rep 1 the Court stated that 'by reason of the rejection by Yugoslavia of the complaints formulated against it by Bosnia-Herzegovina there is a legal dispute between them'. It can be seen that the 'threshold' for a legal dispute is very low!

The jurisdiction of the ICJ is twofold.

1. The Court decides disputes between states. This is the contentious jurisdiction of the ICJ. Only states can be parties to the proceedings.
2. The Court gives advisory opinions at the request of entities which have been given locus standi to this effect.

Judges

The ICJ is made up of 15 judges, five of whom are elected every three years to hold office for nine years, and no two of whom may be nationals of the same state. A quorum of nine judges is required to perform the functions of the Court. Article 2 of the Statute of the ICJ sets out the eligibility requirements for judges. They must be of high moral character and possess the qualifications necessary for appointment to the highest judicial offices in their respective countries or be jurisconsults of recognised competence in international law.

The judges are elected by the General Assembly and by the Security Council from a list of persons nominated by the national groups in the Permanent Court of

Arbitration (PCA). Members of the UN not represented in the PCA may create national groups for this purpose. In making their nominations each national group may nominate no more than four persons, not more than two of whom shall be of their own nationality. The system of election involves independent, simultaneous voting by the Security Council and the General Assembly. Those states which are parties to the Statute of the ICJ but not members of the UN are permitted to participate in the nomination and election procedures. Article 10 of the Statute provides that to be elected candidates must obtain an absolute majority in both the General Assembly and in the Security Council. Article 9 of the Statute of the ICJ requires that in the election procedure both the General Assembly and the Security Council must bear in mind that the ICJ as a whole body must represent the main forms of civilisation and the principal legal systems of the world.

Independence of judges is essential to the proper functioning of the ICJ. Indeed, if the ICJ is to serve any effective purpose it is vital that states have confidence in the integrity of its judges. The Statute of the ICJ reinforces the principle of impartiality and freedom from governmental influence by stating in art 20 that each judge before taking his duties must make a solemn declaration in open court that 'he will exercise his powers impartiality and conscientiously'. Judges are not allowed to perform any political or administrative function or to engage in any other occupation of a professional nature. Under art 17 of the Statute:

> '(1) No member of the Court may act as agent, counsel, or advocate in any case.
> (2) No member may participate in the decision of any case in which he has previously taken part as agent, counsel, or advocate for one of the parties, or as a member of a national or international court, or of a commission of enquiry, or in any other capacity.'

On the basis of the above provision Judge Zaffrula Khan was excluded from participation in the *South West Africa Cases (Second Phase):Ethiopia* v *South Africa; Liberia* v *South Africa* (1966) ICJ Rep 6 because he had played a major role as a member of the delegation of Pakistan to the UN when matters pertaining to South West Africa had been under discussion. In the *Namibia Case* (1971) ICJ Rep 16 South Africa opposed the participation of several judges, including Judge Zaffrula Khan of Pakistan, Judge Nervo of Mexico and Judge Morozov of the Soviet Union. These judges, when members of their national delegations to the UN, had participated in activities directed against South Africa's presence in South West Africa. These objections were overruled by the ICJ. The Court noted that the fact that a judge may have participated in his former capacity as a representative of his government while the subject matter of the dispute was under discussion did not bring art 17(2) of the Statute into application. Being a governmental spokesman in the area of dispute did not necessarily preclude an individual from subsequently exercising judicial impartiality. Judge Zaffrula Khan, excluded from the 1966 case, was no longer prevented from sitting as a judge in the proceedings under consideration as they were entirely separate from the earlier contentious case. However, some members of the ICJ were critical of this decision especially in relation to Judge Morozov who as a previous UN representative of the Soviet Union had played 'a spectacular role in the preparation of Security Council and General Assembly resolutions, the validity of which have had to be assessed by the Court in the present Advisory Opinion'.

Under art 18(1) of the Statute a member of the Court can be dismissed if according to the unanimous opinion of other members he has ceased to fulfil the required conditions.

The Statute also provides for ad hoc judges. Its art 31 states that:

'(1) Judges of the nationality of each of the parties shall retain their right to sit in the case before the Court.

(2) If the Court includes upon the Bench a judge of the nationality of one of the parties, any other party may choose a person to sit as a judge ...

(3) If the Court includes upon the Bench no judge of the nationality of the parties, each of these parties may proceed to choose a judge as provided in paragraph 2 of this Article.'

Thus, the fact that a judge is a national of one of the parties before the Court does not prevent him from continuing to sit. Also in cases where a party has no national representative in the Court, it may appoint a national judge ad hoc for the purpose of the case.

The appointment of ad hoc judges has been criticised as being incompatible with the concept of impartiality and independence of the judiciary. Nevertheless, this practice has been justified as being an incentive to states, who may submit more readily to the jurisdiction of the Court and have more confidence in it if there is a judge of their own choice sitting on the Bench. It has also been said that such judges are useful as they supply local knowledge and a national point of view to the proceedings. The system of judges appointed on an ad hoc basis was strongly criticised by Fitzmaurice (*The Law and Procedure of the International Court of Justice*, Cambridge: Cambridge University Press, 1986) who argued that:

1. those who claim that the presence of such judges increases confidence in the Court argue from an impermissible premise that judges, particularly ad hoc judges, will necessarily espouse the view of their government;
2. once a case has been decided, a judge ad hoc may feel himself free from any obligation of confidence and reveal to his government what was said in the deliberations of the Court.

In practice judges ad hoc usually give judgments in favour of the state which appointed them. Thus where two parties appoint judges ad hoc their votes will usually cancel each other out. Judges, when engaged on the business of the Court, enjoy diplomatic privileges and immunities. Their salary in fixed by the General Assembly and may not be decreased during their term of office.

Article 26 of the Statute provides for the establishment of chambers of three or more members for dealing with a particular case. This procedure was revised in the 1978 Rules and used for the first time in the *Delimitation of the Maritime Boundary in the Gulf of Maine Area: Canada* v *US* (1984) ICJ Rep 246. In this case Canada and the US threatened to withdraw from the case if their wishes as to the composition of the chamber were not met. Their request was complied with by the ICJ. Chambers have been used in subsequent cases, ie: *Case Concerning the Frontier Dispute: Burkina Faso* v *Republic of Mali* (1986) ICJ Rep 554; *Elettronica Sicula SpA (ELSI): US* v *Italy* (1989) ICJ Rep 14; and *Case Concerning Land, Island and Maritime Frontier Dispute: El Salvador* v *Honduras, Nicaragua Intervening* (1992) ICJ Rep 92. Two more chambers were constituted in 2002. This new development offers the parties necessary flexibility in the choice of the judges. Also their case is decided by five judges (in the above cases the chamber was made up of five judges) instead of the ICJ sitting in its full composition of 15 judges (in some cases up to 17 judges if the parties appoint ad hoc judges). However, the establishment of chambers for summary proceedings to deal speedily with a matter by five judges which is envisaged in art 29 of the Statute has never been used.

15.5 Contentious jurisdiction of the International Court of Justice

Access to the ICJ in contentious cases

Before any state becomes a party to a case before the ICJ it must have access to the Court. The ICJ is accessible to states only in respect of contentious cases. Any state in the world has access to the ICJ. There are basically three ways open to a state to have access to the Court.

1. States which are Members of the United Nations. Under art 93(1) of the Charter of the UN all members of the UN are ipso facto parties to the Statute of the ICJ. By becoming a member of the UN a state is bound by the provisions of the Statute of the Court and therefore has access to it. To date 189 states are members of the United Nations.

2. Non-members of the UN. Non-members of the UN may become parties to the Statute under art 93(2) of the Charter of the UN. The conditions of their admission are to be determined in each case by the General Assembly upon the recommendation of the Security Council. In practice the conditions laid down in the first occurrence, namely the request of Switzerland of December 1946, have always been applied. In respect of Switzerland the General Assembly laid down the following conditions:

    '(a) Acceptance of the provisions of the Statute of the International Court of Justice;
    (b) Acceptance of all obligations of a Member of the United Nations under art 94 of the Charter;
    (c) An undertaking to contribute to the expenses of the Court such equitable amount as the General Assembly shall assess from time to time after consultation with the Swiss Government.'

States becoming parties in this way are entitled to nominate candidates for election to the Court and take part in the election, in the General Assembly, of the members of the Court.

In the past Liechtenstein, Nauru, Japan, San Marino and Switzerland were in that category before actually becoming members of the UN.

3. States who are non-parties to the Statute. The conditions for access to the ICJ for such states were determined by the Security Council in 1946. The Security Council stated that:

> 'The International Court of Justice shall be open to a state which is not a party to the Statute of the International Court of Justice upon the following conditions, namely, that such state shall previously have deposited with the Registrar of the Court a declaration by which it accepts the jurisdiction of the Court, in accordance with the Charter of the United Nations and with the terms and subject to the conditions of the Statute and Rules of the Court, and undertakes to comply in good faith with the decision or decisions of the Court and to accept all the obligations of a Member of the United Nations under art 94 of the Charter.'

In the past, such declarations by non-parties were filed by Albania as respondent in the *Corfu Channel Case* (1949) ICJ Rep 4, Italy as a claimant in *Monetary Gold Removal from Rome in 1943: Italy v France, United Kingdom and US* (1954) ICJ Rep 19 and the Federal Republic of Germany as a claimant to the *North Sea Continental Shelf Cases* (1969) ICJ Rep 3.

4. States which have limited recognition from the international community. In the *Case Concerning the Application of the Convention on the Prevention and Punishment of the Crime of Genocide: Bosnia and Herzegovina v Yugoslavia* the Court had to consider, for the first time, the standing of a newly independent state which had only limited recognition from the international community. The state of Bosnia and Herzegovina brought an action against the state of Yugoslavia consisting of Serbia and Montenegro. The applicants alleged that the Yugoslavian government and its armed forces had been guilty of genocide against the peoples of Bosnia and Herzegovina.

The former state of Yugoslavia was a party to the Statute of the Court but the United Nations had refused to recognise the states of Serbia and Montenegro as the successor state to Yugoslavia. Pursuant to a recommendation of the Security Council, the General Assembly decided in Resolution 47/1 of 22 September 1992 that the Federal Republic of Yugoslavia (FRY) 'should apply for membership of the United Nations and that it shall not participate in the work of the General Assembly'. However, the Legal Council of the United Nations stated that the GA Resolution 47/1 did not terminate Yugoslavia's membership. The ICJ decided in the *Case Concerning the Application of the Convention on the Prevention and Punishment of the Crime of Genocide (Second Indication of Provisional Measures): Bosnia and Herzegovina v Yugoslavia* (1993) ICJ Rep 325 to grant a request for provisional measures and in its judgment of 11 July 1996 held that it had jurisdiction to adjudicate the case: see (1996) ICJ Rep 1. After the departure of President Milosovic, the new democratically elected government of the FRY on 24 April 2001 filed an application for revision of the judgment of 11 July 1996, claiming that it had become clear that the FRY was not a successor to the Socialist Federal Republic of Yugoslavia as it was admitted to the UN on 1 November 2000, and thus was, at the relevant time, not a party to the Statute of the Court and was not a party to the Genocide Convention. The application of the FRY was rejected by the ICJ on 3 February 2003.

Jurisdiction of the ICJ in contentious cases

The ICJ can only determine cases with the consent of the state parties. In the *Advisory Opinion on Eastern Carelia* (1923) PCIJ Rep Ser B No 5 the PCIJ stated that: 'it is well established in international law that no state can, without its consent, be compelled to submit its dispute with other states either to mediation or to arbitration, or to any other kind of pacific settlement'. Article 36(1) of the Statute confirms the necessity of a state's consent in the following terms:

> 'The jurisdiction of the Court comprises all cases which the parties refer to it and all matters specially provided for in the Charter of the United Nations or in treaties and conventions in force.'

The words, 'matters specially provided for in the Charter of the United Nations' were included in the draft Statute in the belief that the Charter of the United Nations would provide for compulsory jurisdiction of the Court. Such a proposal was rejected at the San Francisco Conference, but the words were not deleted from the Statute. Consequently, there are no 'matters specially provided for the Charter of the United Nations'.

The ICJ may assert its contentious jurisdiction as follows.

1. On the basis of a special agreement between the parties to submit the dispute to the ICJ.
2. By virtue of a jurisdictional clause. Such a clause has been inserted in numerous international treaties. It provides that in the event of a dispute concerning the interpretation or the application of the treaty, one of the parties may refer the dispute to the ICJ and the other party to the treaty is bound to submit to the Court's jurisdiction.
3. Under the principle of forum prorogatum, ie by tacit agreement between the parties.
4. By virtue of art 36(2) of the Statute which confers on the ICJ the so-called compulsory jurisdiction.

Jurisdiction by a special agreement

This occurs when parties to an already existing dispute agree to submit it to the ICJ.

Such a special agreement is often referred to as a compromis (its name in French). Eleven disputes were submitted to the PCIJ and a number of cases have been referred to the ICJ in this way. The jurisdiction of the Court is defined within the agreement itself and the Court becomes seised of the case by the mere notification of the agreement to its Registrar. In *Maritime Delimitation and Territorial Questions between Qatar and Bahrein (Jurisdiction and Admissibility)* (1995) ICJ Rep 6 the ICJ had to decide whether a unilateral application by a single state was valid if there was an incomplete agreement to submit to the jurisdiction of the Court. The facts in this case were as follows.

A tri-party committee was established among Saudi Arabia, Qatar and Bahrein to prepare a document to be submitted to the ICJ to settle a number of complex matters on sovereignty and the maritime delimitation between Qatar and Bahrein. A dispute arose as to the drafting of the terms of reference. Bahrein wished to submit all disputed matters to the Court for adjudication, while Qatar wanted to submit only a number of selected issues. Nevertheless, the parties did agree on five areas of territory which were the subject of dispute. Ultimately, however, no completed submission was agreed.

At a later meeting of the committee in December 1990, the parties agreed to a further period of the good offices of Saudi Arabia and decided that if these discussions did not produce a settlement by the end of May 1991, then it would be possible to bring the matter before the ICJ for resolution. Minutes of this meeting were signed by the foreign ministers of both Qatar and Bahrein.

No settlement was reached in the stipulated period and Qatar unilaterally applied to the Court for the settlement of a selected number of issues. Bahrein objected that the Court had no jurisdiction unless there was a mutually agreed bilateral submission from both parties.

The ICJ found that the minutes of the meeting of December 1990 amounted to an agreement on which the Court could found jurisdiction. The ICJ stated that the minutes 'do not merely give an account of discussions and summarise points of agreement and disagreement. They enumerate the commitments to which the parties have consented. They thus create rights and obligations in international law for the parties'.

In the circumstances the Court held that it had jurisdiction. On 16 March 2001 the ICJ delivered its judgment in the *Maritime Delimitation and Territorial Questions between Qatar and Bahrein: Qatar* v *Bahrein* (2001) ICJ Rep 40.

Jurisdiction based on jurisdictional clauses

The second basis of jurisdiction is envisaged in art 36(1) of the Statute. It relates to treaties and conventions in force which confer jurisdiction on the Court over disputes arising from them. It has become a general practice to insert into an international agreement, whether multilateral or bilateral, the so-called jurisdiction clause. There are about 400 treaties which confer jurisdiction on the ICJ. For example, in the *Case Concerning the Application of the Convention on the Prevention and Punishment of the Crime of Genocide: Bosnia and Herzegovina* v *Yugoslavia (Preliminary Objections)* (1996) ICJ Rep 1 the ICJ founded jurisdiction on Art IX of the Genocide Convention 1948, and in the *US Diplomatic and Consular Staff in Teheran Case: US* v *Iran* (1980) ICJ Rep 3 it founded its jurisdiction on art 1 of the 1961 Optional Protocol to the Vienna Convention on Diplomatic Relations 1961.

Many treaties and conventions contain clauses conferring jurisdiction on the PCIJ. When the Statute was redrafted in 1945, in order to save such clauses art 37 was added to the Statute of the ICJ. It provides:

> 'Whenever a treaty or convention in force provides for reference of a matter to a tribunal to have been instituted by the League of Nations, or to the Permanent Court of International Justice, the matter shall, as between the parties to the present Statute, be referred to the International Court of Justice.'

Therefore, in order for a treaty which confers jurisdiction on the PCIJ to bestow jurisdiction on the ICJ two conditions must be met.

1. The treaty must still be in force. Normally the treaty will have been registered with the Secretariat of the League of Nations or the United Nations and will have been published by them. However, in some cases it is difficult to determine which of them are still in force. In the *South West Africa Cases (Preliminary Objections): Ethiopia* v *South Africa; Liberia* v *South Africa* (1962) ICJ Rep 319 the Court had to decide whether art 37 of its Statute could apply in respect of the Mandate between South Africa and the League of Nations. The ICJ decided that art 7(2) of the Mandate, which provided for compulsory jurisdiction of the PCIJ in the event of disputes arising between the Mandatory and another member of the League relating to the interpretation and application of the provisions of the Mandate, was still in force taking into account that the Mandate had never been terminated.

2. The states concerned must be not only the contracting parties to the treaty but also be parties to the Statute of the ICJ. This matter was clarified by the ICJ in *Barcelona Traction, Light and Power Company Ltd Case: Belgium* v *Spain* (1970) ICJ Rep 4. In this case Belgium made application to the ICJ on the basis of art 17 of the Spain-Belgian Treaty of Conciliation, Judicial Settlement and Arbitration 1927, which provided that either party had an ultimate right to commence proceedings before the PCIJ in the event of a dispute arising out of its provisions.

   Spain objected to the ICJ's jurisdiction, inter alia, on the ground that Spain became a party to the Statute when admitted to the United Nations in 1955 and was not a party to the Statute for nine years, from the dissolution of the PCIJ until Spain's admission to the UN and, consequently, art 17 of the 1927 Treaty ceased to operate. The ICJ held that art 37 of the Statute was not to be interpreted in this way and that the date on which Spain become a party to the Statute was irrelevant. In this respect the ICJ stated in its 1964 Report that:

'States joining the United Nations or otherwise becoming parties to the Statute at whatever date, knew in advance (or must be taken to have known) that, by reason of art 37, one of the results of doing so would, as between themselves and other parties to the Statute, be the reactivation in relation to the present Court, of any jurisdictional clauses referring to the Permanent Court, in treaties still in force, by which they were bound.'

Jurisdiction of the ICJ based on forum prorogatum

Under forum prorogatum the Court may exercise jurisdiction in those cases where after the applicant state has instituted proceedings the respondent state subsequently consents to submit to the jurisdiction. The consent may be express or implied. In the *Rights of Minorities in Polish Upper Silesia Case* (1928) PCIJ Rep Ser A No 15 the PCIJ stated:

'... there seems to be no doubt that the consent of a state to the submission of a dispute to the Court may not only result from an express declaration, but may also be inferred from acts conclusively establishing it. It seems hard to deny that the submission of arguments on the merits, without making reservation in regard to the question of jurisdiction, must be regarded as an unequivocal indication of the desire of a state to obtain a decision on the merits of a suit.'

Therefore, more is required than the negative fact that the state raises no objection to the Court jurisdiction. The Court will not accept jurisdiction unless there has been real consent by the respondent state. In the *Corfu Channel Case (Preliminary Objections): United Kingdom* v *Albania* (1948) ICJ Rep 15 the UK brought a claim against Albania before the Court by unilateral application. Albania in its reply declared that it:

'... would be within its rights in holding that the Government of the United Kingdom was not entitled to bring the case before the International Court by unilateral application without first conducting a special agreement with the Albanian Government ... However ... it is prepared notwithstanding this irregularity in the action taken by the Government of the United Kingdom, to appear before the Court.'

The ICJ inferred from this reply that Albania voluntarily and indisputably accepted its jurisdiction.

Jurisdiction based on forum prorogatum is rare and so far the Court has only exercised it in three cases: the *Mavromattis Palestine Concessions Case*, the *Rights of Minorities in Polish Upper Silesia* and the *Corfu Channel Case*. On occasions a state has started proceedings before the ICJ knowing that the other party has not accepted the Court's jurisdiction and inviting it to do so. To date this invitation has always been refused.

Compulsory jurisdiction of the ICJ

Article 36(2) and (3) of the Statute describes the compulsory jurisdiction of the ICJ in the following terms:

'(2) The states, parties to the present Statute, may at any time declare that they recognise as compulsory ipso facto and without special agreement, in relation to any other state accepting the same obligation, the jurisdiction of the Court in all legal disputes concerning:

(a) the interpretation of a treaty;

(b) any question of international law;

(c) the existence of any fact which, if established, would constitute a breach of an international obligation;

(d) the nature or extent of the reparation to be made for the breach of an international obligation.

(3) The declaration referred to above may be made unconditionally or on condition of reciprocity on the part of several or certain states, or for a certain time.'

This so-called 'optional clause' is a compromise between the advocates and the opponents of compulsory jurisdiction. Under this article jurisdiction is only compulsory once the declaration is made and then only within the limits of that declaration. However, there is no obligation upon a state to make such a declaration and therefore jurisdiction cannot be regarded as compulsory in the true sense. These declarations are deposited with the Secretary-General of the United Nations and are usually signed by the foreign minister of the state making the declaration or by its representative at the United Nations. At the time of writing 65 states have made declarations recognising the compulsory jurisdiction of the ICJ. It is interesting to note that 12 states have withdrawn their acceptance of such jurisdiction: Thailand did not renew its declaration upon its expiry on 20 May 1960, after it challenged the jurisdiction of the Court in the *Temple of Preah Vihear Case (Preliminary Objections): Cambodia* v *Thailand* (1961) ICJ Rep 17; France withdrew its declaration on 2 January 1974 after the *Nuclear Tests Cases (Interim Protection)* (1973) ICJ Rep 99 brought against her in May 1973; and the US, after unsuccessfully challenging the Court's jurisdiction in the case concerning *Military and Paramilitary Activities in and against Nicaragua: Nicaragua* v *USA (Jurisdiction)* (1984) ICJ Rep 392 brought by Nicaragua in April 1984, withdrew its declaration on 8 October 1985. Taking into account the number of states who are party to the Statute of the Court only a small fraction of them have accepted the Court's jurisdiction under art 36(2) of the Statute. Moreover, four permanent members of the Security Council are not currently accepting the compulsory jurisdiction of the ICJ.

The effects of the declaration recognising the compulsory jurisdiction of the ICJ are as follows.

1. A state's declaration creates bilateral relations with those other states which have also made declarations of acceptance.

2. A state may make a reservation to its acceptance permitting its withdrawal at any time. Unless such a reservation is made, acceptance of the optional clause is irrevocable.

3. Declarations may be made indefinitely, for a fixed term of years, or may be terminable upon notice.

4. If a state withdraws its acceptance, in accordance with such a reservation, it prevents the Court trying future cases against it.

5. Once the Court is seized of a case on the basis of a declaration of acceptance of jurisdiction, the subsequent lapse or withdrawal of the acceptance cannot deprive the Court of jurisdiction. In the *Nottebohm Case (Preliminary Objections): Liechtenstein* v *Guatemala* (1953) ICJ Rep 111 the Declaration of the respondent government, Guatemala, expired a few days after the government of Liechtenstein had seized the Court. It was argued on behalf of Guatemala that upon the expiry of the Guatemalan Declaration the Court no longer had jurisdiction to hear the dispute. The Court rejected this argument and stated that its jurisdiction, once established, cannot be challenged by the subsequent lapse of the Declaration due to the expiry of the period or by denunciation.

6. The contractual relations between the states concerned, and the compulsory jurisdiction of the Court resulting therefrom, come into being on the day the new declarant state deposits with the Secretary-General of the UN its declaration of acceptance.

An important aspect of the optional clause is that the principle of reciprocity applies to the relations between states that have accepted the compulsory jurisdiction of the ICJ. By virtue of art 36(2) of the Statute a state accepting the jurisdiction of the Court does so only 'in relation to any other state accepting the same obligation'.

According to this principle, a state accepts the Court's jurisdiction vis-à-vis any other state only in so far as that state has also accepted the Court's jurisdiction. For example, if state A has accepted the optional clause and state B has not, state A cannot be sued before the Court by state B. If state A makes a declaration subject to reservation Y and state B makes a declaration subject to reservation Z, the Court has jurisdiction to hear disputes between states A and B only in so far as they are not within reservations Y and Z. Therefore, a state cannot enjoy the benefits of the optional clause unless it is also prepared to accept the obligations deriving from it.

The principle of reciprocity applies when a case is submitted to the Court and not before. In the *Right of Passage over Indian Territory Case (Preliminary Objections): Portugal* v *India* (1957) ICJ Rep 125 the Portuguese Declaration accepting the compulsory jurisdiction of the Court contained, inter alia, the following reservation:

> '3. The Portuguese Government reserves the right to exclude from the scope of the present declaration, at any time during its validity, any given category or categories of disputes, by notifying the Secretary-General of the United Nations and with effect from the moment of such notification.'

The Court rejected India's contention that reciprocity applied thus allowing her to take advantage of the reservation in Portugal's Declaration. The reservation gave Portugal the right to reserve its position in respect of categories of disputes notified to the Secretary-General of the UN. But only when Portugal had notified the Secretary-General pursuant to the condition would the reservation become automatically operative against it, in relation to other parties to the optional clause.

The principle of reciprocity contained in art 36(2) of the Statute is quite distinct from the condition of reciprocity set out in art 36(3) of the Statute. The principle in art 36(2) is part of the Statute and applies automatically, while the condition of reciprocity in art 36(3) is optional and is not a part of the Statute. The effect of art 36(3) of the Statute is that a state may add a reservation to its acceptance of the optional clause, to the effect that its acceptance is not to come into force until specified states have also accepted the optional clause. Until named states have accepted the optional clause, the state making such a reservation cannot be sued by any state.

Reservations under art 36(3) of the Statute refer to reciprocity and time. In the early years of the PCIJ it was argued that only reservations in accordance with art 36(3) were admissible. However, it is now accepted that many other reservations may be made and the validity of such reservations is no longer called into question. In the *Case Concerning the Aerial Incident of 10 August 1999: Pakistan v India (Jurisdiction)* (2000) ICJ Rep 12 Pakistan argued, inter alia, that the permissible conditions to which an optional clause declaration may be subject were enumerated exhaustively in art 36(3) of the Statute. The ICJ disagreed. It stated that art 36(3) of the Statute has never been regarded as laying down exhaustively the conditions under which declarations may validly be made, and affirmed its opinion, expressed in previous case law, that states are absolutely free to decide whether or not they wish to make declarations accepting the compulsory jurisdiction of the ICJ either unconditionally and without temporal restrictions, or by qualifying the acceptance through conditions and reservations: *Military and Paramilitary Activities in and against Nicaragua: Nicaragua v US (Jurisdiction)* (1984) ICJ Rep 392.

The most frequently made reservations relate to disputes:

1. for which other methods of settlement of disputes are envisaged;
2. which had arisen before a certain date and concerning certain situations or facts that took place before that date. In general the date in question refers to the time when a state first accepted the compulsory jurisdiction of the ICJ;
3. which are considered as falling within the domestic jurisdiction of that state;
4. in respect of certain states;
5. concerning certain multinational treaties;
6. relating to the law of the sea.

The most important of these reservations are examined below.

Reservations
Reservations relating to matter falling within the domestic jurisdiction of a state.
These are based on art 2(7) of the Charter of the UN which provides that nothing in the Charter 'shall authorise the United Nations to intervene in matters which are essentially within the domestic jurisdiction of any state'. For example, in 1946 the US made such a reservation which became known as the 'Connolly reservation'.

This provided that the declaration accepting the jurisdiction of the Court would not apply to:

> '... disputes with regard to matters which are essentially within the domestic jurisdiction of the United States of America as determined by the United States of America.'

Although the PCIJ held in the *Nationality Decrees in Tunis and Morocco Case* (1923) PCIJ Rep Ser B No 4 that 'the question whether a certain matter is or is not solely within the jurisdiction of a state is an essentially relative question; it depends upon the development of international relations', states are allowed to determine unilaterally what matters are considered to be within their domestic jurisdiction. Such a reservation operates automatically in the sense that once a state which has made it declares that a matter which is the subject of proceedings initiated before the ICJ falls within its domestic jurisdiction the ICJ is deprived of jurisdiction over the dispute.

The validity and application of such reservations came up for consideration in the *Norwegian Loans Case: France* v *Norway* (1957) ICJ Rep 9. France brought a claim against Norway under the optional clause on behalf of French holders of Norwegian bonds. The French Declaration accepting the compulsory jurisdiction of the Court contained the following reservation:

> 'This Declaration does not apply to differences relating to matters which are essentially within the national jurisdiction as understood by the Government of the French Republic.'

Norway which did not make any such Declaration challenged the Court's jurisdiction by relying on the French Declaration. Norway considered that the dispute was within the domestic jurisdiction within the meaning of the French Declaration. The ICJ agreed with Norway. The Court held that:

> 'France has limited her acceptance of the compulsory jurisdiction of the Court by excluding beforehand disputes "relating to matters which are essentially within the national jurisdiction as understood by the Government of the French Republic". In accordance with the condition of reciprocity to which acceptance of the compulsory jurisdiction is made subject in both Declarations and which is provided for in art 36 paragraph 3 of the Statute, Norway equally with France, is entitled to except from the compulsory jurisdiction of the Court disputes understood by Norway to be essentially within its national jurisdiction ...
>
> The Court considers that the Norwegian Government is entitled, by virtue of the condition of reciprocity to invoke the reservation contained in the French Declaration of March 1st, 1949; that this reservation excludes from the jurisdiction of the Court the dispute which has been referred to it by the Application of the French Government; that consequently the Court is without jurisdiction to entertain the application.'

This successful application of the condition of reciprocity led several states which had previously inserted such reservations in their declarations of acceptance to abandon them. In the *Norwegian Loans Case* (above) Judge Lauterpacht in his dissident opinion considered that automatic reservations were invalid as contrary to the fundamental principle of national and international jurisprudence according to which it is within the inherent competence of the court to determine its own jurisdiction. Consequently, an instrument in which a party is allowed to determine the existence of its obligation is not a valid and enforceable legal document of which the Court should take cognisance. This kind of instrument is a declaration of a political nature, not a legal instrument. Lauterpacht further contended that any Declaration under art 36(2) which included an automatic reservation would itself be void, ie it would be insufficient to establish the jurisdiction of the Court. The reasoning behind this conclusion was that the invalid reservation was to be regarded as an essential part of the optional clause declaration. As such, it could not be severable from the declaration as a whole. The only result was, therefore, that the Declaration itself was to be regarded as void. Judge Lauterpacht, together with other members of the Court, returned to consider the matter in the *Interhandel Case*: *Switzerland* v *USA* (1959) ICJ Rep 6. In this case, Lauterpacht in his dissenting opinion, reiterated arguments he advanced in the *Norwegian Loans Case*. In the *Nicaragua Case (Jurisdiction)* (1984) ICJ Rep 551, Judge Schwebel in his dissenting opinion agreed that the effect of the automatic reservation would be to invalidate the entire declaration. The matter of whether or not a reservation should be considered as an integral part of the declaration was examined by the Court in the *Fisheries Jurisdiction Case: Spain* v *Canada (Jurisdiction)* (1998) ICJ Rep 432; 'Case Report *Fisheries Jurisdiction (Spain* v *Canada) (Jurisdiction)*' (1999) 93 AJIL 502. The Court stated that 'declarations and reservations are to be read as a whole': para 47. However, the ICJ's subsequent statement in para 59 seems to suggest that a reservation forms an integral part of a declaration depending upon the circumstances of the case. In this respect the Court said that: 'It follows that this reservation is not only an integral part of the current declaration but also an essential component of it, and hence of the acceptance by Canada of the Court's compulsory jurisdiction'.

Subsequent to the criticism expressed in respect of automatic reservations the Institute of International Law in 1959 called upon governments which had inserted such reservations in their declarations to withdraw them. Some governments had done so. The importance of this reservation has declined, so that in recent time only a small number of declarations contain such a reservation.

Multilateral treaty reservations. Multilateral treaty reservations provide that a state, a contracting party to a multilateral treaty, accepts the compulsory jurisdiction of the Court in so far as all the parties to the treaty which are involved in the dispute are also parties to the case before the Court. This matter arose in the *Nicaragua Case (Jurisdiction)* (1984) ICJ Rep 392. The US included in its Declaration under art 36(2) of the Statute a reservation known as the Vandenberg Reservation, otherwise known as a multilateral treaty reservation. The issues before the Court involved, inter alia, the interpretation of the UN Charter, particularly arts 2(4) and 51. The US argued that as Costa Rica and El Salvador – parties to the UN Charter (and the Charter of the Organisation of American States) and involved in the dispute – were not before the Court, the Court lacked jurisdiction to hear the dispute under the terms of the US Declaration. The ICJ accepted that the Vandenberg Reservation did have the effect of precluding the Court from exercising its jurisdiction in the context of the interpretation of the multilateral treaties. The Court went on to hold, however, that it did have jurisdiction on the basis of customary international law. In the *Case Concerning the Aerial Incident of 10 August 1999: Pakistan* v *India (Jurisdiction)* (2000) ICJ Rep 12 India relied on its multilateral reservation to challenge the jurisdiction of the Court. However, the Court decided neither to elaborate on this argument nor to comment on the response of Pakistan invoking the *Nicaragua* precedent. It is clear from the *Nicaragua Case* (above) that the multilateral treaty reservation will not preclude the Court from hearing the case if a dispute is not based exclusively on the violation of the multilateral convention but is also based on customary law. Multilateral treaty reservations are contained in the Declarations of India, Malta, Pakistan and the Philippines.

Time-limitations and reservations ratione temporis. These reservations clauses are worded in a variety of ways. They may comprise a single clause, for example that contained in the US Declaration, which applies to disputes 'hereafter arising' (that is after 14 August 1946, the date on which the Declaration was made), or they may be double clauses as in the UK Declaration which excludes all disputes arising after the 24 of October 1945 with regards to situations or facts after that date, except disputes with members of the Commonwealth with regards to situations or facts existing before 1 January 1969.

If a Declaration contains a time reservation a state may object in appropriate circumstances to the Court's jurisdiction ratione temporis, that is it may allege that the dispute or the facts upon which it is based occurred outside the period common to both declarations. In its case law the Court has taken the view that for the limitation to be effective the situations or the facts which are the source of the dispute must occur outside the period of acceptance.

In the *Phosphates in Morocco Case (Preliminary Objections)* (1938) PCIJ Rep Ser A/B No 74 T, an Italian national, was assigned in 1918–19 various phosphate prospecting licences in French Morocco. In 1920 France, allegedly in contravention of French Treaty obligations, established a monopoly over phosphate mining, and T's rights were denied recognition by the French Moroccan Mines Department. In 1931 France made a Declaration accepting jurisdiction of the PCIJ over 'any disputes which may arise after the ratification of the present Declaration with regard to situations or facts subsequent to such ratification'. The PCIJ found that the facts and situations giving rise to the dispute were earlier than the 1931 exclusion date. Although the alleged illegality continued after the French Declaration of 1931 the operative event was the creation of the monopoly in 1920. The dispute, the situation and the facts out of which it had arisen preceded the period covered by the French Declaration of Acceptance and thus fell outside the Court's jurisdiction.

Limitation periods for international actions

The Statute of the ICJ contains no express provision relating to a period within which a case must be brought to its attention. However, this is not to say that such a period of limitation does not exist, for clearly the Court would be reluctant to adjudicate disputes that have their origins other than in the recent past.

The issue of a limitation period arose in the *Certain Phosphate Lands in Nauru Case (Preliminary Objections): Nauru* v *Australia* (1992) ICJ Rep 240 where, in a dispute between Australia and Nauru concerning compensation for the rehabilitation of certain mines, the matter arose whether or not the action was time-barred. Australia challenged the admissibility of the application on the ground, inter alia, that Nauru had achieved independence in 1968 and had ample opportunity to initiate proceedings on this matter but had chosen not to do so until 1988.

The Court acknowledged that a delay in initiating proceedings might have rendered an application inadmissible if the delay had prejudiced the rights of the other party. The overriding principle was that it was for the Court to decide 'in the light of the circumstances of each case whether the passage of time renders an application inadmissible'.

A number of factors have to be taken into consideration in assessing whether the circumstances of the case render the application inadmissible, including the relationship between the parties and the steps that had been taken prior to litigation to resolve the matter.

Further, the Court has a responsibility to ensure that any future delay in proceedings does not prejudice the rights of the defending state with regard to both the establishment of the facts and the determination of the content of the applicable law.

It should be noted that, if an action is time-barred, the underlying rights of the parties do not cease to exist. Rather, it is the right of the party raising the action to bring proceedings that is affected. In other words, the rights of the parties under international law do not expire, only their right to vindicate those rights before the Court.

Incidental jurisdiction

Independently of the main proceedings the Court may be called upon to exercise incidental jurisdiction: hearing preliminary objections, determining applications to intervene and ordering interim measures.

Preliminary objections

In numerous cases, before examining the merits of a particular case, the Court has to consider preliminary objections to its jurisdiction. Such objections are usually dealt with in a separate preliminary judgment, but in some cases the objection is 'joined to the merits' and dealt with together with the merits in a single judgment.

By virtue of art 36(6) of the Statute the Court has jurisdiction to determine its own competence and to decide whether or not it has jurisdiction in a particular case. Preliminary objections to the admissibility of the claim can be based on a number of grounds, such as the failure of the claimant state to exhaust local remedies, failure to comply with the procedures required by the treaty or other instrument which confers jurisdiction upon the Court, failure to comply with the nationality of the claim, etc.

In the *South West Africa Cases (Second Phase): Ethiopia* v *South Africa*; *Liberia* v *South Africa* (1966) ICJ Rep 6 Ethiopia and Liberia, two former members of the League of Nations, in 1960 instituted proceedings against South Africa claiming that South Africa had failed to carry out the obligations imposed upon it by the Mandate under which it had agreed with the League of Nations to administer the territory of South West Africa. In its 1966 judgment the Court ruled that South Africa's obligations under the Mandate, in so far as they concerned the treatment of the inhabitants of South West Africa, had been owed to the League of Nations and not to individual members of the League. The Court held that Ethiopia and Liberia had therefore failed to establish any legal right or interest appertaining to them in the subject matter of the claims and thus the Court rejected their claims.

Intervention
The Statute of the ICJ provides for two forms of third-state intervention in cases already before the Court.

1. Article 63: in cases where the main issue in dispute is the construction of a multilateral treaty of which the intervening state is a party. In such cases intervention is as of right although it remains for the Court to determine admissibility – El Salvador's declaration to intervene in the *Nicaragua Case* (above). Intervention of this nature has been allowed by the Court on two occasions: Poland's intervention in the *Wimbledon Case* (1923) PCIJ Rep Ser A No 1 and Cuba's intervention in the *Haya de la Torre Case: Colombia* v *Peru (Judgment)* (1951) ICJ Rep 71.

2. Article 62: this provides that a state may seek to intervene in a case in which it has an interest of a legal nature which may be affected by the decision. In such cases there is no right to intervene the Court decides as a preliminary matter whether or not such an interest exists. The conditions under which the Court will allow a third state to intervene were elucidated in the *Case Concerning Land, Island and Maritime Frontier Dispute: El Salvador* v *Honduras, Nicaragua Intervening* (1992) ICJ Rep 92 in which Nicaragua was given permission to intervene in a dispute between Honduras and El Salvador. Relevant matters are as follows:

   a) the intervening state must prove that its has a legal interest which may, rather than will, be affected by the judgment;

b) the objections of one party or both parties to a dispute to the intervention of a third state will not prevent the ICJ from granting permission to intervene;

c) the intervening state does not become a party to the proceedings and consequently the decision of the Court has no binding effects in respect of its rights;

d) the main purpose of allowing the intervention of a third state is to emphasise to the Court that a third state's rights are likely to be affected by its decision.

Interim measures

Under art 41 of the Statute the ICJ is empowered, if it considers it appropriate, to indicate any provisional measures 'which ought to be taken to preserve the respective rights of each party'

The difficulty facing the Court when deciding the matter of interim measures is that of reconciling the fact that the Court may ultimately decide that it lacks jurisdiction to decide the case with the fact that the party's rights may be irreparably damaged before the decision as to jurisdiction is taken. To avoid this contradiction the ICJ sets out two pre-conditions for the grant of interim protection:

1. the existence of a prima facie case for the exercise of jurisdiction by the Court over the merits of the dispute;

2. the existence of a risk of imminent and irreparable damage to the rights of the party seeking protection.

This test was applied in the *Case Concerning Questions of Interpretation and Application of the 1971 Montreal Convention Arising from the Aerial Incident at Lockerbie: Libyan Arab Jamahiriya* v *USA (Provisional Measures)* (1992) ICJ Rep 114. In this case Libya alleged that the interpretation of Security Council Resolution 748 (1992) imposing certain sanctions in response to Libya's refusal to hand over two Libyan nationals suspected of destroying Pan Am Flight 103 over Lockerbie amounted to a prima facie case over which the Court should exercise its jurisdiction.

Second, Libya argued that the use of sanctions and possible use of force put Libya's interests at a risk of suffering irreparable and imminent damage.

The ICJ declined to find, at that early stage, that the Security Council's Resolution was ultra vires. Neither did the Court find the existence of a risk of imminent and irreparable damage to the rights of Libya. In fact, the Court found quite the reverse. The refusal of Libya to comply with the terms of the Security Council Resolution was more likely to impair the rights enjoyed by the UK and the US than the rights of Libya.

In the circumstances the application for interim protection was rejected and the grant of interim measures refused. The decision of the Court was, however, by a majority with five votes against and strong dissenting opinions were submitted by the minority.

Compliance with interim measures ordered by the Court has always been poor. If a state fails to implement an order of the Court for interim measures of protection, no sanction can be imposed by the Court. The Court merely has power to reiterate the terms of its earlier order through a subsequent order. In the *Case Concerning the Application of the Convention on the Prevention and Punishment of the Crime of Genocide (Second Indication of Provisional Measures): Bosnia and Herzegonina* v *Yugoslavia* (1993) ICJ Rep 325, where Yugoslavia had effectively ignored the Court's first order, the Court could only order Yugoslavia to give immediate and effective implementation to the earlier order.

In numerous cases the ICJ has issued interim measures without ever determining their binding force with regard to the parties to the proceedings. This matter was, for the first time, comprehensively examined by the Court in the *LaGrand Case: Germany* v *United States of America* (2001) 40 ILM 1069 in which, at the request of Germany, the ICJ issued provisional measures calling upon the United states to take all necessary measures to ensure that a German national, Walter LaGrand who was sentenced to death in Arizona, not be executed pending the final decision of the ICJ in the proceedings brought by Germany against the US. He was executed a few hours later on the same day that the ICJ issued provisional measures: *LaGrand* (1999) ICJ Rep 28. The circumstances of this case are unusual: Walter LaGrand and his brother, while living in the US, were arrested in Arizona in 1982 on a charge of armed robbery and murder and later convicted and sentenced to death. During the proceedings before the court in Arizona they were never informed of their rights under the Vienna Convention on Consular Relations 1963 to which both Germany and the US are contracting parties. Under art 36(1)(b) of the Vienna Convention a contracting state is bound to inform a national of another contracting state who is arrested or committed to prison or to custody pending trial or detained in any other manner on its territory that he is entitled to consular assistance of his country. Furthermore, the non-compliance of the US with the Vienna Convention was neither raised during the proceedings against the LaGrand brothers, nor on appeal nor in the post-conviction proceedings in the Arizona courts. It was eventually raised in a federal habeas corpus petition but the petition was rejected on the ground that the matter was not properly raised in the state court. The German government learnt about the matter in February 1999, practically on the eve of the scheduled execution of the two brothers. When the German government filed the proceedings against the US before the ICJ, Walter LaGrand's brother was already executed and Walter LaGrand himself was scheduled to be executed the next day. The German government sought a judgment on the merits against the US and requested the Court to issue provisional measures. In its judgment of 27 June 2001 the ICJ held that it had jurisdiction to adjudicate the matter on the ground of art 1 of the Optional Protocol attached to the Vienna Convention which provides for the Court's jurisdiction over disputes arising out of the interpretation and application of the Convention. The ICJ found the US in breach of the Convention and in breach of its obligation to comply with the order of provisional measures that the Court had issued.

The argument of the US that the submission of the German government in respect of provisional measures was inadmissible, taking into account that Germany waited until the very eve of Walter LaGrand execution to seek the provisional measures and therefore the US had not had enough time to challenge them or to comply with them, was rejected by the Court. The Court stated that although Germany could be criticised for waiting so long, it was nevertheless entitled to invoke the non-compliance of the US with interim measures in view of the irreparable prejudice that appeared to be imminent, that is the execution of Walter LaGrand. Furthermore, the Court stated that the measure of a fax transmission by the US authorities to notify the order of the ICJ to the Governor of Arizona was not sufficient to ensure the compliance with the order. The requirement for the US to take all necessary measures goes further. The ICJ stated that it would, for example, be satisfied by the US Supreme Court granting a preliminary stay of execution order.

The ICJ considered the purpose and the nature of art 41 of the Statute. It found that the purpose of provisional measures is to enable the Court to settle interim disputes by binding decisions, in particular to preserve the respective rights of the parties pending the final decision in the proceedings. Consequently, the ICJ stated 'the power to indicate provisional measures entails that such measures should be binding, inasmuch as the power in question is based on necessity, when the circumstances call for it, to safeguard, and to avoid prejudice to, the rights of the parties as determined by the final judgment of the Court'. In the above decision the ICJ clearly stated that provisional measures are binding and create legal obligations on the addressee.

It is interesting to note that subsequent to the judgment the US instituted measures aimed at ensuring the effective review of every case within the scope of the Vienna Convention on Consular Relations. These measures, however, were judged as being insufficient by the government of Mexico, which on 9 January 2003 instituted proceedings against the US before the ICJ alleging the violation of art 36 of the Vienna Convention in respect of 54 of its nationals who were arrested, detained, tried, convicted and sentenced to death by the US courts without being informed of their right to consular assistance. The government of Mexico requested the ICJ to indicate provisional measures in respect of all Mexican nationals scheduled for execution or to be executed in the US pending final judgment in this case. The US replied that the request submitted by Mexico would be tantamount to a 'sweeping prohibition on capital punishment for Mexican nationals in the USA' and thereby would transform the ICJ into a 'general criminal court of appeal'. On 5 February 2003 the ICJ granted the request: see *Case Concerning Avena and Other Mexican Nationals (Provisional Measures): Mexico v USA* (2003) 42 ILM 309. The Court rejected the argument put forward by the US. However, the ICJ limited the order requesting the suspension of the execution of Mexican nationals to those who had already been identified in the request as being victims of the violation of the Vienna Convention, and not to all nationals of Mexico in the US currently on death row.

The procedure before the ICJ

The procedure before the ICJ is set out in its Statute and in the Rules of Procedure adopted by the ICJ. The latest version of the Rules was adopted on 5 December 2000. In contentious cases the procedure consists of written and oral phases. In the written phase the parties file and exchange pleadings. The oral phase comprises public hearings at which agents and counsel of the parties address the Court. Once the public hearings are over the Court deliberates in camera. The deliberations are secret and usually take about three months. Each decision is taken by an absolute majority of judges present. No abstentions are permitted on any point voted upon. However, if a judge who participated in the proceedings is physically unable to attend the meetings but wishes to vote, he may be allowed to do so, if necessary by correspondence. Also judges who did not participate in the oral proceedings or the deliberations but nevertheless did not miss anything essential may be allowed to vote. If the vote is equally divided, the President of the Court has a casting vote: eg *SS Lotus Case* (1927) PCIJ Rep Ser A No 10 and *South West Africa Cases (Second Phase)* (1966) ICJ Rep 6.

The judgment is delivered at a public sitting held in the Great Hall of Justice of the Peace Palace in the Hague in the presence of all judges who participated in voting on the judgments unless for serious reasons they are preventing from attending. In any case a quorum of nine judges is required for delivery of the judgment. The President of the Court reads publicly the judgment in French or English, ie one of the official languages of the Court. The judgment is divided into three parts:

1. the introduction which contains a summary of the proceedings, the submissions of the parties, the names of the participating judges and the representatives of the parties;
2. the grounds on which the judgment is based;
3. the operative part of the judgment which contains the actual decision of the Court in respect of the disputed matters submitted by the parties.

Since 1978 each judgment must indicate the number and the names of judges constituting the majority. Judges are allowed to express their opinion on disputed matters which are attached to the judgment. These opinions may take three forms:

1. a judge may write a dissenting opinion in which he submits his reasons for disagreeing with the operative provisions of the judgment as a whole or some aspects of it;
2. a judge who voted in favour of the judgment may write a separate opinion in which he may express his disagreement in respect of some or all reasoning of the Court or approve the operative provisions of the judgment on the basis of a different method of reasoning or submit additional reasons for his approval of the judgment;

3. a judge may write a declaration which contains a brief indication of his approval or dissent.

Judgments of the ICJ

The judgment of the Court is binding on the parties to the case and only in respect of that case. For that reason the principle of stare decisis, that is the binding nature of precedents as known at common law, is not used by the Court. In practice the Court often relies on its previous decisions and tries to ensure consistency in its decisions.

A judgment of the Court may, however, affect the interests and rights of a third state. This occurs especially in respect of disputes involving the interpretation and application of multilateral treaties since other contracting parties will, to some extent, be affected by such a judgment. The Court has developed the so-called 'necessary third party rule' to deal with cases involving the determination of the rights and obligations of an absent third party which has not consented to the proceedings. In such cases the Court will decline its jurisdiction. Based on the 'necessary third party' rule the Court refused to deliver a decision on merits in *Monetary Gold Removal from Rome in 1943: Italy* v *France, United Kingdom and US* (1954) ICJ Rep 19 and in the *East Timor Case: Portugal* v *Australia* (1995) ICJ Rep 90. Furthermore, when a case involves the interpretation of a multilateral treaty the Registrar of the Court is required to notify all contracting parties to such treaty of the proceedings brought before the Court. Whether contracting states have been notified or not by the Registrar they may always submit a declaration of intervention and thus ensure that the Court would take into consideration their legal interests while deciding the case.

Judgments of the Court are final and without appeal: art 60 of the Statute. However, at the request of either party the Court may interpret its judgment when there is a disagreement between the parties as to its exact meaning and scope. In some cases the Court has refused to interpret its judgment (eg the *Request for Interpretation of the Judgment of 20 November 1950 in the Asylum Case: Columbia* v *Peru* (1950) ICJ Rep 395), in others it has accepted such a request (eg the *Application for Revision and Interpretation of the Judgment of 24 February 1982 in the Case Concerning the Continental Shelf: Tunisia* v *Libyan Arab Jamahiriya* (1985) ICJ Rep 192).

The Court has also jurisdiction to revise its judgment. Article 61 of the Statute sets out the conditions for revision in the following terms:

'(1) An application for revision of a judgment may be made only when it is based upon the discovery of some fact of such a nature as to be a decisive factor, which fact was, when the judgment was given, unknown to the Court and also to the party claiming revision, always provided that such ignorance was not due to negligence ...

(4) The application for revision must be made at least within six months of the discovery of the new fact.

(5) No application for revision may be made after the lapse of ten years from the date of the judgment.'

So far the Court has never revised its judgment. The *Application for Revision and Interpretation of the Judgment of 24 February 1982 in the Case Concerning the Continental Shelf: Tunisia v Libyan Arab Jamahiryya* was rejected by the Court. The Application filed by Yugoslavia on 24 April 2001 requesting the revision of the Judgment of 11 July 1996 by which the ICJ declared that it had jurisdiction in the *Case Concerning the Application of the Convention on the Prevention and Punishment of the Crime of Genocide: Bosnia and Herzegovina v Yugoslavia* (not yet reported: obtainable from http://www.icj-cij.org) was rejected by the ICJ on 3 February 2003. Yugoslavia (the FRY) argued that the new fact which justifies the revision was the admission of the FRY to the United Nations on 1 November 2000. This demonstrates that the FRY did not continue the international legal and political personality of the Socialist Federal Republic of Yugoslavia (the SFRY), was not a Member of the United Nations and therefore was not a party to the Court's Statute and was not a party to the Genocide Convention. The FRY asserted that since the Court based its jurisdiction on the above-mentioned instruments, in particular art IX of the Genocide Convention, no further basis for the Court's jurisdiction existed or could have existed in the case. The FRY further argued that in its notification to the UN Secretary-General submitted on 8 March 2001, relating to accession to the Genocide Convention, the FRY had made a reservation to art IX. According to the FRY, its accession could not have retroactive effect and even if it did this could not possibly encompass the compromissory clause in art IX taking into account the fact that the FRY never accepted art IX and did not intend to accept it as stated in its notification seeking accession to the Genocide Convention.

The ICJ held that the admission of the FRY to the UN in 2000, four years after the ICJ delivered its judgment, 'cannot have changed retroactively the sui generis position in which the FRY found itself vis-à-vis the United Nations over the period 1992 to 2000'. The ICJ noted that when, on 27 April 1992, the FRY informed the UN that Serbia and Montenegro 'decided to live together in Yugoslavia' the SFRY was transformed into the FRY and thereafter had continued the legal personality of the SFRY. The FRY was never formally expelled from the United Nations: it was only barred from participating in the work of the UN bodies. This 'practical consequence' of the situation of the FRY from 1992 to 2000 could not be regarded as a fact within the meaning of art 61 of the Statute of the ICJ.

15.6 The advisory jurisdiction of the International Court of Justice

The Court has jurisdiction to give advisory opinions. This possibility is open exclusively to organs of the UN and the international organisations. Under art 96(1) of the UN Charter the General Assembly and the Security Council are entitled to make a request for an advisory opinion and by virtue of art 96(2) of the UN Charter other organs and specialised agencies, when authorised by the General Assembly, may also make such a request. At the time of writing five organs of the United Nations and 16 international organisations may ask the Court for an advisory opinion. The General Assembly and the Security Council may submit any legal question for the Court's consideration, while other organs of the UN and international specialised agencies are entitled to consult the Court in respect of legal issues arising within the scope of their activities. In the *Advisory Opinion on the Legal Consequences of the Construction of a Wall by Israel in the Occupied Palestinian Territory* (2004) 43 ILM 1009 delivered by the International Court of Justice on 9 July 2004 the Government of Israel argued that the UN General Assembly exceeded its competence when making the request for an advisory opinion, given that the Security Council was actively engaged with the situation in Palestine. According to Israel, in the light of art 12 of the UN Charter, which provides that:

> 'While the Security Council is exercising in respect of any dispute or situation the function assigned to it in the present Charter, the General Assembly shall not make any recommendation with regard to that dispute or situation unless the Security Council so requests ...'

the General Assembly acted ultra vires when making such a request.

The ICJ answered that a distinction must be made between a 'recommendation' within the meaning of art 12 of the UN Charter and a request for an advisory opinion. These two measures are of a different legal nature. A request for an advisory opinion cannot be regarded as a 'recommendation' referred to in art 12(1) of the UN Charter. Further, the ICJ decided to examine art 12(1) of the UN Charter in the light of the practice of the UN in matters such as this. In this respect the ICJ stated that the interpretation of art 12(1) had evolved. Initially both the Security Council and the General Assembly interpreted this provision as meaning that the General Assembly could not make recommendations on a question concerning the maintenance of international peace and security while the matter was on the Security Council's agenda, given that by virtue of art 24 of the Charter, the Security Council is entrusted with the main responsibility for the maintenance of international peace and security. Subsequently, this interpretation has changed. The ICJ found evidence of the changing nature of the practice in a note of interpretation of art 12(1) given by the UN Legal Counsel at the Twenty-third Session of the UN General Assembly and in the increasing tendency of both the Security Council and the General Assembly to deal in parallel with the same matter. The ICJ stated that the accepted practice of the General Assembly, as it had evolved, was consistent with art 12(1) of the UN Charter. Consequently, the General Assembly did not exceed its competence by adopting Resolution ES–10/14 seeking to obtain an advisory opinion from the ICJ.

The conditions necessary for the Court to exercise its advisory jurisdiction in respect of specialised agencies of the UN were confirmed in the *Legality of the*

Threat or Use of Nuclear Weapons Case (1996) ICJ Rep 90 in which the World Health Organisation (WHO) requested an advisory opinion. These conditions are:

1. the Security Council must authorise the specialised agency to submit such a request;
2. the opinion requested must concern a legal question;
3. the question must be one arising within the scope of activities of the requesting agency.

In the above case the Court rejected the WHO's request on the ground that the third condition was not satisfied. The Court held that although the matters of the effects on health of the use of nuclear weapons and the issue regarding preventive measures to be taken in order to protect the health of populations in the event of such weapons being used were within the scope of the WHO activities, the requested opinion did not concern these matters but focused on the legality of the use of nuclear weapons in the context of their health and environmental effects, a matter which was outside the scope of activities of the WHO. For that reason the Court held the WHO request for an advisory opinion as inadmissible.

The purpose of the advisory role of the Court is to provide legal advice in respect of the submitted matter and not to settle any particular dispute, even though a request is often related to, or has its origin in, an existing dispute. Article 65(1) of the Statute places two limitations upon the Court's advisory jurisdiction:

1. an advisory opinion must be confined to a legal question; and
2. the Court has discretion to decline its jurisdiction if it so wishes (judicial propriety).

Legal question within the meaning of art 96(1) of the UN Charter and art 65(1) of the Statute of the ICJ

In *Western Sahara Case (Advisory Opinion)* (1975) ICJ Rep 12 the ICJ provided a definition of a legal question. It held that questions 'framed in terms of law and rais[ing] problems of international law ... are by their very nature susceptible of a reply based on law ... [and] appear ... to be questions of a legal character'. Very often, a request for an advisory opinion involves a political element. In the *Conditions of Admission of a State to Membership of the United Nations Case* (1948) ICJ Rep 57 the ICJ stated that it examines the question 'only in the abstract form' without taking into consideration the motives which may have inspired the request or the distribution of votes with regard to the relevant resolution. Also, the political implications of the Court's opinion would not deprive it from exercising advisory jurisdiction. The Court has acknowledged many times that questions referred to it often have political significance. This does not, however, deprive them of being, at the same time, legal questions. The Court has emphasised on a number of occasions that it is the nature of things that international law and international politics are inevitably intertwined, but it always stressed that whatever the political aspects of the question 'the Court cannot refuse to admit the legal character of a question which invites it to discharge an essentially judicial task, namely, an assessment of the legality of the possible conduct of states with regard to the obligations imposed upon them by international law': *Legality of the Threat or Use of Nuclear Weapons Case* (1996) ICJ Rep 90.

Also the argument that political pressures on the Court and its members were so great as to make it 'impossible for the Court to exercise its judicial function properly' advanced by South Africa in the *Namibia Case* (1971) ICJ Rep 16 was rejected by the Court. The Court stated that it acts only on the basis of the law, independently of all outside influence or intervention.

In the *Interpretation of the Agreement of 25 March 1951 between the WHO and Egypt Case* (1980) ICJ Rep 73 the Court stated that in situations where political considerations are prominent a request for an advisory opinion may be especially necessary since the requesting organisation would particularly need the Court's advice as to the legal principles applicable to the matter under debate.

In the *Certain Expenses of the United Nations Case* (1962) ICJ Rep 151 the Court was asked to advise whether the costs of the United Nations operations in Congo and in the Middle East constituted expenses of the Organisation that could be apportioned between members of the United Nations.

The legal issues regarding the interpretation of the Charter were bound up with the differing political views of the members of the United Nations as to the UN peacekeeping role. It was argued that the matter was of a political nature and therefore incapable of solution by legal means. The Court decided that political factors did not constitute sufficiently compelling reasons to refuse an Opinion. In this respect the Court stated that:

'It is true that most interpretations of the Charter of the United Nations will have political significance, great or small. In the nature of things it could not be otherwise. The Court, however, cannot attribute a political character to a request which invites it to undertake an essentially judicial task, namely, the interpretation of a treaty provision.'

The fact that the subject matter of a request may also involve the determination of facts by the Court does not affect the advisory jurisdiction of the Court. In the *Namibia Case* (1971) ICJ Rep 16 the Court rejected South Africa's argument that the Court could only answer the question submitted to it by considering the factual issues relating to South Africa's conduct in the disputed territory, and that the Court had no more competence to decide such disputes as to the facts than it had jurisdiction over legal disputes between states. The Court answered that:

'In the view of the Court, the contingency that there may be factual issues underlying the question posed does not alter its character as a "legal question" as envisaged in art 96 of the Charter.'

In the *Advisory Opinion on the Legal Consequences of the Construction of a Wall by*

Israel in the Occupied Palestinian Territory, arguments that the ICJ had no jurisdiction to give an advisory opinion because of the lack of clarity of the terms of the request, and because the request did not raise a 'legal question' within the meaning of art 96(1) of the UN Charter and art 65(1) of the Statute of the ICJ, were dismissed by the ICJ.

The ICJ emphasised that lack of clarity did not deprive the Court of jurisdiction. To the contrary, any uncertainty arising from lack of clarity in the drafting of a question requires clarification, which the Court, by way of interpretation, has frequently provided. The ICJ observed that in the past, both the PCIJ and the ICJ were required to broaden, interpret and reformulate the question submitted (see *Jaworzina, Advisory Opinion* (1923) PCIJ Series B No 8; *Admissibility of Hearings of Petitioners by the Committee on South West Africa, Advisory Opinion* (1956) ICJ Rep 20; *Certain Expenses of the United Nations, Advisory Opinion* (1962) ICJ Rep 151).

The ICJ was also satisfied that the General Assembly's request related to a 'legal question' given that the question concerned the assessment of the legal consequences arising from a given factual situation in the light of the rules and principles of international law. The answer to the question submitted required a reply based on law (*Western Sahara, Advisory Opinion* (1975) ICJ Rep 12). The ICJ stated that the question was not an abstract one but in any event the Court was competent to give an advisory opinion in respect of an abstract question (*Conditions of Admission of a State to Membership in the United Nations, Advisory Opinion* (1966) ICJ Rep 57). The ICJ affirmed that the political motives inspiring the request, the political implications of any advisory opinion, and any political aspects of the legal question were irrelevant to the establishment of its jurisdiction (*Legality of the Threat or Use of Nuclear Weapons, Advisory Opinion* (1996) ICJ Rep 226).

Judicial propriety

By virtue of art 65(1) the ICJ enjoys a discretionary power to decline to give an advisory opinion even if the requirements for jurisdiction are satisfied. This refers to the propriety of the exercise of the Court's judicial function. Only 'compelling reasons' would force the Court to use its discretionary power under art 65(1) of its Statute. In the *Advisory Opinion on the Legal Consequences of the Construction of a Wall by Israel in the Occupied Palestinian Territory* the ICJ emphasised that, as a matter of principle, the Court should not decline to give an advisory opinion given its responsibilities as the principal judicial organ of the UN. The ICJ affirmed that there was no 'compelling reason' which would force the Court to use its discretionary power to decline to give an advisory opinion despite having jurisdiction to do so. The ICJ emphasised that so far it has never, in the exercise of this discretionary power, declined to give an advisory opinion. In the *Legality of the Use by a State of Nuclear Weapons in Armed Conflict* the ICJ refused to accept the request from the World Health Organisation because it lacked jurisdiction and not because it considered that it would be improper and inconsistent with the Court's judicial function to exercise its jurisdiction ((1996) ICJ Report 66).

As to the PCIJ a request for an advisory opinion was refused on the ground of judicial propriety on one occasion only. The refusal was due to the unusual circumstances of the case; namely the question directly concerned an already existing dispute, one of the parties to the dispute refused to participate in the proceedings and that party was neither a party to the Statute of the PCIJ, nor a member of the League of Nations (*Eastern Carelia Case (Advisory Opinion)* (1923) PCIJ Rep Ser B No 5). The ICJ decided in the *Legal Consequences of the Construction of a Wall by Israel in the Occupied Palestinian Territory* to examine the arguments challenging the propriety of the exercise of its judicial function based on the decision of the PCIJ in *Eastern Carelia*. Israel argued that the request concerned a contentious matter between Israel and Palestine, in respect of which Israel did not consent to the ICJ's jurisdiction. The ICJ replied that there is a vital difference between the contentious and the advisory jurisdiction of the ICJ with regard to the consent of a party to a dispute. Whilst in contentious cases consent of all parties to the dispute is necessary in order to establish the Court's jurisdiction, in advisory proceedings the consent of all parties, although desirable, is not necessary taking into account the fact that an advisory opinion has no binding force and is given not to the states but to an international organisation which is entitled to request it. Only when an advisory opinion 'would have the effect of circumventing the principle that a state is not obliged to allow its dispute to be submitted to judicial settlement without its consent' may the issue of lack of consent of an interested state compel the Court to decline its jurisdiction on the basis of judicial propriety (*Western Sahara*).

Further, in the *Advisory Opinion on the Legal Consequences of the Construction of a Wall by Israel in the Occupied Palestinian Territories*, the ICJ found that the principle set up in *Eastern Carelia* did not apply because the question on which the General Assembly requested an opinion was located in a much broader frame of reference than that of the bilateral dispute between Israel and Palestine, and was indeed of direct concern to the United Nations and its responsibility for the maintenance of international peace and security.

The procedure before the Court in respect of advisory opinions is modelled on that for contentious proceedings. The only difference is that when the Court receives a request for an advisory opinion it invites states and international organisations which may provide useful information to present their written or oral statements.

Advisory opinions are of a consultative character and therefore not binding on the requesting entities. It is up to them to decide on the usefulness of an advisory opinion and to choose the appropriate course of action. In most cases advisory opinions have been accepted and acted upon by any state concerned. Some international instruments can, however, provide in advance that the advisory opinion shall be binding.

15.7 Assessment of the International Court of Justice

In the assessment of the ICJ it is very important to note that states are extremely reluctant to submit disputes with other states to any form of international adjudication. Despite cynical views to the contrary, this reluctance is seldom caused by a desire to breach international law with impunity, although the absence of an adjudicatory system is a sore temptation! The distrust of states in respect of international adjudication arises from the fear that judicial decisions are often unpredictable. It is not that international law is uncertain. This is based on the fact that when a particular dispute it is not capable of settlement through diplomatic channels it indicates that the relevant law or facts are uncertain.

States also point to the number of dissenting judgments as evidence of judicial unpredictability. If different judges come to different conclusions, it is surely evident that the outcome of litigation is pure chance! Also, where the law is uncertain, a judge may be influenced by political considerations. However, the fears about the unpredictable nature of international law are, in reality, mere excuses. The most important reason of states' reluctance is that they do not wish to take the risk of exposing serious political issues to the unpredictability of adjudication. An important psychological factor is that states do not like taking other states to court: it may be construed as un unfriendly act. Moreover, if a state loses its case, an inevitable loss of prestige is incurred.

The manifestation of this mistrust can be found in the Statute of the ICJ. First, its contentious jurisdiction is not compulsory as it depends on the acceptance of the optional clause, which in turn is often limited by reservations inserted into a state's declaration of acceptance of the 'compulsory jurisdiction'. Second, under art 59 of the Statute the judgments of the Court have binding force only in respect of the parties to the dispute and only in respect of that particular case. Therefore, the Court's decisions are neither binding in respect of its subsequent cases nor in the event of a similar matter arising between the same parties in the future. Nevertheless, the Court has used its previous decisions in subsequent cases as evidence of the content of international law. Third, art 33 of the Charter of the UN provides for other alternative methods of resolution of disputes between states before referring to the Court.

In assessing the role of the ICJ it is necessary to note that the Court is a part of a collective security system envisaged by the UN Charter that has never materialised. Article 36(3) of the Charter states that 'legal disputes should as a general rule be referred by the parties to the International Court of Justice in accordance with the provisions of the Statute of the Court'. The Court was designed to deter states from resorting to force to settle their disputes. If a party failed to comply with the Court's judgments or interim measures, the Security Council was empowered to take appropriate measures to ensure compliance. Consequently, the ICJ follows upon the decline and the revival of the United Nations, although the Court faced two crises of its own, one in the 1950s in respect of a controversial handling of the *South West Africa Cases* and the other in 1984 when the USA refused to participate in the case brought by Nicaragua and withdrew its acceptance of the Court's jurisdiction on the eve of the filing of the *Nicaragua Case*.

The Court being an institution modelled from, and sustained by, essentially Western ideals of justice tended to be associated with the colonial powers. The Court blotted its copybook very badly in the *South West Africa Cases*. Here Ethiopia and Liberia sought a declaration from the Court to the effect that the Mandate for South West Africa was still in effect, and that South Africa remained under obligations placed upon it under the Mandate and was subject to the supervision of the United Nations. South Africa raised a preliminary objection on the basis of locus standi of the applicants which was rejected by the Court.

After four years of dispute, the Court then said that the applicants did not have locus standi! Between the first and second decision the composition of the Court had changed. In the previous vote a narrow majority had prevailed; in a subsequent vote the Court was equally divided and the President of the Court decided the matter by a casting vote. The volte-face was effected by the Court by recourse to the most specious legal reasoning. This decision of the Court marked the beginning of the disillusionment of the developing countries with the Court and its increasing unpopularity with them.

In the *Nicaragua Case* the Court proceeded with the case (despite US objections and subsequent withdrawal of its acceptance of the Court's compulsory jurisdiction) and rendered a judgment against it. Nevertheless, the US neither complied with its reservation promising to give a six months' notice of its intention to withdraw its acceptance of the Court's compulsory jurisdiction nor with the subsequent judgment. Moreover, the US's veto of the Nicaraguan application to the Security Council for the enforcement of the judgment in conformity with art 94(2) of the Charter of the United Nations did not enhance the Court's popularity. After the end of the Sandinista regime the US and Nicaragua settled the matter. The Court took cogniscence of the settlement in its order of 26 September 1991: (1991) ICJ Rep 47. It must be noted, however, that the Court showed courage and determination when dealing with the US in the *Nicaragua Case*.

Non-appearance of the US did not prevent the Court from giving a judgment against it. The non-appearance of a state is a problem often faced by the Court. In the *Nuclear Tests Cases: Australia* v *France; New Zealand* v *France* (1974) ICJ Rep 253, 457 France did not appear. In the *Fisheries Jurisdiction Case: United Kingdom* v *Iceland* (1974) ICJ Rep 3 Iceland did not appear. In the *Aegean Sea Continental Shelf Case: Greece* v *Turkey* (1978) ICJ Rep 3 Turkey not only failed to appear but also ignored the interlocutory orders. Similarly, in the *Hostages Case* (1980) ICJ Rep 3 Iran failed to appear. Notwithstanding this, the Court proceeded in the absence of defendants and established principles of significant importance to the development of international law.

Since 1946 the ICJ has delivered 79 judgments and 25 advisory opinions on a wide range of issues, the most prominent are examined in this book. Advisory jurisdiction of the Court is a necessary complement to its contentious jurisdiction, taking into account that only states have locus standi in contentious cases and consequently international organisations, including the political organs of the United Nations, need some international forum to voice their concern and to be advised on legal issues relevant to their activities. The advisory jurisdiction of the Court has been very useful in clarifying international law in a non-contentious context.

Since the end of the Cold War the number of cases submitted to the Court has considerably increased. In the 1970s the Court had only one or two cases pending, whereas at the time of writing 21 cases are pending involving both developed and developing states. This is a visible sign of the Court's revival. In the new post-Cold War climate the Court seems well used and may be in danger of having insufficient capacity to deal with all of the matters before it.

The Court has greatly contributed to the development and clarification of international law. In its judgments the Court has always paid attention to the evolving nature of international law and has itself contributed to its evolution.

16

The Use of Force

16.1 Introduction

16.2 The right to wage war

16.3 From partial to total prohibition of wars

16.4 The prohibition of the threat or use of force under the United Nations Charter

16.5 Exceptions to the prohibition of the threat of or the use of force based on self-defence

16.6 Collective self-defence

16.7 Controversial uses of force

16.1 Introduction

International law prohibits the threat of, and the use of, force in international relations. This principle which has acquired the status of ius cogens has developed over many centuries. These developments and their effects are examined in this chapter. The prohibition is not, however, absolute. The UN Charter itself recognises the right to self-defence. Other exceptions, outside the UN Charter, have been established under international law – for example, the use of force by people in the exercise of their right to self-determination. Furthermore, states have invoked a number of justifications for the use of force, some of which have gone unchallenged by the international community. This constitutes a strong presumption in favour of their legitimacy.

16.2 The right to wage war

During the first centuries of Christianity the principal theories on war were formed, which in the Middle Ages gave rise to the foundations of the law of war. The matter whether or not the recourse to war was legitimate was considered from two perspectives: the pacifists condemned any recourse to collective violence irrespective of its objectives and purposes; whilst the doctrine of 'just war' allowed the use of

410

force provided that the 'cause' was 'just'. In the very first centuries of Christianity many authors challenged the presence of Christians in the Roman legions. Tertulien in his work *De Corona*, written in approximately 211 AD, asked the question: 'An in totum Christianis militia conveniat? (Can a Christian, in general, be a part of the army?). He answered in the negative. However, pacifism was rejected when the barbarian invasions threatened the Roman civilisation with which Christianity had identified itself. Augustine of Hippo (354–430) formulated the doctrine of 'just war' in the following terms:

> 'Just wars are usually defined as those which avenge injuries, when the nation or city against which warlike action is to be directed has neglected, either to punish wrongs committed by its own citizens or to restore what has been unjustly taken by it. Further, that kind of war is undoubtedly just which God Himself ordains.'

The doctrine of 'just war' accepted war as a necessary instrument to preserve the Christian civilisation. St Augustine did not advocate war. To the contrary, he considered war as an evil and specified the conditions under which Christians could participate in wars. He also stated that an initially 'just war' may become 'unjust' if pursued to a vindictive excess beyond what is necessary to remedy the original wrong. This was the first expression of the idea of proportionality.

With the conversion of Emperor Constantine the interests of the Roman empire became associated with the interests of Christianity. Consequently, the Catholic Church began distancing itself from its pacifist traditions. By the tenth century Roman Catholicism had become the official religion of all European states. In the Middle Ages the Crusaders' ideal, emphasising that war was justified by the holy cause (that is the rescuing of the Holy Land from the Moslems), associated the Church with warring activities. As the military efforts of the Europeans were directed towards the Moslems, the Church crystallised the customs of warfare between Christian states by imposing limitations. Numerous conciles edicted by the Church defined institutions such as the peace of God and the truce of God which restricted the times for fighting, banned clerical participation and made a distinction between combatants and non-combatants. The doctrine of 'just war' was further refined by St Thomas Aquinas in the thirteenth century in his *Summa Theologica*. He set out three conditions for a just war:

1. only sovereign rulers were entitled to resort to force in defence of the interests of the state;
2. the cause must be 'just' in the sense advocated by St Augustine;
3. some limitations were imposed on the authority of sovereign rulers to make war, namely they had to remedy the original wrong without pursuit to excess. Just wars are those which are not made by ambition or cruelty but in the spirit of love of peace with a view to helping the righteous by vanquishing the evil ones.

These criteria were sufficiently flexible to justify almost any recourse to force!

In the period of the Renaissance the concept of 'just war' was still invoked but its content had changed. It was recognised that war could be just on both sides. Grotius in *De Jure Belli ac Pacis* put the emphasis in the 'ius ad bellum' on the definition of the state of war and the legal consequences flowing from it, rather than on the ideological justification of the justice of the cause. He advocated the settlement of disputes between nations by independent judges and arbitrators to limit the recourse to war. Erasmus represented the pacifist approach based on such philosophical and theological principles as the common humanity and brotherhood of all persons as children of God.

With the development and consolidation of the modern state system the predominant view was that the right of a state to wage war was inherent in the concept of state sovereignty. After the Peace of Westphalia in 1648 the doctrine of just war disappeared from international law. States were sovereign and equal and therefore one state had no authority to judge whether or not the cause of another state was just. By the end of the eighteenth century and throughout the nineteenth century the attitude that it was the right of every state to resort to war prevailed. War was recognised as a legally admissible instrument for attacking and altering existing rights of states independently of the objective merits of the attempted change. War had, therefore, become an instrument of national policy and customary law placed no limitations on the right of states to resort to war. In 1880 Hall stated:

> 'International law has no alternative but to accept war, independently of the justice of its origin, as a relation which the parties to it may set up, if they choose, and to busy itself only in regulating the effects of the relation … Hence both parties to every war are regarded as being in an identical position, and consequently as being possessed of equal rights.'

The first attempts to limit the right to wage war took place at the end of the nineteenth and the beginning of the twentieth centuries at the Hague Peace Conferences of 1899 and 1907. This matter is dealt with elsewhere in this work: see Chapter 18.

16.3 From partial to total prohibition of wars

The major breakthrough took place after World War I with the creation of the League of Nations. and the adoption of the General Treaty for the Renunciation of War 1928 known as the Kellogg–Briand Pact.

The League of Nations

The establishment of international law and a collective security system which would ensure lasting peace and would make World War I the 'war to end all wars', the last war in the history of mankind, was advocated by the US President Woodrow Wilson in his Fourteen Point Plan presented on 8 January 1918 to the US Congress. According to Wilson, in order to oversee the new system:

> '... a general association of nations must be formed under specific covenants for the purpose of affording mutual guarantees of political independence and territorial integrity to great and small states alike': Point XIV in *Selected Literary and Political Papers and Addresses of Woodrow Wilson*, Volume 2, New York: Grosset and Dunlop, 1927.

Under the chairmanship of Wilson, a Drafting Committee was set up to prepare the Covenant and to establish the League of Nations. The Covenant of the League of Nations was included in the Treaty of Versailles 1919 which concluded the peace settlement with Germany. The main purpose of the League was to achieve peace through international law and the maintenance of justice. The Covenant introduced two major innovations in respect of the right to wage war.

First, although the preamble to the Covenant imposed an obligation on its members not to resort to war, the prohibition was not general. It imposed some limitation upon the use of force.

Under art 12(1) of the Covenant if a dispute arose between members of the League they were obliged to submit the matter either to arbitration or to inquiry by the Council and they agreed 'in no case to resort to war until three months after the award by the arbitrators or the report by the Council'.

The three months' 'cooling period' was intended to prevent 'accidental' outbreaks of hostilities. The Covenant expressly outlawed wars of aggression (art 10 of the Covenant), wars which were commenced in breach of art 12(1) of the Covenant, that is when a member state did not submit a dispute to arbitration or to the Council, wars started in defiance of a judicial or arbitral decision rendered under the auspices of the League of Nations (art 13(4) of the Covenant) and wars declared despite the recommendations adopted unanimously by the Council of the League. This possibility was envisaged under arts 15 and 16 of the League. It required that disputes which were not submitted to arbitration or judicial settlement were to be submitted to the Council. If the Council (ignoring any votes of the parties to a dispute) unanimously agreed on a report settling a dispute, the members of the League were bound not to go to war with any party that complied with the recommendations. However, if no such agreement was reached by the Council, the only sanction was the publication of the report, provided its members, unanimously or by a majority vote, agreed to publication. This provision implies that in the situation where the Council could not reach an agreement on a report, members of the League were allowed to take measures which they considered necessary for the maintenance of law and justice (art 15(7)), including the resort to war.

Nevertheless, the above provisions are of major importance as they introduced obligations for the members of the League to settle their disputes by peaceful means and not to resort to war without first exhausting those means.

Second, art 16 of the Covenant introduced another significant innovation. It established the first collective security system and provided for sanctions against a Covenant-breaking member. This provision stated that:

> 'Should any member of the League resort to war in disregard of its Covenants under Article 12, 13, 15, it shall, ipso facto, be deemed to have committed an act of war against all other Members of the League, which hereby undertake immediately to subject it to the severance of all trade or financial relations, the prohibition of all intercourse between their nationals and the nationals of the Covenant-breaking state, and the prevention of all financial, commercial or personal intercourse between the nationals of the Covenant-breaking state and the nationals of any other state, whether a Member of the League or not.'

The system developed by the League of Nations did not work in practice for two main reasons.

1. Not all states were members of the League of Nations. Forty-five original signatories become members by early 1920. At its zenith the membership of the League reached 63 states. Germany was admitted in 1926, the Soviet Union in 1934. However, the United States, the driving force in the creation of the League, refused to ratify the Covenant. The Covenant of the League of Nations failed to obtain the required two-thirds majority before the US Senate.

2. The major disappointment was the failure of members of the League to impose sanctions against a Covenant-breaking state. Under art 16 economic sanctions were intended to be applied automatically and collectively. Article 16 also provided for military sanctions. In this respect, the Council was empowered to make recommendations to its members asking for contributions to such forces. Under art 17 collective measures could also be applied against a non-member state. In practice, even economic sanctions were applied on a selective and optional basis. In 1921 the Assembly of the League adopted a resolution stating that for each member state the imposition of economic sanctions was optional, not mandatory. The system of sanctions was a failure. In 1931 when Japan invaded Manchuria no sanctions were imposed. The League sent a League Commission of Inquiry to the Far East. Apart from a report produced by the Commission, which was adopted by the Assembly and which condemned the act of aggression committed by Japan and refused to recognise territorial changes following the invasion, that is the newly created State of Manchukuo, the League did nothing. However, following the condemnation Japan formally withdrew from the League. No sanctions were imposed when Hitler invaded the Rhineland, Austria and Czechoslovakia. Germany withdrew from the League. Inefficient sanctions were imposed on Italy after its invasion of Abyssinia (now Ethiopia) in 1935. Although 50 members of the League agreed on an embargo on arms and on financial aid to Italy and on certain Italian exports, the most important product, oil, was not the object of an embargo. Furthermore, the League neither blocked the Italian ports nor prevented access of Italy to the sea routes, in particular the Suez Canal, through which its forces in Abyssinia were

kept supplied. All sanctions were revoked in 1936 when Italy was at the point of economic collapse.

The only occasion of apparently serious action by the League of Nations was in 1939 when it imposed sanctions and ultimately expelled the Soviet Union from the League subsequent to the invasion of Finland. However, at that time World War II had started and any action came too late!

The General Treaty for the Renunciation of War 1928 (the Kellogg-Briand Pact)

The comprehensive prohibition of war as an instrument of national policy was achieved under the General Treaty for the Renunciation of War 1928. On 27 August 1928 at the initiative of the French Minister for Foreign Affairs, Aristide Briand, and the US Secretary of State Kellogg representatives of 15 governments signed at Paris the General Treaty for the Renunciation of War and, on the same day, invited other governments to ratify the Treaty. Sixty-three states were contracting states to the Treaty in 1939. The 1928 Treaty is very short. It contains a preamble and two provisions.

Article I states that:

'The High Contracting parties solemnly declare in the names of their respective peoples that they condemn recourse to war for the solution of international controversies, and renounce it as an instrument of national policy in their relations with one another.'

Article II provides for the settlement of international disputes or conflicts 'of whatever nature or of whatever origin' exclusively by peaceful means.

The Kellogg-Briand Pact was enthusiastically endorsed by the international community as a breakthrough in the search for peace. However, it has many shortcomings, the most important being that it does not provide for sanctions against a state who has broken the Pact by resorting to war in violation of its provisions. The Pact was inefficient in preventing conflicts. It was violated many times during the period preceding the outbreak of World War II by contracting states, namely by Japan, Italy, Germany and the Soviet Union. Consequently, the Pact failed to complement the Covenant of the League of Nations by reinforcing the prohibition of the use of force. Other drawbacks included the following.

1. It emerges from the negotiations leading to the adoption of the Pact that contracting states considered as implicitly incorporated into the Pact their right to self-defence. The Pact remains silent on this point.
2. The recourse to war remains lawful as between contracting parties and non-contracting parties.
3. The prohibition of the recourse to war may be taken to imply that not all use of force is covered by the Pact. Also the term 'international relations' may suggest that the resort to war is permitted for the purposes of preserving legal rights.

The Kellogg-Briand Pact has never been terminated. For practical purposes it has, however, been superseded by art 2(4) of the Charter of the United Nations.

16.4 The prohibition of the threat or use of force under the United Nations Charter

The general prohibition of the threat of, or the use of, force in international relations is contained in art 2(4) of the Charter which states that:

> 'All Members shall refrain in their international relations from the threat or use of force against the territorial integrity or political independence of any state, or in any other manner inconsistent with the purposes of the United Nations.'

This provision is complemented by art 2(3) of the Charter which states that:

> 'All members shall settle their international disputes by peaceful means, in such a manner that international peace and security, and justice, are not endangered.'

The purposes of the United Nations are set out in art 1. Therefore, any threat of, or the use of, force incompatible with art 1 is in breach of art 2(4) of the Charter. As the purposes of the United Nations are widely drawn, art 2(4) places a very wide prohibition on the use of force by states. Any use of force by a state outside its own borders is likely to be inconsistent with the maintenance of international peace and security or of promoting friendly relations among nations. The broad interpretation of art 2(4) was approved by the ICJ in the *Corfu Channel Case: United Kingdom* v *Albania (Merits)* (1949) ICJ Rep 4. In this case following an incident when two British warships had been struck by mines while exercising a right of innocent passage in Albanian territorial waters, the UK carried out minesweeping operations (Operation Retail) in the Corfu Channel. The UK argued her action was not in breach of art 2(4) since it 'threatened neither the territorial integrity nor the political independence of Albania. Albania suffered thereby neither territorial loss nor (loss to) any part of its political independence.'

The ICJ rejected the British arguments by stating that:

> 'The Court can only regard the alleged right of intervention as the manifestation of a policy of force, such as has in the past given rise to more serious abuses and such as cannot, whatever be the present defects in international organisation, find a place in international law ...
>
> ... The United Kingdom Agent ... has further classified "Operation Retail" among methods of self-protection or self-help. The Court cannot accept this defence either. Between independent states respect for territorial sovereignty is an essential foundation of international relations.'

The following points regarding art 2(4) should be noted. In the *Nicaragua Case: Nicaragua* v *US (Merits)* (1986) ICJ Rep 14 the ICJ accepted that art 2(4) reflects a rule of customary international law applying to all states whether members of the United Nations or not, and while, as a matter of strict law, the article applies only to resort to force in international relations against another state and does not affect a state's legal right to use armed force in the suppression of internal disturbances, in practice the UN has interpreted a wide range of 'domestic' activities as falling within the purvey of the UN for these purposes.

The article entirely prohibits the use or threat of armed force against another state except in self-defence (art 51) or in execution of collective measures authorised by the Security Council or the General Assembly. The force prohibited is armed force. The general view is that the article does not preclude a state from taking unilateral economic or other reprisals not involving the threat or use of armed force, in retaliation for a breach of international law by another state.

The article talks of the threat or use of force and not of war. Thus, all hostilities are covered even where no formal declaration of war has been issued and the parties have denied that a technical state of war exists.

The meaning of the phrase 'against the territorial integrity or political independence of any state'

The scope of this part of art 2(4) is disputed by writers.

On the one hand, Professor Bowett states:

'The phrase "against the territorial integrity or political independence of any state" may, on one construction, mean that the element of intent is introduced into the prohibition; namely, that the use or threat of force contravenes this obligation only where intended to jeopardise the political independence or territorial integrity of another state. Or, if specific intent is not required, it may mean that at least the use or threat of force must have this effect before being in contravention of Article 2(4)': *Self-Defence in International Law*, Manchester: Manchester University Press, 1958, p152.

Professor Brownlie, on the other hand, argues:

'The conclusion warranted by the Travaux preparatoires is that the phrase under discussion was not intended to be restrictive but, on the contrary, to give more specific guarantees to small states and that it cannot be interpreted as having a qualifying effect.

... The phrase "political independence and territorial integrity" has been used on many occasions to epitomise the total of legal rights which a state has. Moreover, it is difficult to accept a "plain meaning" which permits evasion of obligations by means of a verbal profession that there is no intention to infringe territorial integrity and which was not intended by the many delegations which approved the text. Lastly, if there is any ambiguity the principle of effectiveness should be applied': *International Law and the Use of Force by States*, Oxford: Clarendon Press, 1963, p268.

The definition of aggression

As the organ having the primary responsibility for the maintenance of international peace and security, the United Nations Security Council has the power under art 39 of the Charter to:

'... determine the existence of any threat to the peace, breach of the peace, or act of aggression and shall make recommendations, or decide what measures shall be taken in accordance with Articles 41 and 42, to maintain or restore international peace and security.'

Article 1 of the Charter lists as one of the purposes of the United Nations 'the suppression of acts of aggression'. Therefore, if a state uses aggression this would be a breach of art 2(4). What constitutes aggression is a question for the Security Council to determine in accordance with art 39.

The problem is that a member of the Security Council, when called upon to decide whether or not a particular act is within the ambit of art 39, may be motivated by its own political interests and ideology. Aggression is a subjective concept. In order to overcome this difficulty in deciding whether a particular use of force constitutes a breach of the Charter, the General Assembly in 1974 adopted Resolution 3314 (XXIX) on the Definition of Aggression.

Article 1:

'Aggression is the use of armed force by a state against the sovereignty, territorial integrity or political independence of another state, or in any other manner inconsistent with the Charter of the United Nations, as set out in this Definition.'

Article 2:

'The first use of armed force by a state in contravention of the Charter shall constitute prima facie evidence of an act of aggression although the Security Council may, in conformity with the Charter, conclude that a determination that an act of aggression has been committed would not be justified in the light of other relevant circumstances, including the fact that the acts concerned or their consequences are not of sufficient gravity.'

Article 3:

'Any of the following acts, regardless of a declaration of war, shall, subject to and in accordance with the provisions of Article 2, qualify as an act of aggression:
(a) The invasion or attack by the armed forces of a state of the territory of another state, or any military occupation however temporary, resulting from such invasion or attack, or any annexation by the use of force of the territory of another state or part thereof;
(b) Bombardment by the armed forces of a state against the territory of another state or the use of any weapons by a state against the territory of another state;
(c) The blockade of the ports or coasts of a state by the armed forces of another state; ...
(d) The use of armed forces of one state which are within the territory of another state, with the agreement of the receiving state, in contravention of the conditions provided for in the agreement or any extension of their presence in such territory beyond the termination of the agreement;
(e) The action of a state in allowing its territory, which it has placed at the disposal of another state, to be used by that other state for perpetrating an act of aggression against a third state;
(f) The sending by or on behalf of a state of armed bands, groups, irregulars or mercenaries, which carry out acts of armed force against another state of such gravity as to amount to the acts listed above, or its substantial involvement therein.'

Article 4:

'The acts enumerated above are not exhaustive and the Security Council may determine that other acts constitute aggression under the provisions of the Charter.'

Article 5:

'(1) No consideration of whatever nature, whether political, economic, military or otherwise, may serve as a justification for aggression.
(2) A war of aggression is a crime against international peace. Aggression gives rise to international responsibility.
(3) No territorial acquisition or special advantage resulting from aggression is or shall be recognised as lawful.'

Article 6:

'Nothing in this Definition shall be construed as in any way enlarging or diminishing the scope of the Charter, including its provisions concerning cases in which the use of force is lawful.'

Article 7:

'Nothing in this Definition, and in particular Article 3, could in any way prejudice the right to self-determination, freedom and independence, as derived from the Charter, of peoples forcibly deprived of that right and referred to in the Declaration on Principles of International Law concerning Friendly Relations and Co-operation among states in accordance with the Charter of the United Nations, particularly peoples under colonial and racist regimes or other forms of alien domination; nor the right of those peoples to struggle to that end and to seek and receive support, in accordance with the principles of the Charter and in conformity with the above mentioned Declaration.'

Article 8:

'In their interpretation and application the above provisions are inter-related and each provision should be construed in the context of the other provisions.'

There was great difficulty in formulating the Definition of Aggression and it represents a compromise between those states which favoured the enumerative approach, by which all of the acts that constitute aggression are listed, and those states which favour the general definition approach.

16.5 Exceptions to the prohibition of the threat of or the use of force based on self-defence

The UN Charter expressly mentions an exception to the prohibition of the threat of or the use of force on the ground of self-defence. In this respect the meaning of self-defence under the UN Charter and under customary law must be examined.

Self-defence and self-protection under customary law

Perhaps the most important case on the law of self-defence is the *Caroline Case* (1837) 29 BFSP 1137–1138 which arose out of the Canadian Rebellion of 1837. The rebel leaders, despite steps taken by the US authorities to prevent assistance being given to them, managed on 13 December 1837 to enlist at Buffalo in the US the support of a large number of American nationals. The resulting force established itself on Navy Island in Canadian waters from which it raided the Canadian shore and attacked British ships. The force was supplied from the US by an America ship, the *Caroline*. On the night of 29–30 December a small Canadian force seized the *Caroline*, which was then in the American port of Schlosser, set her on fire and sent her drifting over Niagara Falls. Two US nationals were killed – Amos Durfee, whose body was found on the quay with a bullet through his head, and a cabin boy known as 'little Billy', who was shot while attempting to leave the vessel. The US claimed reparation to which Great Britain (as the colonial power) replied that the destruction of the *Caroline* had been a necessary act of self-defence.

Three years later a British subject, McLeod, who unwisely boasted in the US of his participation in the incident was arrested and tried for murder in New York state. Britain demanded his release on the ground that those who participated in the operation against the *Caroline* had been engaged in the execution of an act of state for which they were not answerable personally in a municipal court.

The US government conceded that the public character of McLeod's acts relieved him of personal responsibility and sought to put an end to the proceedings against him in the New York courts. At the same time, it again disputed the British claim that the case was one of legitimate self-defence and the diplomatic correspondence contains the classical statement of the limits of self-defence.

The two governments, although they disagreed about the facts of the particular case, were entirely agreed upon the principles applicable to armed intervention in self-defence – ie there must be a clear and absolute necessity for the intervention, namely:

1. there must, initially, be a necessity of self-defence, instant, overwhelming, leaving no choice of means and no moment for deliberation; and
2. the acts done in self-defence must not be unreasonable or excessive and the force used must be proportionate to the harm threatened.

On this basis, legitimate self-defence in customary international law has three main requirements:

1. an actual infringement or threat of infringement of the rights of the defending state;
2. a failure or inability on the part of the other state to use its own legal powers to stop or prevent the infringement; and
3. acts of self-defence strictly confined to the object of stopping or preventing the infringement and reasonably proportionate to what is required for achieving this object.

Self-defence under the Charter of the United Nations

Article 51 of the Charter of the United Nations provides:

> 'Nothing in the present Charter shall impair the inherent right of individual or collective self-defence if an armed attack occurs against a member of the United Nations, until the Security Council has taken the measures necessary to maintain international peace and security. Measures taken by members in the exercise of this right of self-defence shall be immediately reported to the Security Council and shall not in any way affect the authority and responsibility of the Security Council under the present Charter to take at any time such action as it deems necessary in order to maintain or restore international peace and security.'

Unlike the Covenant of the League of Nations, the right of self-defence under the Charter system is not left outside the collective system for maintaining peace. Self-defence is recognised to be a necessary exception to the fundamental principle in art 2(4) that resort to force by an individual state is illegal without the prior authority of the United Nations. However, the exercise of the right of self-defence is made subject to the control of the international community – the individual state decides whether or not to use force in self-defence but the propriety of its decision is a matter for the United Nations.

The fact that resort to force in self-defence is lawful without the prior authority of the Security Council is of vital importance from the point of view of the veto. A state may begin action in self-defence without prior recourse to the Security Council and, therefore, no single Permanent Member may veto the action being initiated. Moreover, once the action in self-defence is being taken it requires an affirmative decision of the Security Council to order the cessation of that action. Therefore, action in self-defence under art 51 cannot be barred by the veto and cannot be terminated except by the unanimous vote of the Permanent Members.

The inherent right of self-defence, as it existed in international law before the Charter, was a general right of protection against a forcible threat to a state's legal rights. Article 51, however, speaks only of an inherent right of self-defence 'if an armed attack occurs'.

Does art 51 cut down the customary right of self-defence and restrict it to cases involving resistance to an armed attack by another state?

There is some uncertainty as to the effect of art 51 upon the customary international law right of self-defence. Kelson reads art 51 as meaning that for United Nations members the right of self-defence 'has no other content than the one determined by art 51': *The Law of Nations, A Critical Analysis of Its Fundamental Problems*, London: Steven & Sons, 1950, p914. Brownlie also argues that art 51 says everything and that a state cannot be acting in self-defence unless within art 51: op cit, pp1123 and 264 et seq.

Bowett, however, argues that customary international law remains unless cut down by the Charter. If there is any ambiguity it is proper to look at customary international law:

'It is ... fallacious to assume that members have only those rights which the Charter accords them; on the contrary they have those rights which general international law accords to them except in so far as they have surrendered them under the Charter': op cit, pp185–186.

Supporters of Bowett's view argue that the right of individual self-defence was regarded as automatically excepted in both the Covenant of the League of Nations and the Pact of Paris without any mention of it. The same would have been true of the Charter if there had been no art 51. Indeed, the original Dumbarton Oaks proposals did not contain the art 51 provisions. Committee 1 at the San Francisco Conference, commenting upon art 2(4), reported that 'the use of arms in legitimate self-defence remains admitted and unimpaired': 6 UNCIO, Documents.

Article 51 was inserted in the Charter to clarify the position with respect to collective understandings for mutual self-defence and in particular the Pan-American treaty known as the Act of Chapultepec. The official British government commentary on the Charter reads:

'It was considered at the Dumbarton Oaks Conference that the right of self-defence was inherent in the proposals and did not need explicit mention in the Charter. But self-defence may be undertaken by more than one state at a time, and the existence of regional organisations made this right of special importance to some states, while special treaties of defence made its explicit recognition important to others. Accordingly the right is given to individual states or to combinations of states to act until the Security Council itself has taken the necessary measures.'

Therefore, on the one hand it could be said that art 51 of the Charter is exhaustive and says all there is to know about self-defence. On the other hand, however, it could be said that when art 51 talks about the inherent right of self-defence it goes back to customary international law. Most writers accept the latter view, but there is a difference of emphasis as to how much of the customary law is still extant – and what it says.

The problem is that customary law clearly distinguishes between self-defence, self-preservation and self-help. Prior to the Pact of Paris there was no restriction on the right to wage war and, therefore, states did not always distinguish between self-defence and their other customary rights to use force. For example, in the *Caroline Case* it was unclear whether Great Britain was acting in self-defence or in self-preservation when she attacked the *Caroline*. The Charter, however, refers to the inherent right of self-defence. Therefore, when referring back to customary law does one consider the whole ambit of self-defence, self-preservation and self-help, which mean slightly different things, or is one restricted to clear and unambiguous examples of self-defence?

It must also be remembered that customary international law changes with the practice of states. It is, therefore, no use looking at the nineteenth century and before for the customary law of self-defence. It is argued that one has got to look at the practice of states just prior to the Charter.

Does Article 51 cut down the customary right by restricting forcible self-defence to cases where the attack provoking it has actually been launched?
Article 51 refers solely to situations 'if an armed attack occurs'. The question arises, therefore, as to the legality of anticipatory self-defence. Is an imminent threat sufficient to create a right to resort to force in self-defence or must the victim wait until the aggressor has struck the first blow before it can resort to force in self-defence?

Some authorities have interpreted 'if an armed attack occurs' to mean 'after an armed attack has occurred'. However, this interpretation may be too restrictive. When the article was drafted it is unlikely that there was any intention to cut down the right of self-defence beyond the already narrow doctrine of the *Caroline Case*. That doctrine allows a right of self-defence where there is an imminent threat of attack, and is recognised under art 51 as being an inherent right which continues to exist. In the *Nicaragua Case* (above) the ICJ accepted that the word 'inherent' in art 51 was a reference to customary law. The Court declined, however, to rule one way or another on the question of anticipatory self-defence as this was not required by the case.

Before taking action in anticipatory self-defence the Charter of the United Nations imposes the obligation upon states to settle their disputes by peaceful means, and empowers the Security Council to take the steps necessary to ensure the maintenance of international peace and security. Members have, therefore, an imperative duty to invoke the jurisdiction of the United Nations whenever a grave menace to their security develops carrying the probability of armed attack. However, if the action of the United Nations is delayed or inadequate and the armed attack becomes imminent it would be contrary to the purposes of the Charter to compel the defending state to allow the aggressor to deliver the first and perhaps fatal blow.

This interpretation of the Charter accords with the practice of states and the generally accepted view of international law at the time when art 51 was drafted. For example, it was argued before the International Military Tribunal at Nuremberg that the German invasion of Norway in 1941 was an act of self-defence in the face of an imminent Allied landing there. The Tribunal held that preventive action in foreign territory is justified only in the circumstances laid down in the *Caroline Case*, and that as there was no imminent threat of an Allied landing in Norway the argument must fail.

However, the International Military Tribunal for the Far East had no hesitation in deciding that the Dutch declaration of war upon Japan in December 1941 was justifiable on the grounds of self-defence. When considering the legality of Japan's invasion of Dutch territory in the Far East the Tribunal stated:

> 'The fact that the Netherlands, being fully appraised of the imminence of the attack, in self-defence declared war against Japan on 8 December and thus officially recognised the existence of a state of war which had been begun by Japan cannot change that war from a war of aggression on the part of Japan into something other than that.'

An example of anticipatory self-defence was the pre-emptive attack launched by Israel against the United Arab Republic in June 1967. Following Arab threats to liberate Israeli-occupied Palestine, the Israelis fearing imminent invasion launched an attack against Egypt destroying the Egyptian air force on the ground and cutting off the Egyptian army in Sinai. Israel claimed the action as necessary on the grounds of self-defence and that its pre-emptive strike had removed the threat of an Arab attack against its southern border. However, Israel did rely on pre-emptive self-defence in order to justify its attack on an Iraqi nuclear reactor in 1981. Israel claimed that the Iraqi nuclear reactor under construction was designed to produce nuclear weapons which subsequently would have been used against Israel. The attack was condemned by both the Security Council and by the General Assembly (the General Assembly classified the attack as premeditated and unprecedented act of aggression: Resolution 36/27, 109 votes in favour, two against and 34 abstentions).

The ICJ has consistently refused to make a statement on the issue of pre–emptive or anticipatory self-defence, perhaps because the ICJ has never been directly asked to do so. On the one hand, one understands that the ICJ should limit its judgment to the subject matter of the dispute brought by the parties but, on the other hand, some obiter dicta would have been particularly welcome, taking into account the stand that the USA and its allies have taken on the use of force in international relations. In this respect Judge Elaraby in his Dissenting Opinion in the *Case Concerning Oil Platforms: Islamic Republic of Iran* v *United States of America* (2003) 42 ILM 1334 criticised the ICJ in the following words:

> 'The *Oil Platforms* case presented the Court with the occasion to reaffirm, clarify, and if possible, develop, the law on the use of force in all its manifestations … The Court regrettably missed this opportunity. The judgment refrained from exploring refinements and progressive development of the existing doctrine. Even an obiter dictum was not contemplated. The international community was entitled to expect that the International Court of Justice, on an issue as important as the prohibition of the use of force, would take the opportunity to clarify and enhance the prohibition, and add probative value to the existing jurisprudence.'

The requirement of an 'armed attack'

An examination and comparison of arts 2(4) and 51 indicates that the two provisions are not entirely compatible. Article 2(4) prohibits the threat or use of force. Article 51, in contrast, provides that there is a right of self-defence if an armed attack occurs. The question arises, therefore, as to whether the term 'force' in art 2(4) equates with the term 'armed attack' in art 51. More particularly, under the UN Charter regime is there a right to use force in self-defence in response to a use of force by the other side that does not amount to an armed attack? This question presupposes that a distinction can usefully be drawn between a use of force amounting to an armed attack and one that does not.

Until the decision of the ICJ in the *Nicaragua Case* in 1986, most commentators accepted that a use of force or act of aggression by one state would give rise to a concomitant right of self-defence in the victim state. Any refinement that was required would then involve a discussion of the parameters of the phrase 'the territorial integrity or political independence' of a state. Thus, writers such as Bowett have consistently argued that a use of force against nationals abroad may give rise to a right of self-defence in protection of those nationals because a use of force against nationals abroad amounts to a use of force against the state itself. The ambit of the action in self-defence would then fall to be determined in accordance with the principle of proportionality.

In contrast, writers such as Brownlie have argued that the use of force against nationals abroad will not give rise to a right of self-defence – and, therefore, of intervention – as the use of force against nationals abroad would not constitute a use of force against the territorial integrity or political independence of the state.

The approach of the majority of the Court in the *Nicaragua Case* throws much of this reasoning into doubt and casts a considerable shadow of uncertainty over the right to use force in self-defence. The case arose out of Nicaraguan allegations against the US in respect of a range of activities from the mining of the Nicaraguan ports to the arming, training and directing of the Contra rebels. To these allegations the US raised the defence, inter alia, that they were acting in the collective self-defence of El Salvador and Costa Rica against which, they alleged, Nicaragua had been involved in illegal uses of force.

Considering this argument the Court appeared to limit the right of self-defence to circumstances which amounted to an armed attack. This the Court defined as acts, which because of their scale and effects, would be classified as an armed attack rather than a mere frontier incident. Thus, to amount to an armed attack, the acts concerned must be of a particularly serious nature. While the Court appeared to accept that a use of force amounting to something less than an armed attack may give rise to a right to take counter-measures, they did not discuss this principle at any length.

Sir Robert Jennings, in his dissenting opinion in the case, argued that the Court's distinction between uses of force amounting to an armed attack and those which did not, was 'neither realistic nor just'. He continued:

> 'In this situation is seems dangerous to define unnecessarily strictly the conditions for lawful self-defence, so as to leave a large area where both a forcible response to force is forbidden, and yet the UN employment of force, which was intended to fill the gap, is absent.'

Given the difficulty in distinguishing sensibly between degrees of the use of force, the approach of the Court should be followed with caution and perhaps limited to the facts of the case in issue.

When does an armed attack begin?

To cut down the customary right of self-defence beyond the *Caroline* doctrine does not make sense in times when the speed and power of weapons of attack have greatly increased. For instance, in the case of nuclear missiles, when does an armed attack occur: when the missile lands, when it takes off or when there is the intention to fire it?

In its first Report in 1946 the United Nations Atomic Energy Commission stated:

> 'In consideration of the problem of violations of the terms of the Treaty or Convention (limiting the manufacture of nuclear weapons), it should also be borne in mind that a violation might be of so grave a character as to give rise to the inherent right of self-defence recognised in Article 51.'

Thus it may be argued that art 51 is couched in 1946 terms and has not come to terms with nuclear weapons. Today weapons no longer depend on their being seen and clearly visible and therefore art 51 is not specific enough for the commander in the field who must determine if an armed attack has occurred.

Some writers still argue that anticipatory self-defence is incompatible with the Charter.

They argue that art 51 is an exception to art 2(4) and that it is a general rule of interpretation that exceptions to a principle should be interpreted restrictively, so as not to undermine the principle. They also point out that some collective defence treaties such as the North Atlantic Treaty, based on art 51, provide only for defence against armed attacks, and not for defence against imminent dangers of armed attacks.

A further argument against the right of anticipatory self-defence is that the question whether an attack is imminent is subjective and open to abuse. A state can never be absolutely certain about the other side's intentions and may mistakenly launch a pre-emptive strike in a moment of crisis when no actual threat in fact exists. Also, allowing an aggressor state to strike the first blow may not in practice result in military disadvantage to the innocent state as first strikes in inter-state hostilities are seldom conclusive.

Proportionality and necessity

The requirement of proportionality is not mentioned in art 51. However, customary international law clearly states that force used in self-defence must be proportionate to the seriousness of the attack and justified by the seriousness of the danger. The Court in the *Nicaragua Case* accepted that the requirements of proportionality and necessity were fundamental to any exercise of the right of self-defence.

It is generally agreed that necessity and proportionality means that self-defence must not be retaliatory or punitive. The issue of proportionality and necessity was examined by the ICJ in the *Case Concerning Oil Platforms: Islamic Republic of Iran v United States of America* (2003) 42 ILM 1334.

The actions giving rise to the dispute occurred in the context of an armed conflict between Iran and Iraq which started on 22 September 1980, when Iran was invaded by Iraqi military forces. The war, which lasted eight years, started as a land war but from 1984, when Iraq began attacking oil tankers on their way to and from Iranian ports in order to disrupt Iran's oil export, also affected the Persian Gulf. This so-called 'Tanker War' lasted till 1988. During that time commercial vessels and warships of various nationalities, including neutral vessels, were attacked by aircraft, helicopters, missiles or warships, or struck mines in the waters of the Persian Gulf. Whilst Iran denied any responsibility for these attacks, other than incidents involving vessels refusing a proper request for stop and search, the USA attributed responsibility for some of these incidents to Iran.

The ICJ examined two specific attacks by the USA military forces. The first took place on 19 October 1987. On 16 October 1987 the Kuwaiti tanker *Sea Isle City*, reflagged to the USA, was struck, according to the USA, by an Iranian missile near Kuwait harbour. In response, three days later, the USA attacked and destroyed Iranian offshore oil production installations in the Reshadat (Rostam) complex.

The second took place on 18 April 1988. On 14 April 1988 the warship *USS Samuel B Roberts* struck a mine in international waters near Bahrein. Four days later, in retaliation, the USA attacked and destroyed oil production installations in the Nasr (Sirri) and Salman (Sassan) complexes. The alleged justification for the attacks was presented by the USA to the UN Security Council. The USA claimed that it acted in self-defence. Unlike the incident of 19 October 1987 the attacks on the Salman and Nasr platforms were not isolated operations as they did in fact form part of a much more extensive military operation called 'Praying Mantis', during which the USA attacked other Iranian naval vessels and aircraft.

It is important to note that the Rostam, the Salman and the Nasr complexes were not producing any oil at the time of the USA attacks. These installations were under repair as they had been badly damaged by previous Iraqi attacks.

The ICJ followed the customary international law on the use of force whilst defining and applying the concept of 'an armed attack' and the principle of proportionality and necessity. In respect of the requirement of proportionality, the attack of 19 October 1987 might, had the Court found that it was necessary in response to the *Sea Isle City* incident as an armed attack committed by Iran, have been considered proportionate. In the case of the attack of 18 April 1988, however, which was conceived and executed as part of a more extensive operation entitled 'Operation Praying Mantis' and constituted a response to the mining, by an unidentified agency, of a single United States warship, which was severely damaged but not sunk, without loss of life, the ICJ found that neither 'Operation Praying Mantis' as a whole, nor even that part of it that destroyed the Salman and Nasr platforms, could be regarded, in the circumstances of the case, as a proportionate use of force in self-defence.

The only conclusion that one reaches on the requirements of the principle of proportionality and necessity is that it all depends on the particular circumstances. Each case must be assessed separately in order to establish whether or not, on the factual basis, the use of force can be considered as necessary and proportionate. Also in many cases where a state is justifying the use of force on the basis of self-defence, proportionality and necessity will be of assistance to reject such a justification without embarking upon a more controversial doctrinal dispute regarding the extent of the right to self-defence under customary international law.

The attack giving rise to the right of self-defence need not be directed against a state's territory

For example, art 6 of the North Atlantic Treaty 1949 provides:

> 'For the purpose of Article 5 an armed attack on one or more of the Parties is deemed to include an armed attack on the territory of any of the Parties in Europe or North America, on the Algerian Departments of France, on the occupation forces of any Party in Europe, on the islands under the jurisdiction of any Party in the North Atlantic area north of the Tropic of Cancer or on the vessels or aircraft in this area of any of the Parties.'

In the *Corfu Channel Case* (1949) ICJ Rep 4 the ICJ held that the British warships attacked while exercising their right of innocent passage through Albanian territorial waters were entitled to be at action stations and to return fire if necessary.

Self-defence in the context of the military intervention of the United States and its allies in Afghanistan

On 11 September 2001 four US civilian planes with passengers on board were hijacked from various US airports. They were on internal flights. The hijackers murdered some passengers and crew, took control of the planes and deliberately crashed two of them into the twin towers of the World Trade Centre in New York and one into the Pentagon building in Washington DC. The fourth plane was probably intended to be crashed into Camp David, the summer residence of the US President, but it seems that the passengers and the crew attacked the hijackers and the plane crashed in a wooded area in Pennsylvania. All passengers, crew, thousands of people on the ground and the hijackers died in the attacks.

US President George W Bush blamed Islamic fundamentalists, the Al-Qaeda, led by Osama bin Laden for the carnage. He stated that there was compelling evidence pointing to Osama bin Laden and his organisation's involvement in the attacks. However, for security reasons, this evidence could not be made public.

Al-Qaeda is a terrorist organisation which was founded in the early 1990s and has been led at all times by Osama bin Laden, a national of Saudi Arabia. Al-Qaeda's main objective is to destroy the US and its allies. In February 1998 Osama bin Laden issued a 'fatwa', a decree addressed to all Muslims to fight jihad or 'holy war', which calls for the killing of Americans and their civilian and military allies as a religious duty for each and every Muslim to be carried out in whichever country they are. It is alleged that Al-Qaeda has been responsible for conducting a number of terrorist attacks against the US, in particular the bombing of US embassies in Kenya and Tanzania on 7 August 1998.

Osama bin Laden established a dozen camps for training his militants in Afghanistan. His relationship with the Taliban, the ruling Afghan regime in Afghanistan until the military intervention of the US, started when the Taliban was engaged in a civil war to control the whole of Afghanistan in the 1990s. At that time bin Laden provided the Taliban regime with troops, arms and money to fight its opponents. Once the Taliban won the civil war it provided Osama bin Laden with a safe haven and allowed him to establish training camps.

The Taliban refused many times to extradite Osama bin Laden to the US. It also refused to comply with the UN Security Council Resolutions: see Resolution 1277 (1999), 1267 (1999), 1189 (1998), 1193 (1998) and 1214 (1998) which requested the Taliban to surrender bin Laden so he could be brought to justice. Since 1998 various non-military sanctions were imposed by the Security Council upon the Taliban for harbouring Osama bin Laden and his organisation. In 1999 the Security Council determined that the Taliban's failure to comply with its resolutions constituted a 'threat to international peace and security'.

In the aftermath of the attacks on World Trade Centre and Washington the US President requested the Taliban to hand over Osama bin Laden or to face the consequences. The Taliban regime refused to extradite Osama bin Laden to the US, although it did offer to send him to stand trial before an Islamic court established in a neutral country. It seemed reasonable at the time that the Taliban wanted some evidence of Osama bin Laden's involvement in the September 11 attacks. Further, the possibility of bin Laden having a fair trial in the US seemed rather doubtful given the atmosphere created by the US media and the request by US President to have Bin Laden's 'head on a plate'. The only appropriate forum for a trial of Osama bin Laden is certainly an international court made up of representatives of all major legal systems, including some jurists from Muslim countries.

The UN Security Council strongly condemned the terrorist attacks on the US in two resolutions: Resolution 1368 passed on 12 October 2001 and Resolution 1373 passed on 28 September 2001. Both explicitly recognised the right to self-defence on the part of member states and both determined that the attacks constituted 'a threat to international peace and security'.

On 7 October 2001 the US and its most faithful ally, the UK, started a military intervention in Afghanistan aimed at hunting down Osama bin Laden and bringing him to justice, and destroying his terrorist organisation, Al-Qaeda, and the Taliban regime that had supported them. The US and the UK justified their military action on the ground of the inherent right to self-defence. On the day of commencement of the military intervention in Afghanistan the Chargé d'Affaires of the Permanent Mission of the UK to the United Nations sent a letter to the President of the Security Council informing him that military forces were employed against targets in Afghanistan 'in exercise of the inherent right of individual and collective self-defence recognised in art 51 [of the UN Charter], following the terrorist outrage of 11 September, to avert the continuing threat of attacks from the same source': http://globalresearch.ca.articles/VAR109A.html. The same justification was provided by the US's representative to the United Nations: see the US Ambassador to the UN John D Negroponte's letter of 7 October 2001 informing the President of the Security Council of the commencement of the US military action in Afghanistan, ibid.

The first point which needs to be addressed is whether the military intervention of the US and its allies was authorised by the Security Council; if so, the legitimacy of their action would be established under international law. In this respect it is important to examine Security Council Resolution 1368 (2001) and 1373 (2001). Both Resolutions in their preamble refer to the inherent right of self-defence in the context of terrorist attacks. The matter arises whether or not such a reference may be construed as an authorisation of the Security Council granted to the US to use force. It is important to emphasise a number of points.

1. Resolution 1368 was passed the day after the terrorist attacks took place and at that time it was unclear who was behind the terrorist attacks and whether they were directed from abroad or internally. Resolution 1373 was passed on 28 September 2001 and, although the members of the Security Council had by then had time to reflect upon the matter, the Resolution neither mentions the Taliban nor Osama bin Laden as being responsible for the terrorist attacks on the US.
2. The reference to the right of self-defence was part of the preamble of both Resolutions and not of their operative part.
3. No explicit authorisation is granted in the above Resolutions to the US to use armed force. In the past when the Security Council was authorising the use of force the relevant resolutions were very clear and unambiguous given the seriousness of the measures to be taken against a culprit state.
4. Resolution 1368 explicitly expressed the Council 'readiness to take all necessary steps to respond to the terrorist attacks of 11 September'. Resolution 1373, relying on Chapter VII, calls on all states to 'prevent and suppress the financing of terrorist acts in general and international terrorism in particular by freezing financial assets of persons who commit, or attempt to commit, terrorist acts or participate in or facilitate the commission of terrorism acts'. Furthermore, Resolution 1373 calls on all states to refrain from providing any support to persons or entities involved in international terrorism.
5. Neither Resolution specifies the state against which the US is allowed to use armed force. About 60 states support terrorist organisations. Therefore, it seems preposterous to conclude that the Security Council was authorising the US to use force against all states supporting international terrorism without specifically mentioning any of them and in circumstances where it was uncertain who was behind the terrorist attacks carried out against the US on 11 September 2001.
6. In the letters addressed to the Security Council neither the government of the US nor the government of the UK referred to any existing, actual or implied, authorisation of the Security Council to commence a military intervention in Afghanistan. Certainly, had such an authorisation been in existence both governments would have made an explicit reference to it.

In the light of the above it is submitted that neither Resolution authorised the US and its allies to use force against Afghanistan. The Resolutions have linked the terrorist attacks with the right to self-defence and have consequently recognised that a state may be entitled to invoke the right to self-defence in the context of terrorist attacks, provided that the requirements of art 51 of the UN Charter are satisfied.

By ruling out any authorisation of the Security Council as a possible justification for the military intervention of the US and its allies in Afghanistan the only possible ground for such an intervention in conformity with international law would be the right to self-defence.

The concept of self-defence under international law is the subject of many controversies. However, there is an agreement, in the light of the judgment of the ICJ in the *Military and Paramilitary Activities in and against Nicaragua: Nicaragua* v *US (Merits)* (1986) ICJ Rep 14 at para 176 that art 51 of the UN Charter preserves the pre-existing customary law on the matter. The ICJ stated that:

> 'As regards the suggestion that the areas covered by the two sources of law [art 51 of the UN Charter and customary international law] are identical, the Court observes that the United Nations Charter, the convention to which most of the United States arguments is directed, by no means covers the whole area of the regulation of the use of force in international relations. On one essential point, this treaty itself refers to pre-existing customary international law: this reference to customary law is contained in the actual text of Article 51, which mentions the "inherent right" [in the French text the "droit naturel"] of individual or collective self-defence, which "nothing in the present Charter shall impair" and which applies in the event of an armed attack. The Court therefore finds that Article 51 of the Charter is only meaningful on the basis that there is a "natural" or "inherent" right to self-defence, and it is hard to see how this can be other than of a customary nature, even if its present content has been confirmed and influenced by the Charter.'

From the above it is also reasonable to presume that art 51 refers to customary law prior to the adoption of the UN Charter, and thus not exclusively to customary rules established in the *Caroline Case* (above). In the *Nicaragua Case* (above) the ICJ (in the context of collective self-defence, but nevertheless this also applies to the exercise of individual self-defence) stated that under both art 51 of the UN Charter and customary international law a state claiming the right to self-defence must be a victim of an 'armed attack'. Therefore, for a state to rely on the concept of self-defence it is necessary that 'an armed attack occurs'. In such an event a victim state is entitled to repel an attack that is ongoing or imminent until the UN Security Council can take necessary steps to restore international peace and security.

The attacks on the twin towers of the World Trade Centre in New York and other targets in the US are clearly within the definition of an 'armed attack' committed by armed bands. However, such an attack must be on behalf of a particular state. In the General Assembly Resolution 3314 (XXIX) on the Definition of Aggression art 2(g) qualifies as an act of aggression:

> 'The sending by or behalf of a state of armed bands, groups, irregulars, or mercenaries, which carry out acts of armed force against another state of such gravity as to amount to the acts listed above, or its substantial involvement therein.'

In the *Nicaragua Case* the ICJ stated that an armed attack occurs either when a state directly sends troops into another state or when it sends armed bands 'which carry out acts of armed force against another state [amounting to] actual armed attack by regular forces'. Thus, the crucial matter is whether the terrorists involved in the 11 of September attacks were acting on behalf of the Taliban. First, there is no evidence that either the Taliban or Osama bin Laden was involved in the attacks. The lack of any reference to them in both Security Council's Resolutions as being responsible for the terrorist attacks against the US is, at least, puzzling. Furthermore, as Professor Louis Henkin stated, art 51 is:

> '... limited to cases of armed attack that are generally beyond doubt; a state's responsibility for acts of terrorism is rarely beyond doubt and difficult to prove ... Article 51 gives a right ... to defend against an armed attack. This right does not allow retaliation for armed attack ... or [force] to deter future attacks.'

In the *Nicaragua Case* the ICJ clearly stated that:

> '... while the concept of an armed attack includes the despatch by one state of armed bands into the territory of another state, the supply of arms and other support to such bands cannot be equated with armed attack. Nevertheless, such activities may well constitute a breach of the principle of the non-use of force and an intervention in the internal affairs of a state, that is, a form of conduct which is certainly wrongful, but is of lesser gravity than an armed attack.'

The ICJ concluded that whilst an armed attack gives rise to the exercise of the right to self-defence, the use of force of a lesser gravity cannot allow the use of force in response but may justify the use of appropriate and proportionate counter-measures.

There is no doubt that the Taliban provided support for Osama bin Laden and the Al-Qaeda, mainly by allowing them to stay in Afghanistan and to operate camps for the training of terrorists. However, on the basis of the facts which are commonly known, it is highly improbable that the Taliban was sending members of Al-Qaeda network to the US with a view to committing terrorist acts. It seems that the US was not a victim of 'an armed attack' within the meaning of international law and therefore it has exceeded the limits imposed on the exercise of the right of self-defence.

Self-defence in the context of the unilateral use of force against Iraq by the US and the UK

At dawn on 20 March 2003 the US and its allies, including the UK, launched a military campaign against Iraq despite lack of authorisation to use force from the UN Security Council. Although Iraqi resistance for a few days proved greater than expected, six weeks later all objectives of the US military intervention against Iraq were achieved: the US and allied forces 'liberated' Iraq and the regime of Saddam Hussein was toppled.

In the light of the above the issue of what justifications, if any, can the US government invoke in order to justify its military intervention in Iraq is of crucial importance for the very existence of international law. In this respect it is necessary to examine US Congress Resolution HJ 114, passed on 2 October 2002, which authorised US President George W Bush to use whatever means he deemed necessary, including force, against Iraq. This Resolution states the following reasons for such authorisation.

1. *Iraq has not complied with various UN resolutions.* In this respect it is important to note that it is the role of the Security Council, as the main UN body responsible for maintenance of international peace and security, to deal with the non-compliance of Iraq. For that purpose the Security Council can use all necessary measures, including the use of force under art 42 of the UN Charter. Further, an authorisation from the UN Security Council would have neither allowed a full invasion of Iraq nor the throwing out of Saddam Hussein. Under the UN Charter any use of force must be consistent with the purposes of the UN. The threat that Iraq posed was confined to the possession of weapons of mass destruction and therefore any UN-led military action would have been confined to the removal and destruction of such weapons.

2. *Iraq has stockpiles of chemical weapons, has an advanced nuclear development programme and a substantial biological weapons programme, which are a threat to the security of the US and Iraq's neighbours.* Under UN Security Council Resolution 668, which formalised a ceasefire after the defeat of Iraq in the 1991 Gulf War, Iraq was called upon to destroy, remove and render harmless all chemical and biological weapons and all stocks of agents and components, together with all research, development, support and manufacturing facilities for ballistic missiles with a range greater than 150 km. In order to ensure compliance with the Resolution an international body was set up (UNSCOM) to inspect Iraq's weapons facilities. Since October 1997 Iraq refused to co-operate with UNSCOM, in that Iraq had denied access to the so-called sovereign and presidential sites and had excluded some members of UNSCOM from carrying out inspections on the ground that they worked for intelligence agencies in their respective countries. In 1998 UNSCOM inspectors left Iraq.

Since the 11 September 2001 terrorist attack the US administration has taken a very strong stand against terrorism and rogue states. On 29 January 2002 President George W Bush in his first State of the Union Address said that Iran, Iraq and North Korea 'constitute an axis of evil, aiming to threaten the peace of the world'. Since then the US President focused on Iraq, threatening to launch a military campaign to force Iraq to comply with UN Security Council resolutions. Under the growing pressure from the US, on 16 September 2002 Iraq expressed its willingness to readmit weapons inspectors.

On 8 November 2002 the UN Security Council, after lengthy negotiations, adopted Resolution 1441 which confirmed that Iraq had been in breach of its obligations under relevant UN resolutions. Resolution 1441 warned Iraq that it would face 'serious consequences' for non-compliance and required Iraq to 'immediately, unconditionally and actively' co-operate with weapons inspectors from the UN Monitoring, Verification and Inspection Commission (UNMOVIC) and the International Atomic Energy Agency (IAEA), and to give immediate, unimpeded, unconditional and unrestricted access to, inter alia, 'any and all, including underground, areas, facilities, buildings, equipment, records and means of transport which they wish to inspect'. Also Resolution 1441 required the Iraqi government to provide, within 30 days, full and complete declaration of all aspects of its programme relating to the development of chemical, biological and nuclear weapons. A 12,000-page declaration on weapons of mass destruction was submitted by Iraq to the UN on 8 December 2002, which was immediately challenged by the US.

Until the outbreak of war inspectors from UNMOVIC and the IAEA did not find any convincing evidence. On 27 January 2003 both Hans Blix (in charge of UNMOVIC) and Mohamed El Baradei (from IAEA) reported to the UN Security Council that, apart from a dozen empty chemical warheads and some documents relating to a past nuclear programme, the two months' inspection had brought no conclusive evidence that Iraq was pursuing its weapons programmes. Hans Blix in his report stated that although there was no overt obstruction of the inspectors there was lack of 'pro-active co-operation' from Iraq. The UN inspectors asked the UN Security Council for more time to complete their mission. However, the US administration was unwilling to wait much longer and argued that after 12 years of non-compliance with UN resolutions the burden of proof must be on Iraq.

Within the UN Security Council, apart from the US and the UK, other permanent members voiced their opposition to a quick decision by the US to take military action. They were unconvinced that Iraq posed an immediate danger and argued that inspections, backed up by the threat of force, were sufficient to ensure that Iraq was kept under control. Furthermore, the lack of evidence of any weapons of mass destruction, and the fact that Saadam Hussein was co-operating with the UN inspectors, played an important role in the refusal of the majority of the UN Security Council to adopt a second resolution authorising the use of force against Iraq. Even non-permanent members of the Security Council traditionally within the US sphere of influence – such as Mexico, Chile and Pakistan – did not back the US-led military intervention in Iraq.

The UN inspectors were ordered to leave Iraq 24 hours before the first bombs fell on Baghdad. According to Hans Blix, evidence for war was 'very, very shaky'. On 22 April 2003 Hans Blix accused the US and the UK of deliberately undermining his efforts to locate Iraq's banned weapons before the war. He warned the UN Security Council that only UN inspectors, and not the team being assembled by the US, would be able to provide an objective assessment of any materials that might be found in Iraq. Mr Blix added that it was 'conspicuous that so far [US inspectors] have not stumbled upon anything evident', although he did not rule out that evidence of banned weapons might yet be uncovered (D Usborne, 'Hans Blix v The US', *The Independent*, 23 April 2003, p1).

After the invasion, neither the US team of experts set up to investigate Iraq's programmes on nuclear, chemical, biological and missile weapons (see: Report of the Special Advisor to the Director of Central Intelligence on Iraq's Weapons of Mass Destruction, http://www.cia.gov/cia/reports/iraq_wmd_2004) nor the UN commission that was in charge of disarming Iraq of weapons of mass destruction (see the latest report of UNMOVIC: UN News Service) found any credible evidence of their existence. The failure to uncover any evidence of nuclear weapons or of any significant capability to develop other weapons of mass destruction challenged the US's rationale for invading Iraq.

3. *The US also stated that Iraq posed a threat to its immediate neighbours.* None had complained to the UN Security Council.

4. *Iraq supports terrorists groups and has provided assistance to the 11 September 2001 attacks on the US.* According to Saudi Prince Turki bin Faisal, the former intelligence chief of the Saudi intelligence, Osama bin Laden considers Saddam Hussein 'as an apostate, an infidel, or someone who is not worthy of being a fellow Muslim': S Zunes, 'Foreign Policy in Focus Report: Seven Reasons to Oppose a US Invasion of Iraq', http://www.fpif.org/ papers/iraq2-body.htlm. When Iraq invaded Kuwait in 1990 Osama bin Laden offered to raise an army of thousands of Mujaheddin fighters to liberate Kuwait. Given both the mutual distrust between Saddam Hussein and Osama bin Laden and the incompatible ideologies of Saddam Hussein and Al-Qaeda, the UK government was always very sceptical about there being any connection between them. The US government viewed the situation differently. President Bush on numerous occasions claimed that one could not distinguish between Al-Qaeda and Saddam Hussein. Without providing any evidence, he made statements about a bond between pre-war Iraq and Al-Qaeda. After the US media began demanding proof of the allegations, Dick Cheney admitted, in January 2004, that there was no 'smoking gun' to prove the claim. This issue was conclusively settled when the 11 September Commission released its report investigating the 11 September attacks on the US. The Commission found no credible evidence linking Saddam's regime with Al-Qaeda.

5. *Iraq has demonstrated its continued hostility towards the US by firing on the US and Coalition forces engaged in enforcing UN resolutions and also in the 1993 attempt to assassinate President Bush (Senior).* The non-fly zones over North and South Iraq were created by US, the UK and France as a response to UN Security Council Resolution 688 condemning repressive measures used by the Iraqi government against its minorities: the Kurds in the North and the Shia Muslims in the South. Resolution 688 condemned the action of Iraq against its minorities but did not specify that the Security Council was acting under Chapter VII and did

not contain any authorisation for the creation of such zones. France admitted that the creation of non-fly zones was in breach of international law and had since withdrawn. In 1998 President Clinton authorised three days of bombing of Iraq, and the US and the UK had continued to bomb Iraq whenever Iraqi air defences had locked onto their aircraft. In this respect it can be said that as the setting up of the non-fly zones had no justification in international law Iraq, by firing on the US and the UK aircraft, had exercised its right to self-defence.

In respect of the attempt to assassinate US President George Bush (Senior) there is no conclusive evidence that Iraq was behind it. Furthermore, the attempt took place almost ten years ago and the response of the US is clearly disproportionate and cannot justify a pre-emptive attack on Iraq.

6. *Saddam Hussein's regime should be ousted and a new democratic government should replace that regime.* There is no doubt that Saddam Hussein has committed the worst breaches of human rights, that he used chemical and biological weapons against his own people (the Kurds) and against Iran, and that he certainly posed a threat to international peace and security as in the past he invaded his neighbours unprovoked: Iran and Kuwait. Nevertheless, international law prohibits any intervention in internal matters of a state by any other state, inter alia, art 2(2) of the UN Charter and the 1965 GA Declaration on the Inadmissibility of Intervention in the Domestic Affairs of States and the Protection of Their Independence and Sovereignty. This is reinforced by the judgment of the ICJ in the *Nicaragua Case (Merits)*. Only the Security Council is empowered to authorise the use of force for humanitarian purposes.

It is submitted that the reasons for the authorisation of the use of force by the US against Iraq contained in Resolution HJ 114 of the US Senate are neither justified in law nor in fact. In addition, Resolution HJ 114 is in breach of the US Constitution taking into account the fact that its art 6, clause 2 requires the US to settle all disputes by peaceful means. As a member of the UN the US is obliged to comply with its obligations deriving from the UN Charter, the most important being the prohibition of use of or the threat of force contained in art 2(4) which has become a norm of ius cogens. The US is in breach of the UN Charter unless it can plead self-defence.

It results from the above that the US administration can only rely on the concept of anticipatory self-defence. Whether the anticipatory self-defence is recognised by the international community is doubtful and even if it is it is subject to stringent limitations. Public international law recognises that self-defence can be relied upon only on the clearest evidence of a great emergency and as a measure of last resort. This is not the case in respect of Iraq as there was no evidence of any imminent armed attack to be launched by Iraq against the US, and there is no evidence to link Iraq with the attacks of 11 September 2001. In addition, any military action must be proportional to the seriousness of the attack and justified by the seriousness of its danger. The military action of the US against Iraq has gone beyond the current limits of the concept of self-defence. The perception that the US administration has of self-defence was defined on 17 September 2002 by the US President in his speech on the National Security Strategy of the USA when he stated that 'as a matter of common sense and self-defence, America will act against [...] emerging threats before they are fully formed'.

The consequences of this new comprehension of the concept of self-defence were summed up by Alan Simpson (a UK MP) in the following terms:

'... if the world is being asked to move from a doctrine of containment and deterrence and towards a different doctrine about pre-emptive strikes, regime change, attacks and displacement of potential enemies or unsympathetic regimes, the implications for the planet are enormous': Alan Simpson, Hansard, 24 September 2002, Col 81.

It is also important to note that the International Commission of Jurists (ICJ), a consultative body of the UN, on 18 March 2003, warned the US that any military action without authorisation from the UN Security Council would constitute an act of aggression. The ICJ stated that:

'The ICJ today expressed its deep dismay that a small number of states are poised to launch an outright illegal invasion of Iraq, which amounts to a war of aggression. The United States, the United Kingdom and Spain have signalled their intent to use force in Iraq in spite of the absence of a Security Council Resolution. There is no other plausible legal basis for this attack. In the absence of such Security Council authorisation, no country may use force against another country, except in self-defence against an armed attack': www.ulb.ac.be/droit/cdi/appel_irak.htlm.

Kofi Annan, the current Secretary General of the UN, condemned the US led invasion of Iraq as illegal and in breach of the UN Charter (BBC News, 18 September 2004).

Since the establishment of the UN the international community has never been faced with the situation where two founding members of the UN and two permanent members of the Security Council decided to ignore international law and the fundamental principles of the UN Charter. Both the US and the UK have seriously damaged the UN and NATO and, more importantly, the principle of multilateralism. The US war of aggression against Iraq constitutes a great threat to the rule of international law and has introduced a new world order in which 'might is right'.

No state, even the most powerful in the world, should be careless or arrogant towards the institutions and ideals that have underpinned our civilisation.

16.6 Collective self-defence

Article 51 was introduced into the Charter primarily to safeguard the consistency of the Pan-American regional system of mutual defence with the new regime for maintaining peace established by the Charter. To the South American states the most significant aspect of self-defence was that it could justify collective action. In this respect the Colombian representative said at the San Francisco Conference in 1945:

> '... an aggression against one American state constitutes an aggression against all the American states, and all of them exercise their right of legitimate defence by giving support to the state attacked, in order to repel aggression. This is what is meant by the right of collective self-defence.'

By referring to the 'inherent right of individual or collective self-defence' art 51 has provided a legal basis upon which a number of regional security systems have been founded. However, art 51 does not form part of Chapter VIII which regulates regional arrangements. This is important because Chapter VIII subordinates regional arrangements to the Security Council and specifically directs, in art 53, that enforcement action should not be begun regionally without the Council's approval.

Article 51 was deliberately transferred at the San Francisco Conference from Chapter VIII to Chapter VII with the result that the right of collective self-defence is entirely independent of the existence of a regional arrangement, and is immune from the paralysing effect of the veto.

Mutual assistance treaties for collective self-defence

The North Atlantic Treaty 1949 provides under art 5:

> 'The Parties agree that an armed attack against one or more of them in Europe or North America shall be considered an attack against them all; and consequently they agree that, if such an armed attack occurs, each of them, in exercise of the right of individual or collective self-defence recognised by Article 51 of the Charter of the United Nations, will assist the Party or Parties so attacked by taking forthwith, individually and in concert with the other Parties, such action as it deems necessary, including the use of armed force, to restore and maintain the security of the North Atlantic area.
>
> Any such armed attack and all measures taken as a result thereof shall immediately be reported to the Security Council. Such measures shall be terminated when the Security Council has taken the measures necessary to restore and maintain international peace and security.'

The Inter-American Treaty of Reciprocal Assistance (Rio Treaty) 1947 provides under art 3:

> '(1) The High Contracting Parties agree that an armed attack by any state against an American state shall be considered as an attack against all the American states and, consequently, each one of the said Contracting Parties undertakes to assist in meeting the attack in the exercise of the inherent right of individual or collective self-defence recognised by Article 51 of the Charter of the United Nations ...
>
> (4) Measures of self-defence provided for under this Article may be taken until the Security Council of the United Nations has taken the measures necessary to maintain international peace and security.'

These mutual assistance treaties should accord with the United Nations Charter. Article 103 of the Charter provides that:

'In the event of a conflict between the obligations of the Members of the United Nations under the present Charter and their obligations under any other international agreement, their obligations under the present Charter shall prevail.'

The scope of collective self-defence

Article 51 of the Charter refers to 'individual or collective self-defence'. Professor Bowett argued that this right of collective self-defence is merely a combination of individual rights of self-defence: 'states may exercise collectively a right which any of them might have exercised individually'. Thus, Bowett argued that no state may defend another state unless each state could have legally exercised a right of individual self-defence in the same circumstances. Thus, the USSR could not defend Cuba against attack because an attack on Cuba does not affect the rights and interests of the USSR.

The above view was based mainly on analogies drawn from English law. At the time when Bowett was writing English law did not allow one person to use force in defence of another person unless there was some close relationship between the two parties.

According to Bowett, therefore, if a state is not acting in its own self-defence it can only justify its involvement in the defence of another state if acting under Chapter VIII with the approval of the Security Council. Article 2(4) of the Charter is an attempt to limit conflicts and the maintenance of international peace and security should be in the hands of the Security Council.

State practice and the dicta of the ICJ do not support Bowett's view. Professor Brownlie, for example, argues that state practice shows that if any state asks for assistance, other states may go and help that state to defend itself. For example, the US in justifying its participation in the Vietnam conflict – or, later, justifying the sending of troops to Saudi Arabia – argued, inter alia, that international law permitted a right of collective self-defence even where one party (in this case, the US) did not have an individual right of self-defence.

In the *Nicaragua Case* (1986) ICJ Rep 14 the majority of the Court put forward a two-fold test regarding the exercise of collective self-defence. The state under attack must have declared itself to be under attack, and must request the assistance of the third state. This approach was contested by Jennings in his dissenting opinion:

'Whatever collective self-defence means, it does not mean vicarious defence; for that way the notion is indeed open to abuse ... The assisting state surely must, by going to the victim state's assistance, be also ... in some measure defending itself.'

Jennings, therefore, adopted Bowett's view of collective self-defence, ie that collective self-defence extends to the collective exercise of individual rights of self-defence.

Kelson in his *Law of the United Nations* has pointed out the dangers to world order which are involved in art 51. Two groups of states centred on rival Great

Powers may each decide that resort to force is justifiable in collective self-defence against the other and the exercise of the veto may prevent the Security Council from making a determination under art 39. This may result in a war between two rival groups, each allegedly acting in self-defence, and the Security Council being unable to make a determination even of a threat to the peace.

This difficulty has in some respects been overcome by the Uniting for Peace Resolution which is founded upon the principle that the General Assembly and individual Members have a secondary responsibility for the maintenance of international peace which comes into play when the Security Council has failed to discharge its primary responsibility. Under the Resolution the Assembly may investigate and pronounce upon any resort to force, including alleged acts of self-defence, provided that a two-thirds majority can be obtained.

For example, on 1 February 1951 the General Assembly, acting under the Uniting for Peace Resolution, expressly found that Communist China had itself engaged in aggression in Korea by giving direct aid and assistance to those who were already committing aggression in Korea.

16.7 Controversial uses of force

Since the adoption of the UN Charter member states have, in addition to the right of self-defence, relied on a number of controversial grounds to justify their use of military force. Furthermore, international law itself has evolved in that it allows the use of force by people entitled to exercise their right to self-determination (this matter is dealt with in Chapter 14).

This section examines the possible exceptions to the prohibition of the use of force based on customary international law.

Intervention to protect a state's own nationals and property abroad

Nineteenth-century jurists considered as lawful the use of force to protect the lives and property of nationals. The theory behind this is that nationals of a state are an extension of the state itself. In this way intervention to protect the state's nationals is reconcilable with the theory of self-defence – an injury to the national is an injury to the state. This thesis has, however, been the subject of much debate and controversy, in particular subsequent to the Anglo-French invasion of the Suez Canal in 1956 and the Israeli raid on Entebbe in 1976.

The Anglo-French Invasion of Suez in 1956
In July 1956 Egypt nationalised the Suez Canal Company, a company in which there were considerable British and French interests. On 29 October 1956 Israel invaded Egyptian territory in the area of the Suez Canal zone. France and the UK issued a joint ultimatum to Egypt and Israel demanding that they call a cease-fire, withdraw

their troops from the Suez Canal area and allow British and French troops to be stationed along the Canal. The ultimatum was not complied with and on 21 October British and French troops invaded the Canal area.

Both justified their action on the grounds of the protection of their nationals in Egypt, although other justifications were also invoked such as the danger to shipping in the Canal, the danger to the enormously valuable installation of the Canal itself and the effect on many nations of the blocking of the Canal.

The international community regarded the Suez invasion by the British and the French as illegal.

The 1976 Entebbe raid
On 27 June 1976 an Air France airliner bound for Paris from Tel Aviv was hijacked over Greece. Two of the hijackers were West German nationals and the other two held Arab passports. The airliner was diverted to Entebbe airport in Uganda. The Jewish passengers, some 100 persons, were separated from the other passengers and detained, whilst the others were released. The hijackers demanded the release of some 50 Palestinian terrorists imprisoned in various countries.

Following reports that Uganda was in fact helping the hijackers, on 2 July 1976 Israel flew soldiers to Entebbe and rescued the hostages by force. The hijackers were killed together with some Ugandan soldiers. Extensive damage was caused to Ugandan aircraft and the airport.

Subsequent to the Israeli intervention in Entebbe, two draft resolutions were submitted to the Security Council: one by Tanzania, Libya and Benin condemning Israel for the violation of the territorial integrity and sovereignty of Uganda; and one by the UK and the US condemning hijacking but affirming the necessity to respect the territorial integrity and sovereignty of all states. After much debate within the Security Council neither resolution was adopted: the UK–US resolution failed to obtain the required nine votes in favour; the African resolution was not submitted to a vote.

The right to intervene to protect nationals abroad has been advanced as an alternative ground for intervention in a number of other cases. In December 1989, for example, following the intervention by 20,000 US troops in Panama, one of the grounds advanced by the Secretary of State, James Baker, justifying the action was that US nationals in Panama were under threat. The US similarly advanced such arguments six years previously in justification of the landing of US troops in Grenada. Both interventions were condemned by the UN General Assembly.

It is safe to say that in most cases where a state has relied on the justification that it was protecting its nationals abroad, the main objective of its military action has not been the protection of its nationals!

It is submitted that the right of a state to use force to protect its nationals abroad will not breach art 2(4) of the UN Charter in the following circumstances:

1. when there is a threat of imminent injury or death;
2. when a state in whose territory they are located is unwilling or unable to protect them;
3. when the intervention of a state is exclusively confined to the rescuing of its nationals;
4. when the action must be expected to save more lives than are likely to be destroyed.

There is sufficient evidence in state practice to suggest that there is a right to use force to protect nationals abroad when the above criteria are satisfied. In this respect the main criticism of the US intervention in 1980 intended to rescue the US hostages held in Iran concerned the strategy and tactics used by the US rather than the legality of the mission itself. The rescue mission was stuck in a sandstorm in the Iranian desert during which time much of the equipment was destroyed. Neither Iran nor other countries challenged the legality of the US mission although the ICJ, which at that time was adjudicating the *US Diplomatic and Consular Staff in Teheran Case: US* v *Iran* (1980) ICJ Rep 3, stated in its judgment that it 'cannot fail to express its concern in regard to the United States' incursion into Iran'. This was not because the US rescue mission was contrary to art 2(4) of the UN Charter but because it could 'undermine respect for the judicial process' as it occurred when the Court was deliberating.

Humanitarian intervention

It is necessary to distinguish humanitarian interventions authorised by the Security Council from those undertaken by a state or a group of states without such authority. Since the end of the Cold War humanitarian interventions have been authorised by the Security Council in a number of cases. That is in respect of Somalia, Haiti and East Timor. The actions did not raise any controversy, taking into account the role of the Security Council in the maintenance of international peace and security. In all cases the Security Council decided that there was a threat to international peace and security and took action under Chapter VII of the UN Charter.

The situation is different if a state or a group of states intervene militarily in order to protect the nationals of a third state. Amongst academic commentators the majority opinion is that international law does not allow humanitarian intervention. Operation of the doctrine would be open to abuse since only powerful states could undertake police measures of this sort; and when military operations were justified as 'humanitarian intervention' this was only one of several justifications offered and circumstances frequently indicated the presence of selfish motives.

Article 1 of the Declaration on the Inadmissibility of Intervention in the Domestic Affairs of States and the Protection of Their Independence and Sovereignty adopted in 1965 by the General Assembly clearly prohibits any intervention in internal matters of a state. It provides that:

'No state has the right to intervene, directly or indirectly, for any reason whatever, in the internal or external affairs of any other state. Consequently, armed intervention and all other forms of interference or attempted threats against the personality of the state or against its political, economic and cultural elements, are condemned.'

The topic of humanitarian intervention has been subject to many debates since the intervention of NATO in Kosovo. Before the disintegration of the Socialist Federal Republic of Yugoslavia (SFRY) Kosovo, a province of Yugoslavia, had 2.2 million inhabitants, 90 per cent of whom were ethnic Albanians. Kosovar Albanians enjoyed a large measure of autonomy under the Tito regime. However, from 1989 the autonomy was removed and Kosovar Albanians became targets of the Serb policy of 'ethnic cleansing'.

The situation in Kosovo was of concern to the Security Council. Its Resolution 1160 adopted on 31 March 1998 imposing a mandatory arms embargo also called upon the government of the Federal Republic of Yugoslavia (FRY) and the Kosovar Albanians to work together towards a political solution and stated that failure to achieve it would prompt 'additional measures'. Almost immediately after the adoption of Resolution 1160 violence in Kosovo intensified. In April 1998 the Contact Group for the former Yugoslavia, with the exception of Russia, agreed on the imposition of further sanctions. The UN Secretary-General, Kofi Annan, discussed possible military intervention in Kosovo with NATO. In September 1998 the Security Council adopted Resolution 1199 which determined the situation in Kosovo as a 'threat to peace and security in the region'. Resolution 1199 requested both parties to the conflict to stop hostilities and to return to negotiations. Within the Security Council it become obvious that Russia would not support any further measures against Yugoslavia, in particular measures involving the use of force. Therefore, Resolution 1199 was not sufficient to authorise NATO intervention but the escalation of violence, rape and general 'ethnic cleansing' perpetrated by Serbian forces against Kosovar Albanians living in Kosovo prompted NATO to announce imminent military action against the FRY for failure to comply with Resolution 1199. At that point the FRY agreed on a cease-fire and decided to sign two agreements: one with the Organisation for Security and Co-operation in Europe (OSCE), establishing a verification mission in Kosovo and containing an undertaking of the FRY to comply with the Security Council resolutions; and one with NATO establishing an air-verification mission over Kosovo.

On 29 October 1998 the Security Council adopted Resolution 1203 under Chapter VII endorsing the agreements and urging the FRY to promptly implement them. It also stated that the situation in Kosovo constituted a continuing threat to peace and security in the region. Soon after this Serb forces intensified their policy of 'ethnic cleansing' in Kosovo. In response NATO resumed its threats to intervene. The situation in Kosovo became alarming, an estimated 1.5 million people had been expelled from their homes, 5,000 Kosovars had been executed and some 225,000 Kosovar men were missing. The FRY did not intend to stop atrocities but under NATO's threats started peace negotiations with Albanian Kosovars in Rambouillet,

France in February 1999. Subsequently, the government of Slobodan Milosevic rejected the peace plan for Kosovo and in the face of inaction of the Security Council, paralysed by a threat of the veto by Russia, NATO forces began an aerial bombing campaign against Yugoslav military targets on 23 March 1999. The campaign ended on 10 June 1999 with the withdrawal of Serbian forces from Kosovo and the signing of the Military-Technical Agreement on 9 June 1999. The agreement was notified to the UN Secretary-General who urged both sides to comply. The Security Council adopted Resolution 1244 endorsing the termination of hostilities under the agreement.

In international law there are no convincing legal arguments justifying the legitimacy of the NATO intervention in Kosovo. Nevertheless, as many authors emphasised, the real justification lies in the reaction of the international community to NATO's intervention. The apparent legitimacy of the intervention of NATO has been widely accepted and appears to be based on the following.

1. A draft resolution submitted by Beloruss and Russia to the Security Council with a view to declaring NATO bombing of Yugoslavia illegal was rejected on 26 March 1999 by a majority of 12 votes.
2. On 13 April 1999, at the initiative of the Islamic Conference, the UN Commission on Human Rights adopted a resolution declaring the intervention of NATO lawful by 44 votes in favour, only two against (Russia and Cuba).
3. The General Assembly never condemned NATO's intervention, although it did condemn the US intervention in Grenada in 1983 and Panama in 1989.
4. The Security Council endorsed the agreement between NATO and the FRY in Resolution 1244 (1999).
5. The International Law Commission's Articles on Responsibility of States for Internationally Wrongful Acts clearly allow countermeasures to be taken by any state against a state violating peremptory norms of international law.
6. Another post-factum justification may be provided by the ICJ when, and if, it delivers its judgment in respect of the application brought by Bosnia-Herzegovina against Yugoslavia alleging violations of a number of the basic principles prohibiting the use of force by states, including the provision of assistance by Yugoslavia to anti-governmental forces engaged in acts of genocide in Bosnia-Herzegovina. To date, the International Court has issued two orders indicating provisional measures and a judgment confirming its jurisdiction to deal with the case. In the second order, in respect of the *Case Concerning the Application of the Convention on the Prevention and Punishment of the Crime of Genocide (Second Indication of Provisional Measures)* (1993) ICJ Rep 325 the Court acknowledged that many of the submissions made on behalf of Bosnia-Herzegovina concerning acts of genocide justified the Court's earlier order which declared that:

> 'The Government of the Federal Republic of Yugoslavia (Serbia and Montenegro) should immediately, in pursuance of its undertaking in the Convention on the

Prevention and Punishment of the Crime of Genocide of December 9, 1948, take all
measures within its power to prevent the commission of the crime of genocide.'

The government of Bosnia-Herzegovina has expressly requested clarification of
the rights of states to intervene to prevent genocide. This is clear from the Court's
second order which notes that the case raises three questions relating to
humanitarian intervention:

1. the duties of states to supply weapons to a state confronted with the atrocity of
   genocide within its territory;
2. the obligation of states which are contracting parties to the Genocide Convention
   1948 to intervene to prevent genocide;
3. the duties of contracting states to the Convention to assist a government fighting
   genocidal forces.

The Court did not, of course, in its second order, rule on the merits of the case but
referred on a number of occasions to international condemnation of the acts of
genocide being perpetrated by Yugoslav-sponsored forces. This condemnation gave
considerable support to the Court's decision to merely repeat the substance of its
first order in its second order which the Court considered should be 'immediately
and effectively implemented'.

On 11 July 1996 the ICJ rejected the preliminary objections raised by Yugoslavia
and found that it had jurisdiction on the basis of art IX of the 1948 Genocide
Convention. After the departure from power of Milosevic, on 24 April 2001, the
new, democratically elected government of Yugoslavia submitted a request for the
revision of the ICJ's judgment of 11 July 1996 (obtainable from http://www.icj-
cij.org). The main arguments of Yugoslavia were that before 1 November 2000, the
date on which Yugoslavia was admitted as a new member of the United Nations,
Yugoslavia did not continue the international legal and political personality of the
Socialist Federal Republic of Yugoslavia, was not a Member of the UN, was not a
state party to the Statute of the Court and was not a Contracting Party to the 1948
Genocide Convention. Yugoslavia invoked art 61 of the Statute of the Court in
support of its request. Under that provision an application for revision of a
judgment may be submitted upon the discovery of a new, important fact which was
unknown to the Court and to the party claiming revision when the judgment was
given. Yugoslavia argued that its admission to the UN constitutes such a new fact.
Yugoslavia also requested the Court to suspend its proceedings regarding the merits
of the case until a decision on the application for revision be delivered.

The question whether or not humanitarian intervention by a group of states is
allowed under international law remains unresolved for the time being.

The intervention of NATO in Kosovo is certainly justified on moral grounds.
The international community should not stand by and allow atrocities to be
committed anywhere. Furthermore, the situation in Kosovo had the potential of
spreading conflict in Europe. However, the NATO intervention must not become a

precedent. The monopoly on the use of force is, and should remain, within the exclusive domain of the Security Council. The Kosovo crisis has emphasised the need for the reform of the United Nations in general and the Security Council in particular.

Reprisals

Prior to the adoption of the UN Charter reprisals were lawful under some circumstances which were defined in the *Naulilaa Case: Portugal* v *Germany* (1928) 2 RIAA 1012. In this case, in October 1914, when Portugal was a neutral state during the World War I, three members of a party of German soldiers lawfully in the Portuguese colony of Angola were killed by Portuguese soldiers. On the evidence it was clearly established that the incident arose out of a misunderstanding.

Germany, however, as a measure of reprisal sent a military force into Angola which attacked several frontier posts and destroyed property including the port at Naulilaa. Portugal claimed reparation for damage attributable to the German action. Germany argued that it was a case of legitimate reprisals.

The German plea was rejected by the Arbitrator who stated:

'Reprisals are acts of self-help by the injured state, acts in retaliation for acts contrary to international law on the part of the offending state, which have remained unredressed after a demand for amends. In consequence of such measures, the observance of this or that rule of international law is temporarily suspended in the relations between the two states. They are limited by considerations of humanity and the rules of good faith, applicable in the relations between states. They are illegal unless they are based upon a previous act contrary to international law. They seek to impose on the offending state reparation for the offence, the return to legality and the avoidance of new offences.'

The Arbitrator laid down three conditions for the legitimacy of reprisals:

1. there must have been an act contrary to international law on the part of the other state;
2. the reprisal must be preceded by an unsatisfied request for redress of the wrong committed;
3. the measures adopted as reprisals must not be excessive, in the sense of being out of all proportion to the wrong committed.

While traditional law did recognise that a state could engage in reprisals subject to the above conditions being satisfied, the Charter of the United Nations, in prohibiting the threat or use of force against the territorial integrity or political independence of any state, negated this position under traditional law by making any use of force by a state, including reprisals, illegal. Article 51 of the Charter, however, preserves a state's inherent right of self-defence. It is therefore necessary to distinguish between acts of self-defence which are permitted, and reprisals which are not.

The position of the UN Security Council on reprisals was made clear when it discussed the Harib Fort Incident of 1964. In 1963 and 1964, the British government had complained to the Security Council of a large number of shooting incidents on the Yemeni–South Arabian border and of aerial raids into South Arabian territory from the Yemen. In March 1964, three raids had taken place in which Bedouin and their flocks had been attacked from the air. Thereupon on 28 March 1964 British military aircraft bombed Harib Fort in the Yemen after having first dropped leaflets advising people to leave the area. The Yemen brought the matter before the Security Council.

The British representative denied that the attack had been a reprisal. He argued that:

'... there is, in existing law a clear distinction to be drawn between two forms of self-help. One, which is of a retributive or punitive nature – "retaliation" or "reprisals"; the other, which is expressly contemplated and authorised by the Charter – self-defence against an armed attack.

... it is clear that the use of armed force to repel or prevent an attack – that is, legitimate action of a defensive nature – may sometimes have to take the form of a counter attack.'

He pointed out that aggressive acts from the Yemen had resulted in loss of life and emphasised that the fort at Harib was not merely a military installation, but was known to be a centre for aggressive action against the Federation:

'To destroy the fort with the minimum use of force was therefore a defensive measure which was proportionate and confined to the necessities of the case.

It has no parallel with acts of retaliation or reprisals, which have as an essential element the purposes of vengeance or retribution. It is this latter use of force which is condemned by the Charter, and not the use of force for defensive purposes such as warding off future attacks.'

The Security Council did not accept the UK view and adopted a resolution in which it:

1. condemned reprisals as incompatible with the purposes and principles of the United Nations;
2. deplored the British military action at Harib on 28 March 1964;
3. deplored all attacks and incidents which occurred in the area.

The Security Council has generally taken a stand against reprisals, but during the Cold War it tended to condemn only the more extreme examples. This development has led Bowett to suggest that 'the more relevant distinction today is not between self-defence and reprisals but between reprisals which are likely to be condemned and those which, because they satisfy some concept of reasonableness, are not': 'Reprisals Including Recourse to Armed Force' (1972) 66 AJIL 1.

Bowett lists the following factors which the practice of the Security Council suggests are relevant to the question whether a reprisal is 'reasonable' and hence unlikely to be condemned.

1. The proportionality between the reprisal and the earlier illegal act that causes it.
2. Whether the reprisal is against civilians or the armed forces.
3. Whether the reprisal is one against human life or property.
4. Whether the state against whom it is taken has provoked the reprisal.
5. Whether the reprisal jeopardises the changes of a peaceful settlement by its timing.
6. Whether, at least in the guerrilla context, the state taking the reprisal has exhausted all practical measures for the defence of its territory within its own borders.

Israel has relied less and less on a self-defence argument and has taken action which is openly admitted to be a reprisal. The Beirut raid of 28 December 1969 is the obvious example of an action not really defended on the basis of self-defence at all.

In the Beirut raid 13 civil airplanes valued at over $40 million were destroyed while on the ground at Beirut airport in Lebanon by Israeli commandos. There was no loss of life. The raid was in retaliation for an attack on 26 December of an El Al airplane at Athens airport by Palestine guerrillas. The airplane was damaged and a passenger – an Israeli – killed. Following the Beirut raid in retaliation for the Athens attack the Security Council condemned Israel 'for its premeditated military action in violation of its obligations under the Charter' and considered that Lebanon was entitled to 'appropriate redress for the destruction it has suffered'.

The Israeli Chief of Staff was reported to have stated the purpose as being 'to make it clear to the other side that the price they must pay for terrorist activities can be very high'.

Bowett states that:

'It cannot be expected that the Security Council will ever accept this justification. But there is clearly some evidence that certain reprisals will, even if not accepted as justified, at least avoid condemnation. This shift in argument from self-defence to reprisals may in part be due to the realisation that the self-defence argument is unlikely to be accepted in any event.

It may in larger part be due to a growing feeling that not only do reprisals offer a more effective means of checking military and strategic gains by the other party but also that they will meet with no more than a formal condemnation by the Council, and that effective sanctions under Chapter VII are not to be feared.

Obviously, if this trend continues, we shall achieve a position in which, while reprisals remain illegal de jure, they become accepted de facto. Indeed it may be that the more relevant distinction today is not between self-defence and reprisals but between reprisals which are likely to be condemned and those which, because they satisfy some concept of reasonableness, are not.'

Hot pursuit

In May/June 1977 Rhodesia entered Mozambique territory and attacked bases used by terrorists opposed to the Rhodesian government, up to a distance of 60 miles from the border. It justified its action on grounds of 'hot pursuit'. The concept of hot pursuit exists under the law of the sea and Rhodesia argued that it applied to land offences as well.

The Security Council condemned the action. In the absence of a treaty between the states concerned permitting such action, there can be no right of 'hot pursuit' across land borders. However, such action may have been justified as a 'reasonable' reprisal or an act of anticipatory self-defence.

Annexation of territory

The proscription on the use of force contained in the Charter requires that annexation no longer be considered a basis for the acquisition of territory.

The General Assembly Declaration on Principles of International Law Concerning Friendly Relations and Co-operation among States in Accordance with the Charter of the United Nations 1970 (Resolution 2625 (XXV)) provides, inter alia: the territory of a state shall not be the object of military occupation resulting from the use of force in contravention of the provisions of the Charter. The territory of a state shall not be the object of acquisition by another state resulting from the threat or use of force. No territorial acquisition resulting from the threat or use of force shall be recognised as legal. Nothing in the foregoing shall be construed as affecting:

'(a) provisions of the Charter or any international agreement prior to the Charter regime and valid under international law; or
(b) the powers of the Security Council under the Charter.'

The only possible justification for the temporary occupation of another state's territory would be self-defence, to create a buffer zone along the state's borders on the ground of self-defence against possible future attacks. For example, following the 'June War' of 1967 Israel was left in occupation of large areas of Egyptian and Jordanian territory which not only provided it with a strong bargaining counter but also strengthened the vulnerable boundaries between itself and its Arab neighbours. Nevertheless, self-defence could not justify a purported annexation of such territory and a state incorporating such territory permanently under its national sovereignty.

However, self-defence may be used to retake territory illegally occupied. This justification was used by India in 1961 when it invaded Goa. On 17–18 December 1961 India invaded the Portuguese territory of Goa, Danao and Dui on the Indian sub-continent. On 18 December Portugal asked the Security Council 'to put a stop to the contemptable act of aggression of the Indian Union, ordering an immediate cease-fire and the withdrawal of all the invading forces of the Indian Union'. A draft resolution recalling the terms of arts 2(3) and (4) and calling both for an immediate cease-fire and for the withdrawal by India of its forces was vetoed by the USSR.

India argued that it was merely retaking a part of its country illegally occupied by the Portuguese:

'We are criticised here by various delegations which say "Why have you used force?" The Charter absolutely prohibits force, but the Charter itself does not completely eschew force, in the sense that force can be used in self-defence, for the protection of the people of a country – and the people of Goa are as much Indians as the people of any other part of India.'

17

Collective Security

17.1 Introduction

17.2 The Security Council's role in the maintenance of international peace and security

17.3 The Uniting for Peace Resolution

17.4 Peacekeeping

17.5 Actions by regional agencies

17.1 Introduction

The Charter of the United Nations contains provisions relating to the maintenance of international peace and security. These provisions do not concern lawful or unlawful use of force but relate to measures which may be taken to prevent or terminate the threat of, or the use of, force. The system laid down in the UN Charter confers the main responsibility for the maintenance of international peace and security upon the Security Council. Under Chapters VI and VII of the UN Charter the Security Council decides what type of diplomatic economic or military measures must be taken to prevent or to terminate threats to international peace, breaches of the peace and acts of aggression. To take that decision a unanimous vote (ignoring abstentions) of the five Permanent Members of the Security Council – the US, the UK, France, China and Russia – is required.

The Security Council may rely on regional arrangements or agencies for enforcement action under its authority. When measures involving the use of force are taken every member of the UN is bound, by virtue of art 2(5), to provide assistance to the UN and to refrain from giving assistance to a state against whom the action is directed. This obligation is reinforced by art 25 of the UN Charter which requires all members to accept and carry out Security Council decisions adopted under any chapter of the Charter. Furthermore, under art 103 of the UN Charter, when there is a conflict between the obligations of the members of the UN under the UN Charter and their obligations arising from any other international agreements, the obligations under the Charter prevail.

The Security Council may also impose sanctions against non–member states.

This competence is based on the ius cogens status of the principle of the prohibition of the use of force in international relations.

The system of collective security was conceived with the idea that the Security Council would act unanimously as an international gendarme. Regrettably, the Cold War proved the system to be ineffective and even after the end of the Cold War the agreement of all five Permanent Members of the Security Council to apply measures involving the use of force is not always guaranteed. This was evident when the Security Council failed to prevent widespread and flagrant breaches of human rights and humanitarian law in Kosovo. Because the Security Council has often been deadlocked, the General Assembly has filled the gap. During the Korean war the General Assembly adopted the Uniting for Peace Resolution 1950 (GA Resolution 377 (V) of 3 November 1950) under which it is empowered to recommend collective measures in the situation where the Council is paralysed because of a veto. However, the General Assembly, unlike the Security Council, cannot adopt binding decisions. It may only adopt recommendations on matters of collective security.

The deficiencies of the collective security system were a catalyst for the creation of a new technique to deal with the maintenance of peace and security which was not provided for in the UN Charter – UN peacekeeping. As a result, there are two approaches to situations which endanger international peace and security: the peacekeeping approach and collective security as envisioned by the UN Charter.

Since the end of the Cold War the UN collective security system has undergone important changes in terms of the use of the Security Council's authority to impose sanctions. Chapter VII sanctions were used rarely in the first 45 years of the UN's existence. In the last decade such sanctions have been imposed frequently. Therefore, the matter of their effectiveness, their humanitarian impact on the civilian populations and their effect on third states has become an important consideration for the Security Council. In this respect, the Security Council set up on 17 April 2000 the Working Group on General Issues on Sanctions to develop recommendations on how to improve the effectiveness of sanctions. The Security Council is putting a special emphasis on the so-called 'smart sanctions', that is sanctions which focus on the targeted leadership or group and therefore have little or no effect on civilian populations and third states.

The above topics will be explored in this chapter.

17.2 The Security Council's role in the maintenance of international peace and security

Under art 24 of the UN Charter, the Security Council is invested with primary responsibility for the maintenance of international peace and security. This responsibility includes enforcement actions in the case of threats to the peace, breaches of the peace or acts of aggression under Chapter VII of the Charter.

Under art 39, the Security Council is required to determine the existence of a threat to the peace, a breach of the peace or an act of aggression. What constitutes a 'breach of peace' is not, however, clearly defined and it is up to the Security Council to make a determination on a case-by-case basis. However, the General Assembly Resolution 3314 (XXIX) on the definition of aggression provides some indication as to what is meant by the term 'aggression'. Even though the resolution was adopted by consensus, it remains controversial and it is open to question as to whether it reflects customary international law.

If the Security Council determines that the situation at issue constitutes a threat or a breach of peace or an act of aggression it then decides what measures should be used to maintain or restore peace. Under art 40 of the UN Charter the Security Council may take interim or provisional measures, under art 41 it may apply diplomatic, economic or other sanctions which do not involve the use of force and, if sanctions taken under art 41 fail, it may take military sanctions by virtue of art 42 of the UN Charter. The creation of international military forces for use in applying military sanctions is envisaged in art 43. Such forces have never come into being.

Prior to 1990 the Security Council applied economic sanctions only twice, in 1966 against Rhodesia and in 1977 against South Africa. Since then the Security Council has applied sanctions under art 41 many times. Military sanctions have never been utilised in the form envisaged under art 42 but on a few occasions the Security Council authorised the use of force. In 1966 the UK was authorised to use force if necessary to prevent the breach of an oil embargo imposed against Southern Rhodesia, in 1950 the Security Council in its Resolution of 7 July 1950 recommended that all Members provide military assistance to South Korea under the unified command of the United Nations, in 1990 the Security Council authorised its members to use 'all necessary means ... to restore international peace and security' in the Gulf, and in 1992 the Security Council in its Resolution 794 welcomed the United states offer to help to create a secure environment for the delivery of humanitarian aid in Somalia. The Resolution authorised the US to use 'all necessary means' to achieve the objective of the operation and invited other states to send their contingents of personnel and to contribute in kind or in cash. In 1993 and 1994 the Security Council in its Resolutions 867 and 940 authorised the Organisation of American states to use all necessary means to restore democracy in Haiti. Similar authorisation was given by the Security Council in respect of Rwanda, Bosnia and Herzegovina and East Timor.

Provisional measures

Article 40 of the Charter provides:

'In order to prevent an aggravation of the situation, the Security Council may, before making the recommendations or deciding upon the measures provided for in art 39 call upon the parties concerned to comply with such provisional measures as it deems necessary or desirable. Such provisional measures shall be without prejudice to the rights,

[handwritten marginal note: "look at ICJ advisory opin."]

claims, or position of the parties concerned. The Security Council shall take account of failure to comply with such provisional measures.'

For example, on the Palestine question, art 40 was specifically invoked, ordering a cease-fire and withdrawal. Such provisional measures may provide a basis for the settlement of the dispute without the need for further action by the Security Council. These provisional measures do not prejudice the rights of the parties. They are simply a means of preventing an aggravation of the situation.

One issue arising under art 40 is whether the adoption of a resolution providing for provisional measures creates an obligation upon the parties to whom the resolution is directed. In this respect it is generally agreed that the words 'called upon' when used in art 40 mean 'ordered' and should be read in conjunction with art 25 of the UN Charter. For this reason, to avoid having to take enforcement action against states, the powers under art 40 are rarely used by the Security Council and most resolutions passed are phrased as recommendations and not orders.

The practice of the Security Council suggests that the power to call upon parties to comply with provisional measures under art 40 does not depend upon a prior determination under art 39 of the UN Charter.

Enforcement action under art 41 of the UN Charter not involving the use of armed force

Article 41 provides:

> 'The Security Council may decide what measures not involving the use of armed force are to be employed to give effect to its decision, and it may call upon the Members of the United Nations to apply such measures. These may include complete or partial interruption of economic relations and of rail, sea, air, postal, telegraphic, radio and other measures of communication, and the severance of diplomatic relations.'

Prior to the end of the Cold War the Security Council had taken action under art 41 only twice – with regard to Rhodesia, following the Unilateral Declaration of Independence of 1965, and South Africa in 1977.

In the case of Rhodesia the Security Council called upon all states not to recognise the white minority regime established in Rhodesia following the Unilateral Declaration of Independence and further called upon states to break economic and military relations with the country. These measures were strengthened in Resolution 221 (1966) when the Council imposed selective economic sanctions on Rhodesia that were binding on all states and authorised the UK to use force in the following circumstances:

> 'The Security Council ... (5) Calls upon the Government of the United Kingdom to prevent by the use of force if necessary the arrival at Beira of vessels reasonably believed to be carrying oil destined for Rhodesia, and empowers the United Kingdom to arrest and

detain tanker known as the *Joanna V* upon her departure from Beira in the event her oil cargo is discharged there.'

However, the use of force was not required on that occasion.

The sanctions had no effect on the white minority regime led by Ian Smith because South Africa and Portugal refused to support the UN sanctions.

In the case of South Africa the measures imposed by the Security Council in 1977 were limited to an arms embargo. Security Council Resolution 418 (1977) stated that:

'... all states shall cease forthwith any provision to South Africa of arms and related material of all types.'

Although the Security Council set up a Sanctions Committee, it did not provide for any monitoring mechanism to oversee the effective implementation of the resolution. In Resolution 473 (1980) the Security Council called upon the Sanctions Committee to redouble its effort in the implementation of sanctions. This was further strengthened by Resolutions 558 (1984) and 591 (1986). All sanctions were terminated by Resolution 919 (1994) after the establishment of the first democratically elected government in South Africa.

Since 1990 the situation has dramatically changed. The Security Council has imposed sanctions several times. At the time of writing the following Security Council Committees are supervising the imposition of sanctions.

1. Security Council Committee established pursuant to Resolution 751 (1992) concerning Somalia. Since 1992 a comprehensive arms embargo has been in existence against Somalia. The continuing breaches of the embargo prompted the Security Council to set up a group of experts to investigate the violations and to make recommendations on tightening the arms embargo. At the time of writing the issue of improving compliance with Resolution 751 is on the Security Council agenda.
2. Security Council Committee established pursuant to Resolution 918 (1994) concerning Rwanda. In 1996 the Security Council lifted an arms embargo against the government of Rwanda (Resolution 1011) but retained it against non-governmental forces operating in Rwanda.
3. Security Council Committee established pursuant to Resolution 1521 (2003) concerning Liberia. The Security Council has imposed 'smart sanctions' against Liberia to force the Liberian government to cease support for the Revolutionary United Front (RUF) of Sierra Leone and other armed groups operating in the region. The 'smart sanctions' consist, inter alia, of imposing an arms embargo, a ban on diamonds and timber and a ban on the travel of senior members of the Liberian government.
4. Security Council Committee established pursuant to Resolution 1132 (1997) concerning Sierra Leone. Sanctions have been imposed against the RUF backed by Liberia which fights against the government of Sierra Leone. In the light of

the increased effort of the government of Sierra Leone to control and manage its diamond industry, the Security Council terminated its embargo on diamonds in June 2003.

5. Security Council Committee established pursuant to Resolution 1267 (1999) concerning Al-Qaeda and the Taliban and associated individuals and entities.
6. Security Council Committee established pursuant to Resolution 1518 (2003). The Committee's main task is to identify individuals and entities linked with Saddam Hussein's regime that have removed financial assets or economic resources from Iraq. Resolution 1518 completes Security Council Resolution 1483 adopted in May 2003, which lifted sanctions imposed against Iraq following the invasion of Kuwait and ordered the freezing of all the financial assets removed from Iraq or acquired by Saddam Hussein or other senior officials of his government.
7. Security Council Committee established pursuant to Resolution 1533 (2004) concerning the Democratic Republic of Congo. The Security Council has imposed an arms embargo against all foreign and Congolese armed groups and militias operating in the territory of North and South Kivu and Ituri, and against groups not party to the Global and All-inclusive Agreements operating in the Democratic Republic of Congo.
8. On 15 November 2004 the Security Council unanimously adopted a draft resolution submitted by France imposing sanctions against the government of the Ivory Coast for violating the 2003 ceasefire between the government in the south and the rebels controlling the northern part of the country (Resolution 1572 (2004)).

Mandatory sanctions under art 41 of the UN Charter play an important role in the maintenance of peace and security as they put pressure on states or entities to comply with international law and the objectives of the UN without resorting to force. They are also widely accepted by public opinion.

For each country under sanctions the Security Council sets up a Sanctions Committee to supervise their implementation. The Committee relies on co-operation with states and organisations to provide it with information concerning violations of sanctions. The Security Council has used sanctions for various purposes: in the case of Haiti to restore democracy; in the case of Libya to force Libya to hand over to a foreign jurisdiction two of its citizens, one of whom, Adelbaset al-Megrahi, was convicted on 31 January 2001 by the Scottish Court in The Netherlands for the destruction of Pan Am Flight 103 which crashed at Lockerbie causing death of many people; in the case of the Federal Republic of Yugoslavia to cease the violations of international human rights and humanitarian law; in the case of Sierra Leone to oust the military junta and to restore democracy; in the case of Iraq to force Iraq to comply with Security Council Resolutions 678 (1990) and 688 (1991) adopted in the aftermath of the Gulf War.

It emerges from the above that sanctions imposed by the Security Council are often in place for a very long period of time. The positive effect of sanctions has been acknowledged by the international community. However, there are also negative effects of sanctions, in particular in respect of vulnerable civilian population of a country under UN sanctions and in respect of third states. This matter was considered in the report on *Agenda for Peace* (A/47/277-S/24111) and its Supplement (A/50/60-S/1995/1) prepared by former UN Secretary-General, Boutros Boutros-Ghali. Following his report there has been an ongoing discussion on how to improve the effectiveness of Security Council sanctions and to alleviate their negative effects. One answer to this problem has been the application of the so-called 'smart sanctions' directed against leaders or target groups and consisting of imposing travel bans, freezing of foreign bank accounts of individuals or groups, imposing arms embargos or, as in the case of Sierra Leone, a diamonds embargo. The smart sanctions also have very important psychological effects. It will be impossible for the political elite to blame UN sanctions for hardship suffered by the civilians. In his address to the International Rescue Committees on 15 November 2000, the Secretary-General welcomed the new generation of sanctions. In this respect he said:

> 'If we want to punish, let us punish the guilty. And if we want to bring about change, let us target the powerful, not the powerless. But merely making sanctions "smarter" will not be enough. The challenge is to achieve consensus about the precise and specific aims of the sanctions, and then provide the necessary means and will for them to succeed.'

On 17 April 2000 the Security Council set up a Working Group on General Issues on Sanctions with a view to preparing a document on the use of sanctions by the Security Council as a policy instrument. The current mandate of the Working Group will come to an end in December 2004. The Working Group has examined and agreed on many issues concerning sanctions, such as administration of sanctions, their design, their implementation but, so far, has failed to reach a consensus on the recommended duration and termination of sanctions. Many proposals and recommendations of the Working Group have already been put into practice by the Security Council (see the above Resolution 1521 imposing 'smart sanctions' against Liberia). Nevertheless, 'smart sanctions' are at an early stage of development.

Enforcement action under art 42 involving the use of armed forces

Article 42 states:

> 'Should the Security Council consider that measures provided for in Article 41 would be inadequate or have proved to be inadequate, it may take such action by air, sea or land forces as may be necessary to maintain or restore international peace and security. Such action may include demonstrations, blockade and other operations by air, sea or land forces of Members of the United Nations.'

Strictly speaking, action under this provision has never been taken (eg the UN forces in Korea were created on the basis of a Security Council recommendation following an art 39 determination. Also in the case of the Gulf War the Security Council

Resolution 678, which authorised the use of force, did not refer to art 42 of the UN Charter). However, the Security Council has found a different way to use military sanctions by authorising a state or a group of states or a regional organisation such as NATO to use armed force to restore international peace and order. It is considered that this kind of authorisation is implied in the Security Council's general competence to maintain international peace and security under Chapter VII. Another point is that under art 43 member states are obliged to 'make available ... armed forces, assistance and facilities' on request from the Security Council, whilst under the current solution the contribution to military sanctions is optional.

So far the Security Council has authorised a number of military operations since the end of the Cold War: in the Gulf War, Somalia, Rwanda, Haiti, Bosnia-Herzegovina, East Timor and Liberia. Two of these military interventions are particularly interesting, ie that in Korea in the light of its future implications on the development of international law on collective security and that in the 1990 Gulf War as being the most comprehensive.

The Korean question 1950

Korea became a part of Japan in 1910. In 1943 the Allied powers agreed that it would become an independent state when World War II ended. In 1945 Japanese troops in Korea surrendered to the USSR north of the 38th Parallel and to the US south of it. On 25 June 1950 North Korean armed forces crossed the 38th Parallel into South Korea and fighting broke out. The resulting crisis was immediately debated by the Security Council which (in the absence of the Russian representative) adopted the following series of resolutions.

Security Council Resolution of 25 June 1950:
The Security Council:

'... noting with grave concern the armed attack upon the Republic of Korea by forces from North Korea.
Determines that this action constitutes a breach of the peace.
(I) Calls for the immediate cessation of hostilities; and calls upon the authorities of North Korea to withdraw forthwith their armed forces to the 38th Parallel ...
(III) Calls upon all Members to render every assistance to the United Nations in the execution of this resolution and to refrain from giving assistance to the North Korean authorities.'

Security Council Resolution of 27 June 1950:
The Security Council:

'... recommends that the Members of the United Nations furnish such assistance to the Republic of Korea as may be necessary to repel the armed attack and to restore international peace and security in the area.'

Security Council Resolution of 7 July 1950:
The Security Council:

'(3) Recommends that all Members providing military forces and other assistance pursuant to the aforesaid Security Council resolutions make such forces and other assistance available to a unified command under the United states;

(4) Requests the United states to designate the commander of such forces;

(5) Authorises the unified command at its discretion to use the United Nations Flag in the course of operations against North Korea forces concurrently with the flags of the various nations participating;

(6) Requests the United states to provide the Security Council with reports as appropriate on the course of action taken under the unified command.'

In response to the Security Council Resolutions, 16 member states sent armed forces to Korea.

Some writers are doubtful whether the forces in Korea constituted a UN force. Although they were called a UN force, flew the UN flag and were awarded UN medals by the General Assembly, nevertheless all operational decisions concerning the force were taken by the US. The Commander took his orders from the US, not from the UN.

However, on the question whether the forces in Korea were UN forces, Bowett concludes that: 'There can be no doubt that, in practice, the overwhelming majority of states involved in the Korean action were fully prepared to regard it as a United Nations action involving United Nations Forces': *United Nations Forces*, London: Stevens & Sons, 1964, p47.

The Security Council ceased to play an active part in the conduct of the war after the USSR representative resumed his seat on 1 August 1950. In October China entered the war in support of North Korea. After the USSR had vetoed a draft resolution condemning the Chinese action on 30 November the General Assembly became the organ effectively seized of the question.

The Iraqi invasion of Kuwait

On 2 August 1990, Iraqi armed forces invaded the neighbouring sovereign state of Kuwait and ousted the incumbent Kuwaiti government. The UN Security Council was immediately called into emergency session and on the same day passed Resolution 660 (1990) which condemned the Iraqi invasion of Kuwait, demanded the immediate and unconditional withdrawal of all Iraqi forces from Kuwait and called upon Iraq and Kuwait to settle their international differences by peaceful means.

After Iraq refused to withdraw its troops from Kuwait, the Security Council passed Resolution 661 (1990) of 6 August 1990. This Resolution imposed mandatory sanctions and an embargo on Iraq. Under the terms of the Resolution, all states (not just Members of the United Nations) were prohibited from permitting:

1. trade in commodities and products originating in either Iraq or Kuwait, other than medicine and humanitarian aid;
2. the transportation or transshipment of any Iraqi and Kuwaiti products, by land, air or sea, and the transfer of funds for payment of related transactions;

3. the supply of weapons or any other military equipment; and

4. the grant of financial assistance, credit, or any other economic resources to either Iraq or Kuwait.

In addition, all states were required to take 'appropriate measures' to protect the assets of the legitimate government of Kuwait and the Resolution instructed all states to refrain from recognising any regime set up by the occupying power.

Iraq claimed that the Kuwaiti government had been overthrown by an internal revolution and, on 5 August, a new Kuwaiti government was announced by Iraq. Later, Iraq announced its intention to annex Kuwait, a move which was subsequently renounced by the Security Council in Resolution 662 (1990). Nevertheless, on 28 August, Iraq declared that Kuwait had become its nineteenth province and constitutional amendments were passed to that effect.

After numerous fruitless attempts to achieve a peaceful settlement, on 29 November, the Security Council passed Resolution 678 (1990) which demanded that Iraq 'comply fully with Resolution 660 (1990) and all subsequent relevant resolutions' and authorised 'Member states co-operating with the Government of Kuwait ... to use all necessary means to uphold and implement Security Council Resolution 660 (1990) and all subsequent relevant Resolutions and to restore international peace and security in the area'. The deadline of 15 January was set for Iraqi compliance with the Resolutions of the Security Council.

No Iraqi withdrawal was initiated before the deadline specified in Resolution 678 (1990) and on 16 January 1991 coalition forces from the multilateral forces stationed in Saudi Arabia commenced an aerial bombardment of military installations and strategic targets inside Iraq and Kuwait. After less than a month, the allied forces commenced ground operations to liberate Kuwait, and within four days the territory of Kuwait was surrendered to allied forces.

Resolution 678 (1990) is of particular significance because, for the first time in the history of the United Nations, the use of military force was authorised by the Security Council on the basis of a unanimous affirmative vote among the Permanent Members. However, the multilateral force was not a UN force in the sense of Chapter VII of the Charter, but rather a coalition of military forces organised under the command of the US.

Agreements on the provision of armed forces by UN member states

The basis of the scheme envisaged in Chapter VII lay in the provision to the Security Council of the armed forces necessary to enforce its decisions against recalcitrant states. This was to be effected by agreements between the Security Council and the member states.

Article 43 of the Charter provides:

'(1) All Members of the United Nations, in order to contribute to the maintenance of international peace and security, undertake to make available to the Security Council, on its call and in accordance with a special agreement or agreements, armed forces, assistance, and facilities, including rights of passage, necessary for the purpose of maintaining international peace and security.

(2) Such agreement or agreements shall govern the number and types of forces, their degree of readiness and general location, and the nature of the facilities and assistance to be provided.

(3) The agreement or agreements shall be negotiated as soon as possible on the initiative of the Security Council.'

Therefore, a state is not obliged to take part in military operations under art 42 unless it has concluded a 'special agreement' under art 43. No such agreements have been made. However, the absence of agreements under art 43 does not prevent states agreeing ad hoc to place forces at the disposal of the Security Council in particular cases. For example, as with the United Nations command in Korea 1950.

The Military Staff Committee

Article 46 of the Charter provides that:

'Plans for the application of armed force shall be made by the Security Council with the assistance of the Military Staff Committee.'

Article 47 provides:

'(1) There shall be established a Military Staff Committee to advise and assist the Security Council on all questions relating to the Security Council's military requirements ...

(2) The Military Staff Committee shall consist of the Chiefs of Staff of the permanent members of the Security Council or their representatives ...'

Although established in 1946 the Military Staff Committee has no real function. In practice the existence of this committee has been disregarded by the Security Council and responsibility for carrying out the Council's military requirements has been entrusted to the Secretary-General.

The failure of the Security Council to fulfil its primary purpose of maintaining international peace and security has led to three major developments.

1. The assumption by the General Assembly of the role of determining a breach of the peace, or act of aggression and of recommending action by members including the use of armed force.
2. The development of powerful regional systems outside the United Nations, eg NATO, the Warsaw Pact, the OAS, etc.
3. The development of peacekeeping operations under either Chapter VI or Chapter VII of the Charter, using limited military forces, voluntarily contributed by member states for: observation and fact-finding, eg UNMOGIP (Kashmir), UNYOM (Yemen), UNIFIL (Lebanon), UNDOF (Golan Heights); and maintaining law and order in situations involving an actual threat to the peace, eg ONUC (Congo), UNFICYP (Cyprus).

These developments fall between Chapter VI and Chapter VII, and some writers have advocated a new Chapter VIA which would bring them within the ambit of the UN Charter.

17.3 The Uniting for Peace Resolution

The creation of the unified command in Korea by the Security Council was only possible because of the fortuitous absence of the Soviet representative who had been boycotting the Security Council. As it was unlikely that Soviet boycotts would recur in the future the General Assembly, fearing that the veto would leave the Council powerless to act in a future case of the Korean type, examined methods whereby it could assume some of the responsibilities of the Security Council when the veto prevented it from acting.

As a result of its deliberations the Assembly on 3 November 1950 passed the Resolution on Uniting for Peace: see General Assembly Resolution 377 (V). By the first paragraph the General Assembly resolved that:

> '... if the Security Council because of lack of unanimity of the Permanent Members, fails to exercise its primary responsibility for the maintenance of international peace and security in any case where there appears to be a threat to the peace, breach of the peace, or act of aggression, the General Assembly shall consider the matter immediately with a view to making appropriate recommendations to members for collective measures, including in the case of a breach of the peace or act of aggression the use of armed force when necessary, to maintain or restore international peace and security. If not in session at the time, the General Assembly may meet in emergency special session ... Such emergency special session shall be called if requested by the Security Council on the vote of any seven Members, or by a majority of the Members of the United Nations.'

Following the passing of the Resolution a Peace Observation Commission of 14 Members was established which can be despatched to any troublespot to advise the Assembly of any necessary action, and a Collective Measures Committee of 14 Members was established to co-ordinate the action taken by Members on the Assembly's recommendations.

The justification for the Assembly assuming these powers was that generally the Assembly could do anything by recommendation that the Security Council could do by recommendation or decision. Article 24 of the Charter gave the Security Council primary responsibility for the maintenance of international peace and security. This did not preclude the General Assembly from exercising a secondary or residual responsibility. The foundation of this argument was the wide scope of art 10 of the Charter which enables the General Assembly to discuss and make recommendations on any matter 'within the scope of the present Charter'.

The procedure has been used on several occasions. On 31 October 1956, following the UK and French vote against the resolution in the Security Council proposing measures for the cessation of the military action against Egypt, the Suez question was transferred to the Assembly.

On 4 November 1956, following a Soviet veto in the Security Council, the Hungarian question was referred to the Assembly.

On 17 September 1960, following a Soviet veto in the Security Council, the Congo question was referred by the Council to the Assembly.

On 6 December 1971, the Security Council referred the Bangladesh question to the General Assembly.

Overall the General Assembly held ten emergency special sessions on matters of international peace and security when the Security Council was deadlocked. The result of the sessions on the crises in the Middle East in 1956 and the Congo in 1960, examined below, was the initiation of a new technique of dealing with breaches of international peace, now known as peacekeeping.

BUT IT has happened in 37 years.

17.4 Peacekeeping

Peacekeeping is not mentioned in the UN Charter. It constitutes a practical answer to the malfunction of collective security as envisaged in the UN Charter. During the term of office of Dag Hammarskjöld, as Secretary-General of the UN, peacekeeping was recognised as a sui generis UN contribution to the settlement of international disputes, although de facto peacekeeping operations were carried out on a number of occasions before his entry into office. The UN, retroactively recognised the United Nations Truce Supervision Organisation (UNTSO) created in 1948 to supervise the truce in Palestine as its first peacekeeping operation. Dag Hammarskjöld referred to peacekeeping as belonging to 'Chapter Six and Half' of the Charter. Indeed, peacekeeping represents a middle way between the classical pattern of peaceful settlement of international disputes and collective security measures such as embargos or military actions. Peacekeeping can be described as involving actions to prevent, contain, moderate or terminate hostilities between states or within a state by an organised multinational force comprising soldiers, police and civilians deployed in the conflict area with the approval of the parties involved, or at least the consent of one party and the toleration of the other. Consequently, the parties involved in a dispute, by agreeing on the presence of UN peacekeeping forces on their national territories, show the willingness to avoid military confrontation. The acceptance of UN peacekeeping forces has also an advantage of avoiding the escalation of a conflict as no aggressor is needed to be pointed out when such forces are deployed. Peacekeeping forces are neutral and impartial. Until 1990, they were drawn from small and medium-sized countries not involved in any way in the dispute. UN peacekeepers, as a rule, can use weapons only in self-defence. Therefore, they act more as police than military.

Generally, the political aspects of peacekeeping operations are within the competence of the Security Council, the financial side is within the domain of the

created by GA but given to be ruled by SC.

General Assembly and the Secretary-General directs and manages UN peacekeeping operations and reports on their activities, problems and progress to the Security Council. Peacekeeping operations are established on the basis of Security Council resolutions which also determine their mandates and authorise their deployment. The General Assembly is in charge of the budget of individual operations. Since 1965 the General Assembly considers peacekeeping operations under the agenda item 'Comprehensive review of the whole question of peacekeeping operations in all their aspects'. This item, since 1993, is prepared by the Fourth Committee (one of the six main committees of the General Assembly) which submits reports and drafts resolutions/decisions/recommendations for adoption by the plenary session of the General Assembly.

Since 1948 the UN has set up 59 peacekeeping operations, of which 46 were set up in the years 1990-2004. In October 2004 the UN was maintaining 16 peacekeeping operations, the oldest of these being UNTSO (the UN Truce Supervision Organisation) which was deployed in the Middle East in May 1948 to supervise the truce between Israel and Arab countries subsequent to the armed attack on Israel by Arab countries in 1948. Since then the role of UNTSO has evolved. After the wars of 1956, 1967 and 1973 UNTSO acted as an intermediary between the hostile parties and was used as the means of containing isolated incidents and thus preventing them from escalating into major conflicts. Today UNTSO is attached to the peacekeeping forces in the area: the United Nations Disengagement Observer Force (UNDOF) in the Golan Heights and the United Nations Interim Force in Lebanan (UNIFIL). UNTSO's activities have been spread over territory within five States: Egypt, Israel, Jordan, Lebanon and the Syrian Arab Republic. UNTSO has offices in Sinai, Beirut and Damascus.

At the time of writing the most recent peacekeeping missions include:

1. UNOCI (United Nations Operation in Cote D'Ivoire) which has been deployed since April 2004;
2. MINUSTAH (United Nations Stabilisation Mission in Haiti) which has been deployed since 1 June 2004;
3. UNOB (United Nations Operation in Burundi) which has been deployed since 1 June 2004.

In respect of the current peacekeeping operations 102 countries have contributed personnel which amounts to 62,289 people. The terms and conditions of their service under the UN flag is negotiated between the UN and the governments which volunteer to send its military personnel for a specific mission.

Peacekeeping missions are also dangerous – to date approximately 1,846 personnel have died when serving on missions. This was one of the main reasons for the adoption of the Convention on the Safety of United Nations and Associated Personnel 1994. Under the Convention contracting states are bound to take all necessary measures to ensure the safety and security of UN personnel and premises. Any offender must be prosecuted or extradited.

Peacekeeping has evolved considerably. Its primary task is to prevent further fighting, to act as a buffer between the hostile parties and to help to control an armed conflict. However, each mission has its peculiarities which are taken into account in the determination of the mandate. Sometimes the missions may exceed the traditional peacekeeping principles and become peace-enforcing forces, as happened in Congo in 1960 and in Somalia in 1992. In this respect it is interesting to examine the first two UN peacekeeping operations: in the Middle East in 1956 and in Congo in 1960.

The United Nations Emergency Force in the Middle East (UNEF)

In October 1956 Israel, France and the UK attacked Egypt. On 5 November 1956, after a cease-fire had been agreed, the General Assembly adopted a resolution by which it established a United Nations Emergency Force (UNEF) 'to secure and supervise the cessation of hostilities'. After the withdrawal of the Israeli, French and British troops UNEF was sent to patrol the Israeli-Egyptian armistice line, and to report troop movements near the line. The Force was authorised to fight in self-defence, but was not expected to resist any large scale invasion across the armistice line.

The Force was comprised of contingents of national armies and was founded on the principle of consent. No member state was obliged to provide a contingent unless it consented to do so by means of an agreement between the state and the Secretary-General.

The General Assembly appointed the Commander of the Force, and authorised the Secretary-General to enact regulations essential to the effective functioning of the Force. The Force was paid by the United Nations and took its orders solely from the General Assembly and the Secretary-General.

The Force could not enter the territory of any state without that state's consent. Israel refused to consent to its presence on Israeli territory and the Force therefore operated solely on Egyptian territory. The Force was withdrawn at the request of the United Arab Republic in May 1967.

The United Nations Force in the Congo (ONUC)

On 30 June 1960 the Republic of the Congo was granted independence by Belgium. Within a few days of independence the Congolese army mutinied and law and order broke down, resulting in injury to nationals, aliens and property. On 10 July Belgian troops stationed in the Congo under a treaty of friendship between Belgium and the Congo intervened 'with the sole purpose of ensuring the safety of European and other members of the population and of protecting human lives in general'.

On 12 July the Congolese government cabled the UN Secretary-General requesting 'urgent despatch by the United Nations of military assistance ... to protect the national territory of the Congo against the present external aggression which is a threat to international peace'. On 14 July the Security Council authorised the Secretary-General to provide the Congo with military assistance. In accordance with the Security Council resolution the Secretary-General established ONUC and the first troops entered the Congo in mid-July. The force was not intended to take military action against Belgian troops but to help the Congolese government maintain law and order. The force was modelled on UNEF.

However, by 14 September 1960, the unanimity among the permanent members of the Security Council had disintegrated and disagreement over the extent and nature of ONUC's activities caused the USSR to veto a proposed resolution calling on states not to intervene unilaterally and to act through ONUC. An emergency session of the General Assembly was called under the Uniting for Peace Resolution on 17 September which adopted a resolution requesting:

> '... the Secretary-General to continue to take vigorous action in accordance with the terms of the aforesaid Resolutions (of the Security Council) and to assist the Central Government of the Congo in the restoration and maintenance of law and order throughout the territory of the Republic of the Congo and to safeguard its unity, territorial integrity and political independence in the interests of international peace and security.'

Although the force was originally intended to fight only in self-defence, following the disintegration of the Congolese government the force was authorised to fight in order to prevent civil war and to expel foreign mercenaries. In this respect the force was engaged in extensive military operations against the secessionist movement in Katanga. By the end of 1961, Katangese resistance had been overcome.

ONUC left the Republic of the Congo on 30 June 1964.

The legal basis for the creation of ONUC is obscure and controversial. In the *Certain Expenses of the United Nations Case* (1962) ICJ Rep 151 the ICJ observed:

> 'It is not necessary for the Court to express an opinion as to which article or articles of the Charter were the basis for the resolutions of the Security Council, but it can be said that the operations of ONUC did not include a use of armed force against a state which the Security Council, under Article 39, determined to have committed an act of aggression or to have breached the peace. The armed forces which were utilised in the Congo were not authorised to take military action against any state. The operation did not involve "preventive or enforcement measures" against any state under Chapter VII and therefore did not constitute "action" as that term is used in Article 11.'

It has been suggested that the creation of ONUC constituted 'provisional measures' within the meaning of art 40 of the Charter. This was the view expressed by the Secretary-General in the Security Council Debate of 13–14 December 1960.

Peacekeeping today

Since the end of the Cold War peacekeeping has changed again in terms of the nature of missions, composition of multinational forces and contributions from member states. The tasks of UN peacekeepers have been extended to reconstruction and institution-building in countries devastated by war, including:

1. organising elections: Namibia, Nicaragua, Cambodia, East Timor, Western Sahara;
2. acting as temporary administrative authorities: Cambodia, Kosovo, East Timor;
3. building democracy: Cambodia, Kosovo;
4. providing emergency relief.

For that reason the composition of UN peacekeeping forces has also changed. The participation of both civilian police and civilian staff in peacekeeping operations has considerably increased. For example, the UN peacekeeping forces in Cambodia (UNTAC) employed approximately 3,500 civilian police in 1992–1993 and increased their number to 8,000 by the end of 2000. Also, the number of international civilian staff has substantially increased: in September 2004 approximately 3,896 international civilian staff were serving in peacekeeping operations. Another important change is that peacekeeping forces are increasingly deployed in intra-state conflicts and civil wars and not, as they used to be, in conflicts between states.

Limitations upon the power of the General Assembly

In the *Certain Expenses of the United Nations Case* (above) certain Members of the United Nations fell seriously behind in the payment of the financial contributions assessed to them by the General Assembly under art 17 of the Charter because of their refusal to accept these assessments in so far as they related to the financing of UNEF and ONUC on the ground that both of these forces were unconstitutional and had been created illegally.

The General Assembly requested the advice of the ICJ as to whether the expenses of the two forces were expenses of the United Nations within the meaning of art 17(2) of the Charter.

The main argument against the legality of the creation of UNEF by the General Assembly was that 'action' in the field of international peace and security was the sole prerogative of the Security Council. The General Assembly had argued that art 24 of the Charter only gave the Security Council 'primary' responsibility for the maintenance of international peace and security. This did not therefore preclude the General Assembly from exercising a secondary or residual responsibility, in accordance with its wide general powers under arts 10 and 14 of the Charter. However, it was contended that if the General Assembly did exercise such responsibility it would be in breach of that part of art 11(2) of the Charter which states that any question relating to the maintenance of international peace and security upon which action is necessary must be referred to the Security Council.

The Court, in a majority opinion (nine votes to five) advised that the Security Council had 'primary' and not exclusive authority, and that whilst the taking of enforcement action was the exclusive prerogative of the Security Council under Chapter VII this did not prevent the Assembly from making recommendations under arts 10 and 14. The limitation of art 11(2) does not apply in such cases, since the 'action' referred to in that paragraph means only 'enforcement action' which is in the nature of coercive action directed against a state.

The UNEF action was not, in the Court's view, enforcement action, but rather 'measures' recommended under art 14.

(The validity of the Congo operation was not contested on the same grounds, because it was the Security Council and not the General Assembly which initiated them, therefore the Uniting for Peace Resolution was not in issue. The main argument relating to the Congo was that the UN Secretary-General had exceeded and abused the powers conferred on him. This allegation was rejected by the Court.)

A further problem arising from the Uniting for Peace Resolution is that of the procedure for convening an emergency session.

Article 20 of the UN Charter provides:

'The General Assembly shall meet in regular annual sessions and in such special sessions as occasions may require. Special sessions shall be convoked by the Secretary-General at the request of the Security Council or of a majority of the Members of the United Nations.'

However, the Uniting for Peace Resolution as amended provides that an emergency special session of the Assembly shall be called by a vote of 'any nine members of the Security Council'.

The Soviet Union contested the legality of this on the ground that art 20 governs the convening of emergency sessions and the vote of the Security Council is a non-procedural one to which the veto applies. However, such arguments have not stopped the Assembly from convening to discuss matters, even where the protests of the permanent members have been raised.

17.5 Actions by regional agencies

Article 52 of the Charter of the United Nations provides:

'(1) Nothing in the present Charter precludes the existence of regional arrangements or agencies for dealing with such matters relating to the maintenance of international peace and security as are appropriate for regional action, provided that such arrangements or agencies and their activities are consistent with the Purposes and Principles of the United Nations.
(2) The Members of the United Nations entering into such arrangements or constituting such agencies shall make every effort to achieve pacific settlement of local disputes through such regional arrangements or by such regional agencies before referring them to the Security Council.
(3) The Security Council shall encourage the development of pacific settlement of local disputes through such regional arrangements or by such regional agencies either on the initiative of the states concerned or by reference from the Security Council.
(4) This Article in no way impairs the application of Articles 34 and 35.'

Article 53 provides:

'(1) The Security Council shall, where appropriate, utilise such regional arrangements or agencies for enforcement action under its authority. But no enforcement action shall be taken under regional arrangements or by regional agencies without the authorisation of the Security Council, with the exception of measures against any enemy state, as defined in paragraph 2 of this Article, provided for pursuant to Article 107 or in regional arrangements directed against renewal of aggressive policy on the part of any such state, until such time as the Organisation may, on request of the Government concerned, be charged with the responsibility for preventing further aggression by such a state.

(2) The term enemy state as used in paragraph 1 of this Article applies to any state which during the Second World War has been an enemy of any signatory of the present Charter.'

Article 54 provides:

'The Security Council shall at all times be kept fully informed of activities undertaken or in contemplation under regional arrangements or by regional agencies for the maintenance of international peace and security.'

A regional arrangement or agency must therefore satisfy three conditions stipulated in art 52.

1. It must be concerned with the maintenance of international peace and security.
2. It must be consistent with the Purposes and Principles of the United Nations.
3. It must in some way be regional.

Conflict between regional arrangements and the United Nations

The pacific settlement of disputes

Article 52(2) and (3) imposes upon the parties and the Security Council the obligation to utilise regional procedures for settlement. However, art 52(4) states that 'this article in no way impairs the application of Article 34 and 35'. Therefore it seems that the Security Council's own right to investigate a dispute or situation, and the member states right to appeal to the Council are preserved.

This jurisdictional conflict has led some regional organisations to declare that so far as inter-regional disputes are concerned, the regional procedures have a 'priority' over the Security Council's procedures for settlement. In this way the regional organisations may take action without fear of a permanent member of the Security Council using the power of veto.

Bowett, in an attempt to rationalise the competing claims to jurisdiction places 'disputes' into three categories:

'(1) Disputes involving no actual or potential threat to international peace – here the priority of the regional procedures is undisputed, and the matter ought not to be referred to the Security Council.

(2) Disputes involving a potential threat to international peace – here, the matter seems to fall squarely under Chapter VI of the Charter, so that the rights of the Council under Article 34, and of states under Article 35, are clear. Reference to a regional organisation's procedures becomes a matter of convenience, not of obligation, and much depends on the willingness of the parties to accept such a reference.

(3) "Disputes" which involve an actual threat to peace – here the situation properly belongs in Chapter VII, not Chapter VI, and the "primary responsibility" of the Security Council to deal with the matter is clear: there can be no question of "priority" for regional procedures. Equally, clearly, there is nothing to prevent the Security Council utilising regional procedures to assist in any measures taken under Chapter VII, but they do this subject to the Council's primary responsibility.'

Enforcement action

Article 53 of the Charter provides that 'no enforcement action shall be taken ... by regional agencies without the authorisation of the Security Council'.

This provision constitutes a serious obstacle to regional agencies and in particular to the Organisation of American States (OAS). The US and its allies have attempted to overcome this in a number of ways.

Measures short of the use of force. In 1962 the OAS imposed economic sanctions against the Castro regime in Cuba. The USSR argued in the Security Council that such a measure constituted enforcement action which was illegal without the authorisation of the Security Council. However, the majority of Security Council members considered that economic sanctions did not constitute enforcement action. The OAS was merely doing collectively what any of its members could have done individually – 'Under customary law, every state is at liberty to sever its economic relations with another state'.

Measures involving the use of force: the Cuban Missiles Crisis 1962. The USSR was sending to Cuba missiles and other weapons and materials which could be seen as a threat to US security. On 22 October 1962 President Kennedy announced America's intention to impose a 'strict quarantine on all offensive military equipment under shipment to Cuba'.

(This was essentially a blockade, but a blockade can only exist if there is a state of war and as the term 'war' was not politically acceptable they called it quarantine.) There was a great deal of concern on the part of the US to make what they were doing look to be consistent with international law. Two justifications were possible.

1. Self-defence under art 51 of the Charter: the missiles in Cuba would pose a threat to America. But the action taken by the US would be anticipatory self-defence. They were not only stopping the missiles being fired but were also stopping them being placed in Cuba. Even assuming that there is a right of anticipatory self-defence this must be exercised in accordance with the *Caroline* principle. There had to be an immediate threat and any action taken in self-defence had to be proportionate to the degree of harm threatened.

    It would therefore have been a very dubious case of self-defence and it was argued that if the US relied on self-defence it was not really genuine in showing a legal justification for the quarantine. The US also had to consider the American missiles in Turkey aimed at Russia. Could Russia also attempt to remove these in self-defence? Reliance on art 51 could therefore have created a dangerous precedent which could have been used by many other states. So politically it was felt that self-defence was not the line to take.

2. Regional action under Chapter VIII of the Charter: the quarantine was contrary to art 2(4) of the Charter and therefore it had to be justified. Self-defence could not seriously be used as a justification. The alternative was to ask the Security Council to act under Chapter VII, but Russia would veto. The General Assembly could, of course, then act in accordance with the Uniting for Peace Resolution but it was doubtful that the US would receive the support of the General Assembly. The only alternative therefore was action under Chapter VIII of the Charter. This proved to be the best approach and it was followed.

On 23 October at the suggestion of the US, the Security Council met and discussed the proposed quarantine but took no action. On the same day, the Council of the Organisation of American States adopted a resolution recommending that:

> 'Member states, in accordance with Articles 6 and 8 of the Inter-American Treaty of Reciprocal Assistance, take all measures, individually and collectively, including the use of armed force, which they may deem necessary to ensure that the Government of Cuba cannot continue to receive from the Sino-Soviet powers military material and related supplies which may threaten the peace and security of the Continent and to prevent the missiles in Cuba with offensive capability from ever becoming an active threat to the peace and security of the Continent': 47 US Department of State Bulletin, 1962, p722.

On 23 October the US President issued the following Proclamation:

> 'Any vessel or craft which may be proceeding towards Cuba may be intercepted and may be directed to identify itself, its cargo, equipment and stores and its ports of call, to stop, to lie to, to submit to visit and search, or to proceed as directed. Any vessel which fails or refuses to respond or to comply with directions shall be subject to being taken into custody': 47 US Department of State Bulletin, 1962, p717.

The US Deputy Legal Adviser, Meeker, justified the US action as follows:

> 'The quarantine was based on a collective judgment and recommendation of the American Republics made under the Rio Treaty. It was considered not to contravene Article 2, paragraph 4, because it was a measure adopted by a regional organisation in conformity with the provisions of Chapter VIII of the Charter. The purposes of the Organisation and its activities were considered to be consistent with the purposes and principles of the United Nations as provided in Article 52. This being the case, the quarantine would no more violate Article 2, paragraph 4, than measures voted for by the Council under Chapter VII, by the General Assembly under Articles 10 and 11, or taken by United Nations Members in conformity with Article 51': L Meeker, 'Defensive Quarantine and the Law' (1963) 57 AJIL 515 at 523–524.

The problem was, however, that enforcement action under art 53 could not be taken by regional agencies without the authorisation of the Security Council. The Soviet veto in the Security Council would have ensured that this authorisation was not given. The US therefore argued that the concept of 'enforcement action' subject to prior authorisation by the Security Council does not embrace measures falling short of the use of armed force or taken voluntarily. Enforcement action – the term used in the Charter – meant enforcement action which was compulsory upon a state. If the enforcement action was not compulsory but merely voluntary it would not be enforcement action under the meaning of the Charter. The action taken by the OAS was not therefore enforcement action within the meaning of the Charter because it was only a recommendation to states which was not binding upon them and thus any action taken by them was purely voluntary.

The legal arguments put forward by the US to justify their action are all very dubious in international law. Dean Acheson, a former US Secretary of state for Foreign Affairs, commented:

> 'I must conclude that the propriety of the Cuban quarantine is not a legal issue. The power, position and prestige of the United States had been challenged by another state; and law simply does not deal with such questions of ultimate power – power that comes close to the sources of sovereignty. I cannot believe that there are principles of law that say we must accept destruction of our way of life ... The survival of states is not a matter of law.'

Enforcement actions by regional organisations authorised by the UN Security Council. An example of an enforcement action which was authorised by the UN Security Council was the 1999 intervention by the Organisation of American States (OAS) to uphold democracy in Haiti. Reverend Jean-Bertrand Aristide was elected the President of Haiti in 1990 in the first free election in Haiti's history. After eight months in office his government was overturned in a military coup d'etat and Aristide fled the country. The OAS, of which Haiti is a member, reacted promptly and requested the military government to respect the Haitian constitution. The Organisation took the strongest ever action against Haiti, consisting of severance of diplomatic links and the suspension of all economic, financial and commercial relations except for humanitarian aid. Other measures taken by the OAS involved the denial of access to port facilities to any vessel that violated the embargo, bans on travel and freezing of assets of perpetrators and supporters of the military coup: OAS Resolution MRE/RES 3/92, 17 May 1992. The UN General Assembly fully supported all measures taken by the OAS. The UN Secretary-General appointed a special representative for Haiti who, in July 1993, was successful in securing the Governor's Island Agreement to restore Aristide. The agreement was signed by both Aristide and the military junta. A provision of the agreement provided for a team of US and Canadian advisers to land in Haiti to help to train the Haitian police to observe human rights. Their vessel never reached Port-au-Prince. Angry crowds at the harbour prevented its landing. This prompted the OAS to take military action to impose the agreement. The Security Council in its Resolutions 867 of 1993 and 940 of 1994 authorised the enforcement action by the OAS involving a multinational force from 27 countries to invade Haiti. The operation 'Uphold Democracy' went peacefully as former President Jimmy Carter persuaded the head of the military junta to allow the intervention. The invasion took place in September 1994 and resulted in the restoration of President Aristide to authority.

It is somehow ironic that on 29 February 2004, the UN Security Council adopted Resolution 1529 authorising the deployment of a Multinational Interim Force in Haiti subsequent to the resignation and exile of President Aristide. After flawed elections in May 2000 a growing violent confrontation between the governmental forces and the opposition destabilised the country to the point that the intervention of the UN Security Council became necessary in order to establish public safety and law in Haiti.

What is a regional arrangement?

Not all organisations with membership limited to states in a given geographical area are regarded as regional arrangements within the sense of Chapter VIII.

For example, the North Atlantic Treaty Organisation does not call itself a regional arrangement but is expressed in its Treaty as being an organisation for collective self-defence under art 51 of the Charter. It therefore avoids the control of the Security Council and the Soviet power of veto.

No definition of regional arrangements is given in the UN Charter and there is controversy as to what the phrase actually means. Bowett argues that the real question is not whether a given organisation is a regional arrangement or not, but rather whether particular action is taken as a regional arrangement or not.

18

International Humanitarian Law

18.1 Introduction

18.2 The law relating to the conduct of armed conflicts

18.3 Humanitarian law

18.4 Breaches of international humanitarian law

18.1 Introduction

The traditional distinction in international law between rules concerning the resort to war (the ius ad bellum) and rules governing the conduct of war (the ius in bello) has lost its importance for two reasons.

First, war which was once considered as the normal way to resolve disputes was outlawed in international law, initially by the Kellogg-Briand Pact 1928 and then by art 2(4) of the UN Charter.

Second, the clear–cut distinction between a state of war and a state of peace has become fluid, as in most cases the parties directly involved in hostilities deny that they are at war with each other For example, from 1937 until 1941 there were increasing hostilities between China and Japan although both parties denied any intention of being involved in war to the point of maintaining sham diplomatic relations. In 1956 the UK and France denied that they were at war with Egypt, whilst Egypt declared that it would consider French and British citizens as enemy nationals. The prime minister of the UK officially denied that the UK was at war with Argentina in 1982 and the hostilities were officially referred to as the Falklands Crisis or the Falklands Conflict. The government of the US always refused to acknowledge that it was at war with North Vietnam.

International humanitarian law itself has undergone important changes in the light of the following.

1. International wars have become less frequent, but local wars and internal conflicts occur more often then ever.
2. Wars have become shorter but more destructive taking into account modern military technology. Some weapons, eg nuclear weapons, are too powerful to be used.

3. The development of modern weaponry means that wars are no longer confined to members of armed forces but involve the entire population living in the territory where hostilities are taking place.
4. Modern international law requires that the protection of human rights in peacetime is matched by the necessity of ensuring that individuals are treated with humanity in wartime.

The consequence of the above is that the term 'war' became obsolete in international law. It has been replaced by the term 'armed conflict'. The main objectives of the law of armed conflict is to ensure the humanitarian behaviour of all parties involved by determining the permissible forms, areas and objects of use of force by belligerents against each other and by protecting the most vulnerable non-participants in the hostilities: the civilians, the prisoners of war, the sick and wounded. The definition of the law of international conflicts has two aspects: it limits methods and means of warfare in the light of the principles of humanity and it protects persons who are not or no longer participating in the hostilities. The first aspect relates to the law of armed conflicts and was mainly developed by the Hague Conventions. The second aspect concerns humanitarian law and was primarily regulated by the four Geneva Conventions of 1949. These two aspects converged with the adoption of the 1977 Additional Protocols I and II to the Geneva Conventions, mostly because the law of the Hague was never a subject of a complete consolidation and revision. As a result the 1977 Additional Protocols contain provisions relating to limitations on the methods and means of warfare and thus on the rules governing the conduct of hostilities. For that reason the term 'international humanitarian law' is used to describe both the law of the Hague and the Geneva Conventions. Nevertheless, the two aspects require separate examination.

18.2 The law relating to the conduct of armed conflicts

The cruelty of warfare in antiquity and in the Middle Ages was rarely limited. The winner had it all – the life and all the possessions of the loser, including his wife and children. Only a handful of military leaders and Heads of State imposed a minimum standard of conduct of war upon their soldiers. One such example is provided by Alexander the Great who in 333 BC ordered his soldiers to spare the civilian population of conquered areas and not to intentionally desecrate religious sites. In 70 BC the Roman commander Titus ensured the safe passage of women and children from Jerusalem when it was under siege. In the Middle Ages there were some attempts to civilise the conduct of war, out of necessity rather than humanity. As captured soldiers were normally killed or enslaved (only knights could be freed upon paying ransom) they fought ferociously and desperately to preserve their life and freedom. In order to avoid antagonising and therefore making an enemy desperate, some Christian and Muslim leaders imposed limits on savagery in the conduct of wars. Furthermore, the teaching of Christianity and the rules of chivalry influenced some rulers who imposed on their armies certain rules of warfare. In 1386 King Richard II of England published the Ordinance for the Government of the Army which punished by death certain acts, such as violence against women and unarmed priests, the desecration of Churches and the burning of houses. These kind of rules issued for internal purposes were copied and applied by other nations. Consequently, similar prohibitions can be found in the codes published by Ferdinand of Hungary in 1526, by Emperor Maximilian II in 1570 and by King Gustavus II Adolphus of Sweden in 1570.

In 1625 Hugo Grotius, the father of modern international law, wrote *On the Law of War and Peace*. His work firmly set limits to the way in which hostilities should be conducted between belligerents and established the principle of humanitarian treatment of civilians during armed conflicts. His work influenced his contemporaries as well as future rulers and leaders.

In the Age of Enlightment a new perception of wars changed the manner in which they were conducted. Jean Jacques Rousseau in his *Le Contract Social* wrote that:

> 'War then is a relation, not between man and man, but between state and state, and individuals are enemies only accidentally, not as men, nor even as citizens, but as soldiers … The object of the war being the destruction of the hostile state, the other party has a right to kill its defenders while they are bearing arms; but as soon as they lay them down and surrender they become once more merely men, whose life no one has any right to take.'

Once the objective of a war was identified it became clear that there was no need for unnecessary cruelty and that the civilian population should be protected as it played no role in hostilities. The ideas expressed by J J Rousseau and other writers of the Enlightment gained widespread acceptance.

In the next stage governments started to codify the laws of war for internal use imposing some standards of behaviour on members of their armed forces. During the American civil war, President Abraham Lincoln issued the Lieber Code (Instructions for the Government of Armies of the United States in the Field, General Orders No 100, of 24 April 1863) which was drafted by Professor Francis Lieber and revised by a board of officers. The Code contained provisions relating to 'Protection of persons and especially women, of religion, the arts and sciences. Punishment of crimes against the inhabitants of hostile countries' (arts 31–47), as well as imposing humane treatment of prisoners of war: arts 49–80. Besides being binding on American soldiers, it also influenced the drafting of military regulations of armies of other states. Such rules relating to the customs of war hardened into international customary rules which became gradually incorporated into international conventions.

The first multilateral treaty was the Declaration of Paris Respecting Maritime Law 1856. It was followed by the Geneva Convention for the Amelioration of the Condition of the Wounded in Armies in the Field 1864. Another important codification was the 1868 St Petersburg Declaration Renouncing the Use, in Time of War, of Explosive Projectiles under 400 Grammes Weight which banned the use of such explosive projectiles of a weight below 400 grammes. The Declaration, which is still in force, recognised that some weapons or methods of war which are likely to cause unnecessary suffering should be prohibited. This is one of the fundamental principles of the laws applicable to armed conflicts.

In 1874 the government of Russia convened an international conference in Brussels which adopted the International Declaration Concerning the Laws and Customs of War. Although the declaration never entered into force for lack of ratifications it served as a source for the Regulations attached to the Hague Convention II with Respect to the Laws and Customs of War on Land 1899 (amended by the Second International Peace Conference in 1907, it became the Hague Convention IV), and which contains in its Preamble the famous Martens Clause according to which:

> 'Until a more complete code of laws of war is issued, the High Contracting Parties think it right to declare that in cases not included in the Regulations adopted by them, populations and belligerents remain under the protection and empire of the principles of international law, as they result from usages established between civilised nations, from the laws of humanity, at the requirements of the public conscience': Reprinted in D Schindler and J Toman, *The Laws of Armed Conflicts*, 3rd ed, Dordrecht/Geneva: Martinus Nijhoff Publisher/Henry Dunant Institute, 1988, p70.

The conference had initiated a series of international conferences which provided a forum for discussions between governments and led to the adoption of numerous international instruments in this area. The First International Peace Conference took place in The Hague in 1899 at the invitation of Russia's Czar Nicolas. The Conference adopted:

1. Hague I for the Pacific Settlement of International Disputes;
2. Hague II with Respect to the Laws and Customs of War on Land;
3. Hague III for the Adaptation to Maritime Warfare of the Principles of the Geneva Convention of 1864 on the Laws of War;
4. Hague IV Prohibiting Launching of Projectiles and Explosives from Balloons;
5. Declaration I on the Launching of Projectiles and Explosives from Balloons;
6. Declaration II on the Use of Projectiles the Object of Which is the Diffusion of Asphyxiating or Deleterious Gases;
7. Declaration III on the Use of Bullets Which Expand or Flatten Easily in the Human Body;
8. Final Act of the International Peace Conference 29 July 1899.

Following the First Peace Conference states adopted two further conventions: the Convention for the Exemption of Hospital Ships, in Time of War, from Payment of All Dues and Taxes Imposed for the Benefit of the State 1904 (at The Hague) and the Convention for the Amelioration of the Condition of the Wounded and Sick in Armies in the Field 1906 (in Geneva).

The Second Peace Conference took place in The Hague in 1907. The Conference adopted 13 conventions and one declaration. Most of the conventions have been recognised as customary law. The Conference codified the laws of naval warfare by adopting the following conventions:

1. Hague Convention I for the Pacific Settlement of International Disputes;
2. Hague Convention II on the Limitation of Employment of Force for Recovery of Contract Debts;
3. Hague Convention III Relative to the Opening of Hostilities;
4. Hague Convention IV Respecting the Laws and Customs of War on Land;
5. Hague Convention V Concerning the Rights and Duties of Neutral Powers and Persons in Case of War on Land;
6. Hague Convention VI Concerning the Status of Enemy Merchant Ships at the Outbreak of Hostilities;
7. Hague Convention VII Concerning the Conversion of Merchant Ships into Warships;
8. Hague Convention VIII Concerning the Laying of Automatic Submarine Contact Mines;
9. Hague Convention IX Concerning the Bombardment by Naval Forces in Time of War;
10. Hague Convention X for the Adaptation to Maritime War of the Principles of the Geneva Convention;
11. Hague Convention XI Concerning Certain Restrictions with Regard to the Exercise of the Right of Capture in Naval War;
12. Hague Convention XII Concerning the Creation of an International Prize Court (never ratified);
13. Hague Convention XIII Concerning the Rights and Duties of Neutral Powers in Naval War.

The Hague Peace Conferences did not set up a system to remedy violations of the principles established in the above instruments, rather they tried to impose some limitations on the use of force in international relations. In this respect two conventions were adopted: the Convention Respecting the Limitation on the Employment of Force for the Recovery of Contract Debt and the Hague Convention I for the Pacific Settlement of International Disputes 1899 which set up a Permanent Court of Arbitration (PCA).

The main contribution of the Hague Peace Conferences was that they codified customary law on the conduct of warfare. Consequently, the Hague laws are not only binding between the contracting states but being declaratory of customary international law they are binding on all states. Some of them have been replaced but some are still in force. For example the Hague Convention IV Concerning the Laws and Customs of War on Land and the annexed Regulations are still applicable. Articles 42–56 of the Hague Regulations constitute the principal text applicable to the government of occupied territory and the treatment of property in occupied territory.

The codification of international customary law clearly establishes that the means and methods of warfare are limited by two principles: the principle of humanity and the principle of the protection of non-combatants and civilians.

The principle of humanity

The principle of humanity requires that only those means and methods of warfare are allowed which are justified by military necessities. There is no definition of 'military necessities'. However, their limits are defined by international treaties and customary law.

Four types of rules of warfare derive from the relationship between the principle of humanity and the requirements of military necessities.

1. Rules which prohibit an act which is not justified by the military necessities as it serves no military purpose whatsoever and which violates the principle of humanity, eg such as sadistic acts of cruelty, wanton destruction of property, etc.
2. Rules which prohibit an act which may have possible tactical advantages but which breaches the principle of humanity, eg the use of biological or chemical weapons.
3. Rules which try to achieve a compromise between the two: eg a rule which allows a damaged warship to undergo necessary emergency repairs in a neutral harbour provided that those repairs do not increase her fighting power.
4. Rules which permit an act on the basis of military necessities. Such rules take into consideration the principle of humanity only 'as far as possible'. For example, art 18 of the 1949 Geneva Convention IV provides that 'The Parties to the conflict shall, insofar as military considerations permit, take the necessary steps to make the distinctive emblems indicating civilian hospitals clearly visible to the enemy land, air and naval forces in order to obviate the possibility of any hostile action'.

However, a fifth possibility exists. There are no rules. Military necessities override humanitarian considerations.

Under the principle of humanity certain weapons and certain conduct is prohibited.

Prohibited weapons

Among the weapons of mass destruction – chemical, biological and nuclear – only chemical and biological weapons are banned under international law. The matter of whether or not the use of nuclear weapons is prohibited is still unclear.

Only some conventional weapons are expressly prohibited.

Chemical weapons. A chemical weapon is a weapon that releases chemicals that kill or disable people. There are a great variety of chemicals: some are lethal, such as nerve gas, some merely irritating, such as tear gas. The oldest international agreement limiting the use of chemical weapon is the 1675 Franco–German agreement prohibiting the use of poison bullets. Some provisions of the 1874 Brussels Declaration Concerning the Laws and Customs of War prohibited the employment of poison or poisoned weapons and the use of arms, projectiles or material to cause unnecessary suffering. At the first International Peace Conference in the Hague in 1899 an agreement prohibiting the use of projectiles filled with poison gas was signed. Germany interpreted the agreement literally when it used chemical weapons during World War I. Chlorine gas was released from gas cylinders at Ypres (no projectiles were used). In response the Allied powers also used chemical weapons. The use of chemical weapons during World War I resulted in the death of 91,000 and the suffering of many thousands. The only positive effect of the use of chemical weapons was that seeing their effect on human beings the international community decided to ban them!

The 1925 Geneva Protocol for the Prohibition of the Use in War of Asphyxiating, Poisonous or Other Gases and of Bacteriological Methods of Warfare banned the use of chemical weapons but did not prohibit the development, production or possession of such weapons. During World War II chemicals were not used by either party. Since then only Iraq (other cases are inconclusive) violated the 1925 Geneva Protocol (it used chemical weapons against the Kurdish population and during the war with Iran in the 1980s). After World War II nuclear weapons undermined the importance of chemical weapons.

Further measures were developed within the framework of the Committee on Disarmament. The Eighteen Nations Disarmament Conference which has become the Committee on Disarmament since the late 1960s put on its agenda the issue of chemical and biological weapons. The Committee decided to treat these issues separately. In respect of chemical weapons an ad hoc working group was set up by the Committee in 1980 which after years of deliberations and discussions with representatives of governments and the civil chemical industry produced an evolving draft convention in 1984. This was further elaborated by the draft submitted by Australia in 1992.

On the basis of the above draft, on 3 September 1992 the Conference on Disarmaments at Geneva adopted the final text of the Convention on the Prohibition of the Development, Production, Stockpiling and Use of Chemical Weapons and on Their Destruction (CWC). The CWC entered into force on 29 April 1997. As at 19 November 2004 167 countries had ratified the CWC. Article II(1) of the CWC defines chemical weapons as all chemicals except when intended for purposes not prohibited under the Convention. Schedules to the CWC enumerate chemical weapons (the list is not exhaustive) which are to be verified under the CWC. Under art I(1) of the CWC the contracting states undertake never under any circumstances:

'(a) to develop, produce, otherwise acquire, stockpile, or retain chemical weapons, or transfer, directly or indirectly, chemical weapons to anyone;
(b) to use chemical weapons;
(c) to engage in any military preparations to use chemical weapons;

(d) to assists, encourage or induce, in any way, anyone to engage in any activity prohibited to a state party under this Convention.'

A contracting state is bound under the CWC not only to destroy all chemical weapons under its jurisdiction but also those abandoned by it on the territory of another state party. The destruction must be done in a safe and environmentally friendly manner within ten years of the CWC coming into force. The rate of destruction is determined in the CWC. Also facilities used to produce chemical weapons must be destroyed or converted for uses conforming with the CWC.

The Convention set up the Organisation for the Prohibition of Chemical Weapons (OPCW), which has its seat in The Hague, charged with the supervision of the CWC implementation in contracting states.

The OPCW employs inspectors who, at the request of any contracting party, are entitled to carry out challenge inspections at any facility or location under the jurisdiction of any other contracting party, without right of refusal and at short notice to verify the compliance of that contracting party with the provisions of the CWC.

The destruction of chemical weapons and of facilities used to produce them (or their transformation) is also subject to verification by the OPCW inspectors. Apart from challenge inspections a contracting state may request an investigation if it considers that chemical weapons have been used in any contracting state. If possible, the inspection team should be dispatched within 24 hours after the request was made and submit its first report within 24 hours after its arrival.

Under the CWC the contracting state is entitled to request assistance if attacked or threatened with chemical weapons. The Director-General of the OPCW will examine the request and decide on the further action. The assistance may consist, inter alia, of the supply of detection, protection and decontamination equipment, medical antidotes and treatments, or inspections.

The CWC is the first arms control and non-proliferation treaty which imposes obligations on non-governmental businesses. Even if a contracting state does not manufacture chemical weapons, companies in a contracting state engaged in activities involving certain chemicals may be required to report to the relevant national authority responsible under the CWC for reporting to the OPCW and may be subject to inspections.

Biological weapons. Biological weapons are similar to chemical weapons except that they use microorganisms or biologically derived toxins instead of chemicals. Biological weapons have never been used in wars, although Japan did attempt to use them on a few Chinese villages during World War II. The use of biological weapons as a method of warfare was banned by the 1925 Geneva Protocol for the Prohibition of the Use in War of Asphyxiating, Poisonous or Other Gases and of Bacteriological Methods of Warfare.

The main contribution to the total ban on biological weapons came from the US when on 25 November 1969 President Richard Nixon declared that the US unilaterally and unconditionally renounced all methods of biological warfare using microorganisms and that the US's biological programme would be strictly confined to define defence measures such as immunisation. In 1970 the government of the US extended the ban to toxins. The example of the US was followed by Canada, Sweden and the UK. All declared that they had destroyed their existing stock and expressed their intention not to produce anymore. However, unilateral declarations are binding only on the states that make them. For that reason within the framework of the Committee on Disarmament, negotiations and discussions were conducted in order to produce a binding treaty. The opposition of Communist countries blocked any progress. The breakthrough came on 30 March 1971 with the submission to the Committee by the Soviet Union of a draft convention on the prohibition of biological weapons and toxins. This constituted a step towards a global agreement on the matter. On 16 December 1971 the General Assembly approved the Convention on the Prohibition of the Development, Production and Stockpiling of Bacteriological (Biological) and Toxin Weapons and on Their Destruction (BWC) by 110 votes. The Convention was opened for signature at Washington, London and Moscow on 10 April 1971. It entered into force on 26 March 1975. At the time of writing 151 states have ratified the BWC.

Under the Convention contracting parties are bound neither to develop, produce and stockpile or acquire biological agents or toxins 'of types and in quantities that have no justification for prophylactic, protective and other peaceful purposes' nor weapons and means of delivery. All such material had to be destroyed by contracting Parties within nine months of the Convention's entry into force. The Convention provides for co-operation between contracting states. Review conferences provide a forum for such co-operation. The matter of verification of compliance with the Convention through inspections was discussed at a Special Conference held in September 1994. As a result, an ad hoc group was set up. Initially, its work on a Protocol to the BWC was approved by the contracting parties. This occurred mainly as a result of a growing suspicion that at least eight countries had been carrying out active biological programmes in breach of international law and a concern that terrorist organisations might try to acquire and use biological weapons. In 2001 the work on the Protocol was suspended on the grounds that no measure could provide assurances that such programmes were absent and that the Protocol could be abused for non-BWC related objectives.

Nuclear weapons. It is estimated that the global nuclear stockpile ranges from 24,700 to 33,307 nuclear weapons. There five declared nuclear weapons states are China, France, Russia, the UK and the US. De facto nuclear weapons states are India, Israel and Pakistan; and potential nuclear weapons states are Iran, Iraq, Libya and North Korea. Other countries have no nuclear weapons. There are 433 nuclear reactors in 44 countries. Any country with a nuclear reactor is considered to have the capacity to produce nuclear weapons.

So far any attempt to ban nuclear weapons has been unsuccessful. Many authors argued that the use of nuclear weapons is incompatible with the principle of humanity and the principle of the protection of civil populations. Indeed, customary international law starting with the 1868 St Petersburg Declaration prohibits the use of weapons causing unnecessary suffering. Nuclear weapons are likely to cause unnecessary suffering and to indiscriminately affect combatants and non-combatants. The UN General Assembly, in Resolution 1653 (XVI) of 21 November 1961 and Resolution 984 of 11 April 1995, unconditionally condemned the use of nuclear weapons. At the time of writing the First Committee of the General Assembly (Disarmament and International Security) is preparing a number of resolutions aimed at strengthening the co-operation and commitment of member states towards the total elimination of nuclear weapons.

The matter of the legality of nuclear weapons was the subject of two advisory opinions delivered by the International Court of Justice on 8 July 1996: see the *Legality of the Threat or Use of Nuclear Weapons Case* (1996) ICJ Rep 90. The ICJ was first asked by the World Health Organisation (WHO) to deliver an advisory opinion on the following question:

> 'In view of the health and environmental effects, would the use of nuclear weapons by a state in war or other armed conflict be a breach of its obligations under international law including the WHO Constitution?'

The WHO being an international organisation is entitled to ask the ICJ for an advisory opinion but the matter referred must be within the scope of activities of the requesting organisation: art 96(2) of the UN Charter. The General Assembly, fearing that the question asked by the WHO was not sufficiently connected with the functions of the WHO, decided to ask the ICJ for an advisory opinion on the question: 'Is the threat or use of nuclear weapons in any circumstances permitted under international law?'.

In respect of its jurisdiction the ICJ confirmed that the GA was entitled to ask for an advisory opinion on the matter, taking into account the broad competence of the GA and its long-standing activities relating to disarmament and nuclear weapons. The fact that the question asked was not related to any particular dispute and was expressed in abstract terms did not prevent the ICJ from delivering an advisory opinion. In respect of the WHO, as expected, the ICJ rejected the request for an advisory opinion. The ICJ explained that none of the functions listed in the WHO constitution expressly referred to the legality of any activity hazardous to health, or depended upon the legality of the situations in which the organisation must act. Under art 2 of the WHO constitution its main objective is 'the attainment by all people of the highest possible level of health'. Consequently, the ICJ stated that the WHO's mandate is to deal with effects on health of the use of nuclear weapons, or any other hazardous activity, and to take preventive measures protecting the health of people in the situation where nuclear weapons are used or such activities engaged in. The ICJ found that the request for an advisory opinion was not connected with the effects of the use of nuclear weapons but with the legality of use of such weapons. It held that 'the legality or illegality of the use of nuclear weapons in no way determines the specific measures, regarding health or otherwise (studies, plans, procedures etc), which could be necessary in order to prevent or cure some of their effects.' Further, it was contrary to the principle of speciality, under which international organisations operate in their clearly established fields of competence, to recognise that the WHO had implied powers to address the question of the legality of the use of nuclear weapons. Consequently, the matter was outside the scope of the mandate of the WHO.

With regard to the request of the GA the ICJ held that:

1. there is neither in customary law nor in conventional law any specific authorisation of the threat or use of nuclear weapons (unanimously);
2. there is neither in customary law nor in conventional law any comprehensive and universal prohibition of the threat or use of nuclear weapons as such (by 11 votes to 3);
3. a threat of or the use of force by means of nuclear weapons which is in breach of art 2(4) of the Charter of the United Nations and which fails to satisfy the requirements of art 51 of the UN Charter is unlawful (unanimously);
4. a threat of or the use of nuclear weapons must be compatible with the requirements of the rules of international humanitarian law. Two principles are fundamental in respect of the conduct of military operations: the protection of the civilian population and civilian objects and the prohibition of the use of weapons incapable of distinguishing between combatants and non-combatants; and the principle of humanity which prohibits the use of weapons causing unnecessary suffering. These principles are applicable to any armed conflicts irrespective of whether or not a particular state has ratified them because they constitute intransgressible principles of international customary law. A threat of or the use of nuclear weapons should be compatible with the above rules as well as with specific obligations imposed on a state under treaties and other undertakings which expressly deal with nuclear weapons (unanimously).

The conclusion reached by the ICJ (carried by the President's casting vote) was:

'It follows from the above-mentioned requirements that the threat or use of nuclear weapons would generally be contrary to the rules of international law applicable to armed conflicts, and in particular the principles and rules of humanitarian law.

However, in view of the current state of international law, and of the elements of fact at its disposal, the Court cannot conclude definitely whether the threat or use of nuclear weapons would be lawful or unlawful in an extreme circumstance of self-defence, in which the very survival of a state would be at stake.'

Judge Higgins of the ICJ observed that the ICJ pronounced, in fact, a non liquet on the issue of legality of threat or use of nuclear weapons on the grounds of uncertainty in the present state of law and facts.

Finally the ICJ held that there is an obligation to negotiate in good faith and to achieve complete nuclear disarmament. This obligation is twofold – it applies to the pursuit of negotiations and their conclusion.

The above advisory opinion enhances the importance of the 1968 Non-Proliferation Treaty (NPT). The NPT entered into force on 5 March 1970 and has been ratified by 187 states (April 2003). The NPT creates a framework for controlling the spread of nuclear material and expertise. The main objective of the NPT is to limit the number of states possessing nuclear weapons. Under the NPT states which possess nuclear weapons (those that had manufactured and exploded a nuclear weapon or other nuclear explosive device prior to 1 January 1967), that is the five permanent members of the Security Council, are obliged not to transfer, and the non-nuclear states, not to acquire and not to manufacture, nuclear weapons except for peaceful purposes. The nuclear states are also obliged to negotiate effective measures leading to nuclear disarmament and for general and complete disarmament. The NPT provides for its inspection body – the International Atomic Energy Agency (IAEA), a UN agency, based in Vienna. IAEA is charged with inspecting the nuclear power industry in contracting states in order to prevent any spread of nuclear material and any diversion of nuclear energy from peaceful use to nuclear weapons by a contracting state.

Until 1990 no serious attempts were made by the nuclear powers to meet their obligations under the Treaty. The NPT requires that there be a review and extension conference 25 years after its entry into force. The Review Conference held in 1995 decided to extend indefinitely and unconditionally the NPT, and to take concrete measures to strengthen the non-proliferation regime and to provide assurance of compliance with non-proliferation undertakings. The Conference adopted the Principles and Objectives for nuclear non-proliferation and disarmament which were further examined and developed by the 2000 NPT Review Conference held on April 24–19 May 2000, both of which were aimed at ensuring the full implementation of the NPT as well as its universality. The next Review Conference is scheduled for 2005.

The NPT has been largely successful. The main problem with the NPT is that some countries which are in possession of nuclear weapons are not contracting parties. Israel, India and Pakistan have neither signed the NPT nor the safeguards' agreement with IAEA. North Korea, a contracting party to the NPT, withdrew from IAEA in 1993, although it allowed nuclear inspections in 1999 in exchange for economic aid and the partial lifting of US trade sanctions. However, on 10 January 2003 North Korea announced its immediate withdrawal from the NPT which automatically cancelled the 1992 Safeguards Agreement with IAEA. Subsequently, under international pressure North Korea agreed to enter into six-nation talks (involving South Korea, Japan, Russia, China and the US) on its nuclear weapons programme. From 2003 to September 2004 three rounds of six-nation talks had yielded little. The fourth round was to start in September 2004 but North Korea refused to attend amid speculation that it was waiting to see the outcome of the US presidential election. After the election in November 2004 North Korea agreed to resume six-nation talks. The case of North Korea showed the lack of an effective enforcement mechanism for cases of non-compliance with the NPT and the lack of measures preventing a state from withdrawing from the NPT. Those issues will be on the agenda of the 2005 Review Conference. Another country which has caused international concern is Iran. The US branded Iran as part of an 'axis of evil' along with North Korea and pre-war Iraq and accused Iran of using its nuclear programme to build a nuclear bomb. However, the issue seems to have been resolved peacefully. The government of Iran admitted to the IAEA that it had been secretly developing a broad range of nuclear capacities for the past 18 years in breach of the NPT and promised to fully co-operate with the IAEA. On 26 November 2004 the 35 member IAEA board adopted a resolution condemning Iran for past violations of IAEA rules and welcoming Iran's new pledges of co-operation. Further, the IAEA board, contrary to the US position, decided not to refer the Iranian nuclear issue to the UN Security Council for possible sanctions. Iran agreed to halt its uranium enrichment programme and to allow snap weapons inspections to be carried out by IAEA inspectors.

Another problem facing the international community is that after the collapse of the Soviet Union many of its nuclear storage facilities are not sufficiently protected. There have been attempts to steal and smuggle radioactive substances abroad in exchange for hard currency. The US and IAEA are helping Russia in this area. The Review Conference 2000 urged all states to adhere to the Convention on the Physical Protection of Nuclear Material 1980 and to apply the recommendations provided by IAEA (63 states are party to this Convention). The matter of nuclear safety has been recognised by the Review Conference 2000 as a key element of the peaceful use of nuclear energy. Nuclear safety has been regulated by a number of conventions, inter alia, the Convention on Nuclear Safety 1994, the Convention on Early Notification of a Nuclear Accident 1986, the Convention on Assistance in the Case of a Nuclear Accident or Radiological Emergency 1986, etc.

The most important resolution adopted by the 1995 Review Conference concerned the prospective establishment of a nuclear weapon-free zone in the Middle East. Since 1995 all states of the region of the Middle East, with the exception of Israel, have become contracting parties to the NPT and have placed their nuclear facilities under the full-scope IAEA safeguards. The matter of the potential nuclear-weapon-free zone was referred to the 2005 Review Conference for further recommendation. The five nuclear weapons states committed themselves to support the 1995 Resolution on the establishment of a nuclear-free zone in the Middle East.

Under the NPT nuclear states are bound to conduct negotiations in good faith, to discontinue the nuclear arms race and to achieve nuclear disarmament. In this respect some progress has been made through the Strategic Arms Reduction Treaty process: the 1991 Start I, the 1992 Start II and 1997 Start III Treaties, as well as the Antibalistic Missile Treaty 1972.

Closely related to non-proliferation is the matter of nuclear tests. The ICJ had an opportunity to deliver its judgment on the legality of nuclear weapons tests in the *Nuclear Tests Case: New Zealand* v *France* (1974) ICJ Rep 457, but decided that the action of New Zealand was without object because of the undertaking submitted by France not to carry out further atmospheric nuclear tests. Paragraph 63 of the judgment stated that:

'Once the Court has found that a state has entered into a commitment concerning its future conduct it is not the Court's function to contemplate that it will not comply with it. However, the Court observes that if the basis of this Judgment were to be affected, the Applicant could request an examination of the situation in accordance with the provisions of the Statute.'

When France announced in 1995 its intention to conduct a final series of eight nuclear weapons tests in the South Pacific, New Zealand, on the basis of paragraph 63 of the 1974 judgment, requested the ICJ to resume the 1974 case. Australia, Samoa, Solomon Islands, the Marshall Islands and the Federated States of Micronesia filed an application for permission to intervene. New Zealand also requested provisional measures. In the request reference was made to the order for the indication of provisional measures made by the ICJ on 22 June 1973 ((1973) ICJ Rep 99) aimed at ensuring that France would refrain from conducting further nuclear tests at Mururoa and Fagataufa Atolls. The ICJ restricted the issue it was willing to examine to the following question:

'Do the Requests submitted to the Court by the Government of New Zealand on 21 August 1995 fall within the provisions of paragraph 63 of the Judgment of the Court of 20 December 1974 in the case concerning Nuclear Tests?'

In its order of 22 September 1995 the ICJ dismissed the request submitted by New Zealand and the application to intervene submitted by other states. The Court found that the procedure specified in paragraph 63 was applicable only if circumstances were to arise which affected the basis of the 1974 judgment. This was not the case, taking into account that the 1974 ICJ judgment concerned atmospheric nuclear tests whilst the new tests announced by France were related to a series of underground tests.

France resumed its nuclear tests in 1996 under the fragile coral atoll of Mururoa in the South Pacific but due to international pressure aborted the test series at the sixth test. However, the damage inflicted by the French nuclear tests to the region is enormous. Even the French Atomic Energy Commission admitted that the rock of Mururoa Atoll is threatened with collapse because of sustained nuclear testing: *New Zealand Herald*, 3 March 2001. Global action, inter alia, consisting of the boycotting of French wine and cheese contributed to the termination of the French nuclear tests!

The first attempt to prohibit nuclear tests was the adoption of the 1963 Moscow Treaty Banning Nuclear Weapon Tests in the Atmosphere, in Outer Space and under Water. The Treaty was a failure for two reasons: first, it provided only a partial ban as underground tests was still allowed provided that radioactive debris from underground explosions were kept within the national territories; and, second, many states, including two nuclear powers (France and China), did not ratify the Treaty. In 1974 Russia and the US agreed to limit underground tests to a maximum explosive power of 150 kilotonnes from 31 March 1976, but nuclear tests for peaceful purposes were not included. They were the subject of the 1976 Russia–US Agreement. In 1992 the US Congress declared a moratorium on testing which was later extended by President Clinton. However, some states have continued nuclear tests. The nuclear explosions carried out by India and Pakistan were unanimously condemned by Resolution 1172 (1998) of the Security Council. Both of them declared a moratorium on further testing and signed the Comprehensive Nuclear-Test-Ban Treaty. Indeed, a major step in banning nuclear tests was made by the General Assembly which adopted on 24 September 1996 the Comprehensive Nuclear-Test-Ban Treaty. As at 8 December 2004, 174 states had signed the Treaty and 120 had ratified it. As a prerequisite of its entry into force 44 states believed to have the capacity to build nuclear weapons, however crude, must ratify the Treaty. Eleven states, amongst them China and the US, out of 44 had, as at 8 December 2004, still not ratified the Treaty. It should be noted that the US Senate refused ratification in November 1999 and the US government has no plans to become a contracting party.

The Comprehensive Nuclear-Test-Ban Treaty prohibits any nuclear explosion whether for military or peaceful purposes and establishes an organisation to supervise its implementation. The Treaty includes a Protocol which provides for the international monitoring system, on-site inspections and for confidence-building measures.

Another way leading to the elimination of all nuclear weapons is the establishment of internationally recognised nuclear-weapon-free zones. The UN Disarmament Commission, at its 1999 session, unanimously adopted guidelines on the establishment of nuclear-weapon-free zones on the basis of arrangements freely arrived at by the states of the region concerned: UN DocA/54/42. So far the following arrangements creating nuclear-weapon-free zones have been established:

1. The Treaty on Principles Governing the Activities of States in the Exploration and Use of Outer Space 1966 which prohibits the orbiting, installing and stationing of nuclear or other weapons of mass destruction anywhere in space. Celestial bodies must remain free from all military activities (in force since October 1967).
2. The Antarctic Treaty 1959 which denuclearised the Antarctic.
3. The Seabed Treaty 1971 which prohibits the placing of weapons of mass destruction, or structures for storing, testing or launching such weapons, on the seabed and ocean floor or in their subsoil. It is more limited than the outer space treaty as it neither prohibits nuclear-armed submarines to rest on the seabed nor the placement of military installations within the territorial waters.

4. The Thalelolco Treaty 1967 signed between 21 Latin American states which has made Latin America a nuclear-weapon-free zone. It came into force on 22 April 1968. The Latin American states set up the Agency for the Prohibition of Nuclear Weapons in Latin America in order to ensure compliance of the contracting parties with the Treaty.
5. The Rarotonga Treaty 1985 which came into force on 11 December 1986. It established the South Pacific Nuclear-Weapon-Free Zone. The Treaty set up a Commission to oversee its implementation.
6. The Bangkok Treaty 1995 which created a nuclear-weapon-free zone in South Asia. Contracting states are all states in South East Asia: Brunei, Darussalam, Cambodia, Indonesia, Malaysia, Myanmar, Philippines, Singapore, Thailand, Vietnam, and their respective continental shelves and Exclusive Economic Zones. Also a commission was established to ensure compliance with its provisions.
7. The Pelindaba Treaty 1996, intended to establish a nuclear weapon-free zone in Africa. The Treaty has not yet come into force. It requires 28 ratifications for this to occur. The Treaty will set up a Commission for Nuclear Energy to ensure that contracting states comply with its provisions.
8. The creation of such a zone by the five Central Asian states is being negotiated.

Under nuclear-weapon-free zone treaties the contracting states are encouraged to develop the research, production and use of nuclear energy for peaceful purposes. To the treaties establishing nuclear free zones a protocol is annexed which provides for nuclear power states to signify their co-operation in respecting the treaties. All nuclear power states have done so in respect of all the above-mentioned treaties.

Some states have unilaterally renounced the possibility of becoming nuclear powers although they have the potential to make nuclear weapons: Japan and Germany are amongst them. Also, a number of the former Soviet Republics freely gave up their nuclear weapons.

Conventional weapons. Use of some conventional weapons has been prohibited as being excessively inhumane. The following international instruments specifically ban some conventional weapons.

1. The St Petersburg Declaration Renouncing the Use, in Time of War, of Explosive Projectiles under 400 Grammes Weight 1868. The Declaration was adopted by a conference convened by the Russian government. Its aim was to ban rifle bullets which exploded on impact with a human body, although explosive artillery shells remained lawful.
2. The 1899 Hague Declaration III which prohibits the use of expanding bullets was aimed at banning 'dum-dum' bullets as excessively cruel weapons.
3. Article 23(e) of the Regulations annexed to the Hague IV Convention Respecting the Laws and Customs of War on Land 1907 contains a general prohibition of the use of arms, projectiles or material calculated to cause unnecessary suffering.
4. The Convention on Prohibitions or Restrictions on the Use of Certain

Conventional Weapons Which May be Deemed to be Excessively Injurious or to Have Indiscriminate Effects 1980, also referred to as the Inhumane Weapons Convention (CCW) entered into force on 2 December 1983. As at 19 November 2004 it had been ratified by 97 states. The Convention itself has no substantive provisions. It constitutes an umbrella allowing protocols which ban specific conventional weapons to be annexed. Initially, the CCW contained three protocols which entered into force at the same time as the CCW. Protocol IV and important amendments to Protocol II were added to the Convention as a result of the First CCW Review Conference held in Vienna in 1995. The Second Review Conference which took place in December 2001 set up two Groups of Governmental Experts (GGE) to discuss Explosive Remnants of War (ERW) and Mines Other than Anti-Personnel Mines (MOTAPM). On the basis of proposals submitted by the two Groups state parties agreed at a meeting held in December 2002 to negotiate an instrument on post-conflict remedial measures of a generic nature, such as responsibility for clearance, information sharing, risk education and warnings to civilians in regard to both international and internal conflicts. At a meeting held on 28 November 2003 the state parties to the CCW adopted a new Protocol on Explosive Remnants of War (Protocol V). The Protocol deals with post-conflict remedial measures to be taken by contracting parties in order to reduce the risks of ERW. It covers most types of explosive munitions, with the exception of mines. As of 1 November 2004 three states had ratified the Protocol, which will enter into force six months after obtaining 20 ratifications. At a meeting in November 2004 the state parties to the CCW confirmed their commitment to take further action aimed at strengthening the CCW in 2005 and agreed on follow up work for its two respective working groups (ERW and MOTAPM). The meeting also discussed the possibility of undertaking preparatory work for the 2006 Third Review Conference of the State Parties to the CCW (see http://www.unog.ch/news2/documents/newsen/dc04042e.htm).

Under the CCW the following Protocols have been adopted.

a) Protocol I on Non-Detectable Fragments. This prohibits any weapon the primary effect of which is to injure by fragments which in the human body escape detection by X-rays.
b) Protocol II on Prohibitions or Restrictions on the Use of Mines, Booby Traps and Other Devices (this Protocol was amended by the First Review Conference).
c) Protocol III on Prohibitions or Restrictions on the Use of Incendiary Weapons.
d) Protocol IV which was added in 1995 on Blinding Laser Weapons.
e) Protocol V on Explosive Remnants of War.

As mentioned above, the CCW was reviewed at the 1995 Vienna Review Conference by the contracting parties. The CCW was criticised for not providing a complete codification of customary rules relating to the use of dangerous weapons and so failing to be applicable to a wide range of conventional weapons. However, the majority of states did not want to impose such comprehensive limitations. The Protocols apply only to certain weapons whilst permitting others, similarly harmful, to be used.

Protocol II prohibited indiscriminate use of landmines, booby traps and other devices and, in all circumstances, their deployment against civilians but did not ban them for military purposes. Protocol II also required the recording of the location of minefields and their removal after the termination of hostilities. The main shortcomings of Protocol II were that it did not apply to civil war and it did not impose restrictions on the production and transfer of landmines, booby traps and other similar devices. For the above reasons the Review Conference amended Protocol II. In its amended version it applies to both international and internal wars. Some of the original provisions were strengthened: arts 3–7 introduced more stringent rules relating to their use and the prohibition of the deployment of some of them. Transfer of some mines is restricted by art 8. In view of the shortcomings of the amended Protocol II and taking into account the suffering they cause to civilians, in particular the fact that one-third of the victims are children, public opinion and NGOs put a lot of pressure on governments to ban the future use of landmines.

5. The 1997 Ottawa Convention.

Antipersonnel mines are cheap and easy to use but expensive to find and disarm (about $1,000 per mine). They attracted particular attention because of their use in Angola, Afghanistan, Cambodia and Bosnia. They were used by irregular armed forces and were left without being disarmed. Thus, they are still killing civilians long after the wars have ended. Diana, Princess of Wales, actively supported a campaign to ban them. The campaign resulted in the adoption of the Convention on the Prohibition of the Use, Stockpiling, Production and Transfer of Anti-personnel Mines and on Their Destruction which was signed in Ottawa in 1997. It entered into force on 1 March 1999. The Convention requires that within ten years of its ratification by a contracting state such state shall become a mine-free area and that until the mine clearance is completed a contracting state will take all necessary measures to protect civilians from landmines. As at 1 November 2004 the Convention had been ratified by 143 states. The number of contracting parties is as impressive as are the results achieved under the Convention. By the end of 2003, contracting parties had destroyed 31 million stockpiled anti-personnel mines within the required deadlines. But as the International Committee of the Red Cross (ICRC) emphasised there are an estimated 2,000 million anti-personnel mines stockpiled around the world, mainly by states not parties to the Convention (see Ending the Landmine Era, ICRC Publication, June 2004). Since the entry into force of the Convention the contracting parties including mine-affected countries contributed US$1.1 billion for mine action. The Review Conference of the Convention took place in Nairobi from 29 November to 3 December 2004. The Conference assessed progress achieved under the Convention in the eradication of landmines and set up an action plan to ensure the global elimination of landmines. Only three European countries are not parties to the Convention: Poland, Finland and Latvia. China refuses to ratify it. The target date for ratification by the US is 2006.

Non-proliferation of conventional arms is a very important issue taking into account that such arms are acquired for use in internal repression or international aggression or for terrorist purposes. At international level, efforts to restrict trade in conventional arms have not been successful, although some initiatives have been taken. The UN organised an International Conference from 9–20 July 2001 in New York on the Illicit Trade in Small Arms and Light Weapons in All its Aspects. The Conference proclaimed its opening day the Small Arms Destruction Day. All states were encouraged to destroy, confiscate, collect and seize small arms, light weapons, ammunition and explosives. The Conference adopted a consensus Programme of Action aimed at preventing, combating and eradicating the illicit trade in small arms and light weapons, and containing a wide range of political undertakings at national, regional and global levels.

On 11 and 12 July 1996 representatives from 33 states, among them the US, the UK, Russia, France and Germany, met in Vienna to set up the Wassenaar Agreement on Arms Export Controls for Conventional Arms and Dual-Use Goods and Technology. The main objective of the Wassenaar Agreement is to provide for the exchange of information on the export of dual-use goods and technologies to non-participating states. Participating states report twice yearly on the transfer of arms and specified dual-use items. Refusals of attempts to obtain the specified item are notified. Under the agreement there is a list of reportable items. Participating states are bound to implement the list. There are no restrictions on arms exports as such but the Agreement enhances transparency and contributes to the understanding of the risks associated with the transfer of these items.

More promising is the EU Code for Arms Export of 8 June 1998. It sets up a list of general criteria which a Member state should apply in deciding whether or not an export licence should be granted in a particular case. These criteria are:

1. respect for the international commitments of the EU member states, in particular the UN Security Council sanctions;
2. the respect of human rights in the country of destination;
3. the internal situation in that country;
3. the preservation of regional peace and security which means that a licence should be denied if in a country of final destination there is a clear risk that arms acquired will be used aggressively against another country;
4. the potential effect of the proposed export on the interests of a member state and of territories whose external relations are the responsibility of a member state, its friends and allies;
5. the conduct, in the international arena, of the country of final destination, in particular, its respect for international law, its attitude to terrorism, etc;

6. the existence of risk that the acquired equipment will be diverted within the buyer country or re-exported to terrorist organisations;
7. the compatibility of the export of arms with the recipient country's sustainable development.

The Code has been implemented in all member states. All refused licences, together with an explanation, are notified to other member states. However, the decision to grant or refuse a licence is still left at the discretion of each member state.

The Code complements the EU Programme for Preventing and Combating Illicit Trafficking in Conventional Arms.

Prohibited conduct

Article 23 of the Regulations Respecting the Laws and Customs of War on Land which Regulations are annexed to the Hague Convention IV Respecting the Laws and Customs of War on Land 1907 prohibits the following:

'(a) to employ poison or poisoned weapons;
(b) to kill or wound treacherously individuals belonging to the hostile nation or army;
(c) to kill or wound an enemy who, having laid down his arms, or having no longer means of defence, has surrendered at discretion;
(d) to declare that no quarter will be given;
(e) to employ arms, projectiles, or material calculated to cause unnecessary suffering;
(f) to make improper use of a flag of truce, of the national flag or of the military insignia and uniform of the enemy, as well as the distinctive badges of the Geneva Convention;
(g) to destroy or seize the enemy's property, unless such destruction or seizure be imperatively demanded by the necessities of war;
(h) to declare abolished, suspended, or inadmissible in a court of law the rights and actions of the nationals of the hostile party. A belligerent is likewise forbidden to compel the nationals of the hostile party to take part in the operations of war directed against their own country, even if they were in the belligerent's service before the commencement of the war.'

The above provision was complemented by the 1977 Additional Protocol I to the 1949 Geneva Conventions. The Protocol affirms the principle that the right of the parties to armed conflicts to choose methods or means of warfare is not unlimited: art 35. The Additional Protocol I clarifies and expands some provisions of art 23 of the Regulations. In respect of art 23(d) on quarter, art 40 of Additional Protocol I specifies that it is prohibited 'to order that there shall be no survivors, to threaten an adversary therewith or to conduct hostilities on this basis'. Article 37 of the Protocol replaced the term 'treachery' by 'perfidy' and defined perfidy in the following terms:

'It is prohibited to kill, injure or capture an adversary by resort to perfidy. Acts inviting the confidence of an adversary to lead him to believe that he is entitled to, or is obliged to be accorded, protection under the rules of international law applicable in armed conflict, with intent to betray that confidence, shall constitute perfidy. The following acts are examples of perfidy:
(a) the feigning of an intent to negotiate under a flag of truce or of a surrender;

(b) the feigning of an incapacitation by wounds or sickness;

(c) the feigning of civilian, non-combatant status; and

(d) the feigning of protected status by the use of signs, emblems or uniforms of the United Nations or of neutral or other states not parties to the conflict.'

However, the use of ruses of war has always been lawful. Article 37(2) of Additional Protocol I defines ruses as acts intended to mislead the other party or induce him to act recklessly but which are neither perfidious because they do not invite the confidence of an adversary with respect to protection under the rules of international law applicable to armed conflicts nor constitute infringements of that law. Misinformation and the use of decoys or camouflage are 'ruses of war'.

Additional Protocol I contains new prohibitions. Under art 42 it is prohibited to attack, during their descent, persons parachuting from an aircraft in distress. Once they touch the ground they must be given an opportunity to surrender before being attacked, unless such persons are engaged in a hostile act. However, airborne troops are not protected by this article.

The Protocol also prohibits improper use of distinctive emblems (art 38) such as the emblem of the UN, the red cross, red crescent or red lion and others provided for by the Geneva Conventions or the Protocol. It also prohibits deliberate misuse of internationally recognised protective emblems, signs and signals such as the flag of truce and the protective emblem of cultural property covered by the 1954 Hague Convention. Additional Protocol I extends its protection to cultural objects and places of worship (art 53), to the natural environment (art 55) and to works and installations containing dangerous forces such as dams, dykes, nuclear electrical generating stations (art 56).

The principle of the protection of civil population

The customary rule that civilian population should be protected against the effects of hostilities is expressly recognised by art 48 of Additional Protocol I which states that:

'In order to ensure respect for and protection of the civilian population and civilian objects, the Parties to the conflict shall at all times distinguish between the civilian population and combatants and between civilian objects and military objectives and accordingly shall direct their operations only against military objectives.'

Military objectives are those which by their nature, location, destination or use effectively contribute to the military might of one party. Their total or partial destruction, capture or neutralisation offers military advantages to the other party.

Additional Protocol I prohibits both direct and indiscriminate attacks on civil population (art 51(4)), reprisals (art 51(6)), attacks against objects indispensable to the survival of civilians (art 54), including the use of starvation as a method of warfare (art 54(1)), and 'the use of methods or means of warfare which are intended or may be expected to cause ... damage to the natural environment and thereby to prejudice the health or survival of the population': art 55(1). Also civilians must not be subject to outrages upon personal dignity, tortured, raped, enslaved, used as hostages, or be discriminated against. The belligerents must not allow children under the age of 15 to participate in hostilities or to be recruited into its armed forces.

Article 56 of Additional Protocol I prohibits any attack on works and installations containing dangerous forces even if they are military objectives 'if such attack may cause the release of dangerous forces and consequent severe losses among the civilian population'. Also military objectives located in the vicinity of those works or installations should not be attacked if such attacks will cause severe losses among the civilian population.

The rules examined above are applicable to international and non-international conflicts. However, there are important differences between the 1977 Additional Protocols I and II. Some provisions contained in Additional Protocol I are not reproduced in Additional Protocol II which applies to internal conflicts (eg the fundamental principle that means and methods of warfare are not unlimited, the definition of population, the prohibition of perfidy, the protection of civilian objects). This exclusion is deliberate. Contracting states were reluctant to reinforce the protection of civil population taking into account that wars of liberation were classified as international conflicts. However, the exclusion is loosing its importance in the light of the development of international human rights: see judgment of the Appeals Chamber of the International Criminal Tribunal for the Former Yugoslavia in *Tadic* IT–94–1 'Prijedor', Judgment of 15 July 1999 (obtainable from http://www.un.org/icty/judgment.htm).

18.3 Humanitarian law

Humanitarian law, its origin and content, as well as the contribution of the International Committee of the Red Cross (ICRC) to its actual application, will be examined in this section.

The origin and development of international humanitarian law

The Battle of Solferino between the Austro-Hungarian army and the Franco-Sardinian forces which took place on 24 June 1859 is considered as marking the beginning of international humanitarian law. A Swiss businessman, Henri Dunant, happened to be in the vicinity of the battle. He was appalled by the large number of wounded being left to die because of the lack of medical attention. Together with some local women Henri Dunant organised some medical relief for the wounded, collected them from the battlefield, dressed their wounds, fed them and washed them. He could not forget what he saw. In 1862 he published an account of his experience under the title *Memory of Solferino* in which he made two proposals:

1. for the establishment of a voluntary relief society for the aid of those wounded in battlefields; and
2. for an international agreement on the basis of which such voluntary societies might provide relief for the sick and injured in wartime.

Dunant's proposals led to the creation of the International Committee of the Red Cross (ICRC) which met for the first time on 17 February 1883 and the adoption on 22 August 1864 of the first Geneva Convention for the Amelioration of the Condition of the Wounded in Armies in the Field. By the end of the year the Convention was ratified by France, Switzerland, Belgium, The Netherlands, Italy, Spain, Sweden, Norway, Denmark and the Grand Duchy of Baden. In 1882 the US became a contracting party to the Convention.

The Convention was limited in scope as it applied only to the sick and wounded in land battles. It did, however, establish the fundamental principles of international humanitarian law, such as the neutrality and impartiality of humanitarian aid to the sick and wounded and the protection of military medical personnel. The distinctive emblem of the Red Cross was recognised as an international protective symbol, which was subsequently followed by the Red Crescent, the Red Lion and Sun (Iran) and de facto not de jure the Red Star of David.

The Convention was tested during the Franco–Prussian War in 1870. During that war the ICRC set up the first information agency for families of wounded and captured soldiers. The Prussians and their allies understood and applied the Convention. This was not the case with the French. After the termination of hostilities all parties agreed that a better organised system should be put in place and consequently the Convention was substantially revised in 1906 and 1907. The revised version was applied during World War I. Despite some propaganda claims the Geneva Convention 1907 was well observed by all participants in World War I.

The idea of adopting a Convention protecting the sick, wounded and shipwrecked in naval battles was first proposed in 1868, after the naval victory of the Austrio-Hungarians over the Italians at Lissa in 1868, which emphasised the need for the extension of the Geneva regime to naval warfare. The draft was not successful at that time but was re-examined later by the First Hague Peace Conference and became the Hague Convention III for the Adaptation to Maritime Warfare of the Principles of the Geneva Convention of 1864 on the Laws of War 1899. The Hague Convention was revised in 1907 and, together with the London Declaration on the Rules of Naval Warfare 1909, was applied during World War I.

The next category of persons upon whom the protection of humanitarian law was conferred were prisoners of war. The main provisions applicable to them were contained in the annex to the Hague Convention II with Respect to the Laws and Customs of War 1899, revised by the second Hague Peace Conference. These provisions were applied during World War I and worked reasonably well. However, some gaps were discovered, in particular in respect of repatriation of the POWs after the termination of hostilities. Their revision was urged by the ICRC. On the basis of a draft convention on the treatment of prisoners of war submitted by the ICRC the Geneva Convention on Treatment of Prisoners of War was adopted in 1929. The Convention divorced the treatment of POWs from the Hague law and set up fundamental principles in respect of POWs: they should be treated humanly at all times and be protected, in particular against violence and public curiosity, any reprisals against them are prohibited, they need only provide limited information when questioned etc. The 1929 Geneva Convention was the first to introduce a control mechanism verifying the compliance of contracting states with its provisions.

The 1929 Geneva Convention was applied during World War II. There were serious violations of the Convention on both sides, but in general it was observed, more or less, by the contracting parties. The main problem was with non-contracting parties. Before the outbreak of World War II 46 states had ratified the 1929 Convention, including Germany, the UK, France and the US. However, the Soviet Union had not ratified it. Germany refused to apply the Convention to Soviet prisoners of war. It is believed that of 5.3 million Soviet prisoners of war 3.3 million died. They were treated inhumanely, often sent to concentration camps, and denied food and medical care. The treatment of German prisoners of war by the Soviet Union was similar, although in the case of the Soviet Union it was more lack of care than a deliberate effort to impose inhumane treatment upon them. It is estimated that one million German POWs died in captivity. Also, long after the end of World War II, German POWs were still kept in Russia. Their repatriation was settled in 1955. It took so long because their work in labour camps in Russia was very important for the reconstruction of the Soviet Union.

Before World War II the idea of protecting civilians during hostilities was not popular. In 1934 at the International Red Cross Conference in Tokyo the ICRC submitted a proposal in this respect. An international conference to consider the matter was to be called in 1940. Unfortunately World War II interrupted any work in this area.

Humanitarian law as tested by World War II proved inadequate. It clearly needed a major revision and in any event required adjustment to accord with the Universal Declaration of Human Rights adopted by the General Assembly on 10 December 1948 which recognised the importance of human rights in both peacetime and wartime. Indeed, the interrelationship between international human rights and international humanitarian law has given a new impetus to the development of the latter. Most serious violations of humanitarian law are also violations of human rights. However, with the creation of the United Nations, and the role of the Security Council as a guardian of peace and stability, the UN was not very keen on leading the revision of international humanitarian law. As a result, the ICRC prepared the new treaties and the Swiss government convened the international conference with a view to their adoption. The conference took place in Geneva in 1949 and resulted in the adoption of four Conventions. They were not considered highly relevant, although they were of some importance in wars in Korea and Indochina in the early 1950s.

A new impetus was given to the Geneva regime by the UN in 1968. With new conflicts erupting in 1960s, such as the war in Vietnam, the civil war in Biafra, the conflict between Israel and the Arab states and the wars of national liberation in Africa, the relevance of humanitarian law became obvious. From 1968 the General Assembly adopted a number of resolutions calling for the application of the Geneva Conventions to wars of national liberation, regarding them as international armed conflicts. These resolutions paved the way for the adoption of the two Additional Protocols which were drafted by the ICRC. They were adopted in 1977.

After the end of the Cold War the relationship between humanitarian law and human rights has become even closer as most armed conflicts have occurred internally. During the Cold War internal conflicts, whether religious, ethnic or political, were kept under control by totalitarian regimes or external threats. With the collapse of totalitarian states such conflicts have continued to occur but in the absence of former restraints they have become impossible to tame. It has become clear that only the international community can resolve them. Some attempts at resolving internal conflicts by the UN have been satisfactory, others have failed. The UN was successful in sending observer missions and peacekeeping forces to El Salvador, Cambodia and Mozambique. These operations were based on the consent of the parties involved in the conflict. However, in some conflicts such operations were impossible or inadequate, ie in the former Yugoslavia, Somalia, Rwanda and Sierra Leone.

Since the end of the Cold War the major factors contributing to the development of international humanitarian law have been and remain as follows.

1. The resolutions of the Security Council stating that large-scale violations of human rights and humanitarian law constitute a threat to international peace, taking into account that local armed conflicts have a tendency to become international conflicts and have serious consequences on the international community as a whole: see Security Council Resolution 770 (1992) on Bosnia and Herzegovina; Resolution 794 (1992) on Somalia; Resolution 929 (1994) on Rwanda; Resolution 1244 (1999) on Kosovo. In such circumstances the Security Council is empowered to take all measures at its disposal, in particular measures under Chapter VII of the UN Charter, in order to bring to an end such violations. The Security Council has authorised the use of force in several humanitarian disasters and has set up two international criminal tribunals to deal with the most serious violations of human rights and humanitarian law that took place in the former Yugoslavia and Rwanda.

2. The distinction between international and internal conflicts has lost its importance. For the application of international humanitarian law such distinction was vital as the full Geneva regime applies only to international conflicts. The decision of the International Criminal Tribunal for the Former Yugoslavia in *Tadic* IT–94–1, 'Prijedor', Judgment of 11 November 1999 (Trial Chamber II) (obtainable from http://www.un.org/icty) confirmed that

development. Many rules of humanitarian law applicable to international conflicts have also become customary rules applicable to internal conflicts. As a result, internal conflicts can no longer be considered as internal affairs of the states involved, as they used to be, and therefore excluded from the interventions of the international community. Moreover, internal conflicts are regulated by international rules to a greater extent than previously thought. Since 1968 the UN General Assembly has always called upon parties involved in armed conflicts to respect international humanitarian law and to desist from all breaches without making any distinction between internal and international conflicts. Further, all new treaties adopted since the early 1990s are applicable to both internal and international conflicts. However, the distinction between international and internal conflicts is still there and it is not always possible to apply all rules of the law of international conflict to internal armed conflict.

3. The growing interrelationship between human rights and humanitarian law. Internal conflicts in Cambodia, Rwanda or in the former Yugoslavia demonstrated that armed violence used in internal conflicts has no limitations. Atrocities committed in internal conflicts violate both international human rights and international humanitarian law taking into account their nature and scale. This interrelationship emphasises that it is necessary for international humanitarian law to ensure that victims of internal conflicts are kept safe from the worst horrors of war and to ensure that they can preserve their human dignity in such circumstances.

4. International humanitarian law has been developed not only through decisions of the UN and judgments of the ICJ (see eg the Advisory Opinion of the ICJ of 1966 on the *Legality of the Threat or use of Nuclear Weapons* (1996) ICJ Rep 90) but also through international treaties. There is a growing number of states ready to accept important limitations upon their internal affairs. Among the most important treaties are those banning chemical and biological weapons, landmines, limiting proliferation of nuclear weapons, establishing the International Criminal Court and protecting cultural property in the event of armed conflicts (the Hague Convention for the Protection of Cultural Property in the Event of Armed Conflicts 1954 and the 1999 Second Protocol to the 1954 Hague Convention). Another important development is the adoption on 6 August 1999 by the UN Secretary-General of Rules Concerning the Observance by the United Nations Forces of International Humanitarian Law.

The 1949 Geneva Conventions and 1977 Additional Protocols I and II

The main body of humanitarian law is contained in the four 1949 Geneva Conventions and the 1977 Additional Protocols I and II. The four Geneva Conventions were signed in the Alabama Room at Geneva's town hall on 12 August 1949. As at 8 December 2004 they had been ratified by 192 states, virtually all states taking into account that the current number of member states of the UN is 191.

These Conventions are as follows:

1. Geneva Convention I for the Amelioration of the Condition of the Wounded and Sick in Armed Forces in the Field;
2. Geneva Convention II for the Amelioration of the Condition of Wounded, Sick and Shipwrecked Members of the Armed Forces at Sea;
3. Geneva Convention III Relative to the Treatment of Prisoners of War;
4. Geneva Convention IV Relative to the Protection of Civilian Persons in Times of War.

The necessity of adopting international humanitarian law to changing circumstances both in terms of technological developments and the kind of conflicts that occurred after World War II prompted the ICRC to propose the adoption of supplementary rules to the 1949 Geneva Conventions. In 1974 the Swiss government convened an international conference with a view to reaffirming and developing international humanitarian law. The Conference held four sessions. The ICRC invited certain national liberation movements to fully participate in the work of the Conference although they were not entitled to vote. At its final session on 8 June 1977 the Conference adopted two protocols.

1. Protocol I Additional to the Geneva Conventions of 12 August 1949 and Relating to the Protection of Victims of International Armed Conflicts (Additional Protocol I). As at 8 December 2004 it had been ratified by 162 states.
2. Protocol II Additional to the Geneva Conventions of 12 August 1949 and Relating to the Protection of Victims of Non-International Armed Conflicts (Additional Protocol II). As at 8 December 2004 it had achieved 157 ratifications.

International conflicts

The four Geneva Conventions together with Additional Protocol I apply to international conflicts. Article 2, common to all Geneva Conventions, defines international conflicts as arising between two or more contracting states, even if the state of war is not recognised by one of them. In practice, even if both contracting parties refuse to recognise the state of war the Conventions apply. In order to ensure the largest possible application of the four Geneva Conventions they also apply to all cases of total or partial military occupation even if this occupation meets no armed resistance. If one of the parties to the conflict is not a contracting party to the Conventions, they apply between the remaining contracting parties. Also if a non-contracting party in practice accepts and applies the Conventions all contracting parties involved are bound to observe them in relation to that party. The consequences of non-application of the Geneva Conventions to a non-contracting party who does not accept their de facto application have been attenuated taking into account that most rules of the Geneva Conventions are now regarded as customary international law and therefore are binding irrespective of their ratification by a state.

By art 1(2) of Additional Protocol I that Protocol is applied to situations described in a common art 2 of the Geneva Conventions including 'armed conflicts in which people are fighting against colonial domination and alien occupation and against racist regimes in the exercise of their right of self-determination': art 1(4) of Additional Protocol I. This provision restricts the application of Additional Protocol I to wars against colonial domination which is now a thing of the past. The issues whether Additional Protocol I applies to armed conflicts in the context of self-determination outside colonial and neo-colonial conflicts in still uncertain.

Geneva Convention I. The Geneva Convention I provides detailed rules concerning the protection of the sick and wounded on land. It represents a revised and expanded version of the 1929 Geneva Convention. The Geneva Convention I establishes a fundamental rule that the sick and wounded should be respected and protected in all circumstances. They should be treated humanely and cared for without any distinction based on sex, religion, nationality, political opinions and similar criteria. The wounded and sick of a belligerent who are in enemy hands should be considered as prisoners of war and the provisions of international instruments concerning POWs should apply to them.

Medical units and establishments may in no circumstances be attacked and should at all times be respected and protected by the parties to the conflict. A contracting party is bound to ensure that medical establishments and units, as far as possible, are not situated within the vicinity of military objectives.

Geneva Convention II. The Geneva Convention II contains detailed rules applicable to the sick, wounded and shipwrecked of armed forces at sea. It replaces the Hague Convention X 1907 and Hague Convention III 1899. The Geneva Convention II embodies principles similar to those set out in the Geneva Convention I.

In respect of hospital ships art 22 provides that they may in no circumstances be attacked or captured and at all times should be protected and respected on condition that their names and description have been notified to the parties to the conflict ten days before they are employed.

Geneva Convention III. The Geneva Convention III concerns the treatment of prisoners of war. It has been complemented by 1977 Additional Protocol I which extends the category of persons entitled to the status of combatant and, if they fall into the hands of the enemy, to the status of a prisoner of war and provides some fundamental guarantees in respect of the treatment of persons in the power of a party to the conflict: art 75.

In respect of the status of prisoner of war the most important distinction is between combatants and non-combatants. Only combatants, when captured by an enemy, can claim the status of POW. Article 4 of the Geneva Convention III defines prisoners of war as persons belonging to one of the following categories:

'(1) Members of the armed forces of a Party to the conflict, as well as members of militias or volunteer corps forming part of such armed forces.

(2) Members of other militias and members of other volunteer corps, including those of organised resistance movements, belonging to a Party to the conflict and operating in or outside their own territory, even if this territory is occupied, provided that such militias or volunteer corps, including such organised resistance movements, fulfill the following conditions:

(a) that of being commanded by a person responsible for his subordinates;

(b) that of having a fixed distinctive sign recognisable at a distance;

(c) that of carrying arms openly;

(d) that of conducting their operations in accordance with the laws and customs of war.'

The requirement that combatants must distinguish themselves from the civilian population is intended to protect civilians against the effect of hostilities. Regular armed forces wear uniforms when directly involved in hostilities. Members, of organised resistance movements belonging to a party to the armed conflict, whether or not recognised by the other party, are exempted from wearing uniforms but have a fundamental duty to distinguish themselves from civilians in the manner described above.

Article 4 of the Geneva Convention III also applies to:

'(3) Members of regular armed forces who profess allegiance to a government or an authority not recognised by the Detaining Power.

(4) Persons who accompany the armed forces without actually being members thereof, such as civilian members of military aircraft crews, war correspondents, supply contractors, members of labour units or of services responsible for the welfare of the armed forces, provided that they have received authorisation, from the armed forces which they accompany, who shall provide them for that purpose with an identity card similar to the annexed model.

(5) Members of crews, including masters, pilots and apprentices, of the merchant marine and the crews of civil aircraft of the Parties to the conflict, who do not benefit by more favourable treatment under any other provisions of international law.

(6) Inhabitants of a non–occupied territory, who on the approach of the enemy spontaneously take up arms to resist the invading forces, without having had time to form themselves into regular armed units, provided they carry arms openly and respect the laws and customs of war.'

However, there are situations in occupied territories and in wars of national liberation where a combatant cannot distinguish himself in the manner described above without risking being immediately captured. For that reason Additional Protocol I provides an exception to the above rules, allowing a combatant who cannot distinguish himself from the civilian population to retain his status as a combatant if he carries his arms openly:

1. during each military engagement; and
2. during such time as he is visible to the adversary while he is engaged in a military deployment preceding the launching of an attack in which he is to participate: art 44(3) of Additional Protocol I.

Combatants cannot be punished for the mere fact of fighting, whilst non-combatants taking part in hostilities are subject to penal consequences as they cannot claim the statute of POWs when captured. Thus, a soldier who shoots an enemy soldier cannot be punished, while a civilian who shoots a soldier may be liable for murder. As a rule, combatants when captured may not be punished for the acts they committed during the fighting unless the detaining power would have punished its own soldiers for those acts. For the above reasons for a person captured by enemy forces during an armed conflict it is sometimes a matter of life and death to be recognised as being a POW.

WAR AGAINST TERRORISM AND THE GENEVA CONVENTION III. The matter of the determination of the legal status of persons captured by the US in Afghanistan, in Iraq and in other places as part of the ongoing 'war against terrorism' and subsequently transferred to the US naval base in Guantanamo Bay and other undisclosed places has caused much controversy. There is growing international concern about the legality of their detention, the conditions of detention and the use of military commissions at Guantanamo Bay.

1. Legal status of persons detained at Guantanamo Bay.
   The legal status of persons detained in the US military base in Guantanamo Bay was, to some extent, clarified by the Presidential Order of 13 November 2001 (www.defenselink.mil). According to the order, the President of the US, himself, is the authority to determine which individuals suspected of being members of Al-Qaeda should be transferred to Guantanamo Bay and which should be tried. On 7 February 2002 the US authorities divided the detainees at Guantanamo Bay into two categories: first, members of the armed forces of the Taliban and second, members of Al-Qaeda. In respect of the first category, notwithstanding the official denial of the status of POW to the former combatants of the Taliban, the order states that some of the provisions of the Geneva Convention III will apply to them. Members of the second group have been classified as 'enemy combatants' and have been denied any benefit of the Geneva Convention III. Under the order non-US nationals suspected of being involved in international terrorism can be held indefinitely without trial, or tried by military commission.

   The Presidential Order of 13 November 2001 also authorised the establishment of Military Commissions competent to try terrorist suspects. Subsequent to the above authorisation the US Department of Defence has issued several instructions setting out the applicable law and procedure to be applied by any Military Commission (www.defenselink.mil). To date the President has selected 15 detainees as eligible for trial by a Military Commission of which four have been formally charged and referred for prosecution. Proceedings against them commenced in August 2004.

   In order to decide whether or not persons detained at Guantanamo Bay should be regarded as POWs it is necessary to decide whether the Geneva

Convention III is applicable to the conflict in Afghanistan and Iraq. With regard to the conflict in Afghanistan, both the US (2 August 1955) and Afghanistan (26 September 1956) have ratified the four Geneva Conventions. Consequently, at least from 7 October 2001 (if not from 11 September 2001) when the US started bombing Afghanistan, the four Geneva Conventions were applicable. The fact that the Taliban was not recognised as the de jure government by the US has no bearing either on the applicability of the 1949 Geneva Conventions or on the classification of the conflict as being international in nature.

With regard to Iraq, both Iraq and the US are contracting parties to the four Geneva Conventions and the US government has made many public statements recognising the applicability of international humanitarian law, in particular the III and IV Geneva Conventions, to 'Operation Iraqi Freedom' regarding the invasion of Iraq. Also the UN Security Council Resolution 1483 (22 May 2003) called upon all states to observe their obligations arising from the Geneva Conventions and the Hague Regulations of 1907 with regard to the conflict in Iraq.

Having established the applicability of the Geneva Convention III to both conflicts it is necessary to examine the potential applicability of the relevant provisions of the Convention to persons captured by the US.

Article 4 of the Geneva Convention III sets out the requirements that must be satisfied by a person captured by enemy forces during an international armed conflict in order to be granted the status of a POW. This provision divides combatants into six categories. The first two are relevant to the determination of the legal status of persons captured by the US in Afghanistan and Iraq. The first category concerns members of the armed forces of a party to the conflict. This certainly applies to Iraqi soldiers and to Taliban fighters, but it may not encompass members of Al-Qaeda, who may possibly fit (subject to what is said below) within the second category given the type of activities allegedly carried out by them. The second category covers members of militia or voluntary corps forming part of the armed forces of a state party to the conflict, regardless of whether they operate in or outside their own territory, even if the territory is occupied. Article 4(2) gives them the status of POWs only if they are commanded by a person responsible for his subordinates, they have a fixed distinctive sign recognisable at a distance, they carry arms openly, and they conduct their operations in accordance with the laws and customs of war. Provided that Al-Qaeda fighters acted for the government of Afghanistan or the Government of Saddam Hussein and satisfy the criteria set out in art 4(2) of the Geneva Convention III they may claim the status of POWs.

A particular problem may arise in respect of US citizens who joined the Taliban and Al-Qaeda fighters in Afghanistan. Article 4 of the Geneva Convention III is silent on the issue of nationality. There is, however, case law showing, on some previous occasions, that US citizens fighting with the enemy have not been denied POW status because of their US citizenship (*Re Territo* 156

F 2d 142 (1946)). Such persons may be tried for treason but still retain their POW status. This can be supported by art 85 of the Geneva Convention III which states that persons convicted of war crimes are still entitled to keep their POW status.

Article 5 of the Geneva Convention III is of relevance as to the determination of whether or not a person captured qualifies for POW status. This provision states that in the event of 'any doubts' as to whether an individual is entitled to POW status such an individual should be treated as a POW 'until such time as his status has been determined by a competent tribunal' (on the interpretation of Art 5 of the Geneva Convention III see: Y Naqvi, 'Doubtful Prisoner-of-War Status' (2002) 84 IRRC 571).

It is doubtful that the President of the US can be regarded as a 'competent tribunal' within the meaning of art 5 of the Geneva Convention III (see the case involving Salim Ahmed Hamdan, below).

2. The legality of military commissions.

The rules and regulations governing proceedings before the Military Commission at Guantanamo Bay have been created by the US Department of Defence, are virtually created from scratch without the benefit of the exiting US military federal codes, regulations or case law, and do not comply with international standards for a fair trial. In this respect the Seventh Annual Human Rights Report, released by the UK Foreign and Commonwealth Office on 11 November 2004, repeatedly criticised the Bush administration for the continuing detention of British citizens at Guantanamo Bay. Its chapter on Guantanamo Bay concluded that the Military Commission 'would not provide sufficient guarantees of fair trial according to international standards' (R Beeston, 'Britain Attacks US Abuses in Iraq and Guantanamo Bay', *The Times* 11 November 2004).

The substantive rules applied by the Military Commission disregard the fundamental principles of any criminal legal system given that offences are vaguely described and no precise punishment is prescribed.

There are the following fundamental problems with the operation of the Military Commission.

a) The Commission lacks competence, independence and impartiality. In respect of criminal charges the right to be tried by a competent, independent and impartial tribunal is guaranteed under art 14(1) of the International Covenant on Civil and Political Rights (ICCPR) to which the US has been a contracting party since 1992. Under the Geneva Conventions, art 3(1) (common to them all) requires trials to meet the standards of international justice. The competence of the Military Commission, which is required to deal with complicated issues of domestic and international law including humanitarian law, is seriously undermined by the fact that there is only one lawyer on the Commission panel. The members of the panel are selected by the US military. This combined with the fact that several of its members had intelligence or combat responsibility during the conflict in Afghanistan raise the perception of bias and calls into question the impartiality of the panel.

b) The Commission lacks independent judicial oversight by a civilian court. No appeal to a court independent of the executive branch of the US government is allowed. This departs from the well established principle of civilian review in the US military justice system under which the US Court of Appeals for the Armed Forces, a civilian court independent of the executive branch, deals with appeals from the courts martial. Decisions of the US Court of Appeals for the Armed Forces are subject to review by the US Supreme Court. The Commission's proceedings can be reviewed by a specially created review panel, members of which are appointed by the Secretary of Defence. The US President has the final review of the Commission's convictions and sentences. No appeal is allowed to US federal courts or the US Court of Appeal for the Armed Forces. Consequently, the executive branch is, at the same time, prosecutor, judge, jury and potential executioner given that the Commission can impose the death penalty. At a press conference held by the Pentagon on 21 March 2002 a US Military spokesman stated that individuals tried by the Military Commission but not found guilty would not necessarily be released.

c) There are potential problems relating to the admissibility of coerced confessions in proceedings before the Commission. There is no rule of procedure prohibiting the Commission from using evidence obtained through torture or other forms of coercion. This is itself in breach of art 15 of the Torture Convention 1984 to which the US is a contracting party. Many allegations of torture and ill treatment in Guantanamo Bay and other detention facilities have been confirmed by international human rights organisations such as Amnesty International and Human Rights Watch.

d) Restrictions have been imposed on the right of persons accused to choose their own legal counsel. Such counsel have been assigned to the defendants by the US military. The accused are allowed to have a supplementary civil counsel who, however, has no access to classified evidence or to sessions of the Commission held behind closed doors.

e) Legal counsel assigned to the defendants are not given the protection normally afforded to military lawyers from improper 'command influence'. In addition, the defence teams lack staff and the basic infrastructure to carry out their responsibilities. Human Rights Watch raised these issues subsequent to the first hearings conducted by the Military Commission in August 2004.

f) The accused are not able to fairly examine the evidence against them (see the judgment of US District Judge James Robertson in Hamdan's case, below).

The list of irregularities regarding the substantive and procedural rules of the Military Commission is long.

There is growing opposition to the Military Commission internationally and in the US. There is some hope that this institution will be abandoned and the Presidential Military order previously mentioned rescinded.

On 28 June 2004 the US Supreme Court declared in three separate cases that Guantanamo Bay detainees were entitled to a trial, and that their fundamental human rights had been violated. Contrary to the allegations of the US government that the Guantanamo Bay base is not part of US territory for habeas corpus purposes, the Supreme Court ruled that it is within the US territory and that even if Guantanamo Bay were to be regarded as foreign soil, fundamental human rights would still be applicable to both US and non-US citizens. The Supreme Court in *Al-Odah* v *United States* (not yet reported) ruled that the Guantanamo Bay detainees have fundamental habeas corpus rights. The Court held (by six votes to three) that the right to basic habeas corpus can be exercised in 'all ... dominions under the sovereign's control'. In *Rasul* v *Bush* (2004) 43 ILM 1207 the Supreme Court held that the right to habeas corpus is not dependent on US citizenship. The Court found that the detainees were entitled to bring proceedings challenging their detention as unlawful. In *Hamdi* v *Rumsfeld* (2004) 43 ILM 1166 the Supreme Court ruled that individuals held as 'enemy combatants' were entitled to a fair trial. The court found that, although the US Congress authorised the detention, the Fifth Amendment guarantees the right to challenge that detention before a neutral decision-maker. The US administration responded to the rulings by setting up a combatant status review tribunal to determine the legal status of the detainees. To date 317 cases have been reviewed. Of those 131 have been adjourned, and the findings on all of the remainder but one have been in favour of continued detention.

On 8 November 2004 the Federal District Court for the District of Columbia in the habeas corpus petition of Salim Ahmed Hamdan, a Yemeni national captured in Afghanistan in 2001 and accused of being a member of Al-Qaeda (he was accused of being Osama bin Laden's driver) who was detained at Guantanamo Bay and against whom charges were brought before the Military Commission, ruled that trials by the Military Commission were unlawful under US law and under international law and could not continue in the current form. The Federal Court ruled that Hamdan must be treated as a POW unless and until a competent tribunal determined otherwise. As a POW he may only be tried by court martial under the US Uniform Code of Military Justice, and not by the Military Commission. The Court held that detainees in Guantanamo Bay were entitled to have their status determined by a 'competent tribunal'. The court found that the detainees may be POWs under the Geneva Convention III and were accordingly entitled to the standard protection of military and international law. The Court held that the Military Commission's rules of evidence were in breach of the standards required to achieve a fair trial. As a result of the judgment of the Federal District Court the pre-trial hearings of Salim Ahmed Hamdan were suspended just minutes after they commenced in Guantanamo Bay. At the time of writing it is expected that the US Department of Defence will challenge this judgment. Whatever the outcome of the expected appeal, Judge James Robertson of the US Federal Court in *Hamdan* summarised the danger of the US government's current policy in the following words:

> 'The government has asserted a position starkly different from the positions and behaviour of the United States in previous conflicts, one that can only weaken the United States' own ability to demand applications of the Geneva Conventions to Americans captured during armed conflicts abroad.'

The flaws in the rules and regulations of the Military Commission are very serious but their incompatibility with the Geneva Convention III are even more troublesome. Some of the hundreds of detainees from around 40 countries detained indefinitely in the US naval base in Guantanamo Bay may be entitled to the status of POWs under the Geneva Convention III, in particular the Taliban fighters. Article 102 of the Geneva Convention III provides that a POW can be validly sentenced only by the same courts and by the application of the same procedure as in the case of members of the armed forces of the detaining power. This means that in the US POWs can only be tried by a US Courts Martial according to rules and safeguards provided for in the US Uniform Code of Military Justice, and will have a right to appeal to the US Court of Appeal for the Armed Forces and a further possibility for a case to be reviewed by the US Supreme Court.

Irrespective of whether or not a person is recognised as a POW, he should be treated humanely. The international human rights law continues to apply alongside the international humanitarian law. The US Supreme Court has fully recognised that the threat of terrorism cannot be used as a blank cheque to ignore international law, including the international law of human rights.

THE APPLICABILITY OF THE GENEVA CONVENTION III TO MERCENARIES AND SPIES. Some combatants would be denied POW status under the Geneva regime. Additional Protocol I expressly provides that mercenaries should be regarded as unlawful combatants and thus are not entitled to the status of POW. Article 47 of Additional Protocol I provides a definition of a mercenary. A mercenary is any person who:

1. is recruited abroad to fight in an armed conflict;
2. directly and actually participates in hostilities;
3. is motivated by 'the desire for private gain, in fact, is promised, by or on behalf of a party to the conflict, material compensation substantially in excess of that promised or paid to combatants of similar ranks and functions in the armed forces of that party';
4. has no link based on nationality or residence with the party to the conflict;
5. is neither a member of the armed forces of a party to the conflict nor has been sent by a state which is not a party to the conflict on official duty as a member of its armed forces.

Mercenaries have been used for centuries, and even today the Pope is still employing, as his personal guards, Swiss mercenaries. However, the use and employment of mercenaries changed in the 1960s when highly trained ex-members of special forces of the UK, the US and other European countries were recruited to fight for money in Africa. They were employed by governments to act ruthlessly and fought in a manner devoid of any humanitarian concern. Following the instructions of their employers they violated international law whilst their employers denied any connection with them. The atrocities committed by Colonel 'Mad Mike' Hoare and his five commando units in Zaire on behalf on the breakaway regime of Moise Tshombe, or those of Colonel Bob Denard who appointed himself a military governor of Grande Comore, are examples of conduct which appalled the international community and prompted African countries to introduce art 47 of Additional Protocol I. The above problem has also been dealt with outside the Geneva regime at international level by the Convention against Recruitment, Use, Financing and Training of Mercenaries (Mercenary Convention) 1989 and at regional level by the African Mercenary Convention 1985.

Nevertheless, art 75 of Additional Protocol I, containing fundamental guarantees, covers captured mercenaries and spies as it is applicable to all persons.

Spies, defined in art 46 of Additional Protocol I as persons who clandestinely, or under false pretences, ie not wearing the uniform of their armed forces, gather information in the territory controlled by the other party, are not considered as combatants. However, a spy who after rejoining his own or allied armed forces after successfully completed his mission is subsequently captured is entitled to the status of a prisoner of war and cannot be punished for his previous acts of espionage: art 46(4).

THE TREATMENT OF POWs UNDER THE GENEVA CONVENTION III. POWs are considered as prisoners of a state, the detaining power, and not of the individuals or units that captured them. The detaining power is responsible for their treatment in international law.

The Geneva regime sets out fundamental rules for the treatment of prisoners of war. They must not be treated inhumanely or dishonourably, and they must not be discriminated against on grounds of race, nationality, religious belief or political opinions, or similar criteria. Any measures of reprisal against them are prohibited. They must be protected at all times, in particular against acts of violence or intimidation and against insults and public curiosity. The public display of POWs is prohibited.

The detaining power must maintain prisoners of war adequately and free of charges. The Geneva Convention III contains detailed provisions concerning the conditions of internment of POWs, their labour, financial resources during captivity, relations with the outside world, relations with the military authorities in whose power they are and the termination of captivity.

In respect of this Convention the role of a protecting power is particularly important. A protecting power, any neutral state, should be appointed, at the outbreak of an armed conflict, by each party to a conflict to safeguard its interests. The system of protecting powers was introduced to ensure that parties to an armed conflict comply with the Geneva regime. The main task of the protecting power is to visit prisoners of war and to question them without witnesses. There should be no limitations so far as time or place of visit is concerned on the representatives of the protecting power. In this respect, a detaining power may impose a restriction only as a temporary and exceptional measure justified by imperative military reasons. If judicial procedures are commenced against a POW the detaining power is obliged to inform the protecting power not less than three weeks before the beginning of the trial. The protecting power, in general, looks after the interests of nationals of the party by which it was appointed, who are under adverse control. The protecting powers may also participate in the settlement of disputes.

The main weakness of the system is that the appointment of protecting powers must be mutually accepted by the parties to an armed conflict. As a result, the system has rarely been used. One example is the Falklands war, during which Switzerland acted as the protecting power for the UK and Brazil did likewise for Argentina (no protecting powers were appointed in Korea, Vietnam or in the conflict between Iraq and Iran).

If the parties to a conflict cannot reach an agreement on protecting powers, the ICRC, or any other humanitarian organisation, may step in either to act as a protecting power or to assume humanitarian tasks normally carried out by a protecting power. However, the first possibility is subject to request and the second subject to approval by the detaining power.

The ICRC has a special position. Whether or not a protecting power has been appointed, the ICRC, with consent of the detaining power, is permitted to work for the protection and relief of prisoners of war.

Geneva Convention IV. The Geneva Convention IV was the first international instrument focusing exclusively on the protection of civilians in the time of war. It contains detailed provisions relating to the treatment of civilians who, at a given moment and in any manner whatsoever, find themselves, whether in occupied territory or in internment, in the hands of a party to the conflict of which they are not nationals. It also deals, in a limited manner, with the protection of civilians from the effects of hostilities. This Convention has been extensively supplemented by Additional Protocol I.

In the *Advisory Opinion on the Legal Consequences of the Construction of a Wall by Israel in the Occupied Palestinian Territory* (2004) 43 ILM 1009 the ICJ affirmed the de jure application of the Fourth Hague Convention of 1907, to which the Hague Regulations are annexed, to the Occupied Palestinian Territory, despite the fact that Israel has never ratified it. The ICJ reached this conclusion on the grounds that, first, the Hague Regulations have become part of customary international law and, second, that Israel as a contracting party to the Geneva Convention IV is bound by its art 154 which provides that the Convention is supplementary to ssII and III of the Hague Regulations. The Court found that sIII of those Regulations concerning 'military authority over the territory of the hostile state' was of particular relevance to the situation in the Occupied Palestinian Territory.

Since 1967 Israel has denied the de jure application of the Geneva Convention IV to the Occupied Palestinian Territory. On 22 October 1967 the Israeli Minister of Justice stated that Israel would not regard itself as an occupying power in the territories which its forces had liberated from foreigners. He emphasised that the territories were, 20 centuries earlier, Jewish.

The main legal argument of Israel, however, is based on the lack of Jordanian or Egyptian sovereignty over the West Bank and Gaza prior to their annexation by Israel in 1967. Both Jordan and Egypt are contracting parties to the Geneva Conventions. According to Israel the Geneva Convention IV does not apply, because the territory was not taken over from the territory of a contracting party which would need to be the situation in order to fall within the scope of art 2 of the Geneva Convention IV. Article 2 provides that:

'The Convention shall apply to all cases of partial or total occupation of the territory of a High Contracting Party.'

Israel's refusal to apply the Geneva Convention IV to the Occupied Palestinian Territory has been condemned by the international community as illustrated, inter alia, by numerous UN Security Council Resolutions (see for example Resolution 799 the UN Security Council which states that the Security Council 'reaffirms the applicability of the Geneva Convention IV of 12 August 1949 to all Palestinian territories occupied by Israel since 1967, including Jerusalem').

The ICJ confirmed the de jure application of the Geneva Convention IV to the Occupied Palestinian Territory. The ICJ interpreted both paragraphs of art 2 of the Geneva Convention IV. The Court stated that art 2(1) of the Geneva Convention IV sets out two conditions necessary for the application of the Convention: first that there exists an armed conflict and that the conflict has arisen between two contracting states. Both conditions were satisfied in respect of the Occupied Palestinian Territory, including East Jerusalem, as there was an armed conflict between Israel and Jordan, and both Israel and Jordan were contracting parties at the start of the 1967 war. The ICJ noted that the purpose of art 2(2) of the Geneva Convention IV which refers to 'occupation of the territory of a High Contracting Party' is to ensure that, even if occupation effected during the conflict met no armed resistance, the Convention still applies and the scope of its application was not restricted as determined in art 2(1). The ICJ emphasised that this interpretation was confirmed by the Convention's travaux preparatoires, by the contracting parties to the Geneva Convention IV at their conference on 15 July 1999, by the ICRC, by the UN General Assembly, by the UN Security Council and finally by Israel's Supreme Court in its judgment of 30 May 2004 (*Beit Sourik Village Council* v *the Government of Israel* (2004) 43 ILM 1099).

Having established the applicability of the Geneva Convention IV to the

Occupied Palestinian Territory the ICJ examined whether or not Israel could rely on the 'military exigencies' exception provided for in art 49(1), which states that the prohibition of forcible transfers of population and deportations may be allowed when the security of the population or imperative military reasons so demand. The ICJ held that the exception does not apply to art 49(6) which prohibits not only deportations or forced transfers of population such as those carried out during the World War II, but also any measures taken by an occupying power in order to organise or encourage transfers of parts of its own population into an occupied territory.

Therefore, the establishment of Jewish settlements in the Occupied Palestinian Territory, the ICJ emphasised, was in breach of art 49(6) of the Geneva Convention IV. Also the ICJ stated that Israel could not, while building the wall, rely upon the exception embodied in art 53 of the Geneva Convention IV concerning the destruction of personal property 'where such destruction is rendered absolutely necessary by military operations'.

Additional Protocol I. Additional Protocol I is intended to ensure the widest possible protection of victims of international armed conflicts. It contains provisions concerning the protection of the wounded and sick, the methods and means of warfare, and the protection of civilian population and civilian objects from the effects of hostilities. The main innovations of the Protocol have been discussed above. They are as follows.

1. The rules concerning the protection of civilian population against effects of hostilities which oblige the parties to the conflict to make a distinction between civilian objectives and military objectives, to prohibit reprisals against civilians, to ensure protection of refugees and stateless persons etc.
2. The application of the Protocol to colonial wars. Article 96(3) provides that an authority representing a people engaged in a struggle for self-determination against a contracting state to the Protocol may undertake to apply the full Geneva regime by means of a unilateral declaration. During the Algerian War of Independence the FLN, which was recognised as a provisional government exercising a right of self-determination against the historical colonial aggression of France, made such a declaration. As a result France, as well as the FLN, was bound to apply the four Geneva Conventions to the conflict.
3. The Protocol extended the categories of combatants by adding members of guerilla movements provided they satisfied certain requirements whilst denying the status of a combatant to mercenaries and spies.

Non-international conflicts

Until the adoption of Additional Protocol II only a common art 3 of the four Geneva Conventions ensured some measure of protection to victims of non-international conflicts. This article states:

'In the case of armed conflict not of an international character occurring in the territory of one of the High Contracting Parties, each Party to the conflict shall be bound to apply, as a minimum, the following provisions:

(1) Persons taking no active part in the hostilities, including members of armed forces who have laid down their arms and those placed hors de combat by sickness, wounds, detention, or any other cause, shall in all circumstances be treated humanely, without any adverse distinction founded on race, colour, religion or faith, sex, birth or wealth, or any other similar criteria.

To this end, the following acts are and shall remain prohibited at any time and in any place whatsoever with respect to the above-mentioned persons:

(a) violence to life and person, in particular murder of all kinds, mutilation, cruel treatment and torture;

(b) taking of hostages;

(c) outrages upon personal dignity, in particular humiliating and degrading treatment;

(d) the passing of sentences and the carrying out of execution without previous judgment pronounced by a regularly constituted court affording all the judicial guarantees which are recognised as indispensable by civilised peoples.

(2) The wounded and sick shall be collected and cared for.

An impartial humanitarian body, such as the International Committee of the Red Cross, may offer its services to the Parties to the conflict.

The Parties to the conflict should further endeavour to bring into force, by means of special agreements, all or part of the other provisions of the present Convention.

The application of the preceding provisions shall not affect the legal status of the parties to the conflict.'

The minimum 'safety net' regime set out in common art 3 of the Geneva Conventions has been considerably extended. Additional Protocol II applies to all persons affected by an armed conflict without any discrimination. It requires that all persons not participating directly in hostilities, or who have ceased to participate, must be treated humanely. It contains detailed provisions concerning persons whose liberty has been restricted. The ICRC submitted two proposals with a view to extending their protection: first, the right to be visited by representatives of international impartial humanitarian organisations; and, second, the prohibition of the execution of the death penalty before the end of the conflict. Both proposals were rejected.

The material scope of application of Additional Protocol II is disappointing. It applies to all armed conflicts which are not covered by art 1 of Additional Protocol I subject to two limitations.

1. For the application of Additional Protocol II the dissident armed force must be under responsible control and must exercise such control over a part of its territory as to enable it to carry out sustained and concerted military operations and to implement the Protocol.
2. Additional Protocol II does not apply to situations of internal disturbances and tensions, such as riots, isolated and sporadic acts of violence and other acts of similar nature.

18.4 Breaches of international humanitarian law

Breaches of the rules and customs of war and conventions relating to humanitarian law constitute an international tort and impose the duty of reparation on the tortfeasor. This principle is often impossible to apply in practice (but see the developments in respect of the International Criminal Tribunal for the Former Yugoslavia (ICTY) and the International Criminal Tribunal for Rwanda (ICTR)). The long fight of the ex-American and British prisoners of World War II for compensation from Japan illustrates this point. The Japanese courts and Japanese authorities have neither fully apologised nor compensated the POWs for the inhumane treatment they were subjected to while in Japanese captivity (out of 50,016 British POWs captured by the Japanese during World War II, 12,433 died or were killed in captivity). The main argument of the surviving POWs before the Tokyo District Court was that Japan was in breach of the Regulations Respecting the Laws and Customs of War on Land which are annexed to the Hague Convention IV 1907 and that at the material time international customary law recognised individual rights to claim compensation from a state whose armed forces violated the rules of war. Chapter II of the Regulations concerns the treatment of prisoners of wars. The fundamental principle is that they should be treated humanely. This Convention was ratified by Japan in 1911. Article 3 of the Hague Convention IV provides that a belligerent party who breaches the Regulations is liable to pay compensation and is responsible for all acts committed by persons forming part of its armed forces. Yet, the Tokyo District Court on 24 November 1996 dismissed all claims on the grounds that the 1907 Hague Convention applied only between contracting states and thus could not be applied to individuals and rejected the existence of individual's right to compensation under the customary international law at the material time. In November 2001 the High Court in Tokyo rejected an appeal against the decision. Subsequently, an appeal to the Supreme Court of Japan was filed in April 2003. At the time of writing the matter is still under consideration. The lawsuit seeks an official apology and US $20,000 net per claimant.

However, former British POWs obtained compensation not from Japan but from the British government. On 7 November 2000 the UK government agreed to pay a single ex-gratia payment of £10,000 compensation to each of the surviving POWs, and of £4,500 to widows of the POWs who died, to former members of the Merchant Navy captured and imprisoned and to British civilians who had suffered under Japanese occupation. So far American POWs have neither obtained justice nor compensation.

The four Geneva Conventions contain provisions governing the prosecution of grave breaches of the Conventions: arts 49 and 50 Geneva Convention I; arts 50 and 51 Geneva Convention II; arts 129 and 130 Geneva Convention III; and arts 146 and 147 Geneva Convention IV. They did not establish an international body empowered to search and try persons alleged to have committed grave breaches of humanitarian law. Instead they imposed on the contracting parties the obligation to enact national legislation providing for effective penal sanctions for persons responsible for grave breaches of the Geneva regime and the obligation to enforce such legislation in national courts. For that reason the Geneva Conventions do not specify the punishment for grave breaches of their provisions.

Each contracting party undertakes to search for persons accused of committing grave breaches and try them regardless of their nationality or hand them over for trial to another contracting party provided that the latter has made out a prima facie case. This means that the Geneva Conventions allocate universal jurisdiction to a contracting party in respect of grave breaches. Anyone who is suspected of committing, or ordering to be committed, any of the grave breaches anywhere in the world may stand trial in any contracting state. In practice, contracting states are not interested in enforcing humanitarian law in respect of foreign nationals accused of committing grave breaches when there is no connection whatsoever between that state and the alleged crimes. The handing over of such persons to another contracting state is done through the extradition procedure.

What happens in practice is that a contracting state assumes jurisdiction over members of enemy forces and civilians who fall into its power and are charged with grave breaches of the Geneva Conventions. The accused, including spies and mercenaries, are entitled to fair trial. The Geneva Conventions prohibit any barbarous form of punishment. Under the Geneva Conventions a contracting state is also bound to punish its own nationals accused of committing, or ordering to be committed, grave breaches of its provisions. In practice it is extremely rare for a contracting party to do so and the punishment is more symbolic than real. One example is provided by the trial of Lieutenant Calley and Captain Medina accused of a massacre of civilians in the Vietnamese village of My Lai. The inhabitants were murdered in cold blood, women were raped, mutilated and killed, children and babies were stabbed with bayonets, even corpses were beheaded. Both Calley and Medina were simple solders. The matter of who gave the orders was never established. As a result of a mass-murder enquiry several officers, superiors of Calley, were charged with dereliction of duty and other soldiers were charged with murder. Only one person was convicted: Lieutenant Calley. On 29 March 1971 he was sentenced to hard labour for life. Three days later, he was released from prison on the specific instruction of President Nixon and allowed to appeal. He spent the next three years under house arrest in his own apartment in Georgia. On 9 November 1974 he was paroled a free man.

A recent example of breaches of international humanitarian law is provided by the ill treatment of Iraqi detainees by the US Coalition Forces, in particular in Abu Ghraib prison in Baghdad. Subsequent to complaints from Iraqi citizens, from various international human rights organisations and from the International Committee of the Red Cross (ICRC) on 19 January 2004 Lieutenant General Ricardo Sanchez, the senior US Commander in Iraq, requested US Central Command to investigate the matter. Major General Antonio M Taguba, who was appointed to conduct the investigation, completed his report on 26 February 2004. The Taguba Report found evidence of systematic and illegal 'sadistic, blatant, and wanton criminal abuses ... inflicted on several detainees' in Abu Ghraib prison. Those abuses consisted, inter alia, of physical abuses, videotaping and photographing naked male and female detainees, posing detainees in various sexually explicit positions for photographing, forcing detainees to remove their clothing and remain naked for several hours at a time, a male MP guard having sex with a female detainee, intimidating and frightening detainees using military working dogs, etc (Taguba Report, Part One, Findings of Fact, Para 5). The Report was not made public until graphic pictures depicting US soldiers abusing Iraqi prisoners were aired by CBS on '60 Minutes II' on 28 April 2004.

Whilst the US government has refused to apply the Geneva Convention III to the detainees at Guantanamo Bay captured during 'Operation Enduring Freedom' in Afghanistan, it has never challenged the applicability of the international humanitarian law, in particular the III and IV Geneva Conventions, to 'Operation Iraqi Freedom' regarding the invasion of Iraq. Many procedural and substantive requirements of humanitarian law were breached by the manner of arrest, treatment and detention of Iraqi citizens in Abu Ghraib prison. The most fundamental provisions of the Geneva Convention III were violated in respect of Iraqi POWs which requires the humane treatment of POWs at all times (art 13), prohibits the application of physical and moral coercion against protected persons, in particular to obtain information from them and from third parties (art 31), and prohibits murder, torture, corporal punishment and any other measures of brutality whether applied by civilian or military agents (art 32). Among the detainees in Abu Ghraib prison were civilians. The Geneva Convention IV requires that a distinction must be made between civilians and POWs and that civilians must be treated with dignity and respect (arts 5, 27, 31 and 32). In addition to the violations of the III and IV Geneva Conventions the US was in breach of customary human rights law and many human rights conventions to which the US is a contracting party, such as the International Covenant on Civil and Political Rights and the Torture Convention 1984. Although the US has investigated the violations, and has punished some of the offenders, it remains a fact that the US government did not take any measures as a result of the ICRC or the Taguba Report. It was only when the abuses in Abu Ghraib were made public by the media that the US government decided to act. It is also a fact that the lack of proper supervision and training of US military forces operating in Iraq regarding humanitarian law and international human rights illustrate the difficulty in applying the Geneva Conventions where its enforcement is left to the contracting states.

Article 50 of Geneva Convention I defines grave breaches as acts committed against persons or property protected under the Conventions, and gives a list. They are:

'... wilful killing, torture, inhumane treatment including biological experiments, wilfully causing great suffering or serious injury to body or health, and extensive destruction and appropriation of property, not justified by military necessity and carried out unlawfully and wantonly.'

The remaining Geneva Conventions add to this list specific abuses relating to naval warfare (arts 22, 24, 25 and 27 of Geneva Convention II), to the treatment of POWs (art 13 of Geneva Convention III) and Geneva Convention IV extends the list in art 50 of Geneva Convention I to the following: 'unlawful deportation or transfer or unlawful confinement of a protected person, compelling a protected person to serve in the forces of a hostile Power, or wilfully depriving a protected person of the right of fair and regular trial prescribed in the present Convention, taking of hostages': art 147 of Geneva Convention IV. Similarly, Additional Protocol I further extends the list of grave breaches (art 2, art 85 etc). It also clearly states that grave breaches can be committed not only by acts but also by omission. In respect of Additional Protocol II no grave breaches to its provisions are listed. It is presumed that domestic penal law is sufficient to punish the offenders. Article 6 of Additional Protocol II offers an additional guarantee by restating the general rules on the prosecution and punishment of criminal offences related to armed conflicts.

Grave breaches are always criminal offences punishable through penal proceedings, other breaches which are not considered as grave under the Geneva regime are punished through disciplinary procedures.

In is important to note that the Geneva Conventions and Additional Protocols exclude the possibility of a contracting party derogating from them or that protected persons may contract out of their provisions. Nothing, however, prevents a contracting party from adding to the rights established by the Geneva regime.

The role of the International Committee of the Red Cross (ICRC)

The proposals submitted by Henri Dunant in his book entitled *A Memory of Solferino* attracted the attention of Gustave Moynier, who was a Swiss lawyer and the chairman of a local charity (the Geneva Public Welfare Society). At his initiative a five-member committee was set up to further examine Dunant's proposals. This was the beginning of the International Committee of the Red Cross which initially was called the International Committee for Relief of the Wounded. The first meeting of ICRC took place on 17 February 1863.

The ICRC is a private Swiss organisation made up entirely of Swiss nationals. More than 12,000 people work for it. The ICRC is independent from any government, including the Swiss government, and from any international organisation. It is detached from all political issues relating to conflicts. Its mission is to bring relief and assistance to the victims of armed conflicts and internal violence. Its independence, impartiality and Swiss identity (which ensures its neutrality) are the guarantees of the ICRC's acceptability to all parties involved in armed conflicts or internal disturbances.

The four Geneva Conventions and two Additional Protocols recognise the special status of the ICRC, and allocate special tasks to it. In particular, the ICRC may offer its services as a protecting power if no agreement can be reached between the warring parties as to the appointment of a protecting power. The system of protecting powers has rarely worked. As a result, in fact, the ICRC has assumed, in many international conflicts, the humanitarian functions of a protecting power. Under the Geneva Conventions the ICRC has been granted a general right of intervention in connection with humanitarian matters which it exercises irrespective of whether or not a protecting power has been appointed. The delegates of the ICRC visit prisoners of war, detainees and occupied territories. They interview the POWs and detainees without witnesses in order to ensure that they are being treated humanely. The ICRC makes confidential reports to the authority concerned and if abuses have been discovered urges it to rectify the situation. In 2003 the ICRC visited almost 470,000 prisoners and detainees held in 1,900 places of detention in a total of approximately 80 countries. The ICRC is the only international organisation that has been allowed to visit detainees at Guanatamo Bay.

Since its inception the ICRC has been a driving force behind the development of international humanitarian law. At its initiative the first Geneva Convention for the Amelioration of the Condition of the Wounded in Armies in the Field was adopted in 1864. Since then the ICRC has been active in drafting, negotiating and amending international humanitarian law. On the basis of the ICRC's experience gained on battlefields it has made proposals aimed at improving existing conventions. This resulted in major revisions of international humanitarian law in 1906, 1929, 1949 and 1977. The ICRC is still very much involved in the development of international humanitarian law. In respect of the Geneva Conventions the ICRC is constantly assessing them in order to ensure that they reflect the reality of armed conflicts and internal disturbances. Currently the ICRC is examining the best solution to the issue of POWs refusing to be repatriated after the cessation of hostilities, a matter which is not regulated by international law.

The ICRC has been officially recognised as a guardian of humanitarian law in the Statutes of the International Red Cross and the Red Crescent Movement adopted by them and by the contracting parties to the Geneva Conventions. The main tasks of the ICRC are set out in art 5 of the Statutes. The ICRC makes a direct contribution to the application of humanitarian law by being present wherever there are armed conflicts or internal disturbances.

Another important function of the ICRC is carried out through its Central Tracing Agency (CTA) which maintains records of persons captured, detained, interned, killed and injured. At the request of relatives the CTA provides information such as is in its possession, via the local Red Cross, about missing members of their families. The task of the CTA also consists of exchanging messages between family members, separated by hostilities, who are unable to get in touch because the normal communication channels have broken down or because such persons are detained. In 2003 the ICRC collected and delivered almost 1.3 million Red Cross messages.

The ICRC acts as a neutral intermediary between all parties involved in the conflict urging them to comply with humanitarian law and, if asked, facilitates political negotiations and thus contributes to the restoration of peace and stability.

The ICRC provides medical assistance to the sick and wounded. Its medical activities encompass not only the supply of medical equipment but also of medical personnel when local hospitals are unable to cope with the influx of wounded or when there is no medical personnel at all. The ICRC also takes measures to prevent the local population from becoming sick as a result of poor hygiene. The ICRC technical personnel repair water-supply systems destroyed or damaged by the conflict, and set up safe water-distribution and waste-disposal systems in camps and other settlements in order to prevent the outbreak of epidemics.

The most generally recognised task of the ICRC is the supply of relief aid to POWs, refugees, displaced persons and people in occupied territories in the form of the famous 'Red Cross Parcels'. The ICRC is especially concerned with internally displaced persons. In 2000 the ICRC provided aid for almost five million people displaced by conflicts in 35 situations. However, the distribution of food is a temporary measure. Relief programmes of the ICRC, as far as possible, encompass rehabilitation allowing people to stay in their land and start life anew.

Agricultural tools and seeds, livestock vaccines, etc, when appropriate, are distributed together with food parcels.

Another important task of the ICRC is its work for the understanding and dissimilation of knowledge of international humanitarian law. The ICRC is very persistent in encouraging governments to ratify the Geneva Conventions and Additional Protocols and to implement them. Through its own delegates, national societies, the Swiss government, international organisations and any other available means the ICRC puts this subject on national agendas, and uses all reasonable means to convince reluctant governments to become parties to the 1949 Conventions and 1977 Additional Protocols. Its reward is that almost all countries in the world are now bound by the Geneva Conventions and the ratification of Additional Protocols has increased in the recent years.

In fulfilling its task the ICRC is not alone. The ICRC is the founder of the International Red Cross and Red Crescent Movement, the largest humanitarian network in the world which comprises the following.

1. The ICRC which directs and co-ordinates the international work of the components of the movement in connection with armed conflicts and internal violence.
2. The National Red Cross and Red Crescent societies (national societies) which are considered as 'auxiliary to public authorities' in their respective countries in the humanitarian field. Each society must be approved by the ICRC. They basically work in their own country. In peacetime they provide relief in the case of

disasters and fulfil humanitarian tasks such as caring for the old, sick, poor, etc. In wartime their first-aid personnel become part of the national army medical services. National societies play an important role in disseminating international humanitarian law through conferences, workshops, etc. There are now more than 160 national Red Cross and Red Crescent societies all over the world.

3. The International Federation of Red Cross and Red Crescent Societies (the Federation), which gathers together the national societies. The Federation co-ordinates international assistance from national societies to victims of natural and man-made disasters outside the conflict areas. Its objectives are described in art 2 of its Constitution according to which the Federation is 'to inspire, encourage, facilitate and promote at all times all forms of humanitarian activities by the member society with a view to preventing and alleviating human suffering and thereby contributing to the maintenance and the promotion of peace in the world'.

On 12 August 1999, at the fiftieth anniversary of the signing of the four Geneva Conventions, international figures, including UN Secretary-General Kofi Annan and Prince Hassan of Jordan, gathered in the same room in Geneva's town hall to sign the appeal calling on all nations to eradicate war. Until this occurs the ICRC's presence and exemplary work will continue to be needed.

19

Criminal Responsibility of Individuals under International Law

19.1 Introduction

19.2 The International Military Tribunal (IMT) at Nuremberg

19.3 The International Military Tribunal for the Far East (IMTFE)

19.4 The International Criminal Tribunal for the Former Yugoslavia (ICTY) and the International Criminal Tribunal for Rwanda (ICTR)

19.5 The International Criminal Court (ICC)

19.1 Introduction

The idea of universal justice ensuring that 'no ruler, no junta and no army anywhere can abuse human rights with impunity' (Kofi Annan, UN Secretary-General: see http://www.un.org/law/icc/general/overview.htm) has inspired the creation of the International Criminal Court. The absence of an international mechanism providing for trial and punishment, thus allowing the guilty to continue their life with impunity, has, until now, left the victims and their families without any means of obtaining any retribution or compensation or even moral satisfaction. As José Ayala Lasso, former United Nations High Commissioner for Human Rights said: 'A person stands a better chance of being tried and judged for killing one human being than for killing 100,000!': ibid.

The hope that unprecedented atrocities committed during World War II would never occur again was short-lived. The list of acts of genocide, crimes against humanity and war crimes which have been committed since the end of World War II, for which no individuals have been held accountable, is very long. The worst examples are provided by crimes committed by the Khmer Rouge in Cambodia where an estimated three million people were killed and by Saddam Hussein who, inter alia, ordered in March 1988 a chemical warfare assault against Kurdish civilians living in the town of Halabja (Iraq) in which mustard, cyanide and nerve gases were deployed against the innocent Kurds. Massacres continue in Sudan, the Ivory Coast and many other places.

It took the United Nations 50 years to adopt a convention on the establishment of a permanent international criminal court. The main reason why it took so long to adopt a statute creating a permanent criminal court is that genocide, war crimes and similar serious violations of human rights are most frequently committed in internal conflicts. The principle that the perpetrators of such crimes should be brought before national courts has long been recognised by the international community. However, in the case of internal, or even of international, conflicts, national courts are often unable to try the offenders because governments are often reluctant to punish their own nationals, or because this may jeopardise the existence of fragile democratic structures of a new government of national reconciliation. In some cases national institutions collapsed, as in the case of Rwanda and Cambodia, and there were no appropriate courts!

Before examining the jurisdiction of the permanent International Criminal Court, it is necessary to assess the contribution of its predecessors, the four international criminal courts (the International Military Tribunal (IMT) at Nuremberg, the International Military Tribunal for the Far East (IMTFE), the International Criminal Tribunal for the Former Yugoslavia (ICTY) and the International Criminal Tribunal for Rwanda (ICTR), to the development of international law in this area. Each of the four international criminal courts was created on an ad hoc basis in response to a sense of outrage felt by the international community over atrocities committed by a particular group of people in a particular place and the jurisdiction of each court was subject to limits in terms of time and place.

Furthermore, an ad hoc criminal court was created by the United Nations and the government of Sierra Leone in March 2002 pursuant to UN Security Council Resolution 1315 of 14 August 2000 requesting the UN Secretary-General to start negotiations to set up a special court. The court was established by an agreement between the United Nations and Sierra Leone and not under Security Council resolutions adopted under Chapter VII of the Charter of the UN as in the case of the ICTY and the ICTR. One of the important differences between the Special Court for Sierra Leone and the two international tribunals is that the special court for Sierra Leone tries those accused of atrocities committed in Sierra Leone during the civil war. And unlike the ICTY and the ICTR it has no power to request the surrender of an offender present in a third state. Its jurisdiction rationae materiae encompasses war crimes and crimes against humanity but not the crime of genocide as there is no evidence that such a crime was committed in Sierra Leone. However, some offences under Sierra Leone law were added, such as abusing a girl under the age of 14, abduction of a girl for immoral purposes and setting fire to dwelling-houses or public buildings. The court has the difficult task of resolving the conflict between its jurisdiction rationae materiae and the amnesty granted under the Lomé Agreement by the government of Sierra Leone in respect of crimes under Sierra Leone law committed during the civil war. The Special Tribunal is made up of both national and international judges. National judges are appointed by the government of Sierra Leone whilst international judges are appointed by the Secretary-General of the UN. The court is funded by fixed contributions from member states of the UN. The court has a three-year mandate to find, arrest and try those accused of war crimes committed in Sierra Leone since November 1996.

The first trials commenced in July 2004. As at that date, 11 persons had been indicted (see www.sc-sl.org). If they are found guilty they may be sentenced to prison terms or have their property confiscated but the court has no power to impose the death penalty.

Another new development is the creation of an internationally assisted tribunal in Cambodia. In October 2004 the Cambodian parliament ratified an agreement with the United Nations under which an internationally assisted tribunal will be established in Cambodia to try surviving Khmer Rouge leaders responsible for the death of at least 1.7 million people during the 1975–1979 rule of the Khmer Rouge. So far only two major leaders of the Khmer Rouge have been brought to justice. Ta Mok, former army chief, and Kaing Khek Iev, chief interrogator at Tuol Sleng, are both awaiting trial. Pol Pot, who was the leader of the regime, died in 1998. However, others still live freely in Cambodia. The tribunal will have jurisdiction, inter alia, to review whether or not some leaders of the Khmer Rouge who were pardoned before the tribunal was established should still be immune from prosecution and, if so, the extent of the immunity. This review of immunity will include the case of Ieng Sary, the former Khmer Rouge foreign minister, who was granted a pardon by King Norodom Sihanouk on the ground that he led a mass defection of the Khmer Rouge troops to the government of King Sihanouk in 1996. The agreement prohibits the government from granting amnesty or pardon to individuals who can be investigated or prosecuted for Khmer Rouge crimes. The tribunal will be made up of Cambodian and foreign prosecutors and judges, with Cambodians in the majority.

19.2 The International Military Tribunal (IMT) at Nuremberg

At the end of World War II the allied nations had to decide how to deal with high-ranking Nazis. Some proposed that they should be shot without trial; others that they should be prosecuted and brought to justice before an international court. The latter solution was approved by the US, the UK, France and the Soviet Union (and subsequently by another 19 states) whose representatives signed on 8 August 1945 the London Agreement for the Prosecution and Punishment of the Major War Criminals. This established the International Military Tribunal (IMT) at Nuremberg to bring to justice the major Nazi war criminals. It provided for new and original solutions since there were no legal basis under international law for prosecuting war criminals (although it was submitted that some of the Geneva Conventions, the Hague Conventions and the 1928 Kellogg-Briand Pact provided legal bases for such proceedings).

The Charter of the International Military Tribunal was annexed to the London

Agreement. Under the Charter the charges against the accused were to be brought on any of four counts:

1. conspiracy to wage wars of aggression;
2. crimes against peace;
3. war crimes;
4. crimes against humanity.

The Tribunal consisted of eight judges, two each from: the US, the UK, the Soviet Union and France. For the prosecution there was a team of 23 US attorneys headed by Judge Jackson, seven British barristers and the British Attorney-General Sir Hartley Shawcross, five French advocates and 11 Soviet lawyers. The proceedings were commenced on 20 November 1945 and ended on 1 October 1946.

Charges were brought against 22 defendants, of whom only 21 were present. Bormann, who was never found, was tried in absentia.

There were a number of important matters which challenged the neutrality and the legitimacy of the Nuremberg trial.

1. International law did not provide solid grounds for prosecuting war criminals. In this respect, the most relevant were arts 226–228 of the Treaty of Versailles 1919 establishing the right of allied nations to prosecute and punish individuals responsible for 'violation of the laws and customs of war'. Article 228 stated that 'the German Government recognises the right of the Allied and Associated Powers to bring before military tribunals persons accused of having committed acts in violation of the laws and customs of war'. Under art 227 of the Treaty of Versailles German Kaiser Wilhelm II of Hohenzollern was stated to be guilty of 'supreme offence against international morality and the sanctity of the treaties'. The Allied powers agreed to set up a special international tribunal made up of judges from the US, the UK, Italy and France to try him. However, the Allied powers had never submitted a formal request for the surrender of the Kaiser and the idea of an international trial of the German Kaiser Wilhelm II was abandoned.

   Furthermore, the 1928 Kellogg-Briand Pact which was ratified by both Germany and Japan outlawed war but did not provide for any enforcement mechanism. Thus, the Pact did not provide for criminal sanctions if its provisions were breached. The IMT, based on the idealistic objective of outlawing war in accordance with art 2(4) of the Charter of the United Nations, created brand new laws and applied them retrospectively to the accused contrary to the fundamental principles of any criminal law, that is nulla poena sine lege, nulla crima sine lege, so that the accused might fairly have been able to argue that their trial was in breach of these fundamental principles.

2. It should be noted that the most important Nazi criminals were already dead. Hitler committed suicide on 30 April 1945 and Goebbels, his minister of propaganda, killed himself and his family on 1 May 1945. Himmler and

Heydrich, the principal organisers of the 'final solution' in the course of which six million Jews were killed, were both dead.

One of the most important Nazi criminals captured by the allied forces Reichmarshall Hermann Goering was put on trial despite the fact that there was no documentary evidence linking him conclusively with the 'final solution'. The IMT acquitted only three defendants (Papen, Schacht and Fritzsche), 11 were found guilty on all four counts and condemned to death, the remainder were found guilty and were sentenced to lengthy terms of imprisonment. Reichmarshall Goering was condemned to death but died a few hours before the intended execution by swallowing a concealed cyanide capsule.

3. The defence could neither challenge the legitimacy of the tribunal nor raise some defences. For example, the accused were barred from submitting the argument that the Allied forces themselves committed similar offences (the tu quoque argument – you did it too) such as indiscriminate bombing of civilians in the raids on Hamburg, Berlin and Dresden or waging aggressive war.

4. The defence was seriously handicapped by lack of adequate lawyers, lack of adequate back-up staff, lack of resources etc. It was paradoxical that the accused, Hermann Goering, submitted personally the most effective arguments in his defence.

5. The jurisdiction of the IMT at Nuremberg was based on Germany's debellatio (conquest) and the co-imperium exercised by the occupying powers over Germany.

The main contributions of the IMT at Nuremberg to the development of international criminal law were as follows.

1. The Tribunal established the principle that individuals could be liable under international law. In this respect the judgment of the IMT stated that:

> 'Crimes against international law are committed by men, not by abstract entities, and only by punishing individuals who commit such crimes can the provisions of international law be enforced.'

All the accused argued that states were subjects of international law not individuals and therefore individuals neither had obligations under international law nor could be punished under international law. The accused emphasised that their only obligations were to the Nazi state which was liable under international law. Furthermore, the acts they committed were acts of state and consequently those who carried them out were not liable because of the doctrine of the sovereignty of the state. Both arguments were rejected by the IMT. The IMT stated that:

> '... individuals have international duties which transcend the national obligations of obedience imposed by the individual state [to which they owe allegiance]. He who violates the laws of war cannot obtain immunity while acting in pursuance of the authority of the state if that state in authorising action moves outside its competence under international law.'

2. The Tribunal dealt with the matters of both the official position held by the defendants in the Nazi government and of 'superior orders'. Article 7 of the Charter provided that the official position of the defendant, whether as Head of State or an official in the government would neither exonerate him from responsibility nor mitigate the punishment, whilst art 8 rejected any defence based on the following of orders of the government or of a superior, but accepted that this may be considered in mitigation of punishment. The Nuremberg Tribunal stated in this respect that: 'The true test, which is found in varying degrees in the criminal law of most nations, is not the existence of the order, but whether moral choice was in fact possible'.

   Article IV of the Genocide Convention 1948 confirms that 'persons committing offences under the Convention shall be punished whether they are constitutionally responsible rulers, public officials or private individuals' but an amendment to this provision stating that superior orders should not justify genocide was rejected. Only three international conventions have explicitly dealt with the matters of official position and superior orders.

   a) Article III of the Apartheid Convention 1973. Under this provision individuals are criminally liable, irrespective of whether or not they were members of organisations and institutions or acted as representatives of the state, and irrespective of the motive involved. The preparatory work of the Convention supports the conclusion that neither the orders of superiors nor the official position of the defendant should shield him from criminal responsibility or mitigate his punishment.

   b) The Convention against Torture and Other Cruel Inhuman or Degrading Treatment or Punishment 1984. Its art 2(3) provides that: 'an order from a superior officer or a public authority may not be invoked as a justification for torture'. A defence based on the official position of the defendant is excluded indirectly in its art 1 which describes torture as severe pain and suffering, physical or mental, intentionally inflicted for certain purposes 'when such pain or suffering is inflicted by or at the instigation or with the consent or acquiescence of a public official or other person acting in an official capacity'.

   c) The Inter-American Convention to Prevent and Punish Torture 1985 which explicitly excludes both defences.

From the late 1990s national courts in a number of states (the House of Lords in the *Pinochet* case, the Swiss courts in proceedings against Marcos, the courts of Senegal in proceedings against Hisséne Habré, the French Court of Appeal in proceedings against the Libyan Head of State, Muammar Ghaddaffi, etc) and both the International Criminal Tribunal for Rwanda (proceedings against Jean Kambanda, the prime minister of Rwanda at the relevant time) and the International Criminal Tribunal for the Former Yugoslavia (indictment issued against Slobodan Milosevic) have confirmed that whatever the official position of the defendant in the governmental hierarchy, including that of a Head of State, it will not free that individual from criminal responsibility. However, subsequent to the judgment of the ICJ in the *Case Concerning the Arrest Warrant of 11 April 2000: Democratic Republic of the Congo* v *Belgium* (2002) 41 ILM 536 proceedings against Heads of State still in office were abandoned: in Belgium against Israeli Prime Minister, Ariel Shanon, in 2003, in France against the Libyan Head of State Colonel Ghaddaffi, in 2001, and in the UK against Zimbabwean President Robert Mugabe, in 2004 (an application for an extradition warrant). The Statute of the International Criminal Court firmly reiterates that defences based on an act of state and on superior orders have no effect on the defendant's guilt (see below).

3. Article 6 of the Charter of the IMT stated that individuals could be liable for crimes against peace, war crimes and crimes against humanity. It defined these crimes as follows.

   a) Crimes against peace: namely planning, preparation, initiation or waging of a war of aggression, or a war in violation of international treaties, agreements or assurances, or participation in a common plan or conspiracy for the accomplishment of any of the foregoing.

   b) War crimes: namely, violations of the laws or customs of war. Such violations shall include, but not be limited to, murder, ill-treatment or deportation to slave labour or any other purpose of civilian population of or in occupied territory, murder or ill-treatment of prisoners of war or persons on the seas, killing of hostages, plunder of public or private property, wanton destruction of cities, towns or villages, or devastation not justified by military necessity.

   c) Crimes against humanity: namely, murder, extermination, enslavement, deportation, and other inhumane acts committed against any civilian population, before or during the war; or persecution on political, racial or religious grounds in execution of or in connection with any crime within the jurisdiction of the Tribunal, whether or not in violation of the domestic law of the country where perpetrated.

The definition of war crimes given above was in conformity with customary and treaty law in this area. War crimes constitute violations of the rules applicable to the conduct of armed conflict and were recognised as crimes under international law by arts 45, 50, 52 and 56 of the Hague Convention IV 1907 and arts 2, 3, 4, 46 and 51 of the Geneva Convention Relating to the Amelioration of the Condition of the Wounded and Sick in Armies in the Field 1929.

However, crimes against peace and crimes against humanity were introduced by the Charter of the IMT into international law. In particular, the recognition that the crimes against humanity are so hideous that the international community as a whole is empowered to prosecute and try offenders constituted one of the most important legacies of the IMT. Under the Charter the Tribunal had jurisdiction over crimes against humanity where these crimes were related to war crimes and crimes against peace. As a result, crimes committed by the Nazi regime before War World II were left unpunished.

Both, the crimes against peace and the crimes against humanity raised many controversies, especially in respect of the defendants before the IMT as they were charges with offences which did not exist at the material time. These controversies were resolved shortly after the Nuremberg judgment when the UN General Assembly unanimously adopted Resolution 95 (I) on the Affirmation of the Principles of International Law Recognised by the Charter of the Nuremberg Tribunal 1946. The word 'affirmation' is very important. It suggests that the IMT applied principles which already existed under customary law and thus the IMT had only to 'recognise' them. Consequently the General Assembly confirmed them. Further, the GA asked the International Law Commission (ILC) to codify them taking into account their importance (the ILC codified the Nuremberg Principles in 1950: [1950] UNYB 852). On the basis of the GA Resolution many countries enacted national legislation in order to prosecute lower level Nazi criminals before national courts.

As a result of the fact that the definition of crimes against humanity mentioned genocide an autonomous concept of the crime of genocide has evolved. In Resolution 260 of 9 December 1948 the General Assembly adopted the Convention on the Prevention and Punishment of the Crime of Genocide in which genocide was recognised as a crime under international law which the contracting parties undertake to prevent and punish: art I of the Genocide Convention.

19.3 The International Military Tribunal for the Far East (IMTFE)

The International Military Tribunal for the Far East (IMTFE) was established after the IMT at Nuremberg. The principles set out in the Charter of the IMT were restated in the Charter of the IMTFE, although there were important differences between the two. First, the IMTFE was set up by General Douglas MacArthur who, after the surrender of Japan prompted by atomic bomb attacks on Hiroshima (80,000 died) and Nagasaki (50,000 perished), was conferred virtually dictatorial powers by the Far Eastern Commission made up of representatives of 11 Allied nations. MacArthur, being a citizen of the US, and thus bound by the US constitution was not authorised by Congress to set up an international tribunal. The argument that General MacArthur exceeded his powers by setting up the IMTFE was submitted by the defence in order to challenge the legality of the Tribunal. Another important point was that Emperor Hirohito, to whom all his subjects, including the Japanese wartime Prime Minister Hideki Tojo who was the most important defendant before the IMTFE, owed unconditional obedience, was not on trial. The Emperor was considered by the US as a key element in the post-war reconstruction of Japan and therefore shielded from all blame by the prosecution. Also the defendants dared not involve him in the proceedings. The defence was more aggressive and more outspoken than the defence in the Nuremberg trial because American lawyers, at the request of the Japanese government, represented the defendants! They challenged the retroactivity of the crimes with which their clients were charged and emphasised that there was no analogy between the war crimes committed by Japan and those of Germany, taking into account that in Asia there was no equivalent of the Holocaust. The objective of the war waged by Japan was principally to expand its economic interests. Nobody contested that atrocities were committed by Japanese solders but there was no evidence that they were ordered by Japanese leaders.

The IMTFE divided the defendants into three categories.

1. Class A – encompassed those alleged to have 'planned, initiated, or waged war in violation of international treaties. Twenty-eight Japanese were indicted as class A defendants, including Hideki Tojo.
2. Class B – consisted of those alleged to have violated the laws and customs of war.
3. Class C – consisted of those alleged to have carried out orders to torture and murder.

Tojo and six other defendants were sentenced to death by hanging. General MacArthur to whom an appeal was submitted upheld the sentences.

The decisions delivered by the IMT and the IMTFE were often considered as 'victor's justice' with a vengeance. Whatever the criticism, the establishment of both the IMT and the IMTFE was a necessary answer to atrocities unprecedented in nature and scale committed by the Nazi regime and by Japan. Both tribunals provided an international forum where the accused were held individually responsible under international law for hideous crimes they had committed. It was not perfect justice but there was no realistic alternative. The principles of international law applied by the IMT and the IMTFE were further confirmed, developed and crystallised in an impressive number of international instruments such as the following.

1. The Convention on the Non-Applicability of Statutory Limitations to War Crimes and Crimes against Humanity (General Asembly Resolution 2391 (XXIII) of 26 November 1968, 23 UNGAOR, Supp (No 18), UN Doc A/7218 (1968)).
2. The International Convention on the Suppression and Punishment of the Crime of Apartheid (General Assembly Resolution 3068 (XXVIII) of 30 November 1973, 28 UNGAOR, Supp (No 30), 75, UN Doc A/9030 (1973)).
3. The Principles of International Co-operation in the Detection, Arrest, Extradition and Punishment of Persons Guilty of War Crimes and Crimes against Humanity (General Assembly Resolution 3074 (XXVIII), 28 UNGAOR, Supp (No 30), UN Doc A/9030 (1973)).
4. The four 1949 Geneva Conventions and the two Additional Protocols of 1977.
5. The Convention on the Prevention and Punishment of the Crime of Genocide is

probably the most important of all conventions (General Assembly Resolution 260A, 3 UNGAOR, UN Doc A/810 (1948)).

All the above-mentioned international instruments show that the principles set out in the Charter of the IMT are recognised by the international community as a whole, although they were first applied by a limited number of states at Nuremberg and Tokyo.

The experience of the IMT and the IMTFE, as well as subsequent clarification of customary international law, served as a base for the establishment of two international ad hoc tribunals to deal with acts of genocide and other serious violations of human rights committed in the former Yugoslavia and in Rwanda.

19.4 The International Criminal Tribunal for the Former Yugoslavia (ICTY) and the International Criminal Tribunal for Rwanda (ICTR)

Both Tribunals were created in response to the atrocities committed respectively in the territory of the former Yugoslavia and in Rwanda. Both were set up by the Security Council resolutions adopted under Chapter VII.

1. Resolution 827 of 25 May 1993 set up the International Tribunal for the Prosecution of Persons Responsible for Serious Violations of International Humanitarian Law Committed in the Territory of the Former Yugoslavia since 1991. The Resolution was adopted unanimously.
2. Resolution 955 of 8 November 1994 set up the International Criminal Tribunal for the Prosecution of Persons Responsible for Genocide and Other Serious Violations of International Humanitarian Law committed in the Territory of Rwanda between 1 January 1994 and 31 December 1994. Only Rwanda, which at the time of voting was a non-permanent member of the Security Council, voted against the resolution in order to emphasise, inter alia, its disagreement with the Security Council' s refusal to allow the Tribunal to impose the death penalty.

Each resolution stated that the establishment of an ad hoc international criminal tribunals was aimed at the restoration and maintenance of peace in the relevant region and would, in the case of Rwanda, contribute to the process of national reconciliation.

The ICTY is located at The Hague in The Netherlands. By Resolution 977 of 22 February 1995 the Security Council decided that the ICTR should be located in Arusha, in the United Republic of Tanzania.

Limitations on the jurisdiction of both tribunals

Important limitations have been imposed on the jurisdiction of both tribunals.

1. Ratione materiae: the ICTY may adjudicate cases involving grave breaches of the 1949 Geneva Conventions (art 2 of the Statute of the ICTY), violations of the laws or customs of war (art 3), genocide (art 4) and crimes against humanity (art 5). The ICTR jurisdiction includes: genocide, crimes against humanity, violations of art 3 common to the 1949 Geneva Conventions and of the 1977 Additional Protocol II to the Geneva Conventions. The main focus of the ICTR is the crime of genocide.
2. Ratione tempore: the ICTY has jurisdiction in respect of crimes committed since 1991; the ICTR competence is limited to crimes committed between 1 January and 31 December 1994.
3. Ratione personae et ratione loci: the ICTR has jurisdiction in respect of crimes committed by Rwandans in the territory of Rwanda and in the territory of neighbouring states, and crimes committed by non-Rwandans in Rwanda. The ICTY has jurisdiction over crimes committed in the territory of the former Yugoslavia; the nationality of the victims and the offenders is irrelevant.

The organisation of tribunals and their rules of procedure

The ICTR and the ICTY are made up of three bodies: the three Trial Chambers and the Appeals Chamber; the Office of Prosecutor; and the Registry serving both Chambers and the Prosecutor. Both Tribunals share their chief prosecutor and their appellate chamber. A Deputy Prosecutor for the ICTR has his office in Kigali. He is in charge of two sections: the investigation section which collects evidence in respect of persons suspected of committing crimes falling within the ICTR jurisdiction in Rwanda; and the prosecution section which is made up of trial attorneys who are presenting cases before the Tribunal and legal advisers who provide advice during investigations and prosecutions.

Both Tribunals were established as temporary bodies. However, their mandate has already been extended. The growing judicial backlog of both Tribunals was such that it would take the ICTY alone 15 years to complete its mission. For that reason the initial composition of both Tribunals was amended by Resolution 1329 (2000) of the Security Council adopted on 30 November 2000. The Resolution increases the number of judges for both Tribunals by creating a pool of ad litem judges in order to speed the proceedings before the Tribunals. As a result there are two categories of judges: permanent judges and ad litem judges. The Chambers of each Tribunal are composed of 16 independent judges and a maximum at any one time of nine judges ad litem. Three permanent judges serve in each of the Trial Chambers and a maximum at any one time of six judges ad litem. Each Trial Chamber to which ad litem judges are assigned may be divided into sections of three judges each, composed of both permanent and ad litem judges. A section of a Trial Chamber enjoys the same powers as a Trial Chamber. Seven of the permanent judges are members of the Appeals Chamber. For each appeal five of its members serve in the Appeals Chamber. The decisions of the Appeals Chamber are final on any point of law or procedure.

The nominations for permanent and ad litem judges are submitted by both member states of the UN and non-member states which maintain permanent observer missions at UN Headquarters to the Secretary-General who forwards them to the Security Council. The Security Council establishes a list of nominees taking into account the principle of adequate representation of the principal legal systems of the world. Such a list for permanent judges must contain a minimum of 28 and a maximum of 42 candidates and for ad litem judges the list must contain a minimum of 54 candidates. The lists are then submitted to the President of the General Assembly. Fourteen permanent judges and 27 ad litem judges are elected by the General Assembly by an absolute majority of the votes. No two judges can be of the same nationality. All judges must be persons of high moral character. Their impartiality and integrity must be beyond doubt. They must possess the qualifications required for appointments to the highest judicial offices in their respective countries. The judges are elected for a term of four years. Only permanent judges are eligible for re-election.

The Prosecutor may commence investigations on his own accord or on the basis of information obtained from UN organisations, governments, or other international organisations including NGOs. The Prosecutor is empowered to question suspects, victims and witnesses, to gather evidence and to conduct on-site investigations. The Prosecutor prepares an indictment when convinced that there is sufficient evidence that a person in question has committed a crime within the jurisdiction of the international tribunal. The indictment is then reviewed by a judge of the Trial Chamber. If the judge confirms the indictment he issues an order or warrant of arrest which normally is made public but may be kept secret if there is a possibility that the suspect will try to escape. The actual arrest of the suspect in carried out either by the various peacekeeping forces (eg SFOR in Bosnia, KFOR in Kosovo) or the national authorities of the state in which the suspect is present. All states are obliged to co-operate with the International Tribunal, which has no police force at its disposal and therefore cannot arrest suspects itself. The obligation to arrest an indicted person prevails over national law, including a national constitution (eg the Serbian constitution prohibits the extradition of Serbian nationals). In this respect it seems that there is increasing international co-operation in arresting and transferring suspects to international tribunals. At the time of writing, according to the ICTR the suspects in its custody were arrested and transferred from 15 African states, from European states and the US. For example, in the UK Colonel Tharcisse Muvunyi was arrested and following the withdrawal of legal objections to his surrender to the ICTR was transferred to Arusha. Similar co-operation has been developed by the ICTY. For example, General Momir Talic, the Bosnian Serb Chief of Staff, was arrested in Vienna where he attended a military conference unaware of an indictment issued against him. Also the post-Milosevic government in Belgrade is co-operating with the ICTY. On 28 June 2001 the government of Yugoslavia handed over Slobodan Milosevic to the ITCY at the Hague. On 12 February 2002 the trial of Milosevic commenced before the ICTY. The ICTY

Appeals Chamber decided to join together the three indictments against Milosevic. He was accused of:

1. committing war crimes and crimes against humanity for his role in the expulsion of more than 800,000 ethnic Albanians from Kosovo and in the death of 900 others from 1998–1999;
2. committing war crimes and crimes against humanity for his role in the forcible removal of the majority of the Croats and other non-Serb groups from Croatia from 1991–1992;
3. committing war crimes, crimes against humanity and the crime of genocide in Bosnia-Herzegovina during the Bosnian war, from 1992–1995, by participating in a joint criminal enterprise to forcibly and permanently remove the majority of non-Serbs, namely Bosnian Muslims and Bosnian Croats, from the territory of Bosnia-Herzegovina.

At the commencement of the proceedings against Milosevic in February 2002, the Trial Chamber allowed Milosovic, who had decided to defend himself, to do so (*Prosecutor* v *Milosevic* IT–02–54, 'Kosovo, Croatia and Bosnia'). This decision was revisited by the Trial Chamber in September 2004 because, first, medical problems suffered by the accused resulted in significant delays and, second, because his disruptive behaviour before the court (consisting of making disparaging remarks about the court and harassing witnesses, etc) substantially and persistently obstructed the proper and expeditious conduct of the trial. Milosevic refused to co-operate with the counsels assigned to him by the Trial Chamber and made an interlocutory appeal to the Appeals Chamber. On 1 November 2004 the Appeals Chamber ruled that Milosevic, when physically able to attend the court, must be permitted to take the lead in presenting his case: however, if for health reasons he would be unable to attend the trial then legal counsels appointed by the Trial Chamber would represent him, so that the trial would continue without the participation of Milosevic (for the implications of the above order on trials of other political leaders, in particular, Saddam Hussein, see M P Scharf, 'ICTY Appeals Chamber Decision on Slobodan Milosevic's Right to Self-Representation', Asil Insight, November 2004).

Even though the arrest of Radavan Karadzic or Radko Mladic are still impossible, they and others indicted are not free men. They are confined to their hiding places and cannot leave these places without risking of being arrested.

The Statute of both Tribunals is very similar. The rules of procedure and evidence are almost identical. Both Tribunals exercise concurrent jurisdiction with national courts although under their Statutes the International Tribunals have primacy over national courts and may, at any stage of the procedure, formally request national courts to defer an investigation or proceedings currently before the national courts to the International Tribunal. In this respect on 14 May 1996 the Prosecutor of the ICTY applied to the Trial Chamber for deferral by the Federal Republic of Yugoslavia of all investigations and criminal proceedings concerning

Drazen Erdemovic on the ground that the Prosecutor was carrying out investigations concerning similar facts and legal questions. The Prosecutor was investigating war crimes committed against the civilian population in Srebrenica in July 1995 for which the ICTY had already issued an indictment against Erdemovic, Karadzic and Radko Mladic. The deferral was granted. As a result proceedings against Erdemovic before a court in Novi Sad were deferred to the ICTY. Drazen Erdemovic (see *Erdemovic* IT–96–22 'Pilica Farm', Judgment of 5 March 1998 (Trial Chamber II)) pleaded guilty before the ICTY. He was sentenced to five years' imprisonment. In August 1998 he was transferred to Norway to serve his sentence.

The International Tribunal may, in limited circumstances, retry an individual who has already been tried and sentenced by a national court. This occurs in two situations:

1. under r9(i) when a national court or national prosecuting authorities classified an act as being an ordinary crime whilst the International Tribunal considers that the act in question is a crime within its jurisdiction; and
2. under r9(ii) when the investigation carried out by the national authorities shows 'a lack of impartiality or independence, or the investigations or proceedings are designed to shield the accused from international criminal responsibility, or the case is not diligently prosecuted'.

Dusko Tadic invoked r9(i) and (ii) to challenge the jurisdiction of the ICTY. He argued that proceedings against him had already been commenced in Germany and that the German court should retain its jurisdiction. The Prosecutor answered that an indictment was issued against Tadic when his case was in the midst of trial. No judgment and no sentence had been pronounced against him in Germany. In addition, Tadic was accused of the same offences before both tribunals. As a result in the light of r9(iii) according to which when 'what is in issue is closely related to, or otherwise involves, significant factual or legal questions which may have implications for investigations or prosecutions before the Tribunal', and taking into account that the proceedings in Germany had not reached their final stage, the *Tadic case* (see IT–94–1 'Prijedor') was transferred to the ICTY. The ICTY found Dusko Tadic guilty on five counts of violations of the laws and customs of war and six counts of crimes against humanity. On appeal his sentence was reduced to a maximum of 20 years' imprisonment. On 31 October 2000 he was transferred to Germany to serve his sentence.

Another consequence of the deferral process set out in the Statute and Rules of Procedure of both Tribunals is that many states (eg the US, France, Spain, Turkey, etc) have had to enact legislation implementing that procedure into national law in order to ensure full co-operation with the Tribunals.

A person convicted by the ICTY and the ICTR may be sentenced to imprisonment up to and including the remainder of that person's life, but neither Tribunal has power to impose the death penalty. In determining the sentence the Tribunals take into account such factors as aggravating or mitigating circumstances, including substantial co-operation with the Prosecutor before and after the conviction, and the general practice regarding prison sentences in the courts, respectively, of the former Yugoslavia and Rwanda. Any previous penalty imposed by a court of any state for the same acts which has already been served and the detention period in the Tribunal's custody are also taken into account. The main objectives of a sentence are retribution and deterrence. This was explained in *Furundzija* IT–95–17/1 'Lasva Valley', Judgment of 10 December 1998) (Trial Chamber II) in the following terms:

> 'It is the mandate and the duty of the International Court, in contributing to reconciliation, to deter such crimes and to combat impunity.' (Also confirmed by the Appeals Chamber in Judgment of 21 July 2000.)

Those convicted are to serve their sentences in a country other than their own in order to avoid a situation where a change of regime in their native country might benefit them, to make sure that they serve their full sentence and, in addition, to prevent them from being welcomed back home as heroes and thus avoid punishment. At the time of writing Italy, Finland, Norway, Sweden, Austria and France have signed an agreement with the ICTY and with regards to the ICTR the Republic of Mali and Benin have signed an agreement to provide prison facilities for the enforcement of the ICTR's sentences. A number of African countries are negotiating similar agreements with the ICTR.

The judges of the ICTY at the twenty-second plenary session held in July 2000 acknowledged the right of victims to seek compensation. As a result, the Tribunal President asked the Security Council and the Secretary-General that methods of compensation be considered by the appropriate organs of the UN.

The contribution of the ICTY and the ICTR to the development of international law

Note: all judgments are obtainable for the ICTY from http://www.un.org/icty and for the ICTR from http://www.ictr.org.

Both Tribunals are justly proud of their achievements, not only in having provided some form of restospective justice to victims of atrocities and to their relatives but also in having given important clarifications of international law.

1. Both Tribunals confirmed that the same event may give rise to more than one offence. Each offence which falls within the jurisdiction of the Tribunal (ie genocide, crimes against humanity, violations of art 3 common to the 1949 Geneva Conventions and the 1977 Additional Protocol II) has different elements and the prohibition it contains is intended to protect different interests. For example, the prohibition of genocide is aimed at protecting certain groups from extermination or the threat of extermination, the prohibition of crimes against humanity is intended to protect civilian populations from persecution, and art 3

common to the 1949 Geneva Conventions and the 1977 Additional Protocol II is aimed at protecting non-combatants from war crimes in civil war. Consequently, the same set of facts may be classified as more than one offence. If, for example, an order is given by the government to kill all prisoners of war belonging to the same ethnic group, with the intention of eliminating the group, the crime would constitute both genocide and a violation of common art 3 of the 1949 Geneva Conventions, but may not necessarily constitute a crime against humanity: see *Jean-Paul Akayesu* (ICTR–96–4–T).

This matter was further examined by the Appeals Chamber in *Delalic et al* IT–96–21 'Celebici Camp', Judgment of 20 February 2001 (Appeals Chamber), in which Delalic and Mucic challenged their convictions on the ground that the charges were based upon the same events and it was alleged that both grave breaches of the Geneva Conventions (art 2 of the Statute of the ICTY) and violations of the laws or customs of war (art 3) had occurred. The Appeals Chamber explained that in order to be fair to the accused and taking into consideration that only distinct crimes justify cumulative convictions, such convictions are permissible 'only if each statutory provision [the Statute of the ICTY] involved has a materially distinct element not contained in the other'. The assessment of the elements of the offence must take into consideration all elements of the offence as well as the elements of the legal prerequisites of each article. However, if the offences contain no materially distinct elements the conviction must be based on the offence containing more specific provisions. In the above case a more specific provision was art 2 of the Statute. As a result, the Appeals Chamber dismissed charges under art 3 but upheld charges under art 2.

2. The concepts of internal and international conflict were examined by the ICTY in *Tadic* IT–94–1 'Prijedor', Judgment of 15 July 1999 (Appeals Chamber). The Appeals Chamber found that an armed conflict in Bosnia and Herzegovina was international in nature because the Bosnian Serb forces and the armed forces of the central authorities in Bosnia and Herzegovina acted de facto as organs of the Federal Republic of Yugoslavia. Consequently, their victims were considered as 'protected persons' within the meaning of art 4 of the Geneva IV Convention. The distinction between internal and international conflicts is important because the four 1949 Geneva Conventions and the 1977 Additional Protocol I generally apply to international conflicts, art 3 common to Geneva Conventions and the 1977 Additional Protocol II apply to non-international conflicts whereas the 1977 Additional Protocol II applies when a conflict takes place 'in the territory of a High Contracting Party between its armed forces and dissident armed forces or other organised armed groups which, under responsible command, exercise such control over a part of its territory as to enable them to carry out sustained and concerted military operations and to implement this Protocol.'

In *Tadic* the Appeals Chamber recognised that the distinction between international and internal conflicts is artificial and loses its importance taking into account that fundamental human rights should be guaranteed irrespective of the classification of a conflict and that in fact there are a growing number of international instruments protecting civilians in internal conflicts. However, the Appeals Chamber recognised that the rules applicable to internal and international conflicts have not yet converged and therefore it was necessary for the Appeals Chamber to distinguish between them in order to conform with the principle nullem crimen sine lege. When the Statutes of each Tribunal were drafted the Security Council recognised that it had neither legislative powers nor the competence to punish offenders for crimes which were not criminal offences at the time they were committed. Consequently, the Security Council limited the jurisdiction of the ICTY to well established rules of customary law relevant to armed conflicts: laws and customs of war, grave breaches of the Geneva Conventions, the Genocide Convention 1948 and crimes against humanity. Article 5 of the Statute of the ICTY, as did the Charter of the IMT, linked crimes against humanity with an armed conflict. The Appeals Chamber in the *Tadic* case dissociated the two by stating that:

> '... by requiring that crimes against humanity be committed in either internal or international armed conflict, the Security Council may have defined the crime in art 5 more narrowly than necessary under customary international law. There is no question, however, that the definition of crimes against humanity adopted by the Security Council in art 5 comports with the principle of nullem crimen sine lege.'

Indeed, all doubt should be interpreted in favour of the accused in order to ensure fair and neutral trial and to guarantee the right of the accused to due process.

3. Sexual offences. Both the ICTY and the ICTR have dealt with such offences. The ICTR in the *Jean-Paul Akayesu* case (above) defined rape as an act of genocide and provided its definition in international law as being a:

> '... physical invasion of a sexual nature, committed on a person under circumstances which are coercive. Sexual violence which includes rape, is considered to be any act of a sexual nature which is committed on a person under circumstances which are coercive. This act must be committed:
> (a) as part of a widespread or systematic attack;
> (b) on a civilian population;
> (c) on certain catalogued discriminatory grounds, namely: national, ethic, political, racial, or religious grounds.'

Previously rape was recognised as a crime against humanity and a war crime but not as genocide. The judgment of Trial Chamber II in *Kunarac, Kovac and Vukovic* IT–96–23 and IT–96–23/1 'Foca' rendered on 22 February 2001 constitutes one of the leading decisions on international humanitarian law in respect of sexual violence and enslavement. The defendants were, inter alia, charged with rape as both a crime against humanity and as a violation of the laws and customs of war. This being in respect of Muslim Bosnian woman and girls detained by Serbian forces in camps near the town of Foca in the spring of 1992.

The women and girls were detained in appalling conditions, threatened with guns and knifes and were systematically raped. Some were taken to work in 'quasi brothels' used by soldiers, some were 'rented', others were sold. All defendants denied the charge.

Kunarac was in charge of a reconnaissance unit of the Bosnian Serb army, Kovac and Vukovic were paramilitary leaders. The Court found that the evidence showed beyond any doubt that all defendants knew about the detention centres and knew about the rape and enslavement of Bosnian Muslim women and girls. The Court rejected their defence which was based on the fact that they were following orders of their superiors. The Court stated that: 'the three accused were not just following orders, if there were such orders, to rape Muslim women. The evidence shows free will on their part.'

In respect of rape the Trial Chamber II held that the concept of rape should not be interpreted narrowly and provided its own definition based on comparative studies of national laws and international law. Accordingly the actus reus (the act or omission) of rape in international law is constituted by:

'(a) the sexual penetration, however slight of the vagina or anus of the victim by the penis of the perpetrator or any other object used by the perpetrator; or
(b) of the mouth of the victim by the penis of the perpetrator, where such sexual penetration occurs without the consent of the victim. Consent for this purpose must be consent given voluntarily, as a result of the victim's free will, assessed in the context of the surrounding circumstances. The mens rea is the intention to effect the sexual penetration, and the knowledge that it occurs without the consent of the victim.'

The Trial Chamber II examined the crime of torture and its application to sexual violence. The Chamber stated that there is a difference between the definition of torture under international humanitarian law and under human rights law. In particular, in the Chamber's opinion 'the presence of a state official or of any other authority-wielding person in the torture process is not necessary for the offence to be regarded as torture under international humanitarian law'. The Chamber identified the common elements of the crime of torture under international humanitarian law and under customary international law as:

'(i) the infliction, by act or omission, of severe pain or suffering, whether physical or mental;
(ii) the act or omission must be intentional;
(iii) the act or omission must aim at obtaining information or a confession, or at punishing, intimidating or coercing the victim or a third person, or at discriminating, on any ground, against the victim or a third person.'

Another important point was that the Chamber recognised rape as 'an instrument of terror'. The Chamber refused to classify rape as 'a weapon of war' because there was no sufficient evidence to show that there was a concerted approach or an order given to the Bosnian Serb armed forces to rape Muslim women as a part of their military activities in Bosnia, but acknowledged that rape was used as an instrument of terror by the Bosnian Serb armed forces 'an instrument they were given free rein to apply whenever and against whomever they wished'. Therefore, in the absence of a direct order rape may be considered as an 'instrument of terror'.

Further, the Chamber examined the crime of enslavement and slavery in the context of sexual violence. As a principle, slavery is not regarded as a crime against humanity but as an economic crime. The Chamber classified enslavement as 'a crime against humanity in customary international law consist[ing] of the exercise of any or all of the powers attaching to the right of ownership over a person'. In order to determine whether or not the crime of enslavement took place the following factors should be taken into account 'control of someone's movement, control of physical environment, psychological control, measures taken to prevent or deter escape, force, threat of force or coercion, duration, assertion of exclusivity, subjection to cruel treatment, and abuse, control of sexuality and forced labour'. The Chamber provided a broad definition of enslavement as it emphasised that enslavement did not necessarily require the buying or selling of a human being.

In the above case the Chamber sent a strong message in respect of sexual offences. It stated that although it is always preferabe to prosecute and try those in the higher echelons of power, 'lawless opportunists should not expect mercy, no matter how low their position in the chain of command may be'.

4. The issue of 'command responsibility', that is where the defendant was in a position of command, was examined in *Aleksovsky* IT–95–14/1 'Lasva Valley', Judgment of 25 June 1999 (Trial Chamber I). The accused was a warden of Kaoniki prison where the detainees, inter alia, Bosnian Muslim civilians, were subjected to inhumane treatment or murdered. The Trial Chamber, in order to decide whether the accused was responsible for crimes committed by his subordinates, made reference to art 7(3) of the Statute under which the superior is responsible if three criteria are satisfied.

a) There must be a superior-subordinate relationship. The defence claimed that Aleksovsky was just a warden, while the prosecution claimed that he was in a position of command. The Trial Chamber considered that the term 'superior' encompasses both military and civilian authority. In *Delalic et al* IT–96–21 'Celebici Camp', Judgment of 16 November 1999 the Trial Chamber noted that the factor which determines liability is 'the actual possession, or non-possession, of powers of control over the actions of subordinates. Accordingly, formal designation as a commander should not be considered to be a necessary perquisite for superior responsibility to attach, as such responsibility may be imposed by virtue of a person's de facto, as well as de jure, position as a commander'. However, in the *Aleksovsky* case the Trial Chamber considered that in respect of a civilian authority its power of sanctioning must be interpreted broadly and any analogy with the power to sanction within the military hierarchy should be excluded, otherwise the scope of the doctrine would hardly be applicable to a civilian authority. Therefore, the authority to impose sanctions, de facto or de jure, is not essential. The Chamber emphasised that: 'the possibility of transmitting reports to the appropriate authorities suffices once the civilian authority, through its position in the hierarchy, is expected to report whenever crimes are committed, and that, in the light of this position, the likelihood that those reports will trigger an investigation or initiate disciplinary or even criminal measures is extant'.

b) The superior knew or had reason to know that a crime was about to be committed or had been committed. The Prosecutor argued that under international humanitarian law there is a presumption that the superior must have knowledge of crime whenever it is widespread, notorious and occurs over a long period. The Trial Chamber rejected that presumption. Direct evidence of the superior's knowledge is necessary in order to satisfy this criterion.

c) The superior has failed to take all necessary and reasonable measures to prevent the crime or to punish the perpetrator. This criterion has been interpreted restrictively. Necessary and reasonable measures are those which are within the material possibility of the superior. What is materially possible and reasonable for the superior to undertake must be assessed in the light of circumstances on a case-by-case basis.

The Trial Chamber applied the three criteria to *Aleksovsky* and found him responsible for crimes committed by his subordinates (this was confirmed by the Appeals Chamber, judgment of 24 March 2000).

More recently the Trial Chamber II in the *Kunarac* case (above) applied the above principles, that is that for a superior-subordinate relationship it is not necessary that a commander is designated in any formal manner. Commanding responsibility may be recognised by virtue of a person's de facto as well as de jure, position as a commander. The effective control, even temporary, is the essential element. This means that such a person must 'have the material ability to exercise his power to prevent and punish the commission of the subordinates' offences'. It was proved that Kunarac did not exercise such control.

The second criterion was further explained by the Appeals Chamber in its judgment delivered on 29 July 2004 in *Prosecutor* v *Blaskic* IT–95–14, 'Lasva Valley'. The Appeals Chamber held that 'a superior will be criminally responsible through the principles of superior responsibility only if information was available to him which would put him on notice of offences committed by subordinates'. The above suggests that subjective knowledge is required as a basis for command responsibility. Under art 7(3) (always supposing that criteria 1 and 2 are met) a superior is responsible for acts of his subordinates when 'he knew or had reason to know that the subordinate was about to commit [criminal] acts or had done so'. However, the narrow interpretation of art 7(3) of the Statute must be read in the light of the Appeals Chamber's statement that 'responsibility can be imposed for deliberately refraining from finding out information'. Therefore if a superior deliberately ignores information or is reckless he will still be responsible for acts committed by his subordinate.

5. In *Prosecutor* v *Radislav Krstic* IT–98–33 'Srebrenica-Drina Corps', Judgment of 2 August 2001 (Trial Chamber I) General Krstic was charged with genocide and, in the alternative, with complicity in genocide in relation to the mass executions of the Bosnian Muslim men in Srebrenica between 11 July and 1 November 1995. Notwithstanding the fact that Srebrenica was declared by the UN Security Council a 'safe area' in July 1995, the Bosnian Serb Army (VRS) launched an attack and captured the town. Women, children and elderly people living in Srebrenica were forced to board overcrowded buses and were transported into Bosnian Muslim-held territory. The military-aged Bosnian Muslim men tried to flee the area. Approximately 7,000–8,000 of them were taken prisoner, detained in appalling conditions and subsequently executed. The mass executions took place between 13 and 19 July 1995. There were almost no survivors. Some executions involved a large number of individuals. For example, on 14 July hundreds of Bosnian Muslims were gathered in the Grbavci school (Orahovac) where they were blindfolded and later taken by buses to a field were they were executed. Before the execution was completed machines were already digging a mass grave. After these mass executions measures were taken to cover up the extent of the crimes. All the above crimes were committed in the area controlled by the Drina Corps. General Krstic was the chief of staff and subsequently the Commander of the Drina Corps, a unit of the VRS at the time when these crimes were committed.

    The ICTY found General Krstic guilty of the crime of genocide. This was the first conviction of the ICTY for genocide.

    However, on 19 April 2004 the Appeals Chamber reversed General Krstic's conviction, and instead, on the ground that he did not possess the specific intent required for the conviction as a direct perpetrator of a crime of genocide based on joint criminal enterprise, found him guilty of aiding and abetting genocide. Both the Trial Chamber and the Appeals Chamber provided important clarifications in respect of the crime of genocide. Both Chambers agreed that the crime of genocide was committed in Srebrenica against 'a part of the Bosnian Muslim people as a national, ethnical or religious group'. In Srebrenica the killings involved one gender segment (males) of a part of the overall group (Bosnian Muslims living in Srebrenica). The Appeals Chamber stated that when a genocide conviction concerns a part of a protected group, the part must be a substantial part of that group. The Appeals Chamber specified the factors to be taken into consideration in order to assess whether the targeted part within the specific group was substantial. These are: the numeric size of the targeted part, its prominence within the overall group and the area of the perpetrators' activity and control.

542   *Criminal Responsibility of Individuals under International Law*

The Appeals Chamber found that the VRS's Main Staff had the necessary intent to destroy a substantial part of the Bosnian Muslim population living in Srebrenica. The survival of the Bosnian Muslim population living in Srebrenica as a community was impossible given the execution of the Bosnian Muslim men of fighting age and the forcible transfer from Srebrenica of women and children. However, according to the Appeals Chamber General Krstic's specific intent of genocide was not established. Contrary to the Trial Chamber which found that General Krstic 'shared the genocide intent to kill the men' and participated in a 'joint criminal enterprise' as he was aware that the killing of the Bosnian Muslim men of fighting age would result in the annihilation of the entire Bosnian Muslim community of Srebrenica, the Appeals Chamber found that whilst the issue of participation in a joint criminal enterprise can be established circumstantially, the issue of intent to commit genocide must be established 'unequivocally'. Although the intent can be inferred from the circumstances of the case, evidence must show an individual's specific genocide intent and not just knowledge of the intent of other individuals. Proof of intent to commit genocide, the Appeals Chamber emphasised, is particularly difficult to established. The Appeals Chamber was of the view that:

'... all that the evidence can establish is that Mr Krstic was aware of the intent to commit genocide on the part of some members of the Main Staff, and with that knowledge, he did nothing to prevent the use of Drina Corps personnel and resources to facilitate those killings. This knowledge on his part alone cannot support an inference of genocidal intent.'

The mens rea for the crime of genocide differs from that required for crimes against humanity. In the *Blaskic* judgment the mens rea required for crimes against humanity was described as including 'knowledge on the part of the accused that there is an attack on the civilian population, as well as knowledge that his act is part thereof'. However, the standard of proof required to establish the intent for aiding and abetting genocide is much lower. In this respect it is sufficient to establish that an individual assists the commission of a crime with knowledge of the intent behind the crime. In the case of Krstic the requirement for intent to aid and abet was established. The Appeals Chamber held that given that Krstic was neither a principal perpetrator nor a co-perpetrator of genocide, his sentence should be reduced from 46 to 35 years' imprisonment.

The priority for both the ICTR and the ICTY is to prosecute and punish high-level officials and individuals who have masterminded atrocities. In this respect the ICTR has been more successful. It has in its custody persons who were ministers of the government, leaders of the Parliament and of the dominant political party and regional government at the material time. The biggest achievement of the ICTR was the conviction of Jean Kambanda, the Prime Minister of Rwanda at the relevant time, for the crime of genocide. His conviction was confirmed by the Appeals Chamber.

Both the ICTY and the ICTR are truly international criminal tribunals in terms of their composition, the condition of their establishment and the principles of international law they apply under their respective Statutes. The argument of 'victor' justice cannot apply to them. Both Tribunals have jurisdiction over all parties involved in the conflict. Consequently, the Prosecutor investigates all allegations of atrocities committed by the parties involved in the conflict (eg the ICTY convicted not only Bosnian Serbs but also Bosnian Croats: *Vladimir Santic, Zoran, Vlatko and Mirjan Kupreskic* IT–95–16 'Lasva Valley', Judgment of 23 October 2001.

19.5 The International Criminal Court (ICC)

The creation of a permanent international criminal court finds its origin in art VI of the Convention on the Prevention and Punishment of the Crime of Genocide adopted in Resolution 260 of 9 December 1948 by the General Assembly which provides that persons charged with genocide 'shall be tried by a competent tribunal of the state in the territory of which the act was committed or by such international penal tribunal as may have jurisdiction'. In order to give effect to art VI the General Assembly in the same Resolution asked the International Law Commission (ILC) to undertake necessary study regarding the desirability and possibility of establishing an international court for the trial of persons charged with genocide. The answer from the Commission was that the establishment of such a court was both desirable and possible.

The next step taken by the General Assembly was to set up a committee to prepare proposals relating to the establishment of such a court which submitted a Draft Statute in 1951 and its revised version in 1953. During that time the ILC was working on a Code of Crimes against the Peace and Security of Mankind. The Draft Code constituted a continuation of the work of the ILC pursuant to Resolution 95 (I) of the General Assembly on the Affirmation of the Principles of International Law Recognised in the Charter of the Nuremberg Tribunal: 1sess. Doc A/236 (1947). However, the ILC could not produce the Final Draft as it could not reach agreement on the definition of aggression. The General Assembly suspended consideration of the Draft Statute taking into account that the Draft Code was closely linked with the Statute of the ICC pending the adoption of a definition of aggression. Such a definition was adopted by the General Assembly in Resolution 3314 (XXIX) in 1974.

In 1978 the General Assembly asked the ILC to continue its work on the Draft Code but the Draft Statute was not mentioned.

The International Law Commission was seised again of the Draft Statute in December 1989 when the General Assembly, following a request by Trinidad and Tobago, asked the Commission to resume work on the Draft Statute, and in particular to include drug-trafficking within the jurisdiction of the court. The Draft

Statute was submitted to the General Assembly in 1994. After years of further examination of the Draft by the Ad Hoc Committee on the Establishment of an International Criminal Court a report was submitted to the General Assembly. In 1996 the International Law Commission submitted to the General Assembly its detailed Draft Code of Crimes against the Peace and Security of Mankind (Report of the International Law Commission on the work of its forty-eighth session: UNGAOR, 51st Sess Supp No 10, UN Doc A/51/10 (1996). At that stage the General Assembly set up a Preparatory Committee on the Establishment of an International Criminal Court to prepare a consolidated version of the draft ready for submission to a diplomatic conference. The Draft was duly presented to the General Assembly which at its fifty-second session decided to convene the UN Diplomatic Conference in order to finalise and to adopt the final text of the statute of an international permanent criminal court. The Diplomatic Conference was held in Rome from 15 to 17 July 1998. It approved the Statute of the Court by 120 votes in favour, seven against and 21 abstentions.

The Rome Statute of the International Criminal Court (ICC) entered into force on 1 July 2002. As at 3 May 2004 the number of contracting parties to the ICC was 94. In February 2003 the ICC's governing body, the Assembly of the States Party to the Statute of the ICC, carried out its first election of judges – 18 in number – representing all major legal systems and all the regions of the world. The judges were sworn into office on 11 March 2003. On 21 April 2003 the Assembly elected the chief prosecutor, Luis Moreno Ocampo, who had acquired international recognition whilst acting as a deputy prosecutor in the trials of members in Argentina's military junta in the 1980s.

At the time of writing the ICC is in the course of moving from the preparatory stage to the judicial stage. On 23 June 2004 the Chief Prosecutor opened the first investigation of the ICC. On the referral of the Democratic Republic of Congo the Chief Prosecutor will examine the situation regarding the grave crimes committed on the territory of the Democratic Republic of Congo since 1 July 2002.

The Court has its seat in The Hague but may sit elsewhere when appropriate. The Court has international personality. Its relationship with the UN has been specified in a Relationship Agreement signed on 4 October 2004. Under the Agreement both institutions will co-operate closely and exchange information and expertise. The Agreement provides for an exchange of representatives between the UN and the ICC, gives the ICC the status of observer at the UN General Assembly and ensures UN co-operation if the ICC requests the testimony of UN officials. The last point mentioned means that UN experts on human rights, refugees, members of peacekeeping forces, etc, can supply vital information on issues relevant to the ICC's activities.

The ICC is not an organ of the UN but the Security Council will have power to intervene in the initiation or deferment of the investigation of some cases: arts 16 and 13(b) of the Statute.

Composition of the ICC

The Court is made up of three Chambers: a Pre-Trial Chamber, a Trial Chamber and an Appeal Chamber: art 34(b). Eighteen judges have been appointed to the ICC, four of them will sit in the Appeal Chamber, no less than six judges will sit in the Trial Chamber and no less than six judges will sit in the Pre-Trial Chamber.

The Prosecutor is elected by the General Assembly by an absolute majority vote for a non–renewable term of nine years.

Jurisdiction of the ICC

The Statute reiterates the general principles of criminal law: nullum crimen sine lege, nulla poena sine lege, and the principle of non–retroactivity meaning that no person can be brought before the Court for crimes committed before the entry into force of the Statute. Article 25 confirms individual criminal responsibility. Article 27 states that the official capacity of the accused will have no relevance to his guilt and shall not, in itself, constitute a ground for reduction of sentence. Article 28 deals with the responsibility of commanders and other superiors and confirms the solution recognised in the Statute of the ICTY. Article 33 of the Statute sets out grounds which will exempt the accused, who had committed what would otherwise be a crime within the Court's jurisdiction pursuant to an order of a superior or his government, from criminal responsibility. These are where:

1. a person was under a legal obligation to obey such an order;
2. he did not know that the order was unlawful;
3. the order was not manifestly unlawful. However, art 33(2) specifies that orders to commit genocide or crimes against humanity are manifestly unlawful.

Article 33 sets out general grounds for excluding criminal responsibility.

The most important provisions of the Statute concern the jurisdiction of the Court. The ICC will have complementary jurisdiction to national criminal courts, that is the ICC will have jurisdiction only if the competent national authorities will be unable or unwilling to prosecute. There was no disagreement that the contracting parties should be entitled to refer to the ICC to initiate proceedings against an individual. However, the matter when and whether the Security Council and the prosecutor should be allowed to refer cases to the ICC was a subject of many debates and challenges, in particular on the part of the US (see below).

Under the Rome Statute the jurisdiction of the ICC is based on a two-track system.

1. Track one concerns the situation where the Security Council acting under Chapter VII will refer to the ICC. All states will be bound to comply with the Security Council decision to surrender the indicated person or to supply evidence. The Security Council will use its powers under art 41 of the UN Charter (eg to freeze the assets of the indicted person and his supporters, impose

embargos, etc) and under art 42 (involving the use of force) to enforce the decision. India opposed this solution arguing that the Security Council should have no role in the Court's operation.

2. Track two involves situations where contracting states or the Prosecutor will refer to the Court. There are no enforcement mechanisms in respect of the second track. The Prosecutor's power to initiate investigations is subject to strict safeguards, most of them introduced by the US. Indeed, the biggest obstacle to the establishment and the successful operation of the Court was the US vote against the Statute at the Rome Conference. The US, together with China, Libya, Iraq, Israel, Qatar and Yemen, expressed their opposition in this respect. The main argument of the US was that it wanted a Security-Council controlled Court, whilst all other countries believed that the Court should exercise its jurisdiction over all individuals, irrespective of their nationality, accused of genocide, war crimes and crimes against humanity. The US felt that because of its special position as a world superpower it would be demanded, more than any other country, to militarily intervene in order to prevent humanitarian disasters. Consequently, US nationals, both military and civilian, who will participate in such operations may be prosecuted and tried by the Court. In order to assure the US that this would not happen a number of amendments were made to the Statute of the Court.

a) A referral from the Prosecutor must be authorised by the Pre-Trial Chamber which will decide whether or not there is a reasonable basis on which to continue investigations. The decision of the Chamber is subject to interlocutory appeal to the Appeal Chamber: art 15.

b) The Prosecutor is obliged to notify any state with a prosecuting interest that he intends to commence an investigation and a one month deadline is given to such a state to respond. If that state notifies the Prosecutor that it is investigating the case, the Prosecutor must defer the case to the state's investigation unless he can convince the Pre-Trial Chamber that the investigation is a sham. The decision of the Pre-Trial Chamber is subject to interlocutory appeal to the Appeal Chamber. This solution is in conformity with the principle of the complementary jurisdiction of the ICC: art 18.

c) The Security Council will be entitled to postpone an investigation or a case for up to 12 months, on a renewable basis. This will require an affirmative vote of the Security Council, that is that there is no veto from the permanent members of the Security Council: art 16. The UN Security Council has already exercised its competence referred to in art 16 in Resolution 1422 of 12 July 2002 in the following circumstances. On 30 June 2002 the US vetoed the Security Council Resolution seeking to extend the UN peacekeeping mission in Bosnia-Herzegovina (UNMIBH) and threatened to block future UN missions unless the Security Council would agree to adopt a resolution permanently barring the ICC from initiating proceedings against peacekeepers from non-contracting parties to the ICC. The US government wanted to ensure that US personnel participating in peacekeeping missions would not be subject to unwarranted, politically motivated persecution before the ICC. After a lengthy debate within the Security Council at an open session at which 39 states took part a compromise was reached. On 12 July 2002 Security Council, acting under Chapter VII, adopted Resolution 1422 which suspended any prosecution before the ICC of peacekeepers from non-contracting parties to the ICC for a 12-month period, with a view to renewing it every year on 1 July for further 12-month periods for as long as might be necessary. In exchange the mission in Bosnia-Herzegovina was extended by the Security Council on the same day. Many scholars considered that, first, the Security Council by adopting Resolution 1422 acted ultra vires taking into account that non-participation of some states in peacekeeping missions motivated by a potential prosecution of its personnel by the ICC hardly constituted a threat to peace within the meaning of art 39 of the UN Charter, and that in the case of Bosnia-Herzegovina the jurisdiction of the ICTY prevails over the ICC. Second, Resolution 1422 was inconsistent with the ICC Statute: see C Stahn, 'The Ambiguities of Security Council Resolution 1422' (2003) 14 EJIL 85.

These safeguards combined with the limited jurisdiction of the ICC ratione materiae were judged as insufficient by the US at the Rome Conference. The US made its position very clear regarding the accession to the Rome Statute. On 27 April 2002 the US Under-secretary of State for Arms Control and International Security sent a letter to the UN Secretary-General informing him the US did not intend to become a contracting party to the Rome Statute and accordingly had no legal obligations arising from the signature of the Statute by the US: ASIL, 9 May 2002, p5. In 2003 the US renewed Resolution 1422 for another year. However, in 2004 it abandoned its efforts to renew the Resolution. Instead the US relied on art 98(2) of the Statute of the ICC to make sure that its troops would be immune from prosecution in the ICC. Article 98(2) provides:

'The Court may not proceed with a request for surrender which would require the requested State to act inconsistently with its obligations under international agreements pursuant to which the consent of a sending state is required to surrender a person of that state to the court, unless the Court can first obtain the cooperation of the sending state for the giving of consent for the surrender.'

By November 2004, the US government had entered into 99 of the bilateral agreements contemplated under art 98 of the Statute of the ICC with a view to prohibiting the other party to the agreement from surrendering US personal to the ICC without the US consent. Out of 99 countries which have signed an agreement, 69 are parties or signatories to the Rome Statute. These agreements should be viewed in the context of the American Servicemembers'

Protection Act of 2001 which prohibits US military assistance to states which are contracting parties to the Rome Statute but have not entered into art 98 agreements (see F L Kirgis, 'US Drops Plan to Exempt GIs from UN Court', Asil Insights, July 2004). The bilateral agreements are fiercely opposed by the EU which adopted a common position urging Member States not to enter into such agreements without taking into consideration the EU guidelines on this matter (see Council of the European Union: Council Conclusions and EU Guiding Principles Concerning Arrangements between a State Party to the Rome Statute of the International Criminal Court and the United States Regarding the Conditions to Surrender of Persons to the Court (2003) 42 ILM 240).

The power given to the Prosecutor constitutes the vital element in the functioning of the Court taking into account that the powers of the Security Council may always be blocked by the veto of one of its permanent members. Also, states are rather reluctant to bring proceedings against another state's nationals taking into account the diplomatic or other crises it may lead to. Therefore, when neither the Security Council nor a contracting party to the Statute is willing to initiate investigations, the Prosecutor of the ICC will step in.

In respect of the ICC jurisdiction ratione materiae, crimes within its jurisdiction are genocide, war crimes, crimes against humanity and the crime of aggression. The inclusion of the last-mentioned within the Statute was supported by the UN High Commissioner for Human Rights and Germany. The Commissioner believed that it was necessary to recognise the crimes that constituted a grave breach of international peace and security and to determine the issue of 'individual criminal responsibility for belligerency' (Sarooshi D, 'The Statute of the International Criminal Court, (1999) ICLQ 4000), but the Rome Conference had no time to agree on the precise definition. For that reason art 5(2) provides that once a definition of the crime of aggression is agreed between the contracting parties a review conference will set out conditions under which the Court will exercise jurisdiction over this crime.

Only the most serious violations of human rights of concern to the international community as a whole will be tried before the Court. Each crime is defined. The definitions will be strictly construed by the ICC and any extension by analogy is expressly excluded: art 22(2). In case of ambiguity any interpretation must be in favour of the person under investigation, prosecuted or convicted: art 22(3). The Draft Statute included drug-trafficking within the jurisdiction of the ICC. It was felt, however, at the Rome Conference that investigation of such offences would be beyond the ICC's resources. The inclusion of terrorism was also discussed but no agreement could be reached as to its definition. Nevertheless, it may be possible in the future to include both terrorism and drug-trafficking within the competence of the ICC. In this respect, the states participating at the Rome Conference passed a consensus resolution recommending that the contracting parties consider inclusion of such crimes at a review conference.

The ICC's jurisdiction rationae personae is defined in art 12(2) of the Statute. The ICC's 'competence to obtain jurisdiction over a person will be reliant upon the consent of the state upon whose territory the crime was committed or of the state of nationality of the suspect' insofar are those states are contracting parties to the Statute. The proposal to include the state in which the suspect is physically present and the state of the victim's nationality was rejected at the opposition of the US although the majority of states were in favour of the extension of the ICC's jurisdiction.

It is important to note that the ICC will be funded by a permanent fund from the UN and voluntary contributions from contracting states. This arrangement will ensure the ICC's independence from political influence of any state as the majority of its funding will be drawn from the UN.

The ICC has rightly been called the missing link in the international law order. The necessity to ensure international accountability and to bring to justice perpetrators of genocide, war crimes and crimes against humanity is obvious.

There are many advantages of having a permanent international criminal court, the most important being that many states, when a suspect is present within their jurisdiction, are reluctant to prosecute or extradite him but would have no objection to handing him over to the ICC, an international, impartial and unbiased court. This is especially relevant when the suspect is a leader or a head or a former head of a friendly state (eg Pinochet). The reluctance is frequently based on fear of repercussions from the home state of the suspect, whether economic or diplomatic, or often a state is simply not interested in committing its resources to try foreigners who are accused of having committed atrocities abroad and their victims are not nationals of the state in question.

Another advantage is that the ICC will contribute to the uniform application and interpretation of international criminal law and therefore national courts will certainly rely on its judgments in cases before them. This would minimise the risk of conflicting decisions and varying penalties imposed by national courts.

The importance of the ICC was well summarised by UN Secretary-General, Kofi Annan, in his speech at the Rome Conference when he said:

'By adopting this Statute, participants in the Conference have overcome many legal and political problems, which kept this question on the United Nations agenda almost throughout the Organisation's history. No doubt, many of us would have liked a Court vested with even more far-reaching powers, but that should not lead us to minimise the breakthrough you have achieved … It is an achievement which, only a few years ago, nobody thought possible.'

Glossary of Latin Terms and Maxims

Acta jure imperii – public acts of a state. A state can rely on the immunity from jurisdiction of courts in another state in respect of acta jure imperii.

Acta jure gestionis – private acts of a state, such as trading and commercial activities. A state cannot rely on the immunity from jurisdiction of courts in another state in respect of acta jure gestionis.

Actio in personam – an action against the person, founded on a personal liability.

Actio in rem – in admiralty law, an action directed against a specific thing (as a ship or an aircraft) irrespective of the ownership of it, to enforce a claim or lien upon it, or to obtain, out of the thing or out of the proceeds of its sale, satisfaction for an injury alleged by the claimant.

AD – an abbreviation of Anno Domini meaning the year of our Lord.

Ad hoc – for this, for a particular purpose.

Ad litem – for the suit.

Bona fides – in or with good faith.

Certiorari – to be informed of, to be made certain in regard to, the name of a writ of review or inquiry.

Comitas – courteousness, comity.

Culpa – fault, neglect or negligence, responsibility for wrongdoing.

De facto – in fact, actually, contrary of de jure.

De jure – by right, by law, according to law.

Et cetera (etc) – and other things, and others of the like characteristics and others of the same kind, and the rest, and so on.

Ex aequo et bono – in justice and fairness, according to what is fair and just. The ICJ will apply the principle of ex aequo et bono if instructed to do so by the parties.

Ex officio – from office, by virtue of the office.

Ex parte – on one side only, done for, on behalf of, or on the application of, one party only.

Debellatio – extinction of the international personality of a state by the destruction of the state machinery.

Erga omnes – against everybody.

Fides – faith, honesty.

Forum – a court of justice, a place of jurisdiction, a place of litigation.

Forum prorogatum – prorogation of the court jurisdiction based on the consent of the parties. Under forum prorogatum the ICJ may exercise jurisdiction in cases where after the applicant state has instituted proceedings the respondent state subsequently consents to submit to the jurisdiction. The consent may be express or implied.

Habeas corpus – to produce the body, a court petition which seeks that a person being detained be produced before a judge for hearing to decide whether the detention is lawful. Habeas corpus was one of the concessions contained in the Magna Carta.

Hostis humani generis – an enemy of the human race.

Id est (ie) – that is.

In camera – in private. The deliberations of the ICJ are conducted in private.

Inter alia – among other things.

Inter pares – between peers, between those who stand on a level of equality.

Inter partes – between parties.

Interim – in the meantime. For example, an interim order which is made in the meantime and until something else is done.

Ipso facto – by the fact itself, by the mere fact.

Ius ad bellum – the right to initiate war.

Ius civile – law applicable to relations between Roman citizens.

Ius cogens – imperative, peremptory rules of international legal order. In the hierarchy of norms, imperative rules are superior to any other rules. They are so fundamental that they bind all states and do not allow any exception. A peremptory norm is defined in art 53 of the Vienna Convention on the Law of Treaties 1969 as:

> '... a norm accepted and recognised by the international community of states as a whole as a norm from which no derogation is permitted and which can be modified only by a subsequent norm of general international law having the same character.'

Ius dispositivum – can be disposed of at convenience of the parties concerned. Many municipal laws make a distinction between imperative rules, that is rules referring to public order from which no derogation is permitted and others from which parties in their private transactions can deviate and replace them according to their wishes. Ius dispositivum refers to rules which are capable of being modified by contrary consensual arrangements of individual parties.

Ius fetiale – consisted of religious rules which governed the Roman Empire's external relations and formal declarations of war which, inter alia, recognised the inviolability of ambassadors and was at the origin of the distinction between just and unjust war.

Ius gentium – law of peoples, law of nations. Ius gentium was the answer of the Romans (as Rome expanded) to the necessity of regulating legal relations between Roman citizens and foreigners. A special magistrate, the praetor peregrinus, was appointed in 242 BC who created law called ius gentium acceptable to both Roman citizens and foreigners. This law was the first truly international law, although it essentially regulated relations between private individuals. It was based on the commercial law in use in Mediterranean trade, ius civile (law applicable to relations between Roman citizens) in its less formalistic version, and on principles of equity and bone fides. The distinction between ius civile and ius gentium was obliterated when Roman citizenship was granted to all male inhabitants of the Empire in 212 AD.

Ius in bello – law regulating the conduct of war.

Ius naturale – the law of nature. Law inherent in nature that may be ascertained by reason. Ius naturale was used in the philosophical speculations of the Roman jurists and was intended to denote a system of rules and principles for the guidance of human conduct which, independently of enacted law or of the systems peculiar to any one people, might be discovered by the rational intelligence of man, and would be found to grow out of, and conform to, his nature, 'nature' meaning his whole mental, moral and physical constitution. Cicero in his *De Republica* gave the following definition of natural law:

> 'True law is right reason in agreement with Nature; it is of universal application, unchanging and everlasting; it summons to duty by its commands, and averts from wrongdoing by its prohibitions ... There will not be different laws at Rome and at Athens, or different laws now and in the future, but one eternal and unchangeable law will be valid for all nations and for all times.'

The doctrine of natural law is regarded as a precursor to the concept of human rights.

Ius sanguinis – the law of blood. The principle according to which nationality derives from parentage and thus a newborn acquires the parent's nationality regardless of the place of birth.

Ius soli – the law of the soil. The principle according to which a child born in the territory of a state becomes automatically a national irrespective of the nationality of his parents.

Lex fori – the law of the place where the court adjudicating the case is located.

Lex mercatoria – the law-merchant. With the revival of trade in the tenth century merchants started to travel throughout Europe in order to sell, buy and place orders for various goods. These commercial activities required the establishment of a common legal framework. Out of necessity the European merchants created their own rules of conduct and fair dealing which formed the lex mercatoria.

Lex posterior derogat priori – a later statute takes away the effect of a prior one.

Lex specialis derogat generali – a special statute overrules a general statute.

Lucrum cessans – the loss of prospective profits.

Magna Carta – the great charter. The name of a charter (or constitutional enactment) granted by King John of England to the barons, at Runnymede, on 15 June 1215 and afterwards, with some alterations, confirmed in Parliament by Henry III and Edward I. This charter is regarded as the foundation of English constitutional liberty. Among its 38 chapters are provisions regulating the administration of justice, defining the temporal and ecclesiastical jurisdictions, securing personal liberty and the rights to property.

Mens rea – guilty mind or intention, a criminal intent.

Non liquet – it is not clear. In the Roman courts, when any of the judges, after the hearing of a cause, were not satisfied that the case was made clear enough for them to pronounce a verdict, they were privileged to signify this opinion by casting a ballot inscribed with the letters 'NL', the abbreviated form of the phase 'non liquet'. In the modern context it refers to a hypothetical situation in which in the absence of relevant legal rules a court is unable to give a decision based on law.

Nulla crimen sine lege – no crime without a pre-existing law making the act a crime.

Nulla poena sine lege – no punishment without a pre-existing prohibitary rule of law.

Nullum crimen sine poena – no crime without punishment.

Nuncius – the Pope's legate, the official representative of the Pope at a foreign court or seat of government.

Obiter dictum – a remark by the way, any statement of the law made by the court merely by way of illustration, not necessarily concerning the case or essential to its determination.

Opinio iuris sive necessitates – of the opinion that it is a necessary law. Maxim that a state must perceive a customary practice as one that it is obliged by international law to observe.

Pacta sunt servanda – agreements are to be kept. The legal doctrine that a treaty constitutes a contract between the parties, and that its conditions are binding and must be observed.

Par in parem non habet imperium – legal persons of equal standing cannot have their disputes settled in the courts of one of them. This is founded upon the principle of sovereign equality and independence of states and rests upon the historical proposition that a sovereign could not himself be sued before his own municipal courts, so the sovereign of another state was similarly exempt from the jurisdiction of the local law.

Per se – by himself or itself, in itself, taken alone, inherently, in isolation.

Persona non grata – person not wanted. A receiving state is entitled at any time and without any explanation to declare a head of mission or members of his diplomatic staff as unacceptable – persona non grata. In this event the sending state normally recalls the diplomat concerned. However, if no such step is taken the receiving state may refuse to consider him as being a member of the mission. The declaration of persona non grata may be made either before or after the diplomat's arrival in the territory of the receiving state. There are two main reasons for which a diplomat may be declared persona non grata: his personal behaviour such as the commission of a criminal act or anti-social conduct, or an abuse of his diplomatic status when he acts as a spy, or in any other manner endangers the security and other interests of the receiving state. Also a receiving state may declare a diplomat persona non grata as a retaliation against a sending state which has so declared one of its own diplomats. This practice is quite frequent.

Prima facie – at first sight, on the face of it, so far as can be judged from the first disclosure.

Prima facie case – a showing of sufficient evidence to initially establish a claimant's case. If such a case is made out, the opposing party is then required to respond. It can be overthrown only by rebutting evidence adduced by the opposing party.

Prior – the former, earlier.

Ratio decidendi – the ground of decision.

Ratione materiae – by reason of the matter involved.

Ratione personae – by reason of the person concerned.

Rebus sic stantibus – a name given to a tacit condition, said to attach to all treaties that they shall cease to be obligatory so soon as the state of facts or conditions upon which they were founded has substantially changed.

Res – a thing.

Res derelicta – abandoned property, so as to become open to the acquisition of the first taker or occupant.

Res judicata – a point or question or subject-matter in controversy or a dispute which has been authoritatively and finally settled by the decision of a court, the rule that final judgment or decree on merits by court of competent jurisdiction is conclusive of the rights of the parties in all later suits on points and matters determined in a former suit.

Res nullius – the property of nobody.

Restitutio in integrum – restoration to the original position.

Sine qua non – without which not, an indispensable requisite or condition.

Stare decisis – old decisions. To abide by, or adhere to, decided cases. Policy of courts to stand by precedent and not to disturb a settled point. Doctrine according to which when a court has once laid down a principle of law as applicable to a certain state of facts, it will adhere to that principle, and apply it to all future cases, where facts are substantially the same.

Status quo ante – the state of things as it used to be.

Ultra vires – beyond the powers. An act which is beyond the powers or authority of the person or organisation which took it.

Uti possedetis – whatever you possess is yours. A doctrine which derives from Roman law and which was applied in the context of the decolonisation of Latin America in the nineteenth century. According to the doctrine when Spain was leaving its Latin American territory the boundaries left behind were to be respected and could not be changed under any circumstances. This doctrine has become recognised in customary international law and was applied in the context of later decolonisation.

Index

Old Bailey Press

The Old Bailey Press Integrated Student Law Library is tailor-made to help you at every stage of your studies, from the preliminaries of each subject through to the final examination. The series of Textbooks, Revision WorkBooks, 150 Leading Cases and Cracknell's Statutes are interrelated to provide you with a comprehensive set of study materials.

You can buy Old Bailey Press books from your University Bookshop, your local Bookshop, directly using this form, or you can order a free catalogue of our titles from the address shown overleaf.

The following subjects each have a Textbook, 150 Leading Cases, Revision WorkBook and Cracknell's Statutes unless otherwise stated.

Administrative Law
Commercial Law
Company Law
Conflict of Laws
Constitutional Law
Conveyancing (Textbook and 150 Leading Cases)
Criminal Law
Criminology (Textbook and Sourcebook)
Employment Law (Textbook and Cracknell's Statutes)
English and European Legal Systems
Equity and Trusts
Evidence
Family Law
Jurisprudence: The Philosophy of Law (Textbook, Sourcebook and
    Revision WorkBook)
Land: The Law of Real Property
Law of International Trade
Law of the European Union
Legal Skills and System
    (Textbook)
Obligations: Contract Law
Obligations: The Law of Tort
Public International Law
Revenue Law (Textbook,
    Revision WorkBook and
    Cracknell's Statutes)
Succession (Textbook, Revision
    WorkBook and Cracknell's
    Statutes)

Mail order prices:	
Textbook	£15.95
150 Leading Cases	£12.95
Revision WorkBook	£10.95
Cracknell's Statutes	£11.95
Suggested Solutions 1999–2000	£6.95
Suggested Solutions 2000–2001	£6.95
Suggested Solutions 2001–2002	£6.95
101 Questions and Answers	£7.95
Law Update 2004	£10.95
Law Update 2005	£10.95

Please note details and prices are subject to alteration.

To complete your order, please fill in the form below:

Module	Books required	Quantity	Price	Cost
		Postage		
		TOTAL		

For the UK and Europe, add £4.95 for the first book ordered, then add £1.00 for each subsequent book ordered for postage and packing.
For the rest of the world, add 50% for airmail.

ORDERING

By telephone to Customer Services at 020 8317 6039, with your credit card to hand.

By fax to 020 8317 6004 (giving your credit card details).

Website: www.oldbaileypress.co.uk
E-Mail: customerservices@oldbaileypress.co.uk

By post to: Customer Services, Old Bailey Press at Holborn College, Woolwich Road, Charlton, London, SE7 8LN.

When ordering by post, please enclose full payment by cheque or banker's draft, or complete the credit card details below. You may also order a free catalogue of our complete range of titles from this address.

We aim to despatch your books within 3 working days of receiving your order. All parts of the form must be completed.

Name

Address

Postcode

E-Mail
Telephone

Total value of order, including postage: £

I enclose a cheque/banker's draft for the above sum, or

charge my ☐ Access/Mastercard ☐ Visa ☐ American Express

Cardholder: ....

Card number

☐☐☐☐ ☐☐☐☐ ☐☐☐☐ ☐☐☐☐

Expiry date ☐☐☐☐

Signature: ....Date: ....